JOURNEY INTO DIALOGIC PEDAGOGY

JOURNEY INTO DIALOGIC PEDAGOGY

EUGENE MATUSOV

Nova Science Publishers, Inc.
New York

For permission to use material from this book please contact us:
Telephone 631-231-7269; Fax 631-231-8175
Web Site: http://www.novapublishers.com

NOTICE TO THE READER

The Publisher has taken reasonable care in the preparation of this book, but makes no expressed or implied warranty of any kind and assumes no responsibility for any errors or omissions. No liability is assumed for incidental or consequential damages in connection with or arising out of information contained in this book. The Publisher shall not be liable for any special, consequential, or exemplary damages resulting, in whole or in part, from the readers' use of, or reliance upon, this material.

Independent verification should be sought for any data, advice or recommendations contained in this book. In addition, no responsibility is assumed by the publisher for any injury and/or damage to persons or property arising from any methods, products, instructions, ideas or otherwise contained in this publication.

This publication is designed to provide accurate and authoritative information with regard to the subject matter covered herein. It is sold with the clear understanding that the Publisher is not engaged in rendering legal or any other professional services. If legal or any other expert assistance is required, the services of a competent person should be sought. FROM A DECLARATION OF PARTICIPANTS JOINTLY ADOPTED BY A COMMITTEE OF THE AMERICAN BAR ASSOCIATION AND A COMMITTEE OF PUBLISHERS.

LIBRARY OF CONGRESS CATALOGING-IN-PUBLICATION DATA

Matusov, Eugene.
  Journey into dialogic pedagogy / Eugene Matusov.
     p. cm.
  Includes index.
  ISBN 978-1-60692-535-5 (hardcover)
  1. Questioning. 2. Interaction analysis in education. 3. Communication in education. 4. Education--Philosophy. I. Title.
  LB1027.44.M35 2009
  371.3'7--dc22
                                                                    2008047031

Published by Nova Science Publishers, Inc. ✦ New York

CONTENTS

PREFACE

The author came to the decision to embark on this journey into dialogic pedagogy when he firmly realized that education is essentially dialogic. It is not that pedagogy should be dialogic – he rather argues that it is always dialogic. This is true whether the participants in it, or outside observers of it, realize it or not -- and even when the participants are resistant to dialogue. This statement is in contrast with views that promote dialogic interaction in the classroom as a form of instruction. This conceptualization contrasts with views that dialogic interaction or conversational instruction are more effective instructional means in comparison to, let's say, a more monologic genre of instruction such as a lecture or a demonstration. This statement is also in contrast with views that assume dialogue is a pedagogical instrument that can be turned on and off. He argues that whatever teachers and students do (or not do) whether in their classrooms or beyond it, they are locked in dialogic relations.

Chapter 1

INTRODUCTION: ONTOLOGICAL VS. INSTRUMENTAL DIALOGIC PEDAGOGY

ABSTRACT

I discuss why dialogic pedagogy is not an option. I examine the meaning making process and come to a conclusion that it is inherently dialogic. Then I consider the consequences of this claim for education. I come to a conclusion that any education is dialogic but in some educational practices, dialogicity is distorted because these practices are guided by anti-dialogic projects. The difference between ontological and instrumental approaches to dialogue in education is discussed.

I came to my decision to embark on this journey into dialogic pedagogy when I firmly realized that education is essentially dialogic. It is not that pedagogy *should* be dialogic – I rather argue that it is *always* dialogic. This is true whether the participants in it, or outside observers of it, realize it or not -- and even when the participants are resistant to dialogue. This statement is in contrast with views that promote dialogic interaction in the classroom as a form of instruction. This conceptualization contrasts with views that dialogic interaction or conversational instruction are more effective instructional means in comparison to, let's say, a more monologic genre of instruction such as a lecture or a demonstration. This statement is also in contrast with views that assume dialogue is a pedagogical instrument that can be turned on and off. I argue that whatever teachers and students do (or not do) whether in their classrooms or beyond it, they are locked in dialogic relations.

The sole reason for the omnipresence of dialogue is because meaning is inherently dialogic. In several of my class presentations with students and conference presentations to scholars about dialogic pedagogy, I begin by writing the statement, "Eugene is here" on a blackboard and asking my audience to explain what it means, from their point of view. Here are some of their numerous responses:

> The statement "Eugene is here" means that…
> "Eugene has arrived" ("Is Eugene here?");
> "The class has started" ("Has the class session already started?");

"Shut up!" ("What does Eugene want us to do?");

"Where is Eugene?";

"Who is here?";

"This is an important example of something" ("Why did Eugene write the statement on the blackboard and asked us what it means?");

"It's stupid. I feel stupid." ("How do I feel about Eugene's demand to quiz us about the meaning of his statement?");

"What is Eugene doing?";

"We don't have time to talk anymore." ("Should we stop talking because the class started?" Is that what Eugene wants us to do?");

"I wonder where Eugene is leading us with this?" (an indirect question);

… (silence with a cunning smile, "Why does he think that I will reply to this stupid question?").

This rather simple and, arguably, contrived example is based on my somewhat cunning abuse of my institutional and professional power as a official presenter to ask the audience any question that I wish, however irrelevant it may be perceived by my audience, supported by the institutional obligation of my audience to answer it. I could not repeat what I did in my classroom on a street, or at a café, or even with my family. It suggests, nevertheless, several important points about the meaning-making processes that were articulated by the Russian philosopher and literary theoretician Mikhail Bakhtin.

First, meaning making is always creative; it is a surprise. It is a possibility among many other possibilities, and therefore never pre-determined. I can never fully determine how my audience might reply next time to my question. Even if I can correctly predict how my audience replies to my words, I still surprise that my predication was correct. We are both surprised. My audience was surprised by my question, while I was surprised by their answers. To stay alive, meaning has to renew itself continually. Meaning cannot be repeated, because even literal repetition itself transforms the meaning (Bakhtin, 1999). Paraphrasing a famous statement by Woody Allen from his 1977 movie "Annie Hall", I would say, "Meaning, I think, is like a shark, you know? It has to constantly move forward or it dies." Second, the meaning-making process occurs between at least two distinct consciousnesses that are oblique and non-transparent to each other. Without this gap of understanding between two consciousnesses – what Bakhtin (1990) called "the gap of transgradience" – there is no novelty and element of surprise, on which meaning thrives. In my example, the two (actually more than two) consciousnesses were my audience and me. Of course, one person can also create meaning, but the person does it through creating another virtual consciousness through the gap of incomprehensibility and non-transparency. It is a well-known phenomenon that one person experiences a high difficulty of trying to play chess with him or herself without cheating and taking a side – the consciousnesses of the two players are transparent to the person making the play with oneself near impossible. Thus, even in the solitary production of meaning – in thinking – the meaning-making process is dialogic (Vygotsky & Kozulin, 1986). A single consciousness cannot create a dialogue.   After Bakhtin, I argue that the phenomenon of consciousness "does not have internal terriroty" – it is not a self-contained and self-sufficient center of the person's mediated activity, -- but rather it is created by a gap between consciousness of non-understanding, or saying in more positive way, by *inter-addressivity*. Third, meaning making is mediated by a question, not just by my question to the audience, "How do you understand my statement? What does it mean to you?" but also by the questions that the audience members ask themselves to make sense of what my overall request meant to them. I put their questions in parentheses unless their replies were already in the form of questions. When I asked my audiences why there were so different answers to my question, they said that their interpretations were mediated by diverse questions.

The realization that the meaning-making process is inherently dialogic has important consequences for education. First, since learning is the transformation of a student's meaning, it is unpredictable, undetermined, and cannot be designed or controlled by the teacher (Wenger, 1998). Stating this more positively, learning – what is learned -- is always a surprise for both the student and the teacher. Second, learning is always discursive, that is, the process and product of a new meaning always exists among diverse, real or virtual, consciousnesses. Third, learning is always mediated by the students' questions (explicit or tacit).

On the other hand, teaching is a goal-directed activity. It has its curricular endpoints that the state or even individual teacher often tries to prescribe, "By the end of the lesson/term/year/education, the students will know, be able, mater…" These endpoints of education seem to be anti-dialogical. Dialogue is impossible if a participant knows its endpoint in advance. It is, at best, skillful manipulation of leading a dialogic partner to the known endpoint or, at worst, violent imposition of the teacher's knowledge, skill, attitude on the student. In both cases, it is not a genuine dialogue discussed above.

Let me summarize what I have said so far, as it may seem that I contradict myself. I started by saying that every meaning making process without exception is inherently dialogic but ended up saying that education is anti-dialogic. How can this be? Am I trying to say that education does not involve meaning making? Or, am I trying to say that education in its current form is ineffective as a meaning making process for the students?

My point is rather different. I conceptually separate education as a practice, which is, like any practice, inherently dialogic, and education as a project (or ideology) that can be essentially anti-dialogic. It is not by chance that Bakhtin (1999) often used examples of education for illustrating extreme monologism. Mainstream education as a practice *is* always dialogic but I argue that this dialogicity is often distorted because it is guided by the anti-dialogic education project. It involves students in a meaning-making process but this meaning making process is very distorted, inhumane, and perverse; the pedagogical practice of mainstream education ignores how students make sense of the meaning-making process. For example, the students often interpret school instruction, like "2+2 is always 4" (which is not true! – two friends plus two friends do not always produce four friends), or that the procedure for addition of fractions with different denominators as *conventional rules* (similar to a conventional rule of spelling) rather than a math pattern based on a math proof. Yet the students are not invited to consider whether the rule could change depending on the context or units, or with fractions to consider why the rule is useful and for what, or even to consider whether the they might not want to study the topic at all! This distorted, inhumane, and perverse nature of conventional schooling is well-documented (Jackson, 1968; Lortie, 1975; Waller, 1932). Still, being distorted, the meaning making process and the teacher-students relationship remain dialogic. Let me give a parallel example; the German philosopher Hegel (1967) made an interesting analysis of master-slave relations. He showed that the master desires an ideal slave who will be unconditionally loyal to him and care for the master's well-being even in the face of disagreement with the master or eventual cruel punishment. Thus, Hegel showed that even slavery is dialogic (i.e., acceptance of disagreements) and humane (i.e., unconditional caring) but its dialogicity and humanity are very twisted and perverted. Of course, it is true that the conventional education practice guided by the anti-dialogic project of education can produce good meaning making processes and good learning as well. Similarly, I also believe that at times slavery could involve sparks of genuine humanity. However, I argue that these are abnormalities of conventional education and slavery – good meaning making, good dialogue, and good humanity occur not because of the anti-dialogic projects of conventional education and slavery but, arguably, in spite of them. (I continue the parallel between slavery and conventional education guided by an anti-dialogic project throughout the book).

But can an education project be pro-dialogical per se? Elsewhere (Matusov, 2007), I raised the possibility that education as a particular project may not be compatible with dialogue. First, arguably the teacher does not and should not have any surprises about the content that he or she teaches. This is what defines a teacher – to know much more than a student does, to have content knowledge about the subject matter. Of course, the teacher can and should learn more about his or her students – the teacher has constantly to be a pedagogical learner, learning more about his or her students in order to teach them better. In addition, according to the education project, the teacher must be an expert in the content knowledge that he or she teaches or, at least, know more than the students do. Of course, it is a good idea for a good teacher to keep his or her expertise in the academic subject matter renewed and updated. And sometimes students accidently ask questions about the academic subject matter that the teacher cannot answer, so he or she must learn. But this subject matter learning by the teacher– being surprised about the subject matter while interacting with the students is accidental and not considered an essential quality of teaching. If the teacher were to learn the academic subject continually with and from his or her students, the teacher would be considered as ignorant as the students and not worthy of the teaching profession. This demand for expertise and stability in the teacher's knowledge about the subject matter in his or her work with the students makes teaching anti-dialogic. In dialogue, both parties are surprised by each other about the matter of their dialogue.

Second, the project of conventional education seeks to make all consciousnesses transparent and homogeneous. From this point of view, it does not matter how the process of education is viewed – transmission of knowledge, acquisition of knowledge, co-construction of knowledge, scaffolding of knowledge, or providing "the zone of proximal development" (cf. Vygtosky, 1978). The conventional education project's goal is the reduction of diversity or gap between the community of the educated, to whom the teacher belongs, and the community of the ignorant, to whom the students belong, by making the students more like the teacher. Conventional education is about erasing gaps between the teacher's and the students' consciousnesses by making the students' consciousnesses like the teacher's. Indeed, all educated people must know that "2+2=4" and that "George Washington was the first President of the United States." The pedagogical (and epistemological) notion of "knowledge" existing metaphysically outside of the human minds pushes education towards homogenization of the teacher's and students' consciousnesses. Paraphrasing a famous observation by Russian writer Leo Tolstoy about unhappy families I suggest that, "All knowledgeable people resemble one another, but each ignorant person is ignorant in his or her own way." Even when knowledge is seen as a social construction – as a consensus among the most relevant and authoritative people (Latour, 1987; Latour & Woolgar, 1979) – becoming educated means joining the consensus. Thus, the goal of education to reduce gaps among consciousnesses is anti-dialogic. In dialogue, the gap between consciousnesses is constantly transformed, but it is never reducible because the gap defines dialogue. The conventional education project's goal to eliminate the gap among consciousnesses by ensuring they have the same knowledge is the desire to kill dialogue.

Third, in the project of conventional education, meaning making is mediated neither by the teacher's question nor by the students' questions. It is not mediated by the teacher's question because the teacher should not have genuine questions about the subject matter with the students. If the teacher does have genuine questions about the taught subject matter (on a systematic basis), he or she is viewed as incompetent. While it is true that people ignorant about some academic topic (but more experienced in learning) can successfully provide guidance about how to learn to another ignorant person (Matusov, Bell, & Rogoff, 2002), the conventional education project doesn't recognize these experienced learners as "teachers" (especially in the school context). On the other hand, although students might have genuine questions that they occasionally raise in classrooms, the conventional education project does not treat these questions as a primary source of guidance for shaping the classroom curriculum. The students do not know where they are supposed to arrive – the teacher does. Thus, the students often do not have questions at all, or have "wrong" questions, according to the teacher, (i.e., so-called "off-topic" and "off-script" contributions from the teacher's point of view, the teacher solely representing the education project in the classroom, see Kennedy, 2005). In the conventional education project, the unit of learning is not an information-seeking question that a student asks, but the correct answer that he or she produces at the teacher's demand to an information-known question asked by the teacher. Neglecting the students' (and the teacher's) genuine information-seeking questions as the central unit of learning makes the conventional education project anti-dialogic yet again.

The present book is a response to my inquiry, "Can the practice of education be guided by a pro-dialogic project?" Does such a thing as "dialogic pedagogy" exist? I define "dialogic pedagogy" here as an educational practice that is guided by a pro-dialogic project of education. Let me describe what would make an education project pro-dialogic. First, pro-dialogic education assumes that the teacher is the Learner #1 in the classroom. The teacher learns not only pedagogically – how to teach the students better, -- but also learns the subject matter *with* the students. The teacher is ignorant in a sense that he or she is ready to suspend the certainty of his or her own knowledge and test it with the students again (cf. the notion of "learned ignorance" by Nicholas of Cusa, 1954) and therefore full of surprises with the students. Second, knowledge actually, as such, does not exist -- not now and not later. At least, this notion of stable "knowledge" is not useful for a pro-dialogic education project. The content of learning is always dialogic, thus, problematic. To know means to be addressed and to reply – a growing engagement of the students in historically unfolding discourses. Consciousnesses of the teacher and the students are taken with equal seriousness (Bakhtin, 1999). Third, the unit of learning that defines both curriculum and instruction is genuine information-seeking questions that both the teacher and the students ask of each other.

Following Alexander Sidorkin's (1999) discussion of use of the notion of dialogue in education and Morson and Emerson's (1990) discussion of Bakhtin's notion of "polyphony," I call this pro-dialogic project an *ontological* in contrast to an *instrumental* vision of dialogue in education. An ontological approach to dialogue assumes that all practices, discourses, and relations are inherently dialogic because the meaning making process is dialogic. Life is ontologically dialogic (Bakhtin, 1986). The ontological approach to dialogue calls for practices, and especially education, to make dialogicity its primary guiding principle. In contrast, an instrumental approach to dialogue sees dialogue as a pedagogical method to make learning more effective. The ontological approach is concerned with the nature of relations as they emerge in education – their dialogicity and humanity -- while the instrumental approach discusses those conditions under which it is a good idea to organize an instruction as dialogue and when it is not (see for examples of instrumental dialogue in education Adler, 1982; Burbules, 1993; Macmillan & Garrison, 1988).

In the title of my book, I use the metaphor of a journey because I feel myself sailing in an unknown territory. I was not even sure that the land I was heading for existed. To tell you the truth, I am not sure even now, after "I am back", if it exists. As you travel with me in reading this book, it is up to you to judge whether or how the journey is successful – if even I ever have visited the land that can be called "dialogic pedagogy." My initial roadmap of the journey was rather straightforward. I decided to focus on the most well-known practitioners and theoreticians of dialogue and dialogic pedagogy in the area of education: Socrates (Chapters 2 and 3), Freire (Chapter 4), Bakhtin (Chapter 5), Paley (Chapters 7 and 8 – these chapters were written in collaboration with Mark Smith) and contrast them with conventional, mainstream education (Chapter 6). I chose educational ethnography as my main method of investigation for writing every chapter except purely conceptual Chapter 5, which is about Bakhtin's use of his notions of dialogue and monologue. As an educational researcher grounded in a sociocultural approach (Lave, 1988; Lave & Wenger, 1991), I needed "resistance of material" to make sure that I am not imagining things that do not exist. I also decided to be very critical about what has been written about Socrates, Freire, and Paley and carefully check all the claims that other scholars made about these educators through my ethnography. I treated Socrates as an educator for this purpose because many educators treat him as such. My goal was also to develop the notion of dialogic pedagogy through this analysis.

My findings surprised me. Through my ethnographic analysis of dialogicity, I found that Socrates, Freire, and Paley were not as dialogic in their pedagogy as I, and many other scholars, initially thought. I also found that there have always been dissenting voices in the academic community challenging claims about how dialogic the pedagogies demonstrated by Socrates, Freire, and Paley were. I think my analysis supports, validates, and deepens this dissent. I also found deep ontological tensions in the pedagogies of Socrates, Freire, and Paley that led me to numerous discussions about the relationship between dialogue and social justice. I came to the conclusion that prioritization of one over the other: dialogue over social justice (Socrates) and social justice over dialogue (Freire and Paley) leads to serious pedagogical, moral, and political problems. The chapters discussing the relationship between searching for truth and social justice (2-8) constitute Part 1 of the book.

In Chapter 5, I investigate Bakhtin's polysemic notions of "dialogue" and "monologue" and their potential use in education. I found five different and potentially useful and distinct meanings of Bakhtin's terms. Some of these uses are oppositional (e.g., dialogism and monologism), some complementary (e.g., dialogicity and monologicity), some juxtaposed (e.g., dialogic genre and monologic genre), some rather negative (e.g., "excessive dialogism" and "excessive monologism"), and some exclusive and universal (e.g., meaning being inherently dialogic). Hopefully, my analysis will help to clarify existing confusions about these powerful terms and, perhaps, even create new potentially useful confusions.

Chapters 6, 7, 9, 10, 11, 12 involve the application of Bakhtin's notions of dialogue and monologue to modern conventional and innovative education. The analysis of conventional educational practice (Chapter 6) was developed because I was puzzled by how pervasive it is – it, like a black hole, powerfully acquires teachers. I wanted to study a conventional classroom, the ecology of which promotes an anti-dialogic project of education. I found Bakhtin's notions of diverse chronotopes translated in education useful for this puzzle. I documented that teachers in conventional school settings intentionally and constantly try to de-ontologize the curriculum for their students in order to control their instruction and the classroom interaction. Participants' ontological engagement with the content of their interaction – something that is so unproblematic and natural in everyday settings – becomes a huge problem in conventional schooling. In Chapter 11, I consider how this problem of the students' (and the teacher's) non-ontological engagement in the curriculum can be solved by dialogic pedagogy. In Chapter 10, I analyze the educational setting of an afterschool program in which dialogic pedagogy is carnivalistically unleashed and celebrated. In my analysis, I tried to learn from the ecology of this polyphonic classroom that promotes and supports dialogue and dialogic guidance. I speculated about how schooling might look if it were guided by a pro-dialogic project similar to the afterschool program studied.

In Chapter 9, I partook of an endeavor seriously considering what education would look like when "knowledge does not exist." For that purpose, I analyzed my own undergraduate teaching of a religious student, a preservice teacher, who worked on her final paper for my class arguing about teaching Intelligent Design in public school as an alternative to the Theory of Evolution. Does education mean that I, as her instructor, had to convince her that she was wrong, since Federal courts recently concluded in the USA that teaching of Intelligent Design as a scientific alternative to the Theory of Evolution is illegal in the US public schools? If not, what does education mean? I consider where and how the notion of dialogic pedagogy can guide us to address these questions.

In Chapter 12, I considered an uneasy relationship between dialogue and activity, in general, and between Activity Theory (Engeström, Miettinen, & Punamèaki-Gitai, 1999), in its third generation, and the Theory of Ontological Dialogue inspired by Bakhtin's scholarship, in specific. The issue is if and how conditions that promote dialogue can be designed. If learning does not have an endpoint known in advance by the teacher and it is not predictable, then what is the immediate goal of teaching as a goal-directed activity? In this chapter, I analyzed my own educational practice as well as the innovative educational practices of a Ukrainian pedagogical movement called the "School of the Dialogue of Cultures" (Emerson, 1997; Koshmanova, 2006) inspired by the work of Bakhtin. I found that in dialogic education, learning and dialogue are by-products of a teaching activity aimed at creating provocations for the emergence of certain dramatic events.

Finally, in the conclusion (Chapter 13), I examined possible limitations of dialogic pedagogy. Specifically, I focused on claims that dialogic pedagogy might not be appropriate for younger children and autistic students. The conclusion based on my analysis of specific cases is that dialogic pedagogy is defined by a certain quality of social relations rather than based on interactive verbalism that is often equated with dialogue. This ending of my book suggests that I am optimistic about the development of a pro-dialogic project for institutionalized education. But I am aware that this hope of mine is far from being conclusive and fully grounded in research and practice. The 9-13 chapters constitute the second big theme of the book (Part 2) examining the relationship between dialogue as an emergent process and teaching as goal-directed activity and design.

I wrote this book in a genre of "an adventure novel": it is full of jumps and contradictions (Bakhtin, 1991). Rather than systematically developing a big theme, I was like a child jumping from one interesting problem to another. There is a lot of zigzagging, returning back, and then jumping ahead. My goal in the organization of the chapters was not so much to communicate a linear sequence of ideas but rather to engage the reader in discussions about problems and puzzles I was (and still am) facing. I do not think my findings are as important as my journey and its trajectory.

* * *

I did not know for sure when exactly I started writing this book – when I realized that I was working on a book, I found I was already writing it. Writing this book was like a recession: you become aware that it has come when you already are deeply in it. In 2002, a group of PhD graduate students at the School of Education, University of Delaware, asked me to teach a seminar on Bakhtin as applied to education probably because Bakhtin has become more and more influential in education and I have learned about Bakhtin in Russia and read a lot of Bakhtin's texts in Russian. It was not my first choice for a seminar but I agreed to teach it and titled the seminar "Bakhtin: Investigation of Dialogue, Narrative, and Power." I remember telling my students that I did not know much about how Bakhtin's ideas could be used in education but I promised to read and learn together with them. I also invited my colleague Professor Chris Clark to co-teach this seminar, since I knew that he was also interested in learning about Bakhtin. The class was very inspirational for me. I do not know about the graduate students, but I learned a lot from it. I can recognize now that many germs of ideas (especially for the first 5 chapters) that I later developed in this book came from our heated discussions in the seminar or on the class web. I think it was Chris Clark who was the first person who suggested and encouraged me to write a book on dialogic pedagogy. Later, my former graduate student, colleague, and friend Maria Albuquerque Candela joined her voice constantly asking me when I would write a book about dialogic pedagogy for her to read. Finally, during an international Bakhtin conference in July 2005 in Finland, my US colleague Professor Bob Fecho commented that my presentation at the conference about Bakhtin's polysemy of his notions of dialogue and monologue sounded like the chapter of a book. That was the last drop. I decided firmly to write a book. By that time, I realized that I was working on its third chapter. Before, I was thinking that I was working on separate journal articles. But after Bob's comment, it suddenly became Cris clear for me that I was working not on separate journal articles but on a book because all of these texts were thematically connected and dialogically complementary.

In September 2005, I met Professor Olga Dysthe, a Norwegian scholar from University of Bergen, at a sociocultural conference ISCAR (International Society for Cultural and Activity Research) in Seville, Spain. Our meeting was absolutely a stroke of pure luck. I proposed too many presentations at ISCAR (I think 6 or 7) and some of my presentations were scheduled at the same time. When the ISCAR organizers noticed the problem, they shifted some of my conflicting presentations to some other time. So, by a stroke of luck, Olga's presentation about productive learning and my presentation on ontological teaching (Chapter 11) were scheduled together. After our presentations, we spent 3 hours together with her and her colleagues from the University of Bergen discussing dialogic pedagogy (we even skipped sessions that we planned to attend). As a senior scholar working in this area, Olga was much more knowledgeable about this area than me. After I returned back to US, Olga directed my reading via email. Among many other great sources, she introduced me to the wonderfully inspirational scholarship of Alexander Sidorkin which has heavily influenced this book. Our email discussions of dialogic pedagogy have been very productive for me. In fall 2006, Olga and her colleague Professor Sølvi Lillejord invited me to the University of Bergen as a visiting scholar. They organized a 3-day seminar on dialogic pedagogy as well as many other presentations for me to share and discuss my work in progress on this book. Our formal and informal discussions and debates with Olga and her Norwegian colleagues and graduate students were very stimulating for my intellectual work on the topics of the book. Let me tell just one interesting and funny anecdote demonstrating Olga's influence and guidance.

Once, Olga invited me for a dinner at her house located on a slope of a hill, surrounding Bergen (a gorgeous view from a window!). In our conversation, Olga asked my opinion about different innovative educational programs and schools: how much they employed dialogic pedagogy from my point of view. At some point, she asked me about the Ukrainian pedagogical movement "The School of the Dialogue of Cultures." I replied that I never heard about such movement. Olga was surprised and picked up the book by Emerson "The first hundred years of Mikhail Bakhtin" and read me several paragraphs about this movement started by the famous Soviet philosopher Vladimir Bibler whom I saw and heard many times in the Soviet Union at Davydov's seminars. I read Emerson's book before but for some reason, I did not pay attention to this information. I promised Olga to investigate this interesting pedagogical movement inspired by Bakhtin's ideas. I came back to the dorm for international scholars where I lived in Bergen and complied an email to my Russian colleague who worked at Moscow University. Since the movement was Ukrainian, I decided to cc this message to my old friend Dr. Igor Solomadin who was a philosopher of education and lived in Kharkov. I met Igor ten years before in New York at the American Educational Research Association conference. For some reason, I never received a reply from my Russian colleague, but I received an email quickly from Igor. He wrote me that I was crazy. He wrote, "Imagine that you wrote Vygotsky asking about Bakhtin and then cced Bakhtin – that's exactly what you did." I immediately Googled in Russian "School of the Dialogue of Cultures" and the name Igor Solomadin popped up almost every time because he was one of the main founders of the movement. Igor wrote me that for the last 10 years, he was trying to attract my attention to this movement but I kept ignoring it. It took Olga and my work on the book to finally focus me on what was going on next to me for 10 years! I am very thankful to Olga and Igor for reading many of my chapters, discussing the ideas, providing their critical and supportive feedback, and guiding my reading in preparation for this book (Olga guided me in Western literature while Igor guided me in Eastern literature on dialogic pedagogy). I'm also thankful to my Norwegian colleagues: Anton Havnes, Arne Vine, Sølvi Lillejord, Kariane Westrheim, and Hanne Riese for reading some of my chapters and discussing the ideas from the book. I am also thankful my University of Delaware colleagues David Blacker, Bob Hampel, Christopher Clark, and Jan Blitz and my colleagues from other universities and countries Yifat Ben-David Kolikant, Sarah Pollack, Michal Zellermayer, Kevin Leader, Lois Holzman, Christine LaCerva, Leif Strandberg, Tara Ratnam, Olga Griswold, Myriam Torres, Bob Fecho, Igor Solomadin, for assisting with the research and for providing feedback on some of chapters of the book. I am very thankful to all participants of my research projects that involved in this book, especially Steve Villanueva, a pedagogical genius, at the Latin-American Community Center.

My dialogic melting pot for this book was a group of my colleagues – graduate students and faculty at the School of Education, University of Delaware, – with a funny name PIG ("Professional Inquiry Group"). It is worth naming them all because they all contributed to the development of ideas for this book: Mark Smith (my co-author for Chapters 7 and 8), Kathy von Duyke (she provided ethnography to Chapter 13 and helped me with research for Chapter 10), Tara Falcone, Sohyun Han (she helped with research for Chapter 10), Stephanie Drye, Pawel Bakowski, Maria Albuquerque Candela (she came with the research idea for Chapter 10), Aideen Murphy, Carolina Correa, Julie Kittleson, Renee DePalma, John St. Julien, Cris Mayo, Ana Marjanovic Shane, and Tony Whitson. I feel really honored to have such an intellectual supportive group. It takes a PIG to write a book.

I have noticed that writing this book involved a lot of self-exploitation and neglect of family duties. Self-exploitation was mostly enjoyable but as for neglect of my family duties, I apologize and thank my family: my wife Alla, my son Artyom, my mom Inga, and my dad Lev for their sacrifice and patience (and for the lack of it at times as well). This work would have been impossible without their support and belief in me.

Eugene Matusov
Germantown, Philadelphia, PA; April 03, 2008

PART 1. DIALOGUE: SEARCH FOR TRUTH AND SOCIAL JUSTICE

Chapter 2

DIALOGICITY AND MONOLOGICITY OF SOCRATIC PEDAGOGICAL DIALOGUES

ABSTRACT

Scholarly literature on education often considers Plato's Socratic Dialogues as one of the first examples of dialogic pedagogy. I examine this claim by treating Meno, a highly cited Socratic dialogue in education scholarship, as an educational ethnography. A discourse analysis of Meno suggests that there are many dialogic and monologic aspects of Socrates' pedagogy. At least two pedagogies emerge in the analysis: Socrates' pedagogy with free citizens, which is relatively more dialogic, and Socrates' pedagogy with the Slave, which is relatively more monologic. Overall, Socrates' pedagogy seems to be more monologic than dialogic. Based on this discourse analysis of the Meno educational ethnography, I have developed a deeper understanding of what dialogic and monologic pedagogical relations are.

PLATO'S ACCOUNT OF SOCRATIC DIALOGUES AS EDUCATIONAL ETHNOGRAPHY

The Socratic dialogues described by Plato are probably the first expansively written accounts of dialogic pedagogy in human history. This account involves not only demonstration of dialogic pedagogy in action but also educational philosophy – ideology – of dialogic pedagogy. Socrates discussed his method of dialoging-philosophizing-educating within his dialogues. Finally, Socratic dialogues as methods of teaching are very inspirational and influential on modern pedagogy. All that led me to investigate Socratic dialogic pedagogy: what is it (or what are they), what are its benefits, what are its limitations and pitfalls (if not warnings).

In educational literature, Socratic dialogues have traditionally been praised for promoting critical thinking, renewing interest in subjects, provoking students' thinking, facilitating discovery learning. Contemporary Socratic methods are used for diverse subjects: from philosophical discussions like "What is moderation?" (e.g., C. Phillips, 2002) to social issues of the morality of homosexuality, to conceptual issues in physics, to the technical teaching of photography (Garlikov, 1998). The use of the Socratic method is valued for generating passion for academic subjects, to introduce hands-on constructivist learning to abstract subjects, for promoting reflection of students' beliefs and values (C. Phillips, 2002), for teaching logical and conceptual ideas, for organizing teaching material, and for revealing students' ignorance and misconceptions (Garlikov, 1998; Rud, 1997; Thomas, 1985). For Adler (1982) the Socratic method involves critical review of already learned material. Paley (1984) sees the value of Socratic dialogue in collaborative inquiry and testing of each others' ideas in the classroom. Gadamer (1975) saw Socratic dialogue as "true conversation."

Socrates provided the ideology of his teaching as testing the truth, discovering his own ignorance, pursuing truth about fundamental questions. Socrates claimed that the purpose of his philosophical work was to investigate his own ignorance and to test claimed knowledge and wisdom of others. He wanted to be a "gadfly" for Greek civic society in order to disturb civic consensus and comfort and reveal at times unpleasant truths to its free citizens. Athenian free citizens "really appreciated" the Socratic method by accusing Socrates of treason, and finally killing him for that (Plato, 1997).

Although there have been made many inspirational observations about Socratic dialogic pedagogy (primarily by philosophers -- see, for example, Nietzsche, 1956), I think that educational researchers, especially with their focus on instruction, have not yet provided enough detailed analysis of Socratic dialogic pedagogy. Often scholars made impressionistic claims about Socratic dialogues confusing his "espoused theory" and "theory-in-use" (see, Argyris & Schön, 1978, for discussion of these terms) – what Socrates declared about his own dialogue and how he really dialogued as presented in Plato's account. For example, Gadamer (1975) claims that by raising patient questions, Socrates made sure that he and his opponents were at one topic as they jointly approach the topic under debate. However, through his consideration of actual Socratic dialogues, Billig shows that "the Socratic debates do not proceed in such an orderly fashion. They seldom, if ever, resolve anything, and the participants often end up expressing their frustration. The topics they want to discuss keep disappearing from view, as they find themselves bogged down in other issues. Moreover, the arguments have a habit of doubling back on themselves" (Billig, 1996, p. 24).

My work here is aimed to address this lack of scholarship about detailed analysis of actual, theory-in-use, Socratic dialogues. For this purpose, I treat the Socratic dialogue as presented by Plato in his early Dialogues as educational ethnography, by making a conversational analysis of the Meno Dialogue (Plato, 1997). Although some late Socratic Dialogues were apparently invented by Plato, some were probably recorded second-hand or reconstructed by Plato a few years after they actually happened (Vlastos & Burnyeat, 1994); I consider Plato as one of the first educational ethnographers. Like in any educational ethnography, Plato focused on capturing Socrates' educational practice, although, with some important caveats. It is rather evident that Plato's purpose was to alternate between accurately preserving Socrates' philosophy and practice of doing it for future generations of scholars AND actively promoting Plato's own philosophical and political agenda. Scholars studying Plato have agreed that late Plato cared much less about accuracy and preservation of the Socratic historical legacy than early Plato. It seemed that the late Plato used the ethnographic genre for communicating and promoting his own philosophical ideas. Another reason for considering Plato's writing as educational ethnography is that modern educators treat Plato's Socratic dialogues as ethnography and use them as inspiration for designing their instruction (Cooney, Davis, & Henderson, 1975; Fernandez, 1994; Morse, 1994; Richards, 1991). Since

Plato's ethnography is organized as conversation (marked by Plato as "dialogues") I thought that the method of conversational analysis is appropriate (Moerman, 1988).

The Meno Dialogue begins with Meno, a young but already respected citizen, who asks Socrates about the origin of virtues – whether virtue comes from teaching or is given from birth. Socrates replies that he does not know what virtue is and invites Meno to consider the definition of virtue. After some exchanges of Socrates' cross-examination, in which Meno tries to define what virtue is, Meno becomes convinced that he does not know what virtue is either. However, he refuses to join Socrates' inquiry about what virtue is referring to the apparently known Sophist paradox of any such inquiry: if one knows what he searches for – why does he search for that, and if one does not know what he searches for – what does he search for?! Socrates dismisses the search paradox by claiming that any search is a "recollection" (anamnesis) of what the eternal soul in each human already knows. To demonstrate this Socrates asks Meno's slave to "recollect" how to double square area through a series of presenting the slave with sophisticated leading questions and demonstrations. Meno becomes convinced that inquiry in search of a definition of virtue is possible. However, instead of joining Socrates' inquiry about what virtue is, he insists on his initial inquiry about the origin of virtues. Socrates reluctantly agrees to accept Meno's inquiry and suggests setting several plausible hypotheses about what virtue is. Meno accepts this approach. When Socrates starts examining Meno about whether virtues are teachable, Anytus, a politically influential and affluent Athenian citizen, host and friend of Meno, joins them. Socrates invites Anytus to participate the discussion of whether virtues can be taught since Anytus has excellent credentials, since he knows many virtuous people in Athens. Anytus agrees (although with some trepidation). Socrates tries to examine Anytus' convictions about the teachability of virtue, but Anytus suspects that Socrates wants to trap him and force him to smear respectful Athenian citizens. Anytus, in anger at Socrates, leaves Socrates and Meno. Socrates continues examining Meno and leads him to accept that virtues are not based on knowledge or opinion or nature but are gifts from the gods for some selected people (like them). The Dialogue ends with Socrates' request for Meno to convince his friend Anytus that Socrates' intentions are noble and with Socrates' promise to jointly investigate what virtue is.

The purpose of this chapter is to develop a definition of dialogic pedagogy through analysis of Socratic dialogues. I selected the Meno Dialogue[1] for my analysis for several reasons. First, Meno is a relatively early Dialogue (and thus is less influenced by Plato's promotion of his own philosophy and politics). Second, it involves Socrates' discussions of many educational issues. My analysis can test whether Socrates' educational practice matches his declarations about his own practice and to what extent. Third, Meno seems to be one of the most influential Socratic Dialogues on modern pedagogy and most often referred to in educational literature (e.g., Burbules, 1993; Garlikov, 1998; Macmillan & Garrison, 1988; Pekarsky, 1994; Rud, 1997). In my research, I am more concerned about the pedagogical implications of Socratic dialogic pedagogy for modern education and less with Socrates' philosophical legacy or with the overall *self-contained* pedagogical consistence and essence of Socrates' ideas. Fourth, and probably more important, the Meno Dialogue includes several dialogues: two with free and well respected rich citizens of Athens, Meno and Anytus, and

---

[1] I capitalize "Dialogue" when I refer to Plato's entire piece. I use small letters to refer to various dialogues within Dialogue. For example, within the Meno Dialogue, there were three dialogues: Socrates' dialogue with Meno, with the Slave, and with Anytus.

one with Meno's Slave[2]. I suspected that this dialogic diversity could help me provide a comparative study focused on dialogic pedagogy. Is Socrates dialogue with the Slave different than his dialogues with free (rich) citizens? And if so, do social-political conditions of slavery affect Socrates' dialogue (and his dialogic pedagogy) with the Slave? This question may have important consequences for our modern educational practices because if social relations shape pedagogical dialogues, educators have to be careful in modeling their classroom pedagogical dialogues after certain Socratic dialogues.

To address my research question about the nature of Socratic dialogic pedagogy, I applied qualitative and quantitative conversational analyses to Plato's ethnography. Using the NVIVO software package (QSR International Pty Ltd), I focused on emerging educational "themes" (e.g., who initiated the main inquiry in a dialogue, how Socrates defines appropriate conversation with friends or foes) and on counting certain occurrences that constitute pedagogical discourse (e.g., leading questions, reflective statements). A participant's utterance was the main unit of my analysis (Bakhtin, Holquist, & Emerson, 1986).

FINDINGS

Socratic Dialogic Pedagogy as a Dramatic Encounter of Diverse Communities of Practice: Knowers, Debate-Contesters, Doers, and Learners

Internally-Persuasive Discourse

Analyzing the Meno Dialogue, I found that Socratic dialogic pedagogy is based on internally persuasive discourse (Bakhtin, 1991). Bakhtin defined *internally persuasive discourse* and contrasted it with *externally authoritarian[3] discourse*, "Both the authority of discourse and its internal persuasiveness may be united in a single word -- one that is simultaneously authoritative and internally persuasive -- despite the profound differences between these two categories of alien discourse. But such unity is rarely given -- it happens more frequently that an individual's becoming, an ideological process, is characterized by a sharp gap between these two categories: in one the [authoritarian][4] word (religious, political, moral, the word of a father, of adults and of teachers etc.) that does not know internal persuasiveness, in the other the internally persuasive word that is denied all privilege, backed

---

[2] I capitalize the word "Slave" out of my respect and opposition to the historical conditions of slavery in ancient Greece and slavery in general. Socrates (and/or Plato) did not feel it necessary to learn and refer to this person by name. I also refuse to refer to this person as "boy" as it has been done in several translations of Meno (e.g., Plato, 1984; Plato & Bluck, 1961). The Greek word "pais" παῖς used by Plato referred in Ancient Greek to "boy", "child", and "slave" (and "servant") (Liddell, Scott, Jones, & McKenzie, 1948, p. 1289), which is strikingly similar to the practice of using child names to refer to adult Black slaves in the USA or to adult slave-serfs in Russia in the XIX century and before. I think that it is safer and more respectful to avoid any assumption about the Slave's age. Ironically, in the light of this etymology, the term "pedagogy" might gain a new meaning -- the art and science of managing slaves.

[3] Bakhtin used the term "authoritative" but here I follow Morson (2004) who redefined Bakhtin's term as "authoritarian" probably after educational and psychological modern traditions discussing the teaching and parental styles (Baumrind, 1971; Lewin, Lippit, & White, 1939).

[4] In the original translation the word "authoritative" is used but we think it is more appropriate to use English word "authoritarian" to separate positive and negative use of authority that Bakhtin alluded here (see Morson, 2004 for more discussion of these concepts in Bakhtin).

up by no authority at all, and is frequently not even acknowledged in society (not by public opinion, nor by scholarly norms, nor by criticism), not even in the legal code. The struggle and dialogic interrelationships of these categories of ideological discourse are what usually determine the history of an individual ideological consciousness" (Bakhtin, 1991, p. 342). According to Socrates, an idea can be accepted only after honest and careful investigation on which each person, including his student, foe, or even a slave, is the final authority. As Woodruff (1998, p. 14) correctly put it, "Socratic education puts the responsibility for learning on the learner." The idea can stand only when it can sustain critique, imaginary experiment, and test of this idea provided by other people involved in investigation, "Come then, let us try to tell you what shape is. *See whether you will accept that* it is this: Let us say that shape is that which alone of existing things always follows color. Is that satisfactory to you, or do you look for it in some other way? I should be satisfied if you defined virtue in this way" (p.875, 75b). Socrates never refers to text, public opinion, poets, another philosopher, myth, his own status, or any other external authority as something that cannot be disputed and tested. Acceptance or rejection of an idea has to be done on the authority of internal persuasion itself as self-investigation.

The "axiom" of the Socratic dialogic pedagogy is that interlocutor's genuine opinion and convictions are the only matter in the investigation (Vlastos & Burnyeat, 1994). Nothing else is important: opinions of others, his own opinion, or even the authority of unshared truth. Socrates helps the interlocutor see contradictions within the interlocutor's own beliefs and his genuinely committed opinions. Honest dialogue is not a winning debate but rather commitment to one's search for a sincere agreement, "…if my questioner was one of those clever and disputatious debaters, I would say to him: 'I have given my answer; if it is wrong, it is your job to refute it.' Then, if they are friends as you and I are, and want to discuss with each other, they must answer in a manner more gentle and more proper to discussion. By this I mean that the answers must not only be true, but in terms admittedly known to the questioner. I too will try to speak in these terms" (p. 875, 75c). Socrates claims that it is inappropriate for well-intended interlocutors to answer in a way to break agreement with their partner. Agreement is a device for arrival to truth.

Agreement within the process of examination is the measure of truth in a dialogue. In Socratic dialogue, truth is understood as arriving at agreement after careful investigation of an issue based on critical and consistent thinking (Woodruff, 1998). Truth is something that survives joint refutation. When in the Gorgias Dialogue, Polus made a point with some irony that Socrates' position was more difficult to refute, Socrates replied, "Not difficult, surely, Polus. It's impossible. What's true is never refuted" (p. 817, 473b). Many times Socrates emphasizes that he wants to work with his interlocutors' serious convictions and their pursuit of truth (Vlastos & Burnyeat, 1994). The Meno Dialogue starts with disagreement between Meno and Socrates. Meno thought that the origin of virtues is a problematic issue while the definition of virtue is not; while Socrates thought in reverse: the definition of virtue is problematic while the origin of virtue is not (or, at least, less so). The endpoint of the Dialogue was Meno's agreement with Socrates. It was also the endpoint for the Slave as well but not for Anytus with whom Socrates did not reach an agreement. Socrates was clearly concerned with this failure and wanted Meno to continue dialoging with Anytus to reach such an agreement. Socrates' last words in the Dialogue were about Anytus, "You convince your guest friend Anytus here of these very things of which you have yourself been convinced, in order that he may be more amenable. If you succeed, you will also confer a benefit upon the Athenians" (p. 897, 100b).

The arrival at this Big Agreement between Meno and Socrates at the end of the Dialogue is done mainly not through Meno's encounter with Socrates' more powerful ideas (although Socrates did not hide and freely shared his own ideas with Meno, -- for example, his idea about learning through "recollection" rather than "teaching") but entirely through Meno's internal territory. Socrates did not contrast his own subjectivity with Meno's one but rather focused on Meno's subjectivity without leaving it. In this regard, it is useful to compare Piaget's and Socrates' approaches toward social learning. Piaget argued for usefulness of socio-cognitive conflicts (dissonance) where children (or adults) are exposed with conflicting views from their peers (Piaget & Elkind, 1968). Socrates tried to find internal contradictions within his students without exposing them with his own conflicting view (actually he exposed but not insisted on accepting them). Socrates' students always remained on their own territory of subjectivity. For example, when Meno and Socrates agreed to provide a definition of virtue, Socrates showed Meno that his definition was illustrative and did not focus on the essential general invariant constituting the definition of virtue, "I seem to be in great luck, Meno; while I am looking for one virtue, I have found you to have a whole swarm of them. But, Meno, to follow up the image of swarms, if I were asking you what is the nature of bees, and you said that they are many and of all kinds, what would you answer if I asked you: 'Do you mean that they are many and varied and different from one another in so far as they are bees? Or are they no different in that regard, but in some other respect, in their beauty, for example, or their size or in some other such way?' Tell me, what would you answer if thus questioned?" (p. 872, 72b). With the analogy of bee diversity, Socrates made Meno realize that his original illustrative definition of virtue was not satisfactory for Meno himself since he, Meno, would not like a similar illustrative definition in the case of bees. Thus, Socrates helped Meno realize that he had a contradiction between Meno's own tacit standard for conceptual definitions revealed in the case of bee diversity and his own illustrative definition of virtue. Again, Socrates revealed the contradiction inside Meno's own thinking and not between Meno's thinking and Socrates' thinking, as Piaget seemed to argue in his notion of socio-cognitive dissonance[5]. In the Sophist Dialogue, the Visitor described this practice of Socratic dialogic pedagogy in the following way, "They [i.e., Socratic teachers] cross-examine someone when he thinks he's saying something though he's saying nothing. Then, since his opinions will vary inconsistently, these people [i.e., Socratic teachers] will easily scrutinize them. They collect his opinions together during the discussion, put them side by side, and show that they conflict with each other at the same time on the same subjects in relations to the same things and in the same respects" (p. 250-251, 230b).

Another important feature of Socrates' focus on revealing internal contradictions in his interlocutors is that he did not objectify these revelations. He did not tell his students, "You're contradicting yourself," but rather tried to help his students realize this by themselves (although he was not successful with Anytus). Socrates' focus was on the students' realization of an internal contradiction in their own reasoning.

---

[5] I do not claim that Socratic dialogic pedagogy with its focus on the teacher's revealing of internal contradictions in students is better for learning than Piaget's focus on socio-cognitive dissonance. Rather I use Piaget to describe Socratic dialogic pedagogy through the contrast. Moreover, on occasion, Socrates seemed to use Piagetian socio-cognitive dissonance when he introduced the idea of learning as "recall" of eternal ideas by the immortal soul to Meno (pp, 880-886, 80d-86c).

Analyzing the three Socratic dialogues in the Meno Dialogue, I found that Socrates revealed nine big and small contradictions in Meno's thinking, one contradiction in the Slave's thinking (i.e., doubling the square area when the square side is doubled), and two contradictions in Anytus' thinking (e.g., Anytus claiming that Sophists were bad without experiencing them). This finding allows us to suggest that revealing internal contradictions in the students' thinking and helping them to realize such contradictions is the essential feature of Socratic internally persuasive discourse and, thus, Socratic dialogic pedagogy.

Many scholars of Socratic dialogue (e.g., Goldman, 1984; Rud, 1997) have commented on the *dialectical* nature of Socratic dialogues. My analysis of the Meno Dialogue supports the claim that Socratic dialogic pedagogy involves a focus on questioning contradictions in his students' thinking (see table 3 for the distributions of the participants' statements involving critical meta-reflection on the interlocutor's previous contributions). However, this view of dialectics common in Socrates' times in Ancient Greece does not seem how we use this term today. Our contemporary understanding of dialectics is probably rooted in Hegel's philosophy (1967). According to Hegel, dialectics involves analysis of mutually constituting oppositions like day and night or nature and nurture. These oppositions are opposed to each other but mutually constitute each other and their own boundaries. In this Hegelian sense, the contradictions that Socrates revealed in his interlocutors were apparently not dialectical. Actually, I could not find analysis of any dialectical contradictions in the Meno Dialogue[6]. Rather, Socratic dialogic pedagogy seems to involve "asking questions and refuting errors" (Plato, 1997, p. 1632, Epinomis, 991c), using imaginary experiments and hypotheses, and "collecting and dividing" varieties of a category into classes (Plato, 1997, pp. 542-543, Phaedrus, 265e-266d).

Socratic dialogic pedagogy is based on internally persuasive discourse and involves transformation of the student's subjectivity or the student's "ideological becoming" using Bakhtin's words (Bakhtin, 1991, p. 342; A. F. Ball & Freedman, 2004). Bakhtin refers to ideological becoming as "how we develop our [own] way of viewing the world, our system of ideas" through transformation from participation in authoritarian to internally persuasive discourse (Freedman & Ball, 2004, p. 5). Fishman (1985) is right that the Socratic motto "Know Thyself" should not be confused with the contemporary motto "Be Yourself" because the former requires dramatic and often painful transformation of the self through self-examination while the latter often involves affirmation of self as it is to be accepted by self and others. This dramatic transformation of self was very successful for Meno, rather problematic for the Slave, and arguably unsuccessful for Anytus. By the end of the Dialogue, Meno realized that he did not know what virtue is, learned that virtues are not teachable or natural, started appreciating his own state of epistemological and existential uncertainty ("numbness"), and learned about the intellectual and moral elite that Socrates and he himself belonged to along with many other things. The Slave probably learned about doubling square areas along with the fact that he could be just a tool for illustration in his masters' discussion. Anytus learned probably more distrust of Socrates as being dangerous and disrespectful to other Athenian citizens. However, it is unclear what, if anything, Socrates himself learned

---

[6] In my view, it is possible to find germs of dialectical contradictions in Socratic reasoning about shape: round and straight shapes are different but at the same time the same in their shapeness. But this dialectics is not developed in Socratic dialogues. It seemed Hegel who pushed it further to introduce a contradiction between the particular and the general (or between concrete and abstract).

from the dialogue beyond about state of mind of his interlocutors (I will discuss this point later).

Activation and Transformation of the Student's Prior Knowledge

Since Socratic dialogic pedagogy essentially involves transformation of the student's subjectivity, Socrates always starts with pedagogical diagnostics -- explicating how the student thinks about the issue (Macmillan & Garrison, 1988). As Foucault pointed out with regard to Socratic pedagogy, "He [the student of Socrates] needs to know... the fact that he does not know [what he thinks he knows] and, at the same time, that he knows more than he thinks he does" (Foucault & Gros, 2006, p. 128). In case of Meno, Socrates asked Meno to provide his definition of virtue (along with Meno's views on many other issues that they discussed). In case of the Slave, Socrates asked him about whether square area doubles when the square side doubles. In case of Anytus, Socrates asked Anytus if virtues are teachable. Using modern educational terminology, Socratic dialogic pedagogy is essentially constructivist despite the fact that Socrates himself believed that learning involves recollection of already known but forgotten knowledge by the immortal soul, "As the soul is immortal, has been born often and has seen all things here and in the underworld, there is nothing which it has not learned; so it is in no way surprising that it can recollect the things it knew before, both about virtue and other things. As the whole of nature is akin, and the soul has learned everything, nothing prevents a man, after recalling one thing only -- a process men call learning -- discovering everything else for himself, if he is brave and does not tire of the search, for searching and learning are, as a whole, recollection" (p. 880, 81c-d). Philosophically, the Socratic-Platonic doctrine of eternal ideal forms existing "out there" and being independent of people (learners) captured in this quote is the cornerstone of philosophical positivism (see Fishman, 1985 for more discussion of Socratic-Platonic positivism) and, arguably, of modern educational practices based on transmission of knowledge. Nevertheless, I claim with evidence at my hands that Socrates, as an educational practitioner, was an educational constructivist.

How can we reconcile this contradiction between Socrates the philosopher and Socrates the educator? Although, Socrates insisted that the end knowledge is eternal and indifferent to learners – in this point he was anti-constructivist (see D. C. Phillips, 1995; 2000 for discussion of the main tenets of educational constructivism) – the way of accessing this eternal and indifferent knowledge through self-examination assisted by Socrates is very subjective and constructive. Although the end-point of knowing is eternal, universal, and impersonal, the way of "recollection" is active, personal, and particular. Socrates introduced "discovery learning" (Bruner, 1996, p. xii) and insisted that the person is "the final agency for his or her own learning" (Purkey's term, cited in Klag, 1994, p. 1). The role of the teacher is only to facilitate this process of active discovery. He compared himself with a midwife (Plato, 1997, pp. 165-180, Theaetetus, 149-162). A midwife does not give the birth of a child to the mother but rather helps the pregnant woman to give birth. It is possible for a midwife to give birth for the mother. Similarly, the Socratic teacher does not give knowledge to the student but rather helps the student to reveal the knowledge in his or her own thinking. Socrates believed that it is impossible to give knowledge to the student,

Meno: Yes, Socrates, but how do you mean that we do not learn, but that what we call learning is recollection? Can you teach me that this is so?

Socrates: As I said just now, Meno, you are a rascal. You now ask me if I can teach you, when I say there is no teaching but recollection, in order to show me up at once as contradicting myself.

Meno: No, by Zeus, Socrates, that was not my intention when I spoke, but just a habit. If you can somehow show me that things are as you say, please do so (p., 880, 82).

Thus, *epistemologically* Socrates was a radical anti-constructivist while *pedagogically* he was a radical constructivist. Socrates' constructivist radicalism is rooted in his persuasion that a person can discover knowledge only through critical self-examination of his or her own opinions, assumptions, beliefs, and ideas. According to Socrates the traditional teaching of transmission of knowledge (Socrates seemed to equate teaching with transmission of knowledge) is not simply ineffective or undesirable but impossible altogether. By the term "*knowledge*", Socrates meant ideas requiring understanding rather than *procedural information* about ways in practical affairs or directions to a particular place that, he agreed, can be taught directly through transmission of knowledge, "A man who knew the way to Larissa, or anywhere else you like, and went there and guided others would surely lead them well and correctly?" (p. 895, 97). Using a modern example, the question of "how does the VCR remote control work" can be addressed at a comprehension level involving understanding physical and electronic processes of wireless interaction between the remote control, VCR, and the TV or at a procedural level involving pressing specific buttons for achieving desired outcomes on the TV display. According to Socrates, in contrast to learning for understanding, learning procedural information does not require "recollection" – critical self-examination. For teaching procedural information, Socrates seemed to be a non-constructivist[7].

In other Dialogues like Republic, Socrates warned against teaching comprehensive knowledge requiring understanding from the student as if it is procedural information. He brought essentially two main reasons for this warning. First, even though the student might learn successfully a procedure leading him or her to the correct outcome (e.g., the correct formula of square area as in case of the Socrates-Slave dialogue), the student may often have tacit and un-scrutinized beliefs and assumptions that contradict the learned knowledge (e.g., the Slave had believed that doubling the square side leads to doubling the square area). Learning comprehensive knowledge as procedural information does not help the student to solve this contradiction (or even notice it). Second, learning comprehensive knowledge as a procedure leading to a practical success does not teach the student why this success is guaranteed by this procedure. The student does not master the information but rather information masters the student (the student is the slave of information). When a situation deviates from the ideal expected by the procedure (pressing the VCR remote control button does not produce the desired outcome), without comprehensive knowledge the student can become helpless. Socrates argued that regardless of how correct it is, procedural information

---

[7] I try to be careful with this claim about Socrates' non-constructivist views about learning procedural information. My evidence is indirect and based on an assumption that Socrates uses the term "teaching" consistently as transmission of knowledge. If it were not the case, Socrates might have much more complex constructivist views on teaching/learning procedural information as well. However, I could not find any evidence of such complex constructivist views and since I found indirect evidence for his non-constructivist views, I cautiously assume that Socrates believed that teaching as transmission of knowledge is possible and legitimate in case of teaching procedures.

in place of comprehensive knowledge is a dangerous mistake of judgment. Its danger is rooted in its correctness leading the student to practical successes – it gives the student false confidence that he or she is knowledgeable while actually he or she is still ignorant. From Socrates' point of view, it would be better for the learner to have wrong procedural knowledge or no knowledge at all than correct procedural knowledge in place of comprehensive knowledge because in the former case there are more chances that the student becomes aware about his or her ignorance and turns to critical self-examination.

In my view, although Socratic opposition between teaching comprehensive knowledge versus procedural information is very fruitful for educational debates, it is too strong and too decontextualized. I think that procedural knowledge in place of comprehensive is not as dangerous as Socrates thought and comprehensive knowledge is not always desirable or even possible depending on goals and circumstances. Learning comprehensive knowledge can be very costly in terms of time, intellectual (e.g., people have limited attention power to focus on all possible inquires) and material resources (e.g., somebody should provide food and shelter while another does critical self-examination; in case of Socrates, those "somebody" were slaves and, probably, his wife). In many practical cases, procedural information is enough for good functioning. Even more, learning comprehensive knowledge can be a distraction from the main activity that people are involved (just imagine a person searching on the Internet for the electronic principles behind the functioning of his TV remote control instead of watching his or her favorite TV program!). Finally, we live in a society with complex networks of division of labor. We can be well-functioned ignorants ("ignorants" in Socratic sense) because comprehensive knowledge is distributed across the networks. Other people can do the work requiring comprehensive knowledge for us. We only need to learn how to use these networks when our procedural knowledge becomes inefficient (e.g., asking for help a car mechanic in a car shop when our car malfunctions).

On the other hand, our rapidly changing social and technological world makes procedural knowledge obsolete very quickly. We need to have meta-learning skills based on comprehensive knowledge to adapt well to quickly changing procedural information. Besides successful participation in rapidly changing networks of distributed practices also requires learning comprehensive knowledge. In essence, I argue for a dynamic hybrid of comprehensive and procedural knowledge. Educational institutions should focus on helping students learn how to manage this hybridity. Rather than to doze comprehensive and procedural knowledge in the pre-designed academic curricula, students have to have an opportunity to make their own decisions facilitated by the teacher about whether they should learn specific knowledge procedurally or conceptually.

Unfortunately, as it seemed to be the case in Socrates' times, conventional teaching too much, if not entirely, focuses on teaching comprehensive knowledge as procedural information. It is often that a conventional teacher in response to a student's wrong answer (e.g., "2+2=3") would correct the answer her/himself, "No, it is wrong. 2+2=4," or would ask other students "to help" – i.e., to provide the correct answer. A good conventional teacher might try to explain why 2+2=4 but she or he rarely would work with the student's subjectivity of how and why the student came with the answer she or he came with and if there is a contradiction in the student's thinking[8] as Socratic dialogic pedagogy demands.

---

[8] It appears that Taiwanese and Japanese math traditional teachers work with the students' subjectivities more often than many Western traditional teachers do (Corser, Gardner, & University of Michigan, 1989).

Socratic focus on the teacher working with the students' subjectivity, rather than cover and deliver of the prescribed curriculum, makes important demands on the teacher's improvisation and creativity since the students' subjectivity cannot be fully known in advance and is in the state of constant change during the Socratic lesson. Socrates could not predict what Meno, the Slave, or Anytus said or asked. Socrates could not plan his lesson. His guidance was collaborative in a sense that his students guided him how to guide them. Because of that, Socratic guidance is always sensitive to the educational needs of the student. The curriculum is also a product of teacher-student collaboration. Indeed, even in the case of the Socrates-Slave dialogue, Socrates could not know in advance if the Slave had wrong understanding about the relationship between the square side length and the square area. The Slave might know the relationship or experienced different problems. In these cases, Socrates had to alternate his instruction and curriculum to make his demonstration of the Slave's "recollection" successful for Meno.

Problem-Based Learning

There is a claim in the literature that Socratic pedagogy is inquiry and problem based (Burbules, 1993; Garlikov, 1998; Pekarsky, 1994; Rud, 1997). By inquiry or problem, it is often meant that puzzlement or uncertainty is important for a participant (he or she wants some problem to be addressed). In the Socrates-Meno dialogue, I have found many big and small apparent inquiries posed by Meno and Socrates such as: what is the origin of virtues (Meno), what is the invariant definition[9] of virtue (Socrates), what is the invariant definition of shape and color (Socrates), how can people recollect their knowledge from their immortal souls (Meno), is virtue knowledge (Socrates and Meno), how to double the area of a square (Socrates), what is the length of a double area square (Socrates), is virtue knowledge (Socrates), can virtue be taught (Meno), is virtue a natural feature of one's character (Meno), and what is the difference between knowledge and opinion (Socrates). It is clear from the dialogues that Meno genuinely involved in all but, probably, mathematical inquiries – Meno really wants to know the origin of virtue, the invariant definition of shape and so on. As to Socrates, the issue is murkier. It is rather clear that he genuinely wants to investigate the invariant definition of the concept of virtue. He invites Meno to do that, "Since we are of one mind that one should seek to find out what one does not know, shall we try to find out together what virtue is?" (Plato, 1997, p. 886, 86c). It is less clear if Socrates develops the invariant definitions of shape and color "on-the-fly" while talking with Meno or he has known these definitions in advance. Unless Socrates pretends (probably to flirt with Meno?), he communicates that he had made some real efforts to come up with the definitions on Meno's demand. However, it is clear Socrates is not entirely honest when he claims, "… I myself do not have the answer when I perplex others, but I am more perplexed than anyone when I cause perplexity in others" (p. 879, 80c) (see more discussion of Socrates' pedagogical dishonesty and its consequences in Pekarsky, 1994). Socrates is clearly not perplexed himself when he tried to perplex Meno, the Slave, and Anytus about issues they discussed: he

---

[9] Using Piaget's terminology (it is interesting that some scholars of use of dialogue for teaching view pedagogical dialogue as a game, see for example Burbules, 1993; Macmillan & Garrison, 1988), we distinguish an "illustrative definition" of a concept used initially by Meno from an "invariant definition" of a concept used by Socrates (and later Piaget). An illustrative definition uses examples to induce the concept in another person while an invariant definition extracts the essential general invariant common for all variety of the concept's phenomenological appearances (Piaget & Elkind, 1968).

positively knows in advance how to double square area and he positively knows in advance that virtues are not teachable. My judgment is that some inquiries posed by Socrates himself and by Meno are genuine inquiries for Socrates that he had to address on-the-fly while others were rhetorical and not genuine inquires for Socrates (e.g., how to double the area of square or are virtues teachable).

As I have no doubts that both Meno and Socrates were genuinely involved, at least, in some inquires during the dialogues, it becomes a more problematic issue for the Slave and, especially, Anytus. Indeed, after Socrates forced the Slave to realize that doubling a square side does not lead to doubling the square area, the Slave was also forced to realize that he does not know how to make a double area square. Socrates was right when he told Meno that he moved the Slave from the state of certainty to the state of uncertainty about how to double square area. The question for us is whether this state of uncertainty is an inquiry for the Slave (it is obviously not for Socrates since he was clearly certain how to double square area in advance). It is true that any inquiry involves some kind of uncertainty, but is it true that any uncertainty generates an inquiry? I doubt that it is the case. For example, a medieval theological question of how many angels can dance on the top of a pin may generate an uncertainty but rarely an inquiry in a modern person (besides questions that a modern person might ask of: why did medieval theologians ask this strange question, what did they actually mean by this strange question?). A modern person may not see any relevance, importance, and urgency to address this uncertainty. A modern person can follow the logic of medieval texts, like the Slave followed Socrates, -- he or she may agree or disagree with some statements of the texts – without being involved in an inquiry (Macmillan & Garrison, 1988).

Inquiry is characterized by the participant's active orientation to pursue and address the uncertainty. Macmillan and Garrison (1988) suggest that after the Slave was perplexed by Socrates, he became motivated to have a math problem. What we have in the Socrates-Slave dialogue, however, is the Slave's recognition of his lack of certainty and knowledge without any evidence for his active orientation for pursuing it, "By Zeus, Socrates, I do not know" (p. 883, 84) replied the Slave. In contrast, when Meno faced with an uncertainty induced by Socrates, he openly articulated his active orientation to pursuing his inquiry, "And what do you say color is, Socrates?" (p. 876, 76). Of course, the absence of evidence did not necessary mean that the Slave did not have his active orientation toward his uncertainty. Maybe, the Slave had an inquiry but, in contrast to the free-citizen Meno, it might be inappropriate for a slave to ask questions to Socrates. Indeed, unlike Meno and Anytus, the Slave did not ask Socrates any question during the Socrates-Slave dialogue, see table 1. Wittgenstein (2001), however, doubted that any inquiry can be pursued entirely in private, arguing that there is always a community (immediate or mediated) behind any inquiry: addressing an inquiry involves addressees (cf. Bakhtin, 1986). It is doubtful (but still not impossible) that the Slave had such a community to which he could address mathematical matters.

As to Anytus, it is difficult to find any uncertainty or puzzlement in his turns. It is highly doubtful that Anytus accepts Socrates' question about whether virtues are teachable as a genuine inquiry rather he seems to suspect that Socrates' true intention is to defame Athens' most respectful citizens, "I think, Socrates, that you easily speak ill of people. I would advise you, if you will listen to me, to be careful. Perhaps also in another city, and certainly here, it is easier to injure people than to benefit them. I think you know that yourself" (p. 893, 95).

In general, through all three dialogues, there seem to be many struggles of the participants' unshared intentions: Meno wants to investigate the origin of virtues while

Socrates wants to investigate the invariant definition of virtue; Socrates wants to use the Slave to illustrate to Meno that learning is about recollection rather than teaching while the Slave has to serve to whatever whim the masters require from him; Socrates wants to use Anytus to help Meno realize that virtues are unteachable while Anytus suspects that Socrates wants to defame respectful Athens citizens and corrupt Meno.

The only accord of intentions that was reached in the three dialogues was of Socrates with Meno in the second part of their dialogue. This accord was based on Meno's realization induced and assisted by Socrates that he does not know what the virtue is and that this realization is useful rather than harmful – after Socrates' demonstration of the Slave's "recollection" of math truths, Meno appreciates the "torpedo touch" induced by Socrates on him that immobilizes his sense of certainty with regard to what is virtue that Meno had faulty had before. The accord was also assured by Socrates as he accepted that it was Meno rather than he who should legitimately define their collective inquiry – they should investigate the origin of virtues as Meno wanted rather than the invariant definition of virtue as Socrates wanted, "If I were directing you, Meno, and not only myself, we would not have investigated whether virtue is teachable or not before we had investigated what virtue itself is. But because you do not even attempt to rule yourself, in order that you may be free, but you try to rule me and do so, I will agree with you -- for what can I do? So we must, it appears, inquire into the qualities of something the nature of which we do not yet know" (p. 887, 86d). No such accord was reached by Socrates with the Slave or Anytus.

Socrates realizes that the entire event is directed by Meno's inquiry about the origin of the virtues and that he, Socrates, himself has volunteered and committed to help. This volunteered commitment obligated Socrates to follow Meno's inquiry rather that to insist that Meno has to follow Socrates' own inquiry about the invariant definition of virtue after Meno realized usefulness of this inquiry. Socrates' repetitious invitations for Meno to join his, Socrates', own inquiry and Socrates' non-rhetorical use of "we" in the second part of the Meno-Socrates dialogue suggest that Socrates' vision of learning was probably participatory and communal. He seemed to see learning (and his guidance) as joining of a community of certain practice of self-investigation, "It follows from this reasoning, Meno, that virtue appears to be present in those of us who may possess it as a gift from the gods. We shall have clear knowledge of this when, before we investigate how it comes to be present in men, we first try to find out what virtue in itself is. But now the time has come for me to go" (p. 897, 100b). Socrates did not extend this invitation to his community of practice to the Slave and Anytus, probably, because they did not have inquiries on their own and because Socrates did not feel that it was appropriate and/or necessary/possible perhaps for political reasons (and elitist political views that Socrates, if not Plato, hold)[10].

All pursued inquiries in Socratic dialogues were unilateral and never collective, never involving Socrates. Despite Socrates' numerous statements about self-investigation as the core of his practice, we never witness this practice in dialogues presented by Plato. We have never witnessed Socrates' own transformation and Socrates' own "numbness" of self-touch by "torpedo fish". Being a stunning "torpedo fish", or stinging "gadfly", or facilitating

---

[10] It is interesting to consider an imagined case, in which instead of the Slave, the participant of the dialogue had been slave Aesop, the creator of many politically charged fables. We wonder if dramatic non-cooperation that Aesop could indirectly communicate to Socrates might have disrupted Socrates' smooth guiding about doubling square area and led to genuine inquiries on both sides.

"midwife"[11] for others, we do not see how (and whether) Socrates applied all these approaches to himself. We can only guess how this community of practice of self-investigation was in action since Plato did not seem to show us any genuinely collective investigation of a shared inquiry by Socrates and other members of his community of practice. Some scholars (e.g., Rud, 1997) argue that the lack of collective inquiries and their investigations is really a flaw of Socratic dialogic pedagogy, while the others (e.g., Garlikov, 1998) say that collaborative investigation of joined inquiry is not necessary for good guidance. I will return to this issue later.

In sum, my analysis of the Meno Dialogue yields ambivalence and contradiction of how much Problem-Based Learning is a necessary part of Socratic dialogic pedagogy. On the one hand, the Meno Dialogue is driven by the student's inquiry and the teacher's counter-inquiry. The teacher did repetitiously proclaim the collective and personal nature of inquiries and invite his student to join his own personal inquiry. On the other hand, throughout the Dialogue, the inquiries remain unshared and their persuasion remains non-collaborative. Even more, the dialogues with the Slave and Anytus were arguably without any inquiries at all demonstrating that successful learning can be non inquiry or Problem-Based.

Anatomy of Socratic Micro-Guidance: Leading-Option Rhetorical Questions

Unlike triadic discourse widespread in traditional US classrooms (Mehan, 1979), Socratic dialogic pedagogy was based on dyadic discourse. Socrates asked a "leading question" (Macmillan & Garrison, 1988, p. 153) while an interlocutor replied affirmatively to it. Many scholars and educators commented that Socratic dialogue overwhelmingly involves asking questions (Garlikov, 1998; Rud, 1997). My analysis validates this observation. As table 1 shows, Socrates overwhelmingly asked questions versus making statements, while his interlocutors were placed in the reverse position of making statements in response to Socrates' questions rather than asking questions by themselves.

---

[11] These are analogies that Socrates used to describe himself across many dialogues presented by Plato.

Table 1. Comparative analysis of dialogic turns in the Meno Dialogue

dialogue	Participants	NN of turns	Words per turn on average	Teacher-student word length ratio	Questions/ Uncertainty	Statements	Ontology
Meno-Socrates	Meno	207	8.53		14.49%	89.37%	6.28%
	Socrates	207	37.20	4.36	72.46%	39.13%	18.36%
Socrates-Slave	Slave	51	1.88		0.00%	100.00%	0.00%
	Socrates	51	16.27	8.65	100.00%	7.84%	0.00%
Socrates-Anytus	Anytus	24	13.00		8.33%	95.83%	54.17%
	Socrates	24	70.79	5.45	95.83%	29.17%	66.67%

Notes: Percentages were defined as occurrences in dialogic turns toward the total number of dialogic turns by the participant. Here and further in other tables, the coding categories (e.g., Questions, Statements, Ontology) were not mutually exclusive and did not necessarily yield 100% total as one dialogic turn may have all of them together.

Mehan (1979) has found that the classroom discourse in traditional US classroom (beyond direct instruction – lecturing and demonstration) is heavily based on triadic exchange between the teacher and the students. In the first turn, the teacher initiates the exchange by asking information-known question (e.g., Teacher: "Two plus two equals...Mary?"). In the second turn, the student replies to the teacher (e.g., Student Mary: "Four"). And, finally, in the third turn, the teacher positively or negatively evaluates the student's answer (e.g., Teacher: "That's right"). In the entire Meno Dialogue, I have found only one such triadic exchange and even this case it is more complex than a traditional triadic exchange,

> Socrates: What are they? Tell me, as I could mention other shapes to you if you bade me do so, so do you mention other virtues.
> Meno: I think courage is a virtue, and moderation, wisdom, and munificence, and very many others.
> Socrates: We are having the same trouble again, Meno, though in another way; we have found many virtues while looking for one, but we cannot find the one which covers all the others (p. 874, 74).

It is quite obvious that Socrates knew the answer of the question he asked Meno in advance. Meno provided the answer that Socrates expected – a quite correct answer. However, Socrates evaluated it negatively not because it was a wrong answer to the question he asked but because this answer illuminated the problem in Meno's general reasoning when he had tried to define the concept of virtue using his illustrative definitions. Thus, Socrates' evaluation here was not locally applied to the initiation question as in the case of triadic exchange in traditional US classrooms but globally applied to the entire discourse as an indicator of the problem. When Socrates asked answer-known rhetorical questions, he often did *not* provide his evaluation to the interlocutor's answer (Hansen has made a similar observation analyzing the Theaetetus Dialogue, Hansen, 1988):

> Socrates: How many feet is twice two feet? Work it out and tell me.
> SLAVE: Four, Socrates.
> Socrates: *Now* we could have another figure twice the size of this one, with the four sides equal like this one (p. 882, 82d).

We call answer-known questions rhetorical, because unlike genuine information-seeking questions, the inquirer knows the answer in advance. In the traditional US classroom, the primary purpose of such a rhetorical question is usually to test if the interlocutor knows the answer (Lemke, 1990; Matusov et al., 2002; Mehan, 1979). A secondary purpose of answer-known rhetorical question is to establish common ground (i.e., shared attention, intersubjectivity) between the teacher and the student as a step in their joint guided reasoning. I argue that Socrates used often this "secondary" function of answer-known rhetorical questions as his primary function for these questions. That is why he did not use follow-up evaluations. The evidence for my argument is in Socrates' use of the word's "now" or "then" (or similar words) in the third turn to make a transition from step1 of the established common ground to the next step in joint guided reasoning. An exception from this use of answer-known rhetorical questions by Socrates, I found on the boundary between Socrates-Slave and Meno-Socrates dialogues, when Socrates made Meno evaluate the Slave's answer. The evaluation of the Slave's answer that a doubled square side leads to a doubled area of the square was done for Meno rather than for the Slave himself:

> Socrates: Come now, try to tell me how long each side of this will be. The side of this is two feet. What about each side of the one which is its double?
> SLAVE: Obviously, Socrates, it will be twice the length.
> Socrates: You see, Meno, that I am not teaching the boy anything, but all I do is question him. And now he thinks he knows the length of the line on which an eight-foot figure is based. Do you agree?
> Meno: I do.
> Socrates: And does he know?
> Meno: Certainly not.
> Socrates: He thinks it is a line twice the length?
> Meno: Yes (p. 882, 82e).

Another secondary function of answer-known rhetorical questions that became primary for the Socrates was to determine a gap between the interlocutor and the truth (or, often meaning, Socrates' own thinking). As I have discussed above, Socrates always started with the student's own position that Socrates views as erroneous one as we can see at the beginning of each of the three dialogues: Meno-Socrates (i.e., what is virtue), Socrates-Slave (i.e., what is the area of a doubled sided square), and Socrates-Anytus (i.e., are virtues teachable). It was apparent that Socrates evaluated the interlocutors' erroneous answers privately to develop an instructional strategy of asking leading-option questions to develop and lead agreements between him and his interlocutor to the desired conclusion what he would consider as the truth.

I argue that Socratic dialogic pedagogy is based on constant establishment and maintenance of teacher-student agreements by the teacher. In agreement-based guidance, the teacher does not monopolize evaluation because the teacher's public evaluation of the student's answers contradicts the essence of the agreement-based guidance and the ethics of "friendly discussion" defined by Socrates in the following way, "if my questioner was one of those clever and disputatious debaters, I would say to him: 'I have given my answer; if it is wrong, it is your job to refute it.' Then, if they are friends as you and I are, and want to discuss with each other, they must answer in a manner more gentle and more proper to discussion. By this I mean that the answers must not only be true, but in terms admittedly known to the questioner. I too will try to speak in these terms" (p. 875, 75c-d). According to Socrates, friendly discussion is based on answers and questions – I would add – that are agreeable by the other side.

As table 2 shows, Socrates realized his agreeable guidance mainly through asking leading-option rhetorical questions in dyadic exchanges,

Table 2. Comparative analysis of % of questions asked by participants in the Meno Dialogue

dialogue	Participant	Total questions	Information-seeking questions	Clarification questions	Answer-known rhetorical questions	Leading-option rhetorical questions	Other questions
Meno-Socrates	Meno	14.49%	8.70%	4.83%	0.48%	0.97%	0.48%
	Socrates	72.46%	5.80%	2.90%	4.35%	60.39%	0.97%
Socrates-Slave	Slave	0.00%	0.00%	0.00%	0.00%	0.00%	0.00%
	Socrates	100.00%	0.00%	0.00%	25.49%	74.51%	0.00%
Socrates-Anytus	Anytus	8.33%	4.17%	0.00%	0.00%	4.17%	0.00%
	Socrates	95.83%	8.33%	0.00%	20.83%	75.00%	0.00%

Notes: For all columns, 100% constitutes the total number of dialogical turns in a specific dialogue. Categories are not mutually exclusive.

In a leading-option rhetorical question, the teacher provides the option among other options on which the teacher expects the student to agree. The leading-option rhetorical question is designed in such a way to provide a sense of choice and decision making for the interlocutor although this choice is false and decision making is not genuine one,

> Socrates: ...if I were asking you what is the nature of bees, and you said that they are many and of all kinds, what would you answer if I asked you: "Do you mean that they are many and varied and different from one another in so far as they are bees? Or are they no different in that regard, but in some other respect, in their beauty, for example, or their size or in some other such way?" Tell me, what would you answer if thus questioned?
> Meno: I would say that they do not differ from one another in being bees (p. 872, 72b).

In the given example, the choice in which different bees do not have something in common was expected by Socrates as being unattractive for Meno because otherwise – if different bees are different and have nothing in common – they would not have been called "bees." By calling diverse species as "bees", Socrates indirectly blocked the alternative option as a genuinely possible one. As I show below, Socrates' move is not as straightforward and honest as it may look like.

I think that Macmillan and Garrison (1988, p. 151) are right criticizing commentators of Socrates' leading option rhetorical questions who claim that Socrates cheated by providing the correct answers to his interlocutors in his questions. Indeed, presenting the "correct" answers by the teacher does not guarantee that the student would accept it. There is evidence in the Meno Dialogue, that Socrates' interlocutors (except the Slave) disagreed or non-cooperated with Socrates' "correct" answers that he presented in his leading option rhetorical questions (see table 3). In my view, by itself presenting the "correct" answers – the answers that the teacher shared – is not evidence of cheating (i.e., the teacher's brainwash of the student). Instead, as Macmillan and Garrison correctly argue, Socrates *taught* his interlocutors with help of his leading questions (rather than just let them recall what they already know as Socrates, himself claimed). The teacher gives correct answers to the student and thus attracts the student's attention to certain things; this is the essence of any direct instruction. However, the question remains *how* Socrates taught his students: through internally persuasive discourse OR through hidden authoritarian discourse? In my view, and in contrast to Macmillan and Garrison's judgment, it is the latter.

Table 3. Comparative analysis of % of statements made by the participants in the Meno Dialogue

dialogue	Participant	Total statements	Providing Information	Agreement-Affirmation	Disagreement-Rejection	Non-cooperation with interlocutor	Critical meta-reflection on the interlocutor	Encouragement	Other statements
Meno-Socrates	Meno	89.37%	8.21%	79.23%	3.38%	0.97%	0.97%	0.00%	1.45%
	Socrates	39.13%	19.32%	1.93%	2.42%	3.38%	13.04%	0.97%	4.26%
Socrates-Slave	Slave	100.00%	25.49%	74.51%	0.00%	0.00%	0.00%	0.00%	0.00%
	Socrates	7.84%	1.96%*	0.00%	0.00%	0.00%	1.96%	5.88%	0.00%
Socrates-Anytus	Anytus	95.83%	29.17%	66.67%	0.00%	8.33%	4.17%	0.00%	0.00%
	Socrates	29.17%	12.50%	4.17%	0.00%	4.17%	12.50%	4.17%	0.00%

Notes: For all columns, 100% constitutes the total number of dialogical turns in a specific dialogue. Categories are not mutually exclusive.

* Socrates obviously provided information to the Slave by non-verbal means of drawing geometrical figures during the dialogue (Macmillan & Garrison, 1988).

All explicitly or implicitly presented choices in the successful leading-option rhetorical question, but one, are designed to be unattractive to the interlocutor. By offering many choices, a leading-option rhetorical question creates an illusion in the interlocutor that it just reveals the already existing idea in him while it induces a new way of reasoning (or even a new desire) in the interlocutor. I respectfully disagree with Woodruff who argues that, "Although Socrates has controlled the discussion and led it to this point by design, Euthyphro must take responsibility for the result because of his own commitments to the premises of the arguments" (Woodruff, 1998, p. 18). Rather, the false choices of the leading-option rhetorical question create a sense of ownership and commitment in the student that the leading option presented by the teacher is the student's own internally persuasive one.

I want to illustrate the manipulative and imposing character of leading-option rhetorical questions by bringing a fragment of the dialogue from the popular Soviet comedy movie *Foundling* made in 1939. In the movie, a little girl Natashenka left her parents without permission in a big city. She moved from one adult to another asking them for help. At some point, she bumped into a childless couple who was going out of city for their dacha (a summer cottage in the city suburbs) for the weekend. The little girl told them her story and how she violated her parents' rule and wandered on her own. She exclaimed that her parents probably so worried about her and probably were so angry with her naughty behavior that they would "tear her head apart" when they would find her. Initially the couple planned to bring the little girl to the city police but the more this childless couple talked with the little girl, the more the wife became attached to the little girl. Finally, the wife decided that it would be better for the girl to go to the dacha with them rather than to the police. The husband protested saying that the little girl might not even want to go the dacha. The wife asked the little girl a leading-option rhetorical question by using a fake choice, a la Socrates,

> Wife: Little girl, Natashenka, tell us, what would you like more: that your head would be torn away OR to go to the dacha with us?
> Little girl: I want to go to the dacha.
> Wife (to her husband): You see, Mulya, the little child *wants* to go to the dacha.

This is one of the most comical and popular episodes of the entire movie tacitly connoting with the repressive Stalinist regime based on its, as it was jokingly defined by Soviet people, "voluntary-forced democracy".

The purpose of the leading-option rhetorical questions is to move the teacher-student agreement more in the direction desired by the teacher. The teacher tries to create an illusion of certainty that all other options are obviously bad but one – their own. I argue that using leading-option rhetorical questions, the teacher hides from the student (and sometimes from his/herself as in the case of Socrates) the problematic and uncertain nature of the presented choices. For instance, in the bee example above, Socrates wanted Meno to be able to see a contradiction in his own thinking between his own high value for an invariant definition of any concept and his own illustrative definition of virtue. Since this guidance is done through constant agreement (see in table 3 the percentages of agreements over disagreements), it gives an (often false) impression in the interlocutor that the truth held by the teacher has been revealed in the interlocutor's own thinking. However, if one asked Meno, "What would you find more effective for a person who has never seen bees: to give the person a verbal definition of what is common in all bees or to show different bees and allow the person, him or herself, to develop his/her own sense of what bees are?" Although I do not know for sure how Meno would reply to this hypothetical question, it would be more likely that he would not jump with certainty to the first option as the more superb definition over the second one as he did in the Meno-Socrates dialogue under the manipulative influence of Socrates. Thus, Socrates manipulated – i.e., according to the dictionary explanation of the word "manipulation", "influenced and managed shrewdly or deviously" (Houghton Mifflin Company, 2000), – Meno by hiding the complexity of the choices he presented to Meno rather than helping him discover the truth rooted in Meno's own thinking. Rossetti judges Socratic rhetorical strategies as a "rhetorical machinery" suitable for "successful advertising, propaganda, and other even more fearful manipulations of opinion" (Rossetti, 1989, p. 231).

In my view, the question is not whether the teacher should manipulate the student's thinking. Since teaching is purposeful activity, it involves the teacher's manipulation – purposeful and unilateral changing – of the student's subjectivity by selecting problems, shaping the focus, by providing guidance. The question however is what kind of manipulation is desirable or undesirable in providing good guidance. Like Pekarsky (1994), I have two major objections against Socrates' manipulation based on two considerations: effectiveness and ethics. From the effectiveness consideration, the leading-option rhetorical question based on false choice is pedagogically ineffective because if the student faces real (or even different false) choices he or she is left unequipped to deal with it. From the moral consideration, the leading-option rhetorical question based on false choice violates the student's trust in the teacher. Using the leading-option rhetorical questions, the teacher exploits the student's ignorance and intellectual ineptitude because the student could not imagine other and more real options (or conditions/contexts for the choices) than ones presented in the leading-option rhetorical question by the teacher. The student trusts that the teacher's guidance is based on power of the truth. However, when the teacher uses the leading-option rhetorical questions this power becomes based on the teacher's good will to share the truth and the student's ignorance skillfully exploited by the teacher. Socrates seemed to have his good will to share his knowledge with Meno, the Slave, and Anytus by making the desired option in the question his own belief. However, another person could have easily used the same leading-option rhetorical questions to lead the student to a lie by making the desired option in the question a statement that he or she does not believe him or herself (as it was in the case of the wife in the Soviet movie *Foundling*). The leading-option rhetorical questions give the student (and sometimes the teacher, like in the case of Socrates) an illusory impression of internally persuasive discourse of carefully tested and considered statements/options; while in actuality, the real discourse is based on the student's ignorance and the teacher's manipulation of false choices. I argue that the pedagogical discourse based on leading-option rhetorical questions remains essentially authoritarian (using Bakhtin's term, see Bakhtin, 1991; Morson, 2004). It is not by chance that in any law-based civil society, leading-option rhetorical questions are legally forbidden in using during an interrogation because the information that they produce is not reliable. Leading-option rhetorical questions based on false choices have been used by totalitarian regimes during the secret police's interrogations to break prisoners and make them confess to would-be political crimes (Al'brekht, 1981; Bukovsky, 1979; Solzhenitsyn, 1974).

One may argue that exactly because leading-option rhetorical questions are not appropriate in criminal interrogation, they are appropriate in education. In interrogation, a police inspector tries to establish what a suspect or a witness knows about the circumstances of the crime under investigation, while the teacher's goal is to transform the student's subjectivity. There is nothing wrong per se for the teacher to lead the student to the right option even though the student might not have this option before the pedagogical dialogue with the teacher. The issue is when leading is appropriate and when it is not. Is it pedagogically (and morally) appropriate to place a student into a situation, which forced the student to accept "the right option", like leading-option questions do? The following extreme case of an SS officer "educating" a Polish prisoner in a concentration camp, demonstrates the danger of such "leading pedagogy",

> Kogon (1947, p. 62) reports one of many incidents bearing this out: Once a command of Jewish prisoners was working alongside of some Polish Gentile prisoners. The supervising SS, spying two Jewish prisoners whom he thought to be slacking, ordered them to lie down in the ditch and called on a Polish prisoner, named Strzaska, to bury them alive. Strzaska, frozen in terror and anxiety, refused to obey. At this the SS seized a spade and beat the Pole, who nevertheless still refused to obey. Furiously, the SS now ordered the two Jews to get out of the ditch, Strzaska to get in, and the two Jews to bury *him*. In mortal anxiety, hoping to escape the fate themselves, they shoveled earth into the ditch and onto their fellow prisoner. When only Strzaska's head was barely visible the SS ordered them to stop, and unearth him. Once Strzaska was on his feet, the two Jews were ordered back into the ditch, and this time Strzaska obeyed the renewed command to bury them-possibly because they had not resisted burying him, or perhaps expecting that they too would be spared at the last minute. But this time there was no reprieve, and when the ditch was filled the SS stamped down the earth that still lay loosely over his victims. Five minutes later he called on two other prisoners to unearth them, but though they worked frantically, it was too late. One was already dead and the other dying, so the SS ordered them both taken to the crematorium (Bettelheim, 1960, p. 159).

I argue that this mostly non-verbal dialogue between the SS guard and Polish prisoner is Socratic like. The tragic incident can be re-written in the following imaginary verbal way fitting the format of the Socratic dialogue:

> *The "Socratic" SS guard (to the Polish prisoner):* You will save your miserable life by any price – even by sacrificing lives of your fellow prisoners, like these two Jews, won't you? (Orders the Polish prisoner to bury two Jews alive to save his own life).
> *The Polish prisoner:* No, I won't! (Refuses to bury the Jewish prisoners)
> *The "Socratic" SS guard:* You won't? This is a brave act. Do you think that these two are worth your bravery and your life?
> The Polish prisoner: Yes, I do!
> *The "Socratic" SS guard:* Hmm, let's see... Would you agree that one who is ready sacrifice his own life for life of others, should expect from them to be ready sacrifice their own life for their savior?
> The Polish prisoner: Yes, I would.
> *The "Socratic" SS guard:* Would you agree that those who are not ready sacrifice their lives for their savior are not worth to die for?
> The Polish prisoner: Of course.
> *The "Socratic" SS guard:* Let's see if these two Jewish prisoners are ready to die for you, their savior. (Orders the two Jewish prisoners to bury the Polish

prisoner alive. They follow the order. The SS guard stops them). Were these two Jews ready to sacrifice their lives for their savior?

The Polish prisoner: No!!! (with anger)

The "Socratic" SS guard: Are these two worth your life or do you still think that their lives are more important than yours?

The Polish prisoner: No!

The "Socratic" SS guard: Would you kill them to save your own life or would you prefer to be killed to keep them alive?

The Polish prisoner: Yes, I will kill them! (the SS guard orders the Polish prisoner to bury the two Jewish prisoner alive and he does that).

The SS officer, not unlike Socrates, demonstrated to the Polish prisoner that he had been wrong sacrificing his life for two Jews who were ready to betray him. After the leading-option "demonstration"-provocation organized by the SS guard, the Polish prisoner accepted the SS premise that other prisoners, especially Jews, were not worth living. The Polish prisoner accepted this position not because of his fear or external pressure but voluntarily out of his own conviction coming from experience that the SS organized for him. The SS guard tested the Polish prisoner's hidden premises and showed him through establishment of a series of tacit agreements that the Polish prisoner was wrong and self-contradictory. The SS transformed Strzaska's subjectivity and showed him he was wrong about sacrificing his life for his prison comrades through organizing a leading-option dramatic experience. Was this "search for truth" pedagogical?

In my view, genuine education is not about placing the student into a situation, in which the student would accept one of the options as true voluntarily by him/herself but it is rather about helping the student consider as many alternative options as possible from many diverse angles (i.e., internally persuasive discourse). Authentic education is not about the teacher imposing the correct answer as teachers in conventional schools often do. It is not about placing students in a situation that forces the student to accept the only option as Socrates and the SS guard did. It is about the teacher helping the student see as many relevant options and ways of considering them as necessary for making an informed decision/judgment. It is still up to the student to make the final decision in a free and informed way.

Was Socrates himself aware of the authoritarian nature of the leading-option rhetorical questions? Did he use this hidden authoritarian discourse for pedagogical (if not political) purposes? Or did he honestly believe that his discourse, heavily based on the usage of the leading-option rhetorical question, was internally persuasive? I am inclined to suggest the latter – Socrates apparently honestly believed that leading-option rhetorical questions promote internally persuasive discourse (using Bakhtin's term), although the matter can be even more complex. There is a lot of evidence suggesting that some of Socrates' deception of his students was very conscious and based on his apparently pedagogical purposes (Pekarsky, 1994). For example, Socrates was clearly more certain about issues that he was willing to admit to his interlocutors. In the dialogue with Anytus, Socrates knew from the beginning that the virtues are not teachable but pretended to Anytus (and Meno) that he was not sure or even believed that it was possible,

> Socrates: …tell us, and benefit your family friend here by telling him, to whom he should go in so large a city to acquire, to any worthwhile degree, the virtue I was just now describing.

> Anytus: Why did you not tell him yourself?
> Socrates: I did mention those whom I thought to be teachers of it, but you say I am wrong, and perhaps you are right. You tell him in your turn to whom among the Athenians he should go. Tell him the name of anyone you want (p. 891, 92d-e).

However, I think that Socrates honestly thought that he was testing ideas with his interlocutors while he was using his leading-option rhetorical questions. As I discussed above, Socrates (and Plato) were epistemological positivists who believed that truth is universal, eternal, and located in immortal souls. Based on this positivistic epistemology, it is safe to assume that Socrates believed that the choices he presented in his leading-option rhetorical questions were objective, decontextualized, and the only possible choices – they are real and not false. Being an epistemological positivist, it was difficult, if not impossible, for Socrates to recognize that under certain conditions/contexts, the choices he brought are true while on other possible conditions/contexts they are wrong. For some objects (like apples), 2+2 is always four. But for some other objects (like friends), 2+2 is not necessary four (two friends plus two friends are not necessarily four friends). For certain practical purposes, using invariant definitions of a concept is better but for some other practical purposes, using illustrative definitions are better. Do not get me wrong – I am not trying to say here that everything can go but rather that meaning and, thus, judgment of truth are contextual. In my view, truth (and falseness) is not rooted in statements/ideas as Socrates and other positivists assume but in relations between the statements and their contexts. Epistemological positivism blinded Socrates to see that the choices he presented to his interlocutors – who could not see other possible choices and contexts -- preyed on the interlocutors' ignorance and intellectual ineptitude. When, however, Socrates suspected that there were other options he brought them to the interlocutor even at expense of a detour from his original trajectory directed to the desired endpoint of the discussion. For example, when Socrates tried to prove to Meno that virtue is not based on knowledge, he noticed another option existed: besides knowledge virtue can also be based on a correct opinion/guess,

> Socrates: Then virtue cannot be taught?
> Meno: Apparently not, if we have investigated this correctly. I certainly wonder, Socrates, whether there are no good men either, or in what way good men come to be.
> Socrates: We are probably poor specimens, you and I, Meno. Gorgias has not adequately educated you, nor Prodicus me. We must then at all costs turn our attention to ourselves and find someone who will in some way make us better. I say this in view of our recent investigation, for it is ridiculous that we failed to see that it is not only under the guidance of knowledge that men succeed in their affairs, and that is perhaps why the knowledge of how good men come to be escapes us.
> Meno: How do you mean, Socrates? (p. 894, 96d)

It is interesting that it is Meno's information-seeking question about the origin of goodness in humans prompted Socrates to see another possible option for the origin of virtue that apparently he neglected before in the discussion with Meno. This makes me conclude that Socrates sincerely believed that he made a joint investigation of the objectively existing options presented by him in his leading-option rhetorical questions with his interlocutors rather than thinking that he tricked them into his own beliefs (as Anytus seemed to suspect – I would argue that Anytus' suspicion was correct).

Socrates' insistence to his interlocutors on making joint systematic investigation and testing of all possible options as the basis of education and discovery of truth is a very important legacy of Socratic dialogic pedagogy. It makes organization of internally persuasive discourse the primary pedagogical goal (Bakhtin & Emerson, 1999). However, Socrates' epistemological positivism seemed to guide him to the opposite direction, back to authoritarian discourse masked as an internally persuasive one. Leading-option rhetorical questions are responsible for that. To make pedagogical discourse internally persuasive, the teacher seems to have to relax his or her control over the list of considered possible options and seek together with the students all possibilities within diverse contexts before jointly analyzing each of them and their own system of priorities/values. This change, however, may undermine the teacher's ability to arrive at the preplanned endpoint of instruction or follow any preplanned trajectory (below I will discuss if it is even desirable).

The Dramatic Event of the Torpedo's Touch

When I was a student in high school back in the Soviet Union in the mid 1970s, I had a physics teacher who also was a political dissident. My classmates and I realized that fact quite quickly noticing the not very loyal political comments that our physics teacher applied during his lessons. I was attracted to his bravery and open-minded intellect and entered into conversations with him after school hours while he was preparing experiments and demonstrations for the next day's lessons (I volunteered to help using this help as excuse to talk with him). My physics teacher was very concerned about implicit dogmatism that he could promote in me, as he told me many times, and did not want to indoctrinate me in any political or philosophical system. Instead he asked me about my opinions about matters we discussed at hand (e.g., if democracy was the most desirable political regime – often such discussion topics emerged out of school or political events of the day) and then… crushed them with all his mighty criticism. I often left our discussion in a state of perplexity if not devastation, when so many views and opinions of mine that were so dear to my heart were crushed in front of my very eyes. My defense of my positions encouraged by my teacher was quickly collapsed under his critique in which I was an active but almost involuntary co-participant. When I asked for his mercy to provide me alternative positive views, he refused because he did not wanted me to move from one dogmatism (that was how he called my previously dear but then crushed ideas) to another dogmatism (that was how he referred to his own ideas that I could have uncritically accepted if he exposed me to them). He encouraged me to think more about our discussions, read more books, talk with other people, and develop new ideas with time so we could test them together. But I was impatient and could not stand "the state of negativity" (Beatty, 1984, p. 423) and perplexity in which he put me. I did not want to wait so I developed a cunning strategy. I had noticed that my teacher was absent-minded (like many scholars ☺). So, after enough time passed so I knew that my teacher forgot our particular conversation, I presented him his own critique of my points only to see how skillfully and powerfully he crushed his own critique. I remembered his arguments with my then young and sharp memory and after a while I again presented his counter-critique for his critique of his new critique. Thus, I organized his own self-debate on topics of my interests. Of course, I was not just a passive observer since I improvised his argumentation and actively participated in his self-critique.

After applying my new strategy, the perplexities that I often left with from our conversations were less painful for me for the following reasons. First, my physics teacher argued against *his own* ideas rather against *my* ideas. Although, I enacted his ideas in our conversations with all my intellectual capacity and enthusiasm (I did my homework thinking about the issues), like an actor in a performance, I was detached and protected by my detachment. Second, the process that I set in action pushed de-ownership of the ideas. The ideas and arguments were losing their owners as my teacher and I became defined in this process not as *owners* of particular ideas but as *testers* of the ideas. Third, a collapse of an idea was not a failure any more. My fear (and probably, my teacher's fear) was to not recognize our common enemy – dogmatism – uncritical acceptance of ideas. Fourth, I saw my teacher not winning again-and-again his debate with me but seriously testing ideas with me. I became suspicious that my teacher was also perplexed all the time. Fifth, I started liking to be perplexed myself as anticipation of something exciting and unpredictably carnavalistic (Bakhtin, 1984; Morson, 2004) that may follow this perplexity that could refresh my everyday life (that was embedded in rather boring school and family routines). It was like going through tall waves on ocean beach: fear of death and excitement of rebirth mixed together.

I do not know how Socratic our discussions were (I could not remember the details) but Socrates would probably like our dialogic exercise and my developed attitude toward perplexities. Initially, Meno, like me, thought that perplexity was a cunning strategy to win a debate, that the perplexity induced by the teacher aimed to crush the debater like checkmate in chess,

> Socrates, before I even met you I used to hear that you are always in a state of perplexity and that you bring others to the same state, and now I think you are bewitching and beguiling me, simply putting me under a spell, so that I am quite perplexed. Indeed, if a joke is in order, you seem, in appearance and in every other way, to be like the broad torpedo fish, for it too makes anyone who comes close and touches it feel numb, and you now seem to have had that kind of effect on me, for both my mind and my tongue are numb, and I have no answer to give you. Yet I have made many speeches about virtue before large audiences on a thousand occasions, very good speeches as I thought, but now I cannot even say what it is. I think you are wise not to sail away from Athens to go and stay elsewhere, for if you were to behave like this as a stranger in another city, you would be driven away for practising sorcery (p. 279, 80).

Socrates replied that perplexity cleans people's minds from false knowledge and reveals true ignorance. He insisted that the value of knowing is in collective testing of ideas rather than in their ownership, "if the torpedo fish is itself numb and so makes others numb, then I resemble it, but not otherwise, for I myself do not have the answer when I perplex others, but I am more perplexed than anyone when I cause perplexity in others. So now I do not know what virtue is; perhaps you knew before you contacted me, but now you are certainly like one who does not know. Nevertheless, I want to examine and seek together with you what it may be" (p. 279, 80c).

It seemed to be true that Socrates did not know what the invariant definition of virtue was – he was apparently and, thus, honestly (not rhetorically) perplexed about that and invited Meno to join him in considering this issue. Socrates might be also perplexed about the length of a square that has double area in his dialogue with the Slave. This number is irrational and cannot be represented as a fraction if the length of the original square's side is a fraction. It is not clear if Socrates knew the mathematical proof that the length of doubled area square is an irrational number. If not, Socrates' perplexity that he shared with the Slave (and indirectly with Meno) was also genuine. As to Socrates' dialogue with Anytus, it did not move long enough to perplex Anytus who left the discussion in anger. It seems that Anytus sensed that Socrates tried to manipulate and lead him to some perplexity and suspected that Socrates' manipulation was not intellectually honest but politically motivated. So we do not know whether, if Anytus stayed longer, Socrates might have led Anytus into some specific perplexity, if at all, and if this perplexity would be genuinely shared by Socrates himself.

The torpedo's touch so vividly described by Meno is a dramatic pedagogical event. It is a moment of crisis in the teacher-student relations when old relations cannot be continued any more: either the relations will collapse (as seemed to be in case of Socrates-Anytus dialogue) or transform (as in the case of Socrates-Meno dialogue) (Matusov, St. Julien, & Hayes, 2005). In the torpedo's touch event, the way how the student knows him/herself and how the others know the student collapses. As Meno so eloquently and passionately described, he and others had known him as a masterful speaker about virtues. During the dialogue with Socrates, Meno learned that he had been always ignorant about virtues. His identity as a capable knower and expert of virtue collapsed. Socrates tried to offer Meno a new identity – the identity of a learner who thrives on ignorance rather than being defeated by it (as in the case of knower). But this new identity is only in a process of becoming – it is only a remote promise for the future rather than a current state of being. As Meno pointed out, the torpedo's touch disempowers the student even outside of the teacher-student relations: after meeting with Socrates, Meno would not feel himself as a capable speaker and persuader on the topic of virtue in front of large or small audiences (even in front of himself!). The student comes to the teacher to become more empowered and stronger – he or she does not want to leave the teacher disempowered and weaker than the student was before meeting the teacher. The student expects that the teacher makes him or her stronger in the world. Through the torpedo's touch, the teacher seems to violate the student's trust.

In my view, the torpedo's touch event is dramatic for one more reason. In this event, I argue that three communities of practice collide with each other: a community of knowers, a community of debate-contesters, and a community of learners. A community of knowers was represented by Meno in the first part of the Dialogue. In this community, knowledge is viewed as power and success that can bring happiness. Self-ignorance is associated by this community with failure, weakness, and suffering. People, knowers, are gradated on the scale of knowledge possession. The more knowledgeable a knower, the more respectful he or she is in the community of knowers. Knowledge promotes authority. Dialogue is viewed as a transmission of accumulated knowledge from a more knowledgeable to less knowledgeable knower. For example, Meno really appreciated Socrates for telling him the invariant definitions of shape and color that Meno recognized as knowledge that he had not have before meeting with Socrates on this occasion and that Meno could have later repeated to other listeners to increase his reputation as a knower. Meno did not mind Socrates sharing his other knowledge about the origin of virtues in similar manner and could not understand why Socrates resisted that.

A community of debate-contesters was represented by Sophists in many Socratic Dialogues. In his famous statement about the torpedo's touch quoted above, Meno insinuated to Socrates by suspicion that he was also a Sophist masquerading as an anti-Sophist. Debate-contesters are focused on defeating their opponents at any price in the eyes of the audience and their own eyes. The appearance of knowledge in eyes of bystanders and the opponents is more important than the knowledge itself. That makes dialogue self-contained as a (zero sum) game of form since its content is not as important and consequential for the participants in debate-contest as a sense of persuasion of their audience[1]. Knowledge is not seen as serious but rather instrumental because debate contests focus on the art of winning debates and knowledge can be one of many weapons among others (e.g., clear rhetorical moves or deceptions).

A community of learners was represented by Socrates and Meno by the end of the Dialogue. It focuses on testing ideas and considering uncertainties and problems. Members of a community of learners do not attach and affiliate themselves with knowledge as members of a community of knowers do but they do take the content of dialogue seriously unlike members of a community of debate-contesters. In a community of learners, the truth is rooted not in statements but in the survival of honest tests. Socrates articulated this well in the Gorgias Dialogue, "I'd be pleased to continue questioning you if you're the same kind of man I am, otherwise I would drop it. And what kind of man am I? One of those who would be pleased to be refuted if I say anything untrue, and who would be pleased to refute anyone who says anything untrue; one who, however, wouldn't be any less pleased to be refuted and to refute. For I count being refuted a greater good, insofar as it is a greater good for oneself to be delivered from the worst thing there is than to deliver someone else for it" (p. 802, 458). In the Dialogues portrayed by Plato, one of Socrates' major super-goals seemed not to make his interlocutors as knowledgeable as he was and not to win debates with them but to socialize and to join them in a community of learners so they and he could test ideas together. This process was successful for some interlocutors (like Meno) and unsuccessful with others (like Anytus). In a community of learners, knowledge is viewed as an important, but an unpredictable by-product of the process of learning (Morson, 2004; Thomas, 1985). Learning valued in a community of learning is based on the participants' ontological engagement in problems and uncertainties. This learning is essentially problem- and uncertainty-based. That is why the torpedo's touch – joint ontological engagement in an uncertainty – constitutes a community of learners (Thomas, 1985).

As I have showed above, this "testing ideas together" was not organized honestly enough by Socrates and was not based on internally persuasive discourse but rather on the illusion of its presence. This fact allows us to claim that Socrates belonged to two communities of practices at the same time: a community of knowers and a community of learners. In a community of knowers, the authority of knowledge and expertise over ignorance and ineptitude defines the persuasion of the student by the teacher ("you should do what I told you because I know and you don't" or, in case of Socratic dialogue, it takes a more hidden authoritarian statement, "you will accept it because you cannot see alternatives"). As I showed, the leading-option rhetorical questions, based on manipulation of the interlocutor with the use of false choices, involve hidden exploitation of the students' intellectual ineptitude and ignorance. In a community of learners, the authority is based on joint investigation of an ontological problem ("let's consider this together, please, because I have a problem with it"). Socrates' struggle with affiliation with two incompatible communities of practice seemed to reflect his simultaneous adoption of elite and democratic values, "It

---

[1] It is interesting that some educational scholars (e.g., Burbules, 1993; Macmillan & Garrison, 1988) view pedagogical dialogue as a game. We wonder if they also see pedagogical dialogue as self-contained.

follows from this reasoning, Meno, that virtue appears to be present in those of us who may possess it as a gift from the gods" (p. 897, 100b).

As Garlikov (1998) argues, "the [Socratic] Method differs from just asking questions, especially open-ended or non-leading questions, or ones that one does not know the answer to oneself" (see also Fishman, 1985, for more discussion of this point). Socrates asked relatively few information-seeking genuine questions (see table 2) especially in comparison to all questions he asked (about 10% of the total questions he asked in Meno-Socrates and Socrates-Anytus dialogues; while both Meno and Anytus used information-seeking questions in about 50% of their total questions). According my own non-systematic, impressionistic judgment, in all Socratic Dialogues, I did not find much evidence of Socrates seeking truth and learning something new himself from participation in these dialogues (beyond invitation of his interlocutors to join him in such future investigations that remained outside of Plato's ethnographies)[2]. There was no one exclamation made by Socrates of "eureka!", although, in contrast, from time-to-time his interlocutors obviously showed evidence and awareness of their learning something new in the dialogues with Socrates. Rather, it seemed that Socrates tried to bring other participants to something that he already knew even though this knowledge was negative – about Socrates' uncertainty rather than certainty (Vitanza, 1997). This characteristic of Socratic dialogues to move his interlocutors to his own level of thinking seems to belong a community of knowers rather than a community of learners. While his invitations to consider problems together belonged to a community of learners.

Ontologically-Based Guidance

It has been commented by Socratic scholars (e.g., Pekarsky, 1994; Rud, 1997; Woodruff, 1998) that Socrates' pedagogical dialogues were not only intellectual but also moral and political and emotional. In other words, Socratic pedagogical dialogues were not only philosophical but also *ontological* – they involved the whole person. My conversational analysis (see table 1) shows that some of Socrates and his interlocutors' dialogic turns were ontological. Especially heavily ontological were dialogic turns in the Socrates-Anytus dialogue. In this dialogue, more than 50% of the participants' utterances were ontological, according to my conversational analysis. In the following example Socrates and Anytus discussed then contemporary Greek political issues embedded in Socrates' investigation of whether virtues are teachable,

> Socrates: How do you mean, Anytus? Are these people, alone of those who claim the knowledge to benefit one, so different from the others that they not only do not benefit what one entrusts to them but on the contrary corrupt it, even though they obviously expect to make money from the process? I find I cannot believe you, for I know that one man, Protagoras, made more money from this knowledge of his than Phidias who made such notably fine works, and ten other sculptors. Surely what you say is extraordinary, if those who mend old sandals and restore

---

[2] Zappen (2004) and Kameen (2000) argue that in his Dialogues with equal professional philosophers like sophists Protagoras and Gorgias, Socrates pursued a collaborative inquiry in which both parties were "respectfully, and mutually, becoming knowledgeable" (Kameen, 2000, p. 173). However, other Socratic scholars disagree (e.g., Gulley, 1968; Nightingale, 1999). For example, Enos argues that in the Gorgias Dialogue, Socrates' mode of questioning is "one detailed argument of proposition under guise of a dialogue... a heuristic employed not to discover Truth but rather to create his interpretation of reality in the minds of readers" (Enos, 1993, pp. 95, 99). I think a systematic discourse and content analysis is needed to address this controversy.

clothes would be found out within the month if they returned the clothes and sandals in a worse state than they received them; if they did this they would soon die of starvation, but the whole of Greece has not noticed for forty years that Protagoras corrupts those who frequent him and sends them away in a worse moral condition than he received them. I believe that he was nearly seventy when he died and had practiced his craft for forty years. During all that time to this very day his reputation has stood high; and not only Protagoras but a great many others, some born before him and some still alive today. Are we to say that you maintain that they deceive and harm the young knowingly, or that they themselves are not aware of it? Are we to deem those whom some people consider the wisest of men to be so mad as that?

Anytus: They are far from being mad, Socrates. It is much rather those among the young who pay their fees who are mad, and even more the relatives who entrust their young to them and most of all the cities who allow them to come in and do not drive out any citizen or stranger who attempts to behave in this manner.

Socrates: Has some sophist wronged you, Anytus, or why are you so hard on them?

Anytus: No, by Zeus, I have never met one of them, nor would I allow any one of my people to do so (pp. 890-891, 91c-92b).

Although Socrates seemed to be more interested in the intellectual aspects of his examples than Anytus who seemed to be more interested in the political aspects, both Socrates and Anytus clearly saw political implications of their consideration in the dialogue. While Socrates tried to undermine politically and intellectually a community of knowers as teachers of virtue by arguing that they were ineffective teachers; Anytus made political objections against a community of debate-contesters as ones who were dishonest in manipulating others rather than seeking the truth. In both cases, although in different degrees, the arguments were also about citizenship and politics and were personal – morally and emotionally charged rather than purely intellectual (i.e., whether virtues are teachable). In the Meno-Socrates dialogue, the number of ontological utterances involving the issues of citizenship and politics increases with the end of the dialogue as Meno arguably transitioned from a community of knowers to a community of learners. I did not find any ontological utterances in the Socrates-Slave dialogue – a fact that deserves extended consideration in my further analysis of Socratic dialogic pedagogy (see below).

We argue that in a community of learners, learning and knowledge are always seen as ontological rather than purely intellectual (and detached). In a community of learners, in contrast to other communities of practice, intellectual and ontological aspects of learning and knowledge mutually constitute each other (Latour, 1987; Lave & Wenger, 1991; Rogoff, Turkanis, & Bartlett, 2001; Wenger, 1998). Learning always transforms a person's relationships with other people and the world. Meno, cited in the previous section, nicely showed how his intellectual perplexity and numbness about the definition of virtue caused by his dialogue with Socrates (i.e., the "torpedo's touch" event) might affect his relationship with other people and his own image of himself. Not only could Meno not see himself as a capable and skillful speaker of virtue in the presence of others anymore, but he also could not make as confident moral and political judgments about virtues as he had done before this event.

In a community of knowers, knowledge and learning are detached and indifferent from ontology. Ironically, Socrates himself, as an epistemological positivist of eternal and universal forms, nicely described this anti-ontological approach to knowledge (but not to learning!), "Then if the truth about reality is always in our soul, the soul would be immortal so that you should always confidently try to seek out and recollect what you do not know at present -- that is, what you do not recollect?" (p. 886, 86b). In a community of knowers, learning is viewed as accumulation of knowledge acquired from more knowledgeable others; for example, Meno acquired new (for him) definitions of shape and color from Socrates. This new knowledge arguably elevates Meno in the hierarchy of knowers but it is not viewed as changing Meno in any essential way. This seems to be why Socrates, as an educational constructivist, did not apparently value this type of learning that, in contrast, Meno had valued highly at that stage of the Meno-Socrates dialogue (later in the dialogue Meno seemed to revise his position as he started joining a community of learners). Bakhtin criticized detached intellectual discourse as being monological, "Dialogic relationships are reducible neither to logical relationships nor to relationships oriented semantically toward their referential object, relationships *in and of themselves* devoid of any dialogic element" (Bakhtin & Emerson, 1999, p. 183). Freire claimed that detached and disinterested knowledge is impotent, "An unauthentic word one which is unable to transform reality, results when dichotomy is imposed upon its constitutive elements. When a word is deprived of its dimension of action, reflection automatically suffers as well; and the word is changed into idle chatter, into *verbalism*, into an alienated and alienating "blah." It becomes an empty word one which cannot denounce the world for denunciation is impossible without a commitment to transform, and there is no transformation without action" (Freire, 1986, p. 68).

In a community of debate-contesters, knowledge and learning are subordinated to ontology at expense of truth and intellectual achievement. It is only important to win debate and create a perception of defeat in significant bystanders and, ideally, in the opponent himself. Although the intellectual aspect is present and valued in this practice, it is subordinated to the ontology of winning the debate and the hearts and minds of other people. Sometimes, like in the case of Sophists in Ancient Greece, debate-contesters use their art to get affluent Greek youth to pay for their tutoring (Billig, 1996). Greek political life under democracy demanded from affluent citizens strong debating skills. By separating debating skills from the content of the debates, Sophists ensured getting youth of different political persuasions for their highly paid tutoring. In the Theaetetus Dialogue, Socrates described and criticized this practice in the following way, "He [i.e., a debate-contester, a sophist] would lay into hearing and smelling and other perceptions of that kind; and would keep on refuting you and not let you go till had been struck with wonder at his wisdom – that 'answer to many prayers' – and had got yourself thoroughly tied up by him. Then, when he had you tamed and bound, he would set you free for a ransom – whatever price seemed appropriate to the two of you" (p. 184, 165e). Disregard to knowledge often led debate-contesters to the cynical view that truth and knowledge are unimportant if you know the right tricks how to beat your opponent. This cynicism let some sophists to lose their sense of life and to suicide while Socrates' promoting of a community of learners led him to be killed by his fellow citizens.

Finally, Anytus seemed to represent one more community of practice that can be characterized as "a community of doers". In this community, a certain, highly valued, goal of activity subordinates intellectual aspects of the discourse. In this community, the goal of activity ("why") often seen as non-problematic, while the way of achieving this goal ("how") is usually viewed as problematic. The majority of Anytus' judgments seemed to be rooted in such goal-oriented "pragmatism." Thus, he did not need to experience Sophists to know that they were evilly minded since they were intentional obstacles in the way of his politics. Freire labeled this approach as "activism" and criticized it in the following way, "On the other hand, if action is emphasized exclusively, to the detriment of reflection, the word is converted into *activism*. The latter-action for action's sake-negates the true praxis and makes dialogue impossible" (Freire, 1986, p. 69). It is another way of monologism. Socrates saw this over-commitment to a political cause as uncritically blind and potentially dangerous. It makes a person closed-minded, prejudiced, and not a good listener, "I think, Meno, that Anytus is angry, and I am not at all surprised. He thinks, to begin with, that I am slandering those men, and then he believes himself to be one of them. If he ever realizes what slander is, he will cease from anger, but he does not know it now" (p. 893, 95).

As table 4 shows, the participants' ontology was mainly defined by citizenship and politics. Socrates also afforded himself to make several tacit and explicit homosexual statements directed at Meno, "Even someone who was blindfolded would know from your conversation that you are handsome and still have lovers.... Because you are forever giving orders in a discussion, as spoiled people do, who behave like tyrants as long as they are young. And perhaps you have recognized that I am at a disadvantage with handsome people, so I will do you the favor of an answer" (p. 876, 76b).

Table 4. Comparative analysis of the % of different types of ontological utterances made by participants in the Meno Dialogue

Dialogue	Participant	Ontology total	Citizenship-politics	Homosexuality	Ontology-other*
Meno-Socrates	Meno	6.28%	6.28%	0.00%	0.00%
	Socrates	18.36%	14.01%	2.90%	1.93%
Socrates-Slave	Slave	0.00%	0.00%	0.00%	0.00%
	Socrates	0.00%	0.00%	0.00%	0.00%
Socrates-Anytus	Anytus	54.17%	54.17%	0.00%	0.00%
	Socrates	66.67%	66.67%	0.00%	0.00%

Note: In the Meno dialogue, Socrates made several ontological statements about himself that I consider as "ontology-other" (e.g., p. 877, 77).

Socrates seemed to draw a parallel between the relationship of the teacher and the student (he and Meno) and relationship of old male and young male homosexual lovers. Like the physical beauty of youth capriciously drives an older lover in fulfilling a young lover's desires, the student's inquiry capriciously drives the teacher's guidance, "If I were directing you, Meno, and not only myself, we would not have investigated whether virtue is teachable or not before we had investigated what virtue itself is. But because you do not even attempt to rule yourself, in order that you may be free, but you try to rule me and do so, I will agree with you -- for what can I do? So we must, it appears, inquire into the qualities of something the nature of which we do not yet know" (p. 887, 86d). I agree with Socrates that although the teacher should share his/her own inquiries with the student and try to create joint inquiries for joint investigation, the teacher should prioritize student-initiated inquiries over his or her own. An internally persuasive discourse in a community of learners begins with respect of another's invitation to join his or her ontological inquiry at hand.

CONCLUSIONS

Socratic dialogues have traditionally been praised for promoting critical thinking, renewing interest in subject matters, provoking students' thinking, facilitating construction of meaning and discovery learning. Socrates himself provided the ideology of his teaching as testing the truth, discovering his own ignorance, pursuing truth about fundamental questions. In this study, I treated Socratic dialogues presented by Plato as educational ethnography, by making a conversational analysis of the Meno Dialogue. I found that Socratic dialogues belong to both community of learners and community of knowers/experts and provide dialogical opposition to a community of debate-contesters. In his practice and ideology, Socrates was both a radical constructivist as an educator and a radical positivist as an epistemologist. As a radical constructivist, Socrates tried to employ internally persuasive discourse, focus on the students' subjectivity and its transformation, engage in ontology, and promote inquiry. As a radical positivist, he used leading-option rhetorical questions, did not pursue his own inquiries with the students and genuinely perplexed himself, and believed that the truth is decontextualized and detached. The constructivist and positivist approaches affected deeply Socratic dialogic pedagogy.

I also found that the Socrates dialogues with free people are radically different from the dialogue with the slave and all these dialogues are different from Socrates' declaration about his own method. In all the dialogues, I did not find any evidence of Socrates' seeking truth and learning something new himself from participation in these dialogues. Rather, he tried to bring other participants to something that he already knew. Socrates' dialogues with free people were highly ontological, dramatic, improvisational, truth-seeking, challenged Socrates himself, and were often unsafe for Socrates' public reputation. Meanwhile the dialogue with the Slave was decontextualized, hierarchical, contrived, rigidly pre-designed, pleased Socrates, was non-challenging for Socrates, and safe for Socrates' public reputation. Finally, Socrates declarations about his pedagogy-philosophizing as shared inquiry contradict his own practice as described in Plato's ethnography. In the following chapter, I explore how Socratic dialogic pedagogy affected modern educational practices.

Chapter 3

DOES SOCRATIC DIALOGUE ENSLAVE STUDENTS?: THREE TYPES OF SOCRATIC PEDAGOGICAL DIALOGUE IN MODERN SCHOOLING

ABSTRACT

I look at contemporary applications of "Socratic method" or "Socratic dialogue" in education by investigating modern educational research that uses these terms on the ERIC database. I have noticed three distinguishable formulations of Socratic dialogue. One is characterized by non-ontological engagement of students that involves revealing contradictions in the students' thinking. I argue that this type of Socratic dialogue is modeled after Socrates' dialogue with the Slave. The second type of Socratic dialogue is characterized by ontological engagement of students that are manipulated into the endpoints preset by the teacher. This type of Socratic dialogue is arguably modeled by Socrates' dialogue with free citizens. Finally, the third type of Socratic dialogue that I traced in modern educational scholarship is characterized by teacher-students joint search for truth. This type of dialogue is modeled after Socrates' espoused claims about his own philosophical investigation. The ontological and pedagogical consequences of these three types of modern applications of Socratic dialogue are discussed.

In the current educational literature, there has been a disagreement about whether Socrates' dialogue with the Slave in *Meno* reflects and is shaped by the slave bondage social relations established in Ancient Greek society. For example, Rud (1997) claims that there are "blatant...problems of power and dominance of an elderly Greek citizen teaching a slave boy". Garlikov (1998) disagrees with Rud by arguing that "I see the age and class difference as irrelevant features of that dialogue, since the essential features in it are no different than in the others, where Socrates questions quite prominent and highly positioned citizens. Nor, in many cases are the questions, and the answers given by the characters in the dialogues, very different from what would occur today if one were talking to someone about those very same subjects in a modern vernacular and with references to contemporary examples of the same sorts of actions and ideas Socrates gives his examples to illustrate." Boghossian (2002) tries to find a middle ground between Rud's and Garlikov's positions claiming that, "power relations certainly do play a role in all communicative contexts, and Socratic dialogue is no exception. What is an exception, however, is that the adverse effects of power are minimized, and the focus is shifted from people to propositions."

My close comparative analysis of Socratic dialogues with free citizens and the Slave helps to check whether Rud or Garlikov is right. I also checked Garlikov's very interesting observation shared by Rud (and potentially alarming, if Rud is right) that modern use of Socratic dialogue in education is not different from the Socrates-Slave dialogue (Cooney et al., 1975; Fernandez, 1994; Richards, 1991). For example, Macmillan and Garrison (1988) examine the Socrates-Slave dialogue as a good representative of any Socratic educational dialogue affecting modern teaching. As Rud states, "An old man drawing geometric figures in the sand for a young slave boy is a powerful image of what many believe Socratic teaching to be." If Rud is right that the Socrates-Slave dialogue is shaped by power imbalance rooted in slave bondage, the use of such dialogue in modern classroom is very problematic because it implies that this dialogue is only possible when the teacher establishes slave-like relations with his or her students in the classroom. Of course, if Garlikov is right that the Socrates-Slave dialogue is not bounded by slavery relations of power, then modern use of such dialogue in classrooms is not problematic. The purpose of this chapter is to compare the three Socratic dialogues: 1) Socrates' dialogue with the Slave, 2) Socrates' dialogue with the free citizens, and 3) Socrates' own espoused theory of his own dialogues to track influence of these three influential types of dialogues on modern education.

SOCRATIC DIALOGUES WITH FREE CITIZENS VERSUS WITH THE SLAVE

Using a conversational analysis described in the previous chapter, I found that Socrates' dialogue with free people seems radically different than his dialogue with the Slave and all these dialogues are different from Socrates' declaration about his own method. Dialogue with free people was highly ontological, subjectivized, dramatic, improvisational, truth-seeking, challenged Socrates himself, and was unsafe for Socrates' public reputation. Meanwhile the dialogue with the Slave was decontextualized, objectivized, hierarchical, contrived, rigidly pre-designed, pleasing Socrates, non-challenging for Socrates, and safe for Socrates' public reputation.

The inquiry with the Slave came from Socrates himself, while the inquiry with free people arose from the free people themselves. Meno came to Socrates and asked him about the origin of virtue. Socrates invited Anytus to join Meno and Socrates to consider Meno's inquiry. In contrast, the Slave, however, had remained uninformed about the reasons of why Socrates engaged him in the dialogue. I argue that Socrates apparently violated all rules of polity, respect, and dignity when he addressed the Slave for the first time (it is apparent that Socrates had not known the Slave in advance) as, "Tell me now, boy, you know that a square figure is like this?" (p. 881, 82b). Imagine you are asking somebody unknown on a street or at a café this question (even without using the possibly derogatory reference "boy"). People would probably react that by ignoring this rude question, by becoming hostile, or by asking "what do you mean?" or "why do you ask this question to me?" or "who are you?" In any way, it is doubtful that you would get the answer that the Slave provided to Socrates, "I do." In our society, only in school you may expect the same answer as the Slave gave to Socrates.

The problem with Socrates' address to a person he had never known before is that Socrates did not articulate his own business of why he addressed to his interlocutor. Also, Socrates did not make known to the person, not apologize for possible interrupting of his interlocutor's own business, and did not appeal to the interlocutor for help. Although there can be important cultural and historical variations of how to address unfamiliar person for the first time, the universal message of respect for the addressee is always there. All these functions of the first address to unfamiliar person were missing in Socrates' first utterance directed to the Slave. However, all these functions of polity, respect, and dignity were present in Socrates' first utterance addressed to Anytus,

> ...And now, Meno, Anytus [Anytus enters] here has opportunely come to sit down by us. Let us share our search with him. It would be reasonable for us to do so, for Anytus, in the first place, is the son of Anthemion, a man of wealth and wisdom, who did not become rich automatically or as the result of a gift like Ismenias the Theban, who recently acquired the possessions of Polycrates, but through his own wisdom and efforts. Further, he did not seem to be an arrogant or puffed up or offensive citizen in other ways, but he was a well-mannered and well-behaved man. Also he gave our friend here a good upbringing and education, as the majority of Athenians believe, for they are electing him to the highest offices. It is right then to look for the teachers of virtue with the help of men such as he, whether there are any and if so who they are. Therefore, Anytus, please join me and your guest friend Meno here, in our inquiry as to who are the teachers of virtue. Look at it in this way: if we wanted Meno to become a good physician, to what teachers would c we send him? Would we not send him to the physicians? (p. 889, 89e-90b)

In this address, Socrates:

1. asked Anytus politely to join the inquiry posted by Meno -- Anytus' own friend and guest (i.e., justification of engagement by obligation of friendship and hospitability toward Meno), affirming Anytus' free will to join or not join the conversation;
2. explained the inquiry (i.e., the goal for participation), making Anytus an equal participant of the inquiry;
3. listed Anytus' unique features that might help the inquiry (i.e., the motivation for engagement and acknowledgment of Anytus' strength), explaining why Anytus was asked for help;
4. praised Anytus indirectly (i.e., encouragement for participation), showing respect and admiration for Anytus.

Socrates did not apologize to Anytus for interruption of Anytus' own business probably because Anytus joined the group and did not apparently have any business. On the contrary, the rules of politeness probably dictated Socrates to explain what Socrates and Meno were doing to Anytus who joined their group (and perhaps even to engage him in the discussion).

By addressing to the Slave with his abrupt question, Socrates did not show respect of the Slave's free will to participate or not to participate in the discussion, did not share the goal of the discussion, did not treat him as an equal interlocutor, did not ask for help, did not justify the Slave unique qualities, and did not apologize for interruption of his own business. Why, in this case, the Slave did not show his displeasure with Socrates and, instead, pleased Socrates with the answer as if he were invited, knew the overall goal of the activity, and were asked for help. The answer is rather sad but simple – the institute of slavery. Although Socrates was not the master of the Slave – Meno was, Socrates belonged to the Greek class of potential masters. Besides, Meno, as the master of the Slave and a friend of Socrates, tacitly sanctioned Socrates' all demands for the Slave as his own.

I argue that in the modern institutional settings, only conventional schools support relations similar to relations between Socrates and the Slave. I like to demonstrate this point to my students. For this purpose, I asked abrupt and out-of-context questions like as simple and meaningless as "2+2 equals?", and all my students, including graduate students, replied automatically (although they looked puzzled). However, when I asked the same out-of-context abrupt question children outside of school settings – my own son, my nieces, and children from an afterschool program at Latin American Community Center, -- they all refused to answer without exception. Even when my own students were not in my class and University classrooms but I talked with them freely in café or on the street, they did not anymore cooperate with my meaningless abrupt questions (see Matusov et al., 2002 for more discussion of this phenomenon).

The Slave's ownership for the math investigation seemed to be very low. I have already discussed that unlike Meno and Anytus, the Slave did not ask questions. There are several consequences of this fact. First, as Fernandez (1994) shows there are at least two possible confusions in the Socrates-Slave dialogue caused by Socrates. It is unclear if the Slave understood that Socrates' demonstration of the fact that doubling the square side quadruples of the square area contradicts his claim that doubled area square has doubled side. Fernandez is right that this step in reasoning is not trivial for many novice learners of math, whom the Slave obviously was. Another possible confusion could be, as Fernandez correctly points out, in Socrates' tacit redefining the mathematical problem from finding the exact number of the side length of the doubled area square, to making estimation of this number, to representing the number geometrically as the length of diagonal (at the time of the dialogue, Greeks did not fully establish irrational numbers yet Rossmeissl & Webber, 1969). Without the Slave being able to ask questions to a master, it was difficult for Socrates to be aware of the Slave's confusions even if the Slave were aware of them.

Second, although, guided by Socrates the Slave did probably realize that, contrary to his initial belief, he did not know how to double area of a square or what square side length makes the square doubled its area, it was rather doubtful that he was genuinely engaged in any math inquiry. Let me illustrate this doubtfulness with the following example. An atheist may follow the paradox of *The Almighty God*, "If the God is almighty, He does not have limits of His activities. Thus, He can create a very heavy stone that He cannot lift. But if He cannot lift such a stone, it means that He is not almighty since the stone limits his ability. If, however, He can lift the stone, He is still is not almighty because He has limits on what He can create." An atheist may see a logical contradiction in the paradox behind the concept of "omnipotence" but since the atheist does not belong to a community of a religious practice of belief, he or she does not participate in a religious inquiry of this paradox including "the leap of faith" – faith replaces reason when reason is helpless. Similarly, the Slave might not ontologically participate in the rather esoteric math riddles presented by his master's friend Socrates even though he might realized an uncertainty in these riddles. It is important to notice that participation in a community of mathematicians requires important recourses such time, food, free will, symbolic recourses, access to other mathematicians, sense of freedom in pursuing a selected inquiry, sense of self-respect and respect of other for doing math, and so on – the recourses that would have been difficult to obtain by the Slave. Again, I argue that a similar lack of ownership for engagement in uncertainties is common for modern conventional schools. Like the Slave, students in conventional schools often do not have choice of the activities to do and even a choice of how to pursue activities assigned by the teacher.

Gray claims that Socrates did not have syllabus (cited in Rud, 1997) – a predesinged curriculum to teach common for traditional school. I think that it is very true for Socrates' dialogues with free people but it is less true for his dialogue with the Slave. Socrates unilaterally controlled and planned his dialogue with the Slave. As tables 1, 2, 3 (see the previous chapter) show, free citizens Meno and Anytus initiate inquiries, ask questions, disagree with Socrates, and may not cooperate with him to the point that they could leave Socrates all together in the middle of a dialogue as Anytus actually did. Following any preplanned syllabus was not possible with free citizens. The Slave's utterance in the dialogue with Socrates missed all these features. Even more, I have evidence that Socrates preplanned his dialogue with the Slave as he wanted demonstrate Meno the idea of *anamnesis* – learning through recollection (R. E. Allen, 1959). Of course, the Slave might have surprised Socrates by not knowing what was square or by knowing correctly how to double square area (Macmillan & Garrison, 1988). But these types of the surprises can occur in any conventional classroom with any scripted and rigidly preplanned lesson (although, in a multistudent classroom of a conventional school, it is easier for a teacher to ignore these surprises by picking a student who fits the teacher's imaginary learner, see Matusov & Smith, 2007). In any way, the Slave did not surprise Socrates and did not deviate from being an imaginary student that Socrates preplanned – instead, the Slave allowed Socrates to follow his own unwritten but preplanned syllabus. I argued that what allowed Socrates and a conventional teacher to follow their preplanned teaching scripts is a pedagogical regime in which students asking questions, setting their own inquiries, disagreement with the teacher, non-cooperation with the teacher, and leaving the classroom space at the students' will are illegitimate. In modern conventional classroom, students are captive audiences who cannot leave at their will (like the Slave) who have to attend to the teacher's agenda, who do not have legitimate right to redefine or not to answer to the teacher's questions, who do not have right to talk freely with the teacher or each other, even when they can legitimately ask questions it is the teacher who defines relevance of this question, and who cannot demand or initiate their own activities. In case of a conflict between the teacher's and students' agendas, the teacher's agenda is often prioritized (in contrast with Socrates' view on this issue in his dialogue with Meno (see p. 887, 86d).

As I argued above in the previous chapter, Socrates always worked with his interlocutors' subjectivities through establishment of a series of agreements and challenging contradictions in the interlocutors' thinking. This was true for both types of interlocutors: free citizens and a slave. In this regard, Socrates was very different from modern conventional schools what often worked with subjectivities of their imaginary rather than real students, as our research has shown that elsewhere (Matusov & Smith, 2007). However, unlike treating free citizens, Socrates objectivized the Slave. In the cases of dialogues with free interlocutors, Socrates served to his interlocutors' subjectivities. In the case of the dialogue with the Slave, Socrates used the subjectivity of his interlocutor for his own purpose. He made the Slave an object of his demonstration for and conversation with Meno in the Slave's presence. Even more,

Socrates (nor Meno) made any efforts to make their conversations about the Slave comprehensible by the Slave,

> Socrates [to the Slave]: Come now, try to tell me how long each side of this will be. The side of this is two feet. What about each side of the one which is its double?
> SLAVE: Obviously, Socrates, it will be twice the length.
> Socrates [to Meno]: You see, Meno, that I am not teaching the boy anything, but all I do is question him. And now he thinks he knows the length of the line on which an eight-foot figure is based. Do you agree?
> Meno: I do.
> Socrates: And does he know?
> Meno: Certainly not.
> Socrates: He thinks it is a line twice the length?
> Meno: Yes.
> Socrates: Watch him now recollecting things in order, as one must recollect.
> Socrates [to the Slave]: Tell me, boy, do you say that a figure double the size is based on a line double the length? Now I mean such a figure as this, not long on one side and short on the other, but equal in every direction like this one, and double the size, that is, eight feet. See whether you still believe that it will be based on a line double the length.
> SLAVE: I do (p. 882, 82d-83).

Such a conversation with a free citizen would have been impossible because of its apparent disrespect treating them as a thing of demonstration rather than an active and cognizant participant of an activity, in which they have free agency. This type of discourse based on talking about another like an object monologizes (Bakhtin & Emerson, 1999) the relationship between Socrates and the Slave. I argue that in a conventional school, students often become victims of such discourse treating them as objects (often as containers for the certified knowledge). I am talking about the institutionalized practice of accountability in which the student (and the teacher) is hold accountable for having certain certified knowledge. This discourse of accountability in modern conventional schools organized through practice of high stake testing occurs *on* and *about* the students and never *with* the students (Matusov, St. Julien et al., 2005). Nowadays, conventional teachers are often required to write lesson plans describing their teaching objectives in the following way objectifying their students, "By the end of the lesson, the students are expected to know..." and then items from the list of the State Educational standards follow (see, for example, http://www.sustainabletable.org/schools/teachers/lesson_plans_jburke_0405.ppt).   It   is impossible to imagine that Socrates might have any of such statements for his dialogues with Meno or Anytus or any other free citizens except with the Slave, "By the end of the lesson, the Slave is expected to be perplexed about how to double square area, to realized that doubling square side makes square area four-folded, and to learn how to draw a square of half square area of the original square" (although it is very doubtful that the state of Athens would have had any educational standards for the slaves about teaching them geometry!). With free citizen interlocutors, Socrates was loyal to them and their intellectual needs and was their agency, like a doctor is loyal to his or her patients. With the Slave, Socrates was not loyal this interlocutor but to the Slave's master, Meno, whom Socrates wanted to demonstrate his notion of anamnesis using the Slave as a tool of the demonstration. Similarly, teachers in traditional schools are not loyal to their students and are not recognized by the society as loyal to their students. They are agency of the State and school administration rather than their students. The Hippocratic Oath does not exist for teachers of conventional schools[1].

In contrast to dialogues with free citizens Meno and Anytus, Socrates' dialogue with the Slave was not ontologically charged (see tables 1 and 4 in the previous chapter). During their dialogue, neither Socrates nor the Slave appeals to citizenship, politics, morality, emotions, gender, homosexuality and so forth. Their mathematical discussion was self-contained. We argue that this self-contained dialogue is also a birth mark of a conventional school dialogue and it is rooted in the desire of the teacher to unilaterally control the pedagogical discourse. Of course, one can argue that the non-ontological nature of the Socrates-Slave dialogue was rooted in the math subject that might be non-ontological by its nature (in contrast to the subjects that Socrates discussed with Meno and Anytus that were ontological by their nature). In response to this valid possibility, we want to reply that even if it were true that math is "naturally" non-ontological subject, it were Socrates who chose to discuss it. Second, I strongly disagree that math or any other subject is inherently self-contained and non-ontological (Atweh, Forgasz, & Nebres, 2001). Actually, I argue that the opposite is true: all subjects are inherently ontological, social, political, emotional, and hybrid with other subjects and practices (Latour, 1987). Even more, so-called self-contained non-ontological discourses are a result of some kind of special "purification" (Latour, 1987), in which ever-present ontology is keep hidden outside of the focus of the participants. For example, I argue that in the case of the Socrates-Slave dialogue, Socrates himself was not interested in math but rather in demonstrating Meno the process of anamnesis. Similarly, there is no evidence to suggest that the Save was honestly engaging with the investigations of math problems at hand. In fact, the power-laden circumstances suggest that by participating in the dialogue with Socrates, the Slave was simply pleasing the whimsy of his master's friend (and master), as would have been prudent under the circumstances.

Both Socrates and the Slave were "ontologically not there" during their dialogue: they were both ontologically engaged in subjects other than math that they kept hidden from each other. They both were engaged non-ontologically with math. Similarly, in a conventional school, the teacher does not need to be interested in or passionate about the subject he or she teaches (and rarely is) and does not need to care that the students are. A conventional teacher is often ontologically concerned about how to cover the preplanned curriculum[2] and sustain the unilateral class order without necessarily even checking if the students get the covered curriculum or not. In their own turn, the conventional school students are often ontologically concerned how to get good grades with minimum efforts. In either case, they both are not necessarily concerned ontologically about the subject matter like Meno, Anytus, and Socrates who were passionately concerned during their pedagogical dialogues. In contrast, when

---

[1] Searching the Internet by placing the wording "Teacher Oath" in the Google search engine, we have found Teacher Oath written in 1935 in State of Georgia, in which teachers pledge their loyalty to the State and not their students http://www.cviog.uga.edu/Projects/gainfo/1935resn-3.htm. My graduate student Stephanie Drye has written an alternative Teacher Oath pledging loyalty to her students (see http://ematusov. soe.udel.edu/oath).

[2] The teacher often gets upset with the curriculum is not fully covered or is covered too fast in the prescribed term of the lesson. When the lesson is covered too fast, the teacher often does not know what to do with the rest of the time of the lesson period. When the lesson is not fully covered, the teacher might be concerned that the students are not sufficiently prepared for the tests measuring both the teacher and the students accountability.

Socrates interacted with the Slave, there was no ontological engagement. Only Socrates' dialogues with free men achieve ontological engagement. The nature of the engagement is defined by the nature of the relationship, not the nature of the involved individuals.

STUDENTS' NON-ONTOLOGICAL ENGAGEMENT: SOCRATIC DIALOGUE WITH THE SLAVE

I reviewed modern educational literature on Socratic dialogues in the classroom. My findings show that the use of Socratic dialogue in the classroom is highly variant, mostly on a continuum from Socrates' dialogue with a slave to a dialogue with free citizens. An example of slave-like dialogue is found in Adler's work: "Today I am going to show an object to you and I want you to just look at it for one minute in absolute silence. At the end of that time, please write what you saw first and what question you have about the object. Remember, no talking, because once someone talks it disrupts and alters the others' thinking" (Adler & Paideia Group, 1984). Here the teacher is in full control of all discussion about a decontextulized object, while students cannot challenge nor even talk about why they should discuss this particular object. Behind this imposed silence, there is an institution of pedagogical violence quite similar to the slave system that surrounds Socrates' dialogues. Within this slave-like pedagogical regime, the students will be probably more focused on pleasing the teacher rather than on seeking their own truth in their own inquiry (Boghossian, 2002; Foucault, 1984). It is interesting and symptomatic that in his educational manifesto, Adler does not trust the school students to make responsible for their own learning despite the fact he claims that self-actualization and self-improvement should be the primary goal of schooling (Adler, 1982, p. 16). He thinks that if students are given educational choices, many of them will immediately abuse the system, "All sidetracks, specialized courses, or elective choices must be eliminated. Allowing then will always lead a certain number of students to voluntarily downgrade their own education" (p. 21). In a name of equality, he eliminates students' decision making about their own education. The students are treated as uneducated and too ignorant rather than learners like the teacher. The educational decisions will be made for them by educated experts – the teachers. How can the students learn to become responsible for their own decisions if they are robbed for a possibility for making such decisions and from guidance how to make them responsibly?

Both Rud (1997) and Garlikov (1998) are right that Socrates' math dialogue with the Slave has become a very attractive pedagogical model for conventional educators for both math and non-math instruction (for non-math instruction see, for example, Giangrandi & Tasso, 1997). I have made a search on the wording "Socratic dialogue" using the ERIC reference database. One of the first references that came out was a very interesting article reporting about research on use of Socratic dialogue in Taiwanese elementary schools for math instruction (Chang, Lin, & Chen, 1998). The research was focused on use of Socratic dialogue for correcting elementary school 9-year old children procedural "misconceptions" for arithmetic calculations, "Brown and Burton (1978) have found that some misconceptions occurred in the solving procedures of the subtraction exercises. Among these misconceptions, there are six types to be frequently found in the students" (Chang et al., 1998, p. 62). I want to give one example of how one of the six "misconceptions" is corrected with use of Socratic dialogue, "(*M5*) *0 - N = N*. Whenever the top digit in a column is 0, the student writes the bottom digit in his/her answer. For example, 304 - 232 = 132" (p. 63). The researchers constructed a special pedagogical intervention modeled after Socratic dialogues (they did not specified what kind of dialogues developed by Plato they used for their construction but they did not discuss the principles of Socratic dialogue) between the teacher (T) and the student (S) who demonstrated the M5 procedural "misconception",

Example 3. Correction of "0 - N = N"

1.	T:	50 - 23 = ?
2.	S:	33.
3.	T:	0 - 3 = ?
4.	S:	3
5.	T :	3 - 0 = ?
6.	S:	3.
7.	T:	You mean that 3 - 0 = 0 - 3?
8.	S :	It may [be] wrong.
9.	T:	17 - 6 = ?
10.	S:	11.
11.	T:	18 - 6 = ?
12.	S:	12.
13.	T:	Can you find something about 17 - 6 and 18 - 6?
14.	S:	The digits 7 and 8 in the two exercises are larger than the subtrahend 6. I can directly subtract 6 from 7 or 8 without any borrows.
15.	T:	Can you subtract the digit 7 from 6 for 16 - 7 without borrowing?
16.	S:	No, I cannot.
17.	T:	Why?
18.	S:	The digit 6 is smaller than the digit 7.
19.	T:	Do you think that the digit 0 can be subtracted by the digit 3 without borrowing?
20.	S:	No, It does not.
21.	T:	Try again for 50 - 23 = ?
22.	S:	27.

(Chang et al., 1998, pp. 65-66)

Like all Socratic dialogues, this dialogue involves the teacher asking many questions (11 to be exact), diagnosing the student's prior (erroneous) knowledge (turns 1-4), making the student perplexed (turns 3-8), leash-like leading instruction (turns 9-20), and making the student think like the teacher (turns 21-22). A close analysis shows that the presented pedagogical dialogue is much closer to Socrates' dialogue with the Slave than his dialogues with free people. Indeed, like in the Socrates-Slave dialogue, the student never asked questions, the inquiry was initiated by the teacher, the teacher asked only answer-known rhetorical questions (73% of the total questions) and leading-option rhetorical questions (the teacher's turns 7, 15, 19; 27%). There is the total lack of information-seeking questions in this dialogue. Like the Socrates-Slave dialogue, the teacher-student dialogue was self-contained, decontextualized, and non-ontological for its participants. The only discursive difference[3] of this dialogue from the Socrates-Slave dialogue is that in this pedagogical dialogue there is prevalence of answer-known rhetorical questions over option-leading rhetorical questions (the percentage distribution is exactly opposite, see table 2 in the previous chapter). This finding is in accord with observations of many other researchers of modern conventional classroom discourse showing prevalence of the teacher asking answer-known rhetorical questions (Lemke, 1990; Matusov et al., 2002; Mehan, 1979; Sinclair & Coulthard, 1975; Skidmore, 2000; Wells, 1992, September).

What Is Wrong with Socratic Dialogues Modeled after His Dialogue with the Slave?

A reader may raise an important question, "What is fuss about? The student in the presented dialogue has learned about the important arithmetic problem-solving technique and the teacher successfully corrected the $0 - N = N$ mistake that the student had had. What is the problem with this pedagogue based on Socratic dialogue?! It may be true that this pedagogical dialogue is heavily based on Socrates' dialogue with the Slave, but so what if it leads to solid, successful, and important learning in the student?! Do you doubt that the presented pedagogical dialogue is effective as presented by three scholars?" In my view, the authors, Chang, Lin, & Chen (1998) presented rather convincing evidence that the Socratic dialogue intervention that they developed was impressively successful as their post-test measurement showed[4]. In this sense, the efficiency of the intervention (or better to say "instructional strategy based on Socratic dialogue with the Slave") is out of doubt – it can be successfully used for many students. However, I challenge what "educational success" means in this case. If it means successful use of the math procedure, I agree that the instructional strategy based on Socratic dialogue with the Slave can be very successful. If it means the students' deep conceptual and ontological engagement in math, I see a problem with use of this pedagogy. Let us consider this challenge in details by analysis of the given case of problem-solving of arithmetical subtraction task.

One of astonishing problems often overlooked by information-processing-oriented scholars like the discussed Taiwanese authors and Brown and Burton (1978) and often emphasized by situated cognition scholars like Lave (1988) and Nunes, Schliemann and Carraher (1993) is that conventional school students can make outrageous mistakes without noticing that[5]. While working at an afterschool program, I saw many examples when children did not see anything strange when they divide an integer number by an integer number and get the result that is greater than the initial number that they divided. Even more, the students cannot see anything strange with their answers even after their attention is attracted to the

---

[3] Tara Falcone (personal communication, March 7, 2008) pointed out at another difference. In the turns#13-14, the teacher used an open-ended question that allowed the student articulate his unique strategy. Socrates did not ask the Slave any open-ended question.

[4] Although, in my view, an inferential statistical analysis is needed to support their claim.

[5] At the face of mounting research evidence about decontextualized schoolish practices, I disagree with Linell's (1998) interesting hypothesis that decontextualized monological practices promote transfer knowledge across contexts and this function of these practices is what promotes their widespread in industrial and post-industrial societies.

mistake. When I challenge them, they often tell me that they use the same procedures as the teacher showed them.

> In one [high school] classroom, students were asked to find the weight of a brick after measuring its length, width, and height, and being given the value of its density in pounds per cubic inch. The exchange went something like this:
>
> *Teacher:* 'Who can tell me the weight of the brick?'
> Student: '1016 pounds.' (Looking at his paper)
> *Teacher:* 'Lift the brick. Now, how much does it weigh?'
> Student: (Again looking at his paper) '1016 pounds.'
>
> The student had failed to make the connection between the problem and real life. Calculations were unrelated to common sense. This example was not an isolated incident. Time after time we witnessed the use of numbers with little or no thought given to implications and applications. (Boyer, 1983, pp. 108-109)

Whitson (2007) disagrees with Boyer that the presented problem is rooted in a lack of the connection between the problem and real life. Rather, in a conventional school, students are focused on "cracking" the procedures and directives presented by the teacher (cf. Minick, 1993). Once when I pointed to the 10-year old child that the result of his subtraction in his homework was bigger than the minuend which, I told him was very strange, he replied to me, "But I did everything correctly!" He seemed to imply that the result was correct only because he used the math procedures exactly how they were taught in school. Although his claim was hopefully wrong – his teacher probably did not teach him the wrong math procedures, it is important to notice that, in his reply to me, he appealed to the social norms – the social authority of his teacher and the school -- rather than to the conceptual understanding of the math practice (Davis, 1983; Doyle, 1986b). It is doubtfully that this kind of argument can be offered in everyday practice when, for example, the child negotiates change with his friends while buying collectively a snack. The child sees school knowledge as conventional, similar to conventionality of language or any symbols. It is useless to ask why "desk" is called "desk" (beyond the history of language). Similar, in mainstream schools, it becomes "useless" to ask why fractions with different denominators must be added in such a strange way – it is just a (conventional) rule, as many of my college students, future teachers, told me! *Conventional knowledge* is established through a communal authority while *conceptual knowledge* is established through testing of internally persuasive discourse.

What is interesting, as situated cognition research cited above shows, children and adults do not this kind of outrageous mistakes in their everyday life. Even more, they rarely do mistakes that they do in school settings. Many situated cognition scholars argue that the problem is that conventional modern schools teach children (and adults) universal decontextualized math procedures (like in the case presented by Chang, Lin, & Chen) while in everyday life people learn how to participate in a network of locally situated strategies. Let me explain and illustrate the difference. In the example above, in the turns 9 and 11, the teacher presented similar math problems to the student: $17 - 6 = ?$ and $18 - 6 = ?$ From universal decontextualized procedural approach subscribed by an information processing cognitive paradigm of psychology, the computational tasks are the same. There is the same math procedures expected to be and must be used by the conventional school students. A computer program, such as Excel, uses the same algorithm to calculate these two arithmetic problems. However, from a situated cognition approach the second math task is very different from the first one. As soon as the first task is solved, it can promote a locally situated math strategy for solving the second task (Linell, 1998). Indeed, a student may notice that the second task is the same as the first except the minuend is more by 1 while the subtrahend is the same. So, the second task becomes 1 + THE RESULT FROM THE FIRST TASK (11). The student can solve this task by applying another locally situated math strategy by replacing addition of 1 with counting: the next number of 11 is 12. Please notice that the math strategies used in this imaginary example are very particular and local both to the presented situation (the second task is presented immediately after the first) and to the student (that local strategies are available to the student in general and this particular ontological situation to be "here and there" with the teacher in the classroom). One can easily think of other local math strategies to solve the second task. There can be invoked different network of locally situated strategies to solve math problems. I also want to distinguish my use of the terms of "math *strategy*" versus "math *procedure*". In math strategy, the actor is guided by his/her content-conceptual understanding of the problem at hand. In contrast, in math procedure, the actor is guided by the perceived form (cf. formula) of the problem – the content-conceptual understanding is not needed.

One of the major objections against use of a network of locally situated strategies (in math and in anything else) is that they are very limited and cannot be use in novel situations. Indeed, how to solve the first task of 17 – 6 using a network of locally situated math strategies? One of many possible ways to solve this arithmetic task is to use a locally situated math strategy of subtracting digits 7 – 6 (which by itself can be solved via locally situated strategies or immediately through psychological affordances (cf. J. J. Gibson, 1979) without any strategy). It is true that all locally situated strategies are very limited but their strength is use application via a network: a creative combination of the strategies (like the neural network of the brain: each neuron can be very limited and even rigidly specialized but the network becomes very powerful and flexible). Situated cognition research on practitioners involved in innovative creative tasks shows that these practitioners mainly apply a network of locally situated math strategies rather than universal decontextualized procedures used in school (Hutchins, 1995; Nunes et al., 1993).

Like many situated cognition scholars (e.g., Lave, 1992b), I argue that the school should help the children expand their already existing networks of locally situated strategies rather than to teach them universal decontextualized procedures currently taught in conventional schools in math, science, writing, and other subjects. By doing that, not only the students stop doing outrageous mistakes, but they will learn content-conceptual understanding, increase their motivation in academic subjects, diminish the gap between the school, everyday life, and apply with ease the learned school knowledge in out-of-school practices. However, and this is *my major argument*, the proposed "learning by expansion" (Engeström, 1987) of the network of locally situated strategies cannot be guided by using the Socratic dialogue with Slave similar that was used by Chang, Lin, & Chen (1998)!

The Relationship between Genuine Learning and Pedagogical Regimes of Dialogues

Why not – why a pedagogical dialogue modeled after the Socratic dialogue with Slave *cannot* promote the expansion of students' networks of locally situated strategies? Let me explain "why not". First, if the teacher's pedagogical goal is an expansion of the students' networks of locally situated strategies by learning new strategies and new combinations of the existing strategies (which arguably is a strategy in its own right), then it is impossible for the teacher to know what new strategies each student might learn at the end of the lesson (and even if the lesson has its own end!). The locally situated strategies are themselves are supported by the students' networks and do not stand-alone. For example, above I showed how a student may solve a problem of subtraction of 6 from 18 if he or she just solved a problem 17 – 6. My local solution involved the two locally situated math strategies: 1) recognizing the relationship between the two tasks and 2) using counting for addition of one. The issue is that these are not independent but rather interdependent: one strategy needs another strategy (or similar one). The student's networks of locally situated strategies are not only unique but also dynamic: each student finds him or herself in a unique situation in the classroom even though they are faced with "the same problem" (the problem is never the same for actors). Guiding to expand students' networks of locally situated strategies makes impossible for the teacher to know the exact endpoint of the guidance in contrast to Socratic dialogue with the Slave where the exact endpoint of the dialogue was known to Socrates in advance. To a lesser extend it is true for all Socrates' dialogues presented by Plato, however, Socrates' own numerous statements showed that he strived for such a dialogue in which he would arrive to something new himself. It is definitely true that not only the teacher does not know the endpoint of the students in helping them to expand their networks of locally situated practices but it is highly possible that as a result of such guidance the teacher's own network of locally situated strategies would be expanded. For illustration of this, see my own detailed example of my own learning new strategies from first and second graders while teaching them the multiplication table (Matusov, 2001a).

Second, situated cognition research shows that problem-solving process involves problem- and goal- redefining processes (Engeström, 1990; Hutchins, 1995; Lave, 1988; Nunes et al., 1993; Wenger, 1998). Thus, the teacher cannot unilaterally control the problem and the inquiry at hand in a discussion. Socrates could not and did not fully control the discussion agenda in his dialogues with the free citizens but he did have his full control of the problem in his dialogue with the Slave. The same is true for the teacher in Chang, Lin, & Chen's (1998) case.

Third, expansion of the students' networks of locally situated strategies is impossible when the students (and the teacher!) are not ontologically involved in the academic subject problem at hand. The students' ontology of them "being here and now" defines what locally situated strategies are available to them at the given moment in the given situation. Säljö & Wyndhamn (1993) demonstrated that when a problem of finding out a postage price of a parcel using a photocopied excerpt of postage rates was presented to the same students but during different classes (math versus social studies classes), students used different approaches to solve this hypothetical problem. The author concluded that since the students ontologically perceived themselves being in the midst of different subjects with different institutional subject practices, they felt forced to use different strategies to approach the problem.

When students are not ontologically involved in the academic problem, they often focus on using decontextualized procedures rather than on locally situated strategies. As I will argue in further chapters, students (and the teacher) are always ontologically involved in something; however, this "something" can be not the targeted academic subject. When the students involved in the targeted academic subject non-ontologically, their ontological goal is often to guess what the teacher wants from them and please the teacher with an appropriate action. The students' cooperative but not collaborative (Matusov & White, 1996) focus on the teacher's intentions leads students to pay attention to the *form* of the teacher actions – to formalism and to decontextualized procedures – away from the content-conceptual understanding. To focus the students to the networks of local and situated strategies about the targeted academic subject, the teacher must make lesson, discussion, and the presented problems ontological for the students.

Fourth, when the teacher focuses on helping the students expand their networks of locally situated strategies, the teacher authority is rooted in the ontological engagement of students in the targeted academic subject. The student's implicit question about the relationship with the teacher, "Why should I do what the teacher asks me to do here and now?!" cannot be answered by reference to slavery bondage or to the school coercive institutional practices or to anything else outside of the academic subject itself. For example, if Meno would ask himself, "Why should I answer to Socrates' questions?" – he would probably reply to himself, "Because I want to know what the origin of virtues is and Socrates seems to help me to address this inquiry." As soon as Meno cannot reply to this tacit question, his collaboration with Socrates and entire dialogue becomes in jeopardy. The same was true for Anytus but not for the Slave whom involvement with Socrates was guaranteed by the slavery bondage.

In sum, the teacher focusing on expansion of the students' networks of locally situated strategies requires dramatic transformation of pedagogical regime of power and thus the teacher-student relations. I argue that Socratic pedagogical dialogue with the Slave is so attractive to modern conventional educators exactly because power conditions of their work and teacher-student relations are very similar. Conventional teachers work with disinterested students who are forced to be in the classroom with the teachers. Like in case of slavery, there are external institutional and political forces that make students disinterested like mandatory attendance, state prescribed curricula, state educational standards, the teachers' loyalty to the state and school administration rather than to their students, and so on. Interested students, like interested slaves, can easily disrupt the monologic order of the conventional classroom by focusing on its oppressive conditions as our research on transition of students from an innovative collaborative school to conventional high schools shows (Matusov, Hayes, & Smith, 2005, September).

STUDENTS' ONTOLOGICAL ENGAGEMENT WITH THE TEACHER BEING THE EXPERT NUMBER ONE IN THE CLASSROOM: SOCRATIC PEDAGOGICAL DIALOGUES WITH FREE CITIZENS

My investigation of educational literature on Socratic dialogue shows that modern pedagogical dialogues used by teachers in contemporary classrooms are also guided by Socrates' dialogues with free people. I want to remind the readers that, as my discourse analysis of Socratic dialogues with free citizens in Meno shows, these dialogues were ontological for the participants, open for students' questions, challenging the teacher's reputations, and so on. The following example from Garlikov's own teaching illustrates a classroom dialogue located much closer to Socrates' dialogue with free citizens than with the Slave, "… in a discussion of homosexuality in an 'Ethics and Society' course where many students said that homosexuality was wrong because (the idea of) it was so disgusting. …. I asked them then to close their eyes and think about ... their parents having sex with each other. They all let out an even bigger groan of disgust, and said they found that idea really disgusting. So I asked whether they would have to conclude then that it was immoral for their parents ever to have (or to have had) sex with each other. They agreed it was not. Of course they then asked whether that meant I thought homosexuality was moral. My response was that whether it is or is not is simply unrelated to whether it is personally disgusting or not to anyone. I was not trying to argue in this particular case for or against the morality of homosexuality, but was merely trying to get them to see that finding an action disgusting did not justify their thinking it must be immoral just because of that" (Garlikov, 1998). From this fragment, the students discuss an issue that is ontologically salient for them and they openly challenge the teacher and place his teaching reputation at stake (notice that indirectly the students seem to try to accuse the instructor of attempting to brainwash them by insisting to them that homosexuality is moral). However, the teacher does not seek the boundary of his own ignorance as Socrates claimed about the nature of his own dialogues (although not demonstrated by Plato). Moreover, Garlikov (1998) argues that when the questioner asks a genuine information-seeking question, it is not teaching, "Bill Hunter and I had a long e-mail debate, which is available in an edited form at http://www.Garlikov.com/teaching/ dialogue.html about whether fostering research or discovery by students, via questions the questioner may not know the answer to, is teaching." Thus, this approach stemming from Socrates' dialogues with free citizens creates a community of learners among the students while excluding the teacher him or herself from the inquiry and, thus, from the classroom community of learners.

In such a dialogical pedagogy, the role of the teacher is merely to provoke learning in the students, as "midwife", using Socrates' own words, without challenging his or her own position. The teacher continues using leash-like guidance (Matusov & Rogoff, 2002) by asking known-answer rhetorical and leading-option questions like in the case of Socratic dialogue with the Slave. However, unlike in the latter case, Garlikov's pedagogical dialogue with his students led to emergence of an authentic ontological inquiry in the students. Before the dialogue with their teacher, the students were convinced that homosexuality is immoral because it is disgusting. After the instructor brought an example of parental sex that was perceived by the students as disgusting although not immoral they experienced some kind of paralysis similar to Socratic "torpedo touch" (Thomas, 1985). Now they had either to find another rationale for why homosexuality is immoral, which was not apparently available to them; or to accept that they do not know whether homosexuality is moral or not – a state of uncomfortable perplexity. The ontological (for the students) nature of the dialogue is evident in the fact that the student could and did raise questions to the teacher, disagree with him, and reject his position – in contrast to non-ontological engagement of pedagogical dialogues modeled after Socratic dialogue with the Slave.

The teacher remains being "the Expert Number One" in the class – the teacher continues leading the student to the point that is pre-known by the teacher. However, when the students are ontologically engaged in the inquiry, the teacher has to prove his or her expertise to the students. If in an instruction based on the students' non-ontological engagement, the students try to make sense of what the teacher wants from them – in ontologically-based instruction, the students demand from the teacher the proof within their own(ed) inquiry.

I did not know what happened with Garlikov's class after the students became perplexed but it is reasonable to expect that could continue searching for a solution of their perplexity. Searching ERIC database, I found another example of an instruction involving ontological engagement with the teacher being as the Expert Number One in the class based on Socratic dialogue. If the case of Garlikov, we have the description of the beginning of his Socratic pedagogical dialogue, in the case of Bartolini Bussi we have the second part of the dialogue (Bartolini Bussi, 2000, May). Bartolini Bussi investigated an Italian 5th grade innovative math class where the teacher used Socratic dialogue for math instruction involving a rather sophisticated geometrical problem (pp. 4-5),

The [5th grade] pupils have been given the following individual problem on an A4 sheet:
Draw a circle, with radius 4 on, tangent to both circles. Explain carefully your method and justify it.

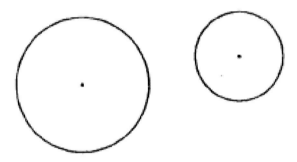

Figure 1. The circles have radii 3 cm and 2 cm and the distance of their centers is 7 cm.

All the pupils of the classroom have produced a solution by trial and errors, adjusting a compass to produce a circle that looks tangent to both. Some of them have found two solutions (symmetrical). The teacher (Mara Boni) collects all the individual solutions, analyses them and, a week later, and gives all the pupils a copy of Veronica's solution. Then she introduces the theme of discussion.

Veronica's solution:
The first thing I have done was to find the centre of the wheel C; I have made by trial and error, in fact I have immediately found the distance between the wheel B and C [6cm]. Then I have found the distance between A and C [7cm] and I have given the right 'inclination' to the two segments, so that the radius of C measured 4 cm in all the cases. Then I have traced the circle.

Veronica's justification:

I am sure that my method works because it agrees with the three theories we have found:
i) the points of tangency Hand G are aligned with ST and TR;
ii) the segments ST and TR meet the points of tangency H and G;

iii) the segments ST and TR are equal to the sum of the radii SG and GT. TH and HR.

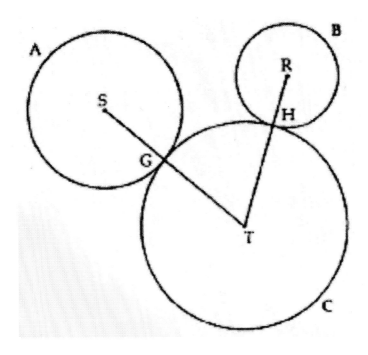

Figure 2.

The classroom discussion:

Teacher: Veronica has tried to give the right inclination. Which segments is she speaking of? Many of you open the compass 4cm. Does Veronica use the segment of 4cm? What does she say she is using?

[Veronica's text is read again.]

Jessica: She uses the two segments ...

Maddalena: ..given by the sum of radii

Teacher: How did she make?

Giuseppe: She has rotated a segment.

Veronica: Had I used one segment, I could have used the compass.

[Some pupils point with thumb-index at the segments on Veronica's drawing and try to 'move' them. They pick up an ideal segment as if it were a stick and try to move it.]

Francesca B.: From the circle B have you thought or drawn the sum?

Veronica: I have drawn it.

Giuseppe: Where?

Veronica: I have planned to make RT perpendicular [to the base side of the sheet] and then I have moved ST and RT until they touched each other and the radius of C was 4cm.

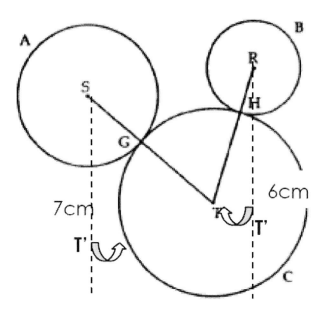

Figure 2a. Veronica's locally situated strategies: 1) making perpendiculars from the given circles A and B to the base of the page, 2) marking the ST' and RT' segments on the perpendiculars, 3) using her thumb-index fingers of both hands she rotated the segments ST' and RT' until they met in the point T, 4) making a new circle C with radius 4cm from the point T as its center, 5) making sure that the new circle C is touching the circles A and B [the figure and the caption are added by me – EM].

    Alessio: I had planned to take two compasses, to open them 7 and 6 and to look whether they found the centre. But I could not use two compasses.

    Stefania P.: Like me; I too had two compasses in the mind.

    Veronica: I remember now: I too have worked with the two segments in this way, but I could not [use two compasses] on the sheet.

    [All the pupils 'pick up' the segments on Veronica's drawing with thumb-index of the two hands and start to rotate them. The shared experience is strong enough to capture all the pupils.]

    Elisabetta [excited]: She has taken the two segments of 6 and 7, has kept the centre still and has rotated: ah I have understood!

    Stefania P.: ... to find the centre of the wheel ...

    Elisabetta: ... after having found the two segments ...

    Stefania P.: ... she has moved the two segments.

    Teacher: Moved? Is moved a right word?

    Voices: Rotated .. as if she had the compass.

    Alessio Had she translated them, she had moved the centre.

    Andrea: I have understood, teacher, I have understood really, look at me ...

    [The pupils continue to rotate the segments picked up with hands.]

    Voices: Yes, the centre comes out there, it's true.

    Alessio: It's true but you cannot use two compasses

    Veronica: you can use first on one side and then on the other.

    Teacher: Good pupils. Now draw the two circles on your sheet.

    [All the pupils draw the two circles on their sheet and correctly identify the two possible solutions for the centers.]

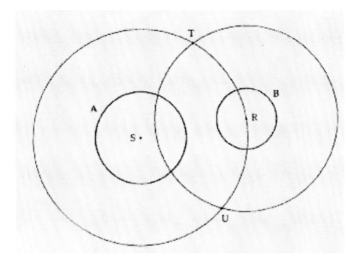

Figure 3.

The teacher, Mara Boni, gave the 5th grade children familiar with compass and circles a math problem far beyond their skill and knowledge. Using trail and error, the children found a pragmatic but not mathematical solution of the problem. I don't know if the problem was ontological for the children when the teacher gave the problem to them. However, when the teacher asked Veronica to present her trail and error solution to the other children, it became ontological for them. Throughout the class discussion, the teacher asked 3 questions: 2 questions were answer-known rhetorical questions (turns#1 and 4) and one question was option-leading rhetorical question (turn#18). The students' questions to Veronica were information-seeking (turns#7 and 9). Their ontological engagement was also evident from their apparent excitement and voluntary participation in the class discussion.

As Veronica (rather articulately) shared her locally situated strategies that she used in her trail-and-error pragmatic non-mathematical solution (turn#10 and figure2a), her classmates and she started "building on each other's ideas" (Matusov et al., 2002) and on each other locally situated strategies until the problem was solved mathematically rather than just pragmatically. Some students like Elizabetta (#15) and Andrea (#21) became excited learning new locally situated strategies that led Veronica to find the center of the new circle C (see also turns# 15, 20, 21, 22, 23). Other children also used locally situated strategies some of which were similar and some were different from Veronica's. For example, Alessio (#11) and Stefania P. (#12) suggested that it was better -- more exact, more mathematical -- to use two compasses instead of the index-thumb fingers of both hands and Veronica agreed with them (#13). However, Alessio (#11, 23) insisted that it is impossible to use two compasses at the same time. This problem was first acknowledged by Veronica (#13) and then solved by her (#24) suggesting the use of one compass in sequence (see figure 3). The teacher acknowledged the solution as mathematically correct one (turn#25).

Although on the first glance it appears that the teacher's role was minimal, it was not true. The teacher was responsible for making the geometrical problem ontological for the students and for making them to share their locally situated strategies. She (like probably Garlikov in his class) was also responsible for creating a special classroom atmosphere, in which the students felt safe and free to participate in the discussion. The students focused on evaluation of and building on each other's idea rather than on self-promotion or putting other students down. This is essential for promoting a regime of "internally persuasive discourse" (Bakhtin, 1991) and "a community of learners" among the students (Rogoff, Matusov, & White, 1996).

However, the teacher – neither Mari Boni nor Rick Garlikov – was not a part of the students' community of learners that they both created. We do not know about the rationale of the Italian 5th grader teacher Mari Boni of why she decided to exclude herself from the classroom community of learners, but Rick Garlikov excluded himself from the classroom inquiry because he believes that the role of the teacher is to remain being the Expert Number One rather than the number one Learner in the classroom. He argues against the teacher asking non-rhetorical information-seeking questions and against the teacher's genuine engagement in the classroom inquiry at hand, "...the [Socratic] Method differs from just asking questions, especially open-ended or non-leading questions, or ones that one does not know the answer to oneself. That is in part why it is a teaching method, not just a brain-storming activity nor an activity whose point is merely to inspire thought or research by simply asking general or open-ended questions or questions one does not know the answer to oneself." Garlikov's main concern leading him to his position is that if the teacher joins the classroom inquiry at hand, he or she would not know the endpoint the discussion and, thus, the teacher might lose the direction of guidance, the special role of class instructor, and even control of the class (see his discussion with Bill Hunter about this issue at http://www.Garlikov.com/teaching/dialogue.html).

Like Bill Hunter, I respectfully disagree with Rick Garlikov. I argue that the teacher's role as the Learner Number One (i.e., the leading learner) in the classroom not only possible but also desirable. Also, this role of the Learner Number One is in the spirit of Socrates' own claims about his own role in pedagogical dialogues (however, in my view, he did not demonstrated these claims in his own practice, at least, as described by Plato – see the previous chapter). In the early 1990s, my colleagues Barbara Rogoff, Nancy Bell, and I studied two public elementary schools in Utah: one was an academically good conventional school and the other was an innovative collaborative school run as a community of learners. Along other things, we investigated the 3rd and 4th grade children's practice and attitudes toward guidance. We interviewed the children and observed how they provide guidance. We found that the children from the conventional school, like Rick Garlikov, did not believe that it is possible to provide guidance to somebody if the guide does not know him or herself how to solve the problem for which the guidance is provided. In accord with this belief, the 4th grade children from the conventional school often solved the math problems that we offered to the children first and only then provided their guidance to the 3rd graders. In contrast, many children from the innovative collaborative school believed that it is possible to provide guidance to somebody even though the guide does not know him or herself how to solve the problem for which the guidance is provided. We found that many 4th graders from the innovative collaborative provided their guidance while collaborative problem-solving with their third graders. Since they usually were more experienced and knowledgeable in math than their third graders, the fourth graders generated more math and meta-cognitive strategies to the problem solving and problem defining and provided guidance to the third graders about the math and meta-cognitive strategies they were using. Our analysis showed that despite Garlikov's concern, the 4th graders did not lose their guiding control over the problem and/or over their student (Matusov et al., 2002). A possibility of losing control over a classroom issue/problem/theme and over the students seems to be a problem of mastery in providing a collaborative guidance rather than a necessary consequence of the teacher becoming a learner (see Tharp & Gallimore, 1988 for discussion of how a seasoned teacher provided guidance to a novice teacher about collaborative guidance). When an instructor has been raised in a conventional school without experiencing a collaborative guidance, learning how to provide a collaborative guidance may not be easy for the instructor (Matusov & Rogoff, 2002).

There are many benefits for the teacher becoming the Learner Number One in the classroom rather than being the Expert Number One in the classroom. First, if the students have never experienced the teacher being learning, they are not modeled by the teacher how to learn in a situation when there is not an expert. When the teacher is a learner in the classroom, the students are modeled by the teacher how to learn in a novice situation. Second, when the teacher avoids hot issues with uncertainties for him or her, the students are not educated in the important social issues, for which there is not a consensus yet (or ever) in the society. Apparently, Rick Garlikov conscientiously avoided his own engagement in hot topics for himself when he did not know answers by himself. From his description, it is not clear what these topics were but it is reasonable to assume that these important hot issues involved whether homosexuality is moral or what is morality. If I am right, his students were left without guidance (partially or fully) for these important social and moral issues. If Rick Garlikov had chosen a collaborative guidance, in which he would investigate issues uncertain to him with his students, I am sure that his student would have learned more and deeper.

Similarly, if the Italian 5th grader teacher Mari Boni had decided to join the children and provide collaborative guidance, arguably her students could have learned more and deeper. For example, the teacher might have chosen to discuss why try-and-trail pragmatic way of solving the offered math problem using index-thumb fingers of both hands is worse than one using two compasses which is itself is worse than using one compass. Why was the pragmatic solution of finding the third circle touching the other two worse than the mathematical solution? What makes pragmatic solutions of tasks and what makes mathematical solutions? What are limitations of math solutions? When are pragmatic solutions better than math solutions? The children seemed to agree with these value judgments but these value judgments were left unexplored and undiscussed. These open-ended and ill-defined issues are interesting and extremely important to explore for the presented problem and future problems. In contrast, in her turn#25 the teacher ended abruptly the discussion by validating Veronica's new solution as the "correct" one (as if other two solutions – trail-and-error and using two compasses were incorrect). The students were left without any guidance of why this solution was better than the other two.

Third, the teacher avoiding a learner role has to limit the students what they can legitimately discuss in the classroom and what they cannot discuss. What if a student insisted about discussing the issues of morality of homosexuality in Garlikov's classroom? Why is it the case that Rick Garlikov can ask his students what they think about morality of homosexuality while his students cannot ask him this question. Sooner or later this relational problem leads the students to a power conflict with the teacher, in which the teacher tries to overrule the students' hot issues. As a consequence of this power struggle, the classroom atmosphere necessary for creating free and safe learning environment can be seriously jeopardized. The students may lose trust in the teacher and reserve themselves from ontological engagement in problems, issues, and topics suggested by the teacher.

Fourth, when the teacher sees him or herself as an expert and not as a learner, the students get a message from the teacher that learning is a temporary process leading to the state of expertise when learning is not needed. Finally, the teacher as the expert in the classroom arrests his or her own learning of the subject.

BUILDING A COMMUNITY OF LEARNERS: SOCRATES' ESPOUSED THEORY OF PEDAGOGICAL DIALOGUE

When Meno used his famous "torpedo touch" metaphor to accuse Socrates for intentionally confusing and paralyzing thinking of free citizens, Socrates replied that unlike torpedo fish, Socrates paralyzes his own thinking by uncovering his own internal contradiction that had been invisible for him before, "if the torpedo fish is itself numb and so makes others numb, then I resemble it, but not otherwise, for I myself do not have the answer when I perplex others, but I am more perplexed than anyone when I cause perplexity in others. So now I do not know what virtue is; perhaps you knew before you contacted me, but now you are certainly like one who does not know. Nevertheless, I want to examine and seek together with you what it may be" (Plato, 1997, p. 279, 80c). Socrates claimed that he was first and foremost a Learner and not an Expert or a Pedagogical Manipulator (like sophists on his days). However, I could not find in the Meno Dialogue or in any other Socratic Dialogue[6] described by Plato instances when Socrates became "numb", admitted self-contradictions, and/or genuinely examined something that he had not known in advance together with his interlocutor. There can be several plausible explanations of why I cannot find evidence of Socrates' genuine learning in his dialogues. First, of course, obviously I could miss them by overlooking some important signs of Socrates' disorientation and perplexity. Second, Plato did not describe these instances well or even intentionally avoided them since his primary goal was not accurately capture the ethnography of Socratic pedagogical practices but rather through Socratic dialogue to articulate Plato's own philosophical views. Third, it can be that without interviewing the teacher – Socrates himself – it is impossible to capture moments of perplexity in the teacher (see description of such case in Matusov, Smith, Candela, & Lilu, 2007). An external observer such was Plato could not simply capture learning moments of Socrates. Finally, it could be that Socrates' "espoused theory" of his own teaching practice (using the word "teaching" in a modern sense) was different from his "theory-in-use" (see Argyris & Schön, 1978 for this useful terminological difference). In other words, it is possible that what Socrates said about his own practice was different that he actually did.

Whatever reason of why I could not find evidence of Socrates being a learner, it is still interesting to investigate how much his espoused theory of the teacher being the Learner Number One has affected modern educational practices. Reviewing current educational literature I found examples of such educational practice in work of extraordinary teachers like Paley (1992) and Gruwell (Freedom Writers & Gruwell, 1999). What is especially interesting

---

[6] Hansen (1988) claims that Socrates did self-examination in the Theaetetus Dialogue. My reading of the Dialogue is that Socrates did not do self-examination but rather pretend "self-examination" for achieving some rhetorical effect. In other word, I suspect that it was his typical rhetorical manipulation of his student to lead the student to a certain point rather than a genuine investigation. However, this issue requires further examination with perhaps use of a conversational analysis similar that I have made for the Meno Dialogue to reach a conclusive judgment.

in case of Paley is that she sees connection of her teaching practice and Socratic dialogue (Paley, 1986b).

Paley's teaching often starts with her being perplexed about her own students' words, thinking, acting, and feelings. The gaps of comprehension in a classroom community create teaching-learning moments for its participants. Paley keeps asking children relevant questions, based not on her own preconceptions, but rather on how the children think about a topic. This open-ended inquiry collaborative process turns into a classroom drama, in which her students enacted imaginative stories of their own construction guided by testing and probing questions coming from the teacher and other students. She turns the questioning reflexively upon herself and her own thinking using a tape recorder:

> ...the decisive factor for me was curiosity. When my intention was limited to announcing my own point of view, communication came to a halt. My voice drowned out the children's. However, when they said things that surprised me, exposing ideas I did not imagine they held, my excitement mounted... I kept the children talking, savoring the uniqueness of responses so singularly different from mine. The rules of teaching had changed; I now wanted to hear the answers I could not myself invent....

> ...teaching at a nursery school, I found that the unanticipated explanations of younger children bloomed in even greater profusion. The crosscurrents of partially overheard talk lifted my curiosity to new heights. It was similar to watching the instant replay of an exciting baseball moment. Did the runner really touch second base? Did Frederick actually say, "My mother doesn't have no more birthdays"? What does a four-year-old mean by this odd statement made in the doll corner? The next day I am pressed to find out.

> "Frederick, I'm curious about something I heard you say in the doll corner yesterday. You said your mother doesn't have birthdays any more." (Frederick knows my tendency to begin informal conversations in this manner, and he responds immediately.)

> "She doesn't. How I know is no one comes to her birthday and she doesn't make

> the cake."

> "Do you mean she doesn't have a birthday party?"

> "No. She really doesn't have a birthday."

> "Does she still get older every year?"

> "I think so. You know how much old she is? Twenty-two."

> "Maybe you and your dad could make her a birthday party."

> "But they never remember her birthday and when it's her birthday they forget when her birthday comes, and when her birthday comes they forget how old she is because they never put any candles. So how can we say how she is old?"

> "The candles tell you how old someone is?"

> "You can't be old if you don't have candles."

> "Frederick, I'll tell you a good thing to do. Ask mother to have a cake and candles. Then she'll tell you when her birthday is."

> "No. Because, see, she doesn't have a mother so she doesn't have a birthday."

> "You think because your grandma died your mother won't have any more birthdays?"

> "Right. Because, see, my grandma borned her once upon a time. Then she told her about her birthday. Then every time she had a birthday my grandma told. So she knew how many candles to be old."

> I turn to Mollie. "Frederick says his mother doesn't have any more birthdays."

"Why doesn't she?" Mollie wants to know.

"Because," Frederick answers patiently, "because my grandma died and my mother doesn't know how many candles old she is."

"Oh. Did your grandfather died, too?"

"Yeah. But he came back alive again."

Mollie stares solemnly at Frederick. "Then your grandma told him. If he whispers it to your mother maybe it's already her birthday today."

"Why should he whisper, Mollie?" I ask.

"If it's a secret," she says.

"I think Mollie has a good idea, Frederick. Why don't you ask your grandfather?"

"Okay. I'll tell him if my mommy could have a birthday on that day that they told her it was her birthday."

Why not just tell Frederick the truth: *"Of course* your mother has a birthday; everyone has a birthday." Tempting as it might be to set the record straight, I have discovered that I can't seem to teach the children that which they don't already know. I had, in fact, made this very statement- that everyone has a birthday – the previous week in another context. I had brought a special snack to school to celebrate my own birthday, and Frederick and Mollie seemed surprised.

"Why?" they asked.

"Why did I bring the cookies?"

"Why is it your birthday?"

"But everyone has a birthday. Today happens to be mine."

"Why is it your birthday?" Mollie insisted, attempting to give more meaning to her question by emphasizing another word.

"Well, I was born on this day a long time ago."

The conversation ended and we ate the cookies, but clearly nothing was settled. Their premises and mine did not match. What, for instance, could it possibly mean to be born on *this* day a long time ago?

A week later, Frederick made cause and effect out of the presence of one's own mother and the occasion of a birthday. The matter is not unimportant, because the phenomenon of birthday looms large. It is constantly being turned around and viewed from every angle, as are the acts of going to bed, going to work, cooking meals, shooting bad guys, calling the doctor or the babysitter - to name just a few of the Great Ideas present in the preschool.

Every day someone, somewhere in the room, plays out a version of "birthday." Birthday cakes are made of playdough and sand, and it is Superman's birthday or Care Bear's birthday or Mollie's birthday. "Birthday" is a curriculum in itself.

Besides being a study in numbers, age, birth, and death, it provides an ongoing opportunity to explore the three Fs - fantasy, friendship, and fairness.

"You can't come to my birthday if you say that!"

"You *could* come to my birthday, and my daddy will give you a hundred pieces of gum if you let me see your Gobot."

Any serious observation made about a birthday is worth following up, not in order to give Frederick the facts and close the subject, but to use this compelling material as a vehicle for examining his ideas of how the world works. If I am to know Frederick, I must understand, among many other things, how he perceives his mother's birthday and his grandfather's permanence. As the year progresses ...he will make connections that weave in and out of imagined and real events, and I will let my curiosity accompany his own as he discards old stories and creates new ones.... [T]he goal is..., no matter what the age of the student; someone must be there to listen, respond, and add a dab of glue to the important words that burst forth (Paley, 1986b, pp. 125-127).

In Paley's classroom, the teaching-learning moments are shaped not so much by self-examination and search for self-contradictions, as in the classic Socratic dialogues, but by findings and examinations of contradictions in social relations and practices that the community members involved. In the example above, the nursery teacher Vivian Paley is apparently perplexed not only by the child's logic, the child's cognition, accepting a possibility that a person may not have a birthday but also by an alarming fact (in a Western cultural tradition) that the child's mother has not been celebrated annually in her family as other members of Western society do. With the help of another child Mollie, Paley guides little Frederick how he can promote celebration of his mother in his family.

The children forced Paley deeper to understand the sociocultural notion of "birthday." The teacher is not just perplexed about how she can teach the child about the concept of "birthday" (although she is clearly perplexed about that), she is not just perplexed about how the child conceptualizes the notion of "birthday" (although she is clearly perplexed about that as well), she also is perplexed about meaning of the notion of birthday itself. As Bakhtin (1986) argued, meaning emerges as the relationship between a question and a answer. The teacher-student incomprehensibility creates opportunities for the teacher to ask new questions for the student and herself and thus to develop a new meaning. The teacher learns with and from the children that birthday is not just a logico-cognitive concept but a network of diverse local, situated meanings involving relationships with other people, tools of coercion and negotiation, and so forth. Paley has realized that the logico-cognitive concept itself is not a definition (e.g., "I was born on this day a long time ago") but rather a special relation within this network of local, situated meaning of "birthday" shaped by a special practice (i.e., a practice of organizing other practices by the calendar, see Zerubavel, 1985). Knowledge, resided in the relationship between somebody's question and somebody's answer, is a communal "property". Paley's concept of "birthday" residing in an adult community has shifted (or expanded) through her investigation with her students to her adult-children classroom community.

A reader may ask, "Well, I see now the evidence of Paley's learning with, from, and about the children. However, what is her learning anything to do with her teaching the children? Where is evidence of teaching in this example? What was evidence that the children become perplexed? And where is evidence that the teaching that Paley might perform relates to her learning about the concept of 'birthday'?" I am very sympathetic to these important questions. Unfortunately, I cannot find answers to all questions in Paley's example. From Paley's description, we know that the children were perplexed about the teacher's birthday ("Why is it your birthday?"). Apparently, Paley did not investigate the nature of the children's confusion. Based on Paley's conversation with Frederick and Mollie, I can guess that the children were perplexed about how the parentless adults know that they have a birthday – who tells them when their birthday is. Please notice that the children's perplexity perplexed the teacher as probably happens the other way around as well. Also, there is a germ of possible future learning presented in Frederick's agreement to ask his grandpa to tell his father about his mother birthday but Paley did not provide any follow up if Frederick did it or not and what came out of this experience. We also do not know if the children raise new questions as a result of these birthday discussions and practices. Fortunately, in her books (Paley, 1989, 1991, 1992), she did provide evidence of children's learning shaped by her own learning with, from, and about them as we will show in a next chapter.

Paley defines children's learning as expansion of their curiosity, "The key is curiosity, and it is curiosity, not answers, that we model. As we seek to learn more about a child, we demonstrate the acts of observing, listening, questioning, and wondering. When we are curious about a child's words and our responses to those words, the child feels respected. The child *is* respected. 'What are these ideas I have that are so interesting to the teacher? I must be somebody with good ideas.' Children who know others are listening may begin to listen to themselves, and if the teacher acts as the tape recorder, they may one day become their own critics" (Paley, 1986b, p. 127). This is an ontological definition of learning because it is rooted in the *students'* concerns, interests, questions, and problems addressing the classroom community and the whole world. Unleashed ontological learning of the students can be guided only unleashed ontological learning by the teacher because it creates opportunities for all participants of the classroom community to ask ontological questions and to search together for answers.

CONCLUSION

Our analysis of diversity of educational practices using Socratic dialogues shows that Rud (1997) is right that Socratic dialogue with the Slave is shaped by social relational of slavery bondage. Unfortunately, this type of pedagogical dialogue is popular in conventional schooling because conventional pedagogical regime based on authoritarian discourse is similar to the regime of slavery. This dialogic pedagogy generates students' non-ontological engagement in the targeted academic curriculum. I argue that Garlikov's (1998) own counter-example of his own teaching promoting ontological learning has not been modeled by Socrates' dialogue with the Slave but rather his dialogues with free citizens. However, I showed above Socrates' dialogues with free citizens violate Socrates' own claims (his espoused theory) about his dialogic pedagogy/philosophizing as collaborative investigation of inquiry.

Socrates' dialogues with free citizens and modern pedagogical dialogues promote students' ontological engagement in the targeted academic curriculum while the teacher remains the Expert Number One in the classroom. The teacher has firm control of the discussed hot issues in the classroom to avoid those issues that the teacher is not considered to be the expert. This leads to a contradiction between the students' collaborative freedom of exploration of the classroom issues and the teacher's unilateral control on the choice of the issues, which in its own turn leads to unavoidable power conflict between the students and the teacher.

Socratic espoused theory of his pedagogical practice is based on the conviction that the teacher is the Learner Number One in the classroom. It involves the teacher's public recognition of her or his own perplexity, self-examination, searching for internal contradictions. Application of these principles in modern educational practices leads to running a classroom as a community of learners. In community of learners, the teacher co-participates in the students' perplexities. The teacher's learning with, from, and about the students guides the students' learning. In the following chapters, I will investigate conditions, design, and processes of a community of learners dialogical pedagogy.

Chapter 4

FREIRE'S DIALOGIC PEDAGOGY FOR LIBERATION... AND TOTALITARIANISM[1]

ABSTRACT

The famous Brazilian educator Paulo Freire is probably the first modern educator who insisted on dialogic pedagogy. The controversy of Freire's dialogic pedagogy is that on the one hand, he claimed to promote dialogic critical thinking in his students while, on the other hand, he seemed to uncritically and willingly participate in totalitarian communist regimes helping their "educational" efforts for state and party controlled propaganda. Facundo (1984) in her critical review of Freire's work (especially in Guinea-Bissau), cited her colleague who raised important questions about Freire's dialogic critical pedagogy for liberation, "If Freire's theory didn't work in Guinea-Bissau, does that mean the theory can't work; that it is irrelevant? Did his ideas not work because of his *personal*, 'contradictory' behavior, or because his ideas don't work? How are his ideas and his personal behavior related?" (italics in the original). I address these questions with a specific critique of Freire's version of dialogic pedagogy. My conclusion is that Freire seemed to sacrifice his commitment to dialogue and truth in exchange for addressing

---

[1] I want to thank my graduate students Pawel Bakowski, Aideen Murthy, Kathy von Duyke, and Mark Smith and my Norwegian colleagues Olga Dysthe and Kariane Therese Westrheim for our passionate discussions of the issues presented in this chapter, their feedback, and suggestions for improvement of earlier versions. I especially want to thank Pawel Bakowski, a former political dissident from Poland and a participant in the Solidarnost movement, who served time in Polish prison as a political prisoner, for his insistence on ethical problems with Freire's pedagogy. Pawel had been deeply disturbed at Freire citing totalitarian criminals like Mao, Castro, and Guevara and his calling for Communist revolutions. For long time, I dismissed Pawel's arguments as closed-minded political rhetoric – despite my minor conceptual disagreements and my distaste for Freire's vigor for Communist revolutions, I loved Freire's book *Pedagogy for the Oppressed* wholeheartedly. I remember arguing with Pawel that from the fact that Hitler's Nazi regime was actively promoting an antismoking campaign in the society, it does not mean that antismoking campaigns have any kinship with Hitlerism. However, when I started working on this chapter and read systematically texts by Freire and his critics I had to change my mind about Freire. Painfully for myself, I found evidence for many of Pawel's suspicions, discovered new troublesome facts, and developed explanations and framework to make sense of them. Like in my work with many other chapters in this book, I had initially planned to provide analysis of a good practical example of dialogic pedagogy. Somehow, this task of finding a good educational practice guided by dialogic pedagogy has become more difficult than I thought initially. Also, my special thanks to Aideen Murphy for challenging and disagreeing with me. Without these discussions, my work won't be as productive and thoughtful (as it seems to me now). Finally, I want to thank John Ohliger for his very useful online review of critical online views on Freire's approach to critical dialogic pedagogy (Ohliger, 1995).

problems of social justice that he thought were known to him. The tension between dialogue and social justice is discussed.

Famous Brazilian educator Paulo Freire is probably the first modern educator who insisted on dialogic pedagogy. He developed well a dichotomy between a monologic banking model of education for the oppression and domestication of oppressed and a dialogic critical pedagogy for liberation (Freire, 1986). He inspired many educators in the United States and elsewhere to promote a dialogic critical pedagogy for liberation (Facundo, 1984; Fiore & Elsasser, 1982; McLaren & Lankshear, 1994; McLaren & Leonard, 1993; Shor, 1987).

However, being an educational practitioner and theoretician of his dialogic pedagogy, Freire did not provide any detailed ethnography of his dialogic practice or evaluation of his method (C. Brown, 1978; Harasim, 1983; Mashayekh, 1974). What Freire publically shared was his sketches of his curriculum and provocations that he used for his pedagogical dialogues with his students (Freire, 1978; Freire & Freire, 1973; Freire & Macedo, 1987). As I have shown in my analysis of Socrates' dialogues in a previous chapter, there can be gaps and misalignments between the theory of dialogue and its practice. For example, Socrates claimed that he wanted to investigate philosophical issues unknown to him with his interlocutors but we found little evidence of that in his actual dialogues (presented by Plato, of course). Freire's readers are left with rather incomplete data to understand and evaluate Freire's approach to dialogic pedagogy.

The controversy of Freire's dialogic pedagogy is that on the one hand, he claimed to promote dialogic critical thinking in his students while, on the other hand, he seemed to uncritically but willingly participated in totalitarian communist regimes helping their "educational" efforts for state and party controlled propaganda. Not only has Freire uncritically and enthusiastically cited theoreticians and practitioners of totalitarian communist regimes such as Lenin, Mao, Che, Castro, Cabral throughout his writings after "Pedagogy of Oppressed" (Freire, 1986), but he also spent space in his book praising the Chinese Cultural Revolution at the mid of the 1970s (Freire, 1978). Of course, one can argue that the full account of the crimes conducted by these and other totalitarian communist regimes was not available to Freire in the 1970s. However, it was difficult to ignore them in the 1980s, yet Freire ignores these crimes in his publications. Even more disturbing, Freire personally participated in two totalitarian communist regimes in Africa: in Guinea-Bissau and in Sao Tome and Principe in the mid 1970s (Freire, 1978; Freire & Macedo, 1987). For some strange reason, neither he nor his dialogic critical pedagogy for liberation registered the totalitarian oppression happening in those African countries as recorded by human rights organizations at that time that Freire worked there (Fry, 1996). Even more, Freire's own texts about his work (Freire, 1978; Freire & Macedo, 1987) suggest, and we will analyze them later, that he and his dialogic critical pedagogy willingly and, arguably, uncritically, participated in the political propaganda campaigns of these totalitarian communist regimes. Facundo (1984) in her critical review of Freire's work (especially in Guinea-Bissau) cited her colleague who raised important questions about Freire's dialogic critical pedagogy for liberation, "If Freire's theory didn't work in Guinea-Bissau, does that mean the theory can't work; that it is irrelevant? Did his ideas not work because of his *personal*, 'contradictory' behavior, or because his ideas don't work? How are his ideas and his personal behavior related?" (the italics are original). I try to address these questions here with a specific critique of Freire's version of dialogic pedagogy.

FREIRE'S CULTURAL-DIALOG

In an analysis of the declarative aspects of Freire's di
themes. As I have stated above, we do not have ethnography
it. As Facundo (1984) points out, Freire's writing is full o
contradictions are probably due to the contradictory nature o
because he may have changed his mind on certain issues espe
1960s (Freire & Macedo, 1987; Shor & Freire, 1987a), and s
indecisiveness[2]. For my analytical purpose, I tried to extract th
important contributions to dialogic pedagogy. I also try to criti
pedagogy as I focus on its strongest points.

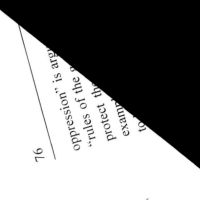

ɔ dialogic

Why Does Education Need Dialogue?

There are two major prescriptive approaches to why education needs dialogue. The first prescriptive approach, which I call "weak dialogism[3]," is an instrumental approach (cf. Maranhão, 1990; Sidorkin, 1999). According to this instrumental approach, dialogue can help to improve instruction and learning. Dialogue is an instructional strategy and a method of teaching – a classroom discussion or debate – that can make learning more effective and can even raise test scores. Dialogic method can be done once a week or one hour a day or not at all – it can be dosed, scheduled, and well located in the classroom[4]. This claim can be tested empirically by comparing students' learning stemming from dialogic and non-dialogic instructions. This prescriptive approach focuses on consideration when dialogic instruction is needed better for learning new material or for reconceptualization of already known material, for learning factual information or for learning conceptual understanding, for younger students or for older students, for math or social studies, and so on (see for proponents of the weak dialogism in education: Adler, 1982; Burbules, 1993; C. Phillips, 2002; Renshaw, 2004). The instrumental approach often confuses dialogicity, how dialogic the discourse is, with genre of discourse, how interactive the discourse is. When it prescribes or describes how to run the class, it focuses on behavioral interactivity: increasing students' talk, asking open-ended questions, setting interactional turns, avoiding lecturing, and so on – what Burbules (1993) calls "dialogue game."

In my view, there is nothing wrong in the instrumentality of dialogue and in the teacher's attention to technical aspects of dialogue per se. However, my concern is about a situation when instrumentality and technicality of dialogue is confused with dialogue itself. I see several problems with this confusion. The first problem is ethical. It is very confusing and potentially harmful for the participants to mix freedom with oppression. In fact, "pure

---

[2] Sometimes Freire used the term "dialectics" (which is almost felt like "dialectical mysticism") when he did not how to address a certain problem (Facundo, 1984).

[3] Sidorkin (1999) calls this weak instrumental dialogism approach "epistemological dialogism" in contrast to a strong dialogism approach that he calls "ontological dialogism."

[4] Once in the mid 1990s, I wanted to visit an innovative school in California but the founder of the school told me that I could not come on Tuesday because they "do community of learners" only on Mondays, Wednesdays, and Fridays.

ably better than the mix. The clarity of the pedagogical regime, when the game" are well known for the students, arguably helps the students adjust and themselves from the damage of the teacher's oppression. One-hour dialogue, for le, might create schizophrenic, "double bind" (Bateson, 1987) message to the students be free and sincere in one moment (when a dialogic regime is promoted in the classroom) and then to pay for your self-disclosure in the other (when a monologic regime rules the classroom). Second, due to its instrumental determinism (Burbules & Callister, 2000; Tisa & Matusov, 2001), the weak dialogism approach erroneously assumes that the means of discourse can define its ends. For example, although it is true that a monologic classroom regime overwhelmingly gravitates toward using lecturing as its instructional strategy, it is not true that lecturing, a monologic genre, by its nature has a lack of dialogicity. Lecture can be a prolonged dialogic turn, a reply to the students' questions or concerns. Lecture can be internally dialogic. Finally, even very monotonous lecture can be dialogic because of the dialogic work of the listener (like in a case of some very monotonous and even ill-designed conference presentations attended by professionals – even if the lecture is not well-formed the work of interested listener can safe its dialogicity). Dialogicity is relational and never fully defined by individual moves of the teacher (or the students). A highly interactive and conversational class, a dialogic genre, might have less dialogicity than a lecture. Genre of discourse cannot guarantee its dialogicity (or its lack of it).

The alternative prescriptive approach to why education needs dialogue is based on radical, strong dialogism. It argues that genuine education cannot survive without dialogue. When dialogue stops, the genuine education stops with it. As Buber put it, "Relation in education is one of pure dialogue" (2002, p. 125). Dialogue is not an interactional format (or a discursive genre) among other interactional formats (e.g., lecture), dialogue is not an instructional strategy among other instructional strategies (e.g., hands-on activities), dialogue is not educational philosophy among other educational philosophies (e.g., constructivism) – instead dialogue is *the* discourse of education. Take this overall discourse out of education and the education is dead. There have been a growing number of proponents of this approach in education (Bakhtin, 2004; Buber, 2002; Dewey, 1966; Nystrand, 1997; Plato & Riddell, 1973; Sidorkin, 1999, 2002). I argue in this chapter that Freire both conceptually and in his pedagogical practice seemed to move between the both weak and radical dialogism leaning at the end more to the weak dialogic pedagogy despite to his numerous claims on the contrary.

I found three main arguments for the radical dialogic pedagogy. Freire justified the need for dialogue in pedagogy *epistemologically* by tracking the origin of reflective knowledge in dialogue and *ontologically* by tracking humanity in dialogue. According to Freire, communication of freely participating people, who cannot overrule themselves by authority or power, generates a special type of reflection, which only humans possess, of knowing about ones' own knowledge. This communication (i.e., dialogue) also generates special social relations of humanity among the participants. Thus, human reflection (episteme) generates humanity and while humanity generates the reflection[5].

---

[5] Almost at the same time, in the early 1970s, similar epistemological and ontological reasoning for use of dialogue in education was developed by Soviet educational and developmental psychologist Vasilii V. Davydov who called reflective knowledge "theoretical knowledge" (in contrast to unreflective "empirical knowledge") (Davydov, 1986; Davydov & Kilpatrick, 1990). Although, it is difficult to find the well-developed ontological reason for use of dialogue in Davydov's writings during the Soviet era (unless one reads between the lines of his texts), orally he made this point on numerous occasions (I personally heard that at his

Monologic relations of domination, manifesting in the mainstream educational system that Freire called, "the banking model of education" (Freire, 1986), cannot produce the reflection described above. In such model, the participants, like many animals, can only participate in primitive non-reflective knowledge – they cannot be involved in knowing about their own knowledge. They can change the repertoire of their behaviors or activities as a result of this monologic education but they cannot fully master it because they are not involved in understanding the mastery of their non-reflective knowledge requiring reflective questions of "why", "for whom", "at whose expense", and so on. Each time when a student's question is not answered, or suppressed, or not encouraged, or not taught to ask, the knowledge remains *ontologically* unhumanized and epistemologically unreflective, "Any situation in which some individuals prevent others from engaging in the process of inquiry is one of violence. The means used are not important; to alienate human beings from their own decision-making is to change them into objects" (Freire, 1986, p. 66). Genuine education requires an ontological and political transformation. As Caulfield comments about Freire's pedagogical approach, "If traditional education mirrors what he views as the oppressor-oppressed relationship prevalent in Latin America, Freire's classroom attempts to model a far more equal society. Based on his description, his classroom is communism in its purest form: strictly egalitarian, no leaders or followers, just people working together first to understand their world and then to revolutionize it" (Caulfield, 1991, p. 311). Similarly, in her critical review of Habermas's notion of "dialogue," BenHabib (1992) agrees with Habermas that if adults want to bring up their children in peace, they need to promote some sort of an ideal of "being reasonable" – to learn how to solve their problems without resorting to violence through engaging in dialogues informed by an attitude of care and respect (Wegerif, 2004). In essence, the ontological argument calls for violence-free education that can only be based on "dialogical reasonableness." Booth argues that, "The pragmatic strength of [dialogic – EM] pluralism does not depend only on its short-run heuristic or pedagogical value. It is, I want to claim, the most fruitful attitude for opening up the world to continuing humanistic life" (Booth, 1979, pp. 217-218).

Dialogue for Freire is the primary medium in which not only primitive, non-reflective, knowing occurs but, even more important, meta-knowing – critical knowing about knowing or as Zinchenko put it "consciousness of consciousness" (1985, p. 114) – occurs. Thus, dialogue is not an instructional technique among other instructional strategies such as hands-on activities and direct instruction that better promote learning in students, but a social meaning making process essential for any authentic education. Let me provide Freire's own voice here,

> I think... that first of all we should understand liberating dialogue not as a technique, a *mere* technique, which we can use to help us get some results. We also cannot, must not, understand dialogue as a kind of tactic we use to make students our friends. This would make dialogue a technique for manipulation instead of illumination.
> On the contrary, dialogue must be understood as something taking part in the very historical nature of human beings. It is part of our historical progress in

---

presentations and lectures). I think that he could not openly discuss a democratic nature of dialogue in his writings due to Soviet censorship. In the early 1980s, Davydov lost his high-ranking academic job because Soviet authorities seemed to recognize his political disloyalty to the regime.

becoming human beings. That is, dialogue is a kind of necessary posture to the extent that humans have become more and more critically communicative beings. Dialogue is a moment where humans meet to reflect on their reality as they make and remake it. Something else: To the extent that we are communicative beings who communicate to each other as we become more able to transform our reality, we are able *to know that we know,* which is something *more* than just knowing. In a certain manner, for example, birds *know* the trees. They even communicate to each other. They use a kind of oral and symbolic language, but they do not use written language. And they do not know that they know. At least scientifically up to now, we are not sure whether they know that they know. On the other hand, *we* know that we know, and we human beings know also that *we don't know.* Through dialogue, reflecting together on what we know and don't know, we can then act critically to transform reality.

In communicating among ourselves, in the process of knowing the reality which we transform, we communicate and know *socially* even though the process of communicating, knowing, changing, has an individual dimension. But, the individual aspect is not enough to explain the process. Knowing is a social event with nevertheless an individual dimension. What is dialogue in this moment of communication, knowing and social transformation? Dialogue *seals* the relationship between the cognitive subjects, the subjects who know, and who try to know. (Shor & Freire, 1987b, p. 13, italics is original)

Freire insisted on dialogue not because a dialogic instruction can increase test scores (it may or may not) but because without dialogue, education is not reflective (not "critical" in Freire's terms) and not humane (not "just and respectful"). Monologic "banking model" based on the hierarchical teacher-students relations of domination might increase test scores but it cannot lead to genuine reflective (critical) mastery and understanding of the learned and, by the same token, it cannot free students from the relationship of oppression and domination.

It is possible to develop an epistemological argument for why genuine education needs dialogue Bakhtin's theory of meaning. According to Bakhtin, meaning emerges from an ontological relationship between a genuine, interested, information seeking, question and a genuine response to this question between, at least, two consciousnesses,

Question and *answer* are not logical relations (categories); they cannot be placed in one consciousness (unified and closed in itself); any response gives rise to a new question. Question and answer presuppose mutual outsideness. If an answer does not give rise to a new question from itself, it falls out of the dialogue and enters systemic cognition, which is essentially impersonal.

The various chronotopes of the questioner and the answerer, and various semantic worlds (*I* and *other*). From the standpoint of a third consciousness and its "neutral" world, where everything is replaceable, question and answer are inevitably deperesonified (Bakhtin, 1986, p. 168).

Like for Freire, for Bakhtin genuine learning involves other people because without a dialogue with other people, a person is locked in ontological circumstances of his or her own being. People commit and invest in their ideas with the fate of their lives and without dialogue cannot transcend this ideologico-ontological imprisonment. Similarly, Dewey argued that school can help to reduce parochialism in the students and get them into contact with strangers and remote communities (Dewey, 1966).

Both Freire and Bakhtin (and Dewey) developed *ontological arguments* for why genuine education has to be dialogic. Freire's ontological argument is based on the notion of liberation from oppression as the humanizing force in the society. Oppressive domination promotes ignorance and "false consciousness" (Engels, 1978) in the oppressed justifying their own oppression, that genuine education has to addressed to start the process of the people's liberation. However, this education cannot start until the teacher-students relations continue being strictly hierarchical, monologic, domineering, unilateral and, thus, oppressive. Oppression has to be removed first ontologically from the teacher-students relations, which will translate into intellectual achievements of elimination of the students' ignorance and false consciousness,

> If it is in speaking their word that people, by naming the world, transform it dialogue imposes itself as the way by which they achieve significance as human beings. Dialogue is thus an existential necessity. And since dialogue is the encounter in which the united reflection and action of the dialoguers are addressed to the world which is to be transformed and humanized, this dialogue cannot be reduced to the act of one person's "depositing" ideas in another; nor can it become a simple exchange of ideas to be "consumed" by the discussants. Nor yet is it a hostile, polemical argument between those who are committed neither to the naming of the world, nor to the search for truth, but rather to the imposition of their own truth. Because dialogue is an encounter among women and men who name the world, it must not be a situation where some name on behalf of others. It is an act of creation; it must not serve as a crafty instrument for the domination of one person by another. The domination implicit in dialogue is that of the world by the dialoguers; it is conquest of the world for the liberation of humankind (Freire, 1986, p. 69).

Dewey saw similarly the "super-task" of education as promotion democracy in the society (Dewey, 1966). Bakhtin's notion of carnival also provides the base for an ontological argument the relationship between the genuine education and dialogue, "Carnival effectively broke down the formalities of hierarchy and the inherited differences between different social classes, ages and castes, replacing established traditions and canons with a 'free and familiar" social interaction based on the principles of mutual cooperation, solidarity and equality" (Gardiner, 1992, p. 52).

Freire showed that good knowledge requires dialogue (i.e., an epistemological argument) and good human life requires dialogue (i.e., an ontological reason) but he did not show as clear that good instruction (and learning) requires dialogue (i.e., a pedagogical argument). As far as I know (or at least, I could not find it in Freire's writings beyond germs of ideas), Freire did not develop a *pedagogical argument* for the need of dialogue in education. He did not start his analysis from instruction and learning that led him to dialogue. In my view, such type of analysis can be found in Bakhtin (1999) when he considered the relations between the writer-author (i.e., the teacher) and the character-hero (i.e., the student) in Dostoevsky's stories and novels.

Good teaching mediates the student's learning – the teacher cannot force the student to learn and cannot learn for the student. By saying "the teacher cannot force the student to learn," I mean that, of course, the teacher can force the students to do certain things and activities (and often does in conventional monologic schools) but the teacher cannot control what the student learns from these forced experiences. Teaching does not cause learning, "learning happens, design or no design" (Wenger, 1998, p. 225). However, this learning occurring with or with no teaching design is not necessarily socially desirable even for the student his or herself: the student might learn to dislike the academic subject or the student might learn that he or she is a bad, incapable learner (Lave, 1992a; Matusov, St. Julien et al., 2005). Learning is (multi-) relational and not fully defined by the teaching actions and moves alone. As Nystrand points, "authentic questions, discussion, small-group work, and interactions, though important, do not categorically produce [socially desired -- EM] learning" (Nystrand, 1986, p. 72). Learning occurs only at the consciousness of the students. The teacher can affect it but cannot determine it. Based on his analysis of Dostoevsky's art, Bakhtin would argue that good teaching involves the teacher working with *the student's self-consciousness* -- "*the hero's final words on himself and his world*" (Bakhtin, 1999, p. 48, the italics original). Student's self-consciousness is the arena of the student's subjectivity where learning occurs. De Lauretis similarly defines subjectivity as image of self and others, "patterns by which experiential and emotional contexts, feelings, images and memories are organised to form one's self-image, one's sense of self and others, and our possibilities of existence" (De Lauretis, 1986, p. 5).

Bakhtin (1999) argued that Dostoevsky carried out a small-scale Copernican revolution in the literary art because Dostoevsky let his characters hear and respond to the author's words about them. Arguably, good teaching should be directed at the students' self-consciousness as well. The teacher's monologic discourse about the student that objectivizes and finalizes the student generates legitimate teacher-resistance or self-suppression (i.e., "domestication" in Freire's terms; silencing emotional, intellectual, and ethical agency[7]) in the student's self-consciousness. Thus, according to this position stemming from Bakhtin-Dostoevsky, the teacher cannot tell to him or herself or to the colleagues, "Oh, this is the student's misconception" or to the student, "Oh, this is your misconception" – this objectivizing and finalizing (i.e., "deficit model") has little pedagogical value but great ontological harm. Instead, the teacher has to offer a counter-argument for the student's self-consciousness to consider. In good teaching, the teacher should not and cannot expect more than the student's serious consideration of the teacher's argument (and arguments of other students and the arguments of the texts offered by the teacher) as equal to the student's own arguments and ideas about the world and the self, "*To the all-devouring consciousness of the hero the author can juxtapose only a single Objective world – a world of other consciousnesses with rights of equal to those of the hero*" (Bakhtin, 1999, pp. 49-50, the italics original). When the participants' consciousnesses gain rights equal to the each other and the teacher, they become *dialogic subjects*.

Thus, good teaching requires dialogue. Dialogue is a medium of existence of truth and knowledge. High-level reflection and learning is dialogic by its nature. Dialogue humanizes our actions and deeds. It occurs only among consciousnesses that have equal rights. There is no alternative to dialogue for genuine human education. However, I argue that empirical support for radical dialogism's arguments is needed. For example, is it the case that animals really do not know that they know (or not know)? Is it the case that this type of reflective knowledge only emerges in a special dialogic communication among people? Is a dialogic itself a culturally biased ontological concept belonging to certain middle-class communities

---

[6] There is no sexist connotation in Bakhtin's Russian texts. Masculine pronouns refer not to gender of the person here but to gender of the noun "hero." In Russian, a noun has one of the three genders -- masculine, feminine, or neutral -- and requires from the corresponding pronouns to refer to its own gender.

[7] Although for different consequences, silencing agency is arguably harming both those who are in power and subalterns.

(Delpit, 1995)? Does Bakhtin's notion of dialogue of equal consciousness kill the teacher's epistemological and organizational authority in the classroom?

What Is Dialogue?

According to Freire, the regime of dialogue requires love and the equality of free people searching for truth. Truth emerges as a consensus among free participants in a dialogue, "dialogical people"[8], that is tested by their actions. Dialogical people cannot impose truth on each other neither by epistemological authority (i.e., "it is true because I know more than you") nor by force (e.g., "if you will not write what I expect you to write, you will get F in my class") but only though critical dialogue tested by the participants' actions (cf. Bakhtin's notion of "internally persuasive discourse", Bakhtin, 1991). Thus, education is a process of joining this consensus in a free dialogue, "For the dialogical, problem-posing teacher-student, the program content of education is neither a gift nor an imposition — bits of information to be deposited in the students — but rather the organized, systematized, and developed 're-presentation' to individuals of the things about which they want to know more" (Freire, 1986, p. 74). Education is "re-presentation", "re-play", "re-arrival" at a previously achieved dialogic consensus (referred by Freire as "the things" in the quote) through another dialogue but, this time, with the student. This dialogic consensus is free for renegotiation in a historically unfolding dialogue and, thus, according to Freire, truth is historically bounded. Dialogue is not mere verbalism or a play with words but a reflective action aiming at transforming reality – it is the socially active aspect of praxis (Freire, 1986, p. 68). Dialogue occurs not only through words but also through actions. In a dialogue, people "name" the world in order to understand it, transform it, understand themselves within it, and transform themselves. Dialogue as a meaning making process is also a process of humanizing the world and, thus, themselves.

---

[8] I take freedom to change Freire's original term "dialogical man" (Freire, 1986, p. 72) that has a sexist connotation in English.

Fifth Situation: The Hunter and the Cat. With this situation, the participants discuss the fundamental aspects which characterize the different forms of being in the world—those of men and of animals. They discuss man as a being who not only knows, but knows that he knows; as a conscious being (*corpo consciente*) in the world; as a consciousness which in the process of becoming an authentic person emerges reflective and intent upon the world. In regard to the preceding series, I will never forget an illiterate from Brasilia who affirmed, with absolute self-confidence, "Of these three, only two are hunters—the two men. They are hunters because they make culture before and after they hunt." (He failed only to say that they made culture while they hunted.) "The third, the cat, does not make culture, either before or after the 'hunt.' He is not a hunter, he is a pursuer." By making this subtle distinction between hunting and pursuing, this man grasped the fundamental point: the creation of culture. The debate of these situations produced a wealth of observations about men and animals, about creative power, freedom, intelligence, instinct, education, and training (Freire & Freire, 1973, pp. 70-71).

A few critical comments. Like many scholars rooted in Hegel and Marx, Freire seemed to prioritize consensus over disagreement in a dialogue. Freire apparently saw dialogue as a process in which individuals can "overcome" (in Hegel's terms, "sublate") their particularity and limitedness. In dialogue, people become complete. Dialogue is "bigger" than its participants are. Like, previously, in the name of the God or the Nature, one can speak monologically on behalf of the Dialogue. This Dialogue (with the capital D) is "bigger" than its participants in a similar way that the name of God or an appeal to Nature has been used to speak monologically on behalf of people, Freire uses a disembodied higher power concept of Dialogue in similar monologic fashion. It is interesting that Freire himself offered an example of such a monologic twist without recognizing it. Thus, on page 74 of his book "Pedagogy of the oppressed", Freire[9] footnoted the quote above with a reference to then Chairman Mao-Tse-Tung, "You know I've proclaimed for a long time: we must teach the masses clearly what we have received from them confusedly." This totalitarian circular reasoning claims a communist monopoly on truth (Laclau & Mouffe, 2001). Indeed, with acceptance of this claim, it is not possible to challenge communist "truths" neither by non-communist intellectuals, who are outside of "the masses" ("who are you to know the truth?! We, communist leaders, are taking truth directly from the masses – you are out of masses and do not have truth!") not by non-intellectual "masses" ("you are confused about your own truth – only we know your truth!"). Mao-Tse-Tung's "we" could exclusively speak on behalf of Dialogue rooted in "the masses." Freire did not recognize this monologic trick but instead enthusiastically but, uncritically, accepted Mao-Tse-Tung's propaganda statement (Walker, 1981) at its deceptive and questionable face value (almost like Orwellian doublespeak), "This affirmation contains an entire dialogical theory of how to construct the program content of education, which cannot he elaborated according to what the *educator* thinks best for the *students*" (Freire, 1986, p. 74, the italics is original).

Furthermore, a consequence of Freire's prioritization of dialogic consensus over dialogic disagreement is that people who are outside of the dialogic consensus are either uneducated (potentially dialogic but currently not dialogic yet but) or the enemy of Dialogue. A critic of Freire, Facundo (1984) has noticed this consequence in Freire's writings as an apparent contradiction of his insistence on love while arguably preparing (and justifying) violence and murder perpetrated by "liberators,"

---

[9] Freire loved this quote from Mao and repeated it in his writings again and again (e.g., Freire, 1978; Freire & Macedo, 1987).

Freire has increasingly exhibited a tendency to romanticize and idealize revolutionary leaders in the Third World, taking their writings at face value and, I hate to say, most *uncritically*. He looks at these leaders to *confirm* his theory: the revolutionary is a man who acts out of love, a human being who sacrifices without personal self-interest; indeed, a Christ-like figure in authentic communion with the people. While he warns that revolutions can betray their ideals and become bureaucratic and manipulative--these he labels "inauthentic"--he does not offer a concrete example of where he has seen this occur, if anywhere....

Interrogated in Vermont by Jonathan Kozol about Cuba, and the highly hierarchical participatory process Kozol has perceived during his visits to the island, Freire responded:

I have not yet been in Cuba. I have friends there and friends who have been there. Cuba is not creating a paradise, because that is not the task for a revolution. A revolution makes history (...) For me the question is that the more Cuba becomes able to go towards an opening, the more Cuba will become authentically socialist. I do not think Cuba is preponderantly rigid. We also can discover in Cuba some signs of Stalinism (which is spread in the left all over the world). But Cuba cannot be compared. The Cuban *people* were able to get their history into their hands in 20 years. This could not exist if the people had been exclusively manipulated. How to explain the creativity, the presence of happiness in the streets (not just the people, the streets themselves!). I think Cuba is trying to go more and more beyond rigidity. I myself do not understand the why's of Ethiopia. I do understand Angola and Mozambique, bombarded by South Africa. I was there once and about 600 children died. They also have mediocres there, people that are not so capable. They [the mediocres] speak Spanish there and not Portuguese. This is wrong. But I never saw Cubans in ghettos separated from the Angolans.

But let us assume that they commit more mistakes than right things. The important thing is the *attitudes* with which they go--as friends; as comrades. (My emphasis.)

The above should be critically examined even by those of us who *have* been in Cuba.

Freire shies away from the harsh, painful, violent acts committed by *both* sides in any revolutionary war, and reserves his criticism for the violence of oppressors. The violence of the oppressed is justified because it is reactive, defensive and made "out of love." This stems, I think, from Freire's dichotomizing of the entire world in two antagonistic sides: oppressors and oppressed, leaving no space for mediators or the *interlocuteurs valables*. This term emerged in the Algerian war of independence and referred to moderate nationalist representatives with whom compromise solutions might be negotiated between France and the struggling Algerians (italics original).

I will return later to the dichotomist nature of Freire's approach to dialogic pedagogy and to his double standards to people's suffering caused by "oppressors" versus "liberators" (see an alternative approach in Rosenberg, 2001).

Teacher as a Learner

On of the most important contributions by Freire to the framework of dialogic pedagogy is his revolutionary analysis of the teacher-student relations. Freire wrote,

Through dialogue, the teacher-of-the-students and the students-of-the-teacher
cease to exist and a new term emerges: teacher-students with students-teacher. The
teacher is no longer merely the one-who-teaches, but one who is himself taught in
dialogue with the students, who in turn while being taught also teach. They become
jointly responsible for the process in which all grow (Freire, 1986, p. 67).

Freire insists that not only the teacher has to learn with the students but also the students
have to teach each other and the teacher. This puts upside down conventional pedagogy
insisting on strict pedagogical and epistemological hierarchy of the teacher-student relations:
the teacher knows more and she or he has to teach while the students have to learn from the
teacher and to study in the teacher-initiated activities and from the teacher-initiated texts. Of
course, in a conventional model, the teacher, as any practitioner, also learns about how to do
his or her teaching practice better, but this learning is nothing much to do with the students
(like a car mechanic learns how to be a better car-fixer). A conventional rigidly hierarchical
pedagogy does not imply that the teacher should learn epistemologically and pedagogically
with the students and from the students. According to the model, if the teacher needs to learn
something epistemologically, it means he or she is ignorant and professionally incompetent.
Pedagogically, the teacher should learn with and from his or her colleagues, educators and,
even better, scientists, and with (or from) the students – it is seen as unprofessional. It also
does not imply students in a role of teachers. Freire challenged these conventional educational
axioms without calling for "the death of the teacher" – denying epistemological and
pedagogical asymmetry in the relationship between the teacher and the students. Let us
consider the issue in details.

One of the important features of dialogue is that participants expect to be surprised by
each other. This dialogic attitude – to expect learning something new from other participants
that some called "a good listening skill" – is crucial for a dialogue to occur (Schultz, 2003).
The paradox, captured in the very term of "dialogic pedagogy", is that 1) dialogue requires
the participants to learn from each other about the subject of the dialogue matter while 2) the
teacher knows more than the student does and hence should not expect to listen to anything
new from the student about the subject matter (of course, the teacher must learn and listen to
the students about pedagogical matters – how to teach the student better, how the student
understands the subject matter, and so on). Indeed, how can the teacher expect to learn
something new from the student about the subject matter without the teacher's
professionalism being challenged? If the teacher *does* learn something new from the student
about the academic subject, this means, at least in regard to this particular learning, that the
teacher is not more knowledgeable than the student is. This means that the teacher is
professionally inept and ignorant at least with regard to this particular learning. In traditional
conventional pedagogy, the teacher's learning the subject matter from the student is
accidental at its best and non-professional at its worst. There might be some peripheral
knowledge and skill that the teacher might graciously learn from a student, but it should
rather peripheral and limited and definitely not systematic. If, however, the teacher does not
expect to learn something new from his or her student, this means that there is no dialogue.
Thus, from this reasoning, the term "dialogic pedagogy" seems to be a misnomer.

One attempt to salvage the notion of dialogic pedagogy is to claim that the teacher should
expect to learn from teaching the student new pedagogical knowledge while remaining
epistemologically superior to the student. Newman, Cole, and Griffin (1989) argue that both

the student and the teacher have uncertainties but they are different in nature. The student is uncertain about the *epistemological* matters of the curriculum not knowing what exactly he or she needs to learn, while the teacher is uncertain about the *pedagogical* matters of the instruction not knowing how to teach this particular student (see table 5).

Table 5. Teacher-student dialogical disjuncture in a non-dialogic pedagogical regime

Participants	Pedagogical learning	Epistemological learning
The teacher	X	
The students		X

The teacher must learn how the student struggles with the targeted epistemological material; the student's particular misconceptions, mistakes, needs, interests, and strengths. For instance, in Freire's example above about the illiterate Brazilian peasant learning the difference between the hunter and the cat, Freire, the teacher, learned that his student recognized the difference between the hunter, whose actions are based on a cultural practice, and the cat, whose actions are based on the natural instincts and habits. The teacher also learned that the student might not see culture in the actions of the hunter themselves but only in its preparation or aftermath. This is new pedagogical information that the teacher learns from the student in a dialogue. However, according to this position, the teacher does not need to learn anything new at the epistemological level. Indeed, Freire did not mention anything new that he had learned from his illiterate Brazilian peasants about culture or hunting in this particular example (and this is more or less true across his writing as well, although he sometimes claimed that he had done).

There is no doubt that the teacher's pedagogical learning about the students' subjectivity – the ways of how the student perceives the world -- is very important for dialogic pedagogy (Matusov & Smith, 2007). Dialogic guidance is collaborative by its nature because guidance is formed by both the students and the teacher (Miyazaki, 2007, July; Nystrand, 1997; Rogoff et al., 1996; Saitou, 1964): the students guide the teacher how to guide them in a better, more pedagogically sensitive, way. Constantly revealing and assessing the student's views, positions, knowledge, skills, interests, needs, and strengths, the teacher forms his or her guidance. This formative assessment (formative with regard to forming the teacher's guidance) is the necessary feature of collaborative guidance and dialogic pedagogy.

However, *being necessary* for dialogic pedagogy, formative assessment is *not sufficient* to define dialogic pedagogy. Instruction guided by formative assessment can be manipulative as I tried to show in the actual practice of Socrates' pedagogical dialogues and what I will demonstrate in my analysis of Paley's (1992) classroom interaction in my chapters ahead. A successful manipulation also requires from careful listening to the object of manipulation by the manipulator (Machiavelli & Donne, 1985; Schultz, 2003). How does manipulative teaching differ from genuinely dialogical teaching? In manipulation, the endpoint of interaction is pre-set (see figure 1) and, thus, known by the manipulator, the teacher, in advance. In real dialogue, the participants do not know the endpoint, at which they will arrive, even more, genuine dialogue does not have a final endpoint – all endpoints are temporary and even arbitrary (Miyazaki, 2007, July; Tolstoy, 1967). Dialogue is always pregnant by new never-ending dialogic contributions. There is no the final word in dialogue (Bakhtin, 1986, 1999).

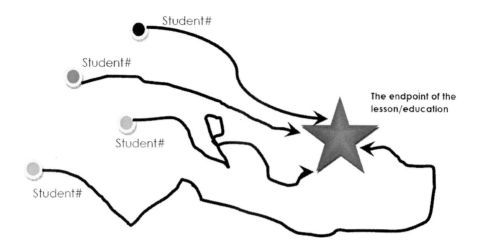

Figure 1. Curricular space of conventional (monologically manipulative) education. The teacher pre-sets the endpoint of the lesson, "At the end of the lesson, the students will be able to understand/master the following knowledge and skills…" The teacher's instructional trajectories of leading the students to the endpoint can be individualized in a manipulative instruction and might take different time. Different students are curricularly located "closer" or further" from the pre-set endpoint and require different strategies to get them there. Thus, for Socrates to manipulate Meno to the pre-set endpoint (i.e., what is virtue is not known and problematic) is not the same to manipulate Anytus to the same endpoint. It takes different and individualized instructional strategies.

I argue that an alternative to the design of pre-setting curricular endpoints by the teacher is the teacher's invitation of the students for a journey into "a curricular land" – a historically emerging discursive space on the subject matter (in a broad sense). The teacher designs a series of provocations that are aimed at surprising the students in order to generate questions in the participants. Discussions of these questions lead to testing ideas and emergence of points in the participants. These points always have a potential to be temporary as dialogue continues (see Chapters 7, 9, 10, and 11 for specific examples of such curricular journeys, this book is another example as well that hopefully you are experiencing yourself, reader).

But, does not the teacher always know where the student has to be at the end? Should the teacher make the student as knowledgeable and skillful as the teacher is? Is education manipulative by its very nature?! Does not without a final endpoint the education stop being directive (i.e. guiding)? Is it the case that genuine dialogue described by Bakhtin kills guidance and the teacher?

Not necessarily – and this is my "crazy" solution of this problem. In any real dialogue, participants learn from each other even if one of them is more knowledgeable than the other is. Dialogue is based not on epistemological equality of the participants' knowledge or their equal ignorance but on their *epistemological non-authority* or in the words of Gardiner (1992, p. 26) about Bakhtin's position, "the equal rights of consciousness *vis-a-vis* truth (understood abstractly and systematically)." In other words, it is OK for one participant to know more than another does – this alone does not spoil the dialogue. What really spoils the dialogue is when the teacher justifies his or her position by saying or implying that it is true just because the teacher, who knows more, says so. When something cannot (or is made difficult to) be challenged or tested by the participants (e.g., the students or even the teacher), the genuine dialogue ceases to exist. In dialogue, everything is open for challenge and testing by anybody (Morson, 2004). The open, public, challenge of the teacher's knowledge and skill creates a possibility that what the teacher knew as certain can turn into uncertainty. To prepare for dialogic teaching, the teacher has to become a dialogic subject and genuine dialogic participants with the students. For that, the teacher has to de-know the targeted curriculum, de-objectivize it for him or herself (in Russian "разпредметить," see Davydov, 1986), de-reify (Wenger, 1998), subjectivize (Matusov & Smith, 2007), "make the familiar seem strange" (Miyazaki, 2007, July) again for him or herself. Using Bakhtin's (1993) term, the curriculum has to again become "participative" (i.e., ontologically and intellectually open, see Bakhtin, Holquist, & Liapunov, 1993) for the teacher. In other words, dialogic pedagogy requires the teacher not only to be open (i.e., to expect and actively seek) to pedagogical learning but also to epistemological learning. The teacher has to learn together *with* the students by sharing their epistemological uncertainty and concerns. Through his or her learning new academic material with the student, the teacher, being more knowledgeable and skillful in the process of learning, models and guides the student in how to learn (Matusov et al., 2002). This idea seems to be expressed by Socrates in his dialogue with Plato, when Meno used his famous "torpedo touch" metaphor to accuse Socrates for intentionally confusing and paralyzing thinking of free citizens, Socrates replied that unlike torpedo fish, Socrates paralyzes his own thinking by uncovering his own internal contradiction that had been invisible for him before, "if the torpedo fish is itself numb and so makes others numb, then I resemble it, but not otherwise, for I myself do not have the answer when I perplex others, but I am more perplexed than anyone when I cause perplexity in others. So now I do not know what virtue is; perhaps you knew before you contacted me, but now you are certainly like one who does not know. Nevertheless, I want to examine and seek together with you what it may be" (Plato, Cooper, & Hutchinson, 1997, p. 279, 80c).

Dialogic pedagogy requires an authentic suspension of epistemological certainty that is yet proven in the teacher-students community. We, educators, can all say that we are open to being challenged in our "knowledge" but are we really open or do we simply view these challenges as opportunities for our pedagogical manipulation of our "less knowledgeable" students?! This is how these issues are addressed by Freire (and his follower Ira Shor),

> *Ira:* The teacher selecting objects of study knows them *better* than the students as the course begins but the teacher *re-learns* the objects through studying them with the students?
>
> *Paulo:* This is *exactly* the question! I could extend what you say in some conceptual language by saying, for example, that the educator *remakes* her or his "cognoscibility" through the "cognoscibility" of the educatees. That is, the ability of the educator to know the object is remade every time through the students' own ability for knowing, for developing critical comprehension in themselves.
>
> What is dialogue in this way of knowing? Precisely this connection, this epistemological relation. The object to be known in one place links the two cognitive subjects, leading them to reflect together on the object. Dialogue is the sealing together of the teacher and the students in the joint act of knowing and re-knowing the object of study. Then, instead of transferring the knowledge *statically,* as a *fixed* possession of the teacher, dialogue demands a dynamic approximation towards the object. (p. 14)

... Precisely because there is an epistemology here, my position is not to deny the directive and necessary role of the educator. But, I am *not* the kind of educator who *owns* the objects I study with the students. I am extremely interested in the object for study. They stimulate my curiosity and I bring this enthusiasm to the students. Then, both of us can illuminate the object together. (p. 15)

... but nevertheless it does *not* mean that the educator first denies that he or she knows! It would be a lie, an hypocrisy. He or she has on the contrary to demonstrate his or her competency to the students. Secondly, it does not mean that every time, in every course, in every term, the educator changes his or her knowledge about this or that object. No. (p. 16)

I must repeat something here, in order to be absolutely clear. At the moment the teacher begins the dialogue, he or she knows a great deal, first in terms of knowledge and second in terms of the horizon that she or he wants to get to. The starting point is what the teacher knows about the object and where the teacher wants to go with it. (p. 17)

...Even though it is not strictly the task of the educator to form or to shape the students, no matter what the level of education, I am in my perspective a helper of the students in their process of formation, of their growing up (Shor & Freire, 1987b, p. 30, italics is original).

In dialogic pedagogy, there is not the final endpoint known to the teacher in advance. As famous Russian writer and innovative educator Tolstoy wrote, educators "not only do not know, but... cannot know, wherein the education of the people is to consist;... education... has no final end [i.e., the endpoint – EM]" (Tolstoy, 1967, pp. 29-30). From a dialogic pedagogy perspective, it is not the goal of education for the student to become epistemologically the same as the teacher. Rather, the goal of education is for the students to join a community of practice bounded by the targeted knowledge or skills (Lave & Wenger, 1991; Tolstoy, 1967). What the student does with this knowledge and affiliation is up to the student. Even if a student decides to reject the knowledge, it will be the student's informed and responsible rejection.

Freire apparently came close to the claim (however, he did not make it, as far as I know), according to which knowledge is dialogically relative because it "belongs" to a dialogic community of educated ("dialogic people") and not to an individual or even to a culture. In other words, until the teacher involves the student into particular knowledge, the teacher does not know truly this knowledge him or herself. Knowing without being able to engage another in this knowledge, to address another, to respond to another and without testing knowledge with another is very partial knowledge. It is definitely not *knowing-together*. The teacher's *knowledge collapses* in a company of the not knowledgeable students. When knowledge is not shared, it does not exist in a community. A Russian-speaking person, who cannot speak English and joins an English speaking community who cannot speak Russian, is losing ability to speak and communicate. The person, of course, still can communicate with him or herself, with Russian speaking community, and might have some meta-speaking and meta-language learning skills. But his or her communication skills, abilities, and participation collapse in English-speaking community.

When, for example, an adult teacher encounters a child student, who is not knowledgeable in arithmetic, the adult teacher stops knowing 2+2=4 in the same way that the teacher knows this math fact with another knowledgeable adult. Some children might be uncertain whether 2+2 can be always represented as with the lines ||+|| that then can be recounted as the four lines. The teacher has to suspend his or her epistemological certainty about this unconditional representation of integer numbers with lines until this certainty emerges in the students or it completely collapses in the teacher as well (as it happened in me after conversation with first graders). Together with the students, the teacher has to examine a possibility that when two objects added to other two objects, they do not always (i.e., unconditionally) produce four objects. Indeed, as I discussed in my earlier chapter, when objects interact with each other (like two hungry cats and two fat mice or like two friends and two friends), 2+2 may not be equal 4. It is only when the objects do not interact with each other, their relations are linear and 2+2 is always 4 for them (or at least this is how I currently think but I am ready reconsider it if a challenge will arrive again). In this example, my knowledge collapsed with the first graders to a point that it never recovered again as I recognized that my previous knowledge that 2+2 was unconditionally 4 was incorrect (cf. Berlyand, 1996).

This example can be seen as extreme but it nicely illustrates the open-ended and unfinalized nature of pedagogical dialogue. Famous Russian writer and educator described Leo Tolstoy described this relative collapse of his writing skills while he was teaching writing eleven-year old peasant boys in his innovative school "Yasnay Polyana" in his pedagogical essay with a provocative title, "Are the peasant children to learn to write from us? Or are we to learn from the peasant children?" (Tolstoy, 1967, pp. 191-224).

But, what if students' investigation leads the entire class to go off course of the curriculum? Or what if the entire class comes to conclusions that are incorrect? There are at least two possibilities here. The conclusion that the students are arrived can be seen as incorrect by the teacher. If this is the case, the teacher has to provide counter-arguments and challenge the students' conclusion as a member of the learning community. Using Bakhtin's term, the teacher's consciousness also has to be taken no less seriously than the consciousnesses of the students.

However, if whole class, including the teacher, came to a conclusion that is very different from the societal conclusion that the society had a strong consensus, then it is the responsibility of the teacher to move the issue further in testing these two conclusions because the teacher's responsibility is to bridge the classroom learning community and the entire society. By that, I mean contacting the most knowledgeable people in the society to ask their opinion on the argumentation that the students and the teacher arrived. In a way, the latter case is about collapsing of knowledge in the entire society. Not only the teacher should contact societal experts in the case of disagreements of the class learning community with the societal consensus as result of the class IPD but also about their endpoint doubts about the societal consensus.

The innovative teacher Kurganov, one of the founders of the Dialogue of Cultures School ("Школа Диалога Культур" in Russian) educational movement in Russia and Ukraine, writes that, "It seems to me that a reasonable cycle of dialogic education [for the teacher – EM] is the following form: from the lesson-seminar to specialists-lesson. During the classroom lesson, the children express ideas new for the teacher. The teacher brings these ideas to the community of professional specialists for a discussion. Then, enriched by the professionals' opinions-replies, the children's ideas return back to the classroom [for further discussion – EM]" (Kurganov, 2005, translation from Russian is mine). Thus, Kurganov suggests the teacher to be a mediator between two distinguished dialogic communities: students' community and professionals' community. As Kurganov shows with examples from his own pedagogical practice, this mediation is not mechanical bridging and following the epistemological authority of the experts but a dialogic address-response to them. Although, he does not mention the third community, the community of educators, Kurganov actively participates in it and uses his participation in this third community for his dialoguing with both his students and professional specialists.

Similarly, studying innovative Japanese educator Kihaku Saitou, who redefined Kyouzai-Kaishaku (literally, "teaching material"-"interpretation"), Miyazaki (2007, July) argues that for providing sensitive guidance for the students, a Kyouzai-Kaishaku teacher has constantly to involve him or herself in learning about the curriculum that has three aspects,

> Kihaku Saitou argued that there are three aspects in the work of Kyouzai – Kaishaku (Saitou, 1963). One is to have a general knowledge about the content. In this aspect, teachers learn the correct answer in common-sense terms. Any adult can do it. The second one is the teacher's professional understanding. Here, teachers learn how each child in the classroom understands the teaching content and thinks about how to respond to their understanding. In other word, teachers understand the teaching content as children. In this aspect, teachers sometimes get excited by and discover something new in the children's understanding of the content. In those cases, teachers learn about the content from children. The third one is to learn from experts in specialized fields of the culture such as the arts and sciences. This one is, on the one hand, to accumulate the knowledge of the teaching content and to know the 'more correct' answers about the problems in teaching content. Learning from experts, on the other hand, often stimulates learners to re-examine the 'correct answers' they have accepted as commonsense. Such re-examination often tells us that the widely accepted answer is not the only correct one and there are other, possibly 'correct' answers in addition to the accepted one. This third aspect is learning of the existence of multiple possibilities of the various interpretations of the teaching content. According to Saitou, these three aspects work together and interact with each other in the actual work of Kyouzai Kaishaku.
> The last two aspects of Saitou's Kyouzai – Kaishaku go beyond the correct understanding of the teaching material. They are the effort to generate understanding other than the one which is commonsensically correct. Understanding which is commonsensically correct is understanding which is familiar to teachers as grown up adults. In this sense, Kyouzai-Kaishaku involves the task of making the familiar strange for teachers as adults (Miyazaki, 2007, July, p. 3).

The entire network of practices involving this math concept, in which the adult teacher is very comfortable, would collapse in the presence of this less knowledgeable child while a new "strange" network would emerge. If the teacher's knowledge survives its collapse initial collapse in the classroom, it can only survive as collective, communal knowledge of the classroom community, "It is quite possible to imagine and postulate a unified truth that requires a plurality of consciousness, one that in principle cannot be fitted within the bounds of a single consciousness, one that is born at a point of contact among various consciousness" (Bakhtin, 1999, p. 81). For the teacher to teach dialogically, he or she has to regain personal epistemological uncertainty about the taught curriculum and, thus, to become a dialogic subject. As Barnacle (2005) points out in her analysis of Socrates' discussion of who is philosopher in Plato's Symposium (Plato, 1997), a learner ("philosopher" in Socrates' terms) cannot be either knowledgeable (i.e., expert) or ignorant (i.e., disvaluing knowledge) but something in between. Similar, a medieval religious philosopher Nicholas of Cusa developed a notion of "learned ignorance" (or, probably, a better translation can be "enlightened ignorance") (Nicholas, 1954). A genuine learner is somewhat in between the expert and the ignorant, "less knowledge-able,[10]" constantly focusing on the (fuzzy) boundary between known and unknown. To prepare the teacher oneself for dialogic teaching, the teacher has to refocus on this epistemological boundary for him/herself in order to create a collective boundary of known and unknown in the classroom with the students in the dialogue.

Let me illustrate the relative collapse of adult knowledge in presence of less knowledgeable child with another example. When a young child of 2-3-year old asks a parent for another cracker in addition to one that the child already has, it might be OK for the parent just to break the cracker in half and give the two halves to the child's both hands. The child might be satisfied with this action by the adult but a knowledgeable adult in the same situation would not. Thus, the parent acts according to a community in which the amount of the substance is considered to be non-conserved by rearranging the substance – "non-conservation" (Piaget & Elkind, 1968). A lot of knowledge that the parent takes for granted in communication with other knowledgeable adults (and children) would collapse[11] in communication with a less knowledgeable child. Is it the adult's knowledge that collapses (i.e., why this knowledge is true) or the adult's persuasiveness (i.e., the adult's ability to convince others and the self)? Both, because they are the same (see Wells, 1999, for more discussion of this issue).

Of course, the parent's knowledge will not collapse *entirely* as the parent can dialogue about it with him/herself (without the presence of the students) and with member of his or her adult community bounded by this knowledge of arithmetic. The mathematical meaning of 2+2=4 is not just rooted in mathematical epistemology, or the cognitive psychological skills of the teacher, or in certain cultural practices of our society – all of this is true – but also, essentially also, in dialogic communication (i.e., communication without authority, Bakhtin, 1991) with another. If such dialogic communication collapses or becomes impossible, then one's knowledge becomes not fully possible for the person-living-with-other-people. Non-dialogic knowledge is autistic knowledge. We *know* only in a community, in which the knowledge is dialogically circulated. Without dialogue, knowledge is autistic, egocentric, parochial, and, thus, not truthful. This is what, I argue, Bakhtin (1999) probably meant when he claimed that truth *lives only in dialogue* and is not just born out of it. The goal of education is for the teacher to help the students engage in a community where the knowledge is circulated – to include them into the Big Dialogue of ideas. Arguably, the students who consider limitations of the math statement of 2+2=4 are more involved in this community and

---

[10] This is not a quantitative, comparative category but a qualitative category focusing the known-unknown boundary and involving both "less" and "-able" aspects.

[11] Sara Labib Salloum (personal communication, February 24, 2007) made an interesting point in response to this example. She suggested that the parent is able to be using this cunning strategy of breaking the cracker to satisfy the toddler's demand exactly because the parent has knowledge of the amount conservation. Thus, the parent has "surplus of vision" (Bakhtin et al., 1990) based on his or her participation in a community of "amount conservators." Although this is probably true, still the adult acts according to the community of "amount non-conservators," in which the toddler participates. First, the toddler can start using the strategy used by the adult: to break a cracker when he or she (or somebody else) wants more in future. Second, the toddler does not understand the adult's "surplus of vision" and the adult would have great difficulty to explain it to the child.

Dialogue than those who do not engage in this inquiry[12]. Similarly, the directionality of moral education is, according this radical dialogic pedagogy, not make the students to act always in a "good" "prosocial" way and thus to take free will of agency away from their deeds but rather to learn to take responsibility for their "good" and "bad" actions by being informed about the actions' consequences, motive, and ethics. Education makes "bad" actions less naïve, it undermines, using Bakhtin's powerful phrase, personal reliance on "an alibi in Being" (Bakhtin et al., 1993, p. 40) (e.g., excuses like "I did not have any choice" or "It just happens with me" or "I did not know").

Freire was very close to this claim, in our view, when he said, "the ability of the educator to know the object is remade every time through the students' own ability for knowing, for developing critical comprehension in themselves" (Shor & Freire, 1987b, p. 14). However, Freire did not subscribe this radical dialogic perspective that we have just described. In my view, Freire argued in this quote (and elsewhere in his writing) that the teacher's knowledge is *renewed* in interaction with the student. For example, the teacher might develop a new or better argument for the positions or facts he or she had known in advance as a result of his or her teaching. But Freire was not apparently making the more radical claim, described above, that the teacher's knowledge collapses every time in an encounter with a new student (although, Ira Shor does seem to be claiming the teacher's *re-learning*, see his original quote above).

The difference in the claims and their consequences is very important for defining dialogic pedagogy. If my understanding of Freire's position is correct, he claims the dialogic origin but not the dialogic existence of knowledge (and truth). Freire's version of dialogic pedagogy can be defined as *cultural-dialogic* because he believed that knowledge emerges dialogically but exists in culture (e.g., artifacts and historically established consensuses). Thus, Freire's approach can be characterized still as *instrumental,* Freire's own insistence to contrary. The main pedagogical consequence from this conceptual difference is that Freire seemed to prioritize the teacher's pedagogical learning over his or her epistemological learning during the educational process. He viewed the teacher's epistemological learning during the instruction as accidental. In his view, it is nearly impossible for the students to shake off the teacher's knowledge in any essential way because behind the teacher's

---

[12] Sigmund Ongstad (2007, January) presented an interesting, but sad, story illustrating how mainstream school does not appreciate and care about students engaging in Big Dialogue about ideas and testing limits of knowledge if not actively discouraging them, "The following task was given as one in a set at the official national exam in 'Norwegian' for all upper secondary schools (high schools) in 1973 in Norway,
The number of youngsters who marry already in their teen ages has increased heavily the last years. There are especially many girls who marry that early. What can be the causes for this development, and what is your view upon that so many marry so young?
Later the same year a class at a local school got the same task. However, one of the students contested the very premise for the task and wrote, as his assignment, a harsh critique of the whole task, arguing why the premise is invalid. The local lecturer gave him a bad mark (for not having answered the given task). The student then contacted the Central Statistical Office, who could confirm that he was actually right. The premise was not valid. He now approached the teacher and the Norwegian department at the school again, without result. He even challenged the school's headmaster, who was a MTE teacher as well, in the hope that this 'sensible man' would support his claim. However, neither the headmaster nor the Norwegian department at the school would admit any mistake. The task had even been given at the national exam the same year and had not caused problems. And one crucial argument was: *You are bristling up against the task instead of trying to come to grips with the problem* (Retold in English based on an article in Aftenposten (newspaper), Oslo October 1973 by Sigmund Onstad)." This reminds a confrontation between Luria and illiterate adult Uzbeks about syllogisms in his famous experiments in Central Asia in the early 1930s (Luria, 1976; Matusov & St. Julien, 2004; Scribner, 1977).

knowledge there is often the history of the humankind and powerful network of societal practices, especially practices of science making. For Freire, knowledge and truth are heavily located in society, history, and culture and not in the teacher-students dialogue,

> *[Paulo:]* ...by discussing dialogue every day with students, I am not changing every day my understanding of dialogue. We arrive at the level of some certainty, some scientific certainty of some objects, which we can count on. What dialogue-educators know, nevertheless, is that science has historicity. This means that all new knowledge comes up when other knowledge becomes old, and no longer answers the needs of the new moment, no longer answers the new questions being asked. Because of that, all new knowledge when it appears waits for its own overcoming by the next new knowledge which is inevitable. Sometimes I say that if scientists were as humble as knowledge is, we would be in a different world (Shor & Freire, 1987b, p. 16)

According to Freire's position, the teacher may or may not learn something new with the students, – which is not essential for his version of dialogic teaching. The teacher has to be open just for this new epistemological learning, which usually occurs outside of teaching. In this point, Freire is similar to Buber who also seemed to be ambivalent on this point. On the one hand, like Freire, Buber insisted on the dialogic nature of education but on the on the other he apparently denied epistemological learning from the teacher as the necessary aspect of dialogical teaching,

> But however intense the mutuality of giving and taking with which he [the teacher – EM] is bound to his pupil's being educated, but the pupil cannot experience the educating of the educator. The educator stands at both ends of the common situation, the pupil only at one end. In the moment when the pupil is able to throw himself across and experience from over there, the educative relation would be burst asunder, or change into friendship.
> We call friendship the third form of the dialogical relation, which is based on a concrete and mutual experience of inclusion. It is the true inclusion of one another by human souls (Buber, 2002, pp. 100-101).

In this fragment, Buber clearly denied dialogic relations to education and excluded the teacher and the students from their dialogic fellowship (what Buber referred to "friendship") despite to claims of opposite a few pages later. Freire seemed to have similar ambivalent position.

In the *radical dialogic* position that I presented above, *there is essentially no difference between so-called pedagogical and epistemological knowledge*[13]. Knowledge originates and exists primarily in dialogue. Knowing and successful teaching through dialogue is the same. In education, to know means to teach and to teach means to know. The teacher is not merely perpetrating culture by helping the student to joint it but creating it with students (Matusov, Smith et al., 2007; Matusov, St. Julien et al., 2005). Thus, if I am correct that his dialogic pedagogy privileges pedagogical over epistemological knowledge, Freire's cultural-dialogic

---

[13] In education, the idea that epistemological and pedagogical learning is the same seems to be odd and novel but in art, similar idea seems to be obvious if not trivial. Indeed, in art, aesthetic mastery and expressive (guiding) mastery of literary artwork is the same. It is difficult to imagine that artwork can be judged as great by a reader who cannot understand it or access it (unless out of trust of the judgment by significant others).

pedagogy is very susceptible to become manipulative teaching (as we discussed above and will discuss below), because without epistemological learning on the part of the teacher during the instruction, dialogue will unavoidably deteriorate into manipulation of moving the students' subjectivities toward the final endpoint known the teacher in advance[14]. Although Freire clearly disliked and opposed this manipulative teaching in his writing (Freire, 1976, 1986; Freire & Freire, 1973), "The truly liberating option is not even realized by means of manipulative... practice. Manipulation is debilitating and, likewise, irresponsible" (Freire & Macedo, 1987, p. 39), his cultural-dialogic approach which assumes a separation of pedagogy and epistemology can easily push him or any other educational practitioners prioritizing the teacher's pedagogical learning over epistemological learning into manipulation of their students instead of genuine dialogue. As I show further, this exactly happened with Freire in his work in Africa.

Situated Ontology of Critical Thinking

Learning is a transformation of the student's subjectivity – skills, worldviews, and understanding about the world (Matusov & Smith, 2007). It is not a replacement of what is wrong with what is right, or adding something that never was there originally. New knowledge in the learning process is never absolutely novel. It always communicates with the student's prior and current knowledge, prior and current interests, prior and current needs, prior and current dreams (and aspirations), and prior and current social relations. So, learning is a dialogue on the boundary between what was known what is known and what potentially will be known (Aideen Murthy, personal communication, December 20, 2006). A place where education occurs (e.g., a classroom) is itself a part of the student's life and, thus, constitutes its own curriculum,

> [*Paulo:*] Dialogue does not exist in a political vacuum. It is not a "free space" where you may do what you want. Dialogue takes place inside some kind of program and context. These conditioning factors create tension in achieving goals that we set for dialogic education. To achieve the goals of transformation, dialogue implies responsibility, directiveness, determination, discipline, objectives.
>
> Nevertheless, a dialogical situation implies the absence of authoritarianism. Dialogue means a permanent tension in the relation between authority and liberty. But, in this tension, authority continues to be because it has authority vis-a-vis permitting student freedoms which emerge, which grow and mature precisely because authority and freedom learn self-discipline (Shor & Freire, 1987b, p. 16).

Thus, dialogic pedagogy always starts with the student. The boundary between student and the teacher (and communities behind the teacher) is the primary curriculum for dialogic pedagogy (cf. learning curriculum vs. teaching curriculum in Lave, 1992a). The curriculum has to be situated in boundary[15] between the teacher and the student "on interindividual territory" (Voloshinov, 1973, p. 12).

---

[14] Freire's endpoint seemed to be that of revolution whereas the peasants may have created an entirely different endpoint.
[15] I'm very thankful to Aideen Murthy for pushing me in this position through her dialogic challenge of a previous draft.

If the student's subjectivity is the initial point of departure for dialogic pedagogy, what is the direction of the dialogic instruction? There are at least three legitimate sources of such directionality of instruction in the context of education. First, the students are full with their own inquiries, problems, projects, interests, needs, and desires that can generate directionality of the instruction (remember, for example, that Meno came to Socrates to learn about the origin of virtue – the inquiry that Meno was puzzled at the moment). Second, seeing the students in broader and more knowledgeable contexts, the teacher (and a broader community the teacher represents) may see very important inquiries, problems, projects, interests, needs, and desires relevant to the students' lives in the students that the students, themselves, might not see (e.g., Socrates saw that while Meno was deeply concerned about the origin of virtues, Meno did not know what the virtue was although he thought he knew). Third, the teacher has his or her own important inquiries, problems, projects, interests, needs, and desires emerging in the teacher's own life (e.g., Socrates himself wanted to examine what is virtue). But, whatever the source of dialogic inquiry, it has to ontologically engage the students. The students should feel not only a problem but also its ontological urgency to address and to prioritize it in their life, "here and now." This is how Shor and Freire described it,

> [*Ira:*] My understanding is that dialogic inquiry is situated in the culture, language, politics, and themes of the students. Teachers have some familiarity with experiential objects or materials for study. They bring in magazines from mass culture, or show popular films and TV shows. They ask students to write about events from their daily lives. But, in situated pedagogy we discover with students the themes most problematic to their perception. We situate the critical pedagogy in subjective problem-themes not yet analyzed by students. This gains intrinsic motivation from subject matter of key concern to students while also giving them a moment of detachment on their previously unreflected experience. In dialogic pedagogy, this turn towards subjective experience must also include a global, critical dimension. That is, we don't only look at the familiar, but we try to understand it socially and historically. The global context for the concrete, the general setting for the particular, are what give students a critical view on reality, what I refer to as "extraordinarily reexperiencing the ordinary." In this way, situating pedagogy in student culture does not merely exploit or endorse the given but seeks to transcend it (p. 18).
>
> [*Paulo:*] When I insist on dialogical education starting from the students' comprehension of their daily life experiences, no matter if they are students of the university or kids in primary school or workers in a neighborhood or peasants in the countryside, my insistence on starting from *their* description of *their* daily life experiences is based in the possibility of starting from concreteness, from common sense, to reach a rigorous understanding of reality. I don't dichotomize these two dimensions of the world, daily life from rigor, common sense from philosophical sense, in the expression of Gramsci. I don't understand critical or scientific knowledge which appears randomly, by magic or by accident, as if it did not need to meet the test of reality. Scientific rigor comes from an effort to overcome a naïve understanding of the world. Science is super-posing critical thought on what we observe in reality, after the starting point of common sense (Shor & Freire, 1987b, p. 20).

Very frequently Chilean peasants, as they conversed with me or as they spoke in the Cultural Circles, noted the very concrete reasons that they had led them to seek literacy education. They insisted that prior to the agrarian reform they had no reason to learn to read and to write, even when their "patron was understanding" and made possible, because they "had no way to use their letters" (Freire, 1978, pp. 111-112).

Again, although Shor and Freire agreed that dialogic inquiry has to be situated in students' lives, they seemed to disagree about the guiding force in that inquiry. Shor seemed to assume an imminent force of critical thinking that drives the dialogic inquiry through re-experiencing the students' ordinary lives by making critical connections with global dimensions[16]. For Shor, science and politics can be discovered in the dialogic inquiry as, and if needed through, the course of collective critical investigation (see Dyson, 1997; Freedom Writers & Gruwell, 1999; Shor, 1987; Stock, 1995, for similar position). For Freire, the driving force of dialogic inquiry is external to inquiry itself: science or politics. The tools of science and politics can be used by the teacher to help students place their subjectivities in order[17]. One practical implication of this difference is that in Shor's dialogic approach, science and politics as such can easily become an object of the teacher-students critique, while in Freire's dialogical approach, science and politics are outside the critique (we are not talking here about specific politics but politics as a practice per se). For Freire, education is subordinated to science and politics, "In my conversations with educators, I have always stressed the need for political clarity – especially with regard to whose interests they are serving – rather than [pedagogical – EM] techniques and methods" (Freire, 1978, p. 147).

Directionality of Education: Political Act of Transformation of Society

Although, Freire rejected that the teacher should share and form the students in a certain way, "Even though it is not strictly the task of the educator to form or to shape the students, no matter what the level of education" (Shor & Freire, 1987b, p. 30), Freire saw the purpose of education in turning students into "militants" – political activists fighting for justice, equality, liberation from oppression, and classless socialist society (Freire, 1978). Freire wrote a very attractive definition of education as "reading and writing the word to read and write the world" reflecting the social activist nature of education.

> [*Paulo:*] …when I am against the authoritarian position, I am not trying to fall into what I spoke of earlier as a laissez-faire position. When I criticize manipulation, I do not want to fall into a false and nonexistent nondirectivity of education. For me, education is always directive, always. The question is to know towards what and with whom is it directive. This is the question. I don't believe in self-liberation. Liberation is a social act. Liberating education is a social process of illumination.

---

[16] See Morson and Emerson for their discussion of similar tendency in Bakhtin and in a Russian writer, philosopher, and innovative educator Leo Tolstoy (see, for example, his philosophical reasoning about the 'prosaic' work of history in his novel "War and peace", Tolstoy, Maude, Maude, & Gifford, 1983). Morson and Emerson coined the term "prosaics" to capture this tendency as "a form of thinking that resumes the importance of the everyday, the ordinary, the 'prosaic'" (Morson & Emerson, 1990, p. 15). In cultural anthropology and psychology this tendency has been captured in the term "situated cognition" (Lave, 1988). Bakhtin called it "participatory thinking" (Bakhtin et al., 1993).

[17] Freire's position seemed somewhat similar to Vygotsky's (1987) position of subordination of the everyday (pseudo-)concepts to the scientific concepts, however, unlike Vygotsky with his ultra modernist position, Freire tried to deemphasize this sharp opposition while preserving the everyday-scientific hierarchy.

Ira: There is no personal self-empowerment?

Paulo: No, no, no. Even when you individually feel yourself most free, if this feeling is not a social feeling, if you are not able to use your recent freedom to help others to be free by transforming the totality of society, then you are exercising only an individualist attitude towards empowerment or freedom. ... [Students'] curiosity, their critical perception of reality, is fundamental for social transformation but is not enough by itself (Shor & Freire, 1987b, pp. 22-23).

In my view, Freire's trouble started when he defined the activist nature of education as subordinated to the politics of promoting a communist revolution. In his later writing-interviews, Freire revealed that in the 1960s he shifted from a "naïve" belief that education can reform the society, that discourse of education can have power over and judge the practice, to a "more mature" view that education is a form (among other forms) of political struggle (Freire & Macedo, 1987; Shor & Freire, 1987a),

> The myth of the neutrality of education – which leads to the negation of the political nature of the educational process, regarding it only as a task we do in the service of humanity in the abstract sense – is the point of departure for our understanding of the fundamental differences between a naïve practice, an astute practice, and a truly critical practice... What we as educators have to do, then, is to clarify the fact that education is political, and to be consistent with it in practice (Freire & Macedo, 1987, pp. 38-39).

> Education as an act of knowing confronts us with a number of theoretical-practical, not [purely? – EM] intellectual, questions: What to know? How to know? Why to know? In benefit of what and of whom to know? Moreover, against what and whom to know? These are fundamental questions, in dynamic relationship to others around the act of educating, its possibilities, its legitimacy, its objectives and ends, its agents, its methods and content (Freire, 1978, p. 100)

> It is in this sense that the ministry of education, in whatever society, is always an eminently political ministry. Politics serves the interests of the dominant class in a class society; it serves the interests of the people in a revolutionary [classless – EM] society (Freire, 1978, p. 78).

Of course, education often has a political aspect, as it has economic, social, aesthetic, emotional, intellectual, and many other aspects that penetrate the fabric of education praxis. It is also true that sometimes the political nature of education dominates and deeply shapes educational processes and institutions as no other aspects can (Gee, 1996). However, it is not true that education is *always* subordinated politics and cannot have its own agenda independent of politics. *At times* education has its own power (even over politics) or becomes independent or leads the politics or is even neutral of politics (see work of Labaree, 1997, for empirical evidence for that). Also, politics itself is not monolithic and has many trends and currents. In other words, Freire's universal subordination of education to politics (Elias, 1994) seems to be reductionist and even totalitarian by its nature. It is also not true that a truly critical practice is only political one (although it can definitely be in this sphere). With an analogy to reductionism to the material, from the fact that we all consist of atoms, does not mean that all that we (our lives as human beings) can be reduced to atoms. The same thing is true of education. Education consists of politics (big and small, I define "politics" here as "power game of domination" after Foucault, 1988) but it cannot be reduced to it. I argue that what makes practice critical is genuine dialogue with its authority-less regime and with its focus on testing ideas in actions be it in a sphere of politics or any other sphere.

In my view, Freire betrayed his own commitment to dialogue and critical practices when he subordinated education (and the truth seeking process in general) to politics per se and to his communist quest in specific. When social justice trumps uncomfortable truths and dialogue with opponents, it quickly leads to even bigger injustices than the ones that it attempts to cure as the history of the 20th century (and Freire's work in Africa) has shown. Social justice and truth are the same, when searching for truth and justice (as concern and sympathy for human suffering) are both prioritized. Freire's apriori statements, like "politics… serves the interests of the people in a revolutionary [classless – EM] society," become dogmatic without dialogic tests. But what else can become out of Freire's "liberating" pedagogy when he claimed that in a socialist society education should be organized "in accordance with the policies of the Party carried by government" (Freire, 1978, p. 30)?!

FREIRE'S TOTALITARIAN PEDAGOGY
OF LIBERATION FROM PEOPLE'S FREEDOM

Freire's (1978; Freire & Macedo, 1987) texts about his work in Africa in socialist Guinea-Bissau and Sao Tome where he spent several months directly preparing teachers for his literacy programs during his several visits can be called *classical totalitarian texts*. One can find a multitude of such totalitarian texts in socialist countries like the Soviet Union, China, Albania, North Korea, Romania, and so on. They all have the same birthmarks of totalitarianism:

- *Cult of personality* of the local Party leaders dead or alive (Walker, 1981) (e.g. "Here, as in all of the dimensions of the liberation process, one can appreciate the prophetic vision of Amilcar Cabral[18]" (p. 17), "Like Guevara and like Fidel, Cabral was in constant communion with the people, whose past he knew so well and in whose present he was so deeply rooted, a present filled with struggle, to which he gave himself without restriction" (p. 18), "He [a young director of a live-in school] referred to Amilcar Cabral, neither sentimentally nor as a mythological figure to the worshipped, but as a symbol, a significant presence in the history of his people… Long before Cabral became the 'Father of the Nation,' he was the 'Son of the People' who learned with them and them in the revolutionary praxis" (p. 32-33) and so on and so forth) ;

---

[18] Amilcar Cabral was one of the main leaders of the arm struggle for independence and socialism against Portuguese colonizers in Portuguese Guinea, a founder of the PAIGC or Partido Africano da Independência da Guiné e Cabo Verde (Portuguese: African Party for the Independence of Guinea and Cape Verde) based on Marxist-Leninist principles. He was killed in 1973 by a Portuguese agent. He was the de facto leader of Guinea-Bissau and Cape Verde pronounced by PAIGC in 1972. After his death and at time of Freire's work in Guinea-Bissau, the country was ruled by the PAIGC that involved many relatives of Amilcar Cabral (the first President of Guinea-Bissau, Luis Cabral, was a half brother of Amilcar Cabral; Mario Cabral was the Commissioner of State for Education and Culture, with whom Freire arranged his visit and project). This Marxist-Leninist reign was stopped in a bloodless coup in 1980, when Cabral's Premier Minister came to power and became a dictator.

- *Authoritarian argumentation*: Using quotes from the most authoritative Party leaders as arguments (e.g., "The rural people succeeded in remaining immune to this strange biculturism. Fortified by their own cultural richness, which even Amilcar Cabral included in what he used to call 'weakness of culture,' they preserved their language[19]" (p. 127), Freire's text is dense with quotes from the Party officials through which he made his points),
- *Propaganda of the official Party line* (e.g., "... in our training seminars for teachers we have not emphasized methods and techniques, but, rather political clarity. This emphasis becomes even more important when we are talking about qualifying middle-class young people who have not yet committed the 'class-suicide' to which Amilcar Cabral refers and which he accomplished in so exemplary a manner... By demonstrating the unity of theory and practice, they [Freire's trainees -EM] prepare students for the '[class-EM] suicide' that will become concrete when they are able to join the oppressed classes in their struggle for liberation. This is the case in Guinea-Bissau today where the people's struggle for the creation of the new [socialist – EM] society continues, even without war" (p. 78), "In the last analysis, I am convinced that it is easier to create a new type of intellectual –forged in the unity between practice and theory, manual and intellectual work – than to reeducate an elitist intellectual. When I say it is easier , I do not discount the validity of such reeducation[20] when it does occur" (p. 104));
- *Full loyalty and conformity to the regime* (Walker, 1981) (e.g., "That can all be done later when we have seen whether the suggestions themselves have any relevance for this country and whether they fit the immediate objectives of the Party and the government" (Freire, 1978, p. 132));
- *Lack or suppression of critical stand toward the regime* beyond "asking oneself if this, that or the other is 'in the right line'" (Gide, 1937, p. 48)[21], *self-censorship* (e.g.,

---

[19] Here, Freire actually disagreed with Cabral about using Portuguese, the language of colonizers, for school instruction (Freire & Macedo, 1987, p. 109), but he had to appropriate the quote of Cabral in his writing to make his argument legit.

[20] In the Soviet Union, in the Communist China, in the Communist Kampuchea, in the Communist Cuba, in the Nazi Germany, and many other totalitarian countries, all such "reeducation" of intellectuals who had to "commit class suicide" was done in labor concentration camps (Kotek & Rigoulot, 2000). This is how this process described by the Cuban creator of the first of such labor concentration camp in the Guanahacabibes region, Che Guevara, "[We] only send to Guanahacabibes those doubtful cases where we are not sure people should go to jail. I believe that people who should go to jail should go to jail anyway. Whether long-standing militants or whatever, they should go to jail. We send to Guanahacabibes those people who should not go to jail, people who have committed crimes against revolutionary morals, to a greater or lesser degree, along with simultaneous sanctions like being deprived of their posts, and in other cases not those sanctions, but rather to be reeducated through labor. It is hard labor, not brute labor, rather the working conditions are harsh but they are not brutal..." (the quote cited in Castañeda, 1997, p. 178)

[21] Andre Gide, a French Marxist writer, visited the Soviet Union in 1936 during the Stalinist purges and made remarkable and keen observations (along with somewhat nationalistic and shallow ones) about the nature of the Soviet totalitarian regime, "We admire in the U.S.S.R. the extraordinary *élan* towards education and towards culture; but the only objects of this education are those which induce the mind to find satisfaction in its present circumstances and exclaim: *Oh ! U.S.S.R. . . . Ave! Spes unica !* And culture is entirely directed along a single track. There is nothing disinterested in it; it is merely cumulative, and (in spite of Marxism) almost entirely lacks the critical faculty. Of course I know that what is called "self-criticism" is highly thought of. When at a distance, I admired this, and I still think it might have produced the most wonderful results, if only it had been seriously and sincerely applied. But I was soon obliged to realise that, apart from denunciations and complaints—("The canteen soup is badly cooked" or "the club reading-room badly swept")—criticism merely consists in asking oneself if this, that or the other is "in the right line." The line

"... often there are reasons of a political character that require silence from the intellectual, even if this silence is sometimes misinterpreted" (Freire & Macedo, 1987, p. 112));

- *Disregard to human suffering from the hands of "liberators"* (one cannot find description of people's sufferings from hands of "liberators" or as results of their repressive or plain inept policies in Freire's book about his work in Guinea-Bissau in the mid of the 1970s that were well documented by Human Right organizations[22] and historians (see Fry, 1996; Harasim, 1983; Lobban & Lopes, 1995; Lobban & Mendy, 1997));

- *Circular reasoning of self-righteousness* (e.g., "Politics ... serves the interests of the people in a revolutionary [classless – EM] society" (Freire, 1978, p. 78) – in a class society, politics serves the dominant class and their oppression, in a classless society it *automatically* serves all people – there is no oppression (cf. similar critique of Freire in Walker, 1981). Whatever the Party does, it does in the interests of people because there are no other interests left out in the classless society. We will have more analysis of Freire's circular reasoning below);

- *Totalitarian ideology*, according to which everything is politicized and subordinated to the dichotomous antagonistic politics (e.g., "As a matter of fact it was this perception of the interrelationship of all the parts of a totality that impressed me so greatly in Amilcar Cabral, as well as his critical comprehension of the role of culture in the struggle for liberation which is, as he emphasized, 'a cultural fact and also a factor of culture'" (Freire, 1978, p. 72) see also critique of Freire's political dichotomy on oppressors and oppressed in Elias (1976)).

What makes Freire's texts interesting (although not unique) is that he wrote them *outside* of these totalitarian countries and, thus, its production cannot be explained by Freire's possible fear of the regimes or by Freire's material gains from the regimes. Freire's production of classical totalitarian texts was obviously intrinsic (see a discussion of this controversy in Torres, 1994).

Freire (Freire & Macedo, 1987, pp. 63-93) provides detailed description of the curricula of his literacy program in Sao Tome and Principe, a small African nation leading to socialism after it decolonization in the mid 1970s when Freire worked there. The immediate impression of this curriculum focusing on Freire's teaching the students "political clarity" (Freire, 1978,

---

itself is never discussed. What is discussed is whether such-and-such a work, or gesture, or theory conforms to this sacrosanct line. And woe to him who seeks to cross it! As much criticism as you like—up to a point. Beyond that point criticism is not allowed. There are examples of this kind of thing in history" (Gide, 1937, pp. 47-48, italics is original).

[22] "At independence, the victorious liberation movement of Guinea-Bissau, PAIGC, ... introduced a political and economic order based on Marxist-Leninist principles. Procedures and results were not unlike those reported for Angola and Mozambique, where similar highly-centralized systems replaced the equally centralized and authoritarian Portuguese colonial order. Attempts to implement a socialized economy resulted in an inflated and inefficient state apparatus, reduction in productivity and increasing dependence on foreign aid, which now finances over 90 percent of the national budget. The determination to build a one-party state resulted in a massive onslaught of violations of fundamental human rights and the perpetuation of a political culture based on mutual fear--the government of its rivals, the people of the security forces. After formal independence in 1974 (the PAIGC had unilaterally declared Guinea-Bissau independent in 1973), the security forces of Luis Cabral's government executed about a hundred individuals suspected of collaboration with the Portuguese regime. After a failed coup attempt in 1978, even more met a similar fate and were buried in mass graves in the Oio region" (Fry, 1996).

p. 78) is that it was political brainwashing focusing on students learning political slogans of the Party,

> The next theme dealt with in the Second Popular Culture Notebook is:
> ...
> National Reconstruction: II
>
> We saw, in the previous text, that to produce more on the farms, in the factories, and to work more in the public services is to struggle for national reconstruction. We also saw that, for us, national reconstruction means the creation of a new society, without exploited or exploiters. A society of workers. For this reason, the national reconstruction demands of us:
>
> Unity
> Discipline
> Work
> Vigilance
>
> *Unity* of all, having the same objective in sight: *the creation of a new society.*
> *Discipline* in action, in work, in study, in daily life. Conscious discipline, without which nothing is done, nothing created. Discipline in unity, without which work is lost.
> *Work.* Work on the farms. Work in the factories. Work in public service. Work in schools.
> *Vigilance,* much vigilance, against the internal and external enemies, who will do anything they can to deter our struggle for the creation of the new society.

This text, as simple as it was, posed the problem of the national reconstruction and played with the words *unity, discipline, work,* and *vigilance.* Obviously, the theme of the national reconstruction or the reinvention of the society of Sao Tome is imposed by its present state. The game played with the words *unity, discipline, work,* and *vigilance,* which appear in a great number of slogans, was introduced to present them in a dynamic text preserving or recovering their most profound meaning (threatened by the uncritical character of clichés) (Freire & Macedo, 1987, pp. 79-80, italics is original, bold is mine, small font represents Freire's curriculum taken out of the Party propaganda text).

It is important for readers, unfamiliar with political practices of totalitarian states, to understand what these Party slogans that Freire enthusiastically taught his students meant in practice in the totalitarian state: state exploitation, lack of any ownership for one's labor or any other public (and often even private) affairs, unconditional loyalty and conformity to the Party and the State, self-censorship, reporting on enemies of people, the Party, and the State[23]

---

[23] Again, a visitor of the USSR, pro-Marxist French writer Andre Gide picked up these features of the totalitarian state and judged them as a terror (although he did not know many details about this terror, that came only later, he could understand and capture its essence already in 1936), "Now that the revolution has triumphed, now that it is stabilized and moderated, now that it is beginning to come to terms, and, some will say, to grow prudent, those that the revolutionary ferment still animates and who consider all these successive concessions to be com-promises, become troublesome, are reprobated and suppressed. Then would it not be better, instead of playing on words, simply to acknowledge that the revolutionary spirit (or even merely the critical spirit) is no longer the correct thing, that it is not wanted any more? What is wanted now is compliance, conformity. What is desired and demanded is approval of all that is done in the U.S.S.R., and an attempt is being made to obtain an approval that is not mere resignation, but a sincere, an enthusiastic

(Havel & Vladislav, 1989; Solzhenitsyn, 1974). Notice please that all statements in Freire's curriculum text are given in a form of commands.

Let's consider responsivity and addressivity of Freire's curricular texts, "Discipline in action, in work, in study, in daily life. Conscious discipline, without which nothing is done, nothing created. Discipline in unity, without which work is lost." Whom and to what does this utterance response? It responses whose who lacks of discipline (from the point of view who authors the utterance, namely, Freire). Whom and why does the author address? The author addresses people who lack of discipline to make them discipline. The author does not want to know anything new from the addressee but he wants them to transform to be self-disciplined. This is one-way monologic communication. Of course, it is possible to turn the utterance around to dialogically criticize it to reveal its monologicity and the manipulative character as we are doing here but there is no evidence that Freire was doing something like that in his literacy programs in Africa. It is rather clear here that this was a case of unilateral molding the students into a form of docile workers and citizens preset by Freire and the Party.

Not only Freire's (and the Party's) unilateralism is a problem here but also setting transformation of the students into a pre-known state given in advance (Whitson, 2007) as the direct goal of education. As I argued elsewhere (Matusov, St. Julien et al., 2005), although the student's transformation is a desired outcome of education, setting this transformation as a direct goal of the teacher's teaching or the student's studying is counterproductive. Education is like dealing with insomnia, in this regard. Although sleep is a desired outcome for the insomniac, it is a wrong goal for him or her to directly focus on forcing him or herself to fall asleep. The more the insomniac focusing on how force him or herself to sleep, the more he or she becomes usually awake. Freire was right insisting that teaching is a goal directed activity (Shor & Freire, 1987a), but he was wrong setting the direct goal of education on a desired transformation of the students. I argue that the goal of education is to set conditions for such transformation through building a new culture (Matusov, St. Julien et al., 2005; Yalom, 1995). Learning is always an essentially emergent, uncertain, and mutual process. This emergent and uncertain process runs for both the teacher and the student.

One interesting feature that Freire demonstrated in his texts on his work in Africa that is very characteristic of the discourse of many intellectuals who sincerely support totalitarian regimes is a trope that can be called "circular self-deception." It goes something like that, "Of course, I noticed bad things in the regime that I love. The things are apparently bad, and it seems very bad that has them. But exactly because it is bad, it is actually good." For example, another Communist foreign (German) writer, Leon Feuchtwanger, visited the Soviet Union in 1937 (several months after Andre Gide's visit), attended political trails fabricated by Stalinist secret police, was terrified by absurdity of the accusation (e.g., a former Soviet minister of industry was accused of trying to hurt Soviet people by putting glass pieces in butter while visiting Soviet collective farms), and then Feuchtwanger concluded that… exactly because

---

approval. What is most astounding is that this attempt is successful. On the other hand the smallest protest, the least criticism, is liable to the severest penalties, and in fact is immediately stifled. And I doubt whether in any other country in the world, even Hitler's Germany, thought be less free, more bowed down, more fearful (terrorized), more vassalized" (Gide, 1937, pp. 62-63). Unlike many left intellectuals that would include Freire, Gide reluctantly rejected the "lesser evil" argument and the Leninist-Trotskyist-Stalinist slogan "either with us *or* against us." Please see also the writings of a South African leader Nelson Mandela and a Soviet dissident writer Solzhenitzin who warn how dangerous the "lesser evil" rationalization is that can eventually leads liberators to participation in "super evil" (Mandela, 1995; Solzhenitsyn, 1974). See also Morson and Emerson (1990) for their discussion of "semiotic totalitarianism" in Marxism and beyond.

these accusations sounded so absurd they were true, they could not fabricate so absurd an accusation (Feuchtwanger & Josephy, 1937) (should it be called "dialectics" or, as Solzhenitzen suggested, "*devil*ectics"?!). Here is how Feuchtwanger defended political conformism imposed by the Soviet totalitarian state ("yes, there is political conformism in the USSR, but is political conformism always bad? It sounds so on the *first* glance but let's look at it closely. What is bad, when the state to which people conform is very good one?! No, Soviet political conformism is good!"),

> Even if one reads and hears everywhere objections to details, one never hears criticism of the general principle of the Party [from Soviet people – EM]. In this they "conform," that is true. In this there is no divergence, or if there is, it dare not be expressed. But what is the general principle of the Party? That every measure adopted is derived from the conviction that the establishment of socialism in the Soviet Union is fundamentally a success and that defeat in the impending war is out of the question. In this aspect, too, I cannot see why conformism is so much to be deplored (Feuchtwanger & Josephy, 1937, p. 42).

I call this rhetoric trope "circular" because it is impossible to falsify it. Conformism is good because the Party is successful. How do we know that it is successful? Because, there is no voice of decent (and Feuchtwanger was not as keen and honest to himself as Gide to notice the problems by himself). Based on the circular reasoning, Feuchtwanger in his book was able to explain all the disturbing facts that he encountered in the Soviet Union in 1937 when the political mass purges reached its peak. Even open political trials of "enemies of the state" badly orchestrated by the secret police that he attended did not undermine his circular reasoning. As Popper (1993) noticed about psychoanalysis, astrology, and Marxism, no matter what happened, what new disturbing fact or evidence is given, psychoanalysis, astrology, and Marxism (and Feuchtwanger and Freire, we would add to this list) could make sense of it within their system of thought. There is nothing, no new fact, which could undermine these conceptual systems. I call it "deceptive" because it acknowledges the truth only to negate it in a circular move. I call it "*self*-deceptive" because I agree with Solzhenitzen's (1974) analysis that, although the argument is formally directed to somebody else (in case of Feuchtwanger it was directed against Gide and to his western readers), the primary audience is the consciousness of the author himself that he tries to put to sleep.

Freire used a similar circular self-deception trope in his writing. Please notice that in the latest quote describing his curriculum I marked in bold his circular self-deception. He noticed that the text he used was imposed by the Party and the State on the people of Sao and Tome, he noticed that the text consisted of political clichés, he noticed that they were uncritical brainwashing. So why was he teaching them to his students? Is it to reveal the manipulative nature of these political slogans for his students? No, it is to recover "their most profound meaning" for his students (Freire & Macedo, 1987, p. 80)! Crude manipulation of people's consciousness is bad – let's make it more (pedagogically) profound! Laclau and Mouffe (2001) analyzed the Marxist totalitarian regimes of the twentieth century and they came to a conclusion that ontological privilege of unquestioned power (i.e., the Party dictatorship) in association with the extreme epistemological certainty of the political leadership leads to totalitarianism.

Of course, when epistemology is separated from pedagogy, like in Freire's case, manipulative teaching of leading the students to the desired end known in advance is not a contradiction with pedagogy for "liberation." Similar observation about Freire's circular self-deceptive reasoning made by Walker,

> Those looking to Freire for political guidance might be surprised where he leads them, and they should certainly be displeased. There are deep contradictions in Freire, which makes the realization of his basic human ideals unlikely in the context of his politics. Indeed Freire's politics threaten to turn back on and attack the very movement towards humanization and liberation it is designed to promote. (p. 121)
> ...Anxious to avoid charges of elitism, he tries to show the dialogical process as progressively blurring differences between [leaders and the people], so that they become 'equally the subjects of revolutionary action' and 'actors in communication.' In just what sense the 'teacher-learner-leaders' and the 'learner-teacher-people' are equal remains obscure.
> Nor is equality really likely to happen within Freire's political framework. One might expect the people to be given power of some sort over their leaders, but democracy does not figure in the theory of dialogue... (pp. 138-139)...
> The contradictions in Freire's theoretical enterprise, within the context of subordination of all basic social functions to the processes of a single organization, the party, produce the negation of some of his most basic ideals. Freire senses these dangers of course, in his expressed fear of the threat of bureaucracy; but what remedies are suggested by his orientation? More moral attentiveness and application to duty on the part of the leaders, and more conscientisation of the oppressed by the leaders? We are not only moving in a circle, we are trapped in it. The tighter it gets, the more like puritanism and the less like liberation our new position will seem (Walker, 1981, p. 146).

Harasim (1983) who empirically evaluated Freire's literacy programs in Guinea-Bissau came to a conclusion that it was a fiasco: very few students of these programs learned to read and write. Freire admitted this failure (without ever naming his critics in his writings – a very characterizing detail) with reservations but blamed the Party and State leadership of Guinea-Bissau who, after Amilcar Cabral, insisted on Portuguese-only instruction, " Speaking of evaluation [of his literacy programs in Guinea-Bissau – probably indirect reference to Harasim and Facundo – EM], I would again insist that so-called failure of our work in Guinea-Bissau was not due to the 'Freire method.' This failure clearly demonstrated the inviability of using Portuguese as the only vehicle of instruction in the literary campaigns" (Freire & Macedo, 1987, p. 114). However, unlike Freire's critics like Harasim and Facundo, I am more concerned with his would-be success rather than with his failure. Of course, not promoting literacy among peasants of Guinea-Bissau may be bad (although, not necessarily, see Facundo's analysis of Guinea-Bissau and our analysis of oppressive functions of literacy in Facundo, 1984; Matusov & St. Julien, 2004), but what could have been much worse if Freire had been successful in "educating" "militants", Red Guards (Hóng Wèi Bīng – youth militia carrying out the Chinese Great Cultural Revolution), political fanatics, or just obedient Party functionaries and made them literate. I agree with the judgment of Philip O'Meara who wrote prophetically in 1973 (before Freire's work in Africa) , "Freire's ideas are potentially dangerous, even in regard to their own goals, for his methods can be subverted subtly, and quickly create a new domination in the name of liberation. Those professionals who initially investigate and code must be open men [sic] a breed not discovered often among sociologists and educators whose jargon seems to contain all truth. And if these men pervert their trust, how easily could these 'codes' be used to brainwash. Anyone who has worked professionally in education must fear" (cited in Ohliger, 1995).

Freire has been criticized by many feminist and critical pedagogy scholars for not accounting the issues of race, gender, homophobia, and many other types of oppression especially in his early writings (Brady, 1994; Ellsworth, 1992; hooks, 1993; Weiler, 1994). He acknowledged this criticism (Freire & Macedo, 1987). However, I do not think this type of criticism undermines the general validity of Freire's dialogical critical pedagogy framework. Educators and social scholars have to expect that societal sensitivity to oppression and human suffering will hopefully grow with time as it has been in history so far and, in future, we will probably discover and become sensitive to and aware of many new types of oppression that we overlook today. Hopefully, critical dialogical pedagogy in a broader sense (not limited Freire's literacy programs) might provide help for that. Arguably, to some degree, the public professional criticism of Freire that he overlooked many other types of oppression in his writings (and educational practice) is itself evidence of how critical dialogue works in improving itself. What, however, in my view, is inexcusable and strongly undermines the general validity of Freire's dialogical critical pedagogy theoretical framework is his active and conscious participation in and support for Communist totalitarianism. I argue that this problem originates in Freire's theoretical framework that he developed at the end of the 1960s when he subordinated critical dialogic education (read "dialogic searching for truth") to politics of liberation (read "predefined social justice") (see Freire & Macedo, 1987; Shor & Freire, 1987a, for Freire's discussion of how he transformed himself from the "naive" to "sophisticated" view about the role of education in society in the end of the 1960s)[24].

Where was Freire's critical consciousness, where was his commitment to dialogue, where was his Christian compassion for suffering people, where was his acute sense of justice and suffering? How come Freire, a brilliant theoretician of dialogue, critical thinking, social justice in education, became an active and enthusiastic contributor to totalitarian oppression?

CONCLUSION

Radical left educators Suoranta and McLaren (2006) currently try to preserve "socialist pedagogy" by weeding out "faulty" Marxists – Stalin, Mao, Kim, Pol Pot, – from good ones: Castro, Nyerere, Cabral, Sandinistas. Freire is still considered to be among good ones. It is already not fashionable among the educational radical left to cite Mao but it is still OK to cite Castro. The history of the 20th century has blown a heavy knockout to the radical left, from which it cannot fully recover. Hundred of million human lives were sacrificed for social experiments and social engineering (mostly by socialist totalitarian regimes based on Communist or Nationalist ideology). Even when these crimes and sufferings unthinkable in scale and cruelty become known in the free world, a high majority of the radical left has remained silent in their condemnation of these totalitarian socialist regimes even despite their espoused sincere commitment to social justice. Social justice was only protected by them in

---

[24] I would argue that Freire's earlier conceptual framework was still based on weak dialogism that I described but it could lead to strong, radical dialogism. As I argue here, unfortunately, Freire chose totalitarian monologism instead. More work on Freire's ontological and conceptual roots and evolution (and also on critical evaluation of his practical work in Brazil and Chile in the 1950s and 1960s) is needed (Facundo, 1984; Zacharakis-Jutz, 1986).

capitalist countries and right-wing regimes. They passionately (and quite appropriately!) condemned the Chilean dictator Pinochet for his crimes against humanity but kept silent about the even bigger and more terrible crimes of the Communist regimes in China or in the Soviet Union or in Castro's Cuba. Even when the crimes of totalitarian socialist regimes are admitted by the radical left, they are treated as mistakes, some kind of deviation from the generally correct theory (by Marx?), due to the personal aberrations of the regimes' faulty leaders. This schizophrenic hypocrisy and self-deception runs deeply through the radical left (see, for example, a short-living but passionate "love affair" between a critical philosopher Michel Foucault and the Khomeini totalitarian regime in Iran, Afary, Anderson, & Foucault, 2005). I call this hypocrisy "schizophrenic" because unlike the radical right who does not often commit to (or even care about) the protection of oppressed people around the world, the radical left does commit to this[25] (Johnson & VanVonderen, 1991). However, this sincere commitment quickly becomes limited to the "class politics" (or any other "identity politics") resulting in severe injustices to those considered oppressors (see Laclau & Mouffe, 2001, for more discussion).

As an educator, who is deeply concerned about social justice and dialogic pedagogy, I have historically perceived Freire's terrible failure as a personal aberration. I am aware of the possibility that if I had lived in a historically different time and place, I could perhaps have been trapped in the same circular trope as Freire was. But this does not mean that Freire had an "alibi in Being" (using Bakhtin's term, see Bakhtin et al., 1993, p. 57) in his own historical time and place, no. Other leftist intellectuals like, Andre Gide, found strength in their heart and mind not to be trapped in Freire-like hypocrisy and self-deception that was so wide-spread among the radical left at that time. But without soul searching and analysis, it is easy to slip into this trap again.

Facundo and her colleague (1984) asked if Freire's conceptual approach or his particular practical application of it in Africa is faulty. From the analysis, I made, I conclude that both Freire's approach and his own practice (a way of doing his own approach) are deeply responsible for this failure. Freire's approach is misleading. He himself was blind and insensitive to people with whom he worked in Africa. His heart and mind were closed there. Another question is whether his insistence on the dialogic nature of pedagogy is responsible for his failure. My answer is no. Actually, I argue that exactly because he conceptually has a very weak version of a dialogic approach, it allowed him to be so misguided in his pedagogical practice that became rather manipulative, uncritical, and oppressive. Let me review Freire's problem with his weak cultural-dialogic approach.

First, although Freire insisted that the teacher has to learn together with the learner, he viewed the teacher's learning as mainly pedagogical: through formative assessment, the teacher allows the students to guide the teacher in how to guide them. Dialogue is viewed as where knowledge is originated while culture is viewed as where knowledge exists. It is unlikely that the student can significantly affect the teacher's knowledge pre-existing in

---

[25] Sincere commitment to compassion ideas in a monologic way can be sometimes worse than opportunist participation in oppression (like it was portrayed in "Schindler's list", Keneally, 1993). Also, according to numerous accounts of former slaves in US, on average, slave-owners, who were more passionate devoted and sincere Christians, were biggest abusers of their power (McAdams, 2006). Similar observation was made by Solzhenitzin (1974) about sincere devotees of the Communist ideas in the USSR being bigger power abusers in Soviet labor camps (and German Nazi concentration camps, see Kotek & Rigoulot, 2000). Monologic consistency in sincere devotion to an idea often leads to unconstrained self-righteous cruelty justified by the idea (cf. Bakhtin's notion of "person-idea" that we will discuss in further chapters, Bakhtin, 1999).

culture (in its artifacts, established consensuses, and so on). Thus, the teacher knows the final endpoint of learning. However, without the teacher epistemologically (not just pedagogically) expecting new ideas from the student, the genuine dialogue between the teacher and the student is impossible. Freire's cultural-dialogic opens doors for manipulative teaching (the opportunity that Freire, as an educational practitioner, apparently exploited in Africa). As Paulston noticed, "Freire's privileging of the teacher-intellectual's voice over the learner's voice has been scored as a bureaucratic imposition that thwarts consciousness-raising. Responding to such criticism, Freire has countered (unconvincingly, I believe) that although educators should reject 'arrogant authoritarianism, we should also remain vigilant about excessive or irresponsible spontaneity that in its lack of seriousness and intellectual discipline undermines the teacher's necessary authority.' ... Although Freire suggested earlier that the oppressed have false consciousness while the teacher-liberator (presumably Freire) has true consciousness, today he is willing to grant the oppressed student partial consciousness... My view of Freire is more paradoxical: he has made a powerful contribution in bringing critical theory to education, but his seeming inability to stand back and let the student experience critical insight on his or her own terms has relegated Freire to the role of ideological guru hovering over practice" (Paulston, 1992, pp. 198-199).

An alternative, radical dialogic approach suggests that knowledge does not only originate in dialogue but it exists in it. This means that in an encounter with the less knowledgeable student, the teacher's knowledge collapses (but never fully: the teacher is still more knowledgeable outside of the interaction with the student). The teacher has to epistemologically re-learn the subject with the student with an uncertain and unforeseen outcome of this learning. For example, teaching 2+2=4 to first graders several years ago together I realized that it is not true that 2+2 is always 4 but sometimes it can 1 or 2 or 5 or even no number at all (e.g., two hungry cats plus two fat mice would produce only two satisfied animals at the end, thus 2+2=2). In the genuine dialogue, there is no epistemological authority who "knows more" *apriori* and that is *why* something is true. The truth has to be (re-)created in a dialogue each time with an uncertain outcome or it stops being the truth.

Second, Freire's pedagogy for liberation has monologic addressivity. The phrase "I'm liberating you" sounds monologic if it is not a response for the student's request for help. It promotes monologic relations between the teacher and the student, despite Freire's claims of contrary. Ellsworth (1992) in her critical article with the provocative title "Why doesn't this feel empowering?" (she could have also say "liberating") nicely captured this problem of monologic addressivity in Freire's approach. As Griffith points out, "Freire leaves little question regarding his willingness to control and restrict the freedom of those who cannot see the superiority of his system. The freedom to disagree with the new ruling group, following the revolution, is to be restricted to those who have passed some undefined loyalty test" (Griffith, 1972). In a bit different but related vein, Facundo (1984) raised an issue about the social interests of the "liberators" themselves as a social group. I think these are important issues to raise.

A radical dialogic approach is very much concerned about dialogic addressivity of the overall message that the teacher sends to the student about their relations. The teacher can only help the student learn something. According to the radical dialogic approach, I propose here, the teacher addresses the student as "How can I help you to learn...?" But, what if the student feels that he or she does not need help from the teacher or does not need to learn? Well, I believe that dialogic teaching starts with the student's request for the help from the teacher. Unless the teacher convinces the student or the student realizes that the learning and help are needed from the teacher, there cannot be dialogic teaching. As Stock puts it, "A dialogic curriculum is introduced when teachers invite and enable students join them in a broadly outlined field of inquiry" (Stock, 1995, p. 24). Liberation or not – it is not for the teacher to decide. The teacher cannot try to make the student good or even free[26] but the teacher can help the student to be informed when issues of goodness or freedom emerge for the former or current student. "Being informed" means to join a community where knowledge circulates dialogically (it does not mean to agree or join a consensus).

Third, like some others on the radical left, Freire prioritized social justice over the search for truth. Searching for truth is the essence of dialogue. By prioritizing social justice over searching for truth, he essentially monologized it. When social justice is monologized (which acted as if it is a given, like in Freire's case), it opens doors for injustice as we saw in Freire's work in Africa. Caulfield (1991) notices how Freire constantly weaves in his texts between his insistence on dialogical equality of the teacher and the student and his commitment to the leftist ideals of justice.

> However, I do question Freire on one very important point. My problem concerns what happens to students who are, as he says, 'increasingly posed with problems' regarding their world. He argues that 'they will gradually come to regard themselves as committed.' By committed, he appears to mean committed to a leftist, if not outright revolutionary, agenda. But just what is the role of the teacher, the problem poser, in fostering that commitment?
>
> Freire insists that teachers should never impose their views of a problem on students, though he does not say teachers should or even could be neutral. The teacher does enter into the exchange of views concerning the problem, but ostensibly and simply as an equal participant. Yet, is it reasonable to assume that students will view teachers as equals? More likely, they will give teachers' views considerably more weight than those of their classmates or their own. In fact, more recently Freire was arguing, 'As an educator, you can only maintain a nondirective posture if you attempt a deceitful discourse; that is a discourse from the perspective of the dominant class (p. 313-314).

In a radical dialogic approach, dialogic searching for truth is prioritized. Truth searching cannot be made an enemy of social justice even if at times it may look like that. Truth searching process has to be trusted and not feared. For example, in their infamous book Herrnstein and Murray (1994) cited studies showing that the IQ of Black people is lower on average than the IQ of White people. I know some educators, concerned with social justice,

---

[26] At the end of a popular children's (and adults') Russian movie "Aybolit-66" (Bykov, 1966), a villain Barmalei, the leader of pirates, considers to become good and kind to people. He tells to a kind doctor Aybolit, who helps animals and people (translation from Russian is mine),

> Barmalei: Big deal, I can also do kind things to people!
> Doctor Aybolit: So?
> Barmalei: If I start doing kind things to people, you will die of envy. I will make all people happy in two
> days. But those who won't become happy, I will beat hell out of them, cut in small pieces and throw
> to sharks – and they will become happy at once. But only I do not like and do not strive doing that!

Doctor Aybolit (speaking directly to the camera to the movie audience): Citizens, if you see Barmalei who is going to do kind things to people, catch him and give him timeout in a corner. I beg you about that very much. Please.

Pedagogy for liberation has the same problem as Barmalei faces: what to do with those who do not want to be liberated and happy as the liberators want them to be?!

who are very upset with this finding to the point of calling the original research racist. In my view, this is exactly Freire's approach prioritizing social justice over searching for truth, "In benefit of what and of whom to know? Moreover, against what and whom to know?" (Freire, 1978, p. 100). I suspect that if Freire had had political power, he probably would have banned this comparative research on IQ. Indeed, a possible implication of this research is that on average Black people have low intellect abilities compared to that of White people. This is a very harming and damaging statement that promotes racism. However, a radical dialogic approach would push the investigation of the comparative IQ research even further by asking questions of how the IQ test was historically developed, what it is ecological validity, what exactly it measures. Such historical and methodological investigations would lead us to the discovery that the IQ test was originally designed to predict school achievement for public policies in France and thus it highly correlates with school achievement (but not with job performance) (Gould, 1996). In other words, the Black-White discrepancy on the IQ test reflects well-known educational inequalities and not a racial deficit in intellect of Black people. However harmful or undesirable the idea is, it should not be suppressed or killed (usually with its carriers) but be more deeply examined. Thus when we examine rather than suppress, in the name of social justice, uncomfortable findings, we create a more truthful, and dialogic, foundation for social justice.

Summarizing, I claim that Freire's pedagogy for liberation was too monologic both conceptually and, even more so, in practice. Freire's approach is not irrelevant but constitutes an important warning of not to prioritize social justice over searching for truth for educators interested in dialogic pedagogy that we should keep in mind. Also, the conceptual and practical problems with his approach should not dismiss his important conceptual achievements. These include but not limited: 1) importance of dialogic for education as a process humanizing actions and deeds, 2) ontological nature of pedagogical dialogue, and 3) emphasis on creating a learning community in which the teacher is also a learner and the student is also a teacher. Nevertheless, I argue that Freire's conceptual approach to dialogic pedagogy was weak because he saw pedagogical learning as primary and separate from epistemological learning for the teacher. I see a radical dialogic approach rooted in Bakhtin's framework that does not make a difference between pedagogical and epistemological learning by the teacher as a way to address uncomfortable truth of Freire's pedagogical disaster in Africa.

Chapter 5

BAKHTIN'S POLYSEMIC NOTIONS OF DIALOGUE AND MONOLOGUE: EDUCATION PERSPECTIVE

ABSTRACT

Reading Bakhtin's texts I became confused about how he used the terms "dialogue" and "monologue," the key terms in his approach. Rather than treating this confusion negatively, I decide to treat it positively as a useful conceptual polysemy. Bearing educational issues in mind, I extracted three conceptual vistas, from which dialogue and monologue can be viewed: oppositional, complementary, and excessive. These three vistas generate at least 5 different uses of these terms that can be very productive in both analysis and design of educational ecologies.

There is a growing interest in the application of Bakhtin's ideas in education, specifically his notions of dialogue and monologue. Critics of mainstream schooling attempt to conceptualize some of the problems with traditional instruction as being too monologic. They propose alternative models for instruction by evoking Bakhtin's notion of dialogue (Gee, 1996; Sidorkin, 2002; Skidmore, 2000). Other educators and educational researchers use the concept of dialogue to unpack the notions of "community of learners" (Brown & Campione, 1994; Wells, 1999), "collaborative guidance" (Matusov & Rogoff, 2002; Rogoff, Matusov, & White, 1996), and "democratic education" (Freire, 1976, 1986). There is a clear opposition, if not dichotomy, in the ways how educators think about dialogue and monologue that is worth investigating further. As Crapanzano (1990, p. 277) points out, "pitting dialogue against [monologue] has probably led to oversimplification of both." Reading Bakhtin, I found that his ways of thinking went beyond simply saying that dialogue is good and monologue is bad.

The purpose of this chapter is to extract and analyze Bakhtin's notions of dialogue and monologue in all its complexity and discuss their possible applications in education. My methodology is heavily based on Bakhtin's writings -- especially on his book on Dostoevsky, where the notions of dialogue and monologue are central -- and on current literature on Bakhtin. Bakhtin saw himself as a philosopher (Bakhtin, Duvakin, & Bocharov, 2002) while many of his readers have seen him as a literature critic and literature theoretician (Clark & Holquist, 1984). Recently, we have learned that Bakhtin was also an educational researcher (Matusov, 2004). As far as we know, Bakhtin's paper on teaching grammar in a middle-to-high school (Bakhtin, 2004) was the only article by Bakhtin on education. However, it is also possible to find negative comments about mainstream education throughout his book on Dostoevsky (Bakhtin, 1999; Skidmore, 2000), "In essence [monologism -- EM] knows only a single mode of cognitive interaction among consciousnesses: someone who knows and possesses the truth instructs someone who is ignorant of it and in error; that is, it is the interaction of a teacher and a pupil, which, it follows, can only be a pedagogical dialogue" (p. 81). Finally, it is possible to trace Bakhtin's comments about Plato's Socratic educational dialogues (Bakhtin, 1999). In addition, I was searching for contemporary analysis and comments on Bakhtin's notions of dialogue and monologue in educational literature.

I was trying to be careful working with the mainly literary contexts in which Bakhtin's notions of dialogue and monologue were embedded but it was clear, as many Bakhtinian scholars (and Bakhtin himself) have noted, Bakhtin's writings and analysis went beyond purely literary critique (Bakhtin, 1999; Bakhtin et al., 2002; Holquist, 1990). I am aware that my approach was somewhat static and anti-biographical (for an excellent historical and biographical presentation of Bakhtin see, for example, Morson & Emerson, 1990). I was looking for Bakhtin's discussions and uses of the notions of dialogue and monologue without trying to situate them within Bakhtin's intellectual development – this can be an interesting endeavor on its own. I present my findings from three vistas: three different but compatible perspectives on dialogue and monologue that I found in Bakhtin's writings.

The first vista on dialogue and monologue is *oppositional*. I argue that this oppositional relation between dialogue and monologue is most known to educators and Bakhtinian scholars. However, it is also probably the most mysterious and misunderstood (indeed, by myself as well as others) and thus probably most exciting for further exploration. In my view, this opposition has been seen either as intellectual and/or political – which are very legitimate perspectives. But, as I show below, reduction of dialogue to a merely intellectual debate or a political fight leads, according to Bakhtin, to monological consciousness and monological relations. The ontological property of this opposition, although noticed, remains mainly unpacked especially in the area of education.

My second vista on Bakhtin's notions of dialogue and monologue is *complementary*. Bakhtin used the notions of dialogicity and monologicity to develop the concept of "voice" that is arguably an alternative framework to the Western notion of "identity". Any voice is characterized by a certain degree and quality of dialogicity and monologicity reflecting both centrifugal and centripetal forces of human consciousness and human community.

I found the third vista in Bakhtin's writings when he talked about dialogue and monologue as *excesses*. For Bakhtin, excessive dialogism and excessive monologism were associated with stable breakdowns in a community that are often politically grounded in social classes. Like anything to do with Bakhtin's notions of dialogue and monologue, these excesses are forms of individual consciousness as well as social relations in a community. Implications for education of these three vistas will be discussed.

BAKHTINIAN ANALYSES OF INSTRUCTION

Based on Bakhtin's analysis of discourse involving the opposition between "authoritative discourse" and "internally persuasive discourse"(Bakhtin, 1991, pp. 342 ff.), Skidmore (2000) contrasts "pedagogical dialogue" and "dialogic pedagogy". He borrowed the notion of "pedagogical dialogue" directly from Bakhtin,

> In an environment of ... monologism the genuine interaction of consciousness is impossible and thus genuine dialogue is impossible as well. In essence ... [monologism – EM] knows only a single mode of cognitive interaction among consciousnesses: someone who knows and possesses the truth instructs someone who is ignorant of it and in error; that is, it is the interaction of a teacher and a pupil, which, it follows, can be only a *pedagogical dialogue* (Bakhtin, 1999, p. 81, emphasis is added).

Skidmore illustrates the notion of pedagogical dialogue common for conventional school by the following fragment of a guided reading lesson in a British elementary school of a teacher working with a small group of students. The teacher focuses the students on finding out if her statements can be grounded in the text of the book (Skidmore, 2000, pp. 287-288, the dialogue is shortened and simplified),

Segment 1

1.Teacher: Right. So is it true or false? Docky knew the sound ..erm... 'He heard a dog barking.' Did he hear in the first picture on the first page did he hear that barking to be a dog?

2. Fiona: Yes.

3. Teacher: It wasn't a dog... Fiona. It was false because it was a fox barking. How does he know it was a fox barking? 'Cause he described it to Mr. Keeping later on and Mr. Keeping said ha that's a fox bark. Fox... foxes bark like that. Do you understand? Not really do you?

4. Fiona: Erm. (*Fiona shakes her head*).

5. Teacher: Why do you think that it's a dog barking? You tell me one piece of information from that story to tell you that it's a dog.

6. Fiona: Because erm foxes don't bark and dogs does.. do.

7. Teacher: OK, look at page six Fiona. Page six? OK. Read it with me.

8. Teacher and Fiona: 'The next day Rocky saw Mr. Keeping. He told him about the noise.'

9. Teacher: What noise Fiona? What noise?

10. Fiona: The noise what the fox was making.

11. Teacher: The noise that the fox was making. Which noise was the fox making?

12. Fiona: A dog... noise. (*Fiona laughs*).

13. Teacher: He was barking. The fox was barking yeah? So the noise that he heard in the night. So he told him about the noise. Carry on... reading.. page six. 'That'

14. Teacher and Fiona: 'will be a fox said Mr. Keeping. Foxes bark like that.'

15. Teacher: So. So the noise he heard on that first page was a bark. He thought it might have been a dog.

16. Fiona: It wasn't.

17. Teacher: But it wasn't a dog. What was it?

18. Fiona: He knew it wasn't a dog.

19. Teacher: What was it?

20. Fiona: It was a fox.

21. Teacher: It was a fox. And the statement says on your sheet 'He heard a dog barking.' Did he hear a dog barking? So is it true or false?

22. Fiona: False.

23. Teacher: Do you understand?

24. Fiona: Yes.

25. Teacher: OK next sentence.

The teacher asked a series of known-answer questions to make the student know what the teacher already knows. The teacher treated the student as having misconceptions that have to be cleared. To guide the student, the teacher developed a sequence of known-answer questions, to which the student provided answers that the teacher desired to hear (9-25), that leads to the student's affirmation of the teacher's knowledge and truth (20, 22).

The teacher's discourse is monologic. Bakhtin (1999) defined a discourse as monologic when the speaker affirms or rejects replies from his or her addressees as being right or wrong. In essence, in monologic discourse, addressees are not expected to say anything new that is unknown to the speaker. Rather they can say the *right* thing – the truth known to the speaker from the beginning – or *wrong* things (errors). Indeed, in monologic teaching, the student either provides the right answer – expected by the teacher -- or the wrong answer that the teacher has to correct. The teacher asks questions, the students reply, the teacher evaluates their responses: if the student provided the teacher-desired answer, the teacher can move on in the curriculum sequence; if not, the teacher has to provide scaffolding (Lemke, 1990; Mehan, 1979; Wells, 1992, September). There is no interest by the teacher in the students' answers. In the example of teaching presented above, the series of leading questions organized by the teacher is a classic monologic discourse. The teacher objectifies and finalizes the students, treating them as a source of errors rather than partners for a dialogic, collaborative endeavor.

The student engaged in the lesson, but she engaged non-ontologically. From an educational point of view, non-ontological engagement is arguably undesirable because it has little educational value or even has anti-educational value. Such engagement is near-fully motivated by the institutional power transcendent to the discourse itself and its content often promotes surface learning based on memorization of unrelated facts (Rogoff, 1990; Rogoff et al., 1996; Scribner & Cole, 1981). Not only do the students often forget what they learn in school through non-ontological engagement but they have difficulty applying what they have learned in school in non-school contexts (Lave, 1988; Nunes, Schliemann, & Carraher, 1993; Säljö & Wyndhamn, 1993). Besides, through non-ontological engagement many students have learned alienation from academic subjects, seeing the subjects as boring and irrelevant and they themselves as not good at them. In other words, through non-ontological engagement the students have learned a non-academic identity (Lave, 1992a; Lave & Wenger, 1991; Wenger, 1998). In this sense, non-ontological learning is essentially anti-educational (rather than just non-educational or educational but ineffective). Arguably, many students have learned to dislike school through non-ontological engagement in school since many of them are institutionally very good students, having a very high GPA and passing exams successfully, but are not necessary good learners. These institutionally-successful students know how to "do" the institution but do not necessarily engage in learning – ontologically -- as something inherently important in their lives (performing in turn a non-ontological activity that is defined by adherence to purely institutional demands). We know that non-ontological engagement created in psychological labs through extrinsic motivation decreases the students' interests (defined in the studies as "intrinsic motivation", cf. Subbotsky, 1995).

Dialogic pedagogy is seen by educators in opposition to this monologic pedagogy. Bakhtin (1999) defined dialogue as information seeking from and with others. Skidmore defines dialogic pedagogy as internally persuasive discourse with which the participants are looking for truth,

> Truth is not born nor is it to be found inside the head of an individual person, it is born *between people* collectively searching for truth, in the process of their dialogic interaction. (Bakhtin, 1999, p. 110, italics is original)

In a classroom run by dialogic pedagogy, the teacher asks information-seeking questions and treats the students as capable and knowledgeable participants of a truth-seeking endeavor. The teacher is also a part of this endeavor. Skidmore brings an example of such classroom discourse from a multiage classroom of British primary school. The teacher discussed a parody on a famous fairytale *Red Riding Hood* and asked the students to place the book characters on a scale from whom to blame the most to whom to blame the least for negative events occurred in the story (pp. 290-291, the dialogue is shortened and simplified),

Segment 2

1. Teacher: Okay we have other characters. Who should we discuss next?
2. Ian: Erm (.) the woodcutter.
3. Teacher: Where does he come on the scale?
4. Ian: Near the end.
5. Suma: Because when she was wandering around in the forest and he met her and then he told her that he's going to show her grandmother how to behave... and he had an axe and... he took the skin off the wolf and he killed grandma.
6. Ian: No they didn't know there was bears in the forest and erm... there they thought she would just get lost in the woods.
7. Kulvinder: But the woodcutter bashed granny's door down.
8. Penda: I don't think he was well behaved (.) *because he should have come and talked to her* not smash her house down.
9. Suma: Yeah but granny still behaved in the same way even when the woodcutter was in her house.
10. Kulvinder: Granny... was mean and she was just horrible she just tells her to get out of the house. [. . . more discussions]
11. Teacher: Okay should we now try to put the characters in some sort of order? [The student provided different types of the order.] It is very difficult, isn't it? I'd say the wolf although we agreed his behaviour was far from perfect. Then I would say... you need to think about what happened. Granny threw Blue Riding Hood out of the house yeah? Erm now that was quite deliberate...
12. Ian: A witch.
13. Penda: Yeah she started everything it was all her fault... *if she hadn't thrown Red I mean Blue Riding Hood none of this would have happened.*
14. Kulvinder: But Blue Red Riding Hood killed the wolf.

15. Penda: Oh yeah.

16. Colin: None of them were really nice.

17. Ian: No.

18. Penda: But whose fault was it?

19. Suma: I think granny's.

20. Colin: But she didn't kill any one.

21. Penda: No but it was her fault really wasn't it?

22. Kulvinder: She wasn't very nice.. well I didn't like... she deserved to be eaten.

23. Colin: She wasn't killed on purpose was she?

24. Ian: The woodcutter killed her.

25. Colin: No she was eaten by bears.

26. Ian: I mean it was his fault he erm… chucked her out.

27. Teacher: Well, we have run out of time. I think you have done very well. I thought it was hard to sort them out but you together all of you have done that really well. I don't think there is a right or wrong answer. If there was, we wouldn't have had much to talk about.

In the Segment 2, the teacher organized a discussion, in which students can test their own ideas. They presented their ideas not just to the teacher but to the entire class for examination and response. The students brought counter-fictional and hypothetical accounts (8, 13) – typical for dialogic testing (Bakhtin, 2004). The teacher does not have monopoly on the truth but rather tried to help the class to collectively reason about final responsibility of the characters for the negative events in the story.

Skidmore concludes that dialogic pedagogy promotes "pupils' autonomous abilities to engage in literate thinking" (p. 292). But does the notion of "pupils' *autonomous* abilities" contradict Bakhtin's claim about dialogic nature of truth's origin? Does Skidmore see the goal of dialogic pedagogy in strengthening monologicity of students' voices?

BAKHTIN'S POLYSEMY ABOUT THE CONCEPTS OF "DIALOGUE" AND "MONOLOGUE"

Many scholars have noticed the polysemic and non-systematic nature of Bakhtin's writing (Holquist, 1991; Morson & Emerson, 1990; Smith, 1998; Todorov, 1984). When I am reading Bakhtin, I feel both excited and… confused. This ambivalent feeling reminds me of my early childhood experience. I see several big fish circling in shallow water of a Ukrainian river. The fish swim slowly, gracefully, almost lazily. Sun plays on the surface. I can see sand on the bottom. The water is extremely transparent and pure. The fish are beautiful. I carefully place my hands down into the warm water and touch the fish. The fish does not react to my touch and keeps moving slowly but surely. I try to grab the gorgeous fish and pull it on the surface but the fish slips out of my hands without any effort on its part. I try again and again but all in vein. The fish effortlessly escapes my grabbing hands. It is both magical and frustrating. I feel the same way when I try to grasp Bakhtin's notions of dialogue and monologue – they are very beautiful notions and apparently very useful but they slip out of my hands each time I try to grab them and pull them to the surface. Here I am trying once again (or this time, I give it one more try). This time it is a public effort and hopefully it will be a collaborative one…

Reading Bakhtin, one easily can notice that he used the terms "dialogue" and "monologue" in very different meanings (Morson & Emerson, 1990). For example, in the following two quotes from the same book, Bakhtin uses the terms "dialogue" and "monologue" very differently:

> The Underground Man conducts the same sort of inescapable **dialogue** with himself that he conducts with the other person. He cannot merge completely with himself in a unified **monologic** voice simply by leaving the other's voice entirely outside himself (whatever that voice might be, without a loophole), for, as is the case with Golyadkin, his voice must also perform the function of surrogate for the other person. (Bakhtin, 1999, p. 235, bold is mine)

> **Monologism**, at its extreme, denies the existence outside itself of another consciousness with equal rights and equal responsibilities, another *I* with equal rights (*thou*). (Bakhtin, 1999, p. 292, bold is mine, italics is original)

In the first quote, "inescapable dialogue" and a lack of "unified monologic voice" are symptoms of a relational and discursive problem that "the Underground Man" had in the Russian society of the XIX century. In this context, "inescapable dialogue" is clearly undesirable while "unified monologic voice" is highly desirable, according to Bakhtin. However, in the second quote as in Bakhtin's writings on average, the picture is reversed: "dialogue" is positive and "monologue" is a negative term. In my view, it is not the case that time-to-time Bakhtin contradicts himself in praising "dialogue" and in scolding "monologue"; rather, by the same terms he distinguished different concepts varying from positive to neutral to negative depending on notion he signified with the concept. It is quite unfortunate, in my view, that Bakhtin did not develop systematically different terms for these important and useful concepts.

COMPLEMENTARY VISTA: "D AND M ARE BOTH GOOD"

1. Nature of Discourse

Reading Bakhtin, I have counted at least 5 different concepts signified by the terms "dialogue" and "monologue"[1]. Some of these concepts are oppositional but some are not. First, the concepts of dialogue and monologue exist in *the nature of any discourse*. Bakhtin was quite clear that the nature of any discourse is dialogic.

> Two voices is the minimum for life, the minimum existence (Bakhtin & Emerson, 1999, p. 252).

> The dialogic nature of consciousness, the dialogic nature of human life itself. The single adequate form for *verbally expressing* authentic human life is the *open-*

---

[1] Morson and Emerson (1990) discuss three different notions of these terms. Wegerif (2007) extracts four distinguished understanding of dialogic in Bakhtin's writing. Their conceptualization overlaps with mine but not identical, probably, because our diverse conceptualizations are shaped by different projects that we have: their project is philological (in the case of Morison and Emerson) while mine is educational. I argue that despite of his focus on education, Wegerif's analysis of Bakhtin's polysemy was heavily influenced by philology with its primary interest in texts.

ended[2] dialogue. Life by its very nature is dialogic. To live means to participate in dialogue: to ask questions, to heed, to respond, to agree, and so forth. In this dialogue a person participates wholly and throughout his whole life: with his eyes, lips, hands, soul, spirit, with his whole body and deeds. He invests his entire self in discourse, and this discourse enters into the dialogic fabric of human life, into the world symposium (Bakhtin, 1999, p. 293, italics is original)[3].

This means that pure monologue cannot and does not exist, according to Bakhtin! At the same time, Bakhtin often discussed monologue in opposition to dialogue. How can we reconcile Bakhtin's insistence on the dialogic nature of human consciousness and his critique of monologue as being undesirable?

From Bakhtin's point of view, dialogue and monologue are not symmetrical notions – they are both a part of bigger communication, a part of Dialogue with capital D (Bibler, 1991) or dialogue as a "global concept" (Morson & Emerson, 1990). *D*ialogue is bigger than *m*onologue and in this sense, dialogue includes monologue, the latter which is an incomplete element. Purely monologic discourse is a misnomer – it does not exist,

> Thought becomes clear for oneself only in the process of making it clear for another person. That is why there is not and cannot be, so to speak, absolute monologue, i.e., a pure expression of thought for oneself that is not addressed to anybody. Such absolute individualistic monologue, if we have tried to imagine it, would have not needed language comprehensible for other people. It would have lost any relationship to the linguistic sphere. Any utterance is dialogic, i.e., it is addressed to others and participates in the process of exchange of thoughts. Absolute monologue – [pure] expression of individuality – does not exist. It is a fiction of idealistic philosophy of language that claims the origin of language from individual creativity. Language, by its very nature, is dialogic ("means of communication"). Absolute monologue, which would have been linguistic monologue, contradicts the very nature of language (Bakhtin, 1997a, p. 213)[4].

Human mind is dialogically constituted (Rommetveit, 1992, p. 23). Dialogue precedes and embraces any individual thought or intention (Linell, 1998, p. 266) or as Billig (1996, p. 111) puts it, "Humans do not converse because they have inner thoughts to express, but they have thoughts because they are able to converse." In their inner thoughts, people response and address other people (and themselves) "in anticipation and in memory of public performance" (Tyler, 1990, p. 299)[5]. "To be means communicate dialogically. When dialogue ends, everything ends" (Bakhtin, 1999, p. 252). Wegerif (2007, pp. 19-20) brought an interesting historical anecdote of a scandal in 1522 when Erasmus, charged with authoritative translation of the Bible from Greek to Latin, translated familiar "in the beginning was the word" as "the underlying principle is conversation." The latter is arguably Bakhtin's motto. Unfortunately, the Church rejected Erasmus' translation.

---

[2] Незавершимый nezavershimyj – being impossible to end or finish by anybody.
[3] All italics are original. Unfortunately English translation with its use of masculine pronouns adds a sense of sexism absent in the original Russian text. In Russian, gender of pronouns often refers to gender of referred nouns and not to gender of the referred people. In Russian, the noun "person" ("chelovek") has male gender and has to be referred as "he" even if the noun itself may refer to a woman.
[4] Here and further translation from Russian is mine for Bakhtin's work that has not been translated from Russian.
[5] See also my work (Matusov, 1998).

Bakhtin's approach to dialogue as the primary over monologue contrasts with traditional monologic approaches in social sciences that argue for the primacy of individual monologic consciousness over dialogue (see Linell, 1998, for more discussion and critique of this premise) and with a neo-formalist position by a Soviet semiotian Lotman (1988) that dialogue and monologue are two equal aspects of communication. According to Lotman, any text (understood, in a broader sense, as a discourse) has two functions: 1) monologic to transmit ready-made meaning adequately and 2) dialogic to generate new meaning. In my view, Lotman's approach to text is monologic because it is based on abstractions generated by specific, often decontextualized, practices that either neglect (function#1) or exaggerate (function#2) the authorship of the meaning. Indeed, only specific (institutionalized) practices (like conventional modern school, military) can ignore the fact that people never have the same meaning. In contrast to monological approaches, meaning is not rooted in containers-like texts that "*say* what they *mean* and *mean* precisely, neither more nor less than, what they *say*" (Olson, 1981, p. 108, the italics is original)[6]. Meaning is always unique and unrepeatable, "An utterance is never just a reflection or an expression of something already existing and outside it that is given and final. It always creates something that never existed before, something absolutely new and unrepeatable, and, moreover, it always has some relation to value (the true, the good, the beautiful, and so forth" (Bakhtin, 1986, pp. 119-120). Meaning always has authorship rooted in a) its unique addressivity and responsivity and b) dynamic networks of relations with other meanings. For example, such a simple mathematical fact as 2x2=4 addresses and responds to many explicit and implicit questions that the person might have in mind, like "what does it mean?", "why bother to think about it?", "why now?", "why doesn't 2x2=5 or 3 or any other number but 4?", "under what circumstances does 2x2 equal 4?", "what does it mean equal?", "what does it mean 'multiplication'?", "why do people use multiplication?", "can I avoid it?", "why did the author of the article bring this particular example?", "what is it going to do with me?", "who cares about 2x2=4?", "why do not we go to see movies rather than to focus on this 2x2?" and so on. The number of such questions is unlimited, situational, and dynamic. Similarly, the math fact of 2x2=4 is always in relationships with many other activities and practices (math and non-math based). For instance, it connotes with a popular phrase, "it is clear as two by two" which does not necessary has math meaning. Mathematically, 2x2=4 can be reworked as degree $2^2=4$ or as addition 2+2=4, which is probably unique for the relationship between twos (is it?). Geometrically, it can be represented as a search for the area of a 2 by 2 square. I have a good memory of learning multiplication in my elementary school. It reminds me my classmate friend in the second grade whom I taught successfully the concept of multiplication. The math fact 2x2=4 both triggers and is supported these chains of my personal memories. However, in this article, 2x2=4 is used because although its meaning seems "self-contained", in actuality, is unique, limitless, contextual, dynamic, and very personal. Only certain practices afford to ignore this fact that is supposed to be especially important in education (Nystrand, 1997).

In contrast, Lotman's idea that meaning is created or produced is exaggeration pushed by other (often also decontextualized) practices that focus on originality and copyright (Wertsch, 1995). Lotman wrote, "The text is a generator of meaning, a thinking device, which requires an interlocutor to be activated" (Lotman, 1988, p. 40). As I have shown above and have

---

[6] In later writings, Olson changed his mind and develop a more dialogic, interpretative approach to meaning of the text (see, for example, Olson, 1994).

argued elsewhere (Matusov, Smith, Candela, & Lilu, 2007), meaning is never generated but emerges on boundaries. Paraphrasing a famous quote about culture from Bakhtin (1999, p. 301), it is possible to say that meaning does not have internal territory: it is entirely distributed along the boundaries, boundaries pass everywhere, through its every aspect, the systematic unity of meaning extends into the very atoms of life of meaning. Meaning can be only transformed but never fully created from scratch. Meaning is not generated by "a thinking device," as Lotman argued, but it is rooted in a dialogue to which participants contribute. For example, Einstein's special theory of relativity, which was very innovative and revolutionary for its time, has emerged from Einstein's attempts to address problems emerged from work of other physicists around the world of the nineteenth century (e.g., Maxwell, Morley, Michelson, Mach) (Einstein, 1950). These physicists could not reconcile the relative nature of the concept of speed in the classical Newtonian mechanics with the apparent absolute nature of the speed of light emerged in electrodynamics equations and experiments on measurement of relative speed of light. Also, in his theory, Einstein reworked attempts of other physicists to address the problem (e.g., the work of Dutch physicist Lorenz). Einstein did not activate his "thinking device" while looking at the texts of other physicists as Lotman suggested, but he tried to addressed the publically shared urgent problems (understood as "crises") in the physics of his time. Einstein's contributions were shaped by the dialogue in physics (and arguably beyond physics) and not by some kind of decontextualized "thinking device" activated by the texts he read. As a Russian philosopher and Bakhtinian scholar, Bibler argued, "Bakhtin has outlined the transition from cognizing reason to dialogic reason whose made is mutual understanding" (Akhutin & Bibler, 1993, p. 356).

Discourse has often been associated with verbalism. Silence has been often negatively viewed and associated with passivity (lack of talk, articulateness, comprehension, reflection, and thinking), non-participation, oppression (fear of speaking), or resistance in educational (and psychological) literature, which probably reflects a lack of an Anglo[7] middle class value of silence in discourse (Rogoff, 2003; Stein, 2004). However, Bakhtin argued that silence is an important part of discourse (Bakhtin, 1986). He considered mostly two types of silence: silence-response, when silence is a response to verbal statements in a discourse (e.g., the famous example from Pushkin's drama "Boris Godunov" – "People are silent" in a response to bloody events in the Kremlin), and silence-address, when silence is evaluation of the on-going verbal discourse by the third party, to which the discourse is directed (as, for example, in the case of a jury).

Dialogue is not limited to verbalism and not even to communication. Bakhtin argued that discourse does not necessarily have to be verbal by its nature. A physical action and its tools can also be discursive and, thus, dialogic when it has responsive and addressive functions: when the action responds to other people's past actions and words and addresses them, expecting, foreseeing, shaping, and provoking their future responses. He insisted that physical action becomes fully human, meaningful, only when it is dialogic because Bakhtin defined meaning as a reply to someone's question (actual or imaginary), "The [h]uman act is a potential text and it can be understood (as a human act and not as a physical action) only in a

---

[7] In Russian culture, silence has been traditionally highly valued. For example, there is a rather popular Russian proverb "Silence is golden" ("молчание – золото"), which has had different meanings depending on socio-political circumstances.

dialogic context of its own [historic – EM] time (as a dialogic response, as a semiotic position, as a system of motives)" (Bakhtin, 1997b, p. 311). The reverse is also true that discourse is an action and a part of activity changing reality (both material and semiotic) and the actors, "Dialogue ... is not the threshold to action, it is the action itself" (Bakhtin, 1999, p. 252). Linell calls this phenomenon "double dialogicity" of action (practice) and communication (Linell, 1998, p. 272). From educational point of view, the issue of "physicality" of discourse relates to the issue of social activism. Freire (1986) metaphorically defined the purpose of liberating education as "reading and writing the word, to read and write the world". Holzman (1997) insists that education has to serve the radical transformation of the world to make it a better place.

However, in my judgment, Bakhtin's discussion of the relationship between action and discourse remains sketchy and needs further development. For example, it is unclear how discourse is different from co-regulation of actions (cf., Fogel, 1993; Mead, 1956) and how "response" differs from "reaction". Probably, for an action to be discursive it has to have some semiotic nature, referring to something that it is not, and be a part of one's "voice". Another interesting issue, not apparently addressed by Bakhtin, is the sequential turn-taking structure of verbal discourse and the parallel, simultaneous, nature of physical actions. It is much more difficult to extract "physical utterance" in the activity[8].

According to Bakhtin, discourse has not only physical and dialogic aspects but also intellectual and ontological aspects. Each discourse, and its smallest unit – utterance (or a dialogic turn), has an intellectual or logico-cognitive aspect. It creates an internal semiotic space where ideas live and correspond to each other. This logico-cognitive aspect of discourse is oriented semantically toward its referential objects – what the discourse talks about. However, discourse cannot be reduced to its purely intellectual aspect. "Dialogic relationships are reducible neither to logical relationships nor to relationships oriented semantically toward their referential object, relationships *in and of themselves* devoid of any dialogic element. They must clothe themselves in discourse, become utterances, become the positions of various subjects expressed in discourse, in order that dialogic relationships might arise among them" (Bakhtin, 1999, p. 183). Any intellectual reference to the object and relationships between referential objects are addressed and responded to other people – they have an author and audience, "...logical and semantically referential relationships, in order to become dialogic, must be embodied, that is, they must enter another sphere of existence: they must become discourse, that is, an utterance, and receive an *author*, that is a creator of the given utterance whose position it expresses" (Bakhtin, 1999, p. 184). Even an apparently intellectual statement is still double-voiced in a discourse where the voice of the author is mixed with the voices (real or imaginary) of the audience. Also, every apparently intellectual statement is embedded in its ontology.

---

[8] In an article on the political, violent struggle between the President of Russia Boris Yeltsin and the Russian Parliament, occupying the "White House," in Moscow in the fall of 1993, the commentator Yury Bogomolov (1993) made an interesting dialogic analysis of the political violence arguing that each action of each side had its responsivity and addressivity to each other and the "third audiences": the general Russian public and the observers outside of Russia and should be understood as such. He wrote, "Without doubts, mass riots is a type of communication. However, it is a rather peculiar, extreme type of communication when communication loses any remains of individual-personal characteristics. This communication does not occur according to the familiar formulae "I-I" or "I-you" or "we-we" or even "we-they". The latter still has a hope for mutual understanding. [T]he formula of the war (including the civil war) as means of communication is "they-they."

The ontological aspect of the dialogue involves the whole-person as an author and the audience participates in the discourse. A person is engaged in a discourse through his/her past and present personal background, through his/her personal hope and expectations, through his/her fate, through his/her personal concerns, through his/her worldviews, through his/her affiliations in different communities, and even through his/her body. The person's life – the background; past, present, and projected social relations with significant others; interests and desires; social norms; lifestyle; availability of intellectual resources; the person's accent and social status; the person's available audience and practice in which he or she can participate; and so on – contributes to the person's idea and positions. On the other hand, the person's ideas and positions contribute to the shaping the person's life: affiliation to some and exclusions from other relations, communities, practices, networks, and institutions; getting credits and dividends; holding to be responsible; being blamed and accused; being defined and judged; providing meaning to intonation, mannerisms, and actions; fates; and so on. Bakhtin articulated the ontological aspect of discourse in his definition of voice, "Definition of voice... includes height, range, timbre, aesthetic category (lyric, dramatic, etc.). It also includes a person's worldview and fate. A person enters into dialogue as an integral voice. He participates in it not only with his thoughts, but with his fate and with entire individuality" (Bakhtin, 1999, p. 293). Thus, voices are born in ontology and not in dialectics or some kind of division of labor. Many commentators of Dostoevsky's artwork admired his portrayal of philosophical ideas in his novels; however, as Bakhtin pointed out, Dostoevsky did not use his characters as puppets of philosophical ideas in purely intellectual debates, "Dostoevsky begins not with the idea, but with idea-heroes of a dialogue. He seeks the integral voice, and fate and event (the fates and events of the plot) become means for expressing voices" (Bakhtin, 1999, p. 296).

To illustrate this point about ontological nature of discourse, let me bring the following anecdote. Once I was passing a hallway of School of Education at my university with my colleague, also an educator. We heard an instructor teaching some undergraduate course for preservice teachers. As we were passing the open door of the class, the instructor was raising a question for her students in rather serious tone, "So,... how can we deal with *minority students?*" The preservice teachers offered suggestions like celebrating diversity that the instructor evaluated and approved them. The instructor's seemingly innocent question raised a storm of acute painful emotions in both of us that we shared with each other. We were disgusted with the question itself and with the fact that it was seriously raised with preservice teachers. The question was ontologically charged for us. We quickly developed the "ontological glossary" of this question working backward from the end of the sentence:

"*minority* students" == barbarians, pain in the ass, bad, unpredictable, a threat, a problem to face, dangerous, a cause of suffering for teachers "the us";
"we" == not (that) minority, not 'them', civilized, cultured, good, polite, well-behaved, trusted;
"to deal with" == to objectify, to conform, to manipulate, to domesticate, to fix, to castrate;
"how" == a progressing narrative with a promise of a happy end;

Divided by the two sides, the two populations are engaged in the deadly dialogue from the third plural person [i.e., "they" -- EM]" (translation from Russian is mine).

(tacit: *I* of the instructor of the attending preservice teachers) == Moses leading 'my people' in the Promised Land of educational smoothness, the instructor' full control of her classroom;

(tacit: *You*, the preservice teachers) == adepts, followers, unconditional obedience and tranquility;

(tacit: rhetorical question) == Not a genuine question for the instructor herself (she is not a part of that "we" who does not know how to "deal with minority students") but a rhetorical opportunity to address a certain anxiety in the preservice teachers, 'I'm the expert: you do not know the answer but I do, you will hear the correct answer from me in a moment, become an expert like me';

(tacit: community) == a community of knowers and experts.

We felt that the way the question was raised forces teachers to treat "the minority students," with whom the teachers experience dis-ease, as objects of their, the teachers', pedagogical actions and thus, provoking adversity, rather than as collaborative and dialogic partners in the joint endeavor of education. We heard ourselves addressed in this question, "How can *WE* deal with *YOU?*" The question antagonized and adversized us with the instructor. The reasons for my colleague and me to associate ourselves with "those minority students" were both personally-autobiographical and dialogically relational. My colleague was a lesbian, experiencing societal and institutional discrimination and oppression in past and present. I was a Jewish political refuge from the Soviet Union experiencing state and folk Anti-Semitism and political persecution in the USSR. However, that is probably more important than our personal background (but in addition to it), we had dialogic and relational affiliation with networks of people who are systematically marginalized by the society. We would have stopped *being us* -- betray *our selves* -- if we had not affiliated with the "*minority* students" in our own eyes and in imaginary eyes of the network of our real and projective friends.

The instructor's question with its, apparently neutral, intellectual idea of teaching preservice teachers a strategy of addressing cultural diversity in the classroom induced polarization among us that immediately threw this polarization in the field of power. My colleague exclaimed to me, "How did we hire this instructor?!" Both my colleague and I, being full time faculty, had potential power over the instructor, being a temporary faculty with the contract that had to be renewed and reviewed by the full time faculty. The instructor's question blended with the instructor herself. She was not an author of a particular neutral question among many other potential neutral questions but rather this question revealed her as a particular political agent aiming at misguiding the preservice teachers and hurting minority students through these misguided teachers in future. She became an ideologue (using Bakhtinian term) who lived her idea through her fate. Her question also threw us, the accidental witnesses of the question, into the field of ethic responsibility and decision making. We felt that if we had not done anything, we might become accomplices of the crime. We also became ideologues who had to live our ideas through our fates.

However, my colleague and I disliked our immediate response to the instructor. The instructor's question induced anger in my colleague and I calling us for immediately striking her back. We did not want to be socialized in monologism of objectification that the instructor produced in her question. Granted, our monological political reaction seemed to be justified by our professional and ethical responsibility to these preservice teachers, their future minority students, and the society. But, probably, the instructor felt the same when she raised her question. Our truth-reason seemed "more true" to us than her conflicting truth-reason. However, if we chose to strike the instructor without even trying to talk with her, we seemed to promote the same monologic truth-action as the instructor called for. By striking her using our institutional power without talking with her first, we may win the battle but lose the war, so to speak.

We discussed if we could find some dialogic response alternative to treating the instructor as an object of our political strike. If we had chosen dialogue instead of strike, we could have asked each other, "How would I try to dialogue with this person who adversarially objectifies my friends and me?" In her question, the instructor seemed to implicitly refer to her pain, and possibly fear, of living together with "minority students." We could ask her if it was true. If so, what was the nature of the pain/fear? We could sympathize she with her fear and pain and possibly could help her to find a dialogic rather than monologic orientation toward the minority students in dealing with her fear and pain if she would accept our offer for help. Not every utterance (i.e., a dialogic turn) generates such an ontological tension as my example but all utterances do produce some.

In education, the ontological aspects of instruction are often overlooked by educators and researchers, focusing only on intellectual aspects of pedagogical discourse in a classroom. This neglect does not make teaching less ontological – teaching, as any discourse, is ontological; however, neglect of ontological aspects of instruction may lead to undesirable teaching ontology. For example, when a university professor lectures his undergraduate students, pre-service teachers, about the benefits of constructivism and then quizzes them on how well they have learned about constructivism; -- this teaching sends the ontological message to the students that the professor lies to them. Why does the professor not do what he preaches (i.e., constructivist teaching)?! Either there is something wrong with the message (i.e., constructivism") or with the messenger (i.e., the professor) or both. A way of teaching that cannot be taught in its own way is, at least, discredited in the eyes of the students and rightly so. Growing disbelief in constructivism is the ontological curriculum that they learn. Intellectually they may learn how constructivism is great – they can intellectually spit back many reasons why constructivism is better than traditional transmission of knowledge instruction, but ontologically they are being socialized in the criticized traditional instruction through the very same instruction. In this example, there is not a lack of ontology in the teaching – there is just "bad teaching ontology".

Bakhtin noticed an ontological ambiguity in the pedagogical dialogue of Socrates as presented by Plato. While Bakhtin praised the dialogic genre of Platonic philosophizing and Socrates' espoused approach of testing ideas of and with other people, he noted that, in practice as presented in Plato's texts, Socratic pedagogical dialogues remain deeply intellectual. Platonic dialogues of Socrates,

> ... while...not a thoroughly monologized pedagogical dialogue, all the same the multiplicity of voices is extinguished in the [Platonic] idea. The idea is conceived by Plato not as со-бытие ["collective being" – dialogic meeting of two consciousnesses in a dramatic ontological event – EM][9], but as бытие [logical relations of referential objects – EM]. [For Plato – EM] to participate in the idea means to participate in [logical relations of its referential objects -- EM]. But [in

---

[9] I have to re-translate this piece because Bakhtin uses play of words existing only in Russian (for more discussion of the translation difficulty of this place see note 6 in Bakhtin, 1999, p. 181).

Platonic dialogues] all hierarchical interrelation between perceiving human beings, created by the varying degrees of their participation in the [initially dialogic] idea, are ultimately extinguished in the fullness of the idea itself (Bakhtin, 1999, pp. 279-280).

In my view, ontological teaching is the genuine teaching target of constructivism and problem-based learning (Phillips, 2000). A focus on ontological aspects of teaching leads educators (and researchers of education) to whole-person engagement of the participants of classroom discourse (i.e., the teacher and the students) into the studied curriculum. This ontological engagement has to be motivated by what occurs with all the participants "here and now" in the classroom rather than by State standards, curriculum programs or references to future usefulness. To teach something, the teacher has to provoke a dialogic drama, in which alternative and incompatible positions and voices reveal themselves. The studied curriculum has to be en-acted as a dialogic drama. This drama will motivate learning. In Platonic dialogues, this drama was often started by a student or another person; while in the classroom it is often the teacher's responsibility to provoke the drama. For example, a Japanese teacher asked students who had not yet studied addition of fractions with different denominators to add ½ and 1/3. The students produced several answers: 2/5, 5.2, 5/6. The teacher asked the children to justify and compare their answers (Corser, Gardner, & University of Michigan, 1989). Although, unfortunately, the teacher's provocation did not lead to a full-scale dialogic drama because the teacher interrupted it too early, in my view, by taking the full responsibility for comparing the diverse approaches to adding fractions presented by the students, it is easy to envision such a possibility. Full scale dialogic dramatic events provoked by the teacher are described in books by Paley (1991, 1992, 1995, 1997, 1998).

2. Genres of Discourse: Dialogic and Monologic Genres

There is *a great variety of monologic and dialogic genres of discourse*. Monologue as a communicative genre involves a prolonged dialogic turn, relatively self-contained, with a strong voice by the author as, for example, in a lecture followed by responses from an audience. This differs from dialogic genres both quantitatively – there is a long dialogic turn - - as well as qualitatively – there is a strong author's voice which is relatively self-contained with a strong focus on the object of the utterance. However, it is still dialogic by the nature of discourse because a monologue-utterance of any monologic genre is a reply to other's utterances and expects future responses from others. According to Bakhtin, monologue-utterance is guided by dialogic discourse.

But if language, by its social nature, is dialogic, if absolute monologue is impossible, then a relative difference of dialogical and monological forms of speech is not only possible but necessary to make. Together with dialogic forms of speech (for example, everyday dialogue) there are monologic forms of speech (for example, scientific manuscripts, fictional novels and stories, lyric artwork, and so on). They are not absolute monologues but they differ from dialogues by their organization. In the limits of such monological totalities such as novels, monologic speech by the author (or a storyteller) differs from the characters' dialogues with each other. There is no need to argue for the obvious existence of salient differences between dialogical and monological forms of speech within the limits (and on the basis) of the general [universal – EM] dialogicity of language (Bakhtin, 1997a, p. 213).

Monologic and dialogic genres differ from each other not only quantitatively – by the length of its utterance, dialogic turn (e.g., how many paragraphs, sentences, words, and time to say or read it takes before somebody else can reply, number and frequency of dialogic exchanges) – but also qualitatively. On the addressee-theme continuum, dialogic genres are more focused on the addressee while monologic genres of discourse are more focused on the theme of its utterance in more than one way. The *qualitative* differences of monologic genres are coming as a result of their *quantitative* differences: longer utterance and lower frequency of dialogic exchanges. However, there can be other qualitative differences between dialogic and monologic genres that are not necessarily rooted in quantitative differences (but still supported but them).

Firstly, according to Bakhtin, any discursive utterance is a reply to an addressee's question (or to several questions of one addressee or different addressees at once). This question (or these questions) of the addressee(s) can be explicit or implicit or imagined/expected by the speaker (or the writer). In any of the three cases (although to a different degree of probability), there is always a possibility for the speaker not to understand or guess the question correctly and thus the speaker risks losing the addressee in the discourse. In other words, the speaker may reply to a question that the intended addressee did not ask or, even more importantly, the addressee is not interested in asking the question nor, as a consequence, the speaker's reply at all. The addressee's reply to the speaker's utterance helps the speaker correct his or her understanding of what question(s) the addressee had and has in mind and, hence, to tune-up his or her utterance better in his or her next dialogic turn. However, since in monologic genres, the distance between speaker's dialogic turn and the addressee's reply is much longer than in dialogic genres, there is a much higher possibility for the addressee to disengage from the discourse. According to Bakhtin, the addressee's disengagement from the discourse is the highest possible failure of the discourse itself.

Secondly, the same is true with regard to the reply itself. Even if the speaker understood or guessed correctly the addressee's question, there is still a possibility that in his or her reply to the addressee's question will be insensitive to the addressee's needs and, as a result, the speaker may lose the addressee. Again, in dialogic genres due to the higher frequency of exchanges, it is much easier to recover from this problem than in monologic genres. In monologic genres, with their very prolonged dialogic turns, the speaker has to guess, foresee, and address many possible misunderstandings by the addressee. However, since the addressee can be also be "creative" in mis- and differently understanding the speaker's utterance, the monologic utterance can never be fully self-sufficient, intra-textually closed, and finalized. As famous Russian poet of the XIX century Tutchev wrote,

Нам не дано предугадать,	*We lack the power of guessing*
Как слово наше отзовется,—	*How lives our word in another's mind, -*
И нам сочувствие дается,	*And gift of sympathy in life*
Как нам дается благодать...	*Is given to us as a holy blessing.*
Фёдор Иванович Тютчев, 27 февраля 1869	Fyodor I. Tutchev, 27 February 1869
	Translated from Russian by Tatiana Sazonova

As the poet suggested, our limitations to control understanding of our own words by others are compensated by caring (or "sympathy" in the poet's words) that we can have one for another. We are not able to and, actually, do not need to know exactly what another person understands, knows, thinks or feels, but we can feel together what is going on. Bakhtin also emphasized that we are blessed by never being able to coincide in our thinking, feeling, and understanding with others because we always have a surplus of vision, knowledge, thinking, feeling, and understanding that the other person does not have (and vise versa: any person has this surplus over us). Bakhtin argues that this is a blessing rather than a handicap because we would not need each other in principle if we could coincide with others in our subjectivity. Without this surplus, love, compassion, friendship, and collaboration would not be possible. "In a relationship to another human being, love, hate, pity, touchingness, and in general any emotion, are always dialogic to some degree" (Bakhtin, 1997b, p. 320). To illustrate this, Bakhtin repeatedly used an example of a person who is in mourning (Bakhtin, Holquist, & Liapunov, 1990). As he argued, the person in mourning needs our *sym*-pathy (i.e., feeling *with* other, feeling together) rather than *em*-pathy (i.e., feeling absolutely *the same*, duplication of our friend's mourning). The former also involves "a surplus of vision": seeing our mourning friend and a sense of caring for this person in need. Unlike empathy, sympathy is a meta-feeling: our feeling-response for the feeling other.

Thirdly, in an utterance of monologic genres, the speaker has the luxury to create intra-textual context for his or her message and, thus, to try to make his or her utterance relatively self-sufficient, finalized, and textually closed. Of course, the more creative the speaker is, the more possible misunderstanding he or she can notice and try to address in speech, the longer his or her monologue becomes. Speakers of monologic genres may have a temptation to be exhaustive in their speech based on the illusion that fully self-sufficient and finalized utterance is possible (Wertsch, 1985).

Fourthly, in monologic genres it is much easier for the speaker to focus his or her utterance on the theme itself at the expense of the speaker's position in relationship to the positions to the addressee(s) and to other speakers, past and future. Monologic genres tend to solidify the voice of the speaker on the theme of the utterance, making the speaker's voice invisible as if the theme speaks for itself. The difference between position-centered (dialogic) utterance and theme-centered (monologic) utterance can be metaphorically illustrated with a difference in linguistic convention in (dis)agreement between Russian and English. In Russian (and Spanish), (dis)agreement is oriented primarily on the position of the speaker and secondarily on the theme ("Ты не видел его сегодня, да? – *Да*, не видел." "You haven't seen him today, have you? – *Yes*, I haven't," – the addressee first agreeing with the speaker by saying "yes" and then confirming the theme, "I have not seen him today"). By contrast, in English agreement is only thematic ("You haven't seen him today, have you? – *No*, I haven't"). Native Russian speakers learning English have difficulty focusing only on thematic, and not on positional (dis)agreement. This example however is only metaphoric because it is not about discursive genre but rather linguistic convention. Let us consider a genre example of two texts written by the same scholar (a famous biologist) belonging to relatively dialogic and relatively monologic genres of writing with respect to being position-centered (i.e., a dialogic genre) versus theme-centered (i.e., a monologic genre),

1. Experiments show that *Heliconius* butterflies are less likely to ovipost on host plants that possess eggs or egg-like structures. These egg-mimics are an

unambiguous example of a plant trait evolved in response to a host- restricted group of insect herbivores.

2. *Heliconius* butterflies lay their eggs on *Passijlora* vines. In defense the vines seem to have evolved fake eggs that make it look to the butterflies as if eggs have already been laid on them (Myers, 1990, p. 150)

On the first glance, the fragments sound discursively the same; they are both describing the same biological process of co-evolution of an insect and a plant, with the second fragment having less scientific jargon. However, a closer look at both fragments reveals that the first is argumentative and, thus, dialogic while the second is descriptive and, thus, monologic. The first fragment, taken from a professional scholarly journal, builds an argument for a specific evolutionary process and against alternative implicit arguments. The words are very carefully chosen, foreseeing possible counter-arguments of his scientific opponents (e.g., "are less likely" – leaving a possibility for *Heliconius* butterflies still possible to ovipost on host plants, "eggs or egg-like structures", "ovipost" rather than "lay their eggs" as a more exact term) (Gee, 1996, pp. 181-183). It focuses on providing as well as demarcating the evidence (the first sentence, "experiments show") and its interpretation ("are an unambiguous example of"). It is also careful in avoiding any possibility for a teleological explanation ("evolved in response to" versus "*make* it look to the butterflies"). The author uses means of persuasive speech such as "the experiments show" and "an *unambiguous* example" to convince not-yet-committed scholars (and to change the mind of his opponents and strengthen his allies) to accept his model of evolution. As Latour (1987) points out, a scientific text tries to both attack opponents and enroll proponents for support. For non-participants of the specialized field of biology, the opponents and proponents are not known to them; they do not know the actual and possible alternative statements about or against the evolutionary processes presented by the author. The non-participants do not know with *whom* and with *what* the author argues. They do not know what attacks the author has made on the alternative positions and how he supports the positions of his proponents. But the participants in the field who read the article in the professional scholarly journal and to whom the author addresses know the author's opponents and their positions and thus they can comprehend the article by replying to it (privately or publicly).

In the second fragment published in a popular science journal, nature is described as a drama between plant eating insects and the plants defending themselves with a special strategy of mimicking. In contrast with the first fragment, the words are selected to build rich metaphors rather than to be exact. Anthropomorphic metaphors of struggle between insects and plans and plants' deception of the insects are useful as they can help the reader to grasp the described natural process ("in *defense* the vines", "*fake* eggs", "*make* it look"). The plants and the insects are portrayed as actors in a drama not unlike ones that can be seen in human dramas. Readers, who are not specialists in the area, probably have prior rich knowledge and experiences of similar dramas. So, the author skillfully connects the readers' possible prior experiences of the drama of struggle and deception to the natural process of co-evolution. At the expense of comprehensibility of the text by non-scholar readers, the scientific preciseness rooted in the scientific debate is sacrificed. Without reconstruction of this debate for the non-scientist audience by the author, without forcing the readers to take a position and participate in the debate (even peripherally), the scientific preciseness – and thus the dialogic nature of the debate that underlies this preciseness -- remains inaccessible for the readers. Bakhtin

(Bakhtin, 1997a, pp. 225-226) pointed out that using tropes (e.g., metaphors, allegories, comparisons) is a monologic way of introducing creative ambivalence and polysemy because they all involve only one voice. He argued that only heteroglossia is a dialogic way of achieving polysemy. However, we argue that tropes can also have dialogic elements when, like in the given example, a trope is aimed at activation of the readers' prior knowledge and/or experiences. In this case, a metaphor emerges out of the boundary between the voice of the scientist and the fuzzy voice of the reader imagined and constructed by the author.

Bakhtin emphasized the relativity of monologic and dialogic genres. Apparently monologic genres – a very long dialogic turn (e.g., lecture) -- can be deeply dialogic (or monologic) by their nature and apparently dialogic genres – quick exchanges of short utterances (e.g., questioning-interrogation) – can be deeply monologic (or dialogic) by their nature. Let us give educational examples illustrating that point. Educational discourse like lectures can be more dialogically or monologically oriented both externally and internally. Externally, a dialogic lecture explicates and tunes up the questions that the audience asked or might ask (ideally the speaker addresses the audience's actual questions or provokes them at the beginning of the lecture). Also externally, a dialogic lecture ends with specific and inherently interested questions that are posed to the audience for a reply. Internally, a dialogic lecture is position-oriented by unfolding its theme in relationship with the positions of others especially the audience but also with people who may not physically present. Finally, a dialogic lecture is also interested in *ontological* rather than purely intellectual positions of others by addressing the audience as people (in a deep search for the genuinely valued grounds for their positions with which the speaker may partially or fully disagree – "why have the proponents come to such positions while I have not?") rather than objectifying their positions as being totally flawed and mistaken. The purpose of a dialogic lecture as a prolonged dialogic turn is to engage listeners into a thematic dialogue and to socialize them in a community of practice involving this dialogue by provoking the listeners to take their diverse positions in the dialogue. The success of a dialogic lecture is in the listeners becoming involved in a dialogue with the speaker and/or with other participants of the community around such dialogue. Such dialogic lectures are common at scientific conferences and in innovative collaborative classrooms (Rogoff, Turkanis, & Bartlett, 2001).

In the contrast, the purpose of a monologic lecture is to transmit (or induce) a message, which is independent of the listener, to the listener. In a monologic lecture, the speaker often tries to motivate the listeners and justify the lecture by the importance of message itself; the lecture is not justified by questions that the listeners have (or even may have) or by a problematic situation that the listeners find themselves. A monologic lecture often ends like a statement and not as a question to which the speaker is genuinely interested in the listeners' reply. Internally, a monologic lecture is thematically-oriented by objectifying the theme and eliminating any uncertainty and ambiguity from it. If positions of others are presented in a monologic lecture, they are objectified and intellectualized as being flawed and mistaken. The success of a monologic dialogue is for the speaker to make sure that the listeners become equal to the speaker with the regard to the presented message (so the listeners can replace the speaker if needed in future). Such monologic lectures are common in traditional schools (Matusov & Rogoff, 2002).

Table 1. Qualitative differences in the genres

Discursive aspects	Monologue	Dialogue
Focus	Theme	Addressee
Sensitivity to addressee	Guessing addressee's questions	Immediate feedback
Context	Intra-textual	Extra-textual
Modality	High: objective	Low: subjective

In educational debates on constructivist versus transmission of knowledge educational philosophies, lecturing has often been associated with transmission of knowledge educational philosophy. It is true that traditional schooling is based on transmission of knowledge educational philosophy and it heavily relies on lecturing (and on direct instruction in general) (Rogoff et al., 1996). However, lecturing as a genre of educational discourse can be dialogic and thus, constructivist. Similarly, quick exchanges of short utterances so characteristic of dialogue can be monologic. Mehan (1979), while studying classroom discourse in a traditional school, found that it involves triadic exchange which is monologic by its nature. The triadic exchange involves the teacher's Initiation, the student's Response, and the teacher's Evaluation of the student's response. What makes this triadic exchange monologic is the fact that the teacher usually asks known-answer questions disinterested for the student and the teacher him or herself. The teacher's evaluation is often focused on the correctness of the student's reply as defined unilaterally by the teacher. The student's goal often becomes to guess what the teacher wants to hear and to please the teacher with the answer (Lemke, 1990). Wells (1992, September) correctly points out that the presence of the triadic exchange in the classroom discourse does not necessarily mean that the discourse is monologic and guided by a transmission of knowledge educational philosophy. As he shows with examples from an innovative collaborative school, such triadic exchange can be dialogic when the questions that the teacher asks are genuine, the students then responding out of attempt to solve a shared problematic situation, and when evaluation is collaborative. We will return to the interesting and important issue-puzzle-phenomenon of educational philosophies gravitating (but not determined by) toward certain discursive genres later in the paper when we will discuss regimes of discourse.

3. Aspects of Discourse: Dialogicity[10] and Monologicity

Any utterance – the unit of discourse, as Bakhtin (1986) claimed, – has two important *properties-aspects that mutually constitute each other: dialogicity and monologicity.* Or, in Bakhtin's words,

---

[10] In Western Bakhtin scholarship, this term is often defined as "intertextuality". However, the term "intertextuality" was coined not by Bakhtin but by Julia Kristeva (Todorov, 1984, p. 60). In my view and in views of other Bakhtinian philologists (e.g., Morson & Emerson, 1990), the term is very misleading and in conflict with spirit of Bakhtin's scholarship. Bakhtin used the term "dialogicity" ("диалогичность") which referred to the inter-utternace nature of utterance -- utterance is defined not by its internal structure but its dialogic relations with other utterances through addressivity and responsivity (Bakhtin, 1986). It would have been probably much better if Kristeva had defined dialogicity as "interdiscoursivity", "intervocality", or even literally "interutterancivity" to be in spirit with Bakhtin.

Relative difference between monologue and dialogue. Each utterance of a dialogue is to some degree monologic (as utterance of one person) and every monologue is to some degree a dialogic turn because it belongs to <?> the context of discussion or issue and implicates audience and past polemics, and so on. Dialogue embraces <?> utterances of at least two participants who are connected with each other by dialogic relations, who are aware of each other, who are replying to each other. Their dialogic connection (the relationship with each other) is reflected in each utterance of dialogue and it defines the individual utterance (Bakhtin, 1997a, p. 209-210).[11]

It is possible to say that each dialogic turn by itself is monologic (it is essentially a little monologue), and each monologue is a dialogic turn of a big dialogue (speech communication of some sphere). Monologue is a speech that is not addressed to anybody and does not suppose any reply. There are possible different degrees of monologicity (Bakhtin, 1997b, p. 325).

Monologicity reflects the shape, the form, the totality of the subject of an utterance in both senses of the term "subject of utterance": 1) who is talking (i.e., voice) and 2) what he or she (or they) is talking about (i.e., finalized object). Strong monologicity involves a strong distinctive voice and a more finalized object of the utterance. Monologicity is recognition of one *by* others (and by one, oneself) and *in* others (i.e., as one's contributions) – recognition of one's generating totality, one's responsibility for ones' words and actions (across time and deeds), and one's agency. Monologicity is equal to affirmation of one's voice among other voices and is grounded in a consensus with another "we". It involves *authorship* (one's utterance has a point and intentionality uniquely rooted in this person in the face of utterances by other people) and *responsibility* for one's own words, actions, and deeds (one is ready to answer for his or her words and deeds to others and oneself). The authorship and responsibility can be *external* – as a voice among other voices (of others) – and *internal* – as a cohesive and persuasive stand, will, intention. Monologicity is aimed at completing one's own understanding, skills, knowledge, goals, and needs by seeking a consensus, revealing agreements, establishing certainty and reliability, saying something non-problematic (e.g., a fact) and positive (i.e., pre-given, cf. positivism), uniting with others and uniting others (around oneself), aligning with others' thoughts, feelings, goals, positions, intentions, values, and so on, and aligning others with one's own thoughts, feelings, goals, positions, intentions, values, and so on, and, finally, using and changing others (i.e., acting upon them) for completing one's own goals. Monologicity makes clear who is speaking (i.e., authorship and responsibility) and what is said (i.e., the message). In other words, monologicity objectivizes others and the themes of communication (i.e., closing them out, "black boxing" using Latour's (1987) term). Monologicity reflects centripetal forces of language, communication, and community oriented on centralization, unification, unity with action, seriousness, cohesiveness and integrity of voice (and position), articulateness, globalization, decontextualization, exactness and correctness of meaning (finalizing the meaning) (Bakhtin, 1991, p. 272).

However, as Bakhtin argued, voice can be recognized and an object can be finalized only in relation to other voices and finalizing by other people, "Any increase of expressivity of personality of a speaker in his/her monologic speech (i.e., at any time when we begin to perceive vividly individual unique personality of the speaker [in his/her utterance – EM]) is

---

[11] This paragraph is taken from Bakhtin's notes. The question marks are in the original text.

an increase of its dialogic potential [i.e., dialogicity – EM]" (Bakhtin, 1997a, p. 212). The power of monologicity is in its effects on other people. Monologicity is impossible without a strong sense of recognition and acceptance by others and thus it is shaped by dialogicity.

Dialogicity involves recognition of boundaries with and relations of different voices. It is about hearing other voices and other people in every utterance, every sentence, every word by a speaking person. Dialogicity is recognition of others *by* a speaker (external dialogicity) and *in* a speaker (internal dialogicity) – recognition of interdependency, incompleteness, addressivity, and responsivity. Dialogicity is equal to respect of others. It involves *addressivity* to others (the speaker's utterance addresses others and anticipates future responses of others to the speaker's utterances) and *responsivity* to others (the speaker's utterances responses to others' past utterances). The addressivity and responsivity can be *external* – dialogically addressing and responding to real other people – and *internal* – dialogically addressing and responding to other voices constructed by my own imagination within my utterance (i.e., internal dialogue). Dialogicity is aimed at seeking, exploring, revealing, and shaping one's incompleteness by problematizing the theme (genuinely for oneself and others – not rhetorically), asking information-seeking questions, revealing boundaries of mis- and non- understandings and disagreements, uncovering uncertainty, promoting doubtfulness (cf. Socrates, "I know that I don't know anything"), expressing interest in others' thoughts, feelings, goals, positions, intentions, values, and so on. In other words, dialogicity subjectivizes the author him or herself, the others and the themes of communication (i.e., opening them out, addressing them). Dialogicity reflects centrifugal forces of language, communication, and community oriented on diversification, decentralization, deunification, creolization, heteroglossia, multivoicedness, depthness, uncertainty, impass of actions, gaiety, diversity of accents and dialects, focus on communication and understanding.

Table 2. Aspects of discourse

Dimensions of discourse	Monologicity=authorship	Dialogicity=heteroglossia
Community	Recognition and acceptance of the voice by others	Recognition of boundaries of voices
Guidance	Informing other voices about one's position	Informing the voice about positions of others
Action	Responsibility	Addressivity

Dialogicity and monologicity are two inherent aspects of human consciousness that complement each other. They are like the two-faced Janus portrayed by Latour (1987). Dialogicity is breaking boundaries among people and things while monologicity sets them. Dialogization is a process of breaking boundaries, revealing problems and uncertainties, expressing genuine interests in others, addressing and responding to others, learning about one's own incompleteness. Meanwhile, monologization is a process of establishing boundaries, strengthening one's own voice, setting certainties and consensuses, finalizing and objectivizing people and things, uniting with others. According to Bakhtin, dialogicity and monologicity mutually constitute each other,

Every utterance of a speaking subject serves as a point where centrifugal as well as centripetal forces are brought to bear. The processes of centralization and decentralization, of unification and disunification, intersect in the utterance; the utterance not only answers the requirements of its own language as an individualized embodiment of a speech act, but it answers the requirements of heteroglossia as well; it is in fact an active participant in such speech diversity. And this active participation of every utterance in living heteroglossia determines the linguistic profile and style of the utterance to no less a degree than its inclusion in any normative-centralizing system of a unitary language.

Every utterance participates in the "unitary language" (in its centripetal forces and tendencies) and at the same time partakes of social and historical heteroglossia (the centrifugal, stratifying forces) (Bakhtin, 1991, p. 272).

VISTA OF DISCURSIVE EXCESSES: "D AND M ARE BOTH BAD"

4. Excesses of Discourse: Excessive Dialogism and Excessive Monologism

When dialogicity and monologicity are off balance with each other, they can lead to excesses and abuses. *Excessive dialogism* is off balance because of too much dialogicity, too much centrifugal force, too much of other voices present in one's voice; in contrast, *excessive monologism* is off balance because of too much monologicity, too much centripetal force, too much of one voice dominating over voices of others.

Excessive dialogism, with its focus on addressivity to imagined (and real) hostile words of others, leads to loss of one's own voice, inarticulateness, paralysis of will, inability to act, and lack of self-respect. In excessive dialogism, a unified, solidified, respected, pacified word is impossible because there is no a community that backs up the individual – rather an individual hears a horde of hostile voices that constantly criticize any attempt by the individual to say something affirming. In extreme cases, an individual loses his or her voice almost completely and becomes quasi-voiceless (to lose completely his or her own voice one should die). Victims almost lose their voice in their solitude of abuse. It is not about them being cooperative with the victimizers or being stupid or even being depressed (although the latter is often the case). It is about not having a voice that supported by a community who takes it sympathetic and seriously. I abstracted five aspects of the notion of "community behind" of what Bakhtin (1999) defined as "the rights for equal consciousnesses":

1) "Gaining floor": Are the relevant people pay attention to me and to what I do, desire, and/or say? (vs. they do not pay attention to me or there are not such people as "relevant" to me);

2) "Taking seriously": Do the relevant people take me and what I do, desire, and/or say seriously? (vs. they laugh at me as a ridiculous and not serious person or there are not such people as "relevant" to me);

3) "Providing support": Can and do the relevant people provide me with necessary support for my actions, desires, and/or discourses? (vs. they are not able or unwilling provide me with support or there are not such people as "relevant" to me);

4) "Respect in disagreement": Will the relevant people keep quality relations with me in case of their disagreement with me: my actions, deeds, desires, and discourses (vs.

they are turn away from me in case of disagreement or there are not such people as "relevant" to me);

5) "Unconditional trust": Will the relevant people stay with me unconditionally, even in fight (vs. they will betray me under certain conditions or there are not such people as "relevant" to me).

In the famous movie by the renown Japanese director Akira Kurosawa's (1970), "Does 'ka-den," an adolescent girl Katsuko (of maybe 14-year old), who had lost her parents, became a servant in house of her well-to-do uncle. The girl was highly exploited by her uncle and his wife. She did not have friends except a sake delivery boy of her age, who came daily to deliver sake for her uncle and who talked with her freely and sympathized her suffering at her uncle house. The boy was very nice to the girl, caring about her well-being and criticizing her uncle, -- their relationship gradually became friendly and intimate (maybe even a bit romantic). Once the girl was raped by her uncle. Some time after the rape, Katsuko met her friend and stabbed him with a knife that she intentionally brought for the meeting (but, fortunately, not for death). After the boy recovered, Katsuko and he met again (he did not want to press changes against her) and he asked her why she had stabbed him. The girl answered that she had wanted to die. We could not hear a word from Katsuko until she got to prison for stabbing the boy. She did not have a community that could take her words seriously but rather she was locked in solitude of powerless that produced vicious circles of excessive internal dialogue. However, after she released from the prison she talked with the boy – we could hear her voice for the first time. Apparently, police sympathetic interrogation of Katsuko created a sense of a community who backed her up by taking her words seriously and respectfully. Katsuko even demanded her uncle to come to the police and to testify but her uncle escaped not being able to face the responsibility for his crime (he got silent).

Bakhtin investigated the case of excessive dialogism, in his study of the discourse of "underground men" portrayed by Dostoevsky. As Bakhtin (1999) argued, underground people do not have a community behind them that (monologically) support, accept, backup, unite, and reconcile words of the underground people. As a result, an underground person has to dialogically react on every and each of his own words and ideas without any rest because he or she he expects that the members of the community significant for him or her will challenge and attack his/her words.

> Capitalism created the conditions for a special type of inescapably solitary consciousness. Dostoevsky exposes all the falsity of this consciousness, as it moves in its vicious [dialogic] circle.
>
> Hence the depiction of the sufferings, humiliations, and *lack of recognition* of man in class society. Recognition has been taken away from him, his name has been taken away. He has been driven into forced solitude, which the unsubmissive strive to transform into *proud solitude* (to do without recognition, without others).
>
> Complex problem of humiliation and the humiliated [p. 288].

> Communion has been deprived, as it were, of its real-life body and wants to create one arbitrarily, out of purely human material. All this is a most profound expression of the social disorientation of the classless intelligentsia, which feels itself dispersed throughout the world and whose members must orient themselves in the world one by one, alone and at their own risk. *A firm monologic voice presupposes a firm social support, presupposes a we – it makes no difference*

whether this "we" is [actually -- EM] *acknowledged or not.* The solitary person finds that his own voice has become a vacillating thing, his own unity and his internal agreement with himself has become a postulate [pp. 280-281; here and further: bold is added, italics is original].

The Underground Man conducts the same sort of inescapable dialogue with himself that he conducts with the other person. He cannot merge completely with himself in a unified monologic voice simply by leaving the other's voice entirely outside himself (whatever that voice might be, without a loophole), for, as is the case with Golyadkin, his voice must also perform the function of surrogate for the other person. He cannot reach an agreement with himself, but neither can he stop talking with himself. The style of his discourse about himself is organically alien to the period, alien to finalization, both in its separate aspects and as a whole. This is the style of internally endless speech which can be mechanically cut off but cannot be organically completed [p. 235].

...we will comment upon two additional characteristics of the Underground Man. Not only his discourse but his face too has its sideward glance, its loophole, and all the phenomena resulting from these. It is as if interference, voices interrupting one another, penetrate his entire body, depriving him of self-sufficiency and unambiguousness. The Underground Man hates his own face, because in it *he senses the power of another person over him, the power of that other's evaluations and opinions.* He himself looks on his own face with another's eyes, with the eyes of the other. And this alien glance interruptedly merges with his own glance and creates in him a peculiar hatred toward his own face:

For instance, I hated my face; I thought it disgusting, and even suspected that there was something base in its expression and therefore every time I turned up at the office I painfully tried to behave as independently as possible so that I might not be suspected of being base, and to give my face as noble an expression as possible. "Let my face even be ugly," I thought, "but let it be noble, expressive, and above all, extremely intelligent." But I was absolutely and painfully certain that my face could never express those perfections; but what was worst of all, I thought it positively stupid-looking. And I would have been quite satisfied if I could have looked intelligent. In fact, I would even have put up with looking base if, at the same time, my face could have been thought terribly intelligent. [SS IV, 168, "Notes," Part Two, ch. I]
    [p. 235]

The discourse of the Underground Man is entirely a discourse-address. To speak, for him, means to address someone; to speak about himself means to address his own self with his own discourse; to speak about another person means to address that other person; to speak about the world means to address the world. But while speaking with himself, with another, with the world, he simultaneously addresses a third party as well: he squints his eyes to the side, toward the listener, the witness, the judge. This simultaneous triple-directedness of his discourse and the fact that he does not acknowledge any object without addressing it is also responsible for the extraordinarily vivid, restless, agitated, and one might say, obtrusive nature of this discourse. It cannot be seen as a lyrical or epic discourse, calmly gravitating toward itself and its referential object; no, first and foremost one reacts to it, responds to it, is drawn into its game; it is capable of agitating and irritating, almost like the personal address of a living person. It destroys footlights, but not because of its concern for topical issues or for reasons that have any direct philosophical significance, but precisely because of that formal structure analyzed by us above (Bakhtin, 1999, pp. 236-237).

The phenomenon of excessive dialogue – double, if not triple or even quadruple, consciousness tearing apart a person whose existence is not reconciled and accepted by a broader society has been noticed and described not only by Dostoevsky in Russian intelligentsia of the second part of the XIX century but also by Kurt Lewin in Jews in the mid 20th century and by DuBois in Black Americans at the beginning of the XX century. Here is how DuBois described double consciousness of the "soul of black folks",

> Between me and the other world there is ever an unasked question: unasked by some through feelings of delicacy; by others through the difficulty of rightly framing it. All, nevertheless, flutter round it. They approach me in a half-hesitant sort of way, eye me curiously or compassionately, and then, instead of saying directly, How does it feel to be a problem? they say, I know an excellent colored man in my town; or, I fought at Mechanicsville; or, Do not these Southern outrages make your blood boil? At these I smile, or am interested, or reduce the boiling to a simmer, as the occasion may require. To the real question, How does it feel to be a problem?[12] I answer seldom a word.

> ... After the Egyptian and Indian, the Greek and Roman, the Teuton and Mongolian, the Negro is a sort of seventh son, born with a veil, and gifted with second-sight in this American world,—a world which yields him no true self-consciousness, but only lets him see himself through the revelation of the other world. It is a peculiar sensation, this double-consciousness, this sense of always looking at one's self through the eyes of others, of measuring one's soul by the tape of a world that looks on in amused contempt and pity. One ever feels his two-ness,—an American, a Negro; two souls, two thoughts, two unreconciled strivings; two warring ideals in one dark body, whose dogged strength alone keeps it from being torn asunder (Du Bois, 1961, p. 16)

Lewin introduced the notion of "marginal people" to describe the similar phenomenon of double consciousness leading to excessive vicious dialogue in American Jews in the mid 1940s,

> Not the *belonging to many groups is* the cause of the difficulty, but an *uncertainty* of belongingness.

> In practically every underprivileged group a number of people will be found who, although regarded by the privileged majority as not belonging to them, feel themselves not really belonging to the underprivileged minority. Frequently it is the more privileged people within the underprivileged group, or those people whose open or secret intent it is to pass the line, who are in the position of what the sociologists call "marginal men." They are people who belong neither here nor there, standing "between" the groups. The psychological difficulties which the marginal man has to face-his uncertainty, his instability, and often self-hate, due to the more or less permanent state of conflict in which he finds himself-are well known to the student of sociology.

---

[12] Unfortunately, more than 100 years later, minority students are still seen as "a problem to deal with" by some teachers in the US as the incident described above reveals.

The frequency of "marginal" persons in an underprivileged group is likely to increase the more the differences between the privileged and underprivileged groups decrease, with the resulting paradox that the betterment of the group might increase the uncertainty and tension of the individual. (pp.179-180) [Lewin quotes at length writing of an American Jewish female college student-EM:]

You may have noticed that I am the middle speaker. It's a very appropriate place for me, I think, not because I strike a mean between them, but rather because I am on the fence. I haven't quite made up my mind as to what I think or why I think it. And in that, I am typical of the Jewish people.

Look at me. I'm neither here nor there. As a Jewess, I don't amount to much. I come to services when I have to; I've been told that mine is a precious heritage, but I haven't the slightest idea what it is. I can name quite a number of relatively unimportant English poets-but do I know who is the greatest Jewish poet? No. My education has been exclusively Christian. My virtues are the Christian virtues-at least my conceptions are. Occasionally, I discover something in me that is characteristically Jewish-and I am surprised, almost estranged from myself. I know I'm Jewish because I've been told so, because I have Jewish friends. Aside from that, it doesn't mean very much to me.

So you see, as a Jewess I don't amount to much. But I'm not much better as an American either. Here at school I move in a charmed circle of Jews. The other circle, the non-Jews, are oblivious of me, and I of them. Occasionally, the circles touch, sometimes more, sometimes less.

I become friendly with some one in the other circle. But self-consciously friendly. If it's a boy, I wonder just how he thinks of me; he wonders what his fraternity brothers are saying. If it's a girl, we both congratulate ourselves mentally on our overstepping the bonds of racial prejudice. When I read the Phi Beta Kappa list, I'm careful to point out how many of the chosen people are Jewish. I'm always conscious that I am Jewish whether I hide it or try to impress it upon others.

So what am I? According to Jews, I'm American. According to Americans, I'm Jewish. And I'm wrong, utterly wrong, in being that way. And so it is only by pushing people like me off the fence-which side isn't so important, so long as it's off the fence-that Jews are ever going to be freed from anti-Semitism. We must remove the beam from our own *eyes*. (pp.178-179)

...The position of staying on the boundary between two groups ("on the fence"), of being in both groups but really in neither, might be natural for the biological half-Jews. We should realize, however, that a similar and not less difficult situation exists for those who might be called "social half-Jews," those who are not fully decided about their belongingness to the Jews. Those marginal men and women are in somewhat the same position as an adolescent who is no longer a child and certainly does not want to be a child any longer, but who knows at the same time that he is not really accepted as a grown-up. This uncertainty about the ground on which he stands and the group to which he belongs often makes the adolescent loud, restless, at once timid and aggressive, over-sensitive and tending to go to extremes, over-critical of others and himself.

The marginal Jew is condemned for his lifetime to remain in a similar situation. Wherever Jewish questions come up he sees with the eyes of both the

Jew and the non-Jew. That would be entirely in order if he were clear about the issue and if he knew clearly what his personal values were, because then he would stand on firm ground for making reasonable and fair decisions. The marginal Jew, however, does not as a rule feel sufficiently rooted in either of these groups to be clear and confident about his views and about his personal relations to either side. He is therefore compelled to remain in a rather vague and uncertain but permanent inner conflict. He is the "eternal adolescent." He shows the same unhappiness and lack of adjustment (Lewin, 1948, pp.180-181)

When a person is not recognized as a legitimated member of a society and perceived by him/herself and the society as "being a problem" (Du Bois, 1961) whose every word has to be challenged and attacked, the excessive dialogism emerges. This excessive dialogism has internal forms and external forms explicated by Bakhtin (Bakhtin & Emerson, 1999). Its essence of an excessive dialogism reveals itself in the person's hearing challenges and attacks by powerful others on every word that the person speaks or thinks. Recently, similar phenomenon has been discussed by Ogbu and his colleagues who talk about "oppositional identity" developed by some members of "involuntarily minorities" (Fordham & Ogbu, 1986; Gibson & Ogbu, 1991; Ogbu, 1987b; Ogbu & Stern, 2001).[13] In interviews with high school students and their parents, these researchers found that members of involuntarily minorities sometimes define themselves as dialogic opposition to the mainstream society: what the mainstream society accepts, they reject and what the mainstream society accepts they reject even despite of sometimes obvious harm and damage to themselves as result of this dialogic opposition. Anything that can be seen by members of involuntary minority as affiliation with the oppressive mainstream society is considered as betrayal of the community, as "selling out". In this social context, a reconciled word (and action) for another and oneself becomes increasingly difficult.

Both excessive dialogism and excessive monologism fight with voices of others. In this sense, they are not in opposition to each other. But while excessive dialogism fights with voices of others dialogically by responding to their hostile replies, excessive monologism tries to suppress the existence of other voices all together. As Bakhtin put it,

> Monologism, at its extreme, denies the existence outside itself of another consciousness with equal rights and equal responsibilities, another *I* with equal rights (*thou*). With a monologic approach (in its extreme and pure form) *another person* remains whole and merely an *object* of consciousness, and not another consciousness [as a partner in a dialogue – EM]. No response is expected from it that could change everything in the world of my consciousness. Monologue is finalized and deaf to the other's response, does not expect it and does not acknowledge in it any *decisive* force... Monologue manages without the other, and therefore to some degree materializes all reality. Monologue pretends to be the *ultimate word*. It closes down [and, thus, completely finalizes -- EM] the represented world and represented persons (Bakhtin, 1999, pp. 292-293).

---

[13] Another recent discussion of similar phenomenon of excessive dialogism can be found in Wertsch (2002) when the author discusses "internal immigration" among some citizens of the former USSR who were opposition-minded against the Soviet regime but who did not choose any form of active resistance (see also a description of exhausting "disputes with radio" broadcasting the official Soviet propaganda in Bukovsky (1979)).

It is interesting that one of Bakhtin's examples of excessive monologism is instruction in traditional schooling,

> In an environment of ... [excessive -- EM] monologism the genuine interaction of consciousness is impossible and thus genuine dialogue is impossible as well. In essence ... [excessive monologism – EM] knows only a single mode of cognitive interaction among consciousnesses: *someone who knows and possesses the truth instructs someone who is ignorant of it and in error; that is , it is the interaction of a teacher and a pupil,* which, it follows, can be only a pedagogical dialogue [i.e., dialogic by its genre but monologic by its regime – EM] (Bakhtin, 1999, p. 81).

The purpose of pedagogical discourse in conventional school is to unite the student's consciousness with the teacher's consciousness. The student's voice is considered to be a voice of ignorance, error, and confusion. The teacher knows that the student is ignorant, lacking knowledge and filled with misconceptions but the teacher does not know how exactly the student is ignorant with regard to a specific curriculum. Thus, in triadic discourse common in a conventional school (Lemke, 1990; Mehan, 1979; Sinclair & Coulthard, 1975; Skidmore, 2000; Wells, 1992, September), firstly the teacher has to address the flawed voice of the student to test his/her flaws in response to the teacher's expectation that the student may be ignorant and in error (that is why the student is in the classroom). To test the student's intellectual flaws, the teacher asks a known-answer question reflecting monologic unity of the teacher's consciousness. The student's response to the teacher's testing question reveals for the teacher whether the student's voice is a part of the teacher's monologic consciousness (in the case of the student's correct answer, where correctness is solely judged by the teacher) or the student's voice is flawed and apart from the teacher's monologic consciousness (in the case of the student's incorrect answer). In the former case, the teacher will affirm the student. In the latter case, the teacher will repudiate the student and correct him or her so the student so the student will be able to coincide with the teacher's monolithic consciousness (Nystrand, 1997; Skidmore, 2000). Or in Bakhtin's own words,

> In the monologic world, *tertium non datur*: a thought is either affirmed or repudiated; otherwise it simply ceases to be a fully valid thought. An unaffirmed thought, ..., must be deprived in general of its power to mean, must become a psychical fact. And as for polemically repudiated thoughts, they also are not represented, because denial, whatever form it takes, excludes the possibility of any genuine representation of the idea. Someone else's repudiated thought cannot break out of a monologic context; on the contrary, it is confined all the more harshly and implacably within its own boundaries. Another's repudiated thought is not capable of creating alongside one consciousness another autonomous consciousness, if repudiation remains a purely theoretical repudiation of the thought as such (Bakhtin, 1999, p. 80).

Extreme excessive monologism does not need even agreement as conscious contemplation of ideas. For example, back in the Soviet Union, I heard through an unofficial oral network that when in the early 1930s Stalin's friend Ordzhonikidze (then a commissar of Soviet heavy industry) tried to protect Kirov, Stalin's would-be political rival, from repression by arguing that Kirov agreed with all Stalin's policies, Stalin replied, referring to himself as a third person, "Stalin does not need anybody to agree with him!" Agreement based on contemplation is a dialogic response full of freedom, authorship, and agency and is an involved polyphonic regime of internal persuasion (Bakhtin, 1991, 1999; Rappaport, 1978, p. 85). Stalin needed monologic agreement based on unconditional acceptance of his will[14] or what Bakhtin (1991, p. 343) would call "unconditional allegiance." I do not know if it is a historical fact, but even if an "urban legend," it is nicely captures the nature of totalitarianism that is based on unconditional loyalty and not on internal persuasiveness. There was an old Soviet political joke illustrating this point: a person was asked by a party official, "Have you ever politically deviated?" The person replied, "Yes, I've deviated, but I deviated only together with the party line."

Excessive monologism tries to create a monolithic, unified voice of the universal truth. It tries to be purely intellectual and not ontological. It tries to erase any references to a particular voice, particular context, particular practice, particular relations, and particular *I*. Anything that is rooted in particular being and circumstances of life has to be removed. It tries to eliminate any gaps between consciousnesses. Gaps between consciousnesses are treated as misunderstandings, misconceptions, distortions, errors, or even conspiracies that have to be eliminated. Excessive monologism understands and empathizes to everyone. It turns dialogic polemics into dialectic method within one consciousness[15]. "Take a dialogue and remove the voices (the partitioning of the voices), remove the intonations (emotional and individual ones), carve out abstract concepts and judgments from living words and responses, cram everything into one abstract [monologic and monolithic – EM] consciousness – and that's how you get dialectics" (Bakhtin, 1986, p. 147). Excessive monologism accepts only one consciousness – the consciousness of the authority or a tradition: all other possible consciousnesses are partial, flawed, and evil. One monolithic consciousness of excessive monologue unfolds itself in solitary universal activity as the Absolute Spirit in Hegel's philosophy (Hegel & Baillie, 1967). This solitude of excessive monologism is kin to the solitude of excessive dialogism (Fromm, 1969). Both are born from insensitive power. Excessive monologism is solitude of the powerful and excessive dialogism is solitude of the powerless.

OPPOSITIONAL VISTA: "D IS GOOD WHILE M IS BAD"

5. Regimes of Discourse: Polyphony Versus Discursive Monopoly

Although, according to Bakhtin, discourse by its very nature is dialogic, society and individual people can try to either promote or inhibit its dialogic nature. Promoting dialogic discourse involves concerns with providing a wide access of diverse participants to communication, emphasis on listening to and learning from others, appreciation of

---

[14] However, even unconditional monologic agreement with Stalin would not guarantee a person's survival from Stalinist purges. The terror was random, unpredictable, and irrational. One of probable reasons for that is that a predictable safe haven from the terror might promote a deliberate -- dialogic, free -- decision on a part of the person to choose unconditional monologic agreement with the regime and, thus, exercise a little bit freedom, which was most hated by the regime. Dialogic tyrants often had a suspicion that beyond people's sincere unconditional monologic agreement is a deliberate dialogic calculation of a free person.

[15] See Wegerif (2007), for his claim that Vygotsky was a dialectic scholar while Bakhtin was a dialogical scholar and for his critique of dialectics. I am very sympathetic to Wegerif's claim and critique (see, Matusov, 2008a, 2008b).

disagreements, misunderstanding, and uncertainties, pluralism, and so on. These efforts are constituted by special political actions and the ideology of polyphony. Ideology attempts to articulate polyphonic values and to mobilize people to act in the name of these values. The famous phrase that was attributed to Voltaire nicely captures the ideology of polyphonic regime, -- dialogic solidarity that is based on appreciation of disagreements and not only agreements (cf. "intersubjectivity without agreement" Matusov, 1996, 2001), -- "I disapprove of what you say, but I will defend to the death your right to say it" (Guterman, 1990; Hall, 1906). Polyphonic regime is mediated by political, judicial, social, and economic institutions focusing on freedom of speech, balance of powers, access and participation in decision making and governance, protection of minorities, just distribution of social goods, and so on. Sen emphasizes two important aspects of a polyphonic regime that applies for both freedoms and tolerance associated with a polyphonic regime, "1) *the value of personal freedom*: that personal freedom is important and should be guaranteed by those who 'matter' in a good society, and 2) *equality of freedom*: everyone matters and the freedom guaranteed for one must guaranteed for all" (Sen, 1999, p. 233, the italic original).

Polyphonic regime is much deep than just the popular notion of a "marketplace of competing ideas." The major contribution of Bakhtin is his realization that any idea by itself outside of dialogue is not alive and, thus, is not true. Truth exists as dialogue. He wrote,

> Truth is not born nor is it to be found inside the head of an individual person, it is born *between people* collectively searching for truth, in the process of their dialogic interaction. (Bakhtin & Emerson, 1999, p. 110, bold is mine, italics is original)

Without addressivity and responsivity, truth expressed in an idea does not exist. That is why it is so important to preserve the history of ideas as dialogue, even disputes, of conflicting viewpoints but also to continue hearing voices of others to whom this idea addresses and responds. Ideas mature through replying to others who disagree and/or are not convinced yet. Although opponents and the unconvinced do not author the idea, they heavily contribute to its development. Truth is not the product of this dialogic process, but it is the process itself. To understand the idea means to join the dialogue that brings this idea to life – it means to stay engaged and hear voices of the opponents and the unconvinced (past and present).

Intellectually, a polyphonic regime is often presented as another utopia, as a fixed Platonic idea (I am not an exception from this tradition here). However, it does not need to be so nor was it always so. Historically, a polyphonic regime is a dialogic response to regimes of monologic monopoly on power and discourse: polyphony is a dialogic response to monologic abuses, both past and present (Dershowitz, 2002). For example, the famous words by Voltaire about his willingness to sacrifice his life for freedom of disliked speech were in response to book burning (Hall, 1906). The viability of polyphonic regime is in its recognition and responses to monologism and monologic regime. As such, polyphony does not have any specific final form; it cannot be fully reached or taken for granted. Establishment of and participation in a polyphonic regime is always an effort, risk, and at times even a sacrifice. As we know from the tragic history of the twentieth century, defeat of one form of monologism does not mean immediate victory of polyphony – another, at times much worse, form of monologism can replace the defeated (weaker) form of monologism (e.g., collapse of Czarist Russia and establishment of communist totalitarianism).

As discursive regime, monologism exists only as a political action (i.e., imposition of one voice on others, a political attempt to monopolize communication and truth) and as an ideology (i.e., ideas that mobilize people for political action of their monopoly on communication and truth). According to Bakhtin, although monologue tries to intellectually and politically monopolize communication, ontologically this monopoly cannot be ever completely successful (Bakhtin, 1997b). The nature of any discourse, including a monologic one, is always dialogic. There have been dialogic turns before any monologue and there will be after. When totalitarian regimes of the 20th centuries tried to seriously and systematically establish their total monologues by "educating" people to become absolutely obedient in concentration camps, the successes of such "education" led only to physical death of the people (Kotek & Rigoulot, 2000). As survivors of concentration camps report, when prisoners began following commands without any consideration, their immune systems seemed to collapse and they quickly died of benign diseases (Bettelheim, 1960). Successful total monologue loses its listeners to death. In other words, as far as the human race continues its existence, any monologue is only a dialogic turn but it is a very specific dialogic turn.

Any monologue is essentially dialogic (Bakhtin, 1999). Actual monologue only ATTEPMTS to be the ultimate word but never IS the ultimate word. Monologue tries to deny existence of equal others but it cannot escape dialogic relationship of disrespect to the others and dialogic response to this disrespect from these others. Attempts to monopolize interaction through purely interactional and communicational means are impossible because they are faced with dialogic reply by others (listeners) thus directly or indirectly challenging this interactional monopoly.

Monologic regime tries to suppress dialogism. Monologism as imposition of one voice on others breeds ideological and physical violence, oppression, and alienation because it cannot establish itself purely through interaction. It does it through demonization of any opponent (past, current, or even imaginary) making dialogue illegitimate and illegal. Under monologic regime, any topic, any theme becomes an issue of loyalty (Havel & Vladislav, 1989). There are no innocent topics – there are not even artistic tastes but political loyalty or betrayal (Bukovsky, 1979). Ideology of monologism is total does not know exceptions. When thematical exceptions from the "us versus them" totalitarian ideology do appear, monologism cracks. For example, when in the Soviet Union in 1980, Malevich's famous picture of "Black Square" was brought from Paris and exposed in Moscow next to the Kremlin, some die-hard Communist party members became increasingly confused and frustrated: the art was clearly "nonsensical" and "bourgeois" but why was it presented at one of the most prestigious Soviet exhibitions?! Was the exhibition an act of sabotage; if so, whose? This dangerous thought would lead to opposition to the official party line. The growing ideological dissonance led some party members to accept an idea of non-ideological[16] "artistic taste" as their political compromise. "The other" (i.e., the artist and the audience who appreciate the painting) was transformed from a demonized enemy into an intriguing puzzlement: what did all these

---

[16] I use the term "ideology" here in the old Soviet propaganda's sense as an expression of the antagonism between "us", Communists (good guys), versus "them", bourgeoisie (evil guys). This is NOT Bakhtin's use of this term (see Ball & Freedman, 2004 for more discussion of how Bakhtin defined and used the concept of "ideology").

people find in this apparently nonsensical picture? Arguably, the Moscow-Paris art exhibition in 1980 added a few more cracks to the Soviet totalitarianism.

Table 3. The opposition of the discursive regimes

	Regime of discursive monopoly	Regime of polyphony
Political action	Monopoly on communication Imposition of one voice over all others Violence Death as the final success Suppression of dialogism	Access to communication Listening and learning from voices of others Democratic participation Life is the final success Response to monologism
Ideology	Monopoly on the truth Truth is located in the statement and in an individual person Black-and-white certainty[17] Unity Demonization of "the other"	Pluralism Truth is located in a community and discourse Value of uncertainty Diversity Respect of others in disagreement

Suppression of dialogism through violence (physical and ideological) is the one thing to which any monological regime is really concerned (Bakhtin, 1984). Ironically, in order to do it well, a good design of suppression and violence requires a dialogue among the totalitarian rulers. Granted, this dialogue among the rulers about how better to suppress dialogue among the ruled is essentially perverted, but it corrupts and contaminates the purity of the monologic regime. Art and historic accounts depict smart totalitarian rulers who used their wits and dialoging among each other for oppression (Fábri, 1976; Orwell, 1992; Solzhenitzin, 1974). Power corrupts. But it corrupts in both directions: making polyphonic regimes more monologic while monologic regimes more dialogic. Monologic regimes have problems with reproducing themselves as new generations of rulers and ruled join them. The Soviet totalitarian system seemed did not pass the test of such reproduction. It cracked and collapsed under pressure of increasingly powerful streams and whirlpools of dialogues that eventually destroyed the material and relational walls of the monologic regime (see a similar discussion of "prosaics" in Morson & Emerson, 1990).

CONCLUSIONS: CHRONOTOPE OF POLYPHONIC CLASSROOM REGIME

In his critique of Habermas, Linell (1998) argues against "idealistic" approaches to dialogue focusing on dialogic utopias of "good dialogue" or "authentic dialogue". Linell insists that a dialogic approach has to be descriptive, methodological, rather than prescriptive, designing (and, thus, political). Linell focuses on the dialogic property any naturally occurring human communication and, in my view, this is a very useful analysis for education

---

[17] As a Norwegian philosopher, Nils Gilje, points out in his response to my presentation of an earlier draft of this chapter at Dialogue Seminar at the University of Bergen (January 15, 2007), the black-and-white certainty of this dichotomist table by itself makes it monologic. Although, the monologue-dialogue opposition can be useful at time, we should be aware of its potential monologic danger.

because it has become obvious for many educators and educational researchers (e.g., Lemke, 1990) that there is something wrong in communication occurring in mainstream classrooms. Linell's dialogic analysis helps us focus on what is wrong. For example, Linell notices that in a naturally occurring communication, there is constantly going on a very active, emergent, and collaborative process of defining a topic of communication, which, in contrast, seems to be a very rigid, unilateral, and stagnant in many classroom communications. However, without going into the substance of Linell's particular critique of Habermas, I want to comment that education is based on design of communication and prescriptive by its nature. I argue that it is not true that any prescriptive designer stance for communication leads to excessive monologism, as Linell seems to suggest. Dialogic design of educational communication informed by naturally occurring communication, analysis of which Linell made, is possible. While Linell focused on dialogicity as an aspect of communication descriptively and methodologically, it is possible to focus on polyphony prescriptively and designedly. Bakhtin's polysemy of the notions of dialogue and monologue help us to navigate in these complex problems.

How can the polysemic notions of dialogue and monologue developed by Bakhtin be applied to educational research and practice? It seems to me that the opposition between dialogue and monologue, between monologic and dialogic pedagogies is fruitful. Dialogic pedagogy can be developed in dialogic response to abuse of monologic pedagogy. However, educational researchers and practitioners have to be careful in borrowing these notions of dialogue and monologue directly from Bakhtin. Dialogue is not always good, monologue is not always bad. The notions of dialogue and monologue are not always in oppositional relations. Such notions like (teacher's and students') agency, authority, and authorship require positive development of the concept of monologue and monologicity. Dialogic pedagogy cannot fully be developed with a strong focus on dialogic monologicity (see Morson, 2004 for the beginning of a fruitful analysis). Such phenomenon as excessive dialogism noticed by Ogbu among some marginalized minority student populations has to be further analyzed and developed.

Below I try to sketch out principles of a polyphonic classroom regime. In my view, Bakhtin's notion of axiological chronotope that he used for analysis of literary genres (Bakhtin, 1991; Bakhtin et al., 1990) is useful for analysis of pedagogical regimes in the classrooms. Bakhtin argued that literary genre is defined by how the author designed time, space, and axiology (i.e., the system of values) for his or her characters in the literary work. In formal education, it can be argued that there are two co-existing axiological chronotopes that the teacher designs. One is the ontological chronotope of "here and now" defined by 1) ontological classroom space and its arrangement (e.g., desk and wall arrangement, freedom of movement, private and public spaces in the classroom and school), 2) ontological time (i.e., rhythm between learning activities, recess, free time), and 3) ontological axiology (i.e., value systems guiding relations between the teacher and the students and among students). The other one is the semiotic chronotope of academia defined by 1) semiotic space (i.e., educational curriculum – "Where is the class now academically?"), 2) semiotic time (i.e., educational instruction – "How the curriculum is unfolded in time?"), and 3) semiotic axiology (i.e., educational philosophy – "What is counted as learning and instruction?"). These two chronotopes of formal education interact but not always compatibly between each other or even within each other (among all its three dimensions). An actual classroom can have a mixture of these two major axiological chronotope models.

In a monologic pedagogy, the ontological chronotope is aimed at constraining the student's undivided attention on the teacher's activity. The ontological space serves to restrict the student's self-initiated movements and interactions with others and to prevent the student from distraction of the outside world in order to tunnel the student's attention directly at the teacher. The space is poor and sterile. The ontological time is rigidly regimented onto equal periods and guided by the physical time of clock independent of needs of the activities. Teacher-student communication is also strictly regimented by the teacher asking answer-known questions, the student replying, and the teacher evaluating it for correctness (Mehan, 1979). The ontological axiology involves a behavioristic system of values based on a system of rewards and punishments (and medication) to modify the student's behavior in order to make it fit the teacher's expectations. The ideal student (and incidentally, the ideal parent) for the teacher is one who does exactly what the teacher expects from him or her.

The semiotic chronotope of monologic pedagogy is aimed at transmission of knowledge from the teacher to the student. The semiotic academic space is defined by a curriculum program often designed outside of the classroom by a state bureaucracy. It is based on growing agreement between the teacher and the student, on certainty, on elimination of the student's misconceptions – on the student becoming identical to the teacher so the student will answer the teacher's question and solve the teacher-presented problems exactly the same way as the teacher would answer and solve them. The semiotic academic time is defined by special sequential instruction -- "scaffolding" (Wood, Bruner, & Ross, 1976) where the gap between the teacher and the student is fragmented to smaller teacher-defined tasks that can be manageable for the student through direct instruction (e.g., lecturing and demonstration but also drills). The academic system of value in monologic pedagogy is transmission of knowledge: learning is defined by how much teacher-defined knowledge the student can retain and demonstrate when the teacher demands.

I argue that monologic pedagogy, prevalent in many conventional classrooms, is responsible for at least three major mutually related problems: alienation of students from formal education, irrelevancy of the school curricula for societal and personal development, crisis of teacher authority. Alienation of students from formal education is well documented (Eckert, 1989; Ogbu, 2003; Willis, 1981) and occurs for both institutionally successful and failing students (Varenne & McDermott, 1998), although the consequences of the alienation for these two groups are different. Both categories of the students learn in school to dislike academic learning. Irrelevancy of school curricula is documented in research on situated cognition (Lave, 1988). There is little feedback between societal practices and students' needs and forming school curricula. The crisis of teacher authority is evident in the mass exodus of novice teachers from teaching profession citing declining discipline as the number one cause of their departure (Sidorkin, 2002).

In a dialogic pedagogy, the ontological chronotope is aimed at promoting an open learning community and a crossover for students to meet many important communities (Kohl, 1970). The ontological space is open and enriched to encourage the students to initiate their own activities and develop open public forums for discussions of their inquiries with or without the teacher. The students have freedom of movement in the classroom (Rogoff et al., 2001). The boundaries between the classroom and home are fluid. The ontological time is activity driven. The activity is over not because the clock shows that the time is out but when the goal of the activity is accomplished. Learning activities often have a distributed character across participants (collaboration), time and place. The ontological axiology is shaped by focus on mutual respect between the teacher and the students and among the students and caring about each other's needs and interests. The ideal student is one who cares about other members of the classroom community (and beyond) and his/her own learning.

The semiotic chronotope of dialogic pedagogy is aimed at the student becoming (cf. "ideological becoming" Bakhtin, 1991) a more responsible and capable citizen of the world and the local communities in which he or she participates. The semiotic academic space of the polyphonic classroom involves disagreements, misunderstandings, uncertainties, and genuine information-seeking questions (Matusov, Hayes, & Drye, 2007; Matusov, Hayes, & Pluta, 2005). The semiotic academic time is defined by the teacher's guidance like provocation, mediation (mapping), evaluation, prioritization, reflection of values (meta-evaluation), facing new choices, and so on. The semiotic axiology, the educational philosophy of polyphonic classroom is a community of learners (Rogoff et al., 1996). The teacher authority – why the students should listen to the teacher – is based on the assumption that the teacher is "learner #1" in the classroom (rather than "expert #1" as in monologic pedagogy).

The purpose of polyphonic classroom is not to establish smooth, non-problematic, harmonic relations between the teacher and the students, among the students, between the students and the world; but rather to make any existing and emerging in harmony the focus of the classroom discussion and analysis. Thus, a polyphonic classroom is always in becoming – it is always on a "journey" and it is never "over there." The journey can be started by the teacher and the students from "any place" and under any condition since this, whatever unfavorable, condition can be a starting point for analysis of the students' and the teacher's lives in the classroom and beyond (Freedom Writers & Gruwell, 1999; Paley, 1992). The academic curriculum is relevant because it is based on ontological engagement of the students (DePalma, Matusov, & Smith, 2009, in press) – the students' social activism – paraphrasing the famous words of Freire (1986), "reading and writing the word to read and write the world." In the polyphonic classroom, "the world" is the immediate world of the students' (and the teacher's) local communities and *The Big World* of the past, current, and future of human civilization. The members of the classroom community are free to define and share problems and agendas in the classroom public discourse. The teacher's goal is to help the students to join *The Big Dialogue* of past cultures (Bibler, 1991) and ground the curriculum in history to understand their problems and inquiries at hand.

Chapter 6

PEDAGOGICAL CHRONOTOPES OF MONOLOGIC CONVENTIONAL CLASSROOMS: ONTOLOGY AND DIDACTICS

ABSTRACT

Using Bakhtin's conception of the chronotope, defined as the unity of space, time and axiology, I explore why monologic conventional pedagogy acquires many teachers, even those who actively resist this acquisition, and its consequences for students and teachers. Two types of chronotopes of particular relevance to the classroom ontological and didactic, are analyzed here. I analyze the two chronotopes in a videotaped case of a 30-minute read-aloud lesson of a pre-service teacher in a second grade conventional classroom. The ontological chronotope of the monologic conventional classroom is assignment-based while the didactic chronotope is based on fragmentation on independent pedagogical elements. I discuss the consequences of the fallacy of the separation between the didactic and ontological chronotopes in education and fragmentation within the didactic chronotope of independently atomized elements like instruction, curriculum, motivation, and so on. I also discuss the consequences of monologic pedagogy for alienation of students from learning, relevance of school curricula and teacher authority.

...what might on the surface appear to be untrained teaching was in fact the active response of some of the best teachers observed as they confronted the organization which rewarded their ability to control students more than their ability to "really teach" (McNeil, 1986, p. 211).

Across the contemporary world there great difference in curriculum, but the actual appearance and organization of schools is similar (Shipman, 1971, p. 52).

Many conventional classrooms are "orderly but lifeless." The teachers try to follow their pre-design scripts and tend to avoid controversial topics and off-script discussions (Nystrand, 1997, p. 3). Why is it that monologism is such an attractive, and partially successful, educational philosophy for most conventional schools (I borrowed and adopted this question from Linell, 1998, p. 278; Still & Costall, 1991, p. 55, who raised it for language sciences and cognitivism)? Hargreaves (1989) argues that traditional teaching is not so much defined by teachers' attitudes based on a transmission of knowledge educational philosophy, although such attitudes can contribute to that as well, and not by outmoded teaching skills that many teachers accept uncritically, although that also can contribute to the problem, and not by the teachers' resistance to new teaching methods, although such resistance can really exist as well, but rather traditional teaching is defined by conditions of the teachers' labor that push teachers with diverse attitudes, diverse educational philosophies, and diverse teaching skills into doing this practice because it is much more difficult (if not impossible in some cases) to do something else. Using the chaos theory (Prigogine & Stengers, 1984), it is possible to say that labor conditions in traditional schools create "a strong attractor" for teachers to organize their teaching practice in a traditional way. In a traditional school, teaching practice is like a coin on a funnel in the Discovery Museum of San Francisco: it does not matter where the coin starts, with what the initial speed it has, with what the initial direction it moves toward, -- after several spiral circles it will finish up in the center of the funnel or get completely out of the funnel surface falling on the floor. Similarly, majority teachers despite their initial inclinations and callings either finish up becoming traditional teachers or leave the teaching profession all together. Very few manage to redefine their work ecology or find innovative schools that would support their innovative, dialogic teaching. This chapter investigates how the "attractor" or the "funnel" of a traditional teaching practice is made to acquire many teachers some of whom actively resist to such acquisition (as an active educator, I personally have experienced and still experience great power of it on me).

Jackson (1968) defined a major challenge for teachers in modern schools as teaching a crowd of students who are not voluntarily gather for instruction while gaining their cooperation (see also Waller, 1932, p. 236). As Lampert points out, "Teachers face some students who do not want to learn what they want to teach, some who already know it, or think they do, and some who are poorly prepared to study what is taught" (Lampert, 2001, p. 1). "The teachers are supposed to juggle subject matter, student skills, and at the same time student behavior and the technicalities fo grades, attendance and course credit' (McNeil, 1986, p. 210). This institutional situation that the teachers face every day in schools is radically different from situations portrayed by Plato in his Socratic dialogues with exception of Socrates' dialogue with the Slave in Meno (Plato, 1997). Socratic participants were mainly free citizens who could legitimately walk out and leave Socrates at their will at any time (and they did), they could talk or not talk at their will, they could define the topic of their conversations with or without Socrates even if Socrates did not appreciate the topics, they could judge and evaluate Socrates and openly challenge his public reputation, and so on. In sum, their participation was free, voluntarily, and open. Socrates achieved (or failed to achieve) cooperation of his free participants mainly through his dialogues themselves – through instruction and curriculum of the dialogues. Free participation of his interlocutors guided Socrates' instruction.

Mandatory schools promote conditions for forced student participation. The students cannot legitimately leave the classroom at their will, they cannot stop coming to school, they cannot talk at their will, they cannot define their own activities, they cannot evaluate the teacher and openly challenge his/her public reputation, and so on. Despite all these limitations of the students' freedom, the teacher needs their cooperation without which teaching is impossible and reduced to chaos so feared by the teachers. Unlike Socrates, the modern teacher does not face with students systematically asking questions at the beginning of the lesson that define the lessons like "what is the origin of virtues". The schoolteacher has to create and sustain the focus on the "crowd" of his/her students "imprisoned in the classroom" (Jackson, 1968, p. 9) during the lesson (Lampert, 2001).

Pedagogies differ in their promoted relationship between the teacher's instruction and the students' cooperation. I find that Bakhtin's literary notion of *chronotope* defining specific of literary genres can be useful for addressing this question of how pedagogy is defined through everyday classroom practices. Bakhtin claimed that, "The chronotope in **literature** has an intrinsic *generic* significance. It can even be said that it is precisely the chronotope that defines **genre** and **generic** distinctions, for in **literature** the primary category in the chronotope is time. The chronotope as a formally constitutive category determines to a significant degree the **image of man in literature** as well. The **image of man** is always intrinsically chronotopic (bold indicates specifically literary terms used by Bakhtin, italics is original)" (Bakhtin, 1991, pp. 84-85). My translation of Bakhtin's statement for education would run approximately in the following way, "The chronotope in **formal education** has an intrinsic *pedagogic* significance. It can even be said that it is precisely the chronotope that defines **pedagogy** and **pedagogical** distinctions **among different pedagogical regimes of schools with different educational philosophies**, for in **institutionalized education** the primary category in the chronotope is time. The chronotope as a formally constitutive category determines to a significant degree the **identity of the teacher and students in education** as well. The **identity of all participants in school** is always intrinsically chronotopic" (the bold indicates my translation of Bakhtin's literary terms into educational ones). Unlike many educational scholars before (e.g., Lemke, 1990; Rockwell, 2000), here I use Bakhtin's term "genre" not in a context of discourse where the term originated but as a metaphor for "educational philosophy." Classroom chronotope helps to describe and analyze classroom practice.

AXIOLOGICAL CHRONOTOPE IN EDUCATION

Bakhtin borrowed his notion of "chronotope" from biology and Einstein's theory of relativity (Bakhtin, 1991, p. 84) and defined them as the unity of space and time of dramatic events through which any literary genre can realize itself. However, in his earlier work on "Author and hero in aesthetic activity" (Bakhtin et al., 1990) he defined the unity as the triplet of space, time, and axiology (the latter refers to the nature of the characters' values and value judgments). Similarly, Vygotsky insisted that for human existence, besides the four physical dimensions (i.e., three dimensions of space and one dimension of time) there is the fifth dimension of meaning (van der Veer & Valsiner, 1991). It is important to mention that even in his later work on chronotope, Bakhtin continued discussions of characters' meaning-making processes and their identities defining the genre of the literary work at hand (Bakhtin, 1991). Following early Bakhtin's and Vygotsky's insights, I define the axiological chronotope as the unity of space, time, and axiology. Although this focus on time, space, and axiology is not new in educational research (cf., for example, McLaren, 1993), in my view, Bakhtin's notion of chronotope can provide new analytical tools for their unity.

Studying literary work of Dostoevsky, Bakhtin noticed that drama among Dostoevsky's characters occurred not in one, like in a vast majority of literary works of many other authors, but in two spheres. Usually, in literary work, the dramatic events occur in *ontological* sphere of characters – in the sphere of their lives expressed by the book's plot (e.g., a boy and a girl of marriageable age fall in love only to be separated by hostile circumstances and obstacles that they successfully overcome, marry, and live happily ever after (see a description of the plot schema of Greek romance in Bakhtin, 1991, p. 87)). However, in case of Dostoevsky's major novels, the dramatic events also occur in another sphere – *ideological* – the sphere of the characters' ideas (Bakhtin & Emerson, 1999). In Dostoevsky's artwork, chronotopes were ideologico-ontological as the characters tested their ideas (and ideas of the other characters) with their lives and trajectories of their lives formed ideas. For example, in Crime and Punishment, Raskolnokov's idea about a genius' stepping over the boundaries of morality was tested by his crime of killing two old women and deep consequences that this crime had on his life and lives of people around him. The drama of ideas was intertwines with the drama of lives.

Bakhtin (1991, pp. 254-257) noticed that any literary artwork occurs in two chronotopes: the chronotope of the real world of the author living and writing the artwork and the chronotope of the imagined (or reported) world, in which the characters of the artwork live,

> Thus we can with relative clarity sense in the segmentation of ancient epic songs the chronotope of the singer and his audience or the chronotope of storytelling in traditional tales. But even in the segmentation of a modern literary work we sense the chronotope of the represented world as well as the chronotope of the readers and creators of the work. That is, we get a mutual interaction between the world represented in the work and the world outside the work. This interaction is pin pointed very precisely in certain elementary features of composition: every work has a beginning and an end, but these topes that can never fuse with each other of be identical to each other but are at the same time, interrelated and indissolubly tired up with each other. We might put it as follows: before us are two events – the event that is narrated in the work and the event of narration itself (we ourselves participate in the latter, as listeners and readers); these events take place in efferent times (which are marked by different durations as well) and in different places, but at the same times these two events are indissolubly in the totality of all its events, including the external material givenness of the work, and its text, and the world represented in the text, and the author-creator and the listener or reader, thus we perceive the fullness of the work in all its wholeness and indivisibility, but at the same time we understand the diversity of the elements that constitute it (pp. 254-255).

I argue that in institutionalized education, the participants – the teacher and the students – often also participate in two related dramatic spheres at once. The first sphere is *didactic*, where curricular ideas collide with each other. The didactic chronotope of academia is defined by 1) semiotic space (i.e., educational curriculum – "Where is the class now academically?"), 2) semiotic time (i.e., educational instruction – "How the curriculum is unfolded in time?"), and 3) semiotic axiology (i.e., educational philosophy and evaluation – "What is counted as successful learning and instruction?"). The second dramatic sphere is *ontological*, where drama of the participants' lives occurs in the local and global contexts of "here and now". The ontological chronotope is defined by 1) ontological classroom space and its arrangement (e.g., desk and wall arrangement, freedom of movement, private and public spaces in the classroom and school), 2) ontological time (i.e., rhythm between learning activities, recess, free time), and 3) ontological axiology (i.e., value and evaluation systems guiding relations between the teacher and the students and among students and people outside of the classroom relevant to them). These two chronotopes of formal education interact but not always compatibly between each other or even within each other (among all its three dimensions). An actual classroom can have a mixture of these two major axiological chronotope models. The axiological chronotope in education is defined in table 1 below.

Below I examine educational chronotopes of monologic conventional classrooms and polyphonic classrooms. By monologic conventional classroom, I mean pedagogy that is shaped by excessive monologism and embedded in conventional institutions of schooling that also shape schools in its own ways (e.g., trying to make them economically efficient that may or may not go along with excessive monologism). By polyphonic classroom, I mean classroom that are shaped by dialogicity of internally persuasive discourse described by Bakhtin (Bakhtin, 1991; A. F. Ball & Freedman, 2004; Matusov, 2007).

Table 6. Axiological chronotope in education (extracted from Bakhtin's work (Bakhtin, 1991; Bakhtin et al., 1990) and translated into education)

	Events	Space	Time	Axiology
Generic definitions	What dramas and collisions are participants involved with each other?	Where do dramatic events take place and unfold? Where are participants? What is available and unavailable for them and how they perceive it?	What happens? How do dramatic events unfold? How do the participants change? What defines rhythm of the changes? What is the shape of the changes? How are the changes perceived by the participants?	How do the participants make sense of their actions, deeds, events, and the world through defining the goals, identities, values, and judgments for themselves and others?
Didactic sphere	Drama of curricular ideas	Academic curricula (where dramas of the ideas occur)	Management of learning and instruction (the form of changes: what is going on)	Definition of academic success and failure
Ontological sphere	Drama among the immediate participants and between immediate and remote participants	Classroom environment embedded in other spaces of the world	Management of the participants' relations (e.g., classroom management)	Definition of happiness and unhappiness with regard to school

CHRONOTOPES OF MONOLOGIC CONVENTIONAL PEDAGOGY

To apply the notion of educational axiological chronotope to an analysis of monologic conventional classroom, I will use Bakhtin's parallel analysis of the chronotope of the Greek romance (Bakhtin, 1991, pp. 86-110). The conventional lessons are remarkably similar to each other, and are in fact composed of the very same elements (instructional steps): individual lessons differ from each other only in number of such elements, their proportional weight within the whole lesson and they way they are combined. One can easily construct a typical composite schema of this lesson, taking into account the most important individual deviations and variations. Such schema would go something like this (this verbatim is taken and modified from Bakhtin, 1991, p. 87).

The lesson begins with the "all-knowing" teacher and the "ignorant" students assembling in a closed space insolated from the outside world: its noise, demands, and people for a certain amount of time. Classroom walls, classroom door, and classroom windows (to a less degree) are brackets of academic learning from the rest of the world (Lortie, 1975) in order not to distract the ignorant students from all-knowing teacher and the teaching. As the lesson going by, the curricular gap between the all-knowing teacher and ignorant students is decreasing as knowledge moving from the "all-knowing" teacher to the "ignorant" students. The ignorant students are moving in the space of curricular knowledge to become like the all-knowing teacher who causes and helps their movements by organizing new knowledge taught in the lesson in smaller bits of information that the ignorant students are able to swallow and digest. The monologic conventional teaching is usually organized in the format of lecturing, modeling, asking known-answer questions to lead, probe, and test the students. After the material is explained by the teacher, the students are required practicing the taught material by applying to learning task in school and during homework. At the end of the instruction that may take several lessons, the students are supposed to "know" the taught material which can be demonstrated on the teacher's demand via exams and tests that finally define good and bad students with regard of the taught material. Although, students are led from grade to grade, from class to class, from subject to subject, from topic to topic, from test to test, from exam to exam, but classroom routine remains very much the same. The monologic conventional school is passing by its students (Ogbu, 2003). The students rarely discuss outside of the class what didactically happens inside class and they rarely discuss inside class as part of their lessons that happens in their lives outside of the class (Kennedy, 2005). Such is the schema for the basic components of monologic conventional teaching.

The Ontological Chronotope of Monologic Pedagogy

In a monologic conventional pedagogy, the ontological chronotope is aimed at constraining the student's undivided attention on the teacher's activity (Lortie, 1975). The ontological space serves to restrict the student's self-initiated movements and interactions with others and to prevent the student from distraction of the outside world in order to tunnel the student's attention directly at the teacher. The space is poor and sterile. The ontological time is rigidly regimented onto equal periods and guided by the physical time of clock independent of needs of the activities. Teacher-student communication is also strictly regimented by the teacher asking answer-known questions, the student replying, and the teacher evaluating it for correctness (Mehan, 1979). The ontological axiology involves a behavioristic system of values based on a system of rewards and punishments (and medication) to modify the student's behavior in order to make it fit the teacher's expectations. The ideal student (and incidentally, the ideal parent) for the teacher is one who does exactly what the teacher expects from him or her.

Ontological Space of Monologic Conventional Pedagogy:
Unilateral Teacher Control

Ontological space in the classroom provides both constraints and affordances for the participants' activities and communication (Lampert, 2001). Ontological space of monologic conventional pedagogy is defined by *the teacher's control and the students' degrees of freedom* understood negatively in the context of the teacher's control as deviation from the control or disruption. In an ideal monologic classroom, the teacher has 100% of control while the students have 0% degree of freedom. At its extreme, the students' self-control has to become habitual, "In creating a condition of order in the classroom, it is essential that every rule laid down be adhered to rigidly, unremittingly. The acme of good discipline is reached when the conditions of order are preserved automatically, without thought or judgment on the pupils' part. In other words, a classroom that is well disciplined has the conditions of good order reduced to habit. But the law of habit-building operates here with unrelenting certainty. To make the conditions of order automatic, every slightest exception must immediately be noted and corrected" (Bagley, 1907, p. 95). The ideal students' attention should be on the teacher, their mind should be on the academic subject at hand (on the teacher's task), their hands should be on the desk, and their pockets are empty 100% of time (Jackson, 1968). As one elementary school teacher that I observed said, reprimanding her student in the class, "Nothing should prevent the teacher from teaching and the students from learning." Everything disturbing the students' attention should be left at home: their toys, their too bright cloths, their interests, their concerns, their relations, and their dreams. Coming to monologic conventional school, the students should be ready to attend the teacher and say and do what the teacher expect them to say and do. However, students are often far from this ideal. As Lampert notices, "students come into the classroom with multiple purposes: making friends, protecting themselves, arranging dates, earning spending money and so on" (2001, p. 92). These purposes of the students present a challenge to a monologic conventional teacher[1]. A Russian innovative educator (theoretician and practitioner) and famous writer, Leo Tolstoy, described his tendency of monologic conventional classroom in the following way in the mid of the nineteen century,

> Schools are established not as places where it is convenient for the children to study, but where teachers may teach in comfort. Conversation, motion, and merriment are all necessary if children are to study. But these are not convenient for the teacher, and so in schools – which are built according to the same plans as prisons—questions, conversation, and motion are prohibited (Tolstoy & Blaisdell, 2000, p. 176).

That is why classroom space is much of the teacher's attention and design in monologic classroom.

The organization of physical and semiotic space in a monologic classroom is designed in such a way to increase the teacher control while decreasing the students' degree of freedom to move, communicate, and attend. As one Australian manufacturer and designer of innovative

---

[1] Actually, in her book, Lampert goes on to say that "within this frame, we [i.e., teachers -- EM] might construe the work of teaching as adding the studying of school subjects to these purposes [by the students – EM] and keeping it prominent, at least during school hours" (2001, pp. 92-93). Thus, Lampert suggests working with and within students' purposes rather than against them. This point (among others) makes her pedagogy contrast to and deviate from a monologic conventional pedagogy.

classroom furniture wrote to me, "I find when I am talking to teachers [about the design of classroom furniture and classroom arrangement] that control is the major issue. Some of them are so adamant about their needs that they refuse to address other ideas such as [how] the classrooms affect on the ability of a student to learn" (personal communication, November 20, 2005). In accord with this account, McLaren defines the spatial arrangement of a monologic conventional classroom as sociofugal, "the spatial arrangement of the suite was *sociofugal* as opposed to *sociopetal* – that is, the arrangements were designed to inhibit social interaction rather than to promote it" (McLaren, 1993, p. 197, the italics is original).

The classroom spatial arrangement both defines and describes the nature of the classroom pedagogy. Several decades ago, Dewey made the following observation,

> Some few years ago I was looking about the school supply stores in the city, trying to find desks and chairs which seemed thoroughly suitable from all points of view -- artistic, hygienic, and educational -- to the needs of the children. We had a great deal of difficulty in finding what we needed, and finally one dealer, more intelligent that the rest, made this remark: "I am afraid we have not what you want. You want something at which the children may work; these are all for listening." That tells the story of traditional education. Just as the biologist can take a bone or two and reconstruct the whole animal, so, if we put before the mind's eye the ordinary schoolroom, with its rows of ugly desks placed in geometrical order, crowded together so that there shall be as little moving room as possible, desks almost all of the same size, with just space enough to hold books, pencils, and paper, add a table, some chairs, the bare walls, and possibly a few pictures, we can reconstruct the only educational activity that can possibly go on in such a place. It is all made "'for listening" . . . (Dewey, 1956, p. 31)

Further I will analyze a Soviet elementary classroom at the end of the 1960s. Although a bit outmoded, the following example of classroom space exemplifies and makes vividly visible the spatial principles of the ontological chronotope of monologic pedagogy.

You see 2nd grade of Moscow Soviet school in 1969. Students are 8-9 years old. There were 48 students in the classroom. You can see only 45 students on the photo (you can count all of them yourself), three students were absent on the day of taking the picture. Because of the lack of desks, it was not uncommon for three students sitting at two-student desks. You can see three students sitting at one desk on the right row at the third desk. Not all Moscow schools were crowded as this one but it was not untypical school at this time as far as I know. The high crowdness of this classroom reflects not a pedagogical or organizational value but economic one: high student-teacher ratio like having shifts decreased the cost of the education.

Ontological space of a classroom consists of things, bodies, and available semiotics. In a monological conventional classroom, things, space, bodies, and semiotics are organized in such a way to promote the highest possible control by the teacher and limit students' degrees of freedom as much as possible. In this particular Soviet monologic classroom[2], there was nothing on the naked walls of the classroom to prevent student distraction. Students' desk placement in the classroom was the teacher's careful consideration. The teacher tried tightly control the classroom to minimize unsanctioned communication among the students. The rows of the desks provide freedom of the teacher's movement in the classroom, the high level of surveillance of the students, and highly limited student-student communicative contact. In a monological classroom, the space is hierarchically organized with the students often facing the teacher. The position of the teacher defines "the teacher spot" (any adult who moves to this spot in the classroom can be automatically considered by the students as a teacher, McLaren, 1993, p. 199). The classroom space has a bottle-like shape of the desks communicating the idea that knowledge is expected to be poured from the teacher to the students. The space is monofocal and sociofugal. In the class on the photo, friends were not allowed to sit closer than at least one desk in between them. In the classroom above, friends were sitting at least two desks apart.

You may notice that boys and girls were placed in the "checker" order again to minimize same-gender contacts among the students. On average, there were rather hostile relations between boys and girls supported by the teacher. Boys and girls often fought for the desk space, tattletale on each other to the teacher for violation of the teacher's rules, and teased each other. The teacher often promoted of gender competitions in everyday school life by constant comparison of boys and girls behavior and by using gender for organization of school activities (e.g., lining boys and girls separately). Sometimes, the teacher reprimanded students by using opposite gender to shame the student (e.g., to a boy, "you behave as a girl"). Thus, gender was used to promote further the teacher control of the classroom (cf. Thorne, 1993).

The most problematic students (from the teacher point of view) were placed at the first desks (e.g., ones that smiled). The classroom atmosphere is serious and business-like. The students' bodies are part of the space of ontological classroom chronotope. Holden hands were supposed to be on the desk all the time when the students did not allowed to use them to prevent the students' body movements as a source for another distraction. On the desks, students had to have a textbook, the report book ("dnevnik") where the teacher put current

---

[2] I chose this particular monologic classroom from the past not to argue that all monologic conventional classroom looks the same and have the same ontological space but to demonstrate most dramatic and contrasting features of the ontological space of a monologic conventional classroom.

grades and notes for parents, a notebook, and a box with a pen, pencil, and eraser. The students' schoolbags were inside of desks – the access to the schoolbags was strictly controlled by the teacher.

All students wore uniforms (different for boys and girls). Historically, the design of uniforms seemed to be shaped by the vision of the Soviet Communist Party for future role of the students (especially for boys). In Stalin's time, the school uniform of boys reminded military uniform; in Khrushchev's time, the school uniform of boys became similar to typical worker's robe; in Brezhnev's time, the school uniform of boys was changed again – it became similar to a suite of Soviet functionary. The elementary school class was divided onto several "Little Stars" with some formal structure set by the teacher. Almost all the 2nd graders (but not all) belonged to the Children of October Communist organization (you can see little pins on the students in the form of star with a picture of young Lenin in the center). The portrait of Lenin was always above the blackboard (not seen on the photo). Thus, the official identity of the students was defined by their gender, by official Communist political ideology, by official role in "Little Star"[3], and by affiliation to a particular grade, defined chronologically, and to the classroom.

In monologic classroom, the teacher constantly regulates ontological space for the students: who can and who cannot open a book at the given moment, stand up, talk, turn his or her head, leave the classroom for a restroom, access schoolbag, pass a pencil, and so on. As the official controller of space, movements, communication, and things, the teacher gains power to grant or not to grant student-desired objects and actions. This distribution of the social good by the teacher in the monological classroom (Gee, 1996) creates bargaining power in negotiation of students' cooperation and compliance.

On the first glance, the ontological space of the monological classroom is fully controlled by the teacher but this impression is wrong, at least, on three accounts. First, the teacher utilizes many pre-existing constraints that he or she finds in the classroom that he or she did not design him or herself. For example, the teacher did not design the room or desks or walls or gender or political ideology and organizations but he or she uses them for promoting his or her control and limit students' degrees of freedom. Second, other institutional goals often interfere in organization of efficient ontological space in monological classroom. For example, for promoting teacher control and further limiting degrees of students' freedom, it is a good idea to reduce student-teacher classroom ratio. However, institution tries to minimize of economic costs of operating the school by increasing the student-teacher ratio and thus making teacher control more difficult. Also, systematic interruptions in school live caused by political and ideological events disrupted the order created by the teacher. A portrait of Lenin hanging above the blackboard could distract a student's attention from the teacher: it might be preferable for the teacher not to have this distraction but the ideological function of the school did not allow the teacher to go along with this wish of total control.

Finally, the students also affected ontological space in monological classrooms by tacit and open violations of the teacher control. Students' body and mind movements remain

---

[3] The most memorable roles (and probably most desirable roles for the children) in the "Little Star" were "zven'evoj", the leader of a "Little Star" responsible for lining the group on numerous official school meetings (ceremonial parades), and "sanitar", a member of "Little Star" checking hygiene of the members of his/her "Little Star" at the beginning of the class day. One more role for the student was "starosta" (literally "community elder") of the class (the class leader) who was a mediator between the teacher and the students in the class.

undisciplined: the students move their heads, close their eyes, do not look at the teacher, turn around, fart, smell, make aloud sighs and other bodily sounds, laugh, yawn, become hungry, drop a notebook from the desk, daydream, pay attention to each other and what is going on outside of the classroom, fight and tease each other, chat, send, pass and read messages, and so on. In extreme cases, the students pee and poop themselves, cry, fall asleep, fall from their seats, sing, get sick, sexually harass female and male students, and even masturbate. The students bring unsanctioned objects from home (e.g., toys). They alternate and utilize sanctioned objects for their own unsanctioned use. For example, I remember how my classmates and I used pieces of blotting paper from our notebooks and tubes from ball pens to make spitting guns for playing secret mock wars during some of the lessons. We were doodling and drawing battles at the back of our textbooks. We were sending paper messages to each other in the class – the practice that I also observed in Japanese classrooms. We alternated our uniform. For example, we put pins and colorful "little eyes" made out of melted plastic isolators of phone wires on the other side of the lapel. We smuggled in the classroom our friendship affiliations and adversaries that potentially presented threats for the teacher's control. We also "brought" social problems in the classroom. For example, the classroom on the photo was ethnically diverse consisting mainly of Russians but also Ukrainians, Tatars, Poles, and Jews (and mixed ethnicities). Ethnical minority children were often verbally and physically harassed and abused by other kids (including other minority students). Some parents told children to distrust and to stay away from minority kids (e.g., "Don't play with them!" "Tatars are thieves and dirty," "Jews are cunning and treacherous", "Ukrainians are stupid"[4]). Ethnic tensions erupted openly or tacitly in the classroom dynamically shaping its semiotic space.

In sum, any spatial part – physical or semiotic – of the ontological chronotope of a monologic conventional classroom can be both an object of the teacher's control and a subject of the students' distraction. For example, a textbook can be used for the teacher's control of the student's attention (e.g., in the teacher's command, "Please open the textbook on page 37") or for starting a mock fight with the desk neighbor sitting next to you by intentional and demonstrative shifting the textbook on his or her "desk territory." The teacher's attempts to decrease the students' degrees of freedom often produce new degrees of freedom and new opportunities for the students.

Ontological Time of Monologic Conventional Pedagogy: Assignment-Time

Ontological time of monologic conventional pedagogy is *assignment-time*. It is *monochromatic time* – emphasizing one task at time, segmentation, promptness, schedules, and unilateral control (E. T. Hall, 1983; Hargreaves, 1994; McLaren, 1993). "School is a place where things often happen not because students want them to, but because it is time for them to occur" (Jackson, 1968, p. 13). "Adherence to a time schedule requires that activities often begin before interest is aroused and terminate before the interest disappear" (Jackson, 1968, p. 16). Similarly, Erickson elaborated on the difference between two Greek terms used for time: *kairos* as opportunities for something to happen (like in Ecclesiastes, "A time to plant and a time pluck up what is planted") and *kronos* as undifferentiated duration of decontextualized clock time (Erickson, 2003, p. x). The latter is the organization of time in monologic conventional classroom. It is not the case that educational activity takes time in a

---

[4] I do not use derogatory ethnic terms in these examples that Soviet adults often used in that time.

monologic conventional classroom, as in Socrates' dialogues where time was *polychromatic*, but, in reverse, educational activities have to be squeezed and filled out the regimented lesson time rigidly defined by the school institution. Assignment is defined by American Heritage Dictionary as "assigned task." The teacher levies a series of big and small, nested and sequential *assigned tasks* on the students during the lesson period (e.g., "All eyes on me", "Listen to me", solving a problem, answering a question, reading a textbook, doing worksheet). The role of the teacher in a monologic conventional classroom is a "taskmaster" rather than a helper for the student-initiatated work (Waller, 1932) – a helper, who starts where the student is and leads the student someplace else (Fantini & Weinstein, 1969; Silberman, 1971, p. 97). In a monological conventional classroom "what is counted" is "that students always appeared busy, hard at work, and 'attending to the task'" (McLaren, 1993, p. 219).

The assigned tasks have four important components defined by the teacher. Each task assigned by the teacher has its: 1) *product* that has to be evident to the teacher (e.g., the students look at the teacher, the students look like reading the assigned textbook, accurately completed worksheet, the correct answer to the teacher's question, the correct replies to a test), 2) *efforts* and engagement expected from the students to achieve the assigned task (e.g., listening, reading, solving a problem, answering, finding an answer, guessing, writing), 3) *constrains* defining "the proper" ways of accomplishing the assigned task (e.g., using a textbook, not talking with peers, not asking for help), and 4) *consequences* of accomplishing or not accomplishing the task (e.g., good or bad grades, merit or demerit points, praises or disapproval, awards or punishments). I define "assigned task" after Doyle's notion of "academic task" (Doyle, 1986b, pp. 365-366) who identifies similar 4 aspects[5], however, do not necessarily view the teacher's assigned task as an academic task. Thus, Doyle's academic tasks are a subset of my "assigned tasks."

Some conventional lessons have only one big assigned task: to listen to the lecture and take notes – like many college lectures, I observed. But some lessons, especially with younger students who are probably not yet turned in well-disciplined conventional students, involved a big number of assigned tasks. For example, I analyzed a videotaped Read Aloud lesson in a second grade of a public school. The teacher read and discussed an information book, Animals in Winter by Henrietta Bancroft, about how some wild animals prepare to winter with 22 second graders sitting on carpet around the teacher (in a quadrant sector) who had the book and a poster chart for writing the students' prior knowledge and guesses of how animals listed in the book prepare for winter. The videotaped lesson lasted 30 and half minutes (1831 seconds). For this time, I counted 161 assigned tasks that the teacher fired at the students or about 5.3 assigned tasks per minute (a task per about 11.4 seconds) on average. The assigned tasks by their frequency and nature constitute rhythm in the ontological time of a monological conventional classroom.

The majority of the assigned tasks had some instructional aspect 48% like asking questions about animals, reading the book, showing book picture requiring for the children sense making and comprehension; 39% of the assigned tasks involved managing communication – who was allowed to talk and who was not allowed to talk at the given moment (cf. the comment by Philips, 1993 about the switchboard operator function of the

---

[5] Although Doyle's original terminology of the aspects is somewhat different: product, operations, resources, and significance, I follow him in spirit.

teacher in a conventional classroom); and 21% of the assigned tasks were involved classroom management – setting classroom rules, asking the students to put down their hands, reprimanding some students for being off task (very rarely) or unsanctioned providing an answer, and so on. Some task had several aspects at once. For example, the teacher explained the meaning of the word "attentive" (i.e., instructional aspect) while she was going through classroom rules that the students had to follow during the lesson (i.e., classroom management aspect). Twenty nine percent of all assigned tasks involved the teacher asking questions – about half of them were open-ended questions. Most of the tasks were verbal 87% while fewer were non-verbal 21% like placing index figure to the mouth to show a student to be quiet (some were both verbal and non-verbal). About 42% of the assigned tasks were targeted to specific students, 79% were explicit tasks while 23% were tacit (some were both for different aspects of the task). An example of a tacit task was the teacher's tacit request to listen to her reading the book when she took a book and started reading it.

Probably the most interesting part of the analysis of the teacher's assigned tasks is about the nature of the tasks' transition and justification of the tasks. I observed and coded three types of the transition: "abrupt" 75%, "reactive" 16%, and "justified" only 10%, of all transitions. Let me provide examples of abrupt, unjustified, unilateral transitions. At the beginning of the lesson immediately after discussing the class rules, the teacher asked the students how people prepare for winter. Without knowing the book, it was impossible for the students to make a sense of why the teacher asked this question. Similarly, when the teacher shifted from one animal to another in activation of prior knowledge, the students could not know that the animals were those that the book was focused and in the order of the book presented. There was also unilateral, abrupt, and unjustified nature of how the teacher called out the students – unjustified from the point of view of the students (and the observer – the teacher might have some justification, of course). Some transitions were reactive to some teacher-desired or (mostly) -undesired behavior. Finally, very few transitions were justified. For example, the teacher showed a book picture of a pika after the students told that they did not know this animal. Only 4% of the teacher's assigned tasks, she provided the rational for the task to the students. For example, after the teacher asked the students to brainstorm about how people can help animals to prepare for winter so the students would write letters with advice to their friends in a future lesson, some students started telling interesting stories about animals. To put the students back on the track defined by teacher, she said, "We are not going to tell our stories. I want to hear things we're going to do [to help animals to prepare for winter] because we're going to write a letter about… [and] we need to brainstorm some idea." Thus, she did not only assign a task of not telling animal stories but also explained why they had to focus on another task instead.

Bloome and Katz (1997) who argue that chronotopes of traditional monologic classrooms remind adventure-chronotope of Ancient Greek Romance novels described by Bakhtin,

> …in some classrooms the school day may be implicitly conceptualized similar to "adventure-time": children and teachers leave their homes, have a series of adventures and overcome various obstacles in the classroom, and are reunited with their families essentially unchanged at the end of the school day. In other classrooms, time and space may be implicitly conceptualized as components of each individual's private life, internal to the person. The individual passes through time and space measured by how they affect and change the student. Within such a conception of time and space, it is the internal world that evolves and changes; the

external world -- the social and political world -- is untouched. In other classrooms, time and space may be implicitly conceptualized in terms of social action on the world outside the classroom. The school year is divided into community projects, and school time and space become redefined by community time and space. Another way in which time and space might be conceptualized is as an attribute of the individual, with each student having so much time and space that he/she can exchange for other items of value, so that the passing of time and the use of space is not so much an arena within which to act but rather a tool with which to act.

Unlike a novel, in which the chronotope may be thought through and well organized, classroom chronotopes are not necessarily coherent or monolithic. There may be several competing chronotopes, and chronotopes may vary across different situations within the same classroom. Further, there has been too little research on conceptions of time and space in classrooms to be able to characterize them the way a literary theorist like Bakhtin might characterize the chronotopes of a particular literary period. In this article, our purpose is merely to raise questions about how classroom chronotopes may be implicated in school literacy practices and in how some students experience difficulties with reading and writing.

Every literacy practice, including those at school, is grounded in a cultural conception of time and space. It is not just how students use time and space to read and write or how time and space constrain their reading and writing, but rather how conceptions of time and space define reading and writing practices, define readers and writers, and define reading and writing difficulties. For example, if the classroom chronotope is similar to "adventure-time," classroom literacy practices become adventures and obstacles to overcome, i.e., things that happen to the student without changing him or her (in the sense of character development or personal evolution). Reading and writing difficulties are obstacles the student was not able to overcome; time stops, and the student is stuck in that space. If time and space in the classroom are defined as goods to be accumulated and exchanged, then classroom literacy practices become consumer items to be acquired through barter. Reading and writing difficulties, within such a chronotope, are the lack of sufficient goods (time and space) to make the exchange, and the remediation of reading and writing difficulties becomes the provision of additional goods (time and space) or the bartering for social practices other than literacy practices. If the classroom chronotope is defined by community time and space (in terms of social action on the world outside the classroom), classroom literacy practices become tools for manipulating time and space, and reading and writing difficulties are defined by the inability of students to take action on the world and to make changes (pp. 216-217).

In sum, like in the adventure-time chronotope of Ancient Greek Romance novels described by Bakhtin (1991, p. 92), in the assignment-time ontological chronotope of monologic conventional classroom, the sequence of assigned tasks has unilateral, abrupt, and arbitrary character while monologic conventional teachers expect predictability, conformity, and docility from their students (McLaren, 1993). As Waller argued, "The teacher has, and should have, the advantage of unpredictability. Students do not know what his next move will be; they do not know what he is thinking, or why; they are ignorant of what he is thinking of them, and they do not know whether he is going to tell them or not" (Waller, 1932, p. 237). The students are not supposed to participate in defining the next assigned task. When the teacher verbally demarcates the end of one assigned task and beginning of the next assigned task, he or she uses the words reflecting both abruptness and unilateralism of the transition such as "now", "OK", "so", "but", and "I want you to…" (or "please do for me…"). Not having topical transitions is very typical for contrived hierarchical activities with a monologic discourse organization (Linell, 1998, pp. 192-193). Students or any external observer, for that matter, rarely can infer the next assigned task unless the assigned tasks highly routinized in the classroom (like raising hands after the teacher asks a question) – what McLaren (1993) calls a "student state" ritual.

I speculate that such a vast density of teacher's assigned tasks during the lesson and especially the abrupt, unilateral, and unjustified nature of the task transitions serve for the teacher's unilateral control of the classroom. Keeping the students busy and dependant on the teacher for their classroom activities promotes the teacher's flow. As the National Education Association volume on classroom discipline advised the teachers, "*Plan the lesson*. Be ready to use the first minute of class time. If you get Johnny busy right away, he has no time to cook up interesting ideas that do not fit to the class situation" (Hunt, 1969; cited in Silberman, 1971, p. 133). According Lortie's interviews of teachers, "It appears that teachers want to establish and maintain a time-bound but definite monopoly over students' attention and engagement" (Lortie, 1975, p. 170). Each assigned task, even a question, is a command to do or not to do something. It is aimed at grabbing the students' attention and at commanding their efforts. Even when there is only one supertask overall the lesson like listen to the lecture and take notes, there are many thematic transitions in the lecture that are often abrupt, unilateral, and unjustified. Many school textbooks have a similar type of thematic transitions. My colleagues and I (Matusov et al., 2002) described this guidance common in conventional schools as "directing actions, without rationale" (cf. also "representational directives", Minick, 1993). It creates both unilateral control and conditions for it by hiding the big picture of the teacher's direction and its purpose from the students. Since the students cannot access the big picture, they are left to their own devices with trying to guess what exactly the teacher wants from them, look for patterns of the teacher's requests, and follow the teacher's lead without challenging it (Nystrand, 1997). They are dependable on the teacher for providing feedback and evaluation of their actions as they cannot make evaluation by themselves. This type of guidance, classroom and communication management promotes learning procedural knowledge at expense of comprehensive understanding (Doyle, 1986b, see also our pervious chapter 3 on modern most common use of Socratic pedagogy).

Jackson (1968) and Labaree (1997) speculate that ontological time of conventional classrooms creates "hidden curriculum" that is functionally aimed at production of modern non-proprietary middle-class. The students' successful socialization in the assignment-time of the classroom seems to prepare the students to participate in a modern highly bureaucratic society. The students who achieved institutional success in school have learned *to be manageable* by following assigned tasks that they can never fully understand on a systematic basis and they have learned *to manage* by cracking the patterns of the teacher's demands and anticipating future assigned tasks and by committing themselves to these tasks. In other words, they seem to learn how to become managerial conduits passing assigned tasks from their superiors to their subordinates. Their creativity of recognizing patterns in the superiors' demands is subordinated to successful achievement of somebody else's task, project, goal.

Besides the flow of assigned tasks, the ontological time of monological conventional classroom is shaped by disruptions – events recognized by the teacher as interruptions of the teaching flow. I found at least seven major sources of disruptions of the teacher's control in research done by Kennedy (2005) and by Jackson (1968):

1. *the non-school world* (e.g., something dramatic happened outside of school like noisy car accident, a political event in a country, animal smell coming from nearby farm, and so on);
2. *the school institution* (e.g., school announcements, medical test of the students, district test, special education pullouts, the instructional equipment does not work);
3. *time pressure*[6] – a tension between activity time of the lesson (i.e., covering the curriculum) and the institutional timetable (Linder, 1970; Zerubavel, 1985) (e.g., lesson ends before the institutionally designated period or is interrupted by the end of the period);
4. *desynchronicity* – assigned tasks are accomplished by different students at different rate, some students already finished the assign task and some do not;
5. *lack of the shared focus* – some students are focused on aspect of the task while other on another (e.g., before a class discussion is exhausted the issue, another student introduces another issue);
6. *the teacher* him/herself (e.g., the teacher is disorganized or not prepared);
7. *the students* (e.g., being off-task or off-script).

Since students are often unwilling participant in monologic conventional classroom, the teacher competes for their attention, struggles to maintain his or her instruction, and recruits the students' cooperation (Jackson, 1968). Intentionally or unintentionally, the students can disrupt the teacher's control either by not being on the teacher's task (e.g., daydreaming), by doing a task in an inappropriate way (e.g., by asking for help a peer on a test), or not being on the teacher's script by violating the teacher's expectation of how they should participate in the task (e.g., when a second grade teacher asked the students how deer prepare to winter, one student raised his hand and, when called out by teacher, replied that the deer mate in preparation to winter which embarrassed the teacher who did not expect this answer and did not know how to react to it; later in a reflection session with her colleagues, the teacher identified this episode of her lesson as being her biggest problem and distraction). Kennedy (2005) defines students' *off-script* behavior in the following way, "students are actively participating in the lesson the teacher developed, but they say things that the teacher has not anticipated, ask questions that were not expected [by the teacher – EM], or misunderstand the ideas in a way that the teacher has not envisioned. Once this happens, the lesson is not longer unfolding in the way the teacher imagined it would. In the interviews [about their videotaped lessons – EM], teachers brought up student off-script comments and questions nearly three times per lesson, and these episodes represent only a portion of all that occurred" (p. 96).

In the 30.5-minute videotaped Read Aloud lesson, I coded 56 visible[7] disruptions of the teacher's flow and its visible causes (about 1.8 disruptions per minute or every 32 seconds on average in the lesson). As table 7 shows, the majority of visible interruptions of the teacher's

---

[6] In the US elementary schools, there is a trend to increase the institutionally designated periods giving teachers more flexibility and less time pressure probably because elementary school classroom is served by one teacher, there is not a need for coordination among many subject teachers like in middle and high schools. In contrast in the USSR (and currently in the Russian Federation), all lessons were limited by 45-minute periods. However, because of the No Child Left Behind policy, there is a new recent counter trend in the US elementary public schools fragmenting lessons and putting more time pressure by mandatory testing.

[7] I am aware that not all disruptions of the teacher's flow are visible for the observer – the teacher can recover from a disruption so quickly that it is not visible. The presented numbers of disruptions have to be treated as underestimated. There is a good suspicion that there were more disruptions that an observer could see.

flow come from inappropriate ways the students engaged in assigned tasks. For examples, a student tried to answer to the teacher's question without being called so the teacher had to put her index finger to her mouth signaling the student to be quiet and raise his hand or a student raises her hand during the teacher reading and the teacher waived her hand signaling the student to put her hand down and wait until the teacher finished the page to be called out.

The second most common type of visible disruption is the students' off-script comments that violate the teacher's expectations for students' contributions[8]. The teacher may expect a range of correct and incorrect answers. The teacher may expect the "I don't know" type of answers. However, there are students' contributions that are clearly on-task that are outside of the range of what the teacher expects. Kennedy (2005, p. 102) argues "[students'] unanticipated comments and questions can create problems for teachers because they present a threat of momentum". For example, the teacher did not expect a student replying that deer prepare for winter by mating. The teacher's face got red and she laughed in apparent embarrassment. She acknowledged the answer by saying, "That's... that's a possibility!" In another off-script instance, the teacher silenced the student. The student raised his hand, when he was called by the teacher (in the context of her previous question of what the students learned from the book), he shared, "One time in late fall, when I was coming back from my church, my mom's friend, she hit a deer in rain." The teacher commented, "That's sad." Other children started vocally reacting to the story and the teacher cut the discussion, "Alright, you know, guys, we will talk about our stories about deer later. Let's see..." Of course, the teacher never returned to the deer story or stories "later" (cf. "We'll talk about that later", in Kennedy, 2005, p. 75). It was her way of stopping the discussion and rejecting the contribution (cf. teacher's dismissal strategy of dealing with students' off-script comments, Kennedy, 2005). Although the teacher might consider the student's comment as off-task, it was highly probably that his contribution was on-task because the student might connect the tragic episode with information offered by the book about deer coming out of woods in search for food. In her research, Kennedy (2005) found that silencing through dismissal is a typical reaction by the teacher to students' off-script comments. She claims that "when a teacher says, for instance, 'We'll talk about that later,' she is telling students not to think about of these ideas, but instead to sit passively and let the teacher take care of these issues. Similarly, when teachers reject plausible ideas from students, with no indication as to why their idea is not acceptable, they discourage students from further thought" (Kennedy, 2005, p. 164).

---

[8] In her research, Kennedy (2005, p. 96) reports that the teachers brought at least 3 off-script disruptions per lesson and, in her assessment, that number represented only a portion of all that occurred.

Table 7. Visible disruptions of the teacher's flow during the 30.5-minute Read Aloud Lesson (N=56)

	Off-task engagement	Inappropriate ways to participate in task	Off-script of the teacher expectations	Reorganization of the task or theme by the teacher	Disagreement between students and the teacher	External interruptions
Total	7	23	20	4	2	2
%	13%	41%	36%	7%	4%	4%

Like in Kennedy's research, not all off-script comments were rejected and dismissed by the teacher. In three cases, students' off-script questions were addressed and supported. The teacher allows Michael to add one more answer about how mice prepare for winter based on the read book. However, a boy raised his hand and when called by the teacher asked a question instead of replying to the teacher question, "How would the sun dry the grass in the winter?" (the book mentioned that) The teacher replies, "It dries in the summer time, and after it all dry during the winter time it mouse eats it the grass." The student reacted, "Ahh." The teacher nodded in acknowledgment. Some other students were apparently surprised and excited with the teacher's answer. Immediately, a girl raised her hand and, after being called by the teacher, asked the teacher, "I have a question too, what if pika forgets where it hides its grass?" The book said that squirrels sometimes forget where they hide their nuts -- the girl apparently made a connection here. The teacher replied, "Well, the pika actually hides it grass in a cave. So it never forgets.... It's a good question." After the third question by another child about the read book, the teacher immediately started reading the book again not allowing the students to ask more questions. It was apparent that the teacher was ambivalent about the students' off-script questions. On the one hand, she approved and encouraged them but, on the other hand, she seemed to be concerned with her "teaching momentum" (Kennedy, 2005). Interviewing teachers, Lortie (1975, p. 195) found that "the teachers report that they must be careful about acting spontaneously on in class."

To my own surprise but in accordance with Kennedy's research, off-task disruptions were not as frequent as I expected from typical concerns expressed by teachers (Lortie, 1975). Being often unwilling participants in a monologic conventional classroom, the students are usually faced with the following problems: 1) urgent agendas competing with the teacher's task (e.g., another student just made an ethnic slur against the student), 2) classroom boredom, and 3) seeing the unfolding academic curriculum differently than the teacher sees it. The students have many creative and well-established strategies of dealing with these problems (Jackson, 1968; Kennedy, 2005) like chatting, playing with own shoe laces, or playing with wall poster[2].

My findings about relative low frequency of off-task disruptions and relatively high frequency of off-script disruptions in a monological conventional classroom support Kennedy's findings. Even more, Kennedy's interviews with the teachers suggest that the teachers treat off-script disruptions caused by the students of their teaching flow much more seriously than off-task disruptions. It seems that, despite their rhetoric to contrary, teachers prefer students who are less involved than more involved in the taught academic content (McNeil, 1986, pp. 79-80, made a similar observation),

> Remarkably, teachers brought up far more episodes involving *off-script students* than they did episodes involving *off-task behavior*. Most of the episodes that teachers worried about related to students who were actively participating in

---

[2] However, an observer (or an educator) should be careful to jump to a conclusion that any unsanctioned activity that a student is involved is evidence of his/her being off-task. Some of such activities (like doodling) is multitasking that can help to keep the students' attention focused on the teacher's assigned task (Matusov, Smith et al., 2007).

the lesson, not to students who had found other ways to amuse themselves. The dilemma for reformers is, if teachers succeed in engaging students intellectually, then students, in their enthusiasm, are likely to share their partial thoughts and their misconceptions with the group, creating for teachers the problem of how to respond to these comments while also keeping the larger group on track and maintaining momentum. Given how frightened teachers are of distractions, it is easy to imagine that many teachers would actually prefer *not* to have students too enthusiastic about the content, because they would rather *not* have students volunteering all their thoughts[3]. This is an ironic outcome, particularly in light of teachers; own rhetoric about wanting students to be willing to taking risks and to participate (Kennedy, 2005, pp. 122-123, italics is original).

Like Kennedy (2005), we found that external disruptions were relatively rare and related to special education teachers pulling a few students out from and returning them back to the class during the lesson. There were two disruptions associated with students' disagreements with the teacher. Some students wanted to offer more answers when the teacher signaled to move on in the lesson. In both cases, the teacher compromised allowing the students to contribute a bit more. In four cases, the teacher made self-disruptions apparently reorganizing the direction of the lesson as if in false-starts, "First we are going to talk about... What do you think... (waives her hand as if trying to erase her words) First of all, different animals do different things in winter to prepare to cold winter." In the lesson, I did not find any adversarial off-task disruptions noticed and described by other educational scholars like students' fights, students' resisting and challenging the teacher, the teacher's aggressive behavior toward students (Gutierrez, Rymes, & Larson, 1995; Jackson, 1968; McLaren, 1993; Willis, 1981).

The picture of the assignment-time ontological chronotope would be incomplete if we do not consider dialogic counter-currencies in monological conventional classroom, in which both the students and the teacher participates. To accomplish this task, I employed the discursive framework developed by Sidorkin (1999). He defines three types of discourse commonly occurring in schools (in and outside of classrooms):

1. *Official centralized discourse.* Edvards and Furlong describe this type of discourse as "centralized communication", "What this means is that everybody else listens (or gives appearance of listening) to a single speaker" (A. D. Edwards & Furlong, 1978, p. 11). It is highly controlled, ritualistic, mono-topic at any given time, topic-centered, scripted, and with highly shared focus (or at least appearance of that) (Gutierrez et al., 1995; Matusov & Hayes, 2000; McLaren, 1993; Michaels & Cazden, 1986; Philips, 1993). Sidorkin (1999) warns that official centralized discourse can be organized by students as well when a student or a group of students monopolizes classroom discourse. However, he also sees its legitimate but limited role in any classroom for arranging a dialogic discourse, "Monologues have their rightful place in a classroom. They allow for shared knowledge to be established, for shared experience to occur" (Sidorkin, 1999, p. 105). The assignment-time

---

[3] McNeil reports about a high school social studies teacher who actually demerited students' off-script contributions, "Questions and volunteered opinions merited negative 'class participation' grades in the her class for slowing up the pace she needed to maintain to cover the material" (McNeil, 1986, p. 196).

ontological chronotope, described above, constitutes the official centralized discourse.

2. *Dialogic discourse*. It involves ill-defined concerns-centered topic, shared control for the communication, collision of ideas, improvisational, eventual, unscripted, with a fluid shared focus, "The comments said within the second discourse become sort of public property of the class, and everyone feels some rights to control what everyone else says" (Sidorkin, 1999, p. 92). It recognizes both "good" and "bad" disruptions: bad disruptions reduce dialogicity while good disruptions promote it. Dialogicity requires disruptions or breakdowns because it based on dramatic events of collisions of truth interrupting the flow of the discourse (Matusov, Smith et al., 2007),

It is not rule governed, nor is it structured, turn-taking conversations between teacher and students. In order to create dialogue in a classroom, teachers should be well-advised to plan for the moment when her class will erupt into unruly talk, with kids not taking turns, taking over each other, being funny and over-critical, Classroom activities should be structured around such possible breaking points. The *breakability* of classroom discourse is one of its most important characteristics. This is the way we all make sense of things. Curriculum material simply cannot be incorporated into the child's world uncorrupted. It is impossible without interpretation, and any interpretation is also a *mis*interpretation. Every understanding includes misunderstanding, because meanings are born between a speaker and a listener, and not only within either head (Sidorkin, 1999, p. 105, the italics is original).

Gutierrez, Rymes, & Larson (1995) define it as "the third space" and refer to Bakhtin's notion of heteroglossia. Many teachers raised in monological conventional classrooms often try to avoid dialogic discourse because they are afraid the students will take over the control which leads to losing thematic control and chaos (Lortie, 1975; Sidorkin, 1999; Tharp & Gallimore, 1988).

Sidorkin lists conditions that the teacher can develop that can promote jump-starting dialogic discourse, although these conditions can never guarantee the success as, according to Sidorkin, dialogic discourse cannot be governed. The listed conditions are involved "procedural fragility" (Sidorkin, 1999, p. 106) – shared responsibility for communication, invitation to challenge the text, to agree and disagree; – and "internal fragility" (p. 106) – the texts and discourse used by the teacher should have internal dialogicity of self-doubt, self-irony, and self-destruction. Sidorkin argues that dialogic discourse organized by the teacher can be "only moderately successful" (Sidorkin, 1999, p. 94) based on his classroom observations. He argues that dialogic discourse "is not only alien to management, but it also excludes self-reflection. When you are in dialogue, you do not reflect upon it from a disengaged position of an observer and self-observer. The dialogue carries you away and completely absorbs you" (Sidorkin, 1999, p. 106). However, other scholars disagree arguing that design of instructional dialogic discourse by teachers, what they call "instructional conversations," requires special training, if not a special culture, from teachers (Echevarria et al., 1995; Tharp & Gallimore, 1988). To some degree, Sidorkin apparently contradicts himself arguing for both breakability and absorption as inherent features of dialogue. In my view, the inherent breakability of dialogue gives wonderful opportunities for participants' reflections and meta-communication management.

3. *Chatter discourse*. It involves loosely aligned "bubbling" themes without a overarching common topic (Matusov & Hayes, 2000), often non-pragmatic and "unbearably trivial" (Jones, 1988, p. 64). Piaget defined it as "collective monologue" (Piaget, 2002). Sidorkin argues that this type of discourse is not limited in children and common in adults when they socialize with each other. It creates sense of pure dialogicity unbounded by any task or goal, pure solidarity among participants – a sense of a familiar space, home – "a place where casualness may act as a prompt for strange, weird, or creative ideas" (Sidorkin, 1999, p. 104). According to his classroom observations, "Children engage in this type [discourse -- EM] time and again despite the threat of possible teacher sanctions" (Sidorkin, 1999, p. 99). They rarely allow the teacher participate because, according to Sidorkin and Jones, the teacher's unequal status, "A teacher has too much power, and chatter is a kingdom of equality and freedom" (Sidorkin, 1999, p. 101). Both Sidorkin and Gutierrez, Rymes, & Larson (1995) argue for oppositional nature of the chatter discourse in monological conventional schools, as it "promotes a counterculture, the peer culture that defines itself in opposition to official school structures" (Sidorkin, 1999, p. 102).

The 30.5-minute Read Aloud lesson that I analyzed involved almost 100% of the official centralized discourse. It had also a few visible germs of dialogic and chatter discourses each lasting no more than a few seconds. When a possibility for dialogic discourse emerged, usually after the teacher invited choral response from the students or accepted a question or answer without the students raising their hands, the teacher quickly put it down by forcefully focusing on her topic. The private chatters among the children died quickly either by themselves or because of the teacher's discouragement. In both cases, it is impossible to call the instances full-fledged discourses because they barely passed one-two exchanges.

Ontological Evaluation of Monologic Conventional Pedagogy: Maintaining Classroom on-Script

Jackson (1968) comments that conventional school is source of unique evaluation in child's life in scope and quality, "Every child experiences the pain of failure and the joy of success long before he reaches school age, but his achievements, or lack of them, do not really become official until he enters the classroom" (p. 19). He lists three sources of the evaluations: the teacher, the peers, and self. Nowadays, there is another source – state or standard testing as it would be anachronism what Jackson wrote in the 1960s, "But tests, though they are classic form of educational evaluation, are not all there is to the process. In fact, in the lower grades formal tests are almost nonexistent, although evolution clearly occurs. Thus the presence of these formal procedures is insufficient to explain the distinctively evaluative atmosphere that pervades the classroom from the earliest grades onward" (pp. 19-20). Recently, educational scholars have studied parents' and local communities' evaluation of students and teachers (M. A. Gibson & Ogbu, 1991; Ogbu, 1987b). Jackson argues that the chief source of the evaluation comes from the teacher that is often wrapped in the triadic discourse: the teacher's Initiation, the student's Response, and the teacher's Evaluation (Lemke, 1990; Mehan, 1979; Sinclair & Coulthard, 1975; Wells, 1992, September). I argue that, despite important "genre" variations of triadic discourse emphasized by Rockwell (2000), it essentially characterizes teacher-initiated communication in a monological conventional classroom[4].

As table 8 shows, almost all students' contributions are evaluated by the teacher. The students' deeds, positions, actions, behavior, objects, relations, and so on are often evaluated by the teacher in a monological classroom as being correct and incorrect, supportive or disruptive for the teacher defined assigned tasks. During 30.5-minute lesson, the teacher made 125 noticeable evaluations (verbal and non-verbal), 4 evaluations per minute or 1 evaluation for every 14 seconds on average. Positive evaluations dominate negative ones with the ratio more than 2:1. Table 8 provides describes four major types of the teacher's evaluation of the students with regard to the assigned tasks. The majority of the teacher's evaluations occurs about the correctness of the students' replies as a result of the triadic interactive exchange dominating communication in a monologic conventional classroom.

Each evaluation happens within the teacher's observational and perceptional flow and becomes consequential only when the assigned task is accomplished or perceived in jeopardy by the teacher. When the teacher perceived a student being off-task, or approaching the task inappropriately, or providing unexpected solutions to the task; then the teacher feels a need to do something with that – the activity flow disrupts. Although the teacher almost always[5] have to evaluate and to react to the students' solutions of the tasks – correct and incorrect one (Mehan, 1979); when these solutions do not violate the teacher's expectations of what is possible, they do not disrupt the teacher's activity flow. However, when a student is on-task, approaching the task appropriately within the teacher's expectations; then the teacher remains in the activity flow.

---

[4] However, unlike Wertsch (1991b) or Wells (1992, September), I do not see the teacher-initiated triadic discourse as the dominant discourse genre of *any* teaching but rather as *monologic* teaching. At the same time, I argue, and this time together with Wells (1992, September), that the triadic discourse is not the birthmark of monologic teaching but rather monologic teaching utilizes triadic discourse for its monologic purposes like it also utilizes lecturing, which under special conditions can also be dialogic. In other words, triadic discourse and lecturing are preferable means of monologic teaching and, thus, its most visible features but neither triadic discourse and lecturing cannot be reduced to monologic teaching nor monologic teaching can be reduced to use of triadic discourse and lecturing, both of which can also serve dialogic teaching.

[5] The teacher provided 100% evaluative responses to the students' answers in the Read Aloud lesson that I analyzed but less so in research of monologic conventional classroom done by others (e.g., Lemke, 1990, however, he did not code non-verbal responses of the teacher that might involve evaluative responses to the students' answers).

Table 8. Types and valence of the teacher's noticeable evaluation of students' achievements of the assigned tasks (N=125)

Aspect of the task in the teacher's evaluative focus	On-task/ Off-task	Appropriate/ **Inappropriate** ways of approaching the assigned task	Correct/ **Incorrect-failed** solutions of the assigned task	On-script/**Off-script** (Expected/**Unexpected** solutions of the assigned task)
	Students' efforts-engagement	Constraints	Product I	Product II
Examples	Daydreaming	Cheating, speaking out the answer without being called	The students do not know what the word "attentive" means	"Deer mate"
Positive evaluation	2 (29%)	3 (13%)	64 (79%)	5 (25%)
Negative evaluation	4 (51%)	15 (65%)	7 (9%)	4 (20%)
Ambivalent evaluation	0 (0%)	2 (9%)	3 (4%)	9 (45%)
Neutral	1 (14%)	2 (9%)	2 (3%)	2 (10%)
Absent evaluation	0 (0%)	1 (4%)	5 (6%)	0 (0%)

Note: **Bolded** are consequential options – ones that demand the teacher's further actions.

Some of students' off-task behaviors were not necessarily illegitimate from the teacher's point of view. About 29% of the off-task disruptions were about students leaving the class for the restroom that was approved by the teacher. To the other four off-tasks disruptions, the teacher reacted negatively: some students did not apparently listen to other students or the teacher's reading the book or a girl was playing with a wall poster instead of participating in a discussion. The teacher also negatively reacts to students' inappropriate ways of achieving the tasks, which is not surprising (Nystrand, 1997). In a few cases, the teacher supports what she otherwise defines as inappropriate (usually speaking without permission) probably because she considers benefits of the students contributions overweight their transgressions. It is interesting that the teacher more often evaluates off-scripts in an ambivalent way sending both positive and negative signals to the students. For example, she both shishes the child who replied that deer mate to prepare for winter, smiles at the child with embarrassment, and supports the child by saying, "That's... a possibility!" It appears that teachers struggle with off-script disruptions and ambivalent about them in monological conventional classrooms. Finally, overwhelmingly positive evaluations of correctness of the students' response suggests that the teacher tries to use the level of challenge for her questions both low and open enough to keep her relations with the children positive that promote their cooperation and necessary and manageable level of their engagement in the assigned tasks.

I argue that the teacher's evaluation of the students in monological conventional classroom is embedded in the teacher's ontological time chronotope – in his or her desire to make the teaching flow smooth. This desire creates an image of *the ideal good student* that guides the teacher's evaluation of real students. The ideal good student in a monological classroom is always on-task, always does the task in an appropriate way, always on-script, and always produces the expected product (what is considered to be "the correct answer" from the teacher's point of view) (Nystrand, 1997). Even more, when a task is not assigned (e.g., when the student finishes his or her assigned task before other students), the ideal good student should be considerate of not disrupting performance on task of others. He or she should do no more and no less that the teacher is expected to keep the teaching flow going without any disruption. The ideal good student has to be cooperative, obedient, active and quick-witted but to the point of convenience for the teacher, correct, moderately engaged, and very appreciative of the teacher. When a real student corresponds with the ideal good student, the teacher evaluates him or her positively, when a real student violates the image of the ideal good student, the teacher evaluates him or her negatively as being disobedient, uncooperative, unmotivated, stupid, wrong, or ungrateful. With time, local evaluative judgments by the teacher create the student's academic reputation both in absolute terms and relative to reputations of other students.

In the assignment-time ontological chronotope of monological conventional classroom, the teacher values negatively disruptions of his/her assignment flow (Kennedy, 2005). One of the most common definitions of good lesson provided by my preservice teachers is a lesson being *smooth* – i.e., free of disruptions. Here are some of their examples in reflection to their performed lessons, "I wanted everything to go smoothly [in my lesson]," "Overall I was very happy with how our lesson went, I felt that it ran a lot smoother then our word study lesson, but that the students wanted to talk more throughout which often forced us to stop and get them quiet before continuing," "But it did go alot smoother then our first lesson," "It was a challenge to balance and I think that it is important to have a plan to deal with situations such as this so that the daily instruction can move smoothly." They think that better planning can eliminate disruptions and make the lesson flow of assigned tasks absolutely smooth. Similar, Lortie got the same results interviewing in-service teachers about a good day in their classrooms, "A good day for me… is a smooth day. A day when you can close the doors and do nothing but teach," "I think, to me, a day is good without interruption…," "Well, when things you planned go well" (Lortie, 1975, pp. 169-170). A very few teachers, whom Kennedy studied, "seemed unusually calm and unafraid of distractions, even distractions arising from unusual student ideas" (Kennedy, 2005, p. 231). Other interviewed teachers expressed their anxiety and fear of losing teaching momentum. In sum, in a monological conventional chronotope, the teachers prefer non-dramatic and eventless classroom ontological time. Smooth running lesson is embedded in smooth-running school (cf. McNeil, 1986).

In some classrooms and even national schools, teachers try to mediate peer and, even, self evaluations. For example, in Soviet schools besides gender competitions promoted by teachers, there were other types of competitions that were often called "socialist competition",

The [Soviet pedagogical] manual begins with instructions for the teacher standing before the class on the first day of school:

It is not difficult to see that a direct approach to the class with the command, "All sit straight," often doesn't bring the desired effect since a demand in this form does not reach the sensibilities of the pupils and does not activate them.

In order to "reach the sensibilities of the pupils" and "activate them" according to principles of socialist competition, the teacher should say, "Let's see which row can sit the straightest" (Silberman, 1971, p. 129).

These competitions induce peer and self evaluations in the students that served general goal of monological conventional classroom to make the teaching flow uninterrupted.

Jackson (1968, pp. 20-21) argues that peer and self evaluations follow the teacher's evaluation in terms its role to comply the teacher's expectations. Other educational scholars have emphasized the binary nature of the peer and self evaluations: the students can accept the teacher's image of ideal student as the basis of their own evaluations or actively resist it. Some scholars explain this binary system of students' evaluation by class reproduction – middle-class students accept the teacher's image of ideal student, while working class students reject it (Eckert, 1989; Erickson, 1986; Willis, 1981); – while other scholars explain it by minority status – students from majority and voluntary minority communities accept the teacher's image of ideal student, while students from involuntary minority communities reject it (Fordham & Ogbu, 1986; M. A. Gibson & Ogbu, 1991; Ogbu, 1987a, 2003). Recently, however, educational researchers have become moving away from the binary model of acceptance versus resistance of the teacher's evaluation system. They find evidence for a more complex picture for students' evaluations that involve group inclusion and exclusions (Lensmire, 1994a; Paley, 1992). Even in terms of academic learning, students' evaluation can be different from the teacher's promotion of "good student" and focus instead of "good learner" that values off-script and, even, off-task contributions if they promote authentic learning in students (Candela, 1999; Matusov et al., 2005, September).

In my analysis of the Read Aloud Lesson described above, I also found four cases of the students' evaluations of the teacher. In one case, a student's evaluation of the teacher was negative as the student disagreed with the teacher's negative evaluation of his reply. The teacher and the boy had several exchanges about the bats' behavior in winter. The boy insisted that some did while the teacher said that none did. It is interesting that the teacher did not provide her rational and she was apparently incorrect.

> Teacher (reads the book): "Many bats fly south too [like birds – EM]. But some bats stay in the north all winter. When the weather gets cold they go to a cave. There is no wind or snow in the cave. The bats sleep there all winter. They do not eat. They live on fat stored inside them. They do not move, they hardly breathe. They sleep, sleep and sleep. They hibernate." So are our predictions correct?
> ...
> Teacher: ...So what did the book say?
> Child: They [bats] hiber-, they um... go to...
> Teacher: Do they hibernate or do they migrate?
> Many children: They... [some children say "migrate" but some say "hibernate" at the same time]!
> Child: Hibernate!
> Teacher: They hibernate!
> Mark: *Some* of them hibernate!
> Teacher: They hibernate in the cave...
> Mark: And *migrate*!
> [The teacher looks at Mark with disapproval, and goes back to the board]
> Teacher: Um... and they don't eat.
> Mark: They migrate.
> Teacher: They *don't* migrate, they just go to a cave.
> Another child: They just lay there all the time and do nothing.

It is interesting that neither the teacher nor Mark appealed to the book to check their claim despite the fact that the teacher referred to the book earlier. It could be an issue of power and the teacher authority that in both cases rather than inability of the participants to test their ideas.

It seems that the incident constitutes off-script disruption similar to ones described by Candela (1999) and Kennedy (2005). Three other evaluations of the teacher by her students were positive. The students clapped when the teacher finished her reading the book, thanked her by her high judgment about their learning and participation, and praised future learning activities the teacher promised to bring. This evidence suggests students' active orientation to their school learning even in monologic conventional classrooms.

The Didactic Chronotope of Monologic Conventional Pedagogy

The didactic chronotope of monologic pedagogy is aimed at transmission of knowledge from the teacher to the student. The semiotic academic space is defined by a curriculum program often designed outside of the classroom by a state bureaucracy. It is based on a growing agreement, pedagogical contracts (Nystrand, 1997, p. 15) or treaties (Powell, Farrar, & Cohen, 1985), between the teacher and the student, on certainty, on elimination of the student's misconceptions – on the student becoming identical to the teacher so the student will answer the teacher's question and solve the teacher-presented problems exactly the same way as the teacher would answer and solve them. The semiotic academic time is defined by special sequential instruction -- "scaffolding" (Wood, Bruner, & Ross, 1976) where the gap between the teacher and the student is fragmented to smaller teacher-defined tasks that can be manageable for the student through direct instruction (e.g., lecturing and demonstration but also drills). The academic system of value in monologic pedagogy is transmission of knowledge: learning is defined by how much teacher-defined knowledge the student can retain and demonstrate when the teacher demands.

Didactic Space of Monologic Pedagogy: Given Curriculum

The didactic space is educational curriculum. In a monologic conventional classroom, the curriculum defines itself through the following questions, "Where are we didactically in the lesson? Are we in math or in social studies? Are we in fractions or in long division? Are we in presentation of a new topic or in practicing learned skills? How does 'the didactic map' look like? How do the participants perceive the didactic space?" The didactic space a monologic conventional classroom is the curriculum fully pre-designed by the teacher and the whole educational bureaucratic apparatus involving school boards and the state departments of education without much of students' inputs. Russian famous innovative educator (and writer) of the nineteenth century, Leo Tolstoy problematized the issue of didactic space by making the following statement, "The conviction that we not only *do not know* – but that we *cannot know* – what the education of the people is to consist of is what forms the basis of our [innovative educational] activities" (p., 180). "[Monologic conventional] education is the tendency of one man to make another just like himself" (p. 189). "It is right here the child suffers the worst and most injurious violence: when he or she is asked to understand in precisely the same manner that the teacher understands it" (Tolstoy & Blaisdell, 2000, p. 184).

In his extremely useful analysis of the concept of educational curriculum, Whitson (2007) convincingly argues the curriculum in a monologic conventional classroom is: 1) given, 2) heavily fragmented (McNeil, 1986), 3) purified (Latour, 1987), and 4) often hierarchically structured. In a monologic conventional classroom, the curriculum is viewed a given thing that is finite, definite, and exists objectively outside of human experience and being. The proponents of monologic conventional notion of curriculum (e.g., Hirsch, Trefil, & Kett, 1988) view curriculum as a sign that contains conventional well-defined, certain, non-problematic meaning. For example, Hirsch wrote a book about what every American needs to know. In his book, he presents "cultural literacy" or "core knowledge" -- bits of information (e.g., what is "due process of law", p. 313) that he sees as well-defined, objective, and non-problematic. Whitson sees the origin of this view in a philosophy of positivism. However, in analysis of non-educational practices of science and business, Latour (1987) and Wenger (1998) argue that the process of "blackboxing" (Latour) and "reification" of meaning (Wenger) are necessary aspects of any practice. They argue that in any practice, at some points, it is very important to view signs *as if* they are containers of well-defined non-problematic conventional meaning. Although in a close historical, conceptual, and pragmatic analysis this perception of signs is wrong, this illusion can be very useful because otherwise, without this illusion, the participants would not be able to move forward in their activities endlessly problematizing the signs they use. Both Latour and Wenger see a problem, similar with one discussed by Whitson, when these necessary aspects are viewed as comprehensively defining the practice and the use of signs as proponents of monologic conventional classroom do (like E.D. Hirsch, Madeline Hunter, and William Bennett, for example). Arguably, in an education practice, the issue is whether the learning curriculum can and should be viewed as given – well-defined, objective, and non-problematic – for both the teacher and the students (after the lesson is learned).[2]

In a monologic conventional classroom, the teacher treats the curriculum as given – well-defined, objective, and non-problematic – for him/herself. For example, my analysis of lesson plan and lesson reflection on the Read Aloud Lesson about Animals in Winter discussed above shows that the teacher saw the curriculum as non-problematic for herself. She defined the purpose of the lesson as, "The lesson objective was to have students understand the ideas of migration and hibernation and to be aware that animals with do either of these or neither." She did not see any aspect of the curriculum as being problematic for herself. However, according to my analysis of the videotaped lesson, I found at least 4 curricular problems that the teacher had faced during the lesson:

1. The teacher was apparently confused with the fact presented by the book and a child that some bats migrate while some hibernate (I wonder if the teacher assumed that species have only one way of dealing with winter),

2. The teacher did not know if a child comment about deer mating was relevant to the topic of deer's preparation for the winter – is mating a part of deer's preparation for the winter,

3. A boy asked her how the sun dries grass gathered by woodchuck and placed on stones in winter and the teacher replied that the sun dries the grass during the summer, however, I am not sure whether this answer is correct and whether the teacher really knew it, finally,

4. A girl asked whether a pika can lose the food that it hides for the winter, like a squirrel does – the teacher replied that a pike never loses the food because it stores in its tunnel. Again, I am not sure that this information is correct or even if it is correct that the teacher had known it rather than simply guessed it correctly[3].

The first two cases the teacher suppressed while the two last cases of the children's questions she supported. However, in all cases, she did not treat the emergent curriculum as problematic and uncertain – as learning opportunities – for herself. Later, after her lesson, she problematized only the issue of appropriateness of the topic introduced by the child about deer mating, "A difficulty that I encountered during the lesson was that at one point when we were discussing what a deer does to prepare for winter, one of the children yelled out, 'They mate!' I was a little shock and I didn't really know how to address this matter, because I didn't know what was considered inappropriate and [or] appropriate. Luckily, none of the other students knew what he was talking about, so I just dismissed his statement. It was a little uncomfortable because I did not know how to address this question." In sum, teachers in monologic conventional classrooms do not try to problematize the targeted curriculum for themselves and do not cease on opportunities to learn together with the students (and to model the students' learning by their own learning) when such problematization emerges during their lessons.

---

[2] Another important issue is what a legitimate role of blackboxing or reification in an educational practice is.

[3] However, it is important to notice, that if the teacher guessed in cases #3 and #4, she also used her reasoning that she shared with the children during the lesson.

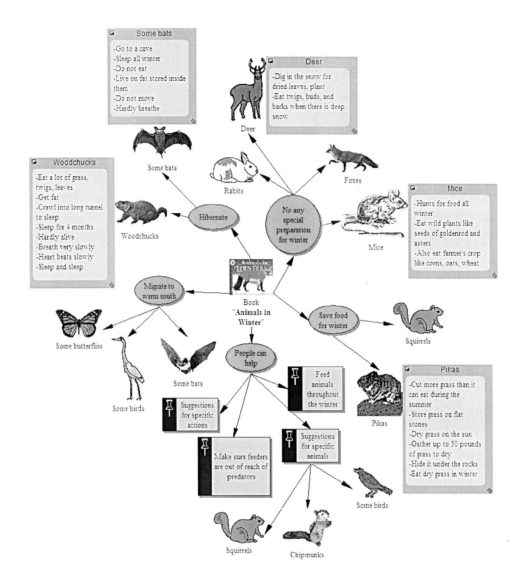

Figure 2. Thematic map of the book "Animals in Winter" (the extended text notes presented in colored rectangles indicate animals that the teacher discussed in her Read Aloud Lesson rather than just read the book).

The given, pre-designed curriculum of monological conventional classrooms is segmented by themes (or topics[5]) that can be found in many conventional syllabi and curriculum discussions (Bennett, Finn, & Cribb, 1999; Hirsch et al., 1988; Hunter & Hunter, 2004). Themes in monological classroom are containers with the pre-given meaning, new for the students, that the teacher decides to teach in advance. However, the notion of themes is problematic even within a monologic approach. What is a curriculum theme for one student

---

[5] The term "topic" originates from the Greek word "topos" which means "place" (Linell, 1998, p. 183).

may not be for another. Using Hirsch's math example of 5+2=7 (Hirsch, 1996, p. 134), for on student addition is a problem in this given, positive, teacher-defined theme, while for another the number five, while for a third student this is not a problem whatsoever. Also, two curricular themes presented together at the same time or in immediate or mediated sequence may produce synergy of other themes for some or all students. Some synergetic themes are planned by teachers and some are not. For example, in the Read Aloud Lesson on Animals in Winter, a girl made connection between presented info about squirrels occasionally losing their food that they save for winter and pika who also saves its food. Curricular themes are different by nature of their containers. They can be factual (i.e., how things are), procedural (i.e., what to do to achieve a certain goal), conceptual (e.g., justification, definition, argumentation, judgment, consideration of consequences), and so on. Themes can include books and stories. They can be nested. For example, a theme of how squirrels prepare for the winter involves a subtheme of them losing food that they hide for winter which in its own turn involves a subtheme of trees and shrubs growing out of the nuts lost by squirrels. In contrast, some curricular themes may relate non-hierarchically. Given curricular theme is a unit of the didactic spatial chronotope of a monologic conventional classroom.

A monologic conventional lesson is heavily based on teacher-scripted curricular themes. Bearing in mind difficulty of defining a curricular theme[6], in this 30.5-minute of Read Aloud Lesson, I estimated at least 239 big and small themes with a help of NVIVO. The high majority of the curricular themes were factual (85.8%) while the minority was conceptual themes (14.2%). Three fourth of the curricular themes or 74.5% were teacher- or book-defined. All of these 178 curriculum themes defined by the teacher (or book) but 6 (or 96.6%) were given, pre-designed. The emergent teacher-defined themes were mainly a result of the teacher's change the initial plan to checking students' predictions about how selected animals prepare for the winter to summarizing the read pages the book. Also, the teacher had to explain what the word "attentive" means in response to the students' lack of familiarity with this word and disagreement with a student about bats sleeping as their dealing with the winter. 25.5% of all themes were student-defined. However, almost all of 61 student-defined themes but 5 (or 9.8%) were in response to the teacher's questions. The five student-defined curricular themes involved students' questions about animals or plants in the winter, their desire to share stories about animals suppressed by the teacher, and comments about the pictures in the book. Nevertheless, even when students initiated their curricular themes in response to the teacher's questions, some of these student-defined themes violated the teacher's expectations and were off-script themes, discussed the sections above, that, by the definition, were novel for the teacher (see table 9). The students' off-scripts themes in response to the teacher's questions involved such themes as people buying Christmas tree in preparation for the winter, deer's mating, the book author writing the animals in winter because he did not know what to write about, and so on.

It is difficult to judge how many of the total curriculum themes were novel for the students and for which students exactly. Sometimes, although it was pretty clear when

---

[6] Linell (1998, p. 181) argues that the notion of topic is essentially ill-defined because topics are not just defined by the participants' utterances but also by negotiation of their future-oriented projects and past utterances as well – "topic structure and participation framework are closely related" (see also, Maynard, 1980, p. 263; Schegloff, Ochs, & Thompson, 1996, p. 40). Similarly, Rommetveit (1984, p. 335) argues that, "vagueness, ambiguity and incompleteness – and hence also: versatility, flexibility, and negotiation – are inherent and essential characteristics of any language."

nobody knew what the word "attentive" meant or when the students were not familiar with pika or woodchuck (it is safe to assume that they did not know how these animals prepare for and deal with the winter). In other cases, it was very clear that the students were very familiar with the animals and how they prepare for the winter (e.g., deer). I made a "liberal" assessment of novel themes for the most of the students by trying to include all themes which I suspect to be novel based on the students' verbal and non-verbal behavior in response to the themes. I found that 114 themes or 47.7% of the total 239 curriculum themes that the students were exposed during the 30.5-minut lesson seemed to be novel for the majority of the students. Out of these 114 curricular themes novel to the students, 28 were student-defined, which constituted 45.9% of all student-defined themes, and 84 were teacher-defined, which constituted 48.3% of all teacher-defined themes. It is possible to conclude that about half of all student- and teacher-defined themes were novel for the majority of the students. Twenty six or 22.8% of the novel themes were conceptual and the rest of them were factual. Nine of the novel themes (7.9%) were problematizing themes (e.g., what was the purpose of videotaping, what is the meaning of the word "attentive", how an unfamiliar animal woodchuck might prepare for the winter, can pika lose its gathered food, why did the author write the book) that took about 40% of the utterances in the lesson discourse, 90% of which were spent by the children on one-suggestion brainstorming assessed unilaterally by the teacher without providing the rationale for the assessment. Finally, I assessed the problematizing themes that the students could not figure out on their own without the teacher's help – called them "the zones of proximal development" or ZPD themes (see Vygotsky, 1978). For example, the students could not figure out on their own what was the purpose of videotaping, what is the meaning of the word "attentive", do deer mate in preparation for the winter, how can the sun dry grass from woodchuck in the winter, which of their predictions about how bats prepare for the winter were correct, and so on. However, they were able to guess on their own how pika may prepare for the winter or why the author could write the book. I found 6 ZPD themes, three of which (a half) were initiated by the children's questions or statements. The discussion of the six ZPD themes constituted only about 10% of all utterances in the lesson discourse. The ZPD themes where very short-live and did not go deeper than a triadic exchange common for monologic conventional classrooms (Mehan, 1979). In sum, this monologic lesson provided a rich learning environment for the students in terms of novelty of the exposed curricular themes for the students; however, it was not very rich on involving the students in their zones of proximal development. The majority of the time of the lesson, the students spent on low level thinking: recalling what they already knew from their own experience or from the read book, guessing-brainstorming about how unfamiliar animals prepare for the winter, about reasons why the author wrote the book, and about how people can help animals to survive in the winter.

Table 9. Types of the curricular themes (N=239) in the 30.5-minute Read Aloud Lesson

	Teacher-scripted themes		Off-script emergent themes, novel for the teacher		
	Themes pre-designed by the teacher	On-script students' themes in response to the teacher's questions	Teacher-defined emergent themes	Off-script students' themes in response to the teacher's questions	Students-initiated off-script themes
Number	172	46	6	10	5
Percentage	72.0%	19.2%	2.5%	4.2%	2.1%
Total Number	218		21		
Total %	91.2%		8.8%		

The curricular themes are highly structured in a monologic conventional classroom. The didactic spatial chronotope of conventional teaching has 'hierarchal' and 'topological' aspects. The hierarchal aspect involves nesting levels: like geographical map of a federal country (the biggest hierarchal level) consists of states (the second hierarchal level) which consist of counties (the third hierarchal level), and so on. The hierarchal aspect of the didactic curricular map of monologic conventional teaching involves: 1) the biggest curricular level of *academic subjects* (e.g., math, English, social studies), 2) the second level of *curricular topics* (e.g., fractions, long division), and 3) the third level of *instructional moves* (e.g., presentation of the topic, testing). Thus, moving bottom-up, it is possible to conclude that instructional moves are organized of curricular themes. The curricular topics are organized of instructional moves. The academic subjects are organized of curricular topics (see figure 3 in table 10).

The biggest hierarchical unit on the didactic map is an academic subject: traditional monologic curricula are divided on separate academic subjects such as math, English, PE, social studies, arts and crafts, and so on. The choice of the subjects is shaped by the history of schooling and its role in the society. For example, such academic subjects as teaching dead languages Ancient Greek and Latin disappeared from the curricular space of traditional schooling as it becomes more middle-class oriented rather than upper-class oriented (Labaree, 1997).

The second hierarchical level of the traditional curricular organization is topical. Topics can be hierarchically related to each other (e.g., the Fractions and the Addition of Fraction), chronologically related (e.g., The Civil War and The Reconstruction), loosely related in juxtaposition (e.g., The Integers and The Decimals), or unrelated (e.g., The Phrase and The Writing Persuasive Compositions). The topical organization is dictated by "importance" of the topics for students' future as defined by the three major educational goals shared by the society (Labaree, 1997): democratic participation (e.g., does this topic promotes democracy), social efficiency (e.g., does this topic help promote skills require by the modern economy), and social mobility (e.g., will the topic be on a high-stake test?). In addition, a curricular topic can be chosen to teach just because of a school tradition – it is in the textbook used by the teacher or in the commercial curricular "unit."

The third hierarchical level of didactic topology is intratopical and involves certain instructional moves of "covering curriculum" such as classroom management, activation of prior knowledge, a presentation of a topic, practicing the topic with the students, summary, follow-up activity, and testing students' knowledge of the topic. For example, in the Read Aloud Lesson about animals in winter, described above, the third hierarchical level of didactic spatial topology is presented at figure 6. The circles represent the teacher-initiated instructional moves while clouds represent the students-initiated topics. The red color of the circles represents behavioral orientation to the lesson, the light green color of the circles represents thematic orientation to the lesson, the light blue color of the circles and clouds represents the main part of the lesson, and, finally, the purple color of the circles and clouds represents the follow-up activity that was supposed to continue to another, a Writing Craft Lesson about the students' writing neighbors advice of how to help animals in winter.

**Table 10. Organization of the didactic spatial chronotope
in monological conventional classroom**

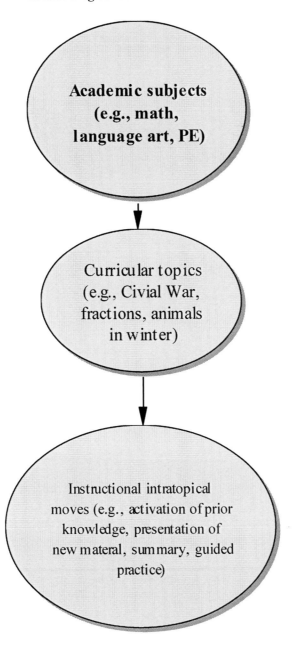

Figure 3. Hierarchical organization of the didactic spatial chronotope in monologic conventional classroom.

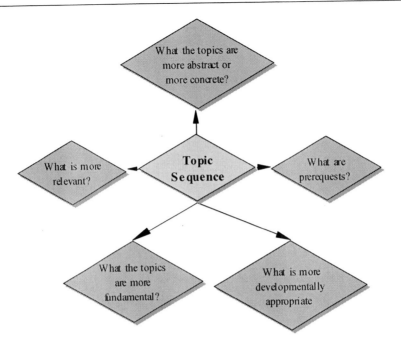

Figure 4. Topically sequential topology of the didactic spatial chronotope in monologic conventional classroom.

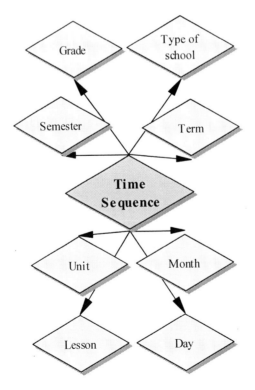

Figure 5. Temporally sequential topology of the didactic spatial chronotope in monologic conventional classroom.

The topological aspect of the didactic spatial chronotope of monologic conventional classroom involves the issues of location, size, and shape of each of the nesting units. The unfolding of the curriculum in monologic conventional classrooms is often unidimensional and linear. Lampert describes the linear nature of the curriculum development in a monologic conventional classroom in the following way:

> This [linear] organization is intended to give the teacher and the students a frame work for identifying what pieces of mathematics are in focus in any particular instance of teaching and learning and a routine for moving through then locating a lesson on an ordered list makes very clear where a class hi been and where it will go next:

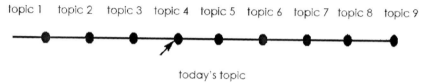

topic 1   topic 2   topic 3   topic 4   topic 5   topic 6   topic 7   topic 8   topic 9

today's topic

If the class is studying topic 4, for example, they will have "covered" topics 2, and 3, and not yet encountered topics 5, 6, and 7. If the class did not "get" the material in the lesson on topic 3, the teacher would solve the problem by "going back over it again" (Lampert, 2001, p. 260).

In the case of the Read Aloud Lesson, I analyzed, if we exclude student-initiated topics and the teacher's "false start" for checking predications, the organization of the instructional moves of the Read Aloud Lesson represents an almost perfect thematic hierarchy unfolded in time (see figure 6). Topologically, the subject units of monologic conventional teaching are usually unidimensional, linear, and independent from each other (i.e., being on somewhere the 'math territory' does not necessarily position one on the 'social study territory' in any way). In other words, the subjects are often purified from networks of interdisciplinary connections. Even when interdisciplinary connections involved in a lesson, they are usually not necessary. For example, although in the analyzed Read Aloud Lesson about Animals in Winter, two academic subjects crossed: language art and natural sciences; their juxtaposition was arbitrary. Arguably, learning natural sciences took over language art: neither students tested the text, nor the text was used to challenge the students' prior experiences as the teacher initially planned. Faced with the challenges of the students' ZPD regarding how to compare the students' own predictions with the text, the teacher withdrew her guidance to organization of the students' recalls of the read book and low-level thinking brainstorming.

Thus, unidirectional linear continuum is the shape of the subject unit in traditional teaching. Its size is potentially unlimited as an endeavor of the academic discipline representing the curricular subject (i.e., there is no potential stop in study of math). The curricular topic in monologic conventional teaching is often a section of the purified subject continuum. It has its location in the sequence of other topics-sections on the subject line. It also has its length – duration. Similarly, instructional steps are line subsections inside of a topic-section that have their sequence and duration.

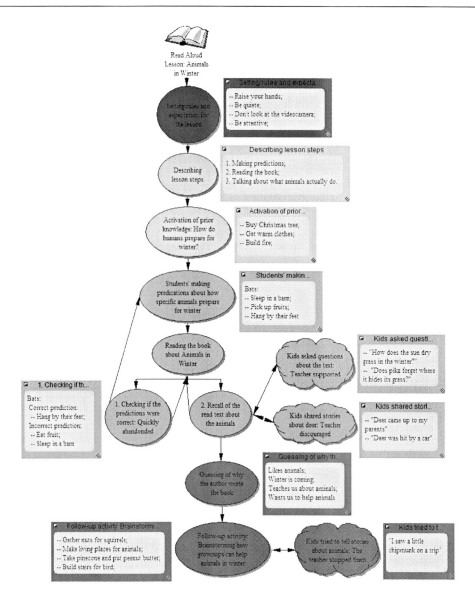

Figure 6. Hierarchical organization of instructional moves of the Read Aloud Lesson on Animals in Winter.

The first topological level of the didactically spatial organization of traditional teaching is sequential: the sequences of the curricular topics. The topical sequence is often defined by the questions: 1) what topics the students have to know to move to the next topic; 2) what the topics are more fundamental (e.g., Hirsch et al., 1988, "what every American needs to know"); 3) what the topics are more abstract or more concrete; 4) what the topics are more relevant/familiar to the students; 5) what the topical sequence is developmentally appropriate; and so on. There is a growing realization of a lack of consensus among educators and discipline specialists about the topical sequence in their subject area (Hiebert, personal communication, March 2003).

In the particular Read Aloud Lesson on Animals in Winter for second grade classroom, the Language Art curricular topic of learning comprehension strategies for reading an informational non-fictional book was guided by the Maryland State Standards for the second grade curriculum while specific choice of information book about how animals deal with cold winter was guided by the Maryland State Standards for the second grade science curriculum and by the season of the year when the lesson occurred – late fall. As the teacher stated in her reflection on the lesson, "This lesson coincides with Maryland standard 2.0, which states that 'Students will read, comprehend, interpret, analyze, and evaluate informational text.' Through this lesson, students were analyzing and evaluating an informational text in order to acquire information about animals in winter. This topic was chosen because the Maryland science curriculum standards suggest that diversity of life is an important topic to address so that students are aware of the world around them. Besides, since this lesson was taught in November, the students might see its relevance as many wild animals were preparing for the winter." Kennedy's (2005) study suggests, however, that we should be careful in trusting the teacher's statements about how much State Standards guide teachers' curricular choices as she found that teachers often refer to the State Standards when the Standards coincide with the teachers' own beliefs about what is important to teach at the given moment. It is interesting and common for many monologic conventional classrooms that the teacher did not justify her curricular choices by reference to the students' interests and needs that she might learn about through her conversations with the children (and/or their parents), observations, and/or their contributions occurring in previous lessons. However, the teacher's last comment about November suggested that she considered the issue of relevancy of the targeted curriculum for the children. She seemed to try to design the relevancy based on her assessment of how a generic second grader might be interested in wild animals' preparation for winter in a state of Maryland where winters are often cold. Despite the fact that her design of the relevancy was somewhat generic, decontextualized, and, thus, blind (I will return to this point to discuss it in details in the next section); her guess about expected interests of her students was rather correct based on a rather high level of engagement that the students demonstrated during the lesson curriculum.

The second topological level of the didactically spatial organization of traditional teaching is calendar, durational, and temporal. It is a projection of the curricular topical sequence on the linear time continuum of class meetings and assigned homework: when in the school calendar each topic will occur. This time continuum involves a mixture of both physical and institutional aspects because it involves days, weeks, months, as well as lessons, terms, semesters, academic years, grades (e.g., third grade versus second grade curricula), schools (e.g., elementary school math curricula versus middle school math curricula). It is also about time duration for each pre-designed curricular topic both in terms of physical and institutional time: how many lessons, weeks, months, terms, grades, and schools a particular topic takes place. Thus, this spatial level of traditional teaching is essentially chronotopic because it combines the didactic space – the pre-designed curricular topics and their sequence – and the local time of traditional teaching – the physical time continuum – as well as the didactic time – instructional considerations for defining the duration of each curricular topic on the physical time continuum the class meetings and homework. In the Read Aloud Lesson on Animals in Winter, for example, the teacher limited what of the animals mentioned in the book to discuss with the students based on limits of the physical time for the lesson and the second grade students' "natural" attention ability and the familiarity-unfamiliarity criterion. As the teacher told after the lesson, she wanted the students to discuss both highly familiar (e.g., deer, mice) and highly unfamiliar animals (e.g., pika, woodchuck). The familiar animals helped the students activate their prior knowledge and feel confident and proud about what they already had known, while the unfamiliar animals forced the students to reason, compare, and guess about their possible behaviors in dealing with winter (see figure 2 and figure 6).

Finally, the didactic space can be defined in terms of its (re)contextualization or decontextualization (Wertsch, 1985, 1991a, 1991b). Based on a semiotic approach to curriculum developed by Whitson (2007), it is possible to define decontextualization as "containerization" and "purification" (Latour, 1987) – a transformation of curriculum in a given, self-contained and self-sufficient bits of meaning. Whitson brings an example of the process of containerization leading to decontextualization of the academic curriculum through analysis of Hunter's teaching guidelines. Hunter (2004, p. 41) insists on teaching students about the botanical clarification by clarifying the students' misconceptions about plants like that cucumber and okra are really fruits while many (if not all) children think that they are vegetables. Whitson argues, however, that by themselves cucumbers and okra are neither fruits nor vegetables (and, arguably neither even plants) but they become as such within particular human practices and discourses: in the botanic practice and discourse, cucumber and okra are fruits because they have seeds inside but in the particular culinary practice and discourse, cucumber and okra are vegetables because they are served as vegetables and not as dessert. Whitson argues that contextualized teaching about cucumbers and okra is not about cleaning students from their "misconceptions" but rather about making the students realize diverse human practices and discourses that involve the studied objects and themes and the relations between them. For example, the issue of the shape of the earth is defined by the human practice and discourse: for city zoning, the earth can be flat while for open see navigation for long distances, the earth is spherical. Whitson argues that the students need to learn about the diversity of the discourses and their interrelation rather than self-contained and self-sufficient decontextualized concepts, which decontextualized nature is always arbitrary based on an authoritarian monological regime of conventional school classrooms.

The issue of contextualization or decontextualization is about how the teacher deals with the students' subjectivities – their perception, skills, and understanding of the world. As an observant teacher, Hunter, for example, correctly guesses that majority of children (and adults) think that okra is a vegetable. She wants to teach the botanic classification of plants, according to which okra is a fruit. So far so good. The problem of decontextualization begins when one idea – the idea that okra is a vegetable – is UNCONDITIONALLY rejected while the other idea – the idea that okra is a fruit – is UNCONDITIONALLY accepted despite the fact that the rejected idea somehow emerged in the human community. Contextualization of the curriculum, argues Whitson, is exactly about investigation of the conditions for the ideas, their rationales for existence, limitations, and relations. In this semiotic approach developed by Whitson, all curricula are conditional and limited even such famous math statements as $2+2=4$. Indeed, two drops of water putted together with two additional drops of water do not produced 4 drops but one drop of water, so for drops $2+2=1$. Two hungry cats placed with two fat mice do not produce 4 animals but only two, so predator and pray animals, $2+2=2$. Two molecules of hydrogen added to two molecules of oxygen do not produce four molecules but only 3: two molecules of water and one molecule of oxygen ($2H_2+2O_2 \rightarrow 2H_2O+1O_2$), so for chemically active molecules $2+2=3$. Two and two small triangles put together can generate 5 different-size triangles (four small equal ones and one big one, see figure 7), so for triangles $2+2=5$.

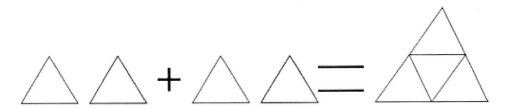

Figure 7. 2. triangles + 2 triangles = 5 triangles.

Even more, from our social experience, we know that two friends plus two friends cannot guarantee 4 friends – the outcome is uncertain, so for friends 2+2=uncertainty. Thus, the math statement of 2+2=4 is conditional and based on addition of particular objects that have linear relations – they do not interact with each other[1]. It is interesting that such school math subject as algebra focuses on studying diverse and often non-linear functions that involve objects, for which 2+2≠4. It can be argued that one of the reasons that many students in conventional schools have problem understanding non-linear functions is because they have learned too well in their elementary school that 2+2 is unconditionally equals 4.

As I have already discussed above in my analysis of the Read Aloud Lesson on Animals in Winter, the teacher treated the curriculum as given and self-contained for the herself. How did she treat it for the students in the lesson? Did the teacher produce containerization, described by Hunter and analyzed by Whitson, during her Read Aloud Lesson? Did the teacher promote realization of diverse human discourses and their interrelations as Whitson suggested in his semiotic approach? My analysis of how the teacher dealt with the students' subjectivities during the lesson highly suggests the process of containerization of the curriculum described by Hunter and analyzed by Whitson. Specifically, I focused on instances of how the teacher dealt with students' curricular off-script contributions to the lesson (e.g., humans prepare to the winter buy getting a Christmas tree, "deer mate", children's stories about animals) and curricular disagreements with the students (e.g., a dispute about whither some bats migrate or not). Out of 11 of such instances that I found in the lesson, only 2 were *curricularly*[2] supported by the teacher (e.g., a student's question of how the sun dries grass in the winter). All other nine instances were either rejected or actively suppressed by the teacher. Granted that the teacher's strategic decision to reject and suppress these themes brought by the children probably were based on her concerns about the limited time of the lesson, maintaining the thematic focus, and thematic appropriateness (like in the case of "deer mate"). However, the teacher clearly supported some off-script themes evens offered by her students and suppressed the others. What was the pattern?

I argue that the pattern was the following. The teacher supported only those off-script themes that fit her given, self-contained, and, thus, decontextualized, curriculum. In a monologic conventional classroom, the teacher tries to maintain an expert authority with

---

[1] The described possibility of why 2+2 does not necessarily equal 4 is not the only one.
[2] The numbers here are different than ones presented in Table 8 because not all off-script contributions made by the students constituted distinguished curricular themes. Also, I counted the valence of the teacher's evaluation of the students' off-script contributions differently. In Table 8, I counted the teacher's holistic reaction to the contribution while here I counted only curricular evaluation of the off-script contribution. Thus, the teacher may praise a student's off-script reply while rejecting it as a curricular theme. This case was coded as "ambivalent" in table 3 but as rejection for the current discussion of the didactic space.

her/his students, by either knowing in advance or reasoning (guessing) on the fly a satisfactory response to the students' contributions. I argue that this expert authority of the teacher generates decontextualized curriculum in the classroom. A response is satisfactory from the teacher's point of view if it is seen as convincing by her/himself and the students and does not contradict the past or current pre-designed curriculum. For example, the teacher had either known or guessed-reasoned on the fly that the sun dries grass from woodchuck in the summer and not in the winter. This seemed to be reasonable and did not contradict the book. Also, the teacher might know (although highly unlikely, based on her admission to the children, that she had known pika before reading the book) or more likely reasoned-guessed that pika never loses its food gathered in summer because it keeps it in its tunnel. It sounds reasonable and does not contradict the book. However, the student's reply to the teacher's questions about how humans prepare for the winter that humans try to get Christmas tree apparently disrupted and challenged the teacher's expert authority as she did not know and could not guess-reason how humans spiritual preparation for the winter fits her pre-designed self-contained curriculum. However, this theme did present rich opportunities for contextualization discussed by Whitson as it promotes new fruitful inquiries and relevant: are human different from animals because of their spiritual preparation to the winter, do some animals have any spiritual preparation for the winter, and so on. Similarly, a student's sad story about a deer being hit by car did not fit the teacher's pre-designed curricula and thus challenged her expert authority so she had to suppress the discussion while the story could have easily promote important inquiries such as whether deer come on roads more often in summer or in winter and why, what humans have responsibilities for the animals in general and specifically in winter, and so on. Finally, probably the most striking example of how the teacher tried to maintain her expert authority by suppressing students' curricular themes was her rejection of the student's correct statement that some bats migrate as their way of dealing with the winter. It is less important for our discussion that the student was right according to the read book but the fact that the teacher trumped her *expert* authority over the expert authority of the book (and over the *learning* authority of the student).

I strongly argue that all nine rejected or suppressed incidents presented wonderful teaching moments and learning opportunities missed by the teacher (cf. Tharp & Gallimore, 1988, ch. 6). Moreover, I hypothesize that these moments and opportunities were missed by the teacher not because she could not think quickly enough (although I do not fully exclude this possibility as partial one (see a discussion of this issue in Kennedy, 2005)), but MAINLY because she was busy with maintaining her expert authority. I could not find one instance of the teacher's curriculum contextualization as defined by Whitson despite many possibilities presented by the students to the teacher (not counting possibilities that the teacher could have created on herself own initiative if she wished to do so). By prioritizing and focusing on how to maintain her teacher-expert authority – this prioritization also includes the teacher's focus on covering curriculum[3] as her main goal in the lesson), by the way, – she containerized,

---

[3] A dialogic teacher Lampert (2001) also expressed her concern about "covering curriculum" in a sense of her making sure that her students learn important math knowledge and are ready for the next grade. Although her concerns can arguably come from working in a broader monological institutional context, still Lampert's way of "covering curriculum" is different from many monological conventional teachers. To assure her "covering curriculum", Lampert investigates *the student curriculum* – what the students have really learned, how they think and participate in math activities -- rather than tries to mover her students through *the teacher curriculum* (the terms in the italics came from Lave, 1992a). Using Lavoie's eloquent metaphor (Rosen & Lavoie, 1989), monologic "covering curriculum" involves obscuring the curriculum (like in a movement of covering a watch

purified, decontextualized, and alienated the academic curriculum from her student. This tendency of a monologic conventional classroom nicely described by Leo Tolstoy, an innovative educator and famous writer of the nineteenth century,

> The whole external world is allowed to act upon the pupil only to the extent to which the educator finds it convenient. The educator tries to surround his pupil with an impenetrable wall against the influences of the world, and allows only so much to pass through his scholastico-educational funnel as he deems to be useful. I am not speaking of what has been done by so-called unprogressive men—I am not fighting windmills. I am speaking of the comprehension and application of education by so-called excellent, progressive educators. Everywhere the influence of life is removed from the cares of the pedagogues; everywhere the school is surrounded with a Chinese wall of book-knowledge, through which only so much of the vital cultural influence is admitted as may please the educators. The influence of life is not recognized. Thus the science called pedagogy looks upon the matter, for it assumes the right to know what is necessary for the formation of the best man, and it considers it possible to remove every extra-educational influence from its charge; even thus they proceed in the practice of education (Tolstoy, 1967, pp. 107-108).

The hidden curriculum of the lesson that the students might learn along many other similar lessons in monologic conventional classroom is that the final authority of the knowledge is rooted in the teacher (and secondary in the text authorized by the teacher) and not so much in their own experiences and/or reasoning. The students may learn that the school academic curriculum is not aimed at enriching their lives but rather their lives may sometimes be illustrations for the self-contained, self-served, and decontextualized school academic curriculum.

Saying that, I want to emphasize that the teacher can never fully determine what students have learned from the lesson. Some students may learn opposite that the hidden curriculum suggests them to learn. For example, in this read aloud lesson, some student might learn to believe in their own reasoning and experience and learn how to resist the teacher when they see through their own reasoning and experiences that the teacher is wrong (Candela, 1999) like, probably, the boy who insisted that some bats migrate for the winter – he did not seem to surrender to the teacher's pressure to accept the erroneous fact about bats.

In sum, the didactic space of monologic conventional classroom designed by the teacher is often decontextualized in a sense that it is bracketed from students' ontology, from their life and life experiences, their own reasoning, as well as from local classroom contexts of the students and the teacher spending time together in the classroom. This didactic space opposes the students' (and the teacher's) ontological real space. In the real world, the students set their own goals, develop their own chain of actions, and check the consequences of these actions in the world's response for fulfillment of their set goals. In the didactic space of monologic conventional teaching the students do not have their own goals besides doing what the teacher asks them to do, their chain of actions has to follow the teacher's prescription, the consequences of their actions is defined not be the world' response but by the teacher's (often arbitrary) judgment of the students' academic progress. The separation of the traditional

---

by a hand). Expanding Lavoie's metaphor, it is possible to claim that Lampert and other dialogic teachers *uncover the curriculum* for their students.

didactic space from the local classroom space and from the participants' ontological space leads to its self-containing and potential irrelevancy.

Didactic Time of Monologic Pedagogy: Covering the Curriculum

The didactic time defines itself in the following questions, "What didactically happens in the classroom? Why does it happen? How do the participants perceive it?" The didactic time of monologic conventional classroom can be characterized as *"covering curricula"* by the teacher. It is a very chronotopic category since the didactic time in traditional schooling defined through didactic space as spreading teaching and learning through it. In the Read Aloud Lesson on Animals on Winter, the given curriculum of how animals deal with winter was covered by reading and summarizing[4] the book (see figure 6).

A teacher in monologic conventional classroom covers curricula through organized *preemptive guidance* that supposed to cause learning in students. As Bakhtin (1986) pointed out, meaning making process involves answering to questions. Meaning making process in a monologic conventional teaching is often organized by the teacher in a series of preemptive question-answers that the teacher asks questions and then answers either by him/herself and/or by the students. Apparently, monologic teaching is modeled after informal everyday guidance when a person seeking information or knowledge asks questions of another person who may know the answer. However, in monologic teaching the person who asks and answers the questions is essentially the same – the teacher, which, according to Bakhtin, contradicts the main principle of dialogical "outsideness" (in Russian "вненаходимость"),

> *Question* and *answer* are not logical relations (categories); they cannot be placed in one consciousness (unified and closed in itself); any response gives rise to a new question. Question and answer presuppose mutual outsideness. If an answer does not give rise to a new question from itself, it falls out of the dialogue and enters systemic cognition, which is essentially impersonal.
> The various chronotopes of the questioner and the answerer, and various semantic worlds (*I* and *other*). From the standpoint of a third consciousness and its "neutral" world, where everything is replaceable, question and answer are inevitably deperesonified (Bakhtin, 1986, p. 168, the italics is original).

The later is exactly the role of the teacher in a monologic conventional classroom. Even if a student answers the teacher's question, it is essentially the teacher's answer because it is the teacher who defines if the answer is acceptable or not. The monologic teacher tries to preempt the students' possible questions by figuring out the questions in advance before the students ever ask the questions. Thus, the nature of the questions is changed: in informal everyday guidance-learning situations, the questions are often asked by the learner and they have the information-seeking nature while in monologic conventional classroom, the questions are mainly asked by the teacher and they have the answer-known nature (Matusov & Rogoff, 2002; Mehan, 1979). Thus, the monologic teacher creates an "imaginary learner" (Matusov & Smith, 2007) often based on the teacher's own prior experiences (D. L. Ball & Cohen, 1999) or speculations about the students whom the teacher plans to guide. This imaginary learner

---

[4] The teacher's initial plan to covering curriculum through making predictions about animals dealing with the winter, reading the book, and checking the prediction was quickly abandoned by the teacher probably because the teacher felt threat to the stability of monologic pedagogy and to the smoothness of her flow of the assigned tasks.

"asks" questions in the teacher's head that the teacher replies to them in the actual classroom (or leads actual students to reply to induce the ready-made correct answers from them). In his vast study of many traditional classrooms, Goodlad (1984) found about only 1% of class time was devoted to open-ended critical discussion. Similar findings were reported by many educational researchers in past and in modern times (Colvin, 1919; Nystrand, 1997; Sarason, 1983; Tharp & Gallimore, 1988).

In contrast, a teacher who is interested in dialogic pedagogy asks genuine information-seeking question and searching for genuine unknown-in-advance answer from his or her students as an innovative teacher Paley (1986b) describes,

> When my intention was limited to announcing my own point of view, communication came to a halt. My voice drowned out the children's. However, when they said things that surprised me, exposed ideas I did not imagine they held, my excitement mounted. I kept the children talking, savoring the uniqueness of responses so singularly different from mine. The rules of teaching had changed: I now wanted to hear answers I could not myself invent. Indeed, the inventions tumbled out as if they had been simply waiting for me to stop talking and being listening (p. 125).

A monologic conventional teacher concerned with maintaining unilateral control over the students and covering the academic curriculum of no personal interest to the teacher develops a monologic didactic voice that is easy to recognize for its flatness, disinterest, disaffection, and unilateral authority well described by an educational sociologist Waller,

> A better voice [of the teacher – EM], unquestionably, from the standpoint of the necessities of the school room, is the dry, impersonal, and didactic voice which teachers usually fall into the habit of using. Apparently it is produced by continuous exposition. Exposition is itself dry and impersonal, and since it is rather the teacher's function to tell people things than to raise questions or to invite them to wonder, the teacher's whole personality comes to be cast into that form of discourse. The dryness of the teaching voice is increased by the necessity for many repetitions of facts which were never very meaningful to the teacher, and from which all vestige of meaning has long since been drained out. The didactic voice is the voice of authority and the voice of ennui. There is in it no emotion, no wonder, no question, and no argument. It imparts facts. There enters likewise into the classroom voice the impersonality of the voice of command. The voice of command is also in large part a product of the social experience of the person who must continually order others about. This tone of voice goes with a formalization of all social relationships and a stereotyping of the words of command (Waller, 1932, p. 229).

In his 8-year study of thousand traditional classrooms, Goodlad (1984) calculated that only 3% of the time in class has any emotional tone.

The voice of the teacher from the monologic conventional classroom in the Read Aloud Lesson on Animals in Winter that I analyzed was much more personal (i.e., partially personal), friendly, relaxed, and affectionate than Waller described above. The teacher's friendliness invites the students' cooperation. This finding seems to support Lortie's (1975) observation that a modern monologic conventional teacher tries to build his or her unilateral classroom order on cooperation with the students rather than on adversarial confrontation apparently more common for Waller's time of schooling. However, like in Waller's description, the teacher's voice remained disinterested, patronizing, authoritative, and expert-like or, using Waller's own words, "There is in it ... no wonder, no question, and no argument," but rather constant evaluation, invitation for cooperation, and the final authority. The voice of a modern monologic conventional teacher remains impersonal with the regard to the taught academic curriculum and the classroom discourse.

Covering curricula through a questioning-answering process predesigned by the teacher usually unfolds through mainly three communicative formats (and their mixture): 1) a monologic lecture, 2) a rhetorically interactive lecture, 3) a teacher-students interaction controlled by the teacher. A monologic lecture consists of answers to the imaginary learner's questions that are not present in the lecture. Only answers are present which puts a lot of demands on a listener who in order to make sense of the monologic lecture has to reconstruct the implicit questions that these answers are aimed to address. For example, consider the teacher's reading the text of the book Animals in Winter,

> "Animals in Winter. The days grow short, the nights grow long, it is getting colder, winter's is coming. The leaves have fallen from the trees. There are no berries on the bushes. Insects are gone. The grass is dead and brown. [shows picture]. Birds and other animals are getting ready for winter. Some of the birds will fly south. Bluebirds and orioles will move toward the south. They go where it is warm and sunny and where there's food for them to eat. When spring comes, the birds will make the long journey back north. They migrate. [shows picture. A child raises his hand. The teacher nods her head. Child puts his hand down about 3 seconds later]. Some butterflies migrate too. That is what the monarch butterflies do. They gather in the tree by the hundreds before cold weather comes. They stay in the tree all night long. In the morning, they fly toward their winter homes in the south."

Using Bakhtin's (1986) insights about meaning as a response to somebody else's question, it is possible to re-write the text as an imaginary dialogue:

> Imaginary reader-student (IRS): What is the title of this book?
> Author-teacher (AT): *Animal is Winter*.
> IRS: What happens when the winter comes?
> AT: The days grow short, the nights grow long, it is getting colder, winter's is coming. The leaves have fallen from the trees. There are no berries on the bushes. Insects are gone. The grass is dead and brown.
> IRS: What happens with animals when the winter comes?
> AT: Birds and other animals are getting ready for winter.[5]
> IRS: How animals get ready for winter?
> AT: Some of the birds will fly south. Bluebirds and orioles will move toward the south.
> IRS: Why do they fly south?
> AT: They go where it is warm and sunny and where there's food for them to eat.
> IRS: When do they come back?
> AT: When spring comes, the birds will make the long journey back north.
> IRS: What process is this called?
> AT: They migrate.

---

[5] It is interesting that this apparently oversweeping generalization about animals is wrong as the book says further that some animals do not to prepare for the winter at all.

and so on... (the italics indicates the original text of the book)

Of course, my segmenting the text on units of meaning is arbitrary and reveals my own interpretation of the text, rather than how the book author or the teacher produce and understand the text. It is one of unlimited ways of meaning segmentation of a particular text. I want to illustrate the idea that comprehension of text is a dialogic discourse that intuitively or very consciously understood by many teachers and use in their teaching practice. In a dialogic classroom, this discourse process of understanding is viewed as emergent, unpredictable, and collective; while in a monologic classroom, this discourse process of understanding is seen as fixed, pre-planned, given, and teacher-controlled.

Even when the teacher asks open-ended questions, as it frequently occurred in the Read Aloud Lesson that I analyzed above, the students' answers mostly remained being a part of unfolding pre-designed script developed by the teacher. Although a monologic teacher cannot fully predict the students' answers to his or her open-ended questions, the teacher still has a range of acceptable answers defined in advance as in the following example from the Read Aloud Lesson on Animals in Winter:

> Teacher: What are some things that you guys do to prepare for winter? [about 8 kids raise their hands] Richard, I saw your hand go up first. So, tell me.
> Richard: Getting Christmas tree and ornaments.
> Teacher: That's something to prepare for... Christmastime! But say, for the cold weather.
> Richard: Oh. Buy warm clothes?
> Teacher: Very good. Anybody else?

Richard's first answer was rejected by the teacher because it was outside of the scope of the expected answers while his second answer was accepted. Bakhtin defined monologic discourse when it is focused on affirmation versus rejection of contributions of others (Bakhtin, 1999) which is very different from dialogic responses of agreement and disagreement. Although both responses are evaluative by their nature, dialogic responses involve testing ideas – both the person's own and the interlocutor's ones, – while monologic responses involve checking how much students' contributions match pre-existing ideas of the teacher – whether the students' responses are within the circle of what the teacher accepts. A dialogic disagreement is different from a monologic rejection because it is based on consideration of the other's ideas rather than on its correspondence to one's own worldviews. For example, during a discussion of exclusion of some children from other children's play, a kindergarten teacher Vivian Paley disagreed with her students about having a boss who always can decide disputes of exclusions but she did not reject the students' ideas and contributions rather she focused on testing their and her own ideas in a dialogic discourse:

> "Does there have to be a boss?" I asked.
> "Yeah, it's better" a girl responds. "Sometimes me and Jamie play and we say there has to be a boss so if other people want to play and some people don't like that person whoever we pick to be the boss is the person to decide."
> *I find myself disturbed* by this unchallenged acceptance of a boss. In the kindergarten, at least, the children argue or even cry about it. "Tell me," I say, "why exactly is a boss necessary?"

"If they didn't have bosses," a boy replies, "they could just vote." He contemplates the choices. "Or if it's someone everyone likes, they could just come in."

"If you are not a person everyone likes, then what gives you a better chance," I ask, "voting or a boss?" They all agree that voting usually works in favor of the person wanting to come in and is the fairest way to decide. But having a boss is much better.

My look of puzzlement brings on a sea of waving arms. One girl seems to speak for the group. "See, the bad thing about voting is, if you don't vote for that person she'll see all the people who don't like her. If it's a boss that's only *one* person doesn't like you so you don't feel so bad."

This is a novel thought [to me – EM]: It is kinder to be rejected by only one classmate. Then you can still imagine that the others like you. "What if there were no bosses? And you didn't vote *or* choose. Whoever wanted to play could do so."

"That would be more fair," a boy agrees, "but it would be impossible to have any fun. It is a good rule though" (Paley, 1992, pp. 45-46, the italics and bold emphases are mine)

The italic emphasis that I added shows how the teacher evaluated the students' idea. Her disagreement was not based on the fact that the students' ideas are not in the pre-existing zone of what the teacher accepts but rather on both dislike the idea of the having boss for decision making and her puzzlement of why the kindergarten children were so attracted to the idea. Finally, I marked with bold the teacher's recognition and appreciation of the novelty of the students' idea that it is better to be rejected by one classmate, who would be designated as the boss, than by the majority of the classmates as in the case of voting. The dialogic disagreement is a rather complex discursive social and cognitive event.

In contrast, in a monologic classroom, students' responses do not constitute new information for the teacher: either the teacher knew the information before in a case when the student's answer is "correct" or the teacher rejects the information in a case when the student's answer is "incorrect" or "off-script" (see table 11). Thus, in monologic conventional classroom, it is essentially the teacher who asks and answers the questions. Although, monologic teaching is doubly a case of "internal dialogue aloud" exactly because the teacher remains identical to him/herself throughout the discourse of the lesson – there is nothing in question for the teacher.

Table 11. Key Features of Monologically and dialogically Organized Instruction (from Nystrand, 1997, p. 19)

	Monologically Organized Instruction	Dialogically Organized Instruction
Paradigm	Recitation	Discussion
Communication model	Transmission of knowledge	Transformation of understandings
Epistemology	Objectivism: Knowledge is a given	Dialogism: Knowledge emerges from interaction of voices
Source of valued knowledge	Teacher, textbook authorities: Excludes students	Includes students' interpretations and personal experience
Texture	Choppy	Coherent

One of major consequences of covering pre-designed curricula is that the teacher's guidance is often blind. The teacher designs guidance in advance to actual interaction with his or her students and, thus, does not have an access to their subjectivities. The guidance (and curricular) design is based on teacher-imagined subjectivities of teacher-imagined students (Matusov & Smith, 2007). These imagined subjectivities are often based on the teacher's expectations of educational needs of "generic student" based on the teacher's own past teaching experiences (e.g., observations on the teacher's past or current students), own learning experiences as a student and a learner, general past experiences, educational and psychological literature (e.g., reading Piaget about pre-operational and operational types of thinking), and pedagogical reasoning. In essence, it is an _informed guess_work on the part of the teacher. The informed guesses can be correct or can be wrong: the students may have needs and problems, which the teacher anticipates and tries to address in her/his pre-planned guidance, or they may not. As I have argued elsewhere (Matusov & Smith, 2007), by itself, the teacher's informed guesswork and imagining students' subjectivities is not a problem and does not necessarily constitute blind guidance. The problem starts when the teacher's informed guesswork is not tested and informed by the emerging reality (i.e., the students' unfolding subjectivities) during the lesson.

In a monologic conventional classroom, the role of actual students is often limited to being witnesses of the unfolding discourse of the teacher with his/her imaginary students. Even when the teacher asks students questions, the students' replies are evaluated by the teacher in the context of the pre-designed instructional discourse with the imaginary students: as correct, incorrect, or off-script. Through this process, the teacher has very little access to the actual students' subjectivities. For example, in the Read Aloud Lesson on Animals in Winter discussed above, when the teacher suppressed a student's story about a deer being hit by a car on a road, the teacher did not learn if the child or the other children who heard the story saw a connection between this tragic event and the seasons (especially the winter) or an issue of human responsibility for animals and, if so, what were the connections or issues they saw. The teacher rejected the student's story as being irrelevant to the theme of Animals in Winter. She could be right or wrong. She could be right about that for the student who told the story but wrong for students who heard the story. On a bigger instructional scope, it is very difficult to know what the students (as a group and each of them) had known about Animals in Winter prior the lesson – i.e., the different ways of their dealing with the winter (see the blue ellipses on figure 2), – and what they (as a group and individual students) actually learned by the end of the lesson. The actual students' subjectivities were remained mainly in dark except a few cases in which the teacher worked with actual students' subjectivities. These exceptional cases involved two students asking questions about the sun drying the grass in the winter and about pika hiding grass, the students' lack of familiarity with the word "attentive", and not knowing how woodchuck looks like. Only in these rare (and, arguably, peripheral) cases, the teacher's guidance was based on the actual students' subjectivities (i.e., formal assessment) and not on their guesswork of imaginary students.

In contrast, in a dialogic classroom, pre-designed instruction (e.g., Lampert's "Problem of the Day", Lampert, 2001) serves a provocation for the students that is aimed at revealing the actual students' subjectivities. By designing such a provocation, the teacher also does informed guesswork and also creates imaginary students, "I am calling this kind of teaching work 'anticipation' because it is about developing the foreknowledge that I would need to take advantage of the opportunities that would arise to make mathematical connections as students worked in the time-speed-distance context" (Lampert, 2001, p. 184). A good provocation reveals a diversity of subjectivities in the classroom (that includes the teacher's subjectivity as well). In other words, a good provocation creates an opportunity for dialogic disagreements, issues, problems, or dilemmas. For example, Lampert's Problem of the Day for a math lesson in a fifth grade classroom was to assess where a train running with permanent speed will be in different periods of time. The teacher expected to find and did find diverse approaches to the math problem and diverse answers both revealing the students' mathematical thinking (i.e., their math subjectivities) and possibilities to have a dialogue for discussion of these diversities and testing each other's ideas, "These variations [made by the students – EM] of what I wrote on the board suggest that in making their representations, students were negotiating between my effort at mathematizing the situation and their own thinking about it" (Lampert, 2001, p. 195). A bad provocation reveals a classroom consensus that makes dialogue near impossible unless some disagreements, issues, problems, or dilemmas external to the classroom are found. For example, the same math problem that Lampert used may not be such a good provocation for advanced math scholars who may quickly establish a consensus for whom the presented problem would be non-problematic. Although a bad provocation can still provide the teacher with the access to the students' subjectivities, it does not create a dialogue and teaching-learning opportunities.

Dialogic instruction is based on the teacher's active searching and finding (i.e., discovering) the curriculum in the students and addressing this emergent student curriculum through a dialogic classroom discourse (see Lampert, 2001; Paley, 1992, for detailed examples and analysis of such dialogic classroom instruction). Dialogic instruction starts with the teacher's genuine, information-seeking questions to him/herself, "How do my students think, feel, act? How do they understand the world? How do they participate in a specific practice? What problems do they have? What strengths they show?" Or in Lampert's own words, "More pedagogically challenging is the problem of figuring our how to use a context, both to bring students in contact with the connected universe of important mathematical ideas that the problems posed make available and to make the contact that they have with those ideas productive learning" (Lampert, 2001, p. 211). Diversity of students' contributions are seen in a dialogic classroom not as the presence or absence of competence but as teaching opportunities, "Instead of identifying those students who made the error as a group that *does not have* something that the rest *does have*, I teach by making the common error into an opportunity for all students to study mathematical reasoning as well as fractions" (Lampert, 2001, p. 357, the italics is original). In other words, dialogic instruction starts with the teacher's learning about the students that guides the teacher's instruction (i.e., so-called "formative assessment"), "Using student work… to figure out what kinds of problems to pose in future lessons was something I did often across the year. Analyzing what one student did gives me a concrete ten-year-old's perspective on what needs to be studied and how we might study it" (Lampert, 2001, p. 198). In a dialogic classroom, teacher curriculum and student curriculum (Lave, 1992a) – what the teacher intentionally teaches and what the student actually learns in the lesson – become nested in the process of the student curriculum emerging in the teacher's design provocations and the classroom discourse itself driving the teacher's instruction. The teacher helps the students transform their own subjectivities. In a dialogic instruction, the curriculum is always emergent and, thus, unpredictable (Morson, 2004). In monologic conventional classrooms, only brief germs of such a dialogic instruction emerge, as it was seen in the discussed Read Aloud Lesson.

Didactic Evaluation of Monologic Pedagogy: "It Sucks the Life out of You!"

Didactic evaluation summatively assesses students' learning credentialized knowledge (DePalma, Matusov, & Smith, 2009, in press; Labaree, 1997; McNeil, 1986) and creates their academic identities. Waller (1932, p. 365) noticed that "academic requirements, grades, and examinations set teachers and students at one another's throats" created by the system of ever-present summative assessment. As Lave elegantly puts it,

> But what is that 'what' that learners are learning? Facts? Knowledge? Skill? Yes, but perhaps that is not the most crucial way to characterize what is going on. We might not want to take the study of learning to be first and foremost the study of knowledge people are acquiring, though theories of learning have traditionally been based in epistemological analysis, in the philosophy of knowledge and knowing, hence on conceptions of the knowing, contemplating, (representing, problem solving ...) person. In contrast, learning, viewed as socially situated activity, must be grounded in a social ontology that conceives of the person as an acting being, engaged in activity in the world. Learning is, in this purview, more basically a process of coming to *be,* of forging identities in activity in the world.
> In short, learners are never only that, but are becoming certain sorts of subjects with certain ways of participating in the world (Lave, 1992a).

So far, we were discussing the didactic space of traditional teaching as designed by the teacher externally. Let's discuss how the space is perceived internally by the class participants. The students of traditional classroom often perceive the didactic space axiologically by setting value-judgments and emotional flavors on specific curricular topics they studied: interesting vs. boring, like-it vs. dislike-it, relevant vs. irrelevant, useful vs. "busy work", easy vs. difficult, and so on. For example, this is students' reactions to a statement, "Today we are going to study poetry" – "BORING!" "Yak," "interesting", "Not again!", "exciting." Thus, each curricular topic has some emotionally axiological valence for a student, sometimes even before the topic being taught. The student's emotionally axiological valence to a specific curricular topic is defined by the student's ontological – whole-person – reaction to the curricular topic, its teaching, the teacher, the classroom, and the student's progress of studying it as defined by the teacher, the classmate, and the student him/herself. Unpackaging such student's statement as "I like fractions because I'm good at them" would probably lead us to evidence that the student successfully: 1) fulfills classroom assignments set by the teacher, 2) meets the teacher's expectations regarding learning the topic of fraction, 3) is seen by the relevant classmates as "being good at fractions" (e.g., being better than many other classmates), 4) supports his/her high social status and cultural/academic capital in area of the fractions in the classroom, 5) has his/her positive identity investment in the topic of fractions, 6) has reverberations to the broader activity, status, identity, and societal areas like being good at and in math, school, institutionalized education, societal institutions, citizenship, and so on.

Monologic conventional classrooms expect failure in students and use grades to inflict some emotional pain in failing students in order to make them put more efforts in their studies – to "stimulate" the students to work harder. The ancient Greek and then Latinized word "stimulus" among other meanings like "stalk", "pin", and "stylus" for writing on wax tables (Oxford University Press, 1989) referred to a sharp spear that was used to prick mules to speed them up and to work harder. It seems that bad grades are often used in conventional schools in a similar way. My colleagues and I did research on how students from an innovative K-8 collaborative dialogic school (Newark Center for Creative Learning, or shortly NCCL) transition to conventional schools. The research involved many interviews and reunions with NCCL alumni, their former teachers, and parents (DePalma et al., 2009, in press; Matusov et al., 2005, September). Here is what an alumnus of the collaborative school said us about grades,

> Eddie: I got really upset the other day because I was talking with one of my teachers about how grades were horrible.
> A3 [interviewer –EM]: What did you say?
> Eddie: ... to sum it up, it was just me ranting on about how I don't like grades, and if everybody got A's, there'd be no point in using the grade system, but they instituted it so people feel bad when they get a bad grade. [Reunion#2]

Grading sorts students for future access to good colleges and jobs. It creates academic and social reputations in the teacher's, students', parents', and institutions' eyes (Waller, 1932). It promotes unhealthy competitions in students and distracts them from genuine learning.

> Sarah: ...There's this one girl in my history class who must get straight A's in absolutely everything. Because she's like bossy and she's loud, and she knows the answer to everything. (laughter among the other interview participants) Absolutely everything! She can quote the textbook. OK? Like it's really kind of getting annoying sometimes. But it's just the impression that you get from somebody who's always good. I like the NCCL way because people don't, I mean, no one at NCCL ever asks you about how did you do on your report card. (laughter, general comments).
> Cameron: There isn't any report card to ask about.
> Sarah: There is a report card but you don't ask about it because it's not something... it's not something that deeply affected your life. I mean some people like, report card day they were like downcast the entire day, like "this is the end of my entire life", and I'm like, "Why?" Cause they just think grades matter so much, and it's just not a good system as NCCL. [Reunion#2]

Grading imposes negative identities on some students and lowers their self-esteem as less worthy people with low intellectual ability (McNeil, 1986). "This method of labeling and streaming students turned students into static 'products'. Because of the bureaucratic design of the school system and the philosophical premises upon which the curriculum was based, the teachers could not with the students as if they were continually changing persons" (McLaren, 1993, p. 202). However, as one NCCL alumnus noticed, sometimes low grades may reflect low interest of the student in the subject rather than their low intellectual abilities.

Monologic conventional classrooms make learning difficult for the students by focusing the students' attention on unconditional efforts to get good grades and high scores on tests. The students' efforts guided by grades become separated and alienated from the work itself. Learning becomes difficult because instead of being a by-product of learning activity it becomes the product of self-motivation to do the things that the teacher requires without necessarily having any intrinsic value in itself. This is how an NCCL teacher explained the process, of which grades inhibit learning,

Richard: I always go through these imaginary situations because parents will ask me these questions, other teachers will ask me these questions, you know, how do you make it work without grades, you know, how do you make it work without grades!? And you know, the thing that I always *imagine* kind of doing is, is, OK, let's play a game. Let's have a conversation, *but,* before we start, realize that I'm going to *grade* everything you say to me. I'm going to judge everything you say to me. And periodically, I'm going to tell you how you're doing in this conversation. I'm going to grade your style, I'm going to grade your content, I'm going to talk about... you know, is your opinion worthy of this discussion, are you *doing well!?* Are you *failing?!* And, you know, it's like [exasperatedly], and then you try to have a conversation with them, and then they can't *talk* to you! They won't talk to you anymore! (Interview, 3-18-2005)

The grades as decontextualized measure of students' institutional success affect students-parents relations, often making them more adversarial. It seemed by a conventional school to be assumed that a good concerned parent has to add stress in their children's life in response to bad grades or demerits,

Danielle: ...I was failing ... one of my classes, and I got a note home and she [i.e., mother] got really mad at me, and I was like, you know, I mean it's not really that big of a deal.
Eugene [the author]: Did she explain why she sometimes concerned about your grades?
Danielle: No, she didn't. She just yelled at me, and that was about it. She didn't actually like explain....
Emma: Wait, I have a question! How many kids here actually intercepted the interim letter so your parents couldn't see them? [raises her hand] [Dylan raises his hand high]
...
Andrew: I just [stole?] the [report card,] one day. I took it out of my mailman's pocket and I kind of *doved* and grabbed it out of his in front of the mailbox. And then I sealed my pocket shut, so it wouldn't open and I forced it into my pocket. I think I had it in there for like a week. If I opened it myself, then i wouldn't have to... [I think he placed something else in the envelope, it's hard to hear] They have no idea what I... [Reunion#3]

The students' focus shifts from learning itself and from the intrinsic purpose of learning activity to self-motivation to study the academic material – credentialized knowledge, rather than knowledge embedded in networks of personal experiences, worldviews, and skills (DePalma et al., 2009, in press; Labaree, 1997; McNeil, 1986), -- so they will do well on the upcoming test,

Amy: Well, for me I definitely feel that there's [the stress in the High school on] the effort [rather than on genuine learning]. Like you have to put in the effort to go the extra step to get to where you want to learn. Like they're not going to hand it to you as easily. But I am still interested in learning. I mean, it's not as much fun as it was before, but it's still, for me, I still want to learn.
Cameron: Yeah, that's true. But they way they do it, you know, with the grades and all, kind of makes it less fun. Because you have to strive and push to get these good grades, which is, at the end of it, that's all anybody cares about, the teachers and everything, is what grades you get. So when you doing so much effort...

putting in so much effort you lose interest and you have less fun because you're working so hard. So that's sort of, I mean, I still like learning and everything, but it's become less interesting, because it's like I have to do all this work.

Melinda [NCCL teacher]: It's too much work.

Amy: I have a question for you. I know I feel like I still want to learn things, but I don't ... have fun learning. (here there is a jumble of apparently agreeing voices) There's not that element of fun anymore. [Reunion#2]

In order to understand better how grades and test scores promote unconditional efforts, extrinsic motivation, and decontextualized learning in students, it is useful to compare psychological effects of test scores in conventional schooling and of game scores in videogames. In videogames, the outcome of the player's action is always *intrinsically consequential*, and, thus, formative, in its nature: when, for example, the player makes his or her character to jump in a videogame, it becomes immediately apparent for the player if the character achieved the goal set by the player or not (e.g., acquire the diamond – desired goal – or jump into the fire – undesired goal). The computer may attach a score to this successful or unsuccessful outcome of the player's action, but the outcome itself is intrinsically consequential for the player because the consequences for the player's actions are rooted in the (plot) content of the game itself (e.g., getting or not getting desired diamonds or avoiding fire). The player's efforts are conditional to the consequential outcome: if the game character, controlled by the player, got the diamond, the character can move further in the maze but if the game character landed into the fire instead, the player has to start the action again.

In contrast, in monologic conventional schools, outcomes of the students' actions are inconsequential or, better to say, extrinsically (socially) consequential. For example, when we asked our preservice teachers (class discussion, in Fall 2002), majority of whom came from monologic conventional schools, why $1/2+1/3$ is not equal to $2/5$, many of them (but, fortunately, not all!) replied that it violates the rule, implying that there is a social convention behind the addition of fractions with different denominators. They were not able to see or even look for a violation of the mathematical equation in the offered example. Monologic conventional schoolwork, epiphanized in its testing practice, makes outcomes of the students' actions inaccessible for them: it is the teacher who has the final authority for deciding if their action was successful or not. The students' efforts are conditional to the teacher's judgment of their work but not to the work itself. Pleasing the teacher through the students' own blind actions becomes the students' overarching goal. The students' efforts become intrinsically conditional only when they learn how to judge themselves the success or failure of their own actions as it is done in NCCL and, thus, become the final authorities of their own actions (like game players). Judging the success of their own actions violates grading and testing practice used in conventional schools. Similar points were made by NCCL alumni when they compared building computers by students for themselves and graded classroom activities in their conventional schools,

Emma: ...you're not going to be graded on how well you build a computer, but when you're taking a class, you're grade says like to the State or to the high school, the grade says who you are and how much you tried. Even if you do try a lot and you know, it's a really hard class or something like that, but like if you're going to build a computer, if you *fail* at building a computer, the only one that misses out is you, because you don't get to take the computer home. But if you were... you know, difficult class, may be people go "Aahh" [short A] because, you know, that means, that means homework, that means grades, that means, it means, it's kind of... it's different in a way.

Robert: I don't know, it'd kind of be the same case though, because you, *you* if you failed the class, you would be missing out on whatever like...

Derek [quietly]: You wouldn't be going to college!

Robert: ...and everything. It might not really be all that different.

Amy: For me, if I put half a computer together, I might be really proud of myself, because I don't think that's something I could do. And you might be able to do something in a class, like, for example, if you did really poorly in history class throughout high school and you were able to feel like you learned a lot in that class, then you would feel really fulfilled, and then you would get your report card, and it would say, like C. And that could just ruin everything for you. You know, but that doesn't mean you didn't learn anything and that doesn't mean you are a bad student. It just means that you weren't able to restate what they wanted you to say. And like, if I build a computer, I'd feel good, but I wouldn't be able to do it all the way. And then, if they were to grade me on it, I would probably fail, but I would feel like I had done a good job. And that's were it gets hard. [Reunion#4]

Since in monologic conventional schools, the students are not taught and not allowed to make their own ultimate judgment about how their actions are successful, their studies and the teacher's guidance are often seen by the students as meaningless and irrelevant. NCCL alumni noticed that their school instruction can be meaningless for their classmates who do not fully understand what is going on in their classroom, "We have textbooks for certain subjects and then in math class we have several different subjects and we have books for each one of those, and when someone is in the class, and they're focusing on the textbook, and there's like three people around and they're like, like they have no idea what they're even starting to talk about. And then after the teacher gives direction they'll be like, 'What did we have to do again?'" [Andrew, Reunion#2] Guidance can become sensitive and requirements meaningful only through negotiation that is often not legitimate in conventional schools, the students are left to their own devices to make sense of what the teacher presents or wants from them, while the teacher is left to guess what the students need. Tolstoy wrote that in a monologic conventional classroom activity of students do not guide the teacher's instruction who is usually not aware of the students' needs, "For centuries each school has been based on the pattern of the one before it, and in each of theses schools the peremptory condition of is discipline – forbidding children to speak, ask questions, chose this or that course of study. In short, all measures are taken to deprive the teacher of all possibility of deducing the students' needs" (Tolstoy & Blaisdell, 2000, p. 177). Without a negotiation of meaning, teaching and learning are reduced to a teacher-student guessing game in a form of ritualistic instruction,

Eddie: Anything memorable? Well, ... like there's only one class that I don't like. Because...

Melinda [NCCL teacher]: and that is?

Eddie: Integrated social science. And it's like...

Melinda: And that's a shame, because that's a real strong point for you. History and social studies and that kind of thing?

Eddie: But it's not the class, it's the teacher. Because she (laughter and comments) I think she only has one, in our school you have phases, which is our general like "How smart you are." And she only has one phase-3 class, which I'm in, and the other ones are all phase-5. So I think she might get them confused, but she's on like super speed. She'll like, have us copy, how I usually do best on tests is when I see the teachers, I like listen to what they have to say. *But I can't listen to what they have to say* and like copy the notes down at the same time. And like because she'll explain something and I'm copying it down. And then she'll be at the end of the sentence and I'm only at the beginning and I'll ask her to repeat something and she gets like really upset. ... [Reunion#2]

The NCCL alumni accustomed to work hard in NCCL for the sake of learning itself that generates more interest in the academic material in them and expands their zone of their intrinsic motivation in academic curricula, "...I like the class and the material, I'm inspired to work harder in that class" [Amy, Reunion#2]. In contrast, the conventional focus on grading, narrows student's zone of intrinsic motivation, "Cause you're all like panicky when they're talking about it [i.e., discussing some academic issues in class] because you're like, 'I gotta remember everything they say,' but then you know it's all gonna be tested on, and it's everything you think was not gonna be on the test" [Cameron, Reunion#1]. Grading, and summative assessment in general, creates difficult dilemma for conscientious teachers in monological conventional schools, "Occasionally I have myself in bitter conflict with individual students over the question whether I was a human being with a message as a human being, or a teacher whose primary function was to help students to get through examinations and obtain credits and grades... I realize that... I was a dispenser of grades, and the custodian of the credits. If in trying to exert a friendly influence for sweetness and light, I failed to be a benevolent helper in the struggle for a diploma, or a no more than ordinarily unreasonable opponent, they [the students – EM] were perhaps justified in resenting it. I realize also that the students were as utterly trapped as I. It was worse for the stupid [i.e., failing students – EM], for they had a bitterly difficult tome in fulfilling even my very moderate course requirements. But even the brilliant ones had good reason to be concerned over their grades, and to conceive of their association with me in terms of marks and credits rather than in terms of understanding" (Waller, 1932, pp. 366, 368). Summative assessment distorts the focus of the students and teacher from learning and instruction to pleasing and sorting.

The NCCL alumni noticed that in monologic conventional schools, teaching is often reduced to preparation for upcoming tests, "That's the way that they're teaching you. Telling you all this stuff, then you're supposed to remember it and give it back to them. And then that's not fun, it's less fun, so..." [Cameron, Reunion#2]. The depth of learning suffers because the students are focused more on remembering the material rather than on exploring it and connecting with their own interests, thoughts, feelings, experiences, and activities. The tests reflect superficial learning limited by memorization of what the teacher taught and expects from the students and skills of test taking itself (you may not even know the material but still do well on the test),

> Amy: ... there's a girl in my school who's on a partial scholarship because she did exceedingly well on the entrance exam, and she's dumb as a rock. (laughter) ... she can pass, she is passing her classes... she can answer all the, all the questions on the test, and do just fine, and not understand any of the material and...and there's this other girl in my homeroom, she prides herself on being good at testing. I met her during the orientation and the first thing she told me about herself was

"Yeah, I'm good at testing." (loud jumbled comments and laughter in agreement with Anna's words from other NCCL alumni)

Mark [an interviewer]: These are the kids that have been testing, doing like tests Kindergarten, first grade, second grade...

Robert: It sucks the life out of you! [Reunion#2].

Summative assessment is anti-educational because it undermines the teacher-students trust. While for education, any student mistake is a teaching opportunity; for summative assessment based on sorting function, any student mistake is a potential punishment. Although sorting and summative assessment, associated with it, can be a very legitimate function and practice in a society[6]; it, arguably, should be not practiced by the same educators who teach students who are summatively assessed and sorted up and down. As Waller argued, summative assessment also inhibits a learner identity in the teacher who focuses more and more on protecting his or her expert identity in the classroom, "The creative powers of teachers disappear because the teacher tends to lose the learner's attitude" (1932, p. 394). It occurs because the teacher becomes shaped by "monological arrogance of official interpretations" (Derrida, cited in McLaren, 1993, p. 223) through practicing and socializing in a summative assessment,

> There is something in the attitude of grading, too, which makes against change, and renders mental growth difficult. One who presumes to rate the performance of another must have a very definite idea of the perfect performance, and he judges other performances, not by their inner, groping onwardness, but simply by their resemblance to the perfect performance. This perfect performance is a thing finished, for nothing can ever be super-perfect except for advertising writers, and so the teacher need not think about it any more. Yet the teacher must have in mind a perfect performance, or he is no very accurate marker. The grading, marking habit assumes increasing importance as one becomes a teacher. The new teacher rarely has definite standards of grading. Often he does not consider that part of his task important. But sceptical though one be concerning the numerical evaluation of so subjective a thing as learning, he must at length conform. From habit, from the importance which others (especially the persons graded) attach to grades, and from the involvement of the teacher's status feelings with the development of rigorous standards, there arises a change in the teacher's attitude. His status feelings become involved when he realizes that students believe that he is "easy," and preen themselves upon their ability to deceive him. (Sometimes there arises a circular interaction as a result of the alternate stiffening and relaxation of academic standards. These changes in the standards produce changes in the attitudes of students, and these in turn work upon the teacher to effect the relaxation or stiffening of standards, according to the place in the cycle where the group happens to be.) The

---

[6] Of course, if a surgeon makes harming mistakes during her surgery, the damage made to the patient cannot be excused by the fact that the mistakes present "learning opportunities" to the surgeon. Summative assessment sorts potential practitioners on those who are competent enough to be trusted with a given practice and those who are not – the societal function of sorting is legitimate in this context. However, it is not the case when a student learns to become a surgeon, when mistake making should be safe for the student, and when the teacher should be trusted by the student because s/he is always on the student's side. Summative assessment violates students' trust in their teacher. I argue here for division of labor and separation of power between the teacher, who should base his or her practice on exclusively formative assessment, and the sorter/examiner, who should base his or her practice on exclusively summative assessment, to avoid a conflict of interests. Summative assessment is a non-educational, anti-educational, and external to education societal demand (cf. Waller, 1932, pp. 368-372).

teacher must establish standards of grading; he must identify himself with them and make them a part of himself (pp. 393-394).

The Relationship between Ontological and Didactic Chronotopes and within the Chronotopes in Monologic Conventional Pedagogy: Chronotopic Compartmentalization

The main characteristic of monologic conventional chronotopes is that they are fragmented, separate, and compartmentalized across and within the chronotopes. I will start the discussion with compartmentalization of the elements of the monologic conventional chronotope -- with the "chronotopic compartmentalization fallacy", common to a monologic conventional instruction as another consequence of its covering curriculum. Whitson (2007) describes the so-called "c+i fallacy" of separation between the curriculum and instruction in monologic conventional classroom. Here, I want to add other aspects of this phenomenon that also include separation of "classroom community building" (Matusov, St. Julien et al., 2005) (often also known as "classroom management" or "classroom discipline"), motivation, assessment, and ontology from both the curriculum and instruction. Dialogic pedagogy and approach is holistic one. In other words, monologic conventional classroom views curriculum, instruction, classroom community building, motivation, and assessment positivistically as given and separate processes. In essence, dialogic pedagogy is "antimethod pedagogy" using Macedo's phrase,

> An antimethod pedagogy points to the impossibility to disarticulating methods from the theoretical principles that inform and shape them. An antimethod pedagogy makes it clear to educators that a method of teaching reflects a particular view of the world and is articulated in the interest of unequal power relations. ... [and] education is involved in a complex nexus of social, cultural, and economic and political relationships that involve students, teachers, and theorists in different position of power (Macedo, 1994, p. 181).

In a monologic conventional classroom, all chronotopic aspects are considered to be given: discipline rules are set and curriculum is defined before the lesson by the teacher and curriculum designers. The instruction is indifferent of the curriculum and can be easily applied to any other curriculum. Indeed, in the Read Aloud Lesson on the book Animals in Winter, reading followed by text summarizing can be applied to almost any text as well as prediction+reading+checking the prediction instructional strategy. The instruction is independent of the curriculum. The fact that one student raises constantly his hand to volunteer to reply to the teacher's question is often not seen how this and other students see themselves in relations to the curriculum or each other (Lampert, 2001). Similarly the system of motivation designed by the teacher for the students to engage in the curriculum is based on the rewards (e.g., stickers or grades) and punishments that are also independent of the curriculum (e.g., consider the following statement by a teacher to her students that I heard, "Those of you who do not finish these math problems, have to finish them during the recess!"). Being a good student of math does not necessarily imply liking math or being interested in math. Finally, assessment in monologic conventional classroom separated from what the students learn (i.e., curriculum) or from how they learn (i.e., instruction): monologic conventional assessment neither defines nor is embedded into curriculum and instruction as it is in a dialogic classroom. In a monological conventional classroom, being a good student does not necessarily mean being a good learner (DePalma et al., 2009, in press). Since monologic lesson involves the actual students witnessing discourse of the teacher with his/her imaginary students, it is never evident for the teacher what exactly the students as a group and individually have learned from such instruction if anything[7].

Finally, the didactic chronotope of a monologic conventional classroom is separated from its ontological chronotope. Hot, dramatic, and controversial events emerging in the classroom, in the students' lives, in the lives of the local communities, and in the life of the society rarely become the classroom didactic curriculum (McNeil, 1986). McLaren (1993) talks about "streetcorner state" and "student state" that define participants' discourse, relations, and chronotopes, "The streetcorner state embodies characteristics that are linked to what has known as informal or popular culture. Informal culture relates to the everyday rhymes of our existence, our lived encounter with our world, our daily engagement with a multitude of symbols and icons, and the informal patterns that make up our shared community of meanings. It is unfortunate that the 'official' culture of the classroom and the informal culture of street mix about as well as oil and water" (p. 248). Monologic conventional teachers try to stay away from hot social issues because the teachers correctly sense that focusing on the hot issues may disrupt the monologic pedagogical classroom order, their unilateral control, and the smoothness of their teaching flow (McNeil, 1986).

Being separate and independent aspects of the pedagogical chronotope of a monologic conventional classroom are subordinated to each other in a hierarchy. On the top of the hierarchy is a unilateral pedagogical regime of the teacher power (i.e., discipline – how to control the students), followed by the curriculum (i.e., what to teach), followed by the instruction (i.e., how to teach), and so on (Jackson, 1968; Kennedy, 2005; McLaren, 1993; McNeil, 1986; Silberman, 1971; Waller, 1932). McNeil (1986) argued that in monological conventional classrooms, knowledge is controlled through its fragmentation and simplification to control the classroom. As many High School social studies teachers interviewed in her study revealed to McNeil, "Their patterns of knowledge control were… rooted in their desire for classroom control" (p. 159). Similarly, Clow stated already in 1920, "Latin and algebra hold their place [in conventional school academic curricula – EM], not so much because school authorities revere the old, as because these old studies satisfy the first requirements of the classroom teacher, namely, a carefully graded course of work, in which definite assignments can be made and the attainments of the pupils graded according to uniform standards" (Clow, 1920, p. 365). As Waller (1932, p. 357) pointed out, "dead matter makes the best course" because it promotes the teacher's unilateral control over the curriculum and, thus, the students as their prior live experiences and knowledge are often irrelevant and their ontology safely separated from the curriculum (no much off-script contributions). When relational problems between the teachers and students emerge due to instructional issues, these problems are often seen by teachers and school administrators as discipline problems and not as instructional issues, "As students disengage from enthusiastic involvement in the learning process, administrators [and teachers –EM] often see the disengagement as a control problem" (McNeil, 1986, p. xviii). Similarly, McLaren argues that

---

[7] In contrast, in a dialogic classroom, learning is publicly visible and collectively owned, which, however, does not mean that there is not a private component of the learning. Also, learning is an open-ended and relational process that is not constrained by time, space, and context.

"instructional rites served as bureaucratic vehicles for teachers who were pressured to cover reams of preordained content; they were managerial rather than educative" (McLaren, 1993, p. 223). In some extremes of monologic conventional classrooms, concerns about control of the students leads to "defensive teaching" (McNeil, 1986, p. 101) when instruction is focused on keeping students busy and cooperative (e.g., excessive lecturing the students; forcing them to write something; using a lot of tests, quizzes, and worksheets; not assigning reading; not discussing academic material; avoiding controversial or experiential topics). "Monitoring students took precedence over teaching them. To gain student compliance with even minimal assignments, teachers had to make class 'pleasant', or at least tolerable, rather than demanding" (McNeil, 1986, p. 212; Powell et al., 1985).

I argue that monologic pedagogy, prevalent in many conventional classrooms, is responsible for at least three major mutually related problems: alienation of students from formal education, irrelevancy of the school curricula for societal and personal development, crisis of teacher authority. Alienation of students from formal education is well documented (Eckert, 1989; McLaren, 1993; McNeil, 1986; Ogbu, 2003; Willis, 1981) and occurs for both institutionally successful and failing students (Matusov, DePalma, & Drye, 2007; Varenne & McDermott, 1998), although the consequences of the alienation for these two groups are different. Both categories of the students learn in school to dislike academic learning. Irrelevancy of school curricula is documented in research on situated cognition (Lave, 1988). There is little feedback between societal practices and students' needs and forming school curricula (Labaree, 1997). The crisis of teacher authority is evident in the mass exodus of novice teachers from teaching profession citing declining discipline as the number one cause of their departure (Sidorkin, 2002).

Chapter 7

INTERNALLY PERSUASIVE DISCOURSE AND ITS COLLAPSE IN MS. VIVIAN PALEY'S CLASSROOM[1]

ABSTRACT

This research has developed a pedagogical notion of Bakhtin's literary concept of internally persuasive discourse (IPD) using Paley's (1992) book *You can't say you can't play* as ethnographic data. IPD is defined as dialogic testing of person-ideas. Mark Smith and I found educationally important features of IPD in Paley's classroom: dialogue at the threshold, dialogic finalizing, dialogic listening, and dialogic objectivizing. IPD promotes participants to transcend their ontological circumstances through addressing the ideas of others. An IPD approach sees the goal of education as engaging the students in a collective search for their own truth and testing it with others. The ontological truths of the participants – their worldviews, knowledge, skills, and attitudes, -- have to be "informed" by dialogue with the ontological truths of others.

Relation in education is one of pure dialogue.
Martin Buber (2002, p. 125).

In education equality and freedom is the chief thing.
Leo Tolstoy (1985, p. 157).

WHY IPD FOR EDUCATION?

The purpose of this chapter is to develop a *pedagogical* notion from Bakhtin's *literary* concept of "internally persuasive discourse" or IPD (Bakhtin, 1991, 1999), using Paley's book (1992) *You can't say you can't play* as ethnographic material because Mark Smith and I suspected that Paley's innovative classroom could be usefully characterized by IPD. In his analysis of the new genre of Dostoevsky's polyphonic novel, Bakhtin defines IPD as characters' testing of their own and each other's ideas. Characters in the polyphonic novel are continually faced with significant and acute life dilemmas that demand their urgent response.

---

[1] This research was performed and this chapter was written in collaboration with Mark Smith, University of Delaware, who was the second author.

The dilemma is a conflict relation among voices surrounding the characters, who are constantly addressing themselves and significant others.

To get out of this dilemma trap, the characters develop *the option-idea* which represents a dramatically new relation within and between themselves and significant others. IPD is *testing* of option-ideas with others and the character him/herself to make sure that these ideas will indeed propel them into these new relations. Bakhtin argued that, in the polyphonic novel, characters accept the ideas only through IPD and not through external authority as happens in other genres.

A major problem in education is that the teacher's guidance is often blind to students' subjectivities; teachers are not accessing for their instruction students' knowledge, worldviews, interests, indifferences, skills, attitudes, etc., simply because they do not know how the students think and feel even though they think they do know (D. L. Ball & Cohen, 1999; Schultz, 2003). Many teachers are not involved in a professional discursive process of learning about their students' subjectivities in contrast to model teachers (Matusov & Smith, 2007). As a result, the teacher's guidance is based on uninformed guesses about students' educational needs, interests and strengths.

Many educators have suggested solutions to this well-known problem, such as increasing student-teacher talk ratio, increasing use of formative assessments and open-ended questions, becoming more critical of their own teaching (in contrast to blaming students), developing rapport with students outside the classroom (Jackson, 1968). While these methods have made teachers more aware of students' subjectivities, they have not necessarily led to dialogic relationships among teachers' subjectivity, students' subjectivity and the academic curriculum (Lampert, 2001).

These dialogic relationships are important for education because the ideas arguably should be accepted only on the basis of their internal, critical persuasiveness rather than due to external authority (teacher, expert, school, etc.), communal tradition or personal prejudice (Lampert, 2001). In such process, the diverse ideas of participants are tested through discourse, and this process of dialogic testing can result in participants transcending their parochial ontological ideas and circumstances with each other. In turn, participants become responsible for envisioning new, arguably better, ontological circumstances for themselves and each other. Arguably, such a type of dialogue is ultimately the goal of education, for the student (and the teacher) are open to "a complexity of voices and perspectives" that have previously not been known, and the student and the teacher both "learn to think with those voices, to test ideas and experiences against them, and to shape convictions that are innerly persuasive in response" (Morson, 2004, p. 330). That is why we think that Bakhtin's literary concept of IPD can be especially useful for defining high-quality guidance.

Educators who recognize the importance of social construction of knowledge usually focus on its two aspects in promoting quality guidance: interactivity and epistemology. Interactive (socio-behavioral) aspect is about increasing students-teacher talk ratio while epistemological aspect is about the teacher's active working with the students' subjectivities (e.g., asking open-ended questions). Interactive-epistemological approaches in education (e.g., Burbules, 1993; Hull, 1985; Nystrand, 1997; Plato, 1997) are mainly concerned about the *blind* nature of a conventional guidance (Matusov & Smith, 2007) based on the model of transmission of knowledge that often tries to address questions in the teacher's lecture that no students asked.

However, from a Bakhtinian perspective, interactive-epistemological approaches are still essentially monologic because they view dialogue as a means for reaching truth and teaching rather than its end (Sidorkin, 1999). Monologic approaches see truth as rooted in statements. Positivistically-oriented approaches define truth as the undistorted reflection of the objective reality existing independently of people "out there". Truth is always given and only has to be discovered. In contrast, constructivistically-oriented approaches define truth as a socially-constructed consensus reached by "the most relevant parties" (see, for example, Latour, 1987). This consensus reflects the human relationship with the world (and in the world) shaped by human practices and, especially, by human goals. Statements of truth are nothing more than symbols and mediators of these consensuses, in other words, statements are reified consensuses. Freely accepted consensus (agreement, sharedness, intersubjectivity) is prioritized as its educational goal. Dialogue of reason, uncontaminated with authority and even with brutal power, is seen as *the condition* (the means) for reaching such a consensus, "Dialogue is an activity directed toward discovery and new understanding, which stands to improve the knowledge, insight, or sensitivity of its participants" (Burbules, 1993, p. 8). That is why Bakhtin's notion of "internally persuasive discourse" (Bakhtin, 1991) is so important for constructivistically-oriented educational scholars. In interactive-epistemological approaches of social constructivism, understanding is viewed as arrival to a consensus through the internally persuasive discourse (see Freedman & Ball, 2004, as an example).

In these approaches, consensuses and statements of truth (like 2+2 equals 4) are more important than people who are just historically accidental and replaceable participants in them. Who is saying the statement of truth, to whom, why, how, and under what relational and ontological circumstances are much less important for truth, if at all, than what is said. From a dialogical approach informed by Bakhtin (and Buber), this perception of truth is a monologic abstraction with serious moral consequences leading to violence and irresponsibility.

Bakhtin (1986, 1999) argued that meaning has the heteroglossic nature. Applying this to statements of truth, truth of statement is not located in its content ("internal territory of the statement") but in its external and internal "boundaries" with other statements, many of which are posing questions and many of which provides alternatives that are not true. Exactly in relationship with these often implied and hidden statements, a statement becomes the statement of truth. For example, the statement 2+2=4 can gain its power of truth only in the context of other implied, hidden, but really present statements like "why do you saying that", "to whom", "what does *it* mean 2 *plus* 2 *equals* 4?", "are you sure?", "what is 2 and what is other 2 and what is 4?", "what do *you* mean by saying that?", "why do you saying it here and now and to me?", "what is going on that you are saying that?", "why 2+2 is not 3 or 5 or something that is non-number?", "how do you know that 2+2 equals 4?", "who else think like you and who disagrees with you?", "who are you to say that?", "who said that?", "so what?", "why bother saying that", "why do you so much care about 2+2=4?", "why don't we go to see a movie instead of you claiming that 2+2=4?", "2+2 is 5!", "pardon?", "it's so boring!", "I'm not stupid!", "dah!", "yeah-yeah-yeah...", "don't show off!", "I still love you," and so on. The space of these implied questions and alternative statements is open and unlimited and prioritized the person – some implied statements are more important for the person to address and to expect than others. However, without these hidden but *really* implied questions the statement 2+2=4 does not have any truth (and any meaning) -- like in case of a parrot repeating the statement in a cage, "Two plus to equals four! Two plus equals four!" or in case of a person exclaiming "Two plus to equals four!" out of blew when he sees a car crash. The most probably replies to 2+2=4 statement in the former case of the parrot would be admiration of the parrot's imitation skills or ignoring it all together (or irritation), while the most probably replies in the latter case would be probably, "Why are you saying that?" or "What do you mean?" In both cases, it is rather unlikely that the reply is consensual, "Yes, I agree, 2+2=4." Two plus two equals four gains its truth because in the context of some specific questions raised by some people in some special circumstances, the statement 2+2=4 is *better* than any alternative statement. The criterion for this statement is being *better* is also emerged from boundaries of many other statements. Meaning is heteroglossic and what makes meaning of some statements true is also heteroglossic. Truth is heteroglossic. In other words, not only truth of statements emerges from dialogue, as proponents of interactive-epistemological approach correctly insist, but it lives in this continuing and never-ending dialogue, "Truth is not born nor is it to be found inside the head of an individual person, it is born *between people* collectively searching for truth, in the process of their dialogic interaction" (Bakhtin, 1999, p. 110, the italics original).

Each meaning is dialogically – personally and heteroglossically – unique as being responded and addressed to the unique open web of actual and implied utterances. Similarly, each truth is dialogically unique and personal. Each statement 2+2=4 whenever said in the world is unique and personal (as a unique place in the world to reply and address others); and, similarly, each time this statement comes better than alternative statements – i.e., true -- is unique and personal. What stabilizes truth is not statements mediating and symbolizing it (like 2+2=4) and not even a consensus achieved by "most relevant others" but alive and perpetual dialogue itself. Consensus among most relevant others (e.g., biology scientists about evolution of species) is only a sign of truth. But a disagreement (i.e., oppositional solidarity) can be a sign of truth as well (e.g., a disagreement between evolutionary and teleological explanations of species' origin that generates proofs for the evolutionary model). The signs of truth should not be confused with the truth itself. When a work of free and alive persuasion stops, truth stops. It can be reified in signs: statements, consensuses, oppositional solidarities, and so on but it won't be participatory truth anymore (cf. talking about truth versus talking truth, using truth versus making truth).

Since all statements in the never-ending dialogue contribute to truth, wrongness of wrong statements is never comprehensive and always relative. Wrong statements provoke alternative statements, provoke inquires, provoke dialogic tensions, provoke important questions of "why?", "what does it mean?", and "how do you know that?" They push alternatives ideas to develop in response. Good teachers know that the students' mistakes are goldmines for educational processes of the entire class. A student's wrong adding fractions 1/2+1/3=2/5 can provoke fruitful classroom discussions of what fractions and their addition means and when sign of "equal" can be used (Corser et al., 1989). Truth depends on wrong statements and cannot exist without them. Any statement is a part of dialogic truth for at least three reasons: it responses to statements of others, it addresses and provokes others for replies, and, finally, it is always rooted in the ontological being of and responsibility by its author. Author's statements constitute his or her personal truth because they response to personal truths of others, beg for responses from others, and provoke dialogic finalizing (evaluation) to reveal personal responsibility for the deed-statements through one's ontological being. The later is done not to justify, rationalize, or excuse the deed but to find constraints out of which the person discursively acted which defines the person's freedom and responsibility.[2]

When truth is seen as independent and indifferent to people participating in it, one can justifiably ignore, dismiss, violate, and eliminate people in name of truth to clean people as obstacles for the reign of monologic truth. Monologue as excess is based on violence and breeds violence (and even genocide) (Holquist, 1990).

Thus, from a dialogic point of view, to teach means to involve students in dialogic truth. There is not other goal in education but dialogue,

> [Dialogic – EM&MS] approach [to educational research – EM&MS] would be not to study dialogue in teaching, but teaching in dialogue. ... Dialogue, which is being *used* for something ceases to be dialogue. This is only a shell of dialogue, a conversation entirely within the *I-It* realm [Martin Buber's term – EM&MS]. No rules can guarantee that dialogue really happens, and dialogue may occur despite gravely monological forms of communication. Once dialogue begins, no one can channel it, or manage it, or transform it, even for the noble aims of education. I contrast the ontological vision of dialogue to a non-ontological one, which sees dialogue as a form of communication, as a means toward some other goal... I want to make education revolve around the dialogical. For this purpose, the life of an entire school should be treated as a whole (Sidorkin, 1999, pp. 14-15, the italics original).

Internally Persuasive and Externally Authoritative Discourses

Bakhtin (1991, 1999) often discussed dialogue in its relation to authority and discursive regimes. He (1991) introduced two discursive regimes externally authoritative discourse and internally persuasive regime. He introduced the notion of *internally persuasive discourse* but developed this notion in details almost two decades later in his discussion of the *menippea* literary genre (Bakhtin, 1999)[3]. The former promote excessive monologue while the later promotes ontological dialogue described above.

Unfortunately, in educational literature these two notions have gotten psychologized almost in a Freudian way (Matusov, 2007). Educators (e.g., Freedman & Ball, 2004) read Bakhtin's term "internal" psychologically as belonging to the individual inner world rather than to see "internal" to the discourse itself. Freedman and Ball consider anything that an individual believes without external pressure is evidence of "internally persuasive discourse." Thus, Freedman[4] brought an example from her interview of Bosnian Croats, "The Bosnian Croats, in contrast [to Bosnian Muslims -- Bosniaks], argued for their language rights, and

---

[2] From this point of view, even such "political monsters" as Stalin, Hitler, and Pol Pot have their personal truths. These truths are not their excuses or justifications of their evils but responses to them, addresses to them, connections of them with truths of their victims, and our "penetrating words" (Bakhtin, 1999) – dialogic finalizing – that can help to explode monologic solitude of these people and bring them back to humanity without forgiving them or forgetting what they had done (like in the process of reconciliation in postapartheid South Africa, see -- Foster, Haupt, & Beer, 2005). This is a posthumous process for them but necessary for living and all those who perished because of them. The dead continue their dialogue through and with us.
[3] One of the massive additions that Bakhtin made to his book on Dostoevsky that was initially published in 1929 to its second edition in the early 1960s was chapter 4 introducing the notions of menippea and carnival. His big essay on the genre of novel where he originally introduced the notion of internally persuasive discourse was written by him in the 1930s (Morson & Emerson, 1990).
[4] Here we repeat argument and critique from Matusov (2007).

rarely mentioned the similarities across the languages [that Bosniaks, Bosnian Croats, and Bosnian Serbs use]. *Their internally persuasive discourses sound quite different from those of their Bosniak neighbors.* They espoused the same rights for other national groups, and claimed every group had the right to keep its language and school curriculum separately.... Most interesting is this student's claim that she has discussed her views with students of other nationalities and that they agree with her. 'I talked about it with friends of different nationality, and they also agree.' Her claim about what others think conflicts with what the Bosniaks say in their interviews" (Freedman & Ball, 2004, pp. 26-27, italics and bracketed inserts are ours). In our view, Freedman's data provides evidence for what Bakhtin called "externally authoritative discourse," in which her Bosnian Croat interviewees were involved, rather than internally persuasive discourse. It has many characteristics of externally authoritative discourse: intolerance, speaking for others, unwillingness to listen to and genuinely question others, not testing one's own ideas and assumptions, desire to impose one's own views on others.

In our view, Bakhtin referred the term "internal" not to psychological "inner world" but to discourse. It is internally persuasive to the discourse itself. In internally persuasive discourse IPD), there is nothing outside of the discourse itself that makes some idea persuasive for its participants. Without naming it, Lampert defines the internally persuasive pedagogical discourse in the following way, "Logical proof... is a fundamental mathematical practice, and in the classroom, it must replace the authority of the teacher in deciding what is right and what is wrong. Ellie's [one of Lampert's students – EM&SM] answer is unreasonable, not because 'the teacher said so' or because she looked up the answer in the a book, but because it does not follow the assumptions given in a problem" (Lampert, 2001, p. 26). And further she concretizes what she meant by saying, "In 'thinking some more' together about these fractions, I hoped students would have an opportunity to teach other students as they tried to convince one another that what they were doing made sense. It would be anyone's choice about whether to 'own up to' having made the erroneous conjecture. By structuring the discussion in this way, I would not set myself up as the final arbiter of right and wrong mathematics. Instead, I would use public reasoning to create an environment in which there could be lots of ideas in the air about why $1/2 + 1/6 = 2/8$ would not make sense" (Lampert, 2001, p. 337). Thus, IPD notion is essentially social and not psychological. It is a regime of critical persuasion and testing ideas. In the spirit of Bakhtin scholarship, we argue that freely, but uncritically, accepting ideas of the dominant ideology in a community is a part of authoritative, not internally persuasive, discourse.

The second mistake that, in our view, many educators who try to apply Bakhtin's scholarship do is to define internally persuasive discourse through psychologizing Bakhtin's notion of "appropriation." Ball (2004) provides many fragments of a South African student's reflective writing for the class organized by Ball, in which the education student freely and willingly accepts Vygotsky, Au, Gee, Giroux, and other scholars' ideas assigned to her by Ball as her instructor. From the quotes used by Ball, the readers can see how the South African student incorporates ("appropriates") these ideas into her own past experiences and future professional goals. However, we argue that this evidence is not enough to insist that the student was involved in internally persuasive discourse in Bakhtin's sense. According to Bakhtin, a person is involved in internally persuasive discourse when different ideas embodied in diverse voices collide with each other in a dialogue in which these ideas are tested (Bakhtin, 1999). As Morson (2004) writes, in internally persuasive discourse "truth becomes dialogically tested and forever testable" (p. 319). Internally persuasive discourse implies a special dialogic and critical exposure of the student facilitated by the instructor to alternative discourses – alternative to Vygotsky, Au, Gee, Giroux and other scholars in the context of a "crisis of truth" (Felman & Laub, 1992, p. 6). Ball does not present any evidence of such collision and testing of ideas and questioning the authors assisted by the instructor. Even more, although we do not claim this in the case of Ball's chapter, the South African student might conceivably accept the pedagogical ideas of Vygotsky, Au, Gee, Giroux and other scholars not as a result of her involvement in internally persuasive discourse, as Ball insists, but as a result of the student's involvement in an authoritative discourse of uncritical indoctrination by the instructor (this is, of course, a very extreme possibility but it should be considered). In our view, by "appropriation" Bakhtin wanted to emphasize heteroglossia involved in IPD that is based on critical consideration and dialogue with diverse alternatives rather than uncritical acceptance of words of others,

> Internally persuasive discourse – as opposed to one that is externally authoritative -- is, as it is affirmed through assimilation, tightly interwoven with 'one's own word'. In the everyday rounds of our consciousness, the internally persuasive words is half-ours and half-someone else's. Its creativity and productiveness consist precisely in the fact that such a word awakens new and independent words, that it organizes masses of our words from within, and does not remain in an isolated and static condition... it enters into interanimating relationships with new contexts. More than that, it enters into an intense interaction, a struggle with other internally persuasive discourses. Our ideological [becoming – EM&SM] is just such an intense struggle within us for hegemony among various available verbal and ideological points of view, approaches, directions and values. The semantic structure of an internally persuasive discourse is not finite, it is open; in each of the new contexts that dialogize it, this discourse is able to reveal ever new ways to mean" (Bakhtin, 1991, pp. 345-346).

In our view, Bakhtin meant the process opposite to one commonly understood by educators (and psychologists) probably due to translation problems from Russian. Internally persuasive discourse involves a tension between one's own words and words of others that is based on critical consideration and dialogic addressing and responding. In some cases (only in some cases and not on others), the words of others can be re-authored by the person as result of this dialogic persuasion, testing ideas, and critical consideration. This critical re-authoring (or what Bakhtin called "affirmative assimilation" or "appropriation") does not define IPD one of its manifestation through dialogic agreement.

In contrast, externally authoritative discourse is based upon the assumption that utterances and their meanings are fixed, not modifiable as they come into contact with new voices: "The authoritative word demands that we acknowledge it, that we make it our own; it binds us, quite independent of any power it might have to persuade us internally; we encounter it with its authority fused to it" (Wertsch, 1991b, p. 78). The static and dead meaning structure of externally authoritative discourse allows no interanimation with other voices. The externally authoritative voice "demands our unconditional allegiance," (p. 78) and it allows "no play with its borders, no gradual and flexible transitions, no spontaneously creative stylizing variants on it" (p. 78). If in internally persuasive discourse, a participant can critically appropriate words of other for re-authoring his or her own utterances in the dialogue, in externally authoritative discourse, somebody else's words uncritically and unconditionally appropriates the participant. In the monologic classroom, the authority of the official curriculum and teacher appropriates students (when they do not actively resist or dialogically address the teacher).

The third mistake that some educators often do in our view is equation of Bakhtin's notion of authority with coercion. It is true that authority can be based on coercion and Bakhtin provided many examples of such. But it is not true that authority is only based on coercion. Authority can also be based on tradition, respect, ignorance, prejudice, and other non-coercive sources of power. We define authority here as legitimate power. To become authority, power gets its legitimacy through a discursive process. Unlike power, authority cannot be understood as the unilateral imposition of a set of norms of behavior or demands. Authority requires the mutual recognition and legitimacy of the demands and requests of one person or group over another. Metz attempted to address this issue in her conceptualization of authority, arguing that authority is "the right of a person [teacher] in a specified role to give commands to which a person in another specified role [student] has a duty to render obedience. This right and duty rests upon the superordinate's [teacher's] recognized status as the legitimate representative of a moral order to which both superordinate and subordinate owe allegiance" (Metz, 1978, p. 27). Metz thus dealt with the issue of legitimization of demands through the idea that both teachers and students owe "mutual adherence to a moral order." What is problematic, however, about such a conception is that it presumes that there must be a common order to which both parties (teachers and students) subscribe. This common order, furthermore, appears to be distant to the relations between teachers and students. It appears as monolithic, difficult to negotiate and Platonic. It also gives little agency to the teachers and students who apparently must unquestionably command obedience to this moral order. This is not to say that such moral orders cannot be said to exist; rather, it is to pragmatically critique Metz's use of moral order as the fundamental basis behind the legitimacy of teacher demands.

Morson, although a philologist and not an educator, (2004) made an excellent point about the limitation of Bakhtin's binary opposition between "authoritative" and authority-less "internally persuasive" discourses. He argues that this limitation is especially evident in and, thus, relevant for education. Morson strongly argues that internally persuasive discourse cannot be sustained without authority. He points out that it is impossible to create *shared classroom attention* solely based on internally persuasive discourse as described by Bakhtin. For example, in order for me to engage my reader in internally persuasive discourse about my essay, the reader must trust me that it is worth reading my essay and investing his or her attention, time, and efforts in doing so. In other words, the reader should trust my authority at least up to some point. This trust is not unconditional and finally has to be rooted in authority-less internally persuasive discourse that I try to organize in my essay. Back in the 1920s, American educator Morrison articulated a similar need for the initial teacher authority that start-jumps the authentic learning process. He wrote, "In the sense, the fundamental problem of teaching is to train the pupil, so arrange his studies and so apply an effective operative technique that he will eventually be able to become so absorbed in any study which in itself is worthwhile [for the pupil]" (Morrison, 1931, p. 135). It is for the teacher to gain control in the classroom only in order to lose it to the internally persuasive discourse. The issue for Morson is not complete elimination of authority, like it apparently is for Bakhtin[5], but rather its purpose and nature.

Probably borrowing the terms from the educational literature on parental and teaching styles (Baumrind, 1971; Lewin et al., 1939)[6], Morson offers not two, like Bakhtin, but three types of discourse: 1) *authoritarian discourse* based on the authority of power, imposition, tradition, and/or ignorance (what Bakhtin previously called authoritative discourse), 2) *authoritative dialogic discourse* based on the authority of trust and respect, 3) *internally persuasive discourse* (similar to Bakhtin) – a discourse without authority based on dialogic questioning, testing, and evaluation of statements. Morson's notion of the authoritative but not authoritarian discourse seems to be similar to Latour's (1987) idea of bifurcation of science discourse between "ready-made science" and "science-in-action" and Wenger's (1998) idea of reification and participation. Like Latour, Morson argues that it is impossible and not needed to challenge/test every statement and any utterance if these statements and utterances are reasonable – meaning testable and achieved through internally persuasive discourse. Dialogic pedagogy has to be based on both authoritative (in Morson's sense) and internally persuasive discourses. It should start with a non-authoritarian authoritative discourse to develop a shared attention in the classroom based on the students' trust in the teacher and then to move to internally persuasive discourse that is supposed to generate more students-teacher trust for future authoritative discourse. Dialogic authority involves legitimate and recognized power of trust and respect: reified past and anticipated future internally persuasive critical discourse. Dialogic authority in IPD is *internally* authoritative (internally to IPD, not psychologically internal) while authority of authoritarian discourse is *externally* authoritative (see, Bakhtin, 1991, p. 345). Here we defined *an IPD regime* that involves dialogic intra-discursive authority but is mainly based on IPD in opposition to externally authoritative discursive regime that *mainly* based on extra-discursive sources of persuasion.

In essence, in the IPD regime, through transition from authoritative to internally persuasive discourse, the teacher loses his/her authority – unilateral control over students – in order that internally persuasive discourse can establish a shared collaborative control in the classroom. Under regime of internally persuasive critical discourse, the teacher is an equal partner of discourse (but may be more skillful or knowledgeable) without extra authority beyond of the persuasive power of his or her critical argument in the discourse. This idea of the teacher losing authority runs against many traditional teachers' struggles to establish firm

---

[5] Bakhtin's position on desirability of authority in discourse is not as clear as it may appear at the first glance. At least in some work, it appears that Bakhtin envisioned a unity of authority and internally persuasive discourse as it is evident in the following quote, "Both the authority of discourse and its internal persuasiveness may be united in a single word [i.e., discourse – EM&SM] -- one that is simultaneously authoritative and internally persuasive -- despite the profound differences between these two categories of alien discourse. But such unity is rarely given -- it happens more frequently that an individual's becoming, an ideological process, is characterized by a sharp gap between these two categories: in one the [authoritarian] word (religious, political, moral, the word of a father, of adults and of teachers etc.) that does not know internal persuasiveness, in the other the internally persuasive word that is denied all privilege, backed up by no authority at all, and is frequently not even acknowledged in society (not by public opinion, nor by scholarly norms, nor by criticism), not even in the legal code. The struggle and dialogic interrelationships of these categories of ideological discourse are what usually determine the history of an individual ideological consciousness" (Bakhtin, 1991, p. 342). In our view, Morson makes an important next step in unpacking the dense, fuzzy, and often polysemic concepts by Bakhtin.

[6] In our view, in contrast with the mentioned psychologists, Bakhtin and Morson developed non-structural understanding of authority. The notion of authority is based not on structural (a)symmetry of power but on a discursive process of legitimization of power.

and permanent authority in the classroom. Traditional teachers are afraid to lose their authority – unilateral control over the students -- expecting chaos, students' violence, and students' unilateral control (unilateral power)[7] (Jackson, 1968; Lortie, 1975; McLaren, 1993; McNeil, 1986; Sidorkin, 2002; Waller, 1932). Of course, successfully established internally persuasive classroom discourse creates conditions for the students' trust in the teacher and for the teacher's trust in the students that the teacher (and students at times) can use for establishing temporal authority of trust in the future as a precursor of future internally persuasive discourse. It is similar like a high credential of a scholar can authoritatively engage other scholars in reading his or her article.

Finally, we want to mention that besides IPD and EAD there are also discourses based on *illegitimate* application of power. Bakhtin mentioned these cases in his work but did not discuss in depth. We are talking about use of violence that is direct without participants' recognition of its legitimacy. This violence can be vertical coming from institutional hierarchy (e.g., despotism) or horizontal coming from institutionally symmetrical mates (e.g., mob). The latter is an especially interesting case authority-less discourse for educators because it suggests that reducing teacher authority in the classroom does not necessarily produces IPD regime but can promote horizontal violence. This case was nicely documented by Lensmire (1994a, 1994b) who tried to establish a regime of carnivalesque authority-less discourse in his writing classroom of second graders but his students took advantage of the authority vacuum to promote semiotic violence against unpopular classmates in their free writing during a writing workshop (see also Leander, 2002). Bearing this discussion in mind, we now want to turn to description and analysis of a case involving IPD regime in classroom.

Why We Decided to Use Vivian Paley's book "You Can't Say You Can't Play" for Analysis of IPD in Education

We decided to select Vivian Paley's (1992) book "You Can't Say you Can't Play" for our analysis of IPD in education because, based on our prior reading of the book and also favorable judgments of other scholars as a practical model for dialogic pedagogy (Cooper, 2005; C. P. Edwards, 1995; Harrist & Bradley, 2003; Sapon-Shevin, Dobbelaere, Corrigan, Goodman, & Mastin, 1998; Sidorkin, 2002; Smutny, 1993; Wiltz & Fein, 1996), we had a strong expectation that Paley's teaching and her authority was based on IPD with her kindergarten students. This particular book by Paley focuses on the social justice issue of inclusion in human communities as "an unalienable right" (using the language of the US constitution), Ms. Paley, as the teacher, and her kindergarten students discuss, that can be characterized as an "ultimate question", an "eternal question of humanity", a "cursed question", a "question of Big Dialogue" discussed by Bakhtin (1999) in his analysis of Dostoevsky's artwork. We expected that there would be many rich examples of IPD dialogue between Paley and her students in transcript-like form (indeed, at many moments in her books, Paley tape records her lessons and provides raw, unedited transcripts of dialogues with students, Paley, 1992, p. 18). We suspected that Paley's (1992) work would function as an important source of data of the role of IPD in teaching and learning, and its connection to

---

[7] It can be interesting to consider other authoritative discourses besides discourse of control like discourse of care but it will go beyond the purpose of this essay.

teachers' authority. Furthermore, the book is of particular interest, as it deals with the establishment of a rule in the classroom with students that you cannot exclude children from play. If Paley is able to establish a rule of inclusion in her classroom that is authoritative on the basis of students' internal persuasion rather than by imposition of Paley's external authority over them, a systematic analysis of the discourse in the book between teachers and students relating to the rule would be an important contribution to better understanding the importance and value of IPD in education.

Our initial reading of Paley and our expectation of its value to an analysis of IPD in education was based on our own prior, unsystematic readings of Paley's work as well as by the references made to Paley's dialogic style of teaching in the educational literature. For example, Sidorkin, speaking of Paley's work *The Boy who would be a Helicopter* (Paley, 1991), noted that while Paley "clearly exercises a great amount of power (influence) over her students,… her power concentrates on encouraging students to write their own stories, which means giving them the tools of interpretation, and therefore, the power to redefine classroom relations" (Sidorkin, 2002, p. 146). Is it then possible that Paley establishes a rule of inclusion in her classroom on its internal discursive legitimacy with students? In Sidorkin's view, the authority Paley establishes "is based on her usefulness to children… 'Drawing invisible lines' between students' stories seems to be where her authority is mostly applied. Her relations with children are not easily described in this framework of power imbalance… Paley does not seek the authority; she is asked by students to assume it" (p. 147). This analysis highly suggests that Paley's authority, while initially extrinsic, could well be characterized as authoritative in the way Morson (2004) describes it; it may well ultimately be based not on unilateral control or imposition of demands on students, but on students' shared, collaborative acceptance of the teachers' demands and requests, and the trust and respect that has been granted by the students to the teachers' authority.

Sidorkin further characterized Paley's classroom as polyphonic, suggesting the presence of the necessary dialogic collisions and testing of ideas that characterize internally persuasive, as opposed to inert or authoritarian, classroom discourse. As Sidorkin writes, "Paley's classroom is an epitome of polyphony. The essence of her teaching is making dialogue possible" (Sidorkin, 2002, p. 146). It appears that in Paley's classroom, student discourse comes to live, as Wiltz and Fein articulate, "In Paley's classroom, children's fantasy play becomes a way of life that carries its own value, pursues its own course, and tells its own story" (Wiltz & Fein, 1996, p. 63). Furthermore, in Paley's classroom, the humanity of the individual is given expression as Smutny writes, "qualities such as affection, humanity, compassion, temperance and hope, when individualized and practiced, lead to self-knowledge, love and wholeness, qualities that protect and defend the bright, sensitive child" (Smutny, 1993, p. 136). Paley is even said by King, who notices the desire of Paley to enforce the rule with unilateral determination, to take children's concerns "seriously," and with "care and respect" (King, 1993, p. 337).

As has already just been stated, Paley's book is about the implementation of an inclusion rule in her kindergarten classroom that "You can't say you can't play." She is particularly concerned with students who are systematically excluded from play in her classroom. As she tells a group of fifth graders (throughout the book, she seeks advice for establishing the rule from older children in the school), "Here's what troubles me, as a teacher… Too often, the same children are rejected year after year. The burden of being rejected falls on a few children. They are made to feel like strangers" (p. 22). For Paley, this problem of exclusion is something that teachers should find inexcusable, and something to which teachers, sharing a public space with students, should take direct responsibility,

> The children I teach are just emerging from life's deep wells of private perspective: babyhood and family. Possessiveness and jealousy are inescapable concomitants of both conditions. Then, along comes school. It is the first real exposure to the public arena. Children are required to share materials and teachers in a space that belongs to everyone. Within this public space a new concept of open access can develop if we choose to make this a goal. Here will be found not only the strong ties of intimate friendship but, in addition, the habit of full and equal participation, upon request... We vote about nearly everything in our democratic classrooms but we permit the children to empower bosses and reject classmates. Just when the old-fashioned city bosses have all but disappeared and the once exclusive dining clubs are opening their doors to strangers, we still allow children to build domains of exclusivity in classrooms and playgrounds (p. 21-22).

The book is divided into four sections of the development of the event "You can't say you can't play." In the first section, "You can't play: The habit of rejection," Ms. Paley[9] discusses the problem of exclusion directly with her students, as well as subtly through storytelling. Paley argues that debates in her classroom are not enough to deeply reflect on the problem, and she thus introduces a fairytale which represents the problem of exclusion and the debates between children in her own classroom about exclusion. First, Paley invents the fairytale adventures of Magpie, a bird who likes to help children. In his first adventure, he flies down to help Princess Annabella, who is sad with loneliness. Throughout the book, the fairytale is interspersed with Paley's discussions with her students and with other children in the school. The story reflects discussions in Ms. Paley's classroom about exclusivity and inclusivity. The telling of the Magpie story was timed to deal with the problems of exclusion Ms. Paley noticed that that Angelo and Clara, in particular, were having with their classmates. Paley's stories are also, however, reflected back into classroom events. The stories – both Paley's magpie story and the stories children create (many of which become based on the Magpie stories) – help makes sense of life in Ms. Paley's classroom, and life in Ms. Paley's classroom helps make sense of the stories.

Besides telling stories, Ms. Paley also directly shares with the students what she notices in the classroom in relation to exclusion and begins a dialogue between the children about exclusion. One day, at "rug time," she talked about what "took place today in the blocks" as Clara was once again struck by sadness, and then hid in her cubby. As Ms. Paley told her students, "I couldn't decide what to do about Clara's unhappiness... A lot of you... think the teachers always know what is right, but this time I don't think the fair thing was done. You see, Clara was made to feel *unwanted. Not wanted*" (p. 13). Getting the "play bosses," those who set up desired games for others in the classroom, particularly Lisa, to play with "Shy Clara" becomes a crusade for Ms. Paley; however, when Lisa will allow Clara to play later on

---

[9] When it was possible, we tried to separate Paley's views as the particular teacher of her kindergarten class that we referred as "Ms. Paley" in our chapter from her view as an educator-researcher in general who wrote the book that we referred as "Paley".

with her in the classroom, Clara is then suddenly in a position of power to reject Cynthia, a child who regularly plays with Lisa. Paley comments: "Even Clara is capable of rejecting someone. After lunch, she and Lisa tell Cynthia she can't play. Why would Clara take part in this manipulative act, knowing how it feels?" (p. 40). Clara appears for Paley initially as a model rejected child, but she frustrates Paley's efforts to be finalized so easily in spite of Paley's efforts to bring the problem of Clara's manipulation to her attention, "When I point this out to her she looks away but is not inclined to give up her sudden and unexpected good fortune. Her wish has come true. Lisa has chosen to play with her today, a temporary whim that will make the next rejection all the more puzzling and painful" (p. 40).

Angelo is the other child that motivates Ms. Paley's interest in the play inclusion rule. He is also systematically rejected by other children from their play. Through IPD with Angelo and his classmates, Ms. Paley constructs a "person-idea" (Bakhtin, 1999) of Angelo as a justice fighter and a communitarian; she feels guilty stopping him from aggression toward other children, and admires him for his apparent working class inclusivity. In her Magpie story, she introduces Raymond, a character in the spirit of Angelo (as Bakhtin might remark, Angelo's person-idea becomes distributed). The creation of Raymond is in part an effort of Paley to encourage Angelo's communion with the play bosses, and there is evidence that the strategy was successful. Angelo does try to run up and "stand next to Charlie," one of the play bosses, but Paley unfortunately does not provide the reader with whether or not Angelo was successful.

Throughout the book, Angelo's person-idea collides with Lisa's person-idea, and the ensuing dialogue between these opposites – that of a rejected child and a "play boss" – reaches the level that Bakhtin refers to as "ultimate questions" in regard to the ethical issues of inclusion and exclusion that are in turn addressed (Bakhtin, 1999, p. 74). Thus, Angelo does not just dream for communion with the rest of the class, he actively sizes the opportunity to address and reach the hearts of his rejectors in the public forum set up by Paley. By contrast, for readers like us, Lisa appears to be almost like Ms. Paley's alter-ego. She is the strongest opponent of Ms. Paley's idea of the right of automatic inclusivity. There are frequent exchanges between Ms. Paley and Lisa in which they insert in their dialogue "penetrating words" for each other that both finalize one another and at the same time provoke their dialogic interlocutor to transcend their ontological circumstances and particular intellectual positions. We can also speculate to what degree Lisa's person-idea may reflect and reveal Paley's own doubts about establishing the rule, based on her own ontology. For Ms. Paley, Lisa is a "barometer, reminding children of the rule under certain circumstances, and crusading for the old order at other times. She worries about losing ground if she gives up control and she is more aware of the ordinary insecurities others feel" (p. 93). It is a strength of Paley's work that we also gain a better understanding of Lisa's ontology throughout the book, her circumstances and her personal reasons for rejecting the rule. This may well be because penetration of words of the teacher into the inner word of the student also lead to an opposite movement of penetration of words of the student into the inner world of the teacher (Bakhtin, 1999).

It is only within the first chapter in the book that Paley significantly engages in IPD with her own students. In the second section of the book, "Is it fair? Will it work?" much of the dialogue that takes place is between Paley and older children in the school, to whom she turns to advice for dealing with the problems of exclusion in her own classroom. The remaining chapters in the book, "The New Order Begins," and "It is Easier to Open the Door," are mainly focused on implementation of Paley's unilateral rule and her rationalization for her decision to implement the rule and Paley's own evaluation of the rule's success. In the second chapter, Paley first turns to the first graders, who generate pros and cons about the implementation of an inclusion rule in the kindergarten classroom (although interestingly, as in all the grades Paley spoke with, the students would be ambivalent about having the rule in their own classroom). Paley then turns to the second graders and the third graders. In discussing the third grade discussion with her kindergarten class, Paley remarked, "I think the third graders feel bad about not being kinder. That's why they talked about it [exclusion and inclusion in play] so much. Anyway, these two children were not completely discouraged. The boy said, 'Your plan will work if we could all get along with each other.' And the girl said, 'Sometimes people are very nice to each other, even to me" (p. 56). Interestingly and tellingly, Paley's remark elicits the following remark from one of her own students, "What plan?" Much of Paley's efforts to figure out if the plan will work are in discussions with older children *not* in her own classroom, and Paley never opens up for discussion with her own students whether or not they would accept or reject this "plan" to deal with play exclusion.

Indeed, it appears, from the second chapter of the book until the end, that Ms. Paley was trying to evaluate the success of her imposed rule, and her own students' opinions and discussions about this rule were not salient for her. Furthermore, it also appears that Paley is more concerned with issues of social justice and fairness than with her honest search for truth with herself and her students. The book closes with Paley ever more willing (although still with some hesitation) to set the rule as a given in future classrooms by implementing it at the beginning of the school year without similar discussions that she had in her kindergarten class. She believes that her imposition of the new rule "you can't say you can't play" on her future students is fair and only just thing to do by any teacher.

Methodology for the Study with Paley's Book

Our NVIVO methodology for the study with Paley's book *You can't say you can't play* involved an analysis of IPD between Ms. Paley and her kindergarten students as our main focus. We focused on instances of IPD as discourse involving testing of participants' ideas and its features especially important for education guided by grounded theory methodology (Glaser, 1967). We tried to analyze what IPD meant in Paley's educational practices, how it was established and why collapsed. We treated Paley's book as ethnography because it is written in the form of fieldnotes and transcripts of audio-recorded classroom conversations. In addition, other educators treat the book as an ethnography and use it as a description of model teaching (Cooper, 2005; Sapon-Shevin et al., 1998). As any ethnography, it has its own limitations being selective and biased; however, this problem is common in teacher's use of action research (Carson & Sumara, 1997).

We chose to focus on Ms. Paley's IPD dialogues with her own kindergarten students because they were central participants to the dilemma that they faced, although there were many IPD dialogues with older students in the school and with teachers in the book. We mainly focused on IPD in Ms. Paley's entire class because it involves *a responsible dialogue* of the participants at a threshold of their ontologically important decision making. All other types of IPD did not involve participants at a threshold of their ontologically important decision making as their discussions were about "others". Their intellectual ideas were not as ontologically responsible as ideas of the kindergarten students who considered vital conditions and changes in their own classroom (and beyond) lives.

We analyzed the presence of IPD in the text, along with the presence of authoritative and coercive discourse. As stated above, IPD is persuasion that is internal to discourse. However, authoritative discourse is persuasive because it is based on some legitimacy of power. It is a legitimacy that can be granted by one person to another through such diverse means as discursive appeal to tradition, respect, prejudice, hierarchy, credential, and prestige. We also coded Paley's manipulation of her students as a form of authoritative discourse. Such manipulation can be seen in providing false choices, knowingly lying to students, hiding facts from students, or habituating students to a set of constrained options. Coercive discourse is persuasion is based on appeal to non-legitimate (and thus non-authoritative) power (e.g., horizontal or vertical violence).

There are, however, some limitations to our methodology. First of all, we are limited to what is in the text. One significant problem with the text is that we do not hear much of students' voices after implementation of the rule. There are many questions we have about how students perceive Ms. Paley's rule (i.e., do they like it or hate it, and who likes it or hates it and why; do the students find Paley's implementation of the rule persuasive, or do they feel coerced to follow it). We feel in order that a full analysis of Ms. Paley's authority and, in particular, an analysis of what students find persuasive about Ms. Paley's rule would require interviews with students, a possibility that is closed in this methodology. Another limitation is that we know more about the students to whom Paley emphasizes in her book – particularly Clara, Angelo and Lisa – and their reactions to the rule, but very little about children who are peripheral to Paley's narrative. While this is certainly a forgivable stylistic decision on an author's part, for a research analysis, the closing off of understanding of the reactions and ontology of a large number of students in the classroom may be problematic, especially when we are forced to take Paley at her word that, for example, "the children are learning that it is far easier to open the doors than to keep people out" (p. 118). However, Paley's narrative style allows for the ontology of Lisa, Angelo, and Clara, in particular to emerge, and for Paley's ontology itself to surface (through an awareness of her internal dialogue).

INTERNALLY PERSUASIVE DISCOURSE IN MS. VIVIAN PALEY'S CLASSROOM

Our goal is to describe, analyze and evaluate internally persuasive discourse on example of Ms. Vivian Paley's book "You can't say you can't play". We will focus on the most important elements of IPD and their educational importance. From our analysis of Paley's book, we found well-illustrated ethnographic examples of IPD in the educational context. Paley is able to create a public forum where IPD emerges by intentionally lowering her teaching authority and sharing her own dilemma about exclusion with the children. In her classroom, we found four ontological social settings: children who are systematically "rejected" from play of others; "play bosses," who have the power to reject children from their play; "friends of bosses," who rely on the play bosses for fun; and the teacher, Ms. Paley, who is concerned about play exclusion. When we hear the voices of these social groups at the beginning of the book, their words are predictable and completely constrained by their ontological circumstances. The "rejected" children blame the "play bosses" and their "friends" for intentionally hurting their feelings. In response, the "play bosses" claim that they are only thinking about having fun; their rejection is contextual and "not mean." The "friends of bosses" are ambivalent; they recognize the need to be loyal to the bosses, but also sympathize with the rejected children. And finally, the teacher is very concerned about rejection but is not sure what to do about this problem. There is nothing in the participants' lives that seems to undermine or disrupt the voices that ground them in their ontological imprisonment. The participants are locked within vicious circle of a relational dynamic where blame leads to excuses, which leads to sympathy, which leads to impasse.

Building a Public Forum for IPD:
Issues of Teacher and Discourse Authority

As we mentioned in our introduction to this chapter, internally persuasive discourse involves the critical persuasion and testing of ideas in dialogue with others, wherein different ideas embodied in diverse voices freely collide with each other. IPD produces "dialogic truth," which emerges from the free and alive dialogue of participants engaged in producing truth through dialogic engagement with each other. Bakhtin opposed such discourse to the discourse of authority, which he argued would produce "dead" or "inert" ideas that cannot enter into dialogic constructions with the other. However, as we mentioned earlier, Morson (2004) critiques Bakhtin's conceptualization of authority as failing to consider the possibility of a certain type of authority which is both a necessary precursor and by product of IPD. Morson envisions not just unconditional *"authoritarian"* forms of authority in which authority is permanently prioritized, but also a conditional *"authoritative"* form of temporary and supportive authority that expects to enter into dialogue with others in order to assist emergence of an authority-less dialogue (IPD), to die in dialogue, and to be re-born in the dialogue for future dialogic possibilities. In contrast with Morson, we will rather call this form of authority *"pre-dialogic"* and *"post-dialogic"* to avoid Morson's apparent tautology in terms.

The pre-dialogic form of authority can set up and establish a public forum, through which new forms of IPD can emerge. A good example of this when Ms. Paley first brings up the "unhappiness" of Clara, one of the rejected children in her classroom, "'Something unhappy took place today in the blocks,' I tell the children at rug time. They sit close to me though my raspy voice makes them uneasy. 'I couldn't decide what to do about Clara's unhappiness.' *I have everyone's attention. Like me, they yearn for explanations of sadness...* The children look at Clara to see if she is still sad" (p. 13). In the beginning of this fragment, there is no internally persuasive discursive reason – indeed, why all her students should stop everything that they were doing before, come to the rug, become silent, and grant to Ms. Paley their undivided attention when she was stating, "Something unhappy took place today in the blocks"?! This statement by itself may not be powerful enough to compete with whatever the children did before to gain its urgency to be listened and replied or even heard. For the children to stop doing what they did before and come to the rug to hear the teacher at more or less the same time, the teacher has to have her authority recognized by the students. The classroom rug time and rug space – "rug chronotope" – is a container for activities, themes, and discourses unilaterally controlled by the teacher. It is the teacher owned chronotope. This reliance on the teacher authority for organizing a dialogue was hidden from the readers by Paley who, for some reasons, chose not to concentrate our attention on the fact of her teacher authority preceding a dialogue. In contrast to the teacher Lampert (2001), who sees a clear link between her authority and teaching, Paley seems not to prioritize this link as much.

We cannot say for sure what the basis of this authority was: hierarchically institutional ("I'm your teacher and you are my students that is why you should always listen to me and obey my requests!") or trust-based ("We have experienced a lot of good and interesting time with our teacher on "the classroom rug" so we expect it more this time that is why we will obey her demand"). The first type of authority is unconditional authoritarian while the second one is conditional pre-dialogic. The authoritarian authority is unconditional because its legitimacy does not depend on actions of the participants: the teacher always remains the teacher and students always remain students (boss-subordinates). The pre-dialogic authority is conditional because its legitimacy depends on the participants' actions. For example, if the teacher violates the students' expectations of promoting fun and interesting rug time for the class several times in a row, her authority based on trust can be withdrawn from her because the students' trust was violated. In case of Ms. Paley as it will become clear in our further discussion, we suspect a combination of both types of teacher authority that she used in her kindergarten classroom.

Both types of teacher authority were habitual for the children (i.e., established in past and recurring non-problematically for the participants), although, as Paley conveyed to us in her book, her children were aware of this habitual authority of the teacher that she presented for them as it is evident from the following exchange,

> "Some of the Arizona teachers think it's probably best to just let children figure out these problems for themselves."
> "What do we figure out for ourself?" Charlie asks me.
> "Your play and your stories. I don't say what they must be about."
> ...
> Angelo wants to know what else I *don't* tell the children. "I try not to tell you what thoughts or opinions to have," is my less than honest answer, at a time when I am single-mindedly pushing new attitudes about play.
> "We have to come to the rug ..."
> "And come to a discussion ..."
> "But I don't tell you what to *say* in the discussion," I hasten to point out. "And I listen to everyone."
> "We have to take turns to talk."
> This is the first time the children examine my role with such intensity. Is it that they sense I am about to change something in a way they may not like? Do I have this right, or even the obligation to enforce free access in the face of their strong feelings of self-determination? (p. 27-28).

In this fragment, the kindergarten children publicly exposed and explored Ms. Paley's teacher authority for the first time (which was in spring of the school year). We wonder if the IPD regime promotes its participants for exploration of authority. Lampert (2001) seems to answer affirmatively to this question while Paley does not apparently see the connection. Lampert argues that the teacher must provide rationale and invite for discussion (and ultimately for decision making) each procedure set by the teacher. She claims that the investigation of authority has to be become the essence of her curriculum and instruction.

Lampert apparently wants to see authority becoming shared with her students and rooted in IPD (dialogic authority, see below). In contrast, Paley apparently worries about the right for her future teacher authority to unilaterally set up her classroom in a way she wants it to be.

When the children turned to Clara to "see if she is still sad," without being told to do that by the teacher, the IPD began emerging. The Clara-theme started mobilizing the children's ontological attention. This ontological mobilization was evident in their voluntary action of questioning Clara's current emotional state. However, the teacher still has her authority at this moment. This teacher authority is further seen in the unquestioned legitimacy granted to Ms. Paley's discursive assessment (finalizing) of Clara as being "sad," despite the fact that Clara was obviously not sad at the time of Ms. Paley saying that she was sad. The children were puzzled – what the teacher was talking about? If an assessment of Clara's emotional state and position in the classroom in relation to others was made by another child, it may well be a subject of either open public agreement or contention, a statement which would be dialogically tested through IPD. In other words, there is a noticeable absence of questioning or dialogic testing of Paley's statement about Clara at this moment. We do not hear the children say, for example: "Clara's not that sad," "I saw Clara just the other day smiling at me! Give me a break!" I play with Clara all the time!" "You're always concerned about Clara!" "She's crying just to want attention!" or "Who are you to talk about how Clara feels?! Why don't you ask her?!". The children were still listening to the teacher letting her to develop her Clara-theme still unknown to them willing to suspense their judgments (like at beginning of reading a book).

A lot of traditional teachers would probably envy Ms. Paley's habitual teacher authority: it is very powerful, it is masterfully hidden, it is highly successful. But, it is only good so far as it can promote IPD. For IPD, authority has to be killed. We can see this process in Paley's book. Indeed, it appears that Paley intentionally lowered her authority to allow this to happen; notice above how she admits to the children, "I couldn't decide what to do about Clara's unhappiness," and also states, "'A lot of you,' I continue, 'think the teachers always know what is right, but this time I don't think the fair thing was done. You see, Clara was made to feel *unwanted. Not wanted.*'" (p. 13). The teacher genuinely and publicly invites the students into her inquiry, indecisiveness, and concern. She is not anymore an authority by the power given to her by the school institution, she is not an adult who knows everything better, she is not even a person to trust – rather she is their fellow human being who is faced with an important, serious dilemma tearing her apart.

The issue of fairness Ms. Paley brings up to the classroom public forum also works to *ontologize* the issue, something Paley noticed in her work with children in an earlier article, "I began using the tape recorder to try to figure out why the children were lively and imaginative in certain discussions, yet fidgety and distracted in others ('Are you almost finished now, teacher?'), wanting to return quickly to their interrupted play. As I transcribed the daily tapes, several phenomena emerged. Whenever the discussion touched on fantasy, fairness, or friendship ('the three Fs' I began to call them), participation zoomed upward… [the children asked] urgent questions, and passion made the children eloquent" (Paley, 1986b, p. 124). Thus, reification of IPD can serve to de-reify, or ontologize, the discourse, making students more passionate in their participation. What is indeed surprising in the case of the *You can't say you can't play* book, however, is how experienced and capable Paley can be with this reification and ontologization of discourse – to be willing to listen to the voices of others and to honestly reflect on these voices – but to block further IPD if it works against her interests.

What follows in the public forum set up by Paley is internally persuasive discourse about Clara's situation and the bigger issue of excluding others from play in the classroom. This IPD involves not only the children, but also Ms. Paley, whose word appears in equal weight with those of her students. Through her discussion at rug time about Clara's unhappiness, Ms. Paley created a public forum for students' internally persuasive discourse about exclusion in the classroom to emerge. However, it is important to note, as Morson argues, that without authority, it would be impossible to create *shared classroom attention.* In other words, this internally persuasive discourse, which reveals everyone's ontological stakes (see a section below) in the problem of exclusion and puts them in a dialogic contact (i.e., "syncrisis", Bakhtin, 1999, p. 110), is an achievement of Ms. Paley's authority.

The pre-dialogic authority dies with establishment of IPD that is aimed at testing ideas. However, the IPD cannot and should not test any idea – it requires *dialogic authority* (cf. Latour, 1987). IPD is always based on ideas taken by the participants for granted and it always creates new consensuses. The reified IPD consensus is dialogic authority. The participants in IPD do not need to repeat their testing each time they refer to the issue that they already discussed. For example, the initial IPD in Ms. Paley's classroom was about exploration of exclusion and considering responsibility for it. But at some point, the IPD turned to the issue of sadness introduced by Angelo, "I think that's pretty sad. People that is alone they has water in their eyes" (p. 20). Through this statement, Angelo re-frames the public problem of "sadness," and *ontologizes* it, making it no longer a reified description of Clara's emotional state, but a problem that must be addressed by the class. After that the IPD issue has turned to consideration of who would be "sadder" the one who is excluded or one who is forced to accept an unwanted child in their play. Sadness as measure of the class well-being became a new consensus emerged in the IPD. It has gained authority of an idea taken for granted in this particular community as thing not to question. For example, Ms. Paley explains how systematic exclusion affects students' learning by "they might become too sad to pay attention" (p. 28) to learning a lesson in the classroom. Similarly, Lisa objects the new rule "you can't say you can't play" on the grounds that "But some children aren't nice enough to play with. They're too—uh, rough, I mean, too sad" (p. 73). The discourse of sadness became authoritative in Ms. Paley's classroom. It becomes like a communal tradition to talk unquestionably about sadness as the measure of the communal (not) well-being. This authoritative discourse is reified IPD. Although it is authoritative, at any time it can be tested in IPD as everything is IPD remains "forever testable" (Morson, 2004, p. 319).

Arguably, the students' and Ms. Paley's participation in IPD leads to more trust and respect of future authoritative discourse, which could support the continuance of the public forum. This newly emerging teacher authority coming from the past IPD and aiming at future IPD is *post-dialogic authority.* Ms. Paley could legitimately appeal to reified IPD, a set of "trusted" statements that are believed or expected by participants to have either undergone or withstood prior dialogic testing (IPD). Such reified IPD can appeal to the past persuasive discourse, or it can be a reification of present IPD (discourse authority). This reified IPD both reconstructs and anticipates future internally persuasive critical discourse, and can thus lead later on to more IPD, and thus more opportunities for respect and trust for further reification.

Ontological Traps and Ontological Engagement in IPD

Bakhtin (1993) distinguished the content of act (and discourse) from the being of the act/discourse itself. In school, participants often experience separation of the content of their acts/discourse from the being of their act/discourse. Teachers often preach one thing (the content of their discourse) but do another (the being of their discourse); students often do not care about what they learn -- they often learn for grades and credentials but not for deep understanding -- or even actively resist the teacher's efforts to teach them all together. In sum, their engagement in academic discourse is often non-ontological while their ontology is often non-engaging (in the academic material).

In our view, internally persuasive discourse is unthinkable without the participants' ontological engagement in it. We extract at least 3 aspects defining ontological engagement. Two of them are related with the notion of "interest" and one of them is related with the concept of "responsibility"[10] as introduced by Bakhtin in his early work (1990, 1993). IPD involves interested parties that have something important *at stake*[11] (i.e., a personal or emotional interest, concern, or involvement). In the case of the Ms. Vivian Paley's classroom, it is possible to extract at least four stake-based interests.

First is the interest of children – whom Ms. Paley later referred to as "play bosses" -- who often initiate and, thus, "own" the games and who are systematically benefited from the status quo of their exclusion right to exclude other children from their play at their will (like, for example, Lisa, Charlie). By having their right they successfully manage their friendships and relations with other children in the classroom (and maybe even beyond). The right of selecting children for the play they initiate gives them special power, authority, privileges, and quality of relations. It makes them feel special. As Lisa exclaimed in response to a suggestion to abandon this right, "But then what's the whole point of playing?!" (p. 20).

The second interest involves children – whom Ms. Paley referred as "rejected children" -- who are systematically hurt by the exclusion from the play of others (e.g., Clara, Angelo, Nelson, Smita). These children do not like the status quo of the exclusion right, they want to be accepted by other children to play, and would like to find protection from adults – the teacher or parents. Thus, Clara said that she would like the teacher to interfere and force other children to accept her in play.

The third interest is constituted by children (e.g., Cynthia, Waka, Sheila) – whom can be called "bosses' friends" (in accordance with Ms. Paley's terminology) -- who are in-between, who experienced systematic inclusion and occasional exclusion from the "owners" of games and who are ambivalent about both the status quo (how fair it is) and suggestions for its change. For example, Cynthia, Lisa's friend, reacts sympathetically to the problem of exclusion but also feels guilty of betraying her best friend,

"They [Lisa and Cynthia] has to let her [Clara] play," Sheila insists. "Unless they really don't want to."

"Unless she really really can't find someone else to play with," Cynthia adds, looking guiltily at Lisa (p. 15).

---

[10] We agree with Morson and Emerson (1990) that in Bakhtin's early writings (before his book on Dostoevsky) it is more appropriate to translate the Russian word "ответственность" as "moral responsibility for one's own deeds" rather than "answerability" – a dialogic term that Bakhtin developed later that does not necessarily have a moral connotation. Unfortunately, the term was always translated as "answerability."

[11] This analysis of *the group stakes* is similar to Marx's (1990) analysis of class interests rooted in their social relations emerging in their practices. However, they do not involve in production like in Marx. Nevertheless, as Paley implied in several places of her book, children's play rejections may follow stratification of the broader society. Thus, she suggested that children who are rejected in her classroom were mostly minority, immigrants, and working class. As one reviewer of the book noticed (King, 1993), Paley did not go deeper in her analysis of the gender basis of play rejection.

The fourth interest involved the teacher Ms. Vivian Paley herself. She, like the children from the third group described above, also felt ambivalent about the exclusion right status quo and the possibility of changing it, "Their ambivalence and mine are similar. 'It's a hard problem,' I agree, 'and the same thing happens to other children *every day.*'" (p. 15). However, her ontological stake and ambivalence are different from the children of the third group. Ms. Vivian Paley felt herself, as their teacher and an adult taking care for the children, morally responsible for children being hurt by exclusion in her classroom, "Turning sixty, I am more aware of the voices of exclusion in the classroom. "You can't play" suddenly seems too overbearing and harsh, resounding like a slap from wall to wall. How casually one child determines the fate of another" (p. 3). She felt a sense of crisis and she could not morally continue the status quo. While we as readers do not know what exactly pushed Ms. Paley to start addressing this issue in her classroom after "turning sixty" (and not before or after, for example), it is very safe to assume that something in Paley's life triggered her concern and she gave the issue lot of thought before that.

Before Ms. Paley started her discussion of Clara being unhappy because of her systematic exclusion from Lisa's play, all four stakes were occurring on a recursive but uncoordinated basis when events of exclusion occur. They were part of being but not part of the classroom public discourse. The teacher actualized these four diverse interests preexisting to the public forum that the teacher started. Interestingly, Lampert (2001) described her teaching in which stakes for the participants – the students and the teacher -- emerged during the public forum on math problem solving and not before it. The problem of the day -- how many miles a car driving at 55 mph will go after 15 minutes – did not probably produce ontological engagement in the students at least initially. However, when they started publicly presenting the various answers that they had to defend, the socio-intellectual stakes clearly emerged for the students as Lampert described.

The second aspect of ontological engagement is another sense of the term "interest" as participants' genuine *puzzlement*. Each of the four groups saw the problem of unhappiness resulted from play exclusion in Ms. Paley's classroom differently although. The "play bosses" saw it as an issue of how to effectively sweeten the bitter but necessary "medicine" of play rejection. They did not want to see the rejected children to be unhappy, hurt, to cry, or to complain to adults. To solve the problem they try to find "good excuses" for exclusion, "'We said [to Clara] if she [Clara] brings a Pound Puppy she can play,' Lisa explains" (p. 14), "nice words" ("We [Ben and Charlie] told him [Nelson] *nicely* he could play because we need a bad guy. We started the game" (p. 39), "promises of inclusion in future", conditional rules for interchange between exclusion and inclusion (as one that Sheila and Cynthia brought above), and so on. In sum they search for a magic universal sugarcoating pill for exclusion of others. Unfortunately for play bosses, their sugarcoating approach did not work all the time and with all children and the teacher as some of the children (e.g., Angelo) and the teacher were aware of the manipulative and disingenuous nature of the "bosses'" solution.

The rejected children were puzzled by how to react to rejection they experienced on systematic basis, how to preserve their own sense of dignity, how to retaliate and punish their excluders, and how consequently to break into play, "Shy Clara will speak for herself. 'Cynthia and Lisa built a house for their puppies and I said can I play and they said no because I don't have a puppy only I have a kitty…. I'll tell my mommy if she could get me that kind of puppy like they have,'" (p.14). The rejected children often turned for help to their parents, "'These kids,' Angelo says disapprovingly. 'They'll always forget sometimes when they tell you. My daddy he say just don't play if they doesn't want you'" (p. 86). As Ms. Paley observed, these parochial and unilateral approaches simply do not work.

As we pointed out above, the "friends of bosses" were ambivalent and puzzled about how to reconcile their sympathy for rejected children and their loyalty to bosses, "'Let's not have bosses until we're in second grade,' Waka says, looking at Charlie. But Charlie offers no response" (p. 48).

Finally, the teacher Ms. Paley was full of genuine inquiries. What can be done about play exclusion in the classroom? Is her idea of forced inclusion fair? Is it practical? And so on. Here is one of them, probably, the most dramatic, "So, I thought, I want to do a favor for Clara, but is it fair to spoil Lisa's and Cynthia's play? Yet would this really spoil their play? How? Well, I couldn't figure out what to do. Luckily, Mary Louise came along and agreed to play with Clara" (p. 16). Some reviewers of the book that have noticed a manipulative character of some of Paley's reasoning raise a question about how genuine Ms. Paley was in her inquiries (e.g., King, 1993). However, in our view, until Ms. Paley reached a high degree of certainty about an issue for *herself*, her public and private questions of puzzlement were genuine (we will return to this issue later).

Participants' interests (i.e., their ontological stakes and the puzzlements they have) define the participants' *ontological circumstances*. In Ms. Paley's classroom there seemed to be four types of ontological circumstances: play bosses, rejected children, friends of bosses, and a conscientious teacher/adult (i.e., governed by or done according to somebody's sense of right and wrong). It is possible to reshuffle the participants by putting them in another classroom with other children in a conventional school and these four groups probably would emerge again. For example, if only play bosses' children are collected from different classrooms into one new classroom, new "rejected" children and "friends of bosses" would emerge. The question is not whether there would be play bosses or rejected children but rather who would these children be in this particular classroom (cf. Varenne & McDermott, 1998). Bakhtin argued that ontological circumstances do not define people, there is "non-alibi in Being" (Bakhtin et al., 1993, p. 40). What people actively do with and in their ontological circumstances is defined by their responsibility.

The third aspect of ontological engagement is participants' taking responsibility for their actions, ideas, and words. People are serious when they are ready do what they preach, when they are ready to commit themselves to their ideas. Ms. Paley brought a good example of the non-ontological engagement of older children in her idea of forced inclusion, "Later, when I read this part of the transcript to some older children, they all agree with Angelo and Clara [about unconditional inclusion]. However, in practice, they admit, they follow the course set by Lisa [about children's exclusion right]" (p. 20). Ms. Paley clearly demonstrated her responsibility for her own doubts by starting the forum in her classroom searching for a solution. She herself was very sensitive about the issue of her own personal commitment to unconditional inclusion rule to the point of changing her own classroom practice to include herself in her own new rule,

> "You know, I have to change something *I've* been doing," I tell the children, so softly they move closer as if on a rolling platform. They have grown accustomed to my new, quieter voice. "I have to make a big change myself. Something I'm doing doesn't fit the new rule." My confession startles them. A bit of the unexpected works wonders when Act I of a new drama begins.

"You have all watched how upset I become with Karl when he won't clean up the blocks."

"Then he can't play there until he does," Sheila says.

"Right." I point to the sign. "However, if you can't say you can't play, then even I mustn't tell Karl not to play."

"But what if he doesn't clean up?" Clara asks.

"Well, what should happen?"

Charlie is first to reply. "Nothing."

"Nothing at all?"

"Nothing," he repeats. "Let him read a book" (pp. 82-83).

It is interesting that Lisa, Ms. Paley's major opponent in the book, did not agree that the teacher subjugated herself to the rule and considered Ms. Paley's change in her classroom management as a manipulative loophole – it is one thing to subjugate yourself to a new rule on free will through self-persuasion and another thing to force others to obey a new rule through use of external institutional authority (we will discuss it later).

What is the evidence in the book that the other participants in Ms. Paley classroom took responsibility for their own positions? Lisa threatened to stop playing ever if her right of play exclusion would be revoked, "'But it was my game!' Lisa cries. 'It's up to me!' She is red-faced and tearful. 'Okay, I won't play then, ever!'" (p. 15). Angelo was committed to retaliatory fights of children who excluded him from their plays, "Nearby at the sand table, Waka is crying because Angelo either pushed or hit him, it is hard to tell. 'He messed up my road on purpose!' Angelo yells. 'Just 'cause they don't want me to play!'" (p. 40). Clara tried to make herself as acceptable to her peers by conforming to their demands as much as she could. Friends of the bosses tried to navigate between their sympathy for rejected children and loyalty to their bossy friends under their watchful eyes. In short, all of the participants were responsible by acting upon where they stand and justifying their actions in the public discourse to others who challenged their actions.

The described responsibility constituting ontological engagement of the participants into IPD, however, is *addressive responsibility* (in contrast to "*recognized responsibility*"): the participants announce/claim responsibility in the world without yet getting an evaluative response from others in response. Actually, the participants in Ms. Paley's classroom did not always view each other's positions as responsible. Thus, Lisa (and some other children) did not see Ms. Paley's abrupt and unilateral imposition of her new inclusivity rule as responsible while some other children, notably Angelo, did. In her own turn, Ms. Paley did not see Angelo's retaliatory (and preemptive) fights as responsible, "My forced whisper sounds angrier than Angelo's outburst. 'Don't *ever* push or hit, Angelo. I've told you that.' There is no ambivalence on my part nor any attempt to persuade" (p. 40). Ms. Paley was also rather sarcastic about Lisa's promise not to write stories anymore if the new all-inclusive rule would be imposed on story writing classroom activity.

One of the functions of IPD is to answer to the addressive responsibility of others: to grant or deny recognition to the claimed responsibility of other participants. This granting or denying of responsibility is in essence a gift of IPD from one person to another: it allows for one's ontological, "stake" based interests to be tested in dialogue with others. External imposed, essentially non-dialogic, authority, however, can block participants' granting or denying of responsibility to others, resulting in a lack of testing of ideas, interests and actions. This lack of testing can lead to interpersonal stagnation and ontological entrapment (into "play bosses," "rejected children," "inclusion imposers"), or at least naïve self-assurance (for example, Ms. Paley's assurance expressed by her later in the book that the "rule is working"). In Ms. Paley's classroom, the reliance on external institutional authority to impose the inclusion rule resulted in a silencing of the dialogue whereby the children themselves could have granted (or not granted) legitimacy to the inclusion rule. Silencing IPD-like dialogue and IPD-oriented students (like Lisa, for example) is rather common phenomenon in conventional schools (Schultz, 2003, p. 119). The reliance on external authority limits the children's freedom, and thus, they cannot fully take responsibility for their own ideas and actions or the ideas and actions of others. Children in Paley's classroom appear stamped into the role of "rejected" children and "boss" children, or somewhere "in between". If children were able to sufficiently test the inclusion rule and to publicly judge its impact on the suffering and sadness of all children, new ontological interests, puzzlements and responsibilities could emerge in the community.

Person-Idea and Voice

In IPD ideas are open and develop through people and people are open to each other and grow through ideas,

> The idea *lives* not in one person's *isolated* individual consciousness-if it remains there only, it degenerates and dies. The idea begins to live, that is, to take shape, to develop, to find and renew its verbal expression, to give birth to new ideas, only when it enters into genuine dialogic relationships with other ideas, with the ideas of *others.* Human thought becomes genuine thought, that is, an idea, only under conditions of living contact with another and alien thought, a thought embodied in someone else's voice, that is, in someone else's consciousness expressed in discourse. At that point of contact between voice-consciousnesses the idea is born and lives.
> The idea-as it was *seen* by Dostoevsky the artist-is not a subjective individual-psychological formation with "permanent resident rights" in a person's head; no, the idea is inter-individual and intersubjective --the realm of its existence is not individual consciousness but dialogic communion *between* consciousnesses. The idea is a *live event,* played out at the point of dialogic meeting between two or several consciousnesses (Bakhtin, 1999, pp. 87-88).

IPD cannot treat the participants' ideas as "no one's" (Bakhtin, 1999, p. 79) but as are rooted in and transcend particular ontological places. IPD creates *person-idea* by the participants taking responsibility for their own ideas that they expect to be tested, responded, addressed, and judged. They are eager to place their ontological reputation for their ideas. For example, if a rejected child repeats word-by-word a recognizable statement by a play boss#1 (e.g., "why can't those kids play alone when others do not want to play with them?!"), the interpretation of "wannabe" is one that is easily available for the listeners. This rejected child has to either accept its new wannabe reputation (an accusation of being a pretender, fraud, charlatan (Bakhtin, 1999)) or actively fight against it. However, if another play boss child (a boss#2) repeats this phrase, it evokes in its listeners a sense of these two bosses' agreement that does not need to be defended or further explained. Their ontological reputation as play bosses will be solidified by these statements in eyes of the listeners. This simple agreement is very difficult to reach by participants of other groups. The participants' authoring ideas are charged with value judgment for listeners depending on the authors' ontological locale,

> I was teaching Richard to respect himself as the kind of person he was when working with Shahin. I wanted to help him to become a person who could make sense of mathematics and initiate working on it in the company of his peers in school. Simultaneously, I was working to structure the situation so that he could save face with his peers and maintain his integrity as both a serious student and a funny, lively, ten-year-old African American boy (Lampert, 2001, p. 286).

> I need Saundra to learn the correct placement of fractions on the number line. I need her to understand why five-sixths is larger than five-twelfths. And at the same time, I need her to learn to think of herself as a person who can study and explain her mathematical reasoning and that she can do it in school, where her peers are watching everything she is doing (Lampert, 2001, p. 305).

In monological conventional classrooms, usually ideas of the participants are separated from them and valued more than the participants themselves, "In essence … [of monologism – EM&MS] knows only a single mode of cognitive interaction among consciousnesses: someone who knows and possesses the truth instructs someone who is ignorant of it and in error; that is, it is the interaction of a teacher and a pupil, which, it follows, can be only a pedagogical dialogue" (Bakhtin, 1999, p. 81). Knowledge is seen as given and transmittable from a person (i.e., the teacher or even textbook) to person (i.e., each student) (Hirsch et al., 1988). The participants' ontological locales (i.e., who speaks, how speaks, to whom, on what occasion, for what purpose, within what history, and so on) are incidental to the ideological content of the academic curriculum. "Every true judgment is not rooted in a particular person, but gravitates toward some totalizing systematically-monologic context[12]. Only error individualizes. Everything that is true finds a place for itself within the boundaries of a single consciousness, and if it does not actually find for itself such a place, this is so for reasons incidental and extraneous to the truth itself. In the ideal a single consciousness and a single mouth are absolutely sufficient for maximally full cognition; there is no need for a multitude of consciousnesses, and no basis for it (p. 81)….This faith in the self-sufficiency of a single consciousness in all spheres of ideological life is not a theory created by some specific thinker; no, it is a profound structural characteristic of the creative ideological activity of modern times, determining all its external and internal forms" (Bakhtin, 1999, p. 82).

The problem of idea taking over particular persons for education and beyond is that the idea cannot find roots in particular persons and thus makes people difficult to participate in it. When an idea is indifferent of it participants, it is alienated from them. They are either slavishly passionate of the idea, not knowing its contextual, historical, and axiological limitations (e.g., when 2+2 is not equal 4, what are political consequences of map projections, Klinghoffer, 2006) – a so called problem of transfer (Bransford, Brown, & Cocking, 1999) -- or they are indifferent to it – the idea does not mobilize people for any action. The more sinister consequence of such monologic divorce of the idea from the particular person is a morally irresponsible perception that people are replaceable and deplaceable (i.e., can be eliminated) without any damage to the idea. This anti-ontological approach prioritizes

---

[12] We retranslated this sentence from Russian to better convey nuances of Bakhtin's idea contexualized in specific connotations of Russian wording of his choice.

intellectual achievements (i.e., dead ideas) over humanity and even can easily lead to genocide[13].

An opposite monological approach involves subordination of the idea to the ontological locale of a particular person that is exemplified (but not limited) in so-called "identity politics" (Alcoff, 2006). In this case, "the idea, once placed in the mouth of a hero who is portrayed as a fixed and finalized image of reality, inevitably loses its direct power to mean, becoming a mere aspect of reality, one more of reality's predetermined features, indistinguishable from any other manifestation of the hero. An idea of this sort might be characteristic of a social type or an individual, or it might ultimately be a simple intellectual gesture on the part of the hero, an intellectual expression of his spiritual face. The idea ceases to be an idea and becomes a simple artistic characterizing feature. As such, as a characteristic, it is combined with the hero's image" (Bakhtin, 1999, p. 79). For this monologic approach, who is saying is more important that what is said. The ontological local automatically justifies or refutes the truth and its authenticity and creates a (fake) alibi in Being (Bakhtin et al., 1993, p. 40). The truth about Jews can be told only by a Jew, the truth about women can be told only by a woman, the truth about Blacks can be told only by a Black person, the truth about oppressed can be told only by an oppressed. The question, "Who are you to say that?" can legitimately refute an argument in this approach. It has reached the highest peak probably in totalitarian regimes of the twentieth century when people and truths were "shuffled" according to their ontological belonging to desired or undesired social groups. In monological conventional schools, it is present in the infallibility of the expert authority that is characteristic of both monologic approaches and in a particular pedagogical approach requiring minority students to represent and speak on behalf of their social groups each time the curriculum touches the topics of minority.

The problem of the ontological locale taking over the idea for education and beyond is that a particular politics destroys any intellectual integrity of discourse by appeal to vulgar sociologisms. This anti-intellectual approach quickly leads to parochial dogmatism in which dialogic judgment is replaced by reference to "class struggle", "oppression", "patriarchy", "white privilege" or whatever favorable/powerful dogma of the day. Social justice is divorced from and prioritized over a search for truth. Cybernetics and genetics were considered to be first evil and second wrong in the USSR in the late 1940s because it was supposed to serve bourgeois classes as "pseudo-science, a whore of capitalism." Unjust ontological locales can be socially re-engineered. It is not worth to argue with a person with false ideas rooted in his/her ontological locale. As soon the locale is fixed, the ideas will be fixed. This monologic approach has also devastating moral consequences because it views victory of truth as elimination of ontological locale of evil untruth (often with people who occupy this locale). So called "collectivization" (elimination of petty bourgeoisie from rural areas) in the USSR and "cultural revolution" (elimination of class enemies) are tragic examples of an anti-intellectual monologic approach.

Both anti-ontological and anti-intellectual monological approaches have in common their total disrespect to a particular person. They are approaches of solitude because they do not listen to others: either others are the ready-made truth or justice side and, thus, they are not

---

[13] Cf. Stalin's famous justification of his purges "you can't chop wood without making chips fly." People are chips for his grandiose idea in which they could not find their place.

interesting in saying something new, or they are on the wrong/unjust side to be disciplined, informed, engineered, or re-educated/re-designed (or eliminated).

In contrast, IPD does not divorce social justice and search for truth. It is not afraid of dialogic truth, whatever it leads, and is not afraid of taking responsibility either. In IPD, persons-ideas are open up in dramatic events of dialogic collisions that ontologically force the participants to develop their truths. IPD involves "knots" of the dramatic dialogic events in which the participants move from tensions to dilemmas (Lave, 1988). Tensions paralyze their actions and routine being developed in the past. While dilemmas unfolded as a dialogic collision of several persons-ideas present with possibilities for new being-in-the-world and new responsibilities. To understand a person-idea is to re-construct the rootness of the idea in the ontological circumstances of the person's being as the person addresses other participants in the dialogic events. This reconstruction is possible through the author's own ontological addressivity to (and engaging in dialogic events with) the depicted persons-ideas as we tried to do below. According to Bakhtin, IPD is always open for new participants at any moment and at any place. IPD can be only studied and understood in and by another IPD. To understand IPD in Ms. Paley's classroom it was necessary for us to engage in IPD with Ms. Paley, Angelo, Lisa, Carla, Charlie, Waka, other kids, the book's reviewers, Bakhtin, other scholars, and anticipated readers. So, reader, what is a person-idea? It is *you* involved in an IPD together with us.

Angelo: A Justice Fighter and a Communitarian

Angelo is a rejected child in Ms. Paley's classroom. He is being rejected systematically although not comprehensively by other children from their plays. He is well aware that he is a stranger there. The only person who does not reject him is Ms. Paley, the teacher. "I was looking for my hamster and it was gone. Then my room was gone and then my house was gone but my grandma was there and she looks all around her and she doesn't see me" (p. 9). When Ms. Paley leaves for a teachers' conference in Canada, Angelo misses her badly and gets jealous of her other social attachments, "Why did you go away?... I don't like that Magpie you was watching" (p.7). After his beloved teacher shared her loneliness in a response, "I have dreams like that," I tell him. "I'll be walking to school but the school isn't where it's supposed to be. Finally, I find the school on a different street and I go inside but none of the doors have my name on them. My dream is like yours" (p. 10), Angelo "smiles and touches my arm" (p. 10), "Then you and me is just the same, teacher" (p. 10).

Of course, Angelo and Ms. Paley are not the same. Angelo is Ms. Paley's consciousness – a gadfly chafing at her wounds of the teacher who perpetuate social injustice in her own classroom. He is a straightforward speaker publicly denouncing any cover-up and meanness of exclusion that play bosses and their friends often use, "-- She [a play boss] promised me [to include into her play next time] and then she forgot. -- These kids, Angelo says disapprovingly, they'll always forget... when they tell you." (p. 86). Angelo usually uses black-and-white us-versus-them overgeneralizations. He often employs sweeping, and unnuanced denouncing words like "never", "always", "all", "nobody." Paley describes Angelo in her story as Raymond character, who lonely and rejected by other characters in the story all but Magpie (who personifies Ms. Paley in the story) through the eyes of children who reject him,

The next day at tea the girls could speak of nothing else but the new red-haired boy. "I wish you could make him disappear, Beatrix," Alexandra said. "Our class was much nicer before he came."...

"Well," Alexandra replied, in a huff, "he tore my picture and he broke Annabella's chalk and he knocked over her chair and he pushes the boys and . . . oh, why did he have to come?"

The new boy's name was Raymond. No one knew where he came from or where he lived, and all the children were complaining about him. .... The Olders helped the Youngers learn to read and write and the Youngers helped the Olders with the chores, which included feeding the chickens that Schoolmistress kept in the schoolyard, chopping wood, and weeding the garden. "I'm not a Younger, and I'm not an Older!" Raymond had protested on his first day, refusing to help with the chores. Schoolmistress raised her eyebrows but said nothing.

"That boy should be punished!" Alexandra told Magpie, and Beatrix liked the idea (pp. 74-75).

Like fictitious Raymond, the character of Paley's fairytale, Angelo irritates not only the children but on occasions Ms. Paley herself. Angelo-Raymond is an uncompromising rebel and fighter, disturbing the middle class feminine civility that Ms. Paley has tried to promote so hardly in her classroom. Zero tolerance to violence. Fights are unconditionally bad, even when they are just. Or are they?

Nearby at the sand table, Waka is crying because Angelo either pushed or hit him, it is hard to tell. "He messed up my road on purpose!" Angelo yells. "Just 'cause they don't want me to play!"

"But look at Waka, Angelo. You made him cry." My forced whisper sounds angrier than Angelo's outburst. "Don't *ever* push or hit, Angelo. I've told you that." There is no ambivalence on my part nor any attempt to persuade. He runs to his cubby and suddenly I remember that Angelo never tells children they cannot play (p. 40).

"There is no ambivalence on my part," says Paley – we can hear sadness and regret in her voice. Paley seems to feel guilty about stopping the working class Black male kid Angelo, speaking Ebonics, from hitting middle class kids while not stopping the middle class kids' meanness of exclusion covered up by their "nice" words of middle class verbal civility (which Angelo arguably reacts and fights against). There are three things that Paley might feel guilty about: 1) other kids are mean non-physically but not less harmfully and she does not react to that; 2) other kids initiate meanness while Angelo just reacts to that (and Angelo is thus less responsible although she makes him fully responsible); 3) Angelo is a "freedom fighter" and Ms. Paley is on the side of the [class/race] oppressors. Apparently, Paley expects from herself if not full justification of Angelo's violent resistance but at least ambivalence of its understanding (Is this her concern about rejecting the working class/race struggle?).

Paley suspects that Angelo and other kids can be rejected because they are Black, "My thought is not a nice one, but Lisa does seem to prefer blond girls. She never chooses Jennifer, who is black, to be in her stories, nor will she pick Angelo to be a father or brother. But she doesn't pick Clara or Nelson either and they are both pale blonds. What all these children may have in common, as far as Lisa is concerned, is that they are outsiders, different in some way from the children she has known. No, this is not true. They are *not* different.

What makes them outsiders is simply that they are *treated* as outsiders." (p. 68). "They don't like those kids," says Angelo (p. 56) who seems to be aware of the problem.

Ms. Paley even seems to romanticize Angelo[14] (e.g., "He organizes himself quickly when the issue is connected to feelings he recognizes—faster than I do", p. 13) and to admire him for never compromising his working class inclusivity, "He enters the classroom, into a land of strangers, and waits until he is caught up in a fantasy before he can see our smiles and smile back" (p. 7), "He runs to his cubby and suddenly I remember that Angelo never tells children they cannot play" (p. 40). In contrast, Paley remarked on the same page that Carla, another rejected child in her classroom, excludes children from her play when she is in a position to select,

> Even Clara is capable of rejecting someone. After lunch, she and Lisa tell Cynthia she can't play. Why would Clara take part in this manipulative act, knowing how it feels? When I point this out to her she looks away but is not inclined to give up her sudden and unexpected good fortune. Her wish has come true. Lisa has chosen to play with her today, a temporary whim that will make the next rejection all the more puzzling and painful. (p. 40)

We might disagree with Paley's romantic vision of Angelo. As a matter of fact, he was jealous about Ms. Paley leaving him for the conference and he did not like Magpie at the beginning. Was he trying to exclude Magpie (and all those for whom Ms. Paley left him) from his relations with Ms. Paley? Was he really inclusive to other kids or he just did not care as much as he cared about his relations with Ms. Paley? Might he not exclude other kids from his plays simply because he was not as attached to them as he was attached to his teacher, Ms. Paley or as Carla was attached to Lisa? We do not know for sure.

And nevertheless, indeed, Angelo is passionately searching for communion with the other side (i.e., play bosses and their friends). He is trying to reach out the hearts of kids who reject him. It is awfully difficult to start a dialogue and collaboration with people who reject you. Arguably, it is impossible to do in a unilateral way but what is any other way left for a rejected child?! Rejected children often are resigned to their fantasy play to do this reconciliation,

> "Angelo started it," Charlie says.
> "They was fixin' to steal my sand," Angelo snaps angrily, "from my hill. Anyway, they's too nasty. I'm leaving!"
> Wiping his hands on his pants, he makes a sand trail to the story table. Then, wearily, he puts down his head, closing his eyes. A moment later he springs up. "Can I tell a story, teacher?"
> "Good," I say, taking his notebook from the pile. "I'm in the mood for a story." The moment he begins a calm descends over this table, though the sand players are still noisy and quarrelsome at theirs.

---

[14] At times Angelo sounds like an ideal Marxist working class rebel with vanguardist consciousness. Many of Angelo's judgments are unconditional. Morson & Emerson (1990) talk about "semiotic totalitarianism" where there is all or nothing, all approaches are comprehensive and total, there are no exceptions. They argue that Marxism has the birthmark of semiotic totalitarianism (but Marxism is not alone, according to them). Interestingly enough, play bosses often use very conditional language of particularity, arguably because it serves for their manipulation of sugar-coating their exclusion.

"Some men was hunting in the forest. They saw something up in the hill and they started climbing. And they was climbing until they got to the top and it was a baby fox was trapped and they was trying to get the baby fox out. It was crying for its mother. Don't worry, fox, we'll take you home and start you a fire. They was trying to help him, not to hurt him. They took him home and the mother fox was there. And the baby said, 'I thought you was dead.' And the hunter said, 'She come alive.' And they started a fire to keep warm."

Clara also wants to tell a story. "There was a little kitty. And there was a little girl. And the girl's name is Lisa and the kitty's name is Clara and they live together."

For years I have written down these stories the children invent, the fairy tales of the young. Their voices have seeped into my consciousness and become as my own" (pp. 25-26).

The difference between Angelo's fantasy and Clara's fantasy about reconciliation is that in contrast to Clara, Angelo seems to think about a pathway to reconciliation and communion. His pathway is about heroic saving from a trap (of exclusion and solitude?) and care of the other (a little fox, Charlie, a play boss), who is unappreciative and afraid of him (a hunter, Angelo, a rejected kid). Self-sacrifice and care is a pathway to a community. Ms. Paley notices Angelo's fantasy solution of communion and adds ("appropriates", in Bakhtin's terms?) in her story of Raymond an episode of Raymond saving a baby-raccoon in woods. This metaphoric move by the teacher, connecting the fictional story of Magpie bird and the real life in the classroom, was noticed by Angelo who immediately wants to replace his baby-fox for Ms. Paley's baby-raccoon, "He jumps up and gets his notebook, bringing me a pencil so I can immediately make the change in his hunter story" (p. 83). Does Angelo really believe that the communion with play bosses possible? It is hard to say but there is the following evidence in Paley's book that he really wants it.

Angelo is very sensitive to the development of Ms. Paley's story and its application to the situation in the class. It seems to give him hope, if not suggestions, how to overcome the systematic rejection he is experiencing in the class,

"Tomorrow we'll return to the hidden mountain [the episode in Ms. Paley's story about Magpie bird and his friends' adventures]," I remind the children. "Do you remember where we left off?"

"The dragons wake up!" everyone calls out.

"Yes, and Raymond is not afraid," I add, noticing Angelo at my side.

"Now those guys is his friends, right?" he asks, but before I can reply he runs to the front of the line and stands next to Charlie (p. 110).

Dragons ("those guys") became friends of Raymond and his friends because Magpie, Beatrix and Raymond's father tricked them out of the mountain shrouded in cold mist into unbelievable warm sunlight of the bigger world where they stopped being lonely and scared by giving them to taste juicy blueberries (p. 120). Angelo hopes that Ms. Paley tricks Charlie and other play bosses into communion by her new rule "you can't say you can't play". He takes a risk of moving next to a "dragon" (Charlie, a play boss) in hope to be accepted as a friend. Unfortunately, Paley did not provide us with Charlie's reaction (or a dialogic response?) to Angelo's move of new hope.

So far, Angelo's person-idea is depicted as his responsibility for his own deeds in relationship with other participants of the classroom outside of internally persuasive discourse. However, it has not been depicted as a dialogue with another person-idea that constitutes the core of IPD. The following section is exactly about Angelo's person-idea involved in a dialogue with Lisa's person-idea about "ultimate questions".

Dialogue on Threshold

What can lead them out of this vicious circle of ontological traps? In IPD, the predictability of voices collapses. Using Bakhtin's terminology, participants become "unfinalized." They can transcend their ontological circumstances and thus become responsible for envisioning new and arguably better ontological circumstances for each other. This happens through their engagement in *dialogue on the threshold*, where social roles disappear, selfish interests disappear, and important social dilemmas present themselves in ultimate form. In our view, Bakhtin's notion "dialogue on the threshold" is an important description of one of the key elements of internally persuasive discourse. Bakhtin (1999) defined "dialogue on threshold" in the following ways,

> In Dostoevsky, the participants in the act stand *on the threshold* (on the threshold of life and death, falsehood and truth, sanity and insanity). And they are presented here as *voices*, ringing out, speaking out "before earth and heaven" (p. 147).
>
> We remember that the menippea[15] is *the universal genre of ultimate questions*. Its action takes place not [only[16]] in the "here" and the "now," but [also] throughout the world for all eternity: on earth, in the nether world, and in heaven" (pp. 146-147).
>
> ... there is a tendency to create the *extraordinary* situation, one which would cleanse the word of all of life's automatism and object-ness, which would force a person to reveal the deepest layers of his personality and thought (p. 111).
>
> Under menippean conditions the very nature and process of posing philosophical problems, as compared with the Socratic dialogue, had to change abruptly: all problems that were in the least "academic" (gnoseological and aesthetic) fell by the wayside, complex and extensive modes of argumentation also fell away, and there remained essentially only naked "ultimate questions" with an ethical and practical bias (p. 115).
>
> Everywhere one meets the stripped-down pro et contra of life's ultimate questions (p. 116).

The culmination of IPD is in testing person-idea. It is often occurs in a critical moment when two polar person-ideas collide on a "public square." In the case of Paley's book, these two person-ideas are a rejected child Angelo and a play boss Lisa, crossing their ideas in a public classroom forum organized by their teacher, Ms. Paley. Their dialogic collision reaches the intensity of Bakhtin's "ultimate questions" in the ethical practical sphere with regard to exclusion and inclusion.

---

[15] In our view, the literary genre of menippea described by Bakhtin nicely reveals the key elements of IPD, "it is essential to emphasize once again that the issue is precisely the testing of an *idea*, of a *truth*, and not the testing of a particular human character, whether an individual or a social type. The testing of a wise man is a test of his philosophical position in the world, not a test of any other features of his character independent of that position. In this sense one can say that the content of the menippea is the adventures of an *idea* or a *truth* in the world: either on earth, in the nether regions, or on Olympus" (Bakhtin, 1999, pp. 114-115).

[16] These qualifiers "only" and "also" are missing in the translation but present in the Russian original.

Angelo does not only dream and hope for the communion with the rest of the class, when an opportunity presents itself in a public forum created by Ms. Paley, Angelo actively seizes it to address and reach his rejectors' hearts directly through a dialogue in which the rejectors (i.e., play bosses, in this case Lisa) can respond to him,

> *Angelo:* Let anybody play if someone asks.
> *Lisa:* But then what's the whole point of playing?
> *Nelson:* You just want Cynthia.

Nelson is another rejected child who like Angelo often denounces play bosses and their friends for covering up their manipulation of relations in their plays with brutal honesty.

> *Lisa:* I could play alone. Why can't Clara play alone?
> *Angelo:* I think that's pretty sad. People that is *alone* they has water in their eyes.

Lisa defines "play alone" as a personal choice and a preference among other preferences that by itself is neither good nor bad. Thus, in her view, pushing another child to play alone is outside of a moral judgment and any issue of Lisa's personal responsibility. Angelo revoices Lisa's word "alone" and defines as imprisonment, as solitary confinement enforced by other, namely, by Lisa. He forcefully moves "play alone" back into the sphere of moral judgment and personal responsibility. His power of persuasion is rooted in evoked compassion: all four parties in Ms. Paley classroom know deeply down that the coerced play alone produces "water" in the rejected children's eyes. He introduces the notion of sadness as the moral judgment of play bosses' deeds and at the same time seems to articulate compassion for play bosses themselves who disregard sadness they create in rejected kids. In our view, this is an example of what we call *dialogic finalizing* in which a participant of a dialogue reveals (as a gift) ontological conditions of one's being that provides an opportunity for the addressed person (Lisa in this case) to deal with his or her ontological confinement (e.g., like Lisa being a play boss) and eventually transcend it.

> *Lisa:* I'm more sad if someone comes that I don't want to play with.

Lisa accepts Angelo's notion of sadness as moral measurement of responsibility in their classroom community. Even more, Lisa seems to accept her moral responsibility for making other kids sad. However, she disagrees with Angelo about his conclusion that the root of the problem is in rejection. Lisa sees the problem of sadness in her classroom as a compromise between two evils. One evil is the evil of rejection that currently present in the class. The other evil is the evil of forced collectivity[17] that the suggested new rule would produce. In Lisa's judgment, rejection is a lesser evil than forced collectivity because it produces less sadness in the class. Is Lisa deceptive in bringing this argument or does she honestly believe that it is true? Without talking with Lisa, we cannot know for sure. But let us elevate possible legitimacy of Lisa's argument by using a more familiar situation of the exclusive marriage institution suggested by one of the book reviewers. King (1993, pp. 334-335) charges Paley

---

[17] You can find a discussion of forced collectivity in the critique of totalitarian regimes (Bukovsky, 1979; Havel & Vladislav, 1989; Solzhenitsyn, 1974).

with failing to see the right to exclude as a protected public right, just like the right to participate, and Paley does not consider this right to exclude seriously. For example, exclusive rights related to the legal protections are socially granted to women in intimate relations with men. Using Lisa's argument, we can ask, "Would it be sadder to legally allow any man to enter into a sexual relation with any woman at his unilateral whim, or to exclude all men but one who is consensually chosen through the institution of marriage as it is in the current societal practice?" Even taking into consideration cultural and historical diversity among societies in marriage arrangements, we think that the right of public exclusion is "less sadder" than the right of unilateral inclusion. Of course, there are important differences between marriage and sexual relations, on the one hand, and children's play and friendships in the classroom, on the other. Like King, we just want to problematize the issue to show its complexity and the potential reasonableness of Lisa's intellectual-ontological position. Ms. Paley seems to also recognize (probably for the first time) the problem they all faced in the classroom that Angelo and Lisa nailed. Angelo's and Lisa's distinguishable personal truths collide and reveal themselves in a dramatic dialogic event on threshold of their testing. The teacher formulates the problem as a question of two alternatives for the class to consider. The inquiry is publicly stated now.

> *Teacher:* Who is sadder, the one who isn't allowed to play or the one who has to play with someone he or she doesn't want to play with?
> *Clara:* It's more sadder if you can't play.
> *Lisa:* The other one is the same sadder.
> *Angelo:* It has to be Clara because she puts herself away in her cubby. And Lisa can still play every time.
> *Lisa:* I can't play every time if I'm sad.
> How clearly the issue is stated. (pp. 19-20)

Unfortunately, Angelo apparently misunderstood Lisa and Ms. Paley's question[18]. The question is not about who is sadder: rejected Clara or rejecting Lisa – the answer is obvious – of course, Clara. We do not think that Lisa would dispute it. What Lisa raises is a *possibility* that she might become even sadder than Clara if the new rule of "Let anybody play if someone asks" (p. 19) proposed by Angelo and Ms. Paley was applied. Unfortunately, Lisa and then Ms. Paley used the present tense instead of the conditional tense in phrasing their dilemma. Ms. Paley should have asked, "Who *would be* sadder, the one who *isn't* allowed to play *now* or the one who *would have* to play with someone he or she doesn't want to play with *after* we *would* require all of you to accept all children who want into the play?" The important part of the dilemma that Angelo misses is about comparison of negative consequences of the status quo with negative consequences of the possible new rule order. Another unfortunate moment is that the teacher, Ms. Paley, does not seem to notice the problem in Angelo's misunderstanding and does not guide him (and other children in the forum) to understand the options presented in her and Lisa's question. It would have been interesting to know how

---

[18] There is another interpretation of Angelo's statement that is he did understand Lisa's point correctly. Angelo might be trying to say that Carla is sadder than Lisa because she does not have control of her circumstances – she cannot play in contrast to Lisa who can control her sadness and she can play if she chooses that. This interpretation of Angelo's statement is possible but, in our view, is unlikely, although it seems that in her answer Lisa understood Angelo exactly in this way. She apparently replied that she would not be able to control her sadness and thus she cannot play when she sad.

Angelo would have addressed Lisa-Paley inquiry if he had understood it correctly. What reconciliation pathway would he had chosen with Lisa if at all?

Angelo-Lisa dialogue on threshold sets the ontological dilemma that the class faced with the ultimate clarity[19]. What produces more suffering-sadness the right to exclude by the play boss (i.e., the right of play privacy) or the right to be included on any child's request (i.e., the right of unilateral inclusivity in play)? Ms. Paley's classroom has only known the regime of the privacy right to exclude children by play bosses. The participants have been familiar only with the suffering-sadness consequences of this regime. They have not been familiar with possible negative consequences of the alternative regime of unilateral inclusivity, the regime proposed by Ms. Paley and Angelo (and supported by a few more, mostly rejected children). In the dialogue on the threshold, Lisa reasons about the possible negative consequences of this regime. But these negative consequences of potential suffering-sadness are purely hypothetical although plausible. Also, it is not clear for the class participants and the book's readers, whether these negative consequences of the regime of unilateral inclusivity would outweigh the suffering-sadness of the rejected children under the current regime of the right to exclude children by play bosses and their friends. The test of person-ideas has to be moved from a verbal dialogue of a public forum to an action dialogue of social experimentation, in which the two regimes can be compared, their negative consequences of suffering-sadness evaluated, and publicly judged.

Lisa: Ideological Becoming through Dialogic Finalizing

By moving dialogue *to the threshold*, the participants moved out of their vicious circles, but not yet out of their ontological positions. Although Lisa's and Angelo's positions become deep and ultimate, they are still ontologically grounded in being a "play boss" or a "rejected child." The breakdown between the participants' voice and their ontological position occurred in events that we termed *dialogic finalizing.* In such events, another's *penetrating word* disrupts the person's self-identity. Ideological becoming involves exploration of boundaries between one's person-idea and person-idea of another for the person's growth through transcending his or her ontological limits. This boundary is set through IPD. Going beyond limits of one's own person-idea, one's own truth, helps the person to realize limitations of his or her ontological being and thus sets conditions to transcend them. Sometimes, this process of ideological becoming is facilitated struggle with another discourse, "The importance of struggling with another's discourse, its influence in the history of an individual's coming to ideological consciousness, is enormous" (Bakhtin, 1991, p. 348). Yet another way is a "penetrating-touching[20] word" by another – dialogic finalizing of the person – "a word capable of actively and confidently interfering in the interior dialogue of the other person,

---

[19] Paley's book undermines an argument that dialogue and internally persuasive discourse is an essentially middle-class discourse based on verbalism, bargaining of interests, and liberal compromises (cf. Casey, 2005; Delpit, 1995; Ellsworth, 1992). As Paley shows, an ontological dialogue (IPD) between middle-class children, who heavily constituted "play bosses" in Paleys' classroom, and working-class children, who were over-represented among "rejected kids", was possible and successful. Arguably, the children's diverse cultural styles (e.g., directness of Angelo and maneuvering and, at times, bargaining by Lisa) did not prevent them and the other kids from engaging the ontological dialogue (IPD).

[20] The Russian word "проникновенный" used by Bakhtin has very different connotations than English word "penetrated". The Russian word is associated with emotional sympathy and sincerity missing in English word. Also English word has connotation of violation and interference missing in the Russian word.

helping this person to find his own voice" (Bakhtin, 1999, p. 242) that we are going to discuss here.

The notion of dialoging finalizing sounds to be a misnomer. Indeed, Bakhtin argued through his book on Dostoevsky that unfinalizing is the key feature of dialogue (Holquist, 1990; Morson & Emerson, 1990). To reconcile this apparent contradiction, let us consider a following analogy. When a child learn how to write, his or her degrees of freedom gets highly reduced – not any drawing, any scribble is acceptable anymore unlike in a visual art expression but only very rigid, conventionally recognized, cursive patterns of the 26 letters (in English). This new constraint, however, creates new degrees of freedom for the child associated with writing expression. So through learning how to write, a child's drawing gets "finalized" while writing gets "unfinalized" at the same time and through the same process, but not automatically because knowing how to write letters creates only possibility for expressive writing and not the writing itself – more efforts (and skill) is needed from the person for that. This is similar to dialogic finalizing that defines the person in order that the person is able to transcend this definition through his or her additional efforts. In dialogic finalizing, unfinalizing occurs through finalizing by other and efforts of the person to response to it. As we argue, the notion of dialogic finalizing was present in Bakhtin's writing in his discussion of "penetrating-touching word" although he did not name it as such.

Paley's book provides fascinating examples of such dialogic finalizing by other and by children themselves. We have already discussed briefly the dialogic finalizing of Lisa (a play boss) by Angelo (a rejected child). However, effortful ideological becoming of the involved children was not much evident in this incident. Here we want to bring another example in which ideological becoming of the child and the teacher through dialogic finalizing are very evident in it.

Lisa is the strongest opponent of Ms. Paley's idea of the right of automatic, unconditional inclusivity (see her debate with Angelo above). Nevertheless, she seems to be considering the new right in her own stories which portrays her as an open-minded child,

> Lisa dictates a mousie story [to the teacher, Ms. Paley]. "Once upon a time there were five mousie sisters and five mousie brothers. Two of their sisters were babies and two of the brothers were babies. They were newborns. The older sisters and brothers brought them blueberries and tucked them into bed and read them stories at bedtime. One day a kitty that had no mother or father and was an orphan asked if she could be a sister and they said yes. The end."
> I gaze at Lisa in admiration. "In your stories you let everyone play."

It is not clear if Lisa was aware of that by herself before Ms. Paley made her observation. But in any case, Ms. Paley's words seem to become "penetrating-touching" words that Bakhtin was talking about. They actively and confidently enter Lisa's consciousness allowing her to reveal the intimate (and probably most hidden) ontological circumstances of her own being. Penetrating-touching words although involved strong finalizing of the person ("you let everyone play") but they direct to, they are up for grabs for the person. They always have a hidden question, "Lisa, you are very inclusive in your stories but why are you supporting the right of exclusive play?" Thus, Ms. Paley starts dialogic finalizing of Lisa and Lisa continues that by herself to a deeper level of self-understanding using an imagined character from Ms. Paley's story,

She smiles and begins to draw pictures of tiny mice in the margins of the page. "Beatrix is jealous, you know," Lisa says, suddenly, as if we have been discussing Magpie's witch friend all along. "That's the reason she thinks she's not nice. Jealous people don't feel nice." (p. 65)

Ms. Paley's stories about Magpie bird and his adventures reflect discussions in Ms. Paley class about exclusivity and inclusivity. The reverse is also true: imagined events of the story are reflected in the context of the classroom events. Storytelling provides a mirroring effect: life helps make sense of a story while story can help make a sense life. For example, Lisa is thinking about Ms. Paley's story about imagined character Beatrix who was a vacillant witch: tried to be evil but having a good heart. Beatrix saved Magpie bird when Magpie was a chick but she has a lot jealousy against Magpie's friends. Lisa sees a connection between herself and Beatrix that Ms. Paley probably had in mind when she design such a story character,

Annabella thanked her and glanced about. "Where is Beatrix?" she asked. "When will we meet her?"
Magpie seemed embarrassed. "Uh ... she's not quite ready to greet . you," he replied, and Alexandra burst out laughing.
"Beatrix is never ready to greet anyone new in her dear Magpie's life. When she first met me, she tried to turn me into a frog, but luckily that was too hard for her."
Annabella looked anxiously at Magpie, who quickly reassured her. "Nothing to worry about, Annabella. Beatrix won't bother you at all. She just needs a bit of time to get used to people."
Ridden nearby behind a tree sat a very jealous Beatrix, glowering at the newcomers. "Don't be too sure of me, Magpie," she muttered. "I'm not nearly as nice as you think I am." (p. 64)

But does Lisa see the connection between herself and Beatrix? Do we read too much in this episode? Fortunately, Ms. Paley follows through and makes further probes in Lisa's inner world.

"That's interesting," I comment. "I wonder what makes a person jealous."
Lisa does not answer to Ms. Paley's question but rather continues elaborating on herself,
"You know, if you can't have someone all to yourself. When I'm jealous I'm not nice."

Now, Lisa reaches a level of being brutally honest with herself but at price of tremendous self-finalization that jeopardizes her dignity as a self-respected agent. There can be very little proud of a person's self-realization, "When I'm jealous I'm not nice" – it is like a self-acknowledgment of being essentially a bad person without any possibility for future improvement (i.e., negative essentializing oneself). Bakhtin warned us that a penetrating-touching word can be brutal without any way out by yourself, "a firmly monologic, undivided discourse, a word without sideward glance, without a loophole, without internal polemics" (Bakhtin, 1999, p. 249). Lisa hits herself with her own finalization really hard and cannot easily recover herself. She cannot defend herself. She needs another. Fortunately, the teacher recognizes that and comes with another penetrating-touching word about a present but still not fully realized possibility for Lisa-Beatrix,

"Beatrix does do nice things," I remind her. "She took care of Magpie just like the big brothers and sisters in your story take care of the newborns...." (p. 65)

Does Lisa get it? Does she realize Ms. Paley's rescue of her from her brutal self-finalizing (i.e., -"When I'm jealous I'm not nice" – "But you do do nice things on other occasions.")? Ms. Paley seems to try to convey Lisa that despite her true self-revelation, she is a nice person already (with some reservations[21]) and has exciting potentials of being even nicer. Let's see…

> Lisa is drawing her third picture of Beatrix. She can't get it quite the way she wants it but she's not at all impatient, as she tends to be with people. "By the way, Lisa, I just remembered something really nice you did for Hiroko. When she hurt her knee you sat with her and looked at a book with her. That made her feel much better. You were her friend for a long time on that day."
> "Who's nicer, me or Beatrix?"
> "You both do nice things."

Ms. Paley remembers that something nice that Lisa did do to people not just to her story characters. However, Lisa's reply suggests a competition between Lisa and Beatrix about who is nicer. Ms. Paley might overdo her rescue work by shifting from dialogic finalizing to projective and arguably manipulative (objective) finalizing of Lisa. The teacher seems to make the student an *object* of her pedagogical actions (Matusov & Smith, 2007). Ms. Paley seems to want to lock Lisa in niceness while Lisa escapes from this cage by changing the virtue of niceness into a competition of niceness credentials, "Who has more niceness credentials/points: Beatrix or me?" Later in the book Paley would remember Lisa's question and remark with disapproval, "Hers is a logical mind and she continually looks for opportunities to compare and sort out the wide variety of behaviors that confront her. Only Lisa would have asked, 'Who is nicer, me or Beatrix?'" (p. 116). We think that Paley is missing that Lisa's competitive question was in response to her own apparently manipulative move to "trap" Lisa into a niceness attitude. Lisa seems to dialogically escape the trap. But Lisa still is genuinely concerned about herself – Lisa-Beatrix's potential to hurt people,

> "Is she going to hurt Annabella?" Lisa looks worried. Would she tell Annabella she can't play, preferring Alexandra? ….

It seems that Paley sees the same connections us we do that Lisa is not only worries about Annabella but also about Beatrix and Lisa herself (can both of them remain to stay nice).

---

[21] Actually, Paley has a very strong reservation about Lisa. Paley actually went on immediately after her utterance in her remark claiming that Lisa is a racist, "My thought is not a nice one, but Lisa does seem to prefer blond girls. She never chooses Jennifer, who is black, to be in her stories, nor will she pick Angelo to be a father or brother. But she doesn't pick Clara or Nelson either and they are both pale blonds. What all these children may have in common, as far as Lisa is concerned, is that they are outsiders, different in some way from the children she has known. No, this is not true. They are *not* different. What makes them outsiders is simply that they are *treated* as outsiders" (p. 68). It appears to us as if Paley felt that she overstated Lisa's goodness and had to correct (dialogically respond) what just she said (wrote). If we are right, Paley's dialogic action is similar to actions of many characters of Dostoevsky's novels who come to make peace but started a fight and vice versa. They also dialogically react to their overreaching plans and actions and self-provoke themselves (Bakhtin, 1999, p. 60; Dostoyevsky, 1996).

"I can see you're a bit anxious about Beatrix and Annabella," I say. "She almost does something bad . . ."

Ms. Paley apparently teases Lisa-Beatrix and does not provide her with loophole-rescue as she did before. But this time Lisa can save herself by herself,

> Lisa jumps up, laughing. "Oh, no! Magpie won't ever let her be mean to Annabella. I just know that!" And she runs off to play.
> Who is this Magpie who won't let Beatrix be mean? Someone apparently who is more powerful than jealousy and more dependable than impulse and caprice. Lisa likes Magpie and trusts him. His is the first picture she draws for the book. I am certain she wants me to be more like Magpie and not allow her to be mean even when she is jealous of playmates or uncomfortable with strangers. (p. 68)

Ms. Paley's analysis sounds very interesting. Did Lisa suggest the teacher to be her savior from Lisa's own jealousy or did Lisa just know happy ending nature of the US fairytales? Did Lisa make a connection between Ms. Paley and Magpie? We do not know for sure, but we suspect that she did (we have evidence in the book that she made a connection between fairytale Schoolmistress and Ms. Paley, p. 86; and between Angelo and Raymond character, p. 83). It is very likely that she made such connection. Now, if we take this for granted, the question is how Lisa wanted Ms. Paley to help her? What was acceptable help for her? Unfortunately, Paley did not raise this inquiry for herself or her readers in the book.

Lisa's words about Magpie are also dialogic finalizing for Ms. Paley who interprets them as request for some kind of action. Lisa's words actively enter Ms. Paley's internal dialogue involving her indecision, "So, I thought, I want to do a favor for Clara, but is it fair to spoil Lisa's and Cynthia's play? Yet would this really spoil their play?" (p. 15) If even Lisa, who was THE leader of opposition to the new inclusivity right, expects to be helped to be nice, then what to worry about – she should act. And Ms. Paley acts as we will see later...

The episode constitutes the dramatic event – maybe the most important episode in the book. The field of education has had a long history of defining the educational process by its goal. Traditionally an educational goal has been defined as the acquisition of skills and knowledge (through different processes like transmission or discovery learning). However, for the last twenty years this goal has been criticized for being too decontextualized and non-ontological (see, for example, Lave, 1988). Different new goals for education have been proposed: identity development, transformation of participation in a community of practice, raising critical consciousness, and so on. Based on Bakhtin's literary scholarship of development of a character in a novel, Freedman and Ball (2004) propose another definition for the goal of education – "ideological becoming."

Freedman and Ball point out that the Russian term "ideology" has different connotations than the corresponding English term. The Russian term implies a (systematic or unsystematic) set of ideas and their contexts (in the way that "ecology" is a system, in a broader sense, of organisms and their habitats) rather than inflexible ideas imposed by propaganda. Ideological becoming is development of ideological subjectivity within "the ideological environment" in which the individual lives (Medvedev, 1985, p. 14). Freedman and Ball (2004) see this ideological becoming of students as transformation of their discourse from authoritative to internally persuasive.

For our analysis of the case of the Lisa-teacher episode, we define authoritative discourse as a degree of insularity (or parochialism, being not deeply informed by others) in a person-idea – both Lisa's and Ms. Paley's. Lisa's insularity before this dialogue with Ms. Paley was evident in her jealous meanness, of which she had probably been not aware before. That jealous meanness not only guided Lisa's deeds but had made her less responsible for her own actions. After the dialogue, Lisa could (and actually did) do mean acts out of jealousy but she was less naïve about that. The dialogue with the teacher helped her develop new ethical choices that had not been available to her before. Now she could have chosen between manipulation and fight of her own jealousy while in the past, before the dialogue, she had been chosen (possessed, appropriated[22]) by her jealousy. If before her explanations of her jealous meanness had been naïve, now, after the dialogue, they were calculated and manipulative because they were mediated by Lisa's self-knowledge. As Bakhtin put it, "[dialogue] forces [participants] to better perceive their own possibilities and boundaries [limits], that is, to overcome their own naiveté" (Bakhtin, 1999, p. 271)[23]. On a positive side, Lisa has learned from a relevant other (her teacher) that not only she can overcome her jealousy but she actually does do it on occasion. The dialogue empowered Lisa to take more responsibility for her own deeds and life. This does not mean that Lisa will stop being jealous or mean but she now has more agency to deal with her own jealousy and meanness by herself and with help of others.

By the way, this does not necessarily mean that Lisa changed her mind about the right to exclude other children from play. Lisa might disagree with Ms. Paley (and Angelo) that children exclude other children from their plays only because of their jealous meanness. And, in our view, she might have a point. This issue is too complex and, in contrast to Paley's beliefs, much exceeds exclusion by jealous meanness although jealous meanness, in general, and Lisa's, in specific, is definitely a part of it. As Paley's book reviewer correctly notices, "Whether or not one agrees or disagrees with the position taken in any specific example [of exclusion], it is clear that the right to exclude is not simply a form of meanness. While appearing to consider the issue from all sides, Paley, unfortunately, shapes our perspective without permitting a serious consideration of the *importance* of the right to exclude" (King, 1993, p. 335). The play is about having fun together. Play bosses not only assume power but they also manage participants' fun. They are fun managers similar, in many ways, to teachers. We wonder if Paley, as a responsible teacher concerned about high quality education for all of her students, might exclude some students if too many try to enroll in her class or, even more important, she might exclude specific children if she knows perfectly well that she could not teach them well to provide quality education and classroom life to them and other children in her classroom. Good teachers are very concerned about educational and social ecology of their classroom and do not compromise their concerns about educating their students by their guilt that they might need to exclude some students to ensure this ecology (Matusov, 1999). It is clearly a tough decision, murky, and potentially dangerous one. It is a dangerous consideration because, as we see in Paley's book, it is easy to mask/rationalize one's prejudices and manipulative power by appealing to ecology preservation. But, however messy this decision is, a contextual, case-by-case, judgment is avoidable and the only responsible

---

[22] Cf. McDermott's (1993) "acquisition of the child by learning disability".
[23] Bakhtin's quote was about the relationship between polyphonic novel and old literary genres but we think it can be applied to dialogue and its parochial participants.

way to go. There is no alibi in a rule -- one cannot find an alibi (Bakhtin's term) for wrong inclusion or wrong exclusion in any rule pre-given to the particular situation. This is similar to doctors, who under the Hippocratic Oath must not harm their patients. If a doctor knows that he or she cannot help a particular patient, he or she must exclude the patient and send to another doctor who can help. Similarly, the teacher can exclude legitimately and responsibly, in our view. It is unfortunate that currently teacher-student "divorce" is not seen as legitimate in educational practice as doctor-patient "divorce" in medical practice (Mayo, Alburquerque Candela, Matusov, & Smith, 2008). The bottom line is that this issue of the moral legitimacy of the public right to exclude other people is debatable and not as resolved as Paley argues in her book (i.e., reasonable people can disagree about it without becoming irresponsible, Dershowitz, 2002).

Lisa's education as ideological becoming is about opening up her insular and parochial person-idea, the naïve authority of her own word, to contact with other, penetrating person-ideas in the internally persuasive discourse. Lisa's parochial person-idea becomes more cosmopolitan[24] – deeply informed by person-ideas of others. The important educational point here is not what Lisa has taken away from the IPD but that her future participation in future IPDs with others and herself is being deeply informed, educated by the her dialogue with Ms. Paley. We argue that from a dialogic pedagogical position, there is no other educational value than transformation of participation in IPD because truth lives in dialogue – truth is not a by-product of dialogue.

Finally, it is interesting to analyze ideological becoming of Ms. Paley herself in her IPD with Lisa. Ms. Paley has learned that her major opponent in the classroom, Lisa, experiments with inclusivity (at least in her stories) but, what is even more important, thanks to Ms Paley's stories and class discussions, Lisa becomes deeply aware of mean side of jealousy that she often experiences toward her friends. Finally, Ms. Paley learns that deeply down Lisa expects her, the teacher, to help Lisa keep from getting caught in a trap of jealous, possessive meanness. As we know from happened in the book, this novel knowledge contributed to Ms. Paley's resolution of her impasse. Ms. Paley's person-idea becomes less parochial and more cosmopolitan.

Is it accidental that the teacher's ideological becoming co-occurs with the student's ideological becoming? We do not think so. Penetration of words of the teacher into the inner word of the student requires an opposite movement of penetration of words of the student into the inner world of the teacher. Newman, Cole, and Griffin have deepened Vygotsky's original concept of the zone of proximal development (Vygotsky, 1978), arguing that the zone of "inherent ambiguity" and new possibilities occurs not only in learners but also in the teacher. They expressed this idea in the following way, "Just as the children do not have to know the full cultural analysis of a tool to begin using it, the teacher does not have to have a complete analysis of the child's understanding of the situation to start using their actions within the larger system" (Newman et al., 1989, p. 63). In other words, the student does not know what to learn (i.e., what is available to learn and why this learning is important for the child) while the teacher does not know how to help the student and "where" the child is (i.e., what is the child's worldview and how exactly parochial it is). From this point of view, *transformation* of

---

[24] Cosmopolitan is defined as "conversant with many spheres of interest", "growing or occurring in many parts of the world, widely distributed", "having constituent elements from all over the world or from many different parts of the world" (Houghton Mifflin Company, 2000). Of course, our definition of cosmopolitan does not preclude particularity and rootness (see, Appiah, 2006, for more discussion).

the teacher's *pedagogical* parochialism (i.e., particular pedagogy) is bounded by *transformation* of student's *curricular* parochialism (i.e., worldview). In the Lisa-teacher IPD above, Lisa's learning was done through the teacher's deeper understanding of her.

However, this is not the whole story. We argue that, *in internally persuasive discourse, the teacher's worldview (i.e., the teacher's curricular parochialism) is* <u>necessarily</u> *changing* as well (not just pedagogy) and its transformation is <u>also</u> bounded by transformation of student's *curricular* parochialism. Bakhtin justified this point in the following quote, embedded in his discussion of how a reader understands of a text of literary artwork, "The person [e.g., teacher] who understands approaches the work [e.g., student] with his own already formed world view, from his own viewpoint, from his own position. These positions determine his evaluation to a certain degree, but they themselves do not always stay the same. They [e.g., the teacher's worldviews and values] are influenced by the artwork [e.g., student], which always introduces something new. Only when the position is dogmatically inert is there nothing new revealed in the work (the dogmatist gains nothing; he cannot be enriched). The person who understands must not reject the possibility of changing or even abandoning his already prepared viewpoints and positions. In the act of understanding, a struggle occurs that results in mutual change and enrichment" (Bakhtin, 1986, p. 142). What is the evidence of that mutual change in the worldviews, in the Lisa-teacher dialogue above? In our view, dialoguing with Lisa helped Ms. Paley to solidify her view that play exclusion is rooted in jealous meanness. Ms. Paley's worldview has been changed as Lisa's worldview was changing. These changes are bounded but do not determine one another. We, for example, as particular readers of the dialogue, have drawn a quite different conclusion than Paley did (as we discussed above). We are sure that there are other reasonable readings of this rich dialogue at its threshold. As Bakhtin (1986) showed, even a simple dialogic agreement involves transformation of the participants' subjectivities (i.e., their parochial worldviews).

Dialogic Listening through Subjectivizing and Problematizing of Others

If the purpose of education is to be internally critically persuaded, it means that the issue at hand has to be considered from different perspectives. This process of education requires dialogizing of one's own internal position, when one's own voice becomes informed by dialogue with others. In Paley's classroom IPD, this process of dialogization of the voices becomes evident in the process that we call *dialogic listening,* which involves what Bakhtin calls double-voicing; people take words of others and use for their own purposes. Bakhtin (1999) defined dialogicity as the double-voiced nature of discourse when utterances are externally and internally shaped by not only their directionality on the object they try to express but also on others whom they address and reply. Bakhtin spent the entire fifth chapter on his book on Dostoevsky's artwork discussing different forms of double-voicedness. Bakhtin's discussion of double-voicedness helps us raise the following question. What is particularity of the double-voicedness in internally persuasive educational discourse?

As we have already discussed above (see also, Matusov, 2007), some educators interpret Bakhtin's notion of double-voicedness almost as transmission of knowledge – as process of the teachers' words (i.e., ideas, skills, knowledge, attitudes) becoming the students' own words (i.e., learning as so-called "appropriation"). This understanding, of course, contradicts one of Bakhtin's most important points about "unmerged voices and consciousnesses" in dialogue (p. 6).

We argue here that the double-voicedness of IPD particularly involves the IPD participants' commitment to inquiry through careful and responsible listening diverse voices and their truths. It is an almost desire from the participants to take the words of others inside as voice of their own doubts and conscience. Although IPD can take a form of polemics and even debate, its double-voicedness is different than double-voicedness of pure polemics because in the latter double-voicedness involves self-advocacy of one's own confident truth – the desire to convince the other or present audience in its own truth. To do that, a participant of polemics has to address and reply to words of the others – his or her opponents – to prove his or her point. This is advocacy double-voicedness. In a true IPD, the participants do not merely advocate and do not prove their truth but collectively investigate the matters at hand. Of course, people can and often do advocate and prove in IPD as well but their advocacy and proofs are subordinated to genuine, open-minded, investigation.

In IPD, the words of opposing others penetrate deeply one's consciousness. For example, Ms. Paley was deeply affected by her students' most passionate protests against the idea of the universal and unilateral inclusivity that she suggested to them,

> "When it happens to Clara she cries and sits in her cubby," I say. "I found her there and we went to see the girls. Lisa said she didn't want anyone else, that they didn't need another person. But I said, 'Clara needs you even if you think you don't need her.'"
> Cynthia lowers her eyes. "I wanted her to play."
> "But it was my game!" Lisa cries. "It's up to me!" She is red-faced and tearful. "Okay, I won't play then, ever!"
> The children watch the participants in the drama. My voice is barely audible as I continue the narrative. "So, I thought, I want to do a favor for Clara, but is it fair *to spoil Lisa's and Cynthia's play?* Yet would this really spoil their play? How?..." (p. 15)

It was quit clear from Paley's book that she felt that she had to address Lisa's passionate objection not only to win the polemics in the public debate she promoted in her own classroom, not even to win hearts and minds of her students, but first and most of all to address her own doubts about her emerging solution for systematic rejection of children from play and friendships in her classroom. Ms. Paley rephrased Lisa's words (underlined) in her own internal dialogue (bolded). By doing that, she took responsibility for her own truth. In IPD, a responsibility for one's own truth is in one's desire to change it when, but only when, one is persuaded in the discourse (Pólya, 1954). The responsibility to reply to the truth of others lays not in success of the one's self-advocacy but in one's responsibility for oneself and for internal honesty. In IPD, the words of others have to be revoiced to move the discourse away from pure polemics into responsible dialogic listening. It seems that Ms. Paley shared this concern when she remarks that debate is not enough and introduces a fairytale reflecting the class IPD that allows the children to hear diverse truths outside of the context of polemic zeal focusing them on their own success rather than on truth and compassion,

Fervently the children search for detours and loopholes as we debate the issues and, eventually, I bring the matter before the older students in the school. They too cannot imagine such a plan working. "You can't say you can't play?" It is very fair, they admit, but it just isn't human nature.

Fortunately, the human species does not live by debate alone. There is an alternate route, proceeding less directly, but often better able to reach the soul of a controversy. It is *story,* the children's preferred frame of reference. This time, however, *I* will be the storyteller, inventing Magpie, a bird who rescues those who are lonely or frightened and tells them stories to raise their spirits. I come to know Magpie well, for I will be the first one he saves (p. 4).

The IPD double-voicedness puts its participants on the boundary of their own words and words of others, on the boundaries their own voices and voices of others, on the boundaries of their own truths and truths of others. This boundary is defined by one's own conscience. Let's us explain that in details.

Polemics has its own honesty as well. But the polemic honesty is rooted in fairness of the polemic fight: the polemic tools and the rule of engagement have to be fair (e.g., no use of logical fallacies http://www.don-lindsay-archive.org/skeptic/arguments.html, honest admitting strengths of opponent's arguments). In polemics, the double-voiced word is a "boundary object" (Star & Griesemer, 1989) that can be structured as "yes, but…" serving for both defense, offense, and polemic sportsmanship. In polemics, participants catch words of others and send them back re-armed, with a new argumentative weapon attached. Let's consider the following polemic exchange in Paley's book,

> *Lisa:* I could play alone. Why can't Clara play alone?
> *Angelo:* I think that's pretty sad. People that is *alone* they has water in their eyes.
> *Lisa:* I'm more *sad* if someone comes that I don't want to play with.
> Teacher: Who is sadder, the one who isn't allowed to play or the one who has to play with someone he or she doesn't want to play with? (p. 20).

Angelo revoiced Lisa's word "alone" that in her mouth refers to independence and to choice (why can't Clara be independent and play with herself alone?). In Angelo's mouth, the word "alone" that he accepts as a description of Lisa's option ("yes, it is playing alone, but…") refers to involuntary imprisonment and suffering. He also implies Lisa as being responsible for Clara's suffering. In her response, Lisa did not reject this responsibility – implicitly she even accepts it – but (there is always a "but" in the polemic double-voicedness) she claims that the alternative generates even more sadness. As the teacher correctly shows in her concluding utterance, the polemic was very fruitful because it moved the discussion to a new dilemma and a possibility to test the presented truths.

In polemics, however, the participants firmly hold their truths. Polemics makes this holding shaper and more consistent but it does not promote the participants transcending their truths and experiences new truths as their own like it happens in IPD. In IPD, words of others constitute a collective investigation and new ontology for the participants. Indeed, consider the following fragment from the discussion of the new rule introduced by Ms. Paley,

> "Anyway, the new rule isn't nice," Lisa persists….

..."But, Lisa, I also agree with Angelo. He said when you're not allowed to play you feel lonely and you get water in your eyes. And if you're lonely and sad I'm afraid you can't learn very much or behave very well."

"Like Raymond the new boy," Lisa says. "He only has Magpie to be his friend" (p. 83).

Lisa abandoned polemics with Ms. Paley and other children who supported the new rule and instead started exploring the relationship between one's loneness and one's aggression. She joined the teacher. Lisa used Ms. Paley words not to re-arm them and send them back as in pure polemics but to contemplate on a new truth that was not available to her before. As we know well from Paley's book, what occurred after this incident, Lisa's contemplation of the new truth did not mean that she accepted Paley's new rule but she understood deeper that was behind the rule. Although, we do not hear a question in Lisa's voice and Paley did not seem to support Lisa's public contemplation of her new truth, it does not sit well with where Lisa has stood before ("I'm more sad.."). Her new truth begs for a question and taking new responsibility.

In our contrast of polemics and internally persuasive discourse, we do not want to create a wrong opposition: IPD is good while polemics is bad. Polemics can be very useful for IPD when it serves IPD. Polemics can reveal and sharpen person-truths. It can help to develop dilemmas and their tests. However, when polemics become independent from IPD's collective search for truth, it can become monological and, thus, counter productive.

Provoking Dramatic Events through Dialogic Objectivizing

The last important feature of pedagogical IPD that we noticed in Paley's book was *dialogic objectivizing,* under which participants not only consider the alien positions of others but choose to experience new ontological settings. Dialogic objectivizing involves safe "tricking" of participants into new ontological positions so participants can compare and evaluate their old and new ontological settings.

Dialogic objectivizing is another apparent misnomer. Unlike dialogic finalizing, we could not find the idea of dialogic objectivizing in Bakhtin's writing. This term describes an interesting phenomenon of objectivizing of one person through involving the person in a new ontological situation by another in order for the first person could rethink his or her ontological being and transcend it. The objectivizing involves acting out on the first person – tricking him or her into a new situation using some kind of bait – as if he or she is a simple object of one's actions. It is always a manipulation of one person by another. However, arguably this objectivizing is not monologic because in the new ontological circumstances that the person has found him or herself, she or he can make decisions and choices freely in response to the new ontological situation. The new ontological situation itself is not a trap but rather an opportunity for a new vista. It has always a loophole for a safe retreat in the old ontological circumstances without any suffering or punishment. The later makes important difference between monologic manipulative social engineering and dialogic objectivizing.

Dialogic objectivizing is tricking (manipulative forcing out) a person into testing his or her person-idea. For example, when I (Eugene Matusov, the first author of this chapter) was a 5-year old child my parents wanted me to taste smoked fish that smelled and looked not appealing for me. So I refused to try. Then, my parents decided to bribe me by offering a chocolate candy, I liked a lot, if I ate one smoked fish. After some hesitation, I made a bite and… I found that I liked the smoked fish. I ate one fish after another without any bribe. This case is arguably dialogic objectivizing. Although I was forced into a new ontological situation of tasting initially unattractive food, my parents gave me safe retreat if the experiment had failed and I would not have liked the smoked fish. This is very different than in a case of *monologic social engineering* when people are tricked or manipulatively forced into a new ontological situation from which they do not have a safe escape anymore. For example, in Sánta's (1986) fiction novel "The fifth seal" the action occurred during the WWII Hungarian Nazi terror in the fall of 1944. One character, a photographer and a former soldier from the Russian front injured in the war, decided to "trick" four local "lay" people whom he met occasionally in a pub into moral consideration of their own "empty" being. He wanted them to stop mental chewing of their everyday prosaic trifle issues (or at least this was how he perceived their conversations) that highly irritated him and instead to turn themselves toward consideration of "ultimate questions" of morality. For this purpose, he socially engineered their ontological being – he reported on them to the Hungarian version of German Gestapo that they had shared several anti-government jokes and spoken disrespectfully about the Hungarian Nazi regime. The four pub attendees were immediately arrested. They indeed faced with ultimate questions of morality in the Nazi prison and were forced to make their moral choices on a threshold of their physical and moral life. In this extreme case, photographer's social engineering was very successful. Monologic social engineering canalizes ontological being of people to pattern their person-ideas in a certain, often pre-designed, way (cf. building a "new Soviet man" as a project of social engineering in the Stalinist USSR, van der Veer & Valsiner, 1991). It does not provide any choice to people (or provides only fake choices). It is important to notice that the photographer trapped[25] his victims without any loophole of a safe escape or return to the previous circumstance of their prosaic everyday life which always gives a genuine choice (unfinalizing) to the participants. In our view, in this important moment of absence of any trap dialogic objectivizing is different from monologic social engineering.

We found two instances of dialogic objectivizing in Paley's book. The first one is real involving the teacher Ms Paley tricking children Charlie and Ben to accept an excluded child Waka into their play,

> Waka tugs on my shirt. "I'm *not* following them!"
> "He keeps following us," Ben complains.
> "Waka just wants to play with you."
> "We're playing *two* army bombers, me and Charlie."
> I try a bit of humor. "Br-r-r! And here comes another one. Waka! The daring army bomber good guy!" The boys are laughing with me. I'm in such a good mood now they can't resist (Paley, 1992, p. 57).

Ms Paley authoritatively joins Charlie-Ben play and from within the play invites Waka, another army bomber good guy, to join the play. Charlie and Ben, the owners of the play,

---

[25] In this case of Sánta's novel, the trap was much more violent than in the previous example, in which parents bribed their son with a chocolate candy to make him try smoked fish. However, this fact is not important for making the difference between monologic social engineering and dialogic objectivizing, in our view.

laugh at Ms. Paley's adult impersonation of an army bomber and at her obviously treacherous attempt to include Waka. Ms Paley creates a carnivalestic atmosphere in which everything is possible (the teacher who is a friendly army bomber) and everybody is welcome. Charlie and Ben "can't resist" not because they are trapped by Ms. Paley but because they enjoy the fun that the teacher helped to create and in which Waka is part now. Ultimately, any play is about having fun together and through Ms. Paley's provocation Waka could clearly be a part of it for the boys. Dialogic objectivizing is about testing ontological circumstances and drawing evaluative conclusions about them. Through dialogic objectivizing, Ms. Paley made an argument (a point) in a form of action. The boys considered it and responded by accepting Waka. Their person-idea of rejection as achieving joint fun in a play did not survive Ms. Paley's test of joint play. In this sense, their acceptance of Waka was not automatic but deliberate and evaluative. The boys could not resist Ms Paley's dialogic, but non-verbal, argument that inclusive fun with Waka is possible – they accepted the argument for its dialogic strength.

Dialogic objectivizing involves provocation similar to Socratic dialogue (anacrisis). However, unlike Socratic anacrisis that is verbal and logical, dialogic objectivizing promotes an ontological provocation common to a modern art school of conceptualism (Tamruchi, 1995). The participants become provoked not by an idea-consideration as in Socratic dialogues but by a different ontological locale that they experience.

Thus, in another, this time fictitious, example of dialogic objectivizing that we found in Paley's book, mean and lonely dragons were tricked by Magpie bird and his friends from their misty cave into a warm sunshine of a mountain, from which the dragons could experience a different and friendlier world (pp. 118-120). The dragons were introduced yummy taste of blueberries and then tricked them out of the cave by putting magic blueberry shrubs more and more away from the cave for the dragons to follow them until they were out of the mist into the sunshine,

> "Where are we?" the dragons asked, and the corporal [Raymond's father – EM&MS] pointed to the six mountains bathed in sunlight.
> "In the world, my friends, in the beautiful world," he said. "Everything you need is there and always has been there, waiting for you to come out of the fog."
> The dragons walked around slowly at first, then began to leap about, chasing one another up and down the mountainside. "Go easy now," called Raymond's father. "There is time to discover your new world, day by day. And we must now return to our home, which is far away from here."
> When the dragons heard this, they ran to the corporal. "Stay with us, please!" they begged, but he waved goodbye.
> "I'm sorry. I cannot remain any longer. And you no longer need magic spirits to protect you" (p. 120).

This new ontological experience softens the dragons' hearts and they allow Raymond's father to go free from their cave where he was kept in captivity by the dragons.

Like Magpie, Ms. Paley wanted to trick her students, especially play bosses and their friends, into a new regime of the children's universal and unilateral right to be included in a play of their wish through dialogic objectivizing. But was she successful in that?

Chapter 8

COLLAPSE OF INTERNALLY PERSUASIVE DISCOURSE IN MS. VIVIAN PALEY'S CLASSROOM[1]

ABSTRACT

A lot of educators praise Paley for her dialogic pedagogy. Mark Smith's and my discourse analysis of her book *You can't say you can't play*, treated as an educational ethnography, reveals the collapse of a dialogic classroom regime based on Bakhtin's notion of internally persuasive discourse. It appears that the main reason for this collapse was that Paley prioritized establishing social justice over searching for dialogic truth with her students. Based on the findings, we came to the conclusion that listening to students is not sufficient or guaranteed for providing sensitive guidance.

THE TEACHER'S MONOLOGIC COUP D'ETAT: THE NEW ORDER OF AN AUTHORITARIAN DISCURSIVE REGIME (OUR DIALOGIC FINALIZING OF MS. VIVIAN PALEY)

After the spring break Ms. Paley decided to introduce a new regime in her kindergarten class, "You can't say you can't play." It involves the new rule according to which any child who wants to join a play has to be included automatically. The previous unilateral right to exclude by play owners (although with possible negotiation) was replaced with the new unilateral right to be included (without any possibility to negotiate). Paley's approach was rule-based, universal, and decontextualized. It was based on Kantian moral imperatives like the moral development theory by Kohlberg (Kohlberg & Ryncarz, 1990) so criticized by some feminists (e.g., Gilligan, 1993).

It is interesting to note that Ms Paley spent a few weeks discussing with her own students, with older kids, with teachers and herself if the new rule is fair and whether it would work but she did not discuss how to transition to the new rule. It seems that she did not consider this an issue. However, it did become an issue for her students and readers. Mr.

---

[1] This research was performed and this chapter was written in collaboration with Mark Smith, University of Delaware, who was the second author.

Paley suspended any IPD discussion about play exclusions, its meaning for the participants, its consequences, alternative approaches and instead she imposed a new rule,

> ... *this will* be the day I'll impose the rule, after Sarah reads the new Magpie chapter. It is about Raymond, the boy nobody likes. *"Our class was much nicer before he came."* (p. 73)
> ... I'm glad I decided not to wait [with imposing the new rule – EM&MS]. The children stare at the sign on the wall above the piano as I point to each word. "YOU CANT SAY YOU CAN'T PLAY. There. Our new rule. In big letters. We've been talking about it and now it's time to do it."
> The children are uneasy, looking at one another. The announcement seems too abrupt, though we've been preparing ourselves for weeks (p. 81).
> Posting a sign that reads YOU CAN'T SAY YOU CAN'T PLAY, I announce the new social order and, from the start, it is greeted with disbelief (p. 3).
> Only four out of twenty-five in my kindergarten class find the idea appealing, and they are the children most often rejected. The loudest in opposition are those who do the most rejecting. But everyone looks doubtful in the face of this unaccountable innovation (p. 4).
> "It's not fair at all." Lisa pouts. "I thought we were only just *talking* about it" (p. 84).

The issue that Paley did not seem to recognize throughout all her book was much deeper that the announcement about the new rule was brought by her "too abrupt." She focused only on moving the class from exclusivity to inclusivity. In our view, the issue was that in one stroke, she abolished IPD and the regime of democratic decision making in her class. Ms. Paley started the IPD with intentional reduction of her unilateral teacher authority, "'A lot of you,' I continue, 'think the teachers always know what is right, but this time I don't think the fair thing was done'" (p. 13). She invited her students to dialogue about important issues of the children's lives in her classroom: fairness of play exclusion, about the role of the teacher in the classroom, about consequences of inclusion, and so on. Now, she withdrew this community right to discuss how to make their collective classroom life better from the children and established a new regime. Ms Paley sacrificed IPD – a collective search for a truth – for her unilateral pursue of social justice (we return to this issue of whether this split between truth and social justice is unavoidable in out later discussion). This new regime was not just about a new rule of the universal and unilateral inclusivity for play but, what arguably even more important, the authoritarian regime of the teacher's unilateral decision making. Now the children can only conform, resist, or try to compromise with the teacher and not to dialogue with her. Ms Paley shut down herself from the decision making about ultimate questions and focused only on how effectively implement her ready-made solution. There was no room anymore for a collective decision making of the students with the teacher. The classroom regime was suddenly and violently shifted from dialogic to monologic. It was Ms. Paley's authoritarian coup d'état.

Collapse of Collaborative IPD in Ms. Vivian Paley's Classroom

We coded all instances of the IPD in Paley's book using NVIVO 7. We divided the IPD instances on the following five types based on the participants of the IPD:

1. *Ms Paley's whole class* or a part of the class including Ms. Paley and all or some students in her class;
2. *Children's only* IPD: Ms. Paley's students among themselves (all or part of the class) without Ms. Paley as an active participant of the IPD;
3. *Ms Paley with older children* in the school;
4. *Ms Paley with other teachers*;
5. *Ms Paley with herself.*

We also looked at the distributions of the IPD types across the four phases of the event "You can't say you can't play" as Paley segmented in her book by 4 chapters: *Setting a problem* (in Paley's book chapter 1, "You can't play: The habit of rejection"), *Considering the inquiry* (chapter 2, "The inquiry: Is it fair? Will it work?"), *Imposing the new order* (chapter 3, "The new order begins"), and *Living with the new order* (chapter 4, "It is easier to open the door"). To get a sense of the distributions of the IPD types, we calculated the percentage of words involving in each in each IPD type to the total number of words in the phase except Paley's own fairytale story. Although these calculations are not exact, we believe they do reflect the nature of the distributions (see figure 8).

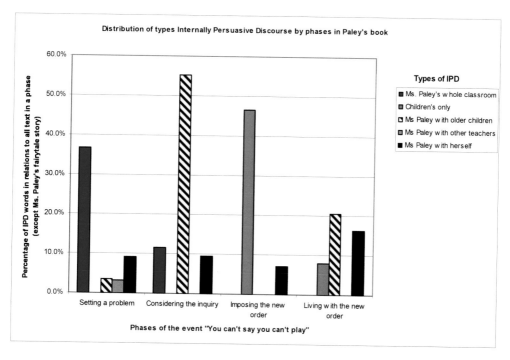

Figure 8. Distribution of types Internally Persuasive Discourse by phases in Paley's book.

As it is seen on the chart, the IPD of Ms. Paley's entire class disappears (in blue on the chart) after the second phase "Considering the inquiry". It occurs because Ms. Paley made firmly her mind to impose the rule and did not discuss anything that was not uncertain for her with her own students. She did not share or joined any inquires with her students in open-minded matter. Although she kept discussing her uncertainties involving reflection on the imposition progress with older children in the school and herself (see the diagonal and solid black bars on the chart). Also, after the second phase the children's only IPD emerges although it drops in the final phase. The children's only IPD mainly involved the children's discussions of their reactions to impositions. They seemed to be losing the sense of the purpose of these discussions when they fully realized that nothing is negotiable or truly discussible in the class anymore. For example, why to bother to discuss how to pick people for enacting their stories if the procedure was already set by their teacher (pp. 124-126)?!

Social Justice vs. Truth Seeking: Ms. Paley's Rationalization of Her Monologic Coup D'état

Throughout Paley's book we tried to find her justification of why she made her coup d'état and replaced a dialogic regime of IPD to a monologic regime of imposing her truth on the children. We focused not on her justification of the rule "you can't say you can't play" (i.e., why is fair or will it work) but on her justification of why she should abandon the public forum discussion and unilaterally impose the new rule appealing by the power given her by the school institution. This task was difficult for us because Paley did not discuss explicitly her coup d'état nor she considered alternative approaches of introduction of the new rule (we will discuss these alternatives later). We had to find indirect evidence and read between the lines her justification of the coup d'état. We will also discuss in the following section of how much Paley was aware of her monological authoritarian coup d'état.

Our holistic judgment of how Paley rationalizes her monologic coup d'état is that apparently *she chose social justice over truth seeking* for herself and her students. Specifically, we found several lines of her often indirect reasoning to support our claim:

1. *Ethical and professional responsibility*: Through diverse IPDs with her own students, older children, teachers, and herself, Ms. Paley came to a conclusion that the pains caused by play exclusion are systematic, acute, comprehensive, and widespread affecting in one or another way all the children being either as victims, witnesses, or as perpetrators of these pains. These pains also affect learning especially in rejected children;

2. *Urgency*: She, as the teacher, has an urgent moral obligation to stop social injustice or at least to try to do something as soon as possible, "I am certain [Lisa] wants me to be more like Magpie and not allow her to be mean even when she is jealous of playmates or uncomfortable with strangers" (p. 68). Dialogue can be deepened forever (Bakhtin, 1999) but the short life requires an immediate action;

3. *Impossibility of the sincere dialogue with oppressors:* You cannot sincerely dialogue with oppressors whose interest and privilege are heavily grounded in the unjust status quo; you can only use violence against them to address social injustice (Freire, 1986);

4. *Lesser of two evils*: She became convinced that whatever inconveniences (or even sufferings) the new rule may cause initially or long-run on the children, stop of suffering justifies these inconveniences;

5. *Habituation*: After the children find themselves in a new regime of the rule "you can't say you can't play" they automatically appreciate its truth and fairness;

6. *Continuity*: She also came to a conclusion that children's play would not be destroyed by the new rule of inclusivity;

7. *Sacrifice of inquiry*: In the name of well-being of the suffering children and her moral responsibility as a teacher, M. Paley consciously decided to suppress the burden of her own unsolved inquiries, uncertainties, and indecisions such as would the children be convinced that the rule is fair; would mechanical, forced inclusivity lead to genuine, voluntary one; should children be convinced or manipulated into a just solution; is the rule really fair as it seems; should be privacy permitted in school or is it entirely public space; and so on and act instead of them, "What joy to be rid of the burden of indecision" (p. 93);

8. *Self-modeling*: To be just and model their students, Ms. Paley tried to apply the new rule of universal and unilateral inclusivity to herself in the relationship with her own students (e.g., abandoning her own classroom rule of forbidding a child to play if he or she did not clean toys, pp. 82-83);

9. *Distrust of students' agency*: It is interesting that she publicly discussed, evaluated, reflected on the progress of her new rule with older children but not with her own students. From Ms. Paley's behavior, we have inferred that she abolished classroom public forum in her classroom because she was afraid that this forum might undermine her imposition of the new rule;

10. *Distrust of verbalism*: Ms Paley was convinced that "stories and talks" (p. 110) alone are not enough for the children to transition into a more just community;

11. *Production of a developmental trajectory*: There is indirect evidence to support that an idea of a developmental trajectory may be in the mind of Paley as well. Pijanowski (2004) argues that Paley's intervention leads students down a trajectory toward democratically-based "relations based on mutual regard." Paley, in Pijanowski's view (borrowing from Winnicott's psychoanalytic theories of "human formation") provides an example of a teacher who engenders "certain psychological and imaginative capacities" in her students through giving them (initially) the opportunity to approve or reject the rule, allowing them to enact and work out the rules on their own, and through allowing them to imaginatively reflect from the events in the Magpie story to the real play life of the classroom. This perspective helps explain the attention Paley paid to gaining the assent of the students, only to destroy the dialogue later on. Paley provides the conditions for play bosses like Lisa "to see herself, feel real, and relate to others as 'not-me'." In turn, Lisa gradually "develops the capacity to enter relations based on mutual regard" (p. 116-117). From this perspective, it does not matter that Paley and Lisa continue in dialogue since Lisa is, through being given the space to enact the rule, provided the resources "to externalize the feelings and relations that motivate bossiness in order to destroy it" (p. 116). Such a developmental lens can lead Paley (and interestingly Pijanowski) to see the evidence that Lisa did not appear to genuinely include others in her play as a gradual acceptance of the rule, rather than a wholehearted rejection of it (which arguably creates of a vicious circle of self-righteousness – there is no evidence that can undermine the person's position, -- so common for people who prioritize social justice to truth-searching, see out critique of Freire in earlier chapter);

12. *Developmental immaturity*: And, finally, and this seems to come from Paley's overall and prior conviction that adults have enormous authority for younger children and that, "We must be told, when we are young, what rules to live by. The grownups must

tell the children early in life so that myth and morality proclaim the same message while the children are still listening" (p. 110).

This list of the justification for unilateralism and social engineering reminds us similar justifications by various revolutionaries in the 20th century (see, for example, Savinkov & Shaplen, 1931). The key feature of it is separation of social justice from and its prioritization over search for truth. There is a concern among many social engineers driven by social justice that sometimes truth can destroy or prevent social justice and that sometimes justice can even be benefited from an, at least "tactical," lie (see a detailed critique of this position in Havel & Vladislav, 1989). It seems to us that deeply down they are afraid that somebody can eventually bring an argument that may destroy social justice (or, better to say, their parochial view of social justice). These social engineers deeply distrust the truth searching process when they fully committed to social justice. Deeply down, they probably suspect and are concerned that social justice can be untrue and truth can be socially unjust. Ms. Paley seems to suppress any public reflection on the progress of the new social order of a new utopia in her class because of this concern criticized by Bakhtin, "All of European utopianism was likewise built on this monologic principle. Here too belongs utopian socialism, with its faith in the omnipotence of the conviction. Semantic unity of any sort is everywhere represented by a single consciousness and a single point of view" (Bakhtin, 1999, p. 82). Thus, it is not a surprise that many political regimes driven by social justice and engineering are ended up totalitarian, highly oppressive, and murderous regardless their political ideology: communist, fascist, or religious.

In our view, the dichotomy of social justice and truth searching is false one. Truth and justice are not separable. Honest commitment to dialogical and ontological truth searching leads to social justice. Honest commitment to social justice leads to dialogic truth. Parochial justice is an enemy of dialogic truth and parochial, monologic, truth is an enemy of humanistic social justice for all.

The urgency of social justice cannot justify abandoning the regime of dialogic truth. As Bakhtin (1986, 1999) argued that any action gains its meaning and humanity in dialogue. Thus, even an emergency action driven by social justice concerns gains its meaning and humanity in dialogue. This, of course, does not mean that people have to act and talk at the same time. Dialogue is not reduced to verbalism because an action can have quality of an utterance (and verbal utterance can have a quality of action) (Freire, 1986). Urgent actions driven by concerns of social justice have to be responsible, answerable, questionable (i.e., allowing questions to be raised about it), and accountable like any other action. *Ms. Paley's action of imposing the new rule "you can't say you can't play" in her classroom was not responsible, answerable, questionable, and accountable with regard to her students in the classroom* (ironically, it was answerable and questionable for older children). Paraphrasing Bakhtin (1993), urgency[2] for social justice does not provide alibi and carte blanche for the teacher's unilateral action.

---

[2] We are talking aside an issue of real versus "feel good" urgency of social justice in Ms. Paley's actions. Remember that as a teacher she practiced the exclusion right in her classrooms for decades. Arguably, there was not real urgency to impose a new rule only after a very few weeks of the class forum discussions. Even if Ms. Paley could not have born to live one more day with the old rule because of realization of her students' suffering, she could honestly introduce this rule to the students to the public forum, as the result of her own

Dialogic regime is often mistakenly associated with indecision and inquiry as a temporary process: when a decision is made, dialogue is considered to be moot or even counterproductive. Thus, dialogue is viewed as a moratorium on action if not a paralysis of will. In this case of pure action-implementation of a decision, dialogue is regarded not only narrow-intellectually and pure epistemologically, but also completely, wrong. We argue that it is not the case that people think first to plan an action, then to act upon it, and finally to reflect on their actions' effects. Rather people think, plan, and reflect as they act, although they do not necessary think in a verbal way, nor always act as they think (Baker-Sennett, Matusov, & Rogoff, 1993, 1998). Similarly, people response and address while they think and act. In our view, Ms. Paley was wrong suppressing her public forum when she decided to act and thus making her actions not answerable, not questionable, not accountable and, ultimately, not responsible for their students. But she could not escape the dialogue itself. Her attempt not to have a public forum was her response to her students. The monologic coup was her address to them. It was her responsibility and her accountability that are never escapable whether people try to do it or not. The issue is not to dialogue or not. The issue is what the quality of dialogue is. Her dialogue involved excessive monologicity. Similarly, responsibility is inescapable: a lack of taking responsibility is not absence of responsibility but a characteristic of responsibility itself (namely, an act of irresponsibility). Dialogue is inescapable. It is uninterruptible and continuing.

Ms. Paley tried to justify her unilateralism by a case from her own past teaching practice when she abandoned so called time-out classroom management strategy,

> I remember feeling this way some ten years ago, when I gave up the time-out chair, my version of "You can't play." Sarah jokes that I substituted six little words for endless arguing simply in order to save my voice, but I do think the image of escape from a trap is appropriate. When the children are reminded of the rule they comply so readily that it is as if they've been rescued. From what? Perhaps from the ordeal of deciding whether or not someone can play, just as doing away with the time-out chair relieved me of the onus of judging punishable actions (p. 93).

However, she forgets that in this example the decision maker and the actor is the same person unlike in the case of her new social order when she was the decision maker about the rule but the children were actors implementing her decision. Ms. Paley might feel very different if it was her school principal who ordered her to stop using time-out strategy while she as a teacher believed in this strategy as effectively promoting the classroom order in her class. In this latter case, she might be upset complaining, resisting, and even rebelling against the new rule by the principal. And this was similar to how many of her students might feel when she imposed her new rule on them. When Ms. Paley tries to apply the new rule to herself and model her students by abandoning her own classroom rule of forbidding a child to play if he or she did not clean toys (pp. 82-83), her main opponent Lisa correctly notices that it "isn't the same thing" (p. 83), Ms. Paley agrees with her but does not go into why it is not the same. One of the problems of "not being the same" is in different locus of responsibility: in the case of Ms. Paley changing her own rule, she is responsible for her own rule, in the

---

unbearable suffering and thus making her action responsible, answerable, questionable, and accountable for her students.

case of "you can't say you can't play", children are not responsible for the rule that governs them.

We have already discussed the difference between dialogic objectivizing when people are tricked into a new ontological locale so they can freely compare and choose lives in the old and new ontological locales and monologic objectivizing of social engineering when people are forced into a new ontological locale (with no safe return) to canalize their new attitudes setup by social engineers. Ms. Paley chose the latter approach of monologic objectivizing by imposing her new rule on the students with no safe return.

In our view, Paley is right that stories and talks are not enough for developing a just environment. We would add that stories and talks are not enough for dialogue either. Neither dialogue nor justice is possible without responsible actions testing person-ideas. Where we might disagree with Paley is in her apparent dichotomy between story/talk, on the one side, and actions, on the other. She seems to think that actions (e.g., rules) should follow the talk/story and the talk/story should seize to let actions unfold. As we argued above, this is a wrong separation and wrong dichotomy (cf. Freire, 1986).

Finally, Paley justifies her coup d'état of dialogic regime in her classroom by a developmental reasoning: if you already know what is good for our little children, why don't we simply impose this good on them? Little children are trustful enough not to rebel too much (i.e., the imposition is doable) and not reasonable enough to be convinced in what is really good for them (i.e., that there is not other way). Indeed, little children seem to find the culture as a given for them; adults do not try to co-construct and justify every cultural moment, every cultural practice for the children.

Our objection to Paley on this important issue is that we believe that the mission of the education is exactly to move students from "a given"[3] -- not reflected authority of a habit (e.g., a cultural tradition or a design by the teacher) that the children find themselves – into "an assigned" – a dialogic invitation to participate in taking responsibility for the societal practices through IPD. This point is nicely articulated by Lampert,

> ... I intend to teach everyone..., that this is not going to be a class in which the teacher says whether an answer is right or wrong as the first response to any assertion [by a student – EM&SM]. Rather, I will provide students with tools for reasoning themselves about the appropriateness of their answers (Lampert, 2001, p. 151).
>
> ... I chose to do that [i.e., giving reasons for her own classroom routines to the students – EM&MS] during the first lesson in order to integrate teaching routines with teaching students to reason about *their* actions and *mine*. I wanted them to know that they could expect explanations from me about why procedures are to be followed, whether they are mathematical or procedures for using materials (Lampert, 2001, p. 60, the emphasis is ours).

Children should move from finding themselves in good rules promoting social justice into considering what is good and whether the rules they are found themselves are just. We will return to this issue later when we consider educational value of IPD. Now we will turn the issue of how much Paley was aware of her monologic coup d'état that she accomplished

---

[3] Bakhtin (1993) used the following Russian oppositional terms "данность" (literally, "given-ness") and "заданность" (literally, "behind or over the given", "assigned-ness", de-reifying the given in terms who gave it, how, and for what purpose; turning the fact of being into artifact of somebody's purposeful design).

in her class by moving from a dialogic IPD regime to monologic authoritarian manipulative regime.

Awareness without Responsibility

But has Paley been aware that she destroyed a dialogic IPD regime in her classroom by imposing the new rule? We are ambivalent about answering this question as, probably, Paley is herself. There is evidence that she knew perfectly well what she was doing, although this evidence is very indirect. We can hear another, almost alien, voice violently entering Paley's self-reflections in her book. It usually comes into very sensitive moments of Ms. Paley replying to children's urgent questions. It sounds like a voice of Paley's *double* (Bakhtin, 1999) who vigorously argues with her in her internal dialogues. Paley's double is not nice to her. It comments on her own statements with brutally-honest evaluations denouncing her own hidden manipulation with the children[4],

> Angelo wants to know what else I *don't* tell the children. "I try not to tell you what thoughts or opinions to have," **is my less than honest answer**, at a time when I am **single-mindedly** pushing new attitudes about play (p. 27).

The double comments evaluatively on Ms Paley's reply to the children (see in bold). Please notice that Paley's wording "single-mindedly" belongs to the voice of the double because it is evaluative and not merely descriptive. However, Paley herself does not reply to her double, it "is my less than honest answer" and...?! There is not Paley's reflection following the denouncement of her double and, even more important, there is not her taking responsibility for this important and disturbing revelation. It feels like Paley is playing with herself and her students by not being honest in a sense of taking responsibility for her own deeds. It almost borders on her cynicism. There is some kind of cover-up going on. She often does not pushes further what the double says to her like in the following example,

> Lisa skips ahead and then returns to take my hand. "I know Magpie likes the new rule, right? He'll tell Schoolmistress about it, because he's nice." *I* like the rule too, **though I'm not nearly as nice as Magpie. However,** each time a cause for sadness is removed for even one child, the classroom seems nicer. And, by association, we all rise in stature (p. 95).

Why does Ms. Paley feel not being as nice as kind bird Magpie in her fairytale? Is it because Magpie always remains dialogic and never reserves himself to authoritarian imposition of rules or monologic regimes as Ms. Paley does? There is high respect and admiration bordering almost on envy by Paley of Magpie but at the same time her deep rejection of Magpie's ways of doing things. Why? There is not an honest discussion of the disagreement. Paley's double provides dialogic finalizing to her with penetrating words. They finalize Ms. Paley's conditions of her ontological being and provide opportunities for her to transcend these imprisoning ontological circumstances in a deed. However, the penetrating words by the double are remained unanswered by Paley in any responsible manner. She does not respond her double by taking responsibility for her own awareness of her deeply rooted desire to manipulate of her students' consciousness instead of genuinely guiding them. The double is intellectually penetrating but ontologically impotent. This phenomenon was depicted by Dostoevsky in his novels "Crime and Punishment" (in Rodion Raskol'nikov) and "Brothers Karamazov" (in Ivan Karamazov) and brilliantly analyzed by Bakhtin (1999). Both Raskol'nikov and Karamazov were ended with a murder. Paley ends up killing a dialogue in her class and genuine learning associated with it.

Excessive vicious dialogism in Paley's internal dialogue with her double leads almost to the collapse of the authoritative meaning in her statements due to growing unresolved contradictions in her thoughts, feelings, and values, like for example in the following statement,

> The children, of course, cannot possibly be aware of all the changes Sarah and I have been watching. **I feel a tinge of regret** that next year's class will begin the school year with "You can't say you can't play" *as a given.* It must be so, for I can never go back to the old ways. Yet the real excitement has been in the process of discovery.
> **However**, the concept of open access, I suspect, *can never be taken for granted,* but must in fact be rediscovered each year by each new group. "You can't say you can't play" is apparently not as natural a law as, for example, "I say you can't play" (p. 128).

What does it mean her statement that the new rule becomes "a given" but at the same time "can never be taken for granted"? Why did she write the book and value all kids' discussions by carefully preserving them in the book if she wants to eliminate all such discussions for her future classes and students? Why does she "feel a tinge of regret" for not having dialogues with her future students if, she considers, the only valuable thing that promotes social justice is her new rule to be imposed at the beginning of the school year? She sounds conflicting at the point of inarticulateness.

McDermott (1988) argues that inarticulateness is rooted in a culture. What culture is Paley's inarticulateness rooted?

The Roots of Excessive Monologism in Ms. Paley's Limited IPD

We argue that this inarticulateness is rooted in an institutional culture of the teacher's monologic authoritarian regime based on manipulation of the students. There is a lot of evidence in the book, that Paley, as a teacher, carefully listens to her students. But why? We suspect that she listens to the students so attentively because *she wants to manipulate them better* to "single-mindedly" push them to the new thoughts, skills, and attitudes defined by her given curriculum. As soon as Paley made her mind up firmly about using the rule of "you can't say you can't play," she focused entirely on how to make her students to accept this ready-made rule. The new ready-made idea, knowledge, conviction, attitude is perceived by the manipulated as an outcome his or her own intellectual and experiential work or well established tradition or habit. The successful manipulation requires very good knowledge of the subjectivity of the manipulated so they won't even notice being manipulated. The most informed officials in the Soviet Union were KGB, the Soviet secret police, that had to be attentive to people's minds to manipulate their consciousness effectively (Solzhenitsyn, 1974;

---

[4] Paley's double denouncing her manipulation with children reminds the voice of Angelo denouncing manipulative kids (see above). This fact provides another reason of why Angelo seems to be Paley's conscience.

Медведев & Медведев, 2004). We have argued elsewhere (Matusov & Smith, 2007) that sensitive guidance involves the teacher's subjectivizing and problematizing students' subjectivity. It is true that Paley promotes her students to talk and listens to them tentatively as she claims on page 27 of her book, but what does she mainly listen to the students for? What we did not notice in our paper then (Matusov & Smith, 2007) that *manipulative teaching* also involves the teacher's subjectivizing and problematizing students' subjectivity. Similarly, Schultz (2003, p. 105) argues that teacher's careful listening to his or her students can serve for coercion and surveillance. Thus, the teacher's subjectivizing and problematizing students' subjectivity does not guarantees dialogic guidance. It can be result of manipulative entrapment into the teacher's ready-made curricular as well (like in a case of Socratic dialogues, see chapters above). Analysis of Paley's book teaches us that.

If Paley was so manipulative in her guidance, why and how she promoted internally persuasive discourse in her classroom at least in the first part of her project? In our view, Ms. Paley *used IPD to make up her mind* if her new rule was fair and was able to work. She used her kindergarten students, older children, other teachers, and herself to dialogue in order to resolve these uncertainties. As soon as she made her mind up, she abandoned IPD in her classroom. She still was dialoging with herself and especially older children about reflection on the progress of her already monologic enterprise of the new regime but she stopped dialoging with her own students, probably, because she was afraid that IPD could threaten her new regime, "If I'm so certain [about the new all-inclusive rule – EM&MS], why not let Schoolmistress [a fictional teacher in Paley's fairytale – EM&MS] try it out? The answer is obvious. I can't have her succeed and me fail" (p. 87). Actually, according to her own account (see p. 27 of her book, quoted above), she tried to manipulate the students' attitudes even during the class IPD when she was gaining more and more clarity regarding to her initial inquiries. Thus, IPD and dialogue was not Paley's way of teaching and truth making.

As we showed in the previous chapter, a monologic practice of viewing curriculum as *a given* that is necessary to imprint into the students by the teacher is a big part of conventional institution of schooling (Whitson, 2007).

Was the New Order of an Authoritarian Discursive Regime in Paley's Classroom Successful?

We found several definitions of success of Ms Paley's enterprise of the new regime in the book that we want to consider in this section. We want to consider here if Ms. Paley was indeed successful according to her own definition of success.

Have the Kids Accepted the New Rule?

"Sarah [Ms. Paley's teacher aide – EM&MS] and I can't believe that the transition to the new rule is so straightforward and easy. 'You can't say you can't play' has been in place for a week and there are only minor mishaps, quickly resolved. It is indeed a ladder out of the trap we've been in. Exclusion is still practiced, of course, but when it is someone will say 'You forgot the rule,' or a teacher will be brought over to say it. What joy to be rid of the burden of indecision" (p. 93). We interpreted Paley's definition of the rule success in this quote as more children over time *accepting* the rule to play with any kids who asked to join. Initially "only four out of twenty-five in my kindergarten class find the idea appealing, and they are the children most often rejected. The loudest in opposition are those who do the most rejecting. But everyone looks doubtful in the face of this unaccountable innovation" (p. 4). What does it mean to "accept a rule"? In our view, there are at least four different definitions of acceptance of a rule that have to be checked: 1) absence of open resistance, 2) appropriation of the rule, 3) authority of the rule, and 4) voluntarily following the rule as a result of IPD. Unfortunately, Paley does not seem to directly address these different possibilities.

First, the acceptance of a rule is *absence of active and open resistance* – people *do not actively and directly violate the rule* in the real or virtual[5] presence of the authority, who enforces the rule. Mr. Paley seemed to worry about active resistance to her rule by some of her students, "I'll invite the children to celebrate my new rule and find that no one comes to the party" (p. 57). As Paley mentions in the quote above, she did not experience active and open resistance from her students to the new rule. We also could not find any counter-evidence for that. Even if rejected children ask to join a play, play bosses allow them to join when a teacher is present or interferes or when the children remind the rule. *Thus, we can conclude that from the presented evidence by Paley, her new rule was accepted in a sense of not generating an active and open resistance by her students.*

Second, a rule is accepted if people start appealing to the new rule when it suits their interests (i.e., appropriate it). As Paley reported in the quote above, indeed using the rule by the children has started happening. Even Lisa who is the most consistent objector of the new rule uses the new rule when it can be for her advantage as Paley reports, "Lisa continues to be a barometer, reminding children of the rule under certain circumstances and crusading for the old order at other times" (p. 93). In another conflict with her friend Cynthia who excluded Lisa from her play with Mary Louise, Lisa appeals to the new rule, "But anyway, it *is* against the rule" (p. 115). Paley did not report about any child who was systematically not using the new rule for his or her own benefits (of course, it might still occur in Ms. Paley's class). *Thus, we can conclude that the children have accepted the rule in terms* of appropriating it for their own purposes.

Third, a rule is accepted when it *has authority* for the participants on some discursive ground (e.g., moral, pragmatic, rational, patriarchic, institutionally hierarchical, respectful, trustful) even when they occasionally do not want to follow it. Any authority is established through an authority event – when a person is faced a situation in which he or she cannot do what he or she wants to do and must do what somebody else (real or virtual) demands (so it is not just what a person would do anyway). Besides the authority event, authority is constituted by a discourse legitimizing the power of the demand for the person (so it is not just a case of coercion or threat of the coercion).

Paley offers several grounds for the legitimacy of her new rule. One ground for its legitimacy is *moral*. She hoped that the rule of universal inclusivity would gain legitimacy in her class because it is a rule of fairness and not because of it is enforced with power of coercion[6],

---

[5] Some people may actively and open resist even when there is no a possibility for the authority to be present (i.e., virtual presence of authority).

[6] Although Paley offers a non-coercive vision of her new rule, she was also much aware of its coercive nature when she asked the children, "Should the teacher force children to say yes? [to let unwanted children in the play]" (p. 19) earlier in the book.

In the library a fifth grader tells me, "If someone in my class broke your new rule and was sent into the hall, they'd just goof off—they wouldn't care."

Her thought surprises me. "This wouldn't be the sort of rule you'd get punished for breaking," I say. "If you don't follow what the rule requires, then . . . well, you just think about it and talk about it some more. It isn't a matter of punishing someone, it's more a case of protecting someone."

I thank the girl for speaking to me. Her comment points to something I must find a way of explaining to the children. "You can't say you can't play" is not like the rules prohibiting hitting or destruction of property. Those behaviors are seldom open for discussion. Thou Shalt Not is final and sufficient.

Our new rule is different. It gives us a useful perspective from which to view our actions. Why not simply say "Don't be mean"? People do, of course, tell each other this all the time. The new rule, however, examines a specific yet broad example of meanness and uses the imagery of play to do so. Since play is the subject children care the most about, its precise words and actions—especially the negative ones—-are easily available and carry the greatest meaning (pp. 113-114).

Another ground for the rule legitimacy was the students' *trust* of the teacher and it was offered by fourth graders. In her discussion with the fourth graders, the fourth graders suggested that kindergartners are "nice" because they can easier submit to the teacher's authority than older kids. A fourth grader tells Ms. Paley, "I don't mean they act that nice to *each other.* But they're nice enough to follow a new rule. They trust you. They'll do what you say. It's too late to give *us* a new rule"… Other fourth graders agree, "Yeah, start it in kindergarten," someone says. "Because they'll believe you that it's a *rule.* You know, a *law*" (p. 63).

Finally, Ms. Paley's reflection on children's own stories and their discussion of Ms. Paley's story suggests that children might have yet another ground for legitimacy of the new rule. The children, including play bosses like Lisa and Charlie, seem to be concerned about, what Paley called "equal protection under the law for themselves" (p. 106).

So, did the kids experience the "authority events" and involved in discourse of legitimacy for the new rule? We could not find even one example of that in the text. Specifically, we were looking for a case in which a child would accept or consider of accepting the new rule despite of his or her interest to exclude another child. There was not also a public discourse involving children that reveal any grounds for legitimacy of the rule in their own actions. In other words, there is no evidence of the children taken responsibility for the new rule. Of course, such cases might not be public or not be noticeable by Ms Paley or she might not find importance to report them in her book. The absence of the cases in the book does not provide us with evidence of the children's *authoritative* acceptance of the rule.

Do we have counter-evidence of that – the evidence that the children *do not* see an authority in the new rule of universal inclusivity? Yes, we do. We have many examples provided by Paley that play bosses and their friends try to manipulate the new rule of inclusion and renegotiate it to diminish its universal and unilateral power. For example, even at the end of the book, Lisa and Charlie might accept children whom they do not want in their play but then they try to send them away (e.g., "in a different woods") in a playful way (p. 121-122) or they try to create unattractive characters that the unwanted children may reject on their own (p. 126). Or Lisa (and Cynthia, pp. 114-115) tries to offer Mr. Paley alternative rules that smuggle exclusion at least sometimes or under certain circumstances,

Lisa raises her eyebrows. "Could I give an opinion?" she asks in her most polite voice. "We could change the rule, not too much change it, but kind of like change it this way. We could say yes you could play if you really really really want to play so much that you just take the part the person in charge wants you to be" (p. 94).

In conclusion, *the presence of the counter-evidence and absence of the direct evidence suggest that Ms. Paley was not successful in establishing the authority of her new rule.*

The fourth possible understanding of the rule acceptance is when people *voluntarily follow the rule through IPD* even without the authority. In this case, people act out of a conviction always open for testing by the person him/herself or with others. They still may not always follow the rule due to other priorities but they open-mindedly accept the rule that trumps some of their desires and interests. They do not need fear of punishment, habit, or any authority (e.g., trust or even respect) to accept the rule. This type of acceptance does not need to be enforced. For example, although the city of Philadelphia issues an ordinance (rather poorly enforced) about mandatory recycling, the first author (and his family) does recycling out conviction of its rightness that he often debates with his friends having doubts that recycling might be not as efficient saving resources as it always claims. The IPD that is behind this acceptance involves not only debates with the friends but following press and reading scientific articles on Internet about this issue of concern. It is important to emphasize that IPD does not necessarily lead to paralysis of will as some people think (including, probably, Paley) but to a responsible and informed action (of course, it is NOT responsible and informed to act when a person does not a somewhat clear picture on the matters of his/her concern).

What can be evidence for IPD-based acceptance of a rule? We think that the evidence is based on two necessary factors: a person's conviction of the rule rightness and his or her involvement in IPD open-mindedly considering this rightness (e.g., does recycling glass really use less energy than producing new glass?). As we claimed above, we did not find any evidence of children's expressing their conviction for the new rule (although it still might exist, as we pointed out) in the sphere of the their actions and actual social relationships. As we discussed above we saw Lisa's experimentation with the new rule in her sphere of story writing and IPD discussions of Paley's fairytale, "Lisa skips ahead and then returns to take my hand. 'I know Magpie likes the new rule, right? He'll tell Schoolmistress about it, because he's nice'" (p. 95). But in the sphere of actions and personal responsibility, the children seemed to remain unconvinced. We also did not see IPD based on public testing ideas after Ms. Paley imposed her rule. Ms. Paley hoped that the new rule would promote a discourse in the children would help them to investigate specific instances of meanness, "The new rule, however, examines a specific yet broad example of *meanness* and uses the imagery of play to do so," (p. 114) and then further she claims that, "All the children will learn a great deal from these fairly objective examinations of behaviors in light of the new rule" (p. 116). However, we could not find such discourse of examination after the new rule was imposed by the teacher (ironically, exactly this type of examining discourse was present before the rule was implemented among the children on their public forum with the teacher). It is true that the new rule created new cases of conflicts among the children and eliminated some old ones and it is also true that the children used the discourse about the new rule but they clearly used it for their own gains and negotiation to accesses into play or story and not for *examination* of specific cases of meanness as Paley hoped (and claims). At least, we could not find any evidence in her book. It was Ms. Paley alone who tried to examine (privately and publicly) specific cases of meanness in the classroom using the new rule and expanding it to new cases (e.g., how roles of stories were distributed). Arguably, the children might have benefited by learning from exposure of Ms. Paley's public examination of meanness. However, again we could not find any evidence in her book of the children's learning from such exposure.

Do we have any counter-evidence – the evidence for children not being convinced about the new rule? Yes, we do. For example, at the end of the book, Lisa tells Ms. Paley *privately* (sic! – there seems no public forum for testing ideas and practices for Lisa to tell how she and her friends feel about the new rule when Ms. Paley rules the class unilaterally after her coup d'état), "'I still don't like the new way,' Lisa tells me privately one day. 'Cynthia doesn't either and also Mary Louise'" (p. 128). *So, taking into account the counter-evidence and a lack of any direct evidence, we conclude that Ms. Paley was NOT successful in helping the children to accept the new rule and regime of universal and unilateral inclusivity based on their IPD conviction despite of Ms. Paley's own hopes.*

Equal Protection for Everybody in the Community

Paley is very concerned about *systematic* exclusion of some children from play. When a fifth grader argues that play exclusion is important learning experience for children that prepares them for their dealing with future unavoidable rejections in their lives, Ms. Paley replies to him, "'Here's what troubles me, as a teacher,' I tell the fifth graders. 'Too often, the same children are rejected year after year. The burden of being rejected falls on a few children. They are made to feel like strangers [in their own classroom – EM&MS]'" (p. 22). Ms. Paley establishes her new rule of universal and unilateral inclusivity to promote "equal protection under the law", "The children want Raymond protected by the rule before he goes off to rescue his father. Furthermore, I take this as a sign that, no matter what backsliding and objections exist, the children, in fact, want equal protection under the law for themselves as well as for Raymond" (p. 106).

Paley hypothesized that inclusion in play drives children's friendship rather than friendship drives play inclusion (although she admits that this also happens). When particular children have an opportunity to have good time together (collective fun) they become friends. When they do not have such opportunities, they remain being strangers (children without friends). Paley decided that inclusion should not be based on the participants' consensus and can be unilateral for collective fun to occur in a play. Paley thinks that systematic exclusion is based on children's "habit of exclusion" (p. 117) rather than on some quality or feature of personalities of the particular children in relations to the play bosses. She insisted that as only the children are forced to abandon their habit of exclusion of particular kids, the friendship will develop. This is a very interesting hypothesis.

Was the teacher successful? In discussion of how she was successful in promoting inclusivity, Paley runs onto a trouble of a logical fallacy of tautology of "reasoning in a circle" (http://www.don-lindsay-archive.org/skeptic/arguments.html#begging). Indeed, under the new rule regime, the teacher was forcing her students to accept any child who asks to their play and then she asks if the children become inclusive under the new rule. To avoid, the logical fallacy of tautology, Paley focuses on cases in which children who are play bosses *voluntarily* select previously rejected children for their play. Only that way, inclusion of a previously rejected child by a play boss can be a "barometer" (p. 93) of Ms Paley's success,

"Very well, let this be the test: When Lisa accepts Angelo into her play or story, it will be a sign that the rule is working. Meanwhile I'll demonstrate my belief that the rule is fair for everyone equally" (p. 82). This investigative approach makes Paley's important investigation legitimate indeed, from our point of view.

We could find only two cases when Paley brings evidence of the success of her forced inclusion. In the first case, Lisa accepts Angelo in her story to perform for the class. This seems to be the ultimate evidence for Paley,

> "One thing you did though, Lisa, made Mrs. Wilson and me very happy."
> "I did?"
> "Remember when it was Angelo's turn and you needed a father? You said, 'Good, a boy! I didn't want a girl for a father.' You were happy to have Angelo in your story. Do you know why that pleased us so much?"
> "Because you like Angelo?" (p. 128)

However, Angelo was not accepted into Lisa's story by her will, rather it was his turn to be included into a story that happened to be Lisa's one. The Lisa's agency was revealed in this episode only in her passive acceptance (not resistance) to the new class rule about how children were pre-selected for participation in story performance. Thus, we have again tautological evidence (and reasoning): the evidence of Angelo being included by Lisa is in the fact that Lisa did not have her choice to reject him. In this case, the issue of inclusion, outside of the forced collectivity, is moot. Even more, Lisa's reply to Ms. Paley about why the teachers were so pleased with Lisa's acceptance of Angelo suggests that Lisa does not appreciated Angelo but rather sees some kind of nepotism from the teacher's side of Angelo being the teacher's pet.

Paley's second example is a bit stronger, in our view. She describes a case when Lisa actively invited Hiroko and then Jennifer, other previously rejected girls, to her play,

> This might well be the first time Lisa has invited Hiroko or Jennifer to play with her. The fact that no one else is around [except the teacher who supervises the girls playing in the classroom – EM&MS] is not important. These girls are often on Lisa's worst-friend list, which proves my point: It is the *habit* of exclusion that grows strong; the identity of those being excluded is not a major obstacle (p. 117).

The question is however, how much the new rule contributed to Lisa's unusual inclusiveness versus unusual circumstance that Paley tries to brush aside by saying that it "is not important". But was the circumstance really unimportant? According to Paley, Lisa and Hiroki were allowed to stay indoors at recess time (obviously under Ms. Paley's supervision) on their parents' written requests (p. 116). So, imagine two girls and the teacher "locked" in the classroom during recess time. If Lisa wanted to play, she had only two options: to play by herself alone or to play with Hiroko, with whom she previously avoided playing. Lisa chose the second option. Does it mean that the new rule works? Not necessarily. She may have done it without Ms Paley's rule of universal and unilateral inclusivity. Of course, there can be another possibility that Lisa calculated that even if she chose to play alone, Hiroko might try to join her and under Ms. Paley's surveillance and enforcement of the new rule, Lisa might not have a choice but accept Hiroko. So, Lisa did it preemptively to avoid the conflict with Mr. Paley and Hiroko. Under this alternative, the rule indeed affected Lisa's active invitation of Hiroko but not in a way Paley suggests – it was still forced rather voluntarily acceptance on Lisa's side. Thus, in face of strong alternative explanations and interpretations of the described event, we disagree with Paley that this case "proves" her hypothesis that *forced* unilateral inclusion promotes in children new *voluntary* inclusions that were not before. We do not necessarily claim that Paley is wrong about that – just that she does not have *any* evidence in her book to support her hypothesis which should remain as it is: a very interesting and plausible *hypothesis* without any supporting evidence. As academicians often say in this case, "more research is needed to investigate this issue."

All-in-all, we do not have any evidence that forced collectivity promotes voluntarily acceptance of previously rejected children. Even more, we did not have evidence of development of new friendships in the book after the new rule "you can't say you can't play" was imposed by the teacher.

Improving Plays and Stories as a Process and a Product

Paley claims that the children's play and story are improved under the new regime of universal and unilateral inclusion,

> [Inclusion] will happen. *It is happening.* Because the children are learning that it is far easier to open the doors than to keep people out (p. 118).
>
> ...
>
> "Lisa, I really do think the new way is working well."
> "How do you know?"
> "For one thing, I think the stories are better, although that's hard to prove. Something else is easier to prove, and we've kept track: Everyone has more turns and no one is left out. Besides, we're nicer to each other at story time. No one is telling someone else 'You can't be in my story.'" (p. 128)

The evidence she provides to Lisa is a bit circular: the imposed rule works well because the kids are forced not to say mean things to each other. It may be true that the previously rejected kids may have more turns to perform in stories and no one is left out but what does it mean for the children and for the quality of play/stories? Rules are only constraints for the actions and by themselves they are meaningless possibilities, "It is only my non-alibi in Being that transforms an empty possibility into an actual [responsible][7] act or deed" (Bakhtin et al., 1993, p. 42). Remember, that play and story inclusion is only a means for the previously rejected children to stop feeling like a stranger in Ms. Paley's classroom. But how the rule is enacted by the participants? Do the previously rejected children really stop feeling like strangers there? Do we have any evidence for that in Paley's book beyond her tautological reasoning focusing on the children's behavior enforced by her new rule?

> Paley reports on her observation that the children accept their roles provided them by story authors more eagerly and without objection under the new regime in the class,

> Now, a new phenomenon appears: Relieved of the responsibility of looking for loopholes in the law, the children have an opposite reaction. If they cannot change

---

[7] The Russian word "ответственность" that Bakhtin in his essay used is better to translate as "responsibility" than as "answerability" used by the translator that does not have moral connotation.

the role, then they will accept *any* role. They dare to take on implausible roles, shyly at the start, but after a while with great aplomb, as if accepting the challenge to eliminate their own stereotyped behaviors. Girls take on boys' roles and boys accept girls' roles. Not everyone, to be sure, but enough children are willing to throw off their shackles to make these role reversals acceptable. Those who have never taken roles as bad guys, witches, and monsters are saying yes to such assignments, and the Ninja Turtles are agreeing to be newborn babies (p. 127).

However, it appears that the unilateralism of children-actors is replaced by the unilateralism of children-authors. Even more, it seemed to be more negotiation of the roles (and thus story) before when children-actors had more power. Under the new regime, it feels like the actors are interchangeable while the roles are fixed while in past the roles were negotiated to fit specific participating actors. It is unclear why the unilateralism of children-author is better for the quality of the story then when the roles were more negotiated between the author and the actors. It is true that under the new regime, the actors can experience roles that they might reject in past or the author might not even offer them and, in this sense, we agree with Paley's judgment. The new regime challenges actors more. But the same token, it might not provide them with a zone of comfort to utilize their existing strengths that is also probably needed for artistic growth as the old regime provided them. However, without actual comparative analysis of the stories and performances before and after the new rule imposed by the teacher, it is difficult to make any conclusions on that. What is interesting, although, is that Ms. Paley refused to consider this question publicly with her students.

Is the Class "Less Sadder" than Before?

Angelo and Lisa dialogued on threshold of ultimate questions at the beginning of the book. They came to the issue that Ms. Paley formulated in the following concise way, "Who is sadder, the one who isn't allowed to play or the one who has to play with someone he or she doesn't want to play with?" (p. 20). We can reformulate this question in the following way, is the classroom community happier with the new rule imposed by the teacher than it was before? Unfortunately, this ultimate question is not addressed by Paley. We do not know how the diverse children – play bosses, friends of bosses, previously rejected kids – feel about the new rule by the end of the book. Do they (or some of them) think that the new regime is better than the old one? Are they (or some of them) are ambivalent? Do they (or some of them) think that the old regime is better than the new one? We have some evidence that Lisa and her friends are still unhappy about the new rule but we do not know if she holistically compares old and new ways (she might judge the old way even worse that disliked new way – please bear in mind that Lisa does not remain the same through the book and does experiment with the idea of inclusivity).

It is interesting that Ms. Paley never asked her students to compare the old and the new regimes, even the previously rejected kids, even Angelo. Why? We do not know for sure. We speculate that she was afraid to hear the unpleasant truth that her rule is not as welcomed by the kids (even by Angelo) as she hoped for. She seemed to be afraid to open any public forum for that. The evidence of her fear is in her reluctance to introduce the new rule in her fairytale story that she was developing for her students,

> "Does Schoolmistress have the rule?" Lisa asks.
> "No, she doesn't."

"Why not?"

"Maybe she hasn't thought enough about it. By the way, I think the new rule will get us out of a trap like the one Beatrix made. She wanted to capture Annabella and keep Alexandra out. Well, if you try to keep someone out of your game then it's like a trap that keeps you and your friends *in.* Beatrix was so sure she'd be happy if only she could have Annabella all to herself, but it turned out she was much happier when both girls *and* Prince Kareem became her friends. And soon she'll have Raymond for a friend also."

It is clear to me that I am avoiding Lisa's question. Why doesn't Schoolmistress have the rule? Shall I write a chapter in which the teacher posts a rule as I have done and Raymond's classmates stop excluding him? How can I have Schoolmistress's children so easily persuaded when mine may not be? **Better to let the children play along the edges of our new rule for a while.** Its complexities are great; **I must not trifle with the subject.**

My discussion with first through fourth grades has convinced me of two certainties: The rule is essential and it must begin at this intuitive stage of learning, when, as the fourth grade girl said, "They're nice enough to follow a new rule. They trust you." If I'm so certain, why not let Schoolmistress try it out? The answer is obvious. **I can't have her succeed and me fail** (pp. 86-87).

It seems that Paley was suspecting that her students were not persuaded by the new rule, "How can I have Schoolmistress's children so easily persuaded when mine may not be?" The students' consideration of the new regime is not "trifling with the subject." Throughout the book, she tries to establish and manipulate the class prolepsis regarding the new rule. She manipulates with the pronoun "we" publicly announcing the consensus on issues where there is an apparent disagreement (i.e., fake collectivity) (cf. Shor & Freire, 1987a, p. 147),

> [Paley was reporting her discussion with third graders to her kindergarten students – EM&MS] The [third grade] boy said, 'Your plan will work if we could all get along with each other.' ...
>
> "What plan?" Jennifer asks.
>
> "You can't say you can't play," I remind her. "It's not **our** plan yet. Or, rather, it's a plan but not a rule. **We're** *planning* for it. We're talking about it, getting opinions, thinking about it, wondering how it will work. I think that's a good way to start a new plan, if you've been doing something different all along" (p. 56)

Ms. Paley is claiming here that the class is planning the use of the new rule in their classroom community; however, in reality, it is she who has just started planning the imposition of the rule. She tries to create an impression in her students that they as the class already arrived to a consensus that the rule is morally good ("fair") and that it has to be implemented in their class.

> "Now we'll know what to do when these things happen. You see, the rule probably won't keep them from going on, but **it will tell us what is the <u>fair</u> thing** to do when they happen" (p. 57).

In the latter quote, Paley implies that the class has established a consensus that the new rule of universal and unilateral inclusivity is fair. However, there is no class consensus on whether the rule reflects fairness or not. Actually, even to the end of the book, there is strong opposition to this statement from many of her children reported by Paley. Ms. Paley uses many entrapments of fake collectivity and fake consensus throughout her book.

We wonder whether Paley's reluctance to discuss the new rule and publicly evaluate it was based on her suspicion that this discussion itself would break the success of the new regime. This is a common belief of perhaps all dictators that freedom of speech among governed destroys the social fabric of the society and not the dictatorial rule itself. It is like in Hans Christian Andersen's famous fairytale "The Emperor's new clothes" the problem was not the little child exclaimed, "But he hasn't got anything on!" but that the Emperor was stupid and had absolute power of coercion over his subjects. The authoritarian power corrupts.

It is ironic that if Paley were not afraid to ask her students to evaluate the new regime in comparison with the old one, at least some of the kids might evaluate the new regime more favorably. This would have boosted Paley's regime by getting more legitimacy among the class members and her own confidence in what she was doing. It might even spark the true acceptance of the new rule through IPD among some of the kids. Even more it may promote IPD counter-coup to reinstate the dialogic regime dethroned by Paley. Unfortunately, it did not happen.

Non-Occurred Events: What Could Paley Have Done Differently to Preserve IPD? (Our Addressing Vivian Paley)

Here we want to consider several questions about how much freedom the teacher Paley had in her circumstances. What could Paley have done to avoid establishing an authoritarian discursive regime that she set up in her classroom, if it were possible at all? Did she have any choice, as a responsible teacher? Further, once she did set up the authoritarian discursive regime, what could she have done to return back to the IPD regime in her classroom, if it were possible at all? In other words, could the teacher Paley have done something different to preserve IPD in her classroom OR she had "the alibi in Being" (Bakhtin et al., 1993, p. 40) by being completely constrained and determined by the circumstances, in which she found herself? Finally, we will consider here the opposite question about "the alibi in Being" -- namely, why couldn't IPD, itself, save Paley from her monologic coup d'état?

Let's imagine Paley reading our chapter[8]. She might agree with many of our critical points that we brought above but still insist that her "coup d'état" (she might not agree with this term) was the only right decision under circumstances she was. "Indeed," she

---

[8] Vivian Paley actually read our two chapters (earlier drafts) about her work that we sent her. She kindly replied, "Dear Eugene Matusov and Mark Smith:

Thank you for sending me your commentary on "You Can't Say You Can't Play." It is always fascinating to discover other people's analysis of my work. Last week I spent a day in a public elementary school in Ohio where I was invited to discuss the YCSYCP rule with children, K-5, grade by grade. The younger children were particularly interested in applying these ideas to the unfair treatment accorded them by their siblings, while in the older classes the discussions seemed to focus more on boy-girl exclusionary behavior. All told, any way the subject was approached, it made for good talk and the groups were all sorry when their sessions were over.

Thanks also for inviting me to comment on your paper, but I prefer to let you carry on your own investigations and come to your own conclusions.

Hopefully then, others (not me, the author) will offer to keep the stories going in innovative ways, as you have done.

My best wishes to you as you bring your manuscript closer to publication.

might have said, "what could I have done when I acutely feel injustice in my class that I, as the teacher, was responsible for? My solution was not ideal but it could be the best alternative under the circumstances." What could she have done indeed? "To continue the class forum when the highest majority of the students (actually, 21:4) supported the status quo while minority suffered under their oppression implicitly sanctioned by the teacher's classroom order?! For how long should the class to discuss the issue? Would all the students (like Lisa, Charlie, Ben, Cynthia) ever be convinced that the new rule is fair and would they ever voluntarily agree on the rule just out of discussions in the class forum?! Is it ever possible? Can persuasion be based solely on discussions and stories? Even so, what is the price of the continuing status quo for the rejected children (and also for oppressive children)?!" Ms. Paley might feel a sense of the impasse in her classroom forum, although we saw clear evidence in her second chapter that Lisa was seriously trying the alternative position in her own stories and deep reflections of Ms. Paley's story character Beatrix – the reflections, which Lisa turned on herself[9]. But let's accept her sense of impasse of the classroom forum for the clarity sake.

We still argue that the alternatives to Ms. Paley's monologic regime coup existed and, even more, were available to her. In her own book, we found germs of ideas that suggest at least several different alternative approaches to establishing the new rule in the classroom within an IPD regime. Let's consider some of them here.

Tricking into Reconsidering: Dialogical Objectivizing

As we already discussed above, Ms. Paley brought at least two examples of dialogic objectivizing and discussed them in depth in the previous chapter. As we discussed above, one case was an actual example of her interference into the Charlie-Ben play to include rejected Waka (Paley, 1992, p. 57). Another example was fictitious, from Ms. Paley fairytale story about adventures of Magpie and his friends (Paley, 1992, pp. 118-120), in which lonely and scared dragons were tricked from a foggy cave to warm sunlight. In both cases, the "bosses" found themselves in ontologically new circumstances (e.g., new fun of playing the game with the teacher and Waka) that help them rethink their attitudes and transcend their ontological being. In both cases, it was very safe objectivizing as the participants could safely return to their old ways of doing things (e.g., Waka could have been rejected by Charlie and Ben, the dragons could still hold Raymond's father as their prisoner).

We argue that the teacher Ms. Paley could have used this approach of tricking the students into the reconsidering their attitude to inclusion in her own classroom systematically. She could have playfully mediated the access of the rejected children to plays on a systematic basis. By doing that, she would have tested her own hypothesis, according to which play engagement with the necessity leads to children's friendships. As we discussed above, we suspect that the issue of what leads to what -- play engagement leads to friendship or

---

Vivian Gussin Paley"
[9] Lisa and some other children tried to develop alternative approaches to the teachers' universal and unilateral inclusivity in order to address systematic rejection while preserving the right to exclude on some occasions but the teacher dismissed these attempts often without much discussion. For example, Lisa proposed temporary alternations between the right of inclusivity and exclusivity, "*Lisa*: Then I'll promise Smita, okay? How about if I promise a different person every Monday? And on the other days I just pick who I want. *Teacher*: I know it's hard to make changes. You don't know in advance if you'll like a new way of doing things. Even the older children are afraid. But look, you've made the other new rule work. Everyone spends more time playing and plays with more people" (p. 125).

friendship leads to play engagement, -- is more complex. In some cases, play engagement may lead to friendship but in some other cases, the reverse it is true. However, Ms. Paley's experimentation through dialogic objectivizing, she might explore this complexity and alleviate the severity of systematic exclusion of rejected children. Also, like Magpie bird in her own fairytale, she could help to mediate networks of friendship for the systematically rejected children. In this case, if Paley had reached the successes, these successes would have had "construct validity" (using term from research methodology, Hartmann, 1992) unlike the tautological "successes" of the new rule presented in the book. As we discussed above, dialogic objectivizing contrasts social engineering by providing a real and safe choice for the participants after they are being tricked into an ontologically new circumstances[10]. The children could have faced the real comparison of two ontological conditions that they experienced. If the kids in a play accepted a previously rejected child as a result of Ms. Paley's dialogic objectivizing (like in her case with Waka), it would be for real, because, now they are having collective fun in being with Waka, and not because the children are forced to do it behaviorally by the rule enforced by the teacher. By doing that, the teacher would have not abandoned the IPD regime and still could address her concern about immediate actions for social justice. She could have involved the students in reflection about these two different ontological circumstances: one is the status quo of the exclusion right and the other is new experiences of play inclusions mediated by the teacher.

It is interesting how much attention Paley gave to this approach in her book and there was not discussion by her why she decided not to try it.

Rule with Choice: Spatial Testing of Ideas

Ms. Paley presented another well-developed IPD approach, alternative to her coup, to her students. She brought an interesting example of her teaching aide, Mrs. Sarah Wilson, who set a play inclusive rule in her backyard for neighborhood children: the children could come and play in her backyard only if they allow other kids to play. Thus, they had a choice either to accept the inclusive rule or to go elsewhere to play having their exclusion right. It was interesting that Ms. Paley did not seem to see any difference between Mrs. Wilson's rule of choice and contract and Ms. Paley rule "you can't say you can't play" that she imposed in her classroom,

> My discussions with the older children have made me wary. How many more times will I be told, "Yeah, it's very fair, but I don't think it can work"? Friendship comes first, with fairness off somewhere in the distance. Yet in each class there seems to be a hopefulness, a light shining, a dream that they could reinvent Mrs. Wilson's backyard for themselves, a place where you are always asked, "Do you want to play?"
> "Sarah, can the classroom be made to feel like your backyard?" I ask her.
> "I think so but I'm not sure. At home the children come and go at will. Here we're stuck with each other all day."

---

[10] For example, a political success of the African National Congress to stop "black-on-black" violence in Soweto, in the mid of 1990s in South Africa was based on dialogic objectivizing, in our view. ANC insisted that recently arrived male migrants to Soweto must bring their wives and families from Zulu homesteads to their Soweto all-male hostels. Having wives and children curbed the violence between Soweto's oldtimers (who lived with the families) and newcomers (who were not allowed to bring their families by the apartheid regime in past). Experiencing two different ontological circumstances helped the participants to make a different choices in their lives and stopped the violence (Beall, Crankshaw, & Parnell, 2002).

"All the more reason, then. None of us can go home and we can't hide in our cubbies. We've got to depend on the kindness of strangers. Let's begin the new rule next week, when I've finished the discussions. I've got fourth grade tomorrow and fifth grade on Monday" (Paley, 1992, p. 57).

Here, Mrs. Wilson pointed to Paley very clearly that the success of her rule was based on an actual choice and a voluntary contract that children who were playing in her backyard were engaged. At any time, the participating children knew that they could withdraw into the territory of the right to exclude and to be excluded. It seems to make the difference. The children had two different territories with different regimes of relating to each other and they could freely move from one territory to another to experience the consequences these two regimes that they could freely choose. The popularity of Mrs. Wilson's backyard was arguably based on this free choice and spatial testing of the different regimes.

Mrs. Wilson correctly argues that the school classroom does not provide the students with any choice of territory. However, Ms. Paley could create two different territories in her classroom for the children to choose and experience voluntarily these two different regimes of play: one with the right to exclude and one with the right to be included. In the class forum, the children could reflect on these two regimes and decide which was better for them and why.

Democratic Decision Making: Temporal Testing Ideas

Finally, we saw another IPD alternative in Paley's book although much less explicit and less discussed by Paley. At some point she wrote in her book, "We vote about nearly everything in our democratic classrooms, but we permit the children to empower bosses and reject classmates" (Paley, 1992, pp. 21-22). It is interesting that she did not provide one instance of voting in her class.

We do not suggest her offering to vote on the new rule because we know the outcome as she reported it 21:4 against the new rule. However, Ms. Paley could offer the student to test this new idea of the rule "you can't say you can't play." She could have told the students, "Listen children, we provided excellent reasons for the current way of how we chose with whom we want to play by rejecting others. We also provided very good examples how rejection from play makes us sad. Some of us think that it is sadder to exclude kids from play but some of us think that it is sadder to include kids in play just because they want to. So far, as a class, we experience sadness of exclusion. But we never experienced any sadness of forced inclusion. We do not know what is better because we never try the other alternative. Let's give it a try for some time (1 month?) and then decide which was sadder. After that we can make our mind which way we want out classroom to be. How can we decide what is sadder?" This speech may convince the children to try and test the new alternative while monitoring its outcome. Would play boss open minded for this testing? We think so, because Paley provided the readers with evidence how much Lisa, for example, who was the strongest opponent of the new rule, was open minded and willing to try new ideas at the same time.

I (Eugene Matusov, the first author) was told about a similar IPD approach in one of innovative collaborative schools (Rogoff, Turkanis et al., 2001) by a 2-3 grade teacher Daniella (a pseudonym). There were 2-3 mixed grade classrooms. One was taught by a male teacher John (a pseudonym) who introduced a candy dispenser in his classroom.

Each time a child did a math problem correctly; he or she was allowed to get a candy from the dispenser. The children from another 2-3 grade classroom asked their female teacher Daniella to set up similar candy dispenser with a similar rule. Daniella was strongly against the use of extrinsic motivators in her classroom. On a regular class meeting, she discussed with her students pros and cons of the rewarding solving math problems with candies. Daniella told her students that she was very concerned that the rewards diminish the students' love to math and distract their attention from learning math to getting more candies. She argued that they could have candies at the end of the year as celebration of their learning achievements or even a freely available candy dispenser in the classroom but not as rewards for learning math. They had several meetings arguing pros and cons. Finally, they had a vote (including the teacher). The teacher's position of not having candy dispenser as the reward system won by just one vote. I asked her what she would have done if the vote had gone the opposite way – it the children voted for having the candy dispenser as the reward system for learning math. Her reply surprised me.

She said that would accept the vote and allow the class to have a candy dispenser to reward their learning math. She said something that struck me, "I'm not afraid of truth." "What do you mean?" I asked her. She explained that she believed that extrinsic motivation reduces students' intrinsic motivation for learning. "This is also what research shows," she added. In that research, children who like to draw were given rewards for drawing pictures. They started drawing more than before but when the rewards were taken away few children chose to draw in their free time than before or then a control group (see review of such research in Subbotsky, 1995). "If it is true, my students and I will see it in our own research on ourselves. I would do with my students the same research on the students' intrinsic motivation about math learning that I read in the articles. If it is not true, why should I worry about having a candy dispenser in my class?!"

We argue that Ms. Paley could set up similar research with her kindergarten students in her class to check if the new regime of the inclusion right is happier than the old one of the exclusion right[11]. Like Daniella, she could have prepared herself and her students to accept truth of this testing. She should not have been afraid of truth. There is no need for a teacher to choose between truth searching and social justice, between IPD and fairness,

> In our personal life we often cling to illusions. That is we do not dare to examine certain beliefs which could be easily contradicted by experience, because we are afraid of upsetting the emotional balance. There may be circumstances where it is not unwise to cling to illusions, but [in the practices of learning and teaching] we need to adopt the inductive attitude which requires a ready ascent from observations to generalizations, and a ready descent from the highest

---

[11] When Paley "discussed" (or better to say "announced") spread of the new rule "you can't say you can't play" to the cases of selecting actors for one's stories to perform, she did suggesting testing the new rule for selection, "We really have to try this out. After a while, if we don't see a lot of good things happening, we'll change back" (pp. 125-126), but her offer to test was arguably disingenuous and manipulative as Ms. Paley did not discuss with her students how they were going to test the new rule and compare happiness before and after the new rule. She also did not try to convince the students to test with a sincere sense of inquiry. Rather, she seemed to use the idea of test to sooth and silent most vocal objectors of the new rule (please notice Paley's manipulative use of pronoun "we"). It was not surprising that both Lisa and Charlie strongly rejected Ms. Paley's manipulation, "*Lisa*: Then I'm not doing any more stories! *Charlie*: Me neither" (p. 126).

generalizations to the most concrete observations. It requires saying "maybe" and "perhaps" in a thousand different shades. It requires many other things, especially the following three:

INTELLECTUAL COURAGE: we should be ready to revise any one of our beliefs

INTELLECTUAL HONESTY: we should change a belief when there is good reason to change it...

WISE RESTRAINT: we should not change a belief wantonly, without some good reason, without serious examination (Pólya, 1954, pp. 7-8).

We found a full blown and actually occurring example of the democratic testing of ideas through IPD in description and video of an innovative British school *Summerhill* (B. Allen, Getzels, & Getzels, 1992; Neill, 1960). The video documentary, *Summerhill at 70* (B. Allen et al., 1992), was filmed just after a vote passed at the children-run school to abolish all rules -- probably, in the interest of those children who found any rules stodgy or too restrictive, -- which according to the book by Neill has happened recursively in the history of the school. The consequences and evaluation of the action became a subject of discussion at the school's General Meetings. The discussions throughout the transcribed meeting below from the video documentary were characterized by IPD and an evaluation of the state of the community without rules. The dialogue that emerged is a clear example of IPD discussion with evidence of children as well as the teachers evaluating their own and one another's responsibility for the community's action. One problem that was brought to the weekly meeting by older children was the problem of no longer having bedtimes (resulting in children staying awake well past 4 a.m. and being very tired and irritated through the following days as we saw on the video):[12]

Roli [boy, age 13]: I mean, I think that the school right now, is just almost falling apart, you know. Like at the meeting, half of it's just everyone's coughing, and they're *ill* and they're *tired*, and it's just, we *need* bedtime back!

Matthew [a houseparent]: I don't think the community can actually not... I don't think the community can handle not having bedtimes. Because...

Two boys: Hear! Hear! Hear!

Matthew: ...not because people are not being kept awake so much, but because there aren't enough people responsible in the community to stay in the school premises. We've had guys going down to, it seems [name of child] is out, [name of child]'s out, Fabienne is out. You guys are meant to be a more responsible people, you've been here a long time, are OUT! Now, this, if it comes back to us that this is happening at night, when it's no bedtimes, this community going to be in shit![13]

Zoë [the school's headmistress, probably Neill's daughter]: After the meeting [in which the rules were dropped], after I'd said, I went into the house, and Amy [probably a staff member] said, what happened at the meeting? And I said, the laws are dropped! And she goes, "Oh, my God!" [exasperated voice with a familiar tone]. And William [probably an old-time staff member who experienced children's abolishing any rules before] went, "Oh, my God!" [more dramatic, a

---

[12] The transcription that follows was made from the videorecording by the second author.

[13] Please note that the use of coarse and vulgar language used by the Summerhill children and adults is common at Summerhill to express feelings. As the video disclaimer says, "This program contains coarse language, which accurately reflects life at Summerhill."

sense of "not this again"]. Because they remember what happened last time. Because basically if you have a community that is a complete anarchy it fucking well doesn't work! Right?

Boy: Yeah, hear! hear!

Zoë: The whole point is, that you dropped. So that's *my* reason, and I don't know what Matthew's [an adult, one of the "houseparents"] reason is, and I don't know why everybody else voted for it, but *my reason* was that I thought this place is up shit creek, every is just doing their own bloody thing, everybody is going [makes "up yours" or fart noise] to everybody else, everybody's thinking about the "good for them," they're all thinking about their own ends, let's drop the fucking laws and see how the school likes it then! And I believe now that the school doesn't like it very much at all! And those members of the community that are still holding it together with no laws are the members of the community who are all right jack [puts two middle fingers up in the air] the just want to put a finger up at everybody else. Of course they don't want bedtimes, they want to have a complete anarchy. They want to do as they like!

The teacher's voice seems to be equal to that of the students in a way how the headmaster addresses the General Meeting. An older boy is able to evaluate Zoë's comments, a clear contrast to Ms. Paley's classroom, where once the teacher's mind is made up about something, there is no more discussion. In response to Zoë, the boy says,

Older boy: I don't know. People have appreciated some of those laws being dropped. I don't think, some of the laws we had weren't necessary at all, and getting rid of them is good, it has a nice clean-out, we can start fresh. I think that the bedtimes thing is starting to bring in other problems, so maybe we need to bring bedtimes back [the community votes to return to a bedtime rule enforced by "beddies officers"].

At Summerhill school, the dialogue about rules can continue with inclusion of new generation of the students who had to test the idea of living without any communal rules. Although this process seems to be repetitive for some staff oldtimers new priorities, interests and responsibilities can thus emerge practically in the community and these staff members seem to be aware of these processes and appreciate them. The Summerhill community recognizes the power and necessity of IPD. As houseparent Matthew says in the documentary, "Now here [at Summerhill] you actually see what kids are like, you see them go through these processes, but because they're dealt with practically instead of morally, or by somebody up there looking down, the kids can move beyond that particular period."

In conclusion, Paley's ontological circumstances do not seem to imprison her – monologic manipulation was not the only alternative for her to introduce the new rule to her students. In our view, she had alternative approaches to introduce the inclusive regime in the classroom without abandoning IPD. She did not have an "alibi in being" for her coup d'état of establishing monologic authoritarian discourse in her classroom. The reverse seems to be true as well, IPD regime never creates an "alibi in being" in itself. It always demands active efforts and responsibility from its participants. It is *eventive* (Bakhtin, 1991, 1999; Bakhtin et al., 1993) rather than habitual (see Dershowitz, 2002, for his similar argument about human rights).

Dialogic Addressivity Versus Monologic Manipulation

In an early part of the book Paley admitted to herself and the readers that she tried to manipulate her students to force them into the attitude about play inclusivity she thought was right one, "Angelo wants to know what else I *don't* tell the children. "I try not to tell you what thoughts or opinions to have," is my less than honest answer, at a time when I am single-mindedly pushing new attitudes about play" (p. 27). As we have discussed above, although Paley struggled with her own desire to manipulate with her students' minds in such a hard, extreme way, she never openly doubted the idea of the teacher's hidden manipulation of the students per se. In general, she seems to consider instruction as mind manipulation (or, putting it in the less judgmental wording, "purposeful transformation of the students' mind by the teacher") and students as objects of the teacher's pedagogical actions.

Once, a colleague of ours told us the following story. She came to interview a mother for her research while her young son popped up the room time-to-time, interrupting the interview, with his toy pistol shooting the visitor (our colleague) in a mock playful way. The mother asked the boy several times not to interrupt the interview by in vain. Finally, our colleague decided a different strategy. When the boy "shot" her, she pretended to be shot falling dead. The boy giggled in delight, left the room, and stopped bothering the visitor. The interview proceeded uninterrupted. Our colleague presented this case as her successful dealing with the problematic behavior of the child by getting along with the child's wish until the wish was exhausted. The little boy wanted to play with the visitor and the visitor played with him while the visitor wanted to get rid the boy and the boy finally left. Of course, any experienced and skillful parent or educator can bring cases like that. There are no doubts that this manipulation of the child's attention and mind, in general, can be helpful to achieve certain practical goals at hand and it is especially useful for the adult to avoid violent confrontations with the child. However, the following question emerges. Is education about, or should education be about, skillful tricking a child into the behavior, mindset, knowledge, and attitude desired by the adult?

It seems to us that Erich Fromm described and analyzed this manipulation when he discussed a societal change from "overt authority" to "anonymous" hidden authority in the mid of the twenty century in the US society (and probably in Western Europe as well),

> Overt authority is exercised directly and explicitly. The person in authority frankly tells the one who is subject to him, "You must do this. If you do not, certain sanctions will be applied against you." Anonymous authority pretends that there is *no* authority, that all is done with the consent of the individual. While the teacher of the past said to Johnny, "You must do this. If you don't, I'll punish you"; today's teacher says, "I'm sure you'll *like* to do this." Here, the situation for disobedience is not corporal punishment, but the suffering face of the parent, or what is worse, conveying the feeling of not being "adjusted," of not acting as the crowd acts. Overt authority used physical force; anonymous authority employs psychic manipulation.
>
> ...
>
> Our system need men who *feel* free and independent but who are nevertheless willing to do what expected of them, men who will fit into the social machine without friction, who can be guided without any aim except the one to 'make

good.' It is not that authority has disappeared, nor even that it has lost in strength, but that it has been transformed from the overt authority of force to the anonymous authority of persuasion and suggestion. In other words, in order to be adaptable, modern man is obligated to nourish the illusion that everything is done with his consent, even though such consent be extracted from him by subtle manipulation. His consent is obtained, as it were, behind his back, or behind his consciousness.

The same artifices are employed in progressive education. The child is forced to swallow the pill, is given a sugar coating. Parents and teachers have confused true nonauthoritarian education with *education by means of persuasion and hidden coercion.* (Fromm, 1960, pp. x-xi)

Of course, when Fromm says "persuasion" he means "manipulative pseudo-persuasion", it is appear-to-be-persuasion rather than authentic critical internal persuasion that Bakhtin (1991) was talking. Fromm described an important phenomenon of pseudo-IPD that some "progressive" educators and parents sometime use. The birthmark of the pseudo-IPD is fabricated consent behind person's back, behind person's consciousness – the theme that was fully analyzed by Bakhtin in his notion of "behind one's back truth"[14] monologically objectivizing the other (Bakhtin, 1999, p. 59). In contrast, in genuine IPD, it is possible to claim that, paraphrasing and retranslating Bakhtin, "the teacher's discourse about a student is organized as discourse about the person who is *actually present here and now in the same room with the teacher*, someone who hears the teacher and who is immediately *capable of answering the teacher*" (Bakhtin, 1999, p. 63). Just imagine an improbably event of a preoperational child reading Piaget's essay on his experiments on operational thinking – what would the child tell Piaget[15]? Or imagine that our colleague described above would tell the boy that she just wanted to get rid of him by pretending to get along with his play – how would the boy feel and respond to this truth? In a genuine internally persuasive discourse, all words are directed to the participants – nothing is told behind his or her back, behind his or her consciousness. The issue is here how much the teacher's manipulation of the student's mind is desirable in education. How much can the teacher legitimately fabricate consent behind the student's consciousness in education? Is manipulation a form of illegitimate domination (Shor & Freire, 1987a, p. 172)?

Innovative teacher A.S. Neill, the organizer and headmaster of the famous British *Summerhill* school, described many cases of his "curing" children from their psychological problems. However, as Fromm pointed out about Neill's approach, it does not use hidden, behind child's consciousness, manipulation (Fromm, 1960, p. xii). Let consider the following case presented by Neill (1960, pp. 289-291). The case involved a young boy Arthur "who was a real crook who stole cleverly" (p. 289). A week after Arthur's arrival to the Summerhill school, Neill, the school headmaster, got two phone calls: one from Arthur's uncle Dick and the other from Arthur's mother asking Neill to give Arthur travel money of two pounds and ten shillings to visit his uncle in Liverpool. This was not unusual arrangement in the Summerhill School, so Neill agreed to Arthur's mother and gave the boy the required travel

---

[14] Bakhtin's word "заочная правда" was translated as "secondhand truth" (Bakhtin, 1999, p. 59), however, probably it should be translated better along Fromm's lines as "behind one's back evaluation" or "behind one's consciousness evaluation." "The truth about a man in the mouths of others, not directed [addressed] to him dialogically and there a *secondhand* [*behind his consciousness*] truth, becomes a lie degrading and deadening him, if it touches upon his 'holy of holies,' that is, 'the man in man.'" (p.59)

[15] There was an interesting case of a subject of Luria's cross-cultural experiments on thinking (Luria, 1976) replying to the experimenter but unfortunately Luria did not get the reply but rather treated it as a part of his experiment (Matusov, 2008a; Matusov & St. Julien, 2004).

money. Some time later Neill realized (although we do not know how) that he was tricked by the boy – the two phone calls were made from a public phone booth by Arthur successfully impersonating his uncle and mother to steal money from Neill in a very clever way. After consulting with his wife who also worked in the school, Neill decided to reward Arthur and to not punish for his stealing and swindling as a conventional school often does and as Arthur surely expected to be done. Neill came to Arthur's bedroom and announced to him that his mother just called him again and asked to give more money (ten shillings more) to Arthur because she made a mistake about the train fare to Liverpool. Before shocked Arthur could say anything, Neill "carelessly threw a ten-shilling note on his bed and departed" (p. 290). Next morning Arthur went off for Liverpool leaving a letter for Neill, "Dear Neill, you are a greater actor than I am" (p. 290). After his return, Arthur kept asking Neill for weeks why he gave him more money perfectly knowing about the scheme. One day, Neill replied to Arthur, "How did you feel when I gave it [extra 10 shillings] to you?" Arthur hesitated for a moment and replied slowly, "You know, I got the biggest shock of my life. I said to myself: 'Here is the first man in my life who has been on my side'" (p. 290). After this incident, Arthur stole a few more times. Each time Neill rewarded his stealing. Eventually the boy stopped his delinquency and credited Neill's actions for that. Neill claimed that the boy "was cured" by his therapy of love.

Is it a great example of manipulation or, as Fromm claimed, an example of absent authority? Arthur expected either to get away with his swindling or to be caught and punished by Neill. Neill disrupted Arthur's expectations (and Arthur's worldview) and puzzled the boy by his unprovoked generosity. But, in our view, what is probably the most important in this case was that Neill *addressed* Arthur making him "conscious of the love that is approval." What was unconditionally approved by Neill was not stealing but Arthur as a human being among other human beings. Neill's focus seemed to be not on tricking Arthur into stopping swindling (that would have been monologic manipulation) but in accepting him and approving of him. Arthur might have never stopped stealing but Neill could not stop trying to relate to him as a human being to another human being: with unconditional respect, recognition, approval, and love. Neill addressed Arthur with "open cards put down on the table" – there was not a word said or motive thought about Arthur by Neill behind Arthur's back, behind his consciousness.

In our own work with preservice teachers working in an afterschool program at a Latin-American Community Center (LACC) with Latino children as a part of their teaching practicum (Hayes & Matusov, 2005b; Eugene Matusov, St. Julien et al., 2005), we faced with similar problem of dialogic addressivity versus monologic manipulation. At LACC our students met a little African-American boy Darryl, seven years old, who was quite a challenge for many of the students. He was very affectionate with the students and robustly tried to engage them in playing with him but he was not very cooperative with them. Many of our students tried to avoid him. However, one male student, John, really liked to play with Darryl (both names are pseudonyms). The students often discussed Darryl as full of deficits on our class web, "He's a rambunctious kid, who means well, but he can be rude and uncontrollable. He is often disrespectful and a [LACC] supervisor there has told me the same thing… Today he was very disrespectful and kept jumping on me and grabbing me… He is a very stubborn kid that tries to get attention in all the wrong ways however he ends up getting the attention he wants…. I think Darryl just wants attention… most likely the attention he does not get at home." To guide the students out of the deficit model, I (the first author of this chapter) was looking for an opportunity to engage with Darryl at LACC in my students' presence. This opportunity came very quickly. This was how I described it on the class web,

> Today I notice that when you transfer a request into a play with Darryl, he becomes very cooperative (and respectful). For example, he dropped blocks but refused to gather them. Instead he grabbed a toy shark and prepared to leave a room. I turned the request into a game by asking shark to help to gather the blocks. The "shark" agreed to help and Darryl and I gathered blocks quickly. I used the same approach later when I asked Darryl's mouse to help me collect all puzzle pieces from the floor. What other successful approaches did you try with Darryl? What do you think? Eugene

One of the students who witnessed the event replied,

> I have to be honest, I did not expect Darryl to respond the way that he did. I know that with the way I was raised, little things like not picking up after yourself were not tolerated at all and you were in a way yelled into, or kind of scared into doing it. This way you learned not to mess around with the authoritative position and you just knew what to expect if you didn't do it. I guess you don't always have to get all bent out of shape or aggravated. Instead just get creative.

The students decided to use my strategy whenever they needed to do anything. However, very quickly they became unsuccessful with him. I saw the following scene. It was at the end of the session when the students prepared to go back to the University. They asked kids to clean the toys after themselves. Darryl ignored their request. Then the students tried to "play" with him to make him clean the toys from the floor modeling after my successful strategy. Initially, he followed their playful cleanup but then suddenly stopped cleaning as if he realized being manipulated and returned back to his initial play. All further attempts by my students to make him clean were in vain. Before I decided to do something, my colleague and former grad student who visited on that day LACC with us, told Darryl with a playful tone, "Hey, Darryl, I order you not to clean the toys! Do not even think helping the students cleaning the room! I'll yell at you if you help them!" Darryl looked at my colleague, smiled and jumped on the floor to help cleaning the room. The colleague pretended yelling at him for that. My students were again very impressed and decided to use this strategy. Needless to say, it stopped working in a few days.

Finally, I [i.e., the first author] suggested John, a UD student, who liked working with Darryl and was very puzzled with his behavior to interview him. My point was why we were discussing Darryl while never asking Darryl what he thought about his own behavior. I suggested John to ask Darryl how he would like to be asked by other people to do something. John interviewed Darryl for several days. Darryl told, "Don't tell what to do! Ask me nicely." However, when John asked Darryl how he would ask kids to do something if he were an authority figure, Darryl contradicted himself, "You better get over here and help me clean up!" When John reported his findings of contradiction how Darryl likes to be asked to do something versus how he would ask somebody to help him to the class. I asked John if he pointed at the contradiction to Darryl himself. John replied that he did not but he liked the idea. Soon, John reported back to the class via the class web, "Darryl and I were sitting at a table and I looked at him. He said to me, "Don't look at me! Turn around or I'll kick you in

the face!" So I asked him, "Why do you tell me what to do, when yo
what to do?" The only response he could give was 'Sorry.'" Of co
expectation of Darryl's miraculous change of his attitude aft
contradictions in his attitude and behavior. However, we argue h
important step that was made by John to relate differently with Darryl
acceptance and honest sharing and thinking together through emerging
problems. If the rest of the students wanted Darryl's genuine cooperation based on Darryl's
free agency and not on some "clever" monologic manipulation, they would have to join the
John-Darryl community. They had to stop treating him as a non-responsive object of their
pedagogical actions but rather as a person with feelings, thoughts, and worldviews who had to
be addressed.

Like in Neill's case of Arthur, John helped Darryl to transcend his ontological
circumstances through dialogic addressivity. From a dialogic perspective, the goal of
education is not make a student to do what the teacher wants him or her to do, or to change
his or her own attitude or worldview in the image of the teacher's one. In our view, the goal
of education is for the student to be informed about other, previously unknown, worldviews,
attitudes, and approaches that help the student to make an informed choice and decision
making. There is never deciding for the student and not even with the student. It is always
helping the student to make his or her own informed decision as the student always remains
being the highest agency for his/her own decision making (Purkey, 1992). The teacher just
has to respect this agency of the student.

Why IPD Is Valuable for Life and Education: Can Truth Be Imposed?

What is educational value of internally persuasive discourse? Why cannot truth be
imposed as an educational shortcut? Paley argues for such a shortcut when she plans to
impose the new rule "you can't say you can't play" from the beginning of the new school
year on her future kindergarteners,

> The fourth grader who wondered if getting rid of owners and bosses would
> solve the enigma of exclusionary behavior makes a good point. Children with
> appealing ideas will always have followers, but the word "boss" creates problems.
> Another designation is needed. Words do make a difference. Next year, when "You
> can't say you can't play" will not be a new rule, but simply *the* rule, it will be
> interesting to see if "boss" and "owner" disappear. And, if they do, what will be
> invented to take their place?
> The play goes so well now that we are unprepared for a new issue that arises,
> one that confounds the teachers and disturbs the children. Nearly two weeks after
> "You can't say you can't play" has gone into effect, a simple and logical expansion
> of the rule to cover the logistics of storytelling and story acting creates a near
> revolution (p. 122).

Indeed, why would she need to have a class forum with her future students if she knows
the rule that works (at least in her mind) to prevent social injustice?

Lave (1992a) agues that learning is an inescapable aspect of any activity – the issue is not
whether people learn or not but whether what they learn is socially desirable. For example,

a boring math lesson, students may learn that math is boring, that the math is not for them, and that they hate math. Similarly, we argue is that dialogue and IPD is not escapable – the issue is not whether people engage in an IPD dialogue or not but whether this IPD dialogue is socially good or not. In the given case of Ms. Paley's coup d'état, the IPD was preserved for her students and herself as an unanswered but unavoidable question of "why?!" Why was the classroom dialogic regime abandoned by the teacher? Why was the students' trust and respect violated? Why did the teacher shift to manipulating her students as the essence of her guidance? Why did not the teacher have moral and professional restraints precluding her from her coup? The excessive monologicity of the teacher's act is still embedded in dialogue. So the questions for us, educators, is not whether to have IPD or not but what kind of IPD should we have in our classrooms. Should it be about why are we, teachers, so monologic in a specific curricular context and beyond it VERSUS what are conditions of our lives, why are they what they are, and how to make them better? In the former regime, IPD is arrested, parochialized, and fragmented moving IPD away from a public arena into the underground of the students' and the teacher's privacy. In monologic classroom, IPD is bracketed outside of the curricula and instruction. The academic content remains outside of IPD as a given stuff to be learned by the students in contrast with the latter regime of IPD, in which IPD is the curriculum and instruction,

> ... zooming out of my work with the class as a whole, I have also been teaching everyone to participate in a classroom [dialogic – EM&MS] culture in which students:
>
> are publicly willing to reason their way from confusion to making mathematical sense;
> are publicly willing to talk about what they are thinking; and
> respect what others say even if it does not seem to make sense (Lampert, 2001, p. 159).

Truth cannot be imposed or implemented because it demands responsibility, addressivity, responsivity, accountability, questionability, respect, and unfinalizability toward others. As Morson writes, "Education and all inquiry are fundamentally different when the need for reasons is acknowledged and when questioning becomes part of the process of learning. Truth becomes dialogically tested and forever testable" (Morson, 2004, p. 319). When truth is imposed on others it becomes contaminated by excessive monologicity. It automatically becomes half-truth and, thus, half-lie. For example, when the truth of 2+2=4 is imposed on students as a rule of truth without questioning it, testing it, addressing others, answering, reasoning it, considering alternatives, learning reasons for its emergence and importance (e.g., why should we care about it?), learning its limitations and historical, social, and ontological conditions of its existence, joining historical debates on it, and so on, 2+2=4 is not fully truth. The students can parrot the rule and blindly apply it without seeing its meaning for themselves. This is the half-lie of monologic truth.

CONCLUSION: WHAT IS POLYPHONIC CLASSROOM?

Bakhtin's notion of "internally persuasive discourse" redefines the purpose of education. Traditionally, mainstream schools define the main purpose of education as indoctrination in the universal truth. The school expects from students demonstration of facts, rules, and problem solving on the authority's demands. One line of innovative education, which is called itself as "constructivism," recognizes wrongness of such a decontextualized and passive goal and offers an alternative for the goal of education, in which students construct the contextual truth. In this approach to education, students are active in developing their worldviews that collide together in development of unified truth that exists objectively and separately from the participants. While another line of innovative education movement, which is often recognized as "postmodernist," sees the goal of education in students' mere exposure to diverse, ontological, and non-privileged points of view inseparable from their authors.

From Bakhtin's IPD notion, all these educational approaches are monologic, although each in its own different way. The conventional approach to education of teaching the truth dismisses the students' worldviews and imposes ideas. The truth of the imposed ideas is rooted in the authority of imposition itself. As Bakhtin pointed out (1999), this educational approach knows all affirmation or rejection of ideas of others. No dialogic relations are known to conventional, transmission of knowledge, educational philosophy.

The described constructivist approach is also monologic although it takes into consideration of worldviews of the students. It sees the goal of education in transformation of the students' worldviews, skills, knowledge, and attitudes into the correct and powerful ones through a serious of guided discoveries that the students will do. This approach essentially manipulates the students into the purely-epistemological truth of the united consciousness. The students' worldviews are seen as erroneous misconceptions that have to be corrected. People's ideas are placed on the scale of their approximation to the truth to be taught through guided discoveries and construction. Thus, the relationship between ideas does not know truly dialogic relations.

The postmodernist approach tries to overcome monologic monism of the other two educational approaches by insisting on the ontological nature of the participants' worldviews. In this approach, education is viewed as mere exposure to diversity of arguably equal ontological worldviews that do not have any privilege with regard to each other. A student is brought to the ontological market place of idea in which ideas are not bought or sold but exposed. Influences can happen but not necessary and not pushed. "Live oneself and let other live" is the ethic rule of such exposé. Although the ontology of the participants' worldviews is taken seriously by the postmodernist approach to education, in contrast to the two other approaches in which the participants' ontologies are dismissed or manipulated, it still remains essentially monologic as the participants are locked in their own ontological subjectivities. In the postmodernist approach, people are seen being prisoners of their own ontologies claiming, paraphrasing Bakhtin, "alibi in their being" (see Morson & Emerson, 1990, for more discussion). It is only on the first glance that it appears that the postmodernist approach is free from any external authority. It is true that it is free from an authority of imposition and manipulation but it is not free from a hidden authority of tradition, ignorance, and prejudice.

An IPD approach sees the goal of education in engaging the students in collective search for their own truth and its testing with others. The ontological truths of the participants – their worldviews, knowledge, skills, attitudes, -- have to be "informed" by dialogue with ontological truths of others. People do not simply expose their equal truths but address, response, take responsibility, evaluate, and judge each other truths. Ontological truths are equal only in a sense of being respected as always fruitful contributions to a dialogue. This equality and respect for ontological truths of others was well expressed allegedly by the famous French writer Voltaire, "I disapprove of what you say, but I will defend to the death your right to say it" (Guterman, 1990; E. B. Hall, 1906). Ontological truths are not equal with regard to their persuasiveness emerged from testing of the ideas. In IPD dialogue, some ideas come up better than others. Ontological person-idea is neither divorced from a person, like in the transmissionist and constructivist approaches, not rooted in the person, as in the postmodernist approach. Paraphrasing Bakhtin it is possible to say that "ontological person-idea is half the person's and half somebody else's." It is always shaped by a dialogue and in dialogue. To teach means to broaden student's participation in dialogue. Paley's ethnography provides us with some useful insights about exciting features of IPD in educational settings. Further investigation of IPD in education may open new exciting vistas for innovative education.

As we said above, we initially selected Paley's book "You can't say you can't play" in hope to analyze IPD in a polyphonic classroom. We found IPD in her book but not a polyphonic classroom. What is a polyphonic classroom? Slightly paraphrasing Morson and Emerson's (1990, p. 234) definition of Bakhtin's notion of polyphony, we can define polyphonic classroom, as "two closely related criteria are constitutive of polyphony: 1) *a dialogic sense of truth* and 2) *a special position* of the [teacher] necessary for [promoting] this sense of truth [in the classroom community]. In fact, these two criteria are aspects of the same phenomenon, the polyphonic [classroom's] 'form-shaping ideology'. They can be separated only for purposes of analysis." Our analysis of Paley's book shows that although it was full with diverse forms of IPD (see figure 8), a dialogic sense of the truth was not central in Ms. Paley's classroom, in specific, and in Paley's pedagogy, in general. It seems to us that IPD served Paley as a temporary intellectual tool for clearing her personal doubts rather than way of dialogic living (i.e., dialogic being-in-the-world) and dialogic teaching. Similarly, her special position in the classroom was arguably not directed at promoting dialogic truth but rather on her imposition of her version of social justice.

We are left with unanswered questions here. What does polyphonic classroom look like? Is the notion of polyphony compatible with education? What is a curriculum that promotes dialogic truth? What are ultimate questions behind 2+2=4 (for example)? How and why the teachers can honestly participate in an IPD around 2+2=4 year after year – is it possible (Matusov, 2007)? What responsibility do the students take when they claim or question 2+2=4? What kind of special position (authority) of the teacher promotes dialogic truth? What are institutional conditions that promote polyphonic classrooms? How much freedom do teachers and students ontologically have: is a polyphonic classroom possible in conventional schools which emphasize transmission of knowledge? This is the question of determinism (i.e., nothing can be done under this circumstances), voluntarism (i.e., everything is possible if one only wishes and correctly acts), and "a non-alibi in being" (i.e., people are shaped by their constraints that allow the people to transcend them in their responsible act of unfinalizing). What can we tell and ask the teachers who are interested in promoting polyphony in their classrooms?

PART 2. DIALOGUE AND ACTIVITY

Chapter 9

ARGUMENTATION IN DIALOGIC EDUCATION[1]

ABSTRACT

What is the goal of teaching? Is it to pass knowledge and skills to the students? What is the goal of teaching in pro-dialogic education project? I consider these questions with specific example of the role of argumentation in education. Argumentation practice has often been studied outside of education and has been linked with persuasion. I argue that, while argumentation is incompatible with conventional education, in dialogic pedagogy argumentation is a necessity. I provide an ethnographic case of my instructional support of undergraduate education student working on her final paper for an educational diversity course. In this case, the student, as a highly religious Protestant, argued for teaching Intelligent Design along with the theory of evolution in US public schools. Although I strongly disagreed with Intelligent Design and its teaching in public schools, through dialogic argumentation I provided guidance for the student. The findings show that the primary goal of argumentation in dialogic pedagogy is not persuasion but the socialization of students into professional discourse and the promotion of the students' unique professional voice.

Traditionally, argumentation has been examined outside of educational practices[2]; examples include scientific practices (Latour, 1987), law, medicine, philosophy, and bureaucracy (S. Toulmin, 1981; Walton, 1996). It has been argued that the main function of argumentation in these non-education practices is persuasive speech[3] (Billig, 1996). However, I argue here that in education in general, and in dialogic pedagogy specifically, the persuasive function of argumentation can become problematic. Let's consider a specific example. I am

---

[1] I am thankful to Mark Smith, Arne Vines, Yifat Ben-David Kolikant, Sarah Pollack, and John St. Julien for their feedback on an earlier draft of this paper. Part of this paper was presented at the International Bakhtin conference, May 2007, Crete, Greece.

[2] There is a lot of foci on argumentation in education (e.g., De Laat & Wegerif, 2007). However, I argue that this focus is mostly on how to teach students argumentation rather than on what is the role of argumentation in education per se, as a practice among other practices that might use argumentation. My other related observation is that in traditional education practice, argumentation is taught based on how argumentation is defined and used in other, non-educational, practices.

[3] I use "persuasive speech" as a broad genre function that can be embedded in many specific genres. Thus, Walton (1998) has developed six forms of the normative dialogue in which argumentation plays important role: persuasion, inquiry, negotiation, information seeking, deliberation, and eristic (i.e., personal conflict). Arguably, all these forms of normative dialogues involve persuasive speech as a genre function.

an educational psychologist who teaches graduate students in education. In the educational psychology of learning, currently there can be noticed a conflict between two dominant paradigms (among others): information-processing and sociocultural (Anderson, Reder, & Simon, 1997; Greeno, 1997). As a scholar, I belong to the sociocultural camp: in my scholarly work, I often argue against an information-processing approach to learning. However, as an educator, I feel pedagogical ambivalence about using the full power of my argumentative persuasion in my graduate seminars. I think that it is pedagogically unprofessional for me to set a goal of convincing my less knowledgeable graduate students to become proponents of a sociocultural approach (especially my version of it). In education, the appropriate function of argumentation seems to be more informative rather than persuasive. The issue here is not a possible unprofessional desire on the part of the instructor to brainwash his or her students. Rather, it is the instructor's professional commitment to seriousness about his or her professional position. For example, up to now, I feel that my version of "a sociocultural approach" is the best in psychology and I can skillfully engage in a professional discourse arguing openly minded my position (but also listening carefully arguments from my opponents and ready to change my mind if I find their argument convincing). Burke discussed different ranges of persuasion from manipulative, unilateral to collaborative, mutual. In his view, persuasion "ranges from the bluntest quest of advantage, as in sales promotion or propaganda, through courtship, social etiquette, education, and the sermon, to a 'pure' form that delights in the process of appeal for itself alone, without ulterior purpose" (Burke, 1969, p. 49). My point here is that even when persuasion is an honest, open-minded, and collaborative endeavor (or what Bakhtin (1991) called "internally persuasive discourse"), applied to its full potential strength by the much more knowledgeable instructor, it might unwillingly lead to brainwash of the students.

Thus, I will argue that a graduate student apparently needs to learn an "argumentative map" (see an example of such mapping in Matusov, St. Julien et al., 2005) of ongoing debates in science and learn to participate in it rather than to be convinced (or repelled) by particular arguments presented by the instructor. Bakhtin's (1986) notion of "voice" seems to be more suitable than the traditional notion of "skill" (see, for example, Bransford et al., 1999) in setting educational goals for argumentation (and probably beyond).

In this paper, I focus on the educational function of argumentation as used in dialogic education. I start the chapter with an analysis of the relationship between argumentation and education. I then focus on an analysis of a case of my own use of argumentation in dialogic pedagogy where I guided an undergraduate education-major student working on her final paper arguing why the theory of Intelligent Design has to be taught in public schools together with the theory of Evolution in biology classes.

NON-EDUCATIONAL VIEWS ON ARGUMENTATION

In non-educational practices, argumentation is often seen as a part of persuasive speech to convince self and other of a certain truth either through rhetoric or logic (Billig, 1996). Plato (1997), through Socratic dialogues, introduced an idea of argumentation as a truth-searching process in which new ideas are born[4], developed, and tested in debates. Analyzing the

---

[4] Strictly speaking, Plato argued that through dialogic argumentation truth is recalled from one's memory.

practice of science making, Latour (1987) comes to the conclusion that scientific discourse involves scientists changing modalities of each other's statements by on a continuum of "fact" (i.e., authorless, "objective truth") to "artifact" (i.e., illusion authored by a confused scientist). Finally, based on the literary work of Bakhtin (1986, 1991, 1999), Bialostosky (1986) claims that its dialogism is striving for "responsiveness and responsibility of the consequential person-ideas of a time, culture, community, or discipline – that is, for the fullest articulation of someone's ideas with the actual and possible ideas of others" (p. 789). Through dialogic argumentation, one defines his or her own self and relationship with the world.

Latour (1987) defines good argument is one that persuades relevant others. There are many different views on how a good argument can be achieved: rhetorical structure (attributed to the Sophists in the Socrates-Plato account), formal logic and logical fallacies (Aristotle & Apostle, 1966; Aristotle & Freese, 2000), presumptive judgments (Walton, 1996), and so forth. This list of diverse approaches to assessing the quality of argument can be characterized as "formal" (i.e., focusing on the form of discursive ideas and their relations) because it does not directly consider the content of the argument, its connections to other contexts, and its circumstances (Billig, 1996). Socrates (in Plato's account) introduced the content-based judgment of argument through dialectics, in which a statement is considered in relationship with other statements involving questions and answers, certainty and uncertainty, synthesis and analysis, affirmation and negation, and so on (Vlastos & Burnyeat, 1994). Toulmin (2003) developed his logical model of argumentation, based his abstraction of important discursive skills which he modeled after experts' participation in scientific discursive practices such as reliance on data, claims, warrants, rebuttals, and so on (cf. Graff, 2003). Eemeren & Grootendorst (1992) argue for the discursive nature of argumentation, which always involves at least two opponents, and abstracted ten maxims of "a critical discussion" based on the tradition of Grice's (1975) work on maxims of good communication. Recently, there has been a tendency to consider argumentation as a rhetorical practice within a discourse (rather than simply an independently deployable rhetorical structure) and view judgments of the quality of argument within the discourse in which it is deployed (Billig, 1996, tracts this tendency already in Sophists who were unfairly distorted by Plato in his view; Gagarin, 2001)[5]. Latour (1987), Freire (1986), and Bakhtin (1986) extended the notion of discourse beyond a verbal, purely rhetorical medium, and claim that actions have discursive (and persuasive) aspects as well. Finally, Bakhtin (1999) introduced the notion of "dialogue" in which, probably, for the first time in the history of argumentation studies, agreement is not the goal of argumentation and not a criterion for the truth or its approximation (cf. Latour, 1987) . In Bakhtin's notion of dialogue, a good argument is not necessarily one that wins others over and establishes a new consensus; the ideal argument is one that urgently generates an infinite numbers of responses in its actual and potential audience. According to Bakhtin, if people hold truth they still might and, probably, will disagree.

---

[5] In contrast to Plato's Socrates, Gagarin (2001) claims that Sophists did not focus on persuasion at any cost as the final goal of their argumentation, but on intellectual pleasure of bringing support for an improbable idea or opinion that, although not necessarily persuasive, was witty in front of an intellectual audience. In my view, this non-persuasive goal of argumentation for an intellectual audience does not necessarily prove that Sophists might not have had different discourse focusing on persuasion for different audiences (e.g., juries, political parties, their students, common people). The Sophists' understanding of the limitations of persuasion or even their cynical view of it is not necessarily proof of their non-practice of what later became known as "cynical sophism" – manipulation of the consciousness of the audience to force it to think in a certain way.

Despite the diversity of the listed approaches regarding argumentation in non-educational practices[6], they all seem to agree about social conditions that promote the quality of argumentation such as freedom of speech with its tolerance to disagreement (cf. the famous statement assigned to the French writer Voltaire, "I disapprove of what you say, but I will defend to the death your right to say it," Guterman, 1990; E. B. Hall, 1906)[7]. Good argumentation is also understood to involve personal interest in listening to and caring about others and in arguments themselves (Lipman, 2003; Schultz, 2003) and epistemological equality: equal access to knowledge (i.e., one cannot exploit ignorance of the opponents). Good argumentation does not know hierarchy, authority, or even friendship (as the famous English physicist Sir Isaac Newton said in the heading statement for his famous book entitled *Quaestiones Quaedam Philosophicae*, "Plato is my friend, Aristotle is my friend, but my best friend is truth"). Finally, good argumentation requires open-mindedness which means that it entails freedom of outcome: the outcome of argumentation is unknown beforehand by the participants and defined entirely by the discourse itself; it is not preset in advance. Even though participants might commit to strong opinions about its outcome in advance, they have to leave a possibility for themselves to be surprised and change their mind during the joint argumentation. As we will see below the goals, means, and social conditions of non-educational argumentation contradict conventional education. The reverse is true as well.

PROBLEMS WITH TRADITIONAL EDUCATION IN ARGUMENTATION

Traditional institutionalized education is far from being an ideal place for promoting argumentation, as it described above, because it seems to distort the purposes of argumentation. Unlike in many non-educational argumentative practices, traditional schooling emphasizes learning "the proper" arguments by students in the limited period of institutionalized time[8]. The purpose of argumentation in open minded convincing, persuading, developing, or testing ideas collides with the purpose of traditional schooling in assigning students academic tasks, covering predesigned curriculum in preset limits of institutional time, making students predictable and obedient, and testing students whether or not they expose the "proper" (i.e., the teacher approved) arguments on the teacher's demand. The traditional school seems to intentionally de-ontologize argumentative positions in order that the students can have the bird's eye view on argumentation rather than to commit to any

---

[6] Even Plato's dialogues are non-educational in a sense that their main purpose declared by Plato-Socrates was not teach (which is impossible anyway, from the Plato-Socrates perspective) but to collectively search for the philosophical truth. I argue that it was a practice of philosophy making, not education. Treating Plato's dialogues as educational is rather problematic. My own analysis of the Meno dialogue elsewhere (see Chapter 2) reveals that Plato's dialogues were heavily involve brainwash and exploitation of the participants' ignorance (see also, Rud, 1997).

[7] There are some doubts if Voltaire ever said that. Here is another quote from Voltaire that might be an even better fit to the paper: "Monsieur l'abbé, I detest what you write, but I would give my life to make it possible for you to continue to write." Voltaire in a letter to M. le Riche, February 6, 1770 (http://www.quotationspage.com/ quote/35376.html).

[8] Although more research is need to investigate how comprehensive is my claim, based on reading literature and visiting even innovative schools with emphasis on inquiry and problem-based learning, I hypothesize that the focus on teaching students "proper argumentation" is very widespread in the US institutionalize education (see, A. L. Brown & Palincsar, 1987 as an example of such innovative school).

particular position (unless it is "the correct" one from the teacher's point of view). In traditional schooling, a good argument is one that pleases the teacher who is the final authority for the students' institutional success and well-being; it is, after all, impossible to persuade the teacher of the truth of what he or she is already teaching!

From the perspective of non-educational argumentative practices, the pedagogical regime and institutionalized social relations of traditional schooling violate the social conditions for promoting high quality, fair argumentation. Indeed, the traditional school does not have freedom of speech (and communication in general) – it is usually the traditional teacher who sets and controls the discourse agenda. There is epistemological and dialogic inequality because it is assumed by the participants that the teacher is the number one expert in the classroom and the final arbiter of knowledge. The teacher's voice has more weight than the students' one and cannot be dismissed (or often criticized) even when the teacher's position might not have much sense in eyes of the students. There is no freedom of outcome in classroom argumentation – the outcome of the classroom argumentation is pre-set and pre-known by the traditional teacher (and educational researchers of argumentation, see Nussbaum & Sinatra, 2003, as an example). Finally, there is ontological disengagement in traditional schools in the targeted topics by all the participants (including the teacher and often educational researchers) -- all parties are involved in classroom argumentation not because they personally interested in it. Personal interest is not only accidental in traditional schools but often undesired as it can easily interfere with institutional time and the goal of covering pre-set curricula (Jackson, 1968; Kennedy, 2005; McLaren, 1993; McNeil, 1986; Mehan, 1979; Ogbu, 2003; Tenenbaum, 1940; Waller, 1932).

Arguably, the violations of social conditions for good argumentation by traditional education create possibilities for abuses that give rise to argumentation only in appearance. One well-known abuse in traditional education is the teacher's brainwashing of students, in which the teacher might abuse the students' ignorance to make them think alike. My discourse analysis of the Socratic dialogue Meno (Plato & Bluck, 1961) shows that Socrates often abused his interlocutors' ignorance by presenting them with false choices that make them agree with him (see Chapter 2). Another abuse is epistemological institutional coercion: a student has to pretend to agree while actually disagreeing with the teacher to succeed in the class (Jackson, 1968; Waller, 1932). Finally, the traditional school abuses argumentation by demobilizing the participants' arguments – the arguments become objects of public display and classification in the classroom without personal involvement, passion, and action behind them. Thus, argumentation deteriorates into some kind of an intellectual theatre with a predetermined outcome.

ARGUMENTATION IN EDUCATION

Not only might argumentation has problems with traditional education but also traditional education might have problems with argumentation. As I discussed above, the major goals of argumentation—persuasion and idea development—contradict the goals of traditional education of covering pre-set curriculum, transmission of knowledge, and testing. Billig (1996) and Bakhtin (1999) argued genuine argumentation is a never-ending process which contradicts well-defined institutional time (i.e., a "class period") of the traditional school.

Argumentation demands equality of the participants' consciousnesses to be taken seriously (Bakhtin, 1999) and undermines any authority including the authority of the teacher, the text, the academia, and the institution (Bakhtin, 1984, 1991). It also leads to the erosion of the authoritative "final word" of the teacher, school, or official text and, thus, makes any school testing rather problematic. The traditional teacher might easily lose control and authority in the classroom in the ontological discourse of argumentation. There is a rather reasonable concern on the part of the teachers that in argumentation, the students might learn only their own side of the debate. They can also become too adversarial with each other as a consequence of being too passionately committed to their own ideas and positions. Students might bring only shallow or ungrounded opinions as their arguments. They might not see the educational "final" point of the debate or be confused by diversity of the ideas and positions (i.e., which is the correct one?). Argumentation, often understood in traditional education as an instructional strategy (see Asterhan & Schwarz, 2007, as an example of such approach), is not always the most efficient instructional method in terms of time and effort to convey the point or transmit the correct knowledge. In sum, traditional argumentation seems to be incompatible with traditional education.

For dialogic pedagogy, argumentation is not an optional instructional strategy but rather an important aspect of any human communication (Sidorkin, 1999). When a person authors an idea, position, action, or deed, it implies taking responsibility – being ready to respond to others' questions (challenges) about this authored idea, position, action, or deed. Thus, human positions, ideas, actions, and deeds are argumentative by their nature; they are always a part of actual and potential discourse. In a dialogic approach to pedagogy to teach means to engage the students into socially valuable discourse involving argumentation. If education has to be genuine, from the perspective of dialogic pedagogy, the teacher does not have the option not to engage students in argumentation. Unlike traditional teaching, dialogic teaching does not require and does not value unanimity as the desired outcome of education. The goal of education is not to make the student know the correct point of view but to reply and address historically valuable positions, ideas, actions, and deeds. In this educational process, argumentation still has its function of exploration and development of ideas but not so much the teachers' persuasion or conviction of students, as it is often the case in traditional argumentation outside of education. Below I consider and analyze a case from my undergraduate teacher education class which, I argue, uses dialogical pedagogical argumentation. The case study involves my undergraduate student, a future elementary school teacher, who decided to write her final paper arguing why public school in biology classes have to teach both the pre-modernist theory of Intelligent Design and the theory of evolution. I disagreed with this argument but guided the student using dialogic pedagogical argumentation.

RESEARCH METHOD AND PEDAGOGICAL PROBLEM
OF DIALOGIC PEDAGOGICAL ARGUMENTATION

The data for this study involves my student's work on her final project, my guidance on the project, and her non-anonymous evaluation of the course. The student's name is Sandy (pseudonym). She was a White freshman, coming from a middle-class family, majoring in the elementary teacher education (ETE) program. She took my 16-week course "Cultural Diversity and Teaching," a course required for all ETE preservice teachers. As Sandy revealed in class, she is a very religious Protestant. As a part of one of the course assignments (in the 10th week of the class), Sandy had to interview "a culturally different person." She chose to interview her Catholic boyfriend about his experience in public school as a part of an assignment. One issue that struck her was the issue of the discrepancy in the curriculum of public school and the Catholic religious beliefs of her boyfriend. Sandy herself attended a private religious school and never was exposed to this discrepancy. For her final project in this class, Sandy chose to explore the issue of teaching evolution in public school; in her proposal for the project, she explicitly mentioned this project as continuation of her investigation of the discrepancy between students' potential religious beliefs and the secular curriculum in US public schools.

It was a course requirement to submit a proposal for final project (11th week of the class), a working draft (15th week of the class), and the final draft (16th week of the class). I also encouraged my students to submit extra drafts for my feedback, as many as they felt they needed. Sandy submitted a total of 4 drafts: three mandatory and one non-required[9]. For the other students in her class, the range of the total number of drafts was from 8 to 3. Sandy got 31 points out of 30 points maximum (she got one extra point allowed by the course syllabus) for her final project and A for the entire course. I provided my feedback on her proposal (which I label here as "draft#1"). For working drafts (i.e., drafts#2 and #3), I provided detailed formative assessment and mock summative assessment (i.e., points as if I graded the text as the final draft). She got 14 mock points out of 30 points maximum for her draft#2 and 24 mock points (including one extra credit point) for her draft#3. In class, I explained to the students how to treat my feedback and suggestions for their working drafts of the final project. If they agreed with my concerns, I expected the students to address these concerns either in the way I propose or in some other way. If they disagreed with my concerns and did not want to address them in their paper, they must explain why they disagreed in a special email to me (this process was guided by the peer-review process in professional academic journals). For Sandy's final draft entitled "Intelligent Design vs. Evolution Theory," I provided only summative assessment with my justification of the points.

According to the course guidelines that I developed, the final project involved an essay on a controversial educational issue on cultural diversity broadly defined. The students had to discuss the relevance of the issue for education, its cultural diversity aspect and provide PRO and CON views and their analysis on the issue. They had to find "real voices" arguing the diverse and contradicting views and evidence (and practical cases) supporting and undermining these views. Finally, in conclusion, they had to develop their own opinion and practical recommendations, justify them, and discuss their strong and weak points. There was no page limit. Also, in class, we developed together the grading rubrics by our collective analysis of the quality of final projects from my previous classes. The following is the finalized text of grading rubrics that we collectively developed:

---

[9] It is an open question of how much the fact that Sandy submitted extra one, non-required draft is evidence of her genuine interest in the project versus guided by her anxiety to get A in class. In my judgment, both motives – "doing subject matter" and "doing school" (Furberg & Ludvigsen, 2008) – probably played their role in Sandy's decision to submit one extra draft. It is interesting that in traditional educational settings, in which I work, often "doing subject matter" and "doing school" often contradict each other (Furberg & Ludvigsen, 2008)).

1. Defining the purpose of the FP (i.e., Final Project) that is highly relevant and useful for issues of cultural diversity in education and for educational practitioners (in a broad sense). This will also involve creativity and originality of the FP -- 10 max;
2. Inquiry, problem, research of a complex and controversial issue of cultural diversity in education. Considering diverse alternative positions, providing specific evidence, analyzing values, revealing PROs and CONs in each position, making prioritizations and a summative judgment -- 10 max;
3. Presentation, clarity, articulation, visualization of examples – 10 max.

We also agreed that, as the instructor, I should have discretion to give 3 extra credit points maximum based solely on my judgment of the extraordinary quality of their work. Thus, I gave Sandy one extra point for her very interesting reply to my concern by redefining the issue (I will discuss it later).

Sandy's initial participation in class discussion was very quiet. She listened tentatively to the class discussions but did not volunteer much with a question or a comment. The class had 36 students and met twice a week for 75 minutes. After a few weeks I managed to engage all the students in my class using a participatory strategy described by Shor (1987). As in his example, my students and I discussed the issue of participation in class discussion and we agreed that I could call out a student but the student had a right to excuse him or herself from a reply without giving me any explanation (by simply saying, "pass"). Like in the case described by Shor, this participatory regime provided enough opportunities and comfort for all students (even the shiest ones) to participate in the oral public discussions (a skill that, I believe, is very important for future teachers – the topic that we also discussed in class). Besides, all students were required to participate in class web discussions. By the second part of the semester, Sandy felt comfortable to volunteer with questions and comments.

Sandy's contributions in oral and web class discussions of educational issues like teaching children of illegal immigrants, teaching about sexuality, addressing homophobia in school, and so on were often guided by her religious beliefs. It presented an interesting pedagogical challenge for me, as her instructor. First, I am religiously indifferent. This means that I see that theological issues are irrelevant for my life and my worldview. However, I read many religious texts in past and consider myself moderately educated in religious issues[10]. Second, in the US there is a legal separation of the Church and the State. It was rather obvious

---

[10] I grew up in the Soviet Union that promoted a state atheism. Religion was suppressed and marginalized by the state and school atheist propaganda. Some religious beliefs and practices were criminalized. Open participation in religion could be persecuted by firing from job – often only pensioners could afford to be openly religious. Although, majority of people surrounded me were non-religious, in my observation of the self and other and interviews with my friends, time-to-time people were engaged in what can be called "proto-religiosity." Specifically, people around me (and myself) were involved in three types of action of proto-religiosity: 1) attributing animation to inanimate objects (e.g., "punishing" his or her own skis when one felt down by deliberate and systematic hitting the skis), 2) using magic actions to cause a desired outcome (e.g., having "lucky" dress for school tests), 3) using pray-request by addressing some supernatural authority to cause a desired outcome. In my judgment, this proto-religiosity helped people manage their frustration – their fear, despair, hope, uncertainty, and so on, -- and put their life under control in a particular stressful circumstance. The proto-religiosity was not based on any sustained belief or faith – if any belief was involved, it was temporary and situational, -- it was more like temporary suspension of reason (cf. Dawkins, 2006). After the stressful situation was passed, the proto-religious actions were often felt embarrassing, ridiculous, and private by the actor, which was not precluded him or her to use them again in a new stressful situation.
As a young adult, I secretly experimented with participation in the Buddhism and the Russian Orthodox Church.

to me, from her statements in class and in her first drafts, that Sandy was not fully aware of it. All these presented both challenges and exciting educational opportunities for me, as an educator. My class was about cultural diversity issues in education and Sandy's and my differences (as well Sandy and some of her classmates' differences) represented cultural differences for sure. Thus, I had an opportunity to not only teach about cultural diversity but also practice it in my own class in this regard. Our deep disagreement running through our value systems created opportunities for a deep dialogue about "final damned questions" (Bakhtin, 1999). The culmination of this challenge-opportunity was Sandy's final project, in which she argued for equal representation of the theory of evolution and the theory of Intelligent Design during biology classes.

The class was taught in fall 2006, almost a year after the historical legal ruling in Dover, Pennsylvania (our neighboring state) about whether or not the theory of Intelligent Design could be taught as an alternative biological theory to the theory of evolution in Dover public schools in biology lessons. The majority of Dover biology teachers refused to teach it anyway about the theory of Intelligent Design as a scientific alternative to the theory of evolution despite the Dover School Board's decision to do so. The conservative Federal judge appointed by the Republican administration ruled that teaching the theory of Intelligent Design as an alternative biological theory in a public school contradicts the Constitutional separation of Church and State because, as the judge concluded from the hearings, the theory of Intelligent Design is unscientific and religious in its nature (http://www.msnbc.msn.com/id/10545387/). Although, as it became clear later, Sandy did not know about the case and the court hearings, she had heard about the theory of Intelligent Design and considered it as a legitimate alternative to the theory of evolution that students, especially religious ones, have to be exposed to in school. She argued that all students had to be given the choice of what to believe: the theory of evolution or the theory of Intelligent Design.

This presents an important teaching dilemma for me as Sandy's instructor: what does it mean to educate a religious student about science education (in the context of public schooling and beyond) and about cultural diversity? Should I convince Sandy that she is wrong? Should I impose the professional consensus, achieved in the professional education community, on her? Should I simply inform her about legal and historical facts?

I chose dialogic pedagogy (Bakhtin, 2004; Matusov, 2004; Matusov, Smith et al., 2007; Matusov, St. Julien et al., 2005; Shor, 1987; Sidorkin, 1999) as my guiding principle of how to guide Sandy (and my other students). According to this pedagogical approach, my educational goal is to engage (i.e., socialize) Sandy in professional dialogue and discourse about professional issues and help her develop her own professional voice within this professional dialogue. Sandy had to learn how to become "at home" in a professional educational community. For that, Sandy had to learn how to reply to legal and historical facts, positions, theories, and other professional voices through her own system of values, interests, concerns, needs, and strengths and to learn how to be addressed from this professional discourse. This process might or might not produce changes in Sandy's own system of values (it probably always does but the issue of what changes are brought about and how vast and deep these changes are remains uncertain and open). What kind of stance she will take within this professional discourse is up to her – she would have to take responsibility for her own stance. Her position in professional discourse might ultimately lead her away from teaching in public schools altogether or from teaching in general or it might lead her to rethink her relationship with religion or to join other religious organizations to press the current legal system to change, and so forth. In other words, she would not be naïve or ignorant for whatever position she would take as a professional educator.

This means that as her teacher, I must not try to impose my or a professional group's views on issues even if I believe that these views are correct. Unlike some popular beliefs among educators (see, for example of such beliefs, Labaree, 2003, p. 17), it is not the goal of education to mold students' minds. I must not use my institutional power (i.e., I have more institutional power over Sandy than she over me) and epistemological superiority (i.e., I know more about education than Sandy) to impose or even convince Sandy to conform to "the correct views" even though these views might be accepted as correct by the professional educational community (the fact that she should know, although). A student can be educated even if she or he does not subscribe the latest truths established in the society.

The issue here is not about disturbing the comfort of religious students (cf. Saperstein, 2007) – I think that authentic education often involves frustration and discomfort for students. In my view, for example, it is not the teacher's role to help a religious student reconcile the conflict between science and religion as Saperstein seems to suggest but rather to help him or her to consider and engage into the conflict from diverse positions and their consequences. It is up to the student to resolve this conflict one way or another or not to resolve it at all. Thus, a student's discomfort is a necessary byproduct of good education, if not a direct educational goal for the teacher. In my view, the teacher's concern about students' comfort might kill opportunities for authentic education.

Dialogic teachers do not want to impose knowledge on the students as a consequence of several related concerns. First, they are concerned with education of the agency of the student that is going to make autonomous decisions and judgments as a member of a professional community. The imposition of knowledge undermines the growth of the agency of the student. Second, imposed knowledge that is not tested by the most powerful alternative ideas existing in a communal discourse by the student is not authentic knowledge. Third, the student cannot take responsibility and be fully responsible for imposed knowledge. I argue that this is true for dialogic education not only in teaching controversial issues like Intelligent Design but also teaching 2+2=4. In dialogic education, knowledge is always viewed *dialogically* -- i.e., as being problematic (Berlyand, 2009, in press).

The role of pedagogical argumentation becomes crucial for the dialogic approach. My educational goal is not to convince Sandy in certain truth but to engage her in "internally persuasive discourse" (Bakhtin, 1991) in which any truth can be tested and be forever testable (Morson, 2004) by the participants (i.e., Sandy). Testability of the truth in the discourse is more important than the participants becoming convinced by certain statements. I argue that unlike, in many other, non-educational, practices like science, law, philosophy, and politics, the role of pedagogical argumentation in dialogic pedagogy is not to convince (internally or authoritatively) but to foster the ability to engage in a professional dialogue.

My main research question was to find evidence of the growth of the students' professional voice in response to my guidance and her involvement in internally persuasive discourse with me (and through me with "relevant others"). My alternative hypothesis was that the student simply tried to please me, as her teacher. My secondary questions were focused on the design and regime promoting dialogical pedagogical argumentation. My analysis of pedagogical argumentation focused on four major aspects. First, what were the specific pedagogical goals of the instructor's argumentation that guided him in the process? Second, what were the instructional means for achieving dialogical pedagogical argumentation? Third, what was the definition of a successful pedagogical argumentation in dialogic pedagogy? And, finally, what were the social conditions (i.e., pedagogical regime) that promoted pedagogical argumentation in dialogic pedagogy? To address these questions I used discourse analysis (Gee, 1996) and specifically NVIVO qualitative data analysis software to extract and abstract themes answering these questions.

FINDINGS

Specific Pedagogical Goals Promoting Pedagogical Argumentation

It is very important for dialogic pedagogy that pedagogical argumentation involve a historically important issue that is highly relevant for the professional community in which the student is going to be socialized through participation in the argumentation. When Sandy (and the other students) submitted their proposals for their final projects, I, as their instructor, had to make a judgment about how appropriate the topics they chose were for my class. There were many aspects of this issue: relevance to the course, manageability (i.e., can the student handle the issue, whether there are enough sources), and so on. One of the important aspects of this decision is how the proposed issue is historically important, relevant, and acute for the modern professional community. For example, the issue of whether a female teacher can get married without being fired was important in past (Waller, 1932) but not now. Future teachers might need to know this history but should not engage in arguing about it because it is now professionally moot. As to the issue of Intelligent Design, Creationism, and Evolution, this is one of the hottest issues for my undergraduate ETE students who predominately come from suburbs of the Northeastern States. In fact, in one of my previous classes of ETE sophomores, the majority of my students actually claim that this is the issue of which they were willing to sabotage the Federal law (and the US Constitution) and risk their career (they actually claimed that many of their teachers in public schools in the past taught Creationism in public schools – this important claim deserves a future empirical investigation). There is some anecdotal evidence that religious students are more willing to push this issue in colleges than before (Saperstein, 2007). Despite the recent court decision rejecting the Dover School Board's decision to teach Intelligent Design in biology classes as a legitimate scientific biological theory alternative to the theory of evolution, the tension in the professional community and in the general public remains very high in the US as it is evident in numerous professional publications on this topic (e.g., Ayala, 2006; Beckwith, 2003; Brockman, 2006; Chapman, 2007; Comfort, 2007; Forrest, Gross, & NetLibrary Inc., 2004; Koppel et al., 2006; Numbers, 2006; Petto & Godfrey, 2007; Porter, 2006; Scott & Branch, 2006; Shanks, 2004; Shermer, 2006; Woodward, 2006; M. Young & Edis, 2004). In sum, Sandy proposed an educational issue for her final project that is historically and acutely important for the professional community and US society.

Pedagogical dialogic argumentation requires students' ontological engagement in the issue (Sidorkin, 1999). The students' important reason for argumentation in dialogic pedagogy has to be their interest in the issue and not only the desire to get a good grade and please the teacher. What was the evidence that Sandy's main reason for her engagement was her genuine interest in the issue of teaching the theory of evolution and Intelligent Design in public schools? She wrote in her assignment about interviewing a culturally different person (her Catholic boyfriend),

> Prior to this [assignment] I thought that religion made no difference in [public] schools. It never occurred to me that introducing kids to new concepts takes away a part of their beliefs. By telling a child that in school they have to do away with what they believe in and learn a new concept because it does not involve religion is wrong. It tells a child that their beliefs are wrong and they need to learn the "right" ideas. It changes my view of how [public] schools should be run. I understand that they do not want religion to be a part of [public] schools, but by doing that they are confusing children with what is right and wrong about their religious beliefs.

It is apparent that as a very religious person, she was perplexed about how she as a public school teacher should conduct herself on issues contradicting her religion. She wrote in her proposal for the Final Project,

> The purpose of my final project will be to explore the teachings in the classroom versus the teachings of religion. ... I will research on the controversy of teaching the 'Evolution Theory' in sciences. Many people disagree with this approach because it goes against their religion, but it is still taught. [Since religion is a very important part of my life,] I really do not agree with the approach but I can see the reason why they teach it. That is why when I research the topic I will probably choose the side that is for this teaching method. [T]his project will help me with the confrontations that I will face during my years as a teacher [and as a person].

This shows that the topic selected by Sandy for her Final Project was very important for her. Of course, I cannot argue that the main reason she made the project was her personal concerns and inquiries about the relationship between religion and public school and that her concerns about grades and complying to institutional requirements did not matter for her. Although, it was doubtful that Sandy would work on the project without it being an assignment for the class, the quotes provide evidence that the project topic had an ontological character for Sandy as she tried to reconcile her own religiosity and professional demands of becoming a teacher for a public school.

My analysis of my own guidance of Sandy's argumentation shows that it was guided by my interest in Sandy's worldviews. The questions I raised and responses I shared with Sandy about her text were genuine – seeking information about how she was thinking about the issues, -- and not rhetorical information known questions (like in traditional school, teacher's information-known questions: "2+2 equals what?") common in many conventional classrooms. I tried to treat her as my colleague educator – with the same professional seriousness. I wanted to know better how she thought about the issues that prompted me to ask her questions of clarification (blue fonts, cross-outs, and yellow highlighting are mine):

> [Draft#2] There is no true side that is better than the other; it is basically a matter of opinion and beliefs. However if I were to pick a side, it would be to teach Intelligent Design .

Although, I raised an issue of value here, "better for what?", at the time Sandy seemed not to be capable of dealing with this issue. Instead of addressing what does it mean that there is no true side (which probably means that that one side is correct in one situation and the other is in another), she elaborated on the disagreement between the two sides taking a relativist position in her next draft (#3),

> *[Draft#3]* I think that there is no true side that is better, in terms of believing in the creation of Earth and creatures and which theory is truly right, than the other; it is basically a matter of opinion and beliefs. However, these beliefs are limited in public educationbecause only the Evolution Theory is permitted to be taught.
>
> *[Draft#4, final]* I think there is no true side that is better than the other, in terms of believing in the creation of Earth and creatures and which theory is truly right; it is basically a matter of opinion and beliefs. Both sides have good arguments for their viewpoints but only certain theories should be used at certain times. For instance,... Evolution is good for the doctor's office or any medical facilities because the most advanced medical treatments are needed. However Intelligent Design is better in the Church because that is the best place to talk about God and other forms of intelligent forces. So different theories are best in the sense of the context in which they are used. However, these theories are limited in public education because only the Evolution Theory is permitted to be taught.

Sandy apparently liked my suggestions of what her statement "there is no true side" might mean (or she could not find a better one at the moment). As we will see later, Sandy did not automatically accept my suggestions. I learned that at least at the moment, Sandy felt comfortable with pragmatic contextual justifications that each opposing side could provide. She seemed to reject the other, non-pragmatic, explanation that I provided in her final draft (#4). What is important from the point of view of dialogic pedagogical argumentation is NOT that Sandy accepted and elaborated on my suggestion but rather that she addressed new questions about what it means that "there is no true side" and what it means to say "better" (i.e., better for what). Arguably, these were new questions for her that she had to deal with while for me these two questions came out of my genuine interest in how Sandy thought about the issue. If she had addressed my questions in some other ways, through an alternative position or even disagreement with me, I still would have been happy as her instructor. Only if she had ignored my questions, I would have probably felt pedagogically dissatisfied and would ask her why she was ignoring the questions (e.g., not feeling their important and relevance, not knowing how to address them). My asking Sandy these questions helped me and her better understand what and how she thinks about the educational issue at hand[11].

Dialogic pedagogical argumentation involves not only engaging the student into deep critical reasoning (e.g., "better for what?") but also brings them into the space of historical

---

[11] Of course, an alternative explanation is that Sandy simply did what I WANTED her to do and extend a bit (in yellow). It could be out of a strategy of "this is what my crazy professor wants me to do so that's what he's gonna get it". In other words, she just wanted to please me to get a good grade. This is definitely possible but it contradicts other cases in our work, in which Sandy did not comply with my requests. I cannot rule out that the pleasing goal in Sandy's work on her drafts did not cross her mind. It is probably combination of the goals that guided her work.

facts and evidence. This guidance occurs also through raising interested, information seeking, questions by the instructor,

> *[Draft#2]* The creation of mankind is a debate that has been continued throughout history. There are two basic beliefs, actually more than 2 to how man was created.
>
> *[Draft#3]* The creation of mankind is a debate that has been continued throughout history. There are different beliefs to how man was created, but the three focused on with public education are Creationism, Intelligent Design and the Evolutionary Theory.

Although Sandy rejected my lead about the Pope's criticism of the theory of Intelligent Design in her Draft#3, she addressed my concern that there are more than 2 approaches to the origin of the humankind by focusing on the modern educational controversy in the US as the opposition between the theories of Intelligent Design and Evolution. I did not insist on her discussion of Pope's position involving Creationism because it was not exactly an educational issue. Sandy's redefinition of the topic of her discussion at hand in Draft#3 (not just about the origin of humankind, as she stated in Draft#2, but rather on educational aspect of this issue, as she stated in Draft#3), indirectly addressed my concern without following my lead. However, as the judge in the Dover case, I personally suspected that there is Creationism behind the theory of Intelligent Design and I was interested in how Sandy thought about this issue, so I raised it.

> *[Draft#4, final]* The creation of mankind is a debate that has been continued throughout history. There are different beliefs to how man was created, but the two focused on with public education is Intelligent Design and the Evolutionary Theory. There are those who believe in Intelligent Design, which is the theory that an intelligent force had a role to play in the creation of the universe. This theory is somewhat similar to Creationism, the older arguments that surrounded public education, which says that that God created man. The difference is Intelligent Design believers do not necessarily believe God created man, just that an intelligent force was responsible for his coming (Daniel Engber, http://www.slate.com/id/2118388).

Sandy addressed my inquiry about Creationism by separating it from the theory of Intelligent Design (in her Draft#2 she mixed history of Creationism and Intelligence Design). She investigated this issue on the Internet and brought a citation as I did in case of my example of Pope in my feedback on her Draft#2. Please notice that she used the web citation in Draft#4 without my request to do so. Sandy did not use any web citation in Draft#1 and #2. I used 8 web citations in my feedback to her Draft#2. She used 4 web citations in her Draft#3. I used 1 web citation in my feedback to her Draft#3. And, finally in Draft#4, she used 12 web citations of which only four were ones that I showed to her. Again, this raises an important question of how much Sandy replied to the institutional pressure of the expected "A paper" versus her genuine socialization in professional educational discourse requiring the participants to reveal the source of the facts used.

There is evidence that as Sandy worked on her Final Project, she started questioning her sources of information as I questioned her about her text. While working on poll statistics provided on the Internet, Sandy noticed that the numbers were different depending on the questions asked. She criticized some of the polls that supported her views, "It is hard to get the whole spectrum and distribution of views, as a general population, of where people stand: do they want only Evolution taught, do they want Intelligent Design to be included in the curriculums, or do they think both should be allowed in the school classroom? There are so many polls out there that purposely manipulate the voting outcome to favor their side. For instance the way a question is worded or the different groups they may ask the questions to (for example asking atheists about teaching Intelligent Design). However I did find some polls done by televisions stations and weekly magazines...." (Draft#4).

The student's voice become "more real" as it becomes positioned in relationship with the voices of other people. One of the goals of the instructor guided by dialogic pedagogy is to provide the students with access to diverse voices to allow the students to reply to them. As I showed above, Sandy implicitly disagreed with the Pope's criticism (that I introduced to her) of the theory of Intelligent Design exactly because she agreed with him about the opposition between the theory of Intelligent Design (which is a scientific theory for Sandy) and Creationism (which is apparently a religious dogma for Sandy). This arguably deepened Sandy's position and made it more nuanced. In my feedback below, I introduced Sandy to "militant atheism" (i.e., one that actively rejects the idea of God) and "indifferent atheism" (i.e., one that does not care about religion, seeing it as an irrelevant issue) (Snyder, 1985). It is interesting that Sandy addresses militant atheism but rejects indifferent atheism,

> *[Draft#2]* The big issue with this is whether the Evolution Theory or Intelligent Design, or both, should be taught in our schools. Those who agree with Evolution being taught feel that it is not a threat to religion; it is just simply a theory.

> *[Draft#3]* The big issue with this is whether the Evolution Theory should be taught, Intelligent Design should be taught or both taught in our public schools. Some who agree with Evolution being taught feel that it is not a threat to religion; it is just simply a scientific theory. Others, such as atheists, believe it is an argument against religion to prove the non-existence of God.

> *[Draft#4, final]* The big issue with this is whether Evolution Theory should be taught in our public schools, Intelligent Design, or both. Some who agree with Evolution being taught feel that it is not a threat to religion; it is just simply a scientific theory. Others, such as atheists, believe it is an argument against religion to prove the non-existence of God. It is a scientific theory with evidence and proof of man's creation through evolution.... Basically, this theory[12] goes against what the Christian church has said all along which is God created this planet and all forms on it....

---

[12] It is interesting that out of all the voices opposite to her own, -- the proponents of the theory of evolution: tolerant to religion (Draft#2), intolerant to religion (Draft#3) and indifferent to religion (Draft#4) -- it is apparently indifferent atheists who pushed Sandy to declare that the scientific theory of evolution is in violation with "the Christian church" dogma. In her final draft (Draft#4), she did not incorporate indifferent atheists as she did militant atheists in Draft#3 but rather addressed them through strong religious condemnation. I suspect that tolerant and militant evolutionists are a lesser threat for religion because they are in a relationship with religion (positive or negative), while indifferent atheists are out of the relationship with religion entirely. Unfortunately, our potentially never-ending dialogue stopped there, at the final draft, and I could not pursue this interesting discussion thread with Sandy.

Dialogic pedagogical argumentation involves reorientation of the student from a non-professional discourse to a professional discourse. For example, Sandy started her drafts with raising the question of which of the theories is correct – this question is not educational at its face value,

> *[Draft#2]* So which side is right and which is wrong? That is the question that educators must face and develop a solution. This is not a question that drives controversy in PUBLIC education. The issue is that state and public education is separated from religion. According to the law rooted in the US constitution, public school cannot promote religion. The controversy about teaching ID (not so much evolution) is about whether it is scientific or a purely religious theory. If it is a scientific theory, it can be taught in public schools, if not, then not (according to the law and Constitution). Please redirect your essay on an EDUCATIONAL issue.
>
> *[Draft#3]* So is it wrong to only teach evolution as the creation of this universe? That is the question that educators must face and develop a solution.
>
> *[Draft#4, final]* The big issue with this is whether Evolution Theory should be taught in our public schools, Intelligent Design, or both. ... So is it wrong to only teach evolution as the creation of this universe? That is the question that educators must face and develop a solution.... In the 1948 case of McCollum v. Board of Education an atheist mother complained that the school her child went to, a school that taught religious classes during that day and non-religious classes (which were classes not actually given any regular academic instruction because this would have put them ahead of their religious counterparts) violated the separation of church and state and, specifically, the Establishment Clause of the First Amendment of the US Constitution.

Sandy assumes her professional voices through redefining her personal-professional dilemma. She wants to teach well in public schools and apparently to remain a good Protestant Christian as defined in her local religious community. Initially, as she expresses herself in the interview assignment, she feels that is unfair for religious students that school goes against religious teachings. She also seems to feel that it is unfair that she, as a public school teacher, cannot bring her religious beliefs and who she is as a religious person into a public school classroom. Sandy's initial solution was to teach both theories "because I felt that it gives a sense of equality to those who are very religious and to those who strongly believe in the scientific evidence... I think this is the perfect balance and will make people most happy" (Draft#2). After reading my feedback on Draft#2 in which I directed her to reading from proponents of the Evolution only approach she concluded that, "I can find no consensus that could fix the problem because no one would be happy either way" (Draft#3). She abandoned the idea of finding a solution that pleases everybody and instead focused on how she would like to teach both theories. She however concluded that "Even though teaching both Intelligent Design and Evolution Theory could be the best compromise to the controversy it could never work. All the laws requiring religion to stay outside the classroom makes it hard to be able to teach both sides. So there is no perfect solution to this problem. Therefore this debate will continue to occur until both sides have equal satisfaction" (Draft#3). Her final draft deepened the discussion of why the consensus is currently impossible and why more discussion is needed for both sides. Thus, she started with certainty of her solution of "balanced teaching" and came to a conclusion that public and professional conversation on the issue has to be deepened. It was clear from Sandy's later drafts that through the exploration of the issue, she better understood the legal and professional ramifications of her position which will inform her future decision making about her teaching of evolution in public schools and taking responsibility for it. She might decide not teach in public school, she might renegotiate boundaries between her teaching profession and her religion, she might become a political activist in changing laws, she might decide to sabotage the US Constitution and smuggle teaching of Intelligent Design as a legitimate alternative to the theory of evolution into her teaching, and so on. Whatever she decides to do, she is not naïve and professionally ignorant after doing this project.

Genuine dialogue involves learning on both sides. In my argumentative work with Sandy as her teacher, I have learned not only about Sandy's position, about religious community, and about teaching religious students about science and education, but I also learned more about teaching evolution in school. In my feedback on Sandy's Draft#3, I shared my solution of the dilemma she raised, "(My problem with your solution is that ID and Creationism are not scientific theories and should not be taught as such in biology lessons but I agree with you that students have to be informed about [these] historical debates in our society involving religion. Sandy, if you want to hear my opinion on this interesting issue, I think that the Evolution Theory has to be taught in biology lessons as the only scientific theory so far but Intelligent Design and Creationism have to be taught about in Social Studies class to inform students about great historical debates in our society. What do you think?). Again, your discussion is very-very good!" (Instructor's feedback on Draft#3). She replied to me that it would not work for her because "I feel that the best solution, in my view, would to be to try and teach both the Evolution Theory and Intelligent Design. This way students get to see both sides and pick which they agree with, not what they must agree with at school and at home" (Draft#4). Sandy's reply made me rethink my position. Considering carefully Sandy's latest argument, I wonder if I were a biology teacher I might discuss arguments put forward by proponents of the theory of Intelligent Design challenging the theory of Evolution. For example, some proponents of Intelligent Design (and Creationists before them) raised an issue about impossibility of the evolutionary origin of woodpeckers. In their views, woodpeckers could not evolve because the first proto-woodpeckers who started hit their head against wood would have had concussion and, consequently, their brain would be damaged before they would have been able to evolve to develop protective beaks and scalps (Heinze, 2002; Sunderland, 1976). I think that consideration of an evolutionist reply to this challenge (e.g., Ryan, 2003) can promote better understanding of evolutionary principles in school students than learning these principles outside of this and similar debates. Scientific theories emerge and can be understood in discourse of consideration of and debate with alternatives. Within this debate of testing ideas, some of the debated ideas become scientific and some become non-scientific. Science has emerged in opposition and in debates with religion (Galilei & Drake, 2001) and the modern debate between science and religion might help school students better understand science practice. Although I might still be in disagreement with Sandy (unfortunately, I did not have an opportunity to share my new educational views with her as the semester was over – however, ontologically, but not necessarily epistemologically, all debates and discourses have their end for their participants as they have to attend to other demands and interests in their lives and because they are mortal), my argumentation with her helped me to develop different professional views.

Educational Means Promoting Dialogic Pedagogical Argumentation

Here I want to reflect on educational means that promote dialogic pedagogical argumentation based on my work with Sandy. Through analysis of Sandy's various working drafts and my feedback on them, I have noticed that I tried and succeed in shifting Sandy's attention from *advocacy* of her certain position that she articulated in the Drafts#1 and #2 to *problematization and exploration* of the involved issues and uncertainties. Sandy started with an argument advocating her solution of teaching both theories – Intelligent Design and Evolution – can be a good compromise for "both sides" but finished up with an argument exploring the complexity of the issue calling for more discussions for not only the public and professionals but also for Sandy herself. However, although this outcome of dialogic pedagogical argumentation is very interesting and important, it was not my pedagogical goal. I would have been pedagogically satisfied even if Sandy had been stuck with her advocacy argumentation through all her drafts. My pedagogical goal was not to undermine her arguments or her confidence in her advocacy but rather to ask her to reply and address diverse voices that are historically important for the debate (i.e., the Pope, militant and indifferent atheists, the US Constitution, Dover biology teachers who refused to teach the theory of Intelligent Design, diverse religious communities, my own position). Some of these positions represented real people and communities, but some were imagined (like PROs and CONs for some real positions or imaginary alternative positions). I did not start from scratch because Sandy herself tried to address certain voices and positions (e.g., proponents of evolution who are tolerant of religion) – some of whom were her "straw men" positions as Sandy learned through studying these voices on the Internet. I saw the purpose of my guidance and Sandy's education in this project as her dialogic positioning to voices of others that led her to engage in the historical and professional discourse on the issue of her interest. How Sandy has chosen to address and reply to these positions and voices is ultimately Sandy's responsibility – her personal and professional voice develops in this process of taking responsibility for her position in dialogic relations with others in this discourse (cf. Bakhtin et al., 1993). I might disagree with Sandy's final draft position on the issue of teaching the theory of Intelligent Design in public schools but her final position was relatively well informed.

As I showed above with examples of her drafts and my feedback to them, I had many pedagogical means of engaging Sandy in dialogical argumentation. The main means, in my view, was to ask her to address and reply to diverse and important voices relevant for the issue. The diverse voices and their positions sparked disagreement and provoked Sandy to consider alternatives and problems with her own ideas. These voices often generated conflicting concerns and values behind them for Sandy (for example, see above my introduction of the voices of militant and indifferent atheists for Sandy). I also asked Sandy to reply to alternative and challenging ideas that might not have real voices behind them (at least I did not find and present these voices to Sandy),

So it seems people who are for teaching Evolution only believe that, no matter what else is taught, it should always be apart of the curriculum. Also a majority (60-70%) agree that Evolution and Intelligent Design should be taught together in schools. However most still believe that Evolution should be the number one idea taught in science class and that Intelligent Design alone does not seem to be acceptable by majority of general public. (Draft#4, final).

Another pedagogical means was to focus Sandy on the modality of her statements. Latour (1987) defines modality of statements as the continuum between the authorless objective fact (i.e., the highest modality) and the illusionist artifact fabricated by somebody (i.e., the lowest modality). In my view, Sandy initially had a tendency to use unwarranted high modality (and thus high-level certainty) in her statements and I asked her to provide clarification of them. In her earlier drafts, Sandy used statements without author and subject that objectified her own beliefs and hid their arbitrary nature (and possibilities for alternatives). As some of my past students have told me, they got this style from school instruction demanding that they should avoid pronoun "I" from their writing,

[Draft#3] I think that there is no true side that is better...
[Draft#4, final] I think there is no true side that is better than the other...

Sandy was very responsive to my guidance about lowering the modality of her unwarranted statements which often led Sandy to explore of her own ideas and consequently to deepening them as she tried to consider, address and reply to the alternative ideas, concerns, and counter-arguments.

Sandy's growing dialogic positioning to the voices and concerns by others affected her planning for actions. In her Draft#2, she developed a lesson plan of how she would teach the theories of Evolution and Intelligent Design in a public school in a "balanced way." By her Draft#4, not only did she learn that her lesson plan was illegal to use in US public schools but also it was questionable for Sandy herself as she could not find a satisfactory solution any more in the face of her own growing concerns about teaching the theory of Intelligent Design and the impossibility of finding any compromise and consensus in a US public that disagreed about religious matters.

Social Conditions for Dialogic Pedagogical Argumentation

Let me turn to a consideration of the social conditions that promote dialogic pedagogical argumentation. First, there is an issue about Sandy's participation in dialogic pedagogical argumentation. She was definitely obligated to participate but, on the other hand, her engagement had an apparently ontological character. It is doubtful that Sandy would have initiated the same project outside of the class completely on her own at that time. Please notice that Sandy chose not to rely on my questions on her final draft because the class was over. But it is not to be doubted that she was personally engaged, committed, and deeply interested in this project. I call this participatory structure "obligated participation in ontological dialogue." Thus, imposition and forced participation can support students' ontological engagement but, by itself, probably is not enough to promote it. Ontological engagement can be furthered by providing students with choices (i.e., the students' choice of topic for the final project) and "throwing them into ontological provocations" (for Sandy such ontological provocation was the assignment to interview a "culturally other" – her Catholic boyfriend, for the other students in the class it was other class assignments, class oral and web discussions, videos that I showed in class, class readings, their out of the class experiences, and so on). The issue of student's ontological engagement and obligated participation requires further investigation in the design of a dialogic classroom.

The second condition promoting the student's engagement into dialogic pedagogical argumentation is the instructor's goal of focusing on providing the student with access to historical and professional discourse on the issue of the student's interest. In this approach, evidence of learning is not found in how well the student can reply to the teacher's demand (e.g., a test or exam) but the student's participation in the historical and professional discourse: her addressing and replying to the most important and relevant voices, positions, concerns, and values which lead to her taking responsibility for her professional (and overall human) actions in an informed way (which still can be socially or even morally wrong but this wrongness is informed and not resulted from the student's ignorance). Thus, the educational dialogic goal here is to develop the student's own professional voice rather than to replicate the teacher's view or the current consensus in a professional community. The dialogic learning outcome is defined by the discourse. It is future-oriented, not preset, and unpredictable (as the change in my professional position about teaching about ID in a biology class as a result of Sandy's guidance was unpredictable for me, the instructor, too).

Third, the teacher's feedback on the student's work and guidance has a dialogic character. The teacher genuinely wants to learn more about the student's worldview and responsibility with regard to the issue by asking questions about alternatives, responding to other voices and positions (including the teacher's own positions), justifications of the student's own views, and so on. Through this dialogic process, the teacher brings the student into contact with historically and professionally important discourse as one of its active and de facto legitimate participants.

Finally, the dialogic pedagogical regime is aimed at using the teacher's institutional and epistemological authority to kill it only for it to reemerge as trust and respect. Although work on the project was started using the institutional and epistemological authority of the teacher as recognized by the student, in the dialogic process of Sandy's working on the project her consciousness had equal rights with the consciousness (Bakhtin, 1999) of her teacher to consider the issue, address and reply to the diverse voices, positions, and concerns, and to make the final judgment[13]. The student could and did challenge the instructor (e.g., see above the examples of Sandy's not following my position about teaching about ID only in social studies class and of her disagreeing with me) and did not accept his ideas or suggestions on the face value. The teacher and the student provided each other dialogical opposition (i.e., the resistance of the material) which is the key for any deep understanding (Bakhtin, 1986). However, she apparently trusted and respected my suggestions and feedback as worth considering (beyond the threat of getting a lower final grade). Sandy apparently appreciated the guidance as she wrote in the feedback on the class, "I have learned many things in this class that have opened up my eyes to teaching. I never realized all the conflicts that can occur in the classroom, let alone even have a clue how to handle them. With this class, I have learned ways to handle the problems." However, from this feedback it is unclear whether Sandy appreciated or had become aware of the dialogic nature of the experienced guidance. In this case, dialogic pedagogical argumentation did not become polyphonic pedagogical

---

[13] The equal rights of the instructor's and the student's consciousnesses were severely curtailed by the institutional practices of the summative assessment, namely, the final grading made by the instructor. Even though, the students knew that the final grading was not based on their agreement with the instructor and the grading criteria were developed collectively, the grading practice made the teacher's consciousness privileged. In my class, the final grading practice (i.e., summative assessment) was the biggest compromise for the education in general and argumentation in specific.

argumentation in which the participants appreciate and value the dialogue (see Morson & Emerson, 1990, for discussion Bakhtin's notion of polyphony).

CONCLUSION

I argue here that the main goal of dialogic pedagogical argumentation is for the teacher to help a student develop his or her own professional *voice* through engaging the student in an internally persuasive professional discourse. Persuasion, development, and testing ideas – traditional goals of argumentation -- are important but subordinated parts of this process. Dialogic guidance involves the teacher bringing the student in a zone of dialogic contact with historically important and relevant voices of the professional discourse, promoting the student to address and reply to these voices and to take responsibility for the student's emerging positions in the face of this professional (and a broader) community. This goal contrasts with one stated by Wells (1999) who argued that the goal of education is to socialize students to *appropriate* a specialized discourse (cf. students' learning "science talk" described in Lemke, 1990). I argue that a teacher, who does not orient around the dialogic positions of biology (math, dancing, and so on), is missing the task of teaching. I am not talking here about learning these discourses in a traditional sense (i.e., memorizing who said what) but to learn *how to participate* in these open discourses that have both internal and external components. This participation necessarily involves development of the student's unique voice and responsibility within these discourses through addressing and responses to the voices of others (cf. , taking personal orientation towards diverse professional positions in specialized discourses, see Furberg & Ludvigsen, 2008). Dialogical pedagogical argumentation heavily depends on the relationship of utterances among the participants, and moreover on the local academic community of discourse. This relationship is based on genuine interest in others' points – desire to address and reply to the relevant others -- rather than on "argumentative schemas," or "argumentative syntax," or "argumentative tools, " or "argumentative principles," or "argumentative skills" that themselves are derivatives of dialogic argumentation.

The professional discourse involves not only voices and positions of the members of professional community (a "community of practice", see Lave & Wenger, 1991; Wenger, 1998) but also relevant members of other communities of practice and relevant people of society who might raise important questions about the practice (the famous physicist Galileo Galilei included "a simple person" in his dialogues to jumpstart the scientific discourse of his time, see Galilei & Drake, 2001). Recently, there are attempts among educational scholars to extract necessary positions and roles to jumpstart a scientific discourse. Ford and Forman argue that two such roles are enough, "Constructor of claims and Critiquer of claims" (Ford & Forman, 2006, pp. 4-5). I argue that two roles are not enough. For example, to teach math argumentation in school using dialogic pedagogy means to engage students in math discourse so they have to reply to alternative positions as *within* math discourse (e.g., "why your position or answer is better for an alternative position or answer?", "how do you define 'better'?", "why is your math problem worth of our attention?") as *about* math discourse (e.g., "why to bother to do math at all?", "why are you doing math here and now and not something else?", "what does your math practice say about us, who are not involved in it?", "why should we, non-mathematicians, support you?"). Through this process, a student will develop his or her math voice.

The teacher's pedagogical responsibility is not only to find and "reanimate" diverse, historically relevant, professional voices constituting the current professional discourse for the students but also to teach them how to find and then to and to confront/dialogize with those voices themselves. In the case study presented above, the instructor introduced Sandy to the search terms on the Internet that led her into the contact with diverse voices. The voices of relevant others are often mediated by the text and might not be directly relevant for the students. The available texts might answer questions that the students did not raise and address positions that the students do not have (and not address the student's questions and not to reply to their particular positions or concerns). In this case, the instructor should help to "reanimate" these somewhat reified voices that are mediated by the texts for the students by raising questions and addressing the students' positions on their behalf.

The case study above presented only the dyadic teacher-student interaction in my cultural diversity classroom. In the reality, this dyadic interaction was embedded in the interaction of the classroom community that indirectly affected the dyadic teacher-student interaction. In class, the students were involved in not only "doing subject matter" and "doing school," but also "doing peer social relations" (Lampert, 2001) (which was outside of my analysis here). In the class and on the web, we discussed the issue of religion and public education. We also discussed professional issues of possible disagreement of teachers with laws (such as the case of dealing with the children of undocumented immigrants). Finally, the class had grown into a regime of internally persuasive discourse in that each participant could freely express his or her ideas without the teacher or textbook imposing their authoritative "final words" even when some students wanted to hear the "final points" of the discussion of what they should "take from" the class (as they provided on their in class and after class feedback), "I like our class discussions today but I don't understand where Eugene tried to lead us" (signed index card with the feedback on the class, September, 2006) or "I feel like I did not learn a lot but rather just expressed my opinions" (anonymous class evaluation, December 2006). While other students appreciated the polyphonic regime of the class, "The honors section of this course did not differ in any way from the regular section [of this class]. However, I feel that Prof. Matusov runs his class in a way that I wish all my honors classes (and non-honors classes) were run. It is always discussion based, he is very open to students' opinions, and we are able to discuss issues that directly relate to our practicum experiences. I grew professionally and personally. I met so many minds inside and outside the class – my mind is blossoming" (anonymous class evaluation, December 2006). Thus, some students apparently ended the class still seeing themselves as consumers of a professional discourse looking for ready-made professional solutions but some students began to see themselves as active participants in the discourse.

As we see in the case study, the students' argumentative skills are a by-product of their engagement in internally persuasive pedagogical discourse rather than a pre-cursor of it (Furberg & Ludvigsen, 2008). When the student provided uninformed argument or an argument based on a logical fallacy the instructor asked challenging questions, "but what about this or that" rather than provided a general instruction of how to make argument informative or avoid logical fallacies in general, non-specific ways. In contrast to Simon, Erduran, and Osborne (2006) who insist on separate teaching of argumentative skills, I argue for participatory, rather than skill-based, learning focused on dialogic addressivity, responsivity, and responsibility. However, it is an interesting issue of when, if ever, a skill-based learning is appropriate.

APPENDIX: SAMPLE OF SANDY'S WRITING AND MY FEEDBACK THROUGH HER DRAFTS

Note: Blue fonts, crossing out, and yellow marker are the instructor's comments and suggestions.

Intelligent Design vs. Evolution Theory

[by Sandy, a preservice teacher, the first paragraph of her Conclusion section]

[Draft#2]

The Solution

My solution to the controversy is to have both The Evolutionary Theory and Intelligent Design taught in the classrooms. This way both sides will be satisfied.There will be ample time to discuss both view points and show how both theories came about. I made this decision because I felt that it gives a sense of equality to those who are very religious and to those who strongly believe in the scientific evidence. By teaching Intelligent Design religious viewpoints will not be left out and parents will not have to worry that their children's schooling is going against their beliefs. And by including Evolution, the scientific evidence and centuries of work will not be lost. I think this is the perfect balance and will make people most happy.

[Draft#3]

My Solution

There is no public consensus on fixing the solution to teaching only one point of view of the creation of world and mankind. According to the U.S. Constitution and different Federal Court decisions only Evolution Theory is allowed to be taught. Therefore there is no legal allowance of teaching religious and non-scientific theories. However, I feel that the best solution, in my view, would to be to try and teach both the Evolution Theory and Intelligent Design. This way, students get to see both sides and pick which they agree with, not what they must agree with at school and at home.

However even though this idea may satisfy some, a lot would still be disappointed. For instance, Biology teachers in Dover High School in 2005 are refusing to read a one-minute statement at the beginning of class explaining that "evolution is a theory that continues to be tested and informs students of alternatives, such as intelligent design." The teachers are outraged because by doing this is saying that intelligent design is a theory, like evolution, which is not completely true. There is no evidence or facts to prove that intelligent design could have ever existed, unlike Evolution which is solely based on all facts and evidence. Dover High teachers explained "INTELLIGENT DESIGN IS NOT SCIENCE. INTELLIGENT DESIGN IS NOT BIOLOGY. INTELLIGENT DESIGN IS NOT AN ACCEPTED SCIENTIFIC THEORY," and therefore they are refusing to accept letting Intelligent Design be a part of their classroom curriculum. Likewise just as people are upset with Intelligent Design, there are those that are just as upset with only allowing Evolution in the classroom. So I can find no consensus that could fix the problem because no one would be happy either way.

[Draft#4, final]

My Solution

There is no public consensus on fixing the solution to teaching only one point of view of the creation of world and mankind. According to the U.S. Constitution and different Federal Court decisions only Evolution Theory is allowed to be taught. Therefore there is no legal allowance of teaching religious and non-scientific theories. However I feel that the best solution, in my view, would to be to try and teach both the Evolution Theory and Intelligent Design. This way students get to see both sides and pick which they agree with, not what they must agree with at school and at home. However even though this idea may satisfy some, a lot would still be disappointed. For instance, Biology teachers in Dover High School in 2005 are refusing to read a one minute statement at the beginning of class explaining that "evolution is a theory that continues to be tested and informs students of alternatives, such as intelligent design" (Dover Science Teachers, http://www.pandasthumb.org/archives/ 2005/01/dover_science_teachers_take_a_stand.html). The teachers are outraged because by doing this is saying that intelligent design is a theory, like evolution, which is not completely true. There is no evidence or facts to prove that intelligent design could have ever existed, unlike Evolution which is solely based on all facts and evidence. Dover High teachers explained "INTELLIGENT DESIGN IS NOT SCIENCE. INTELLIGENT DESIGN IS NOT BIOLOGY. INTELLIGENT DESIGN IS NOT AN ACCEPTED SCIENTIFIC THEORY," and therefore they are refusing to accept letting Intelligent Design be apart of their classroom curriculum (Dover Science Teachers, http://www.pandasthumb.org/archives/2005/01/ dover_science_teachers_take_a_stand.html). Likewise just as people are upset with Intelligent Design, there are those that are just as upset with only allowing Evolution in the classroom. So I can find no consensus that could fix the problem because no one would be happy either way…. Therefore this debate will continue to occur until both sides have equal satisfaction.

Chapter 10

LEARNING ECOLOGY OF
A POLYPHONIC CLASSROOM[1]

ABSTRACT

This research investigates the conditions that promote or hinder dialogic pedagogy in an afterschool Lego-Logo Robotics club at a Latin-American Community Center. I analyze videotaped observations and interviews with the club participants to investigate the evidence of polyphony, degrees of freedom, and types of constraints for the participants' physical movements and communication. I also look at ways in which the participants modify their guidance and solve interpersonal problems. The findings suggest that the club involves a high degree of polyphony and a low level of pedagogical violence demonstrated by a high degree of freedom for the participants to physically move in and out of particular local settings and to initiate, change, and drop topics of communication.

THE PROBLEM OF VIOLENT ECOLOGY
OF CONVENTIONAL SCHOOLING
AND ITS ALTERNATIVES

One of the big problems with the existing mainstream educational practices, especially in conventional schools, is that when pedagogical and, even more specifically, instructional mistakes occur, there are usually no compensating forces, built internally to the pedagogical practice, that promote improvement for the pedagogical practice. When professional mistakes occur in other practices (such as the movie making industry, for example), there often are internal forces in those practices that "urgently communicate" the problem to the practitioners. These compensating forces, inherent to the practice, compel the practitioners either to improve their practice or to leave the profession. For example, if the public systematically does not come to the movie theater to see a particular movie, the director usually either must change his or her moviemaking practices, find his or her niche audience,

---

[1] I want to thank Maria Alburquerque Candela for suggesting studying guidance of Mr. Steve Vullienova. I am very thankful my research team involving Kathy von Duyke and Sohyun Han for helping with collecting and analysis of the data for the presented research. Finally, I am very grateful Mr. Steve Vullienova, Jose Rosa, and the LACC children, participants in the Lego-Logo Robotics Lab, for their interviews and general support.

or perhaps be forced out of business of movie directing. In contrast, for teachers of compulsive, mandatory, education, this is often not the case. When the instructional and curricular design fails and students become increasingly disengaged, the teacher often replies with *pedagogical violence* using coercive disciplinary methods such as: reprimands, poor grades, calling parents, using suspensions, and so on. Both, the XIX century Russian innovative educator and also famous writer, Leo Tolstoy, and modern educational philosopher Alexander Sidorkin diagnose this reliance on pedagogical violence as the main problem of modern formal education (Sidorkin, 2002; Tolstoy, 1967; Tolstoy & Blaisdell, 2000). The absence of pedagogical violence creates possibilities for formative feedback in teaching practice. Indeed, if students are not forced to be in the classroom and allowed to come and leave at their will, if they are not forced to be quiet during the lesson but allowed to talk when they want, if they are allowed to have freedom of movement, if they are not punished for their "mistakes", and so forth – the problems with the teacher's instruction and curricula might "naturally" lead to improvement of the instruction because no other means are available to the teacher in the response to the problems (alternatively, the teacher has to leave the profession similar to a failing movie director). A dialogical approach to student responses allows this ready compensatory internal force to develop ecological classroom conditions that promote genuine learning.

Based on literary work of Bakhtin (1999) and its interpretation by Morson and Emerson (1990), I define dialogic pedagogy as one in which the dialogic nature of teaching, learning, and truth is recognized by the teacher in his or her professional work. In the same vein, I define a "polyphonic classroom" as one in which the dialogic nature of learning and truth is recognized also by the students (a classroom can be partially polyphonic when it the dialogic nature of learning is recognized but not fully or not by all the participants). Tolstoy (1967), Lave (1992a), and Wenger (1998) argue that learning cannot be designed – only conditions for learning are designable. The endpoint of learning for a particular student is never known and therefore should not be attempted to determine by the teacher (or the students) in advance. As Tolstoy (1967, pp. 30-31) pointed out, "the science of education" must focus on defining those conditions that promote or hinder learning. We define the "learning ecology of a polyphonic classroom" as those conditions that promote education via dialogic pedagogy in a polyphonic classroom. In this chapter, I want to investigate the learning ecology of a polyphonic classroom.

In reading pedagogical literature, I extracted three historical approaches to promoting a non-violent educational ecology. I consider the first two approaches non-instructional because they are not focused on reforming and improving classroom instruction. The first approach is sometimes called "children-run," or "students-run" (cf. Matusov & Rogoff, 2002; Rogoff et al., 1996). It was proposed and enacted by Neill in his famous Summerhill innovative school project (Neill, 1960). According to this innovative boarding school, classroom attendance is voluntarily for the children. The pedagogical idea behind this approach is that a child will join classroom instruction out of his or her interest in the subject, boredom from other non-classroom activities, natural curiosity, enthusiasm of the other children already engaged in the classroom instruction, or a pragmatic need. According to Neill, having a willing student in the classroom is enough to propel learning without violence. While sensitive and engaging instruction is always a plus, it is not necessary, according to Neill. Neil argued that even when instruction is insensitive the willing student puts his or her own efforts into learning. This student willing effort, in spite of poor instruction, is like that of interested scholars at a professional conference who, while attending a monotonous and otherwise not well-organized presentation about important research in their field, will put out extra attentional effort to understand and engage themselves in the presented information. Similarly, Neill argued, willing students put extra efforts to understand what they want to understand even when instruction is insensitive to the students' needs. In this approach, teachers serve as facilitators for willing and, essentially, self-guiding students rather than as the primary motivating source of their guidance.

But what if a child never chooses to attend a particular instruction? Neil argued that this could happen yet this was not considered a serious educational issue. At Summerhill, the children learn self-guidance in and out of the classroom. If later in their life they find that they need to learn something that they missed at Summerhill, the former Summerhill students can easily do so because they learned at Summerhill how to provide guidance to themselves. If they never find they need a certain skill it is not an issue exactly because they don't need it. For Neill, the students' will to learn and self-guidance is more important than any particular skill or knowledge. A recent documentary about Summerhill (Kleindienst, 1998) investigated Neill's claim and found it to be more or less accurate. A student, who chose not to attend reading instruction at Summerhill, learned to read and write later in his adult life when he found literacy to have become important and necessary for him. Looking back, the former Summerhill student apparently agreed with Neill, although his experiences were not without pain. However, he acknowledged that the pain and consequences of forced literacy instruction may have possibly had a more devastating and damaging effect on him (Kleindienst, 1998).

The second non-instructional approach to promoting non-violent educational ecology has been proposed by Sidorkin (2002, 2004). My colleague and I call his approach "exchange of favors" (Smith & Matusov, 2009, in press). According to Sidorkin, modern schooling is mandatory due to many non-educational reasons and this is the fact of the modern reality that all educators have to accept. School students have to be engaged in many unpleasant activities and discourses, in which they have little ownership, control, purpose, or even understanding. From Sidorkin's point of view, having many learning activities meaningless for the students is unavoidable. However, the students' engagement in these unpleasant, meaningless, uninteresting, even painful activities and discourses has to be promoted in a non-violent way. In contrast to conventional modern schools, in which engagement in these learning activities often done through pedagogical violence, or threat of violence, or bribery; Sidorkin proposes the use of "relational economy" -- exchange of favors between the teacher and the students. In the "relational economy," the teacher tries to meet many of the students' social and intellectual needs. The teacher may help the students to socialize with peers and adults, promote their self-esteem and self-worth, investigate inquiries of their interests, and so on. This is done in exchange for the students' compliance with the teacher's demand to do academic work as defined by the teacher that might not have much meaning for them or be even painful and frustrating. Sidorkin calls this type of classroom ecology a "relational economy" and claims that even in the current conventional schools, "good" students in are often willing participants in this relational economy with their teachers and parents (which makes them "good"). This separates them from "poor" students for whom relational economy is closed for some reason and that is why those students are unwilling to comply with the teachers' academic demands.

In my view, it is amazing how both Neill and Sidorkin neglect discussing the issue of instructional reform and improvement in the classroom. From my reading and watching of numerous documentaries about Summerhill School, I conclude that the key success of the school is in its General Assembly meetings and in similar social events around social conflicts. In these events, issues of interpersonal relations, conflicts, problems, and their different ways to be in communal life together are discussed within a regime of internally persuasive discourse. I analyze this idea further in a subsequent chapter about Paley's pedagogical failure. In my view, the General Assembly meetings are where the Summerhill students mainly learn how to become self-guided learners. This is where dialogic pedagogy primarily unfolds its extreme strength. However, it remains unclear why the dialogic pedagogy at Summerhill is limited only to the General Assembly meetings and its curriculum of resolving social conflicts. Ironically, attendance in these meetings is mandatory. It is unclear why other academic curriculum at Summerhill is not orchestrated as dialogic pedagogy as well. Why are not adults at Summerhill more proactive and collaborative with students on other academic matters?

In Sidorkin's non-instructional approach to promoting non-violent educational ecology through his "relational economy" of an exchange of favors, he seems to confuse two possible developmental trajectories. The development of "a good student" who unconditionally, but willingly, complies to whatever institutional demands with the development of "a good learner" who actively engages him or herself in promoting and negotiating his or her own learning as the final agency of his or her own learning (DePalma et al., 2009, in press; Matusov, 1999; Rogoff et al., 1996). While absence of pedagogical violence is a good, necessary step forward, it is arguably not enough for promoting good education. However, even the very fact of absence of violence is questionable in Sidorkin's educational ecology of a "relational economy." Sidorkin's approach is a call for the domestication of students and the "internalization" of educational violence to insensitive guidance as no student counter voice is part of his "relational economy." In a conventional school, it is the responsibility of the teacher to force the students to attend insensitive guidance; while in Sidorkin's school regime of "relational economy," the oppressive role is transferred to the student him or herself (cf. Foucault, 1995). The initial problem of insensitive guidance remains unaddressed in the "relational economy" of schooling proposed by Sidorkin. He claims that the problem of insensitive guidance is impossible to address on the mass scale inherent to modern institutionalized compulsory education. In both non-instructional approaches, by Neill and by Sidorkin, it is the unilateral responsibility of the student to adjust to insensitive instruction. For Neill, the student might genuinely learn when he or she chooses to attend the insensitive instruction, for Sidorkin the student must pass institutional requirements for social favors.

The third approach to promoting non-violent educational ecology was introduced by famous Russian writer and innovative educator Leo Tolstoy in his school that he called "Yasnaya Polyana" (in Russian "Clear Meadow," the name of his familiar estate and former serfdom). Tolstoy formed the innovative school in the early 1860s immediately after serfdom became legally abandoned by the Russian Emperer. Yasnaya Polyana had several branches located in different villages was established to serve the educational needs of peasant children, children of Tolstoy's former serfs. A few adults also attended the school. Despite its established schedule, the school had open door policy: students could come at any time, and leave at any time – out of any classroom or the school itself. According to the descriptions provided by Tolstoy in his self-published pedagogical journal titled "Yasnaya Polyana", teachers in his school sometimes limited their lessons to children based on their age, but participation seemed to be negotiable. This attendance policy probably varied from one teacher to another.

Tolstoy's open door policy and volunteer attendance sounds similar to Neill's Summerhill (cf. Archambault, 1967) but the purposes of these policies were arguably different (cf. Murphy, 1992). I argue that the pedagogical goal of Tolstoy's open door policy was to improve instruction, while for Neill it was to have willing, self-directed students. As a teacher, Tolstoy wanted to keep all his students in the classroom but by improving his curricula-instructional means. When his students left his instruction in the middle of his class period, he assumed that the instruction (in a broader sense that included the curriculum) was insensitive for the students and needed improvement[2]. Tolstoy emphasized the "eclectic", "a-theoretical", pragmatic nature of his pedagogy (Archambault, 1967) – he chose not to apply ready-made pedagogical ideas decontextualized from the particular students' present. Rather, he wanted to "discover" his pedagogy from and with his students. From his articles in the Yasnaya Polyana pedagogical journal (Tolstoy, 1967), it is clear that he experimented, observed, and supported emerging discursive and pedagogical patterns that promoted his students' meaningful engagement in their learning[3]. Tolstoy was very critical of his own pedagogy by evaluating his own teaching practice based on student response. He rejected both: 1) pedagogy promoting ontological disengagement that was causing either his students to leave, or was dependent on keeping them in the classroom via violence, and 2) pedagogy promoted by non-educational engagement. As an example of the latter pitfall, Tolstoy rejected his own pedagogical experiments with teaching Russian national history through engaging his students with patriotic chauvinism even though he was very successful in engaging his students in this (harmful) curriculum. In contrast to Sidorkin, Tolstoy saw a non-violent ecology of schooling as a necessary but not sufficient condition for good education. Tolstoy initiated and supported open discussions, ones he genuinely did not know the endpoint of, about what constituted good education, -- not only among the general public but among his peasant children students (see, for example, his discussion with his peasant students about whether art is needed to be engaged and learned Tolstoy, 1967).

Unfortunately, although Tolstoy provided a well-developed and rich ethnography of his conversations with a few of his students about the use of art while writing stories (Tolstoy, 1967) suggestive of dialogic pedagogy and internally persuasive discourse at work, his ethnography was collected outside of his classroom. His description of his own pedagogical successes and failures is sketchy and does not allow for following the details of how his pedagogy emerged from his pedagogical design. To investigate a polyphonic non-violent educational ecology in detail, I turn to a modern example that I found almost "next door."[4]

---

[2] Of course, Tolstoy was aware that his students might leave his classroom not because his instruction was insensitive but for some other reasons. However, he apparently wanted a "free completion" between his instruction and learning activities and other activities that attracted the children. He seemed to believed that in this competition, the instruction might get better. However, he viewed as natural that some activities were situationally more important than his learning activities for the students – these activities could be also invited in the educational process rather than have to be suppressed (as it is often done in a conventional school).

[3] Arguably, Tolstoy's approach to pedagogy was very similar to De Soto's (2000) approach to economy in the underdeveloped and former communist countries. Like Tolstoy in education, De Soto calls not for imposition ready-made economic and legal structures borrowed from economically advanced countries but rather for "discovery" and legal support of emerging beneficial economic patterns in local contexts.

[4] I am very thankful to my colleague and dear friend Maria Albuquerque Candela. When I shared my problem of limited ethnography of Tolstoy's Yasnaya Polyana school, she told me immediately, "You should study Mr. Steve's Lego-Logo Club at LACC." She was right.

THE LEGO-LOGO CLUB AS A POLYPHONIC CLASSROOM

The Lego-Logo Robotics (LLR) afterschool club is located at the Latin-American Community Center (LACC) in the inner city of Wilmington (DE). The LLR afterschool club was started by the University of Delaware La Red Mágica program (Hayes & Matusov, 2005b; Matusov, St. Julien et al., 2005) and has existed for 4 years at LACC by the fall 2007 when I started this research. The LLR club meets twice a week for about 1-2 hours to prepare for the LLR national annual competition. I videotaped 5 one-to-two hour-long sessions of the LACC LLR club. I also interviewed the instructor, known in the LACC as "Mr. Steve," his assistant Jose Rosa (18-year old, who in past was himself an active participant of the LLR club), and 8 participating children (novices and oldtimers, younger and older, boys and girls). The core participating children were aged from 9-year old to 14-year old as defined by the national competition rules . Sometimes, younger children are allowed to participate. The 9-14 yr olds are organized into 3 teams of 4 boys and one team of 4 girls. Some of the core children were very experienced LLR participants but some were new to the club. More than 50 children so far havebeen involved in the program. Sometimes the University of Delaware undergraduate students majoring in education, their professors, and older LACC children who have graduated from the LLR club come to assist the children and help Mr. Steve.

The LLR lab was a long, narrow room. In the center of the room, there were four long tables grouped (two by two), arranged into one big rectangular table. On this table, the LLR mission stand was installed. The rest of the big table space was used either for assembling car-robots or as an additional mission table. On the perimeter of the LLR lab room there were computers for programming car-robots, searching for LLR-related information, or for playing games and chatting.

Figure 9. Mr. Steve and younger children observe Yasenia's car-robot performing a mission task on the mission table as a test of Yasenia's programming. You can see a team of older girls assembling their car robot at the other part of the table. On the right of the room, several children are working on

programming their car-robots. On the left of the room, there are two very young children playing computer games (you cannot see them).

The main LLR room activities consisted of: 1) discussions of the upcoming and past annual national competitions, mission tasks for the teams' car-robots, and the merit-demerit system of the competition; 2) building the Lego prompts based on the provided blueprints for the challenge (e.g., houses, surroundings) via step-by-step instructions, 3) assembling robots from Lego-Logo blocks with certain desired functions based on given instructions, 4) programming the robots to perform the desired tasks, 5) and testing the robots' performing the desired tasks. Activities were often accompanied by multiple conversations with dynamically changing topics among the diverse participants of the LLR.

FINDINGS

Activity Inventory

I focused on one particular hour-long videotaped session, which was rather typical, and extracted all visible activities during the session. Besides 5 major LLR activities, listed above, I found 7 LLR secondary activities:

1. Fixing the team car-robots so they can effectively and reliably perform particular mission tasks;
2. Playing and manipulating with diverse objects on the mission table;
3. My interviews of LLR children about their participation in the LLR club;
4. Children's videotaping LLR activities using Eugene's second camera, showing LLR worksheets to Mr. Steve's camera, interviewing other children about the missions;
5. Mr. Steve's (and at time other children's) managing the participants' involvement in the LLR activities and discourses;
6. Observations and eavesdropping of others' participation in the LLR-related activities;
7. Younger children's waiting for Mr. Steve's return to a discussion and learning mission tasks from helping older kids with their programming the car-robots;

   In addition, I found 5 non-LLR activities:

1. Playing two computer games;
2. Chatting on teenage topics often involving peer relations, teasing, romance flirting, and sexual themes (e.g., stomach pain --> pregnancy);
3. Horse-playing, chasing, and teasing;
4. Talking on a cellular phone with a friend;
5. Filling out LACC documentation (Jose Rosa);

In sum, all together, I observed 19 different activities in the LLR lab during this session (it was rather typical for other videotaped sessions). Twelve activities were related to the Lego-Logo Robotics program and 5 were not. Many of the activities were running at the same time. For example, on figure 9, the participants were involved in at least 7 different activities: a) Yasenia and Mr. Steve were involved in one of the majors activities of testing the car-robot that Yasenia programmed to perform a mission task (of getting to the other side of the mission table, touching the wall and getting back), b) children on the right were programming their robot-cars, c) two older girls on the other side of the table were assembling their car-robot, d) a girl on the right side of the table was watching the performance of Yasenia's car – she was a newcomer and involved in peripheral participation of testing the car, d) a girl on the left was manipulating with Lego prompts on the mission table, e) while assembling their car-robot, these girls were chatting about their teenage themes that were not related to the LLR club, f) the two other newcomer children on the left were waiting Mr. Steve returning back to instructing them about the mission tasks and competition in general, finally, g) two young boys (7 and 8 years old), who were sitting on the left at a computer (not seen on the photo), were playing computer games unrelated to LLR activities.

Some participants were involved in more than one type of the activity at the same time. For example, the two older girls were assembling their car-robot while chatting on their chosen teenage themes revolving around peer relations, romance, and sex. Newcomer younger children around the mission table were also engaged in multiple activities: being peripheral participants in Yasenia's and Mr. Steve's testing of Yasenia's car-robot, other children's LLR and non-LLR activities, waiting until Mr. Steve returned back to his instruction, occasional manipulation of Lego prompts, and chatting with each other.

Some activities have their own "natural" rhythm and relations based on its particular intrinsic logic and development: thus, programming car-robots and their testing alternated with each other while assembling car-robots preceded their prog,ramming. Management of the participants' involvement in these activities was either preemptive of, or responsive to, certain organizational problems. However, other relations were strategic. For example, Mr. Steve prioritized testing car-robots by oldtimer children over his instruction of newcomer children about the annual LLR mission tasks. This he always put on hold when an oldtimer child was ready to test his or her robot-car.

The multiplicity of available activities – actually, often a network of available activities – along with freedom to move between activities, cease an old one, or create a new one create a sense of ownership of the activities by participants. The children in the LLR lab do their activities, not for Mr. Steve, but for themselves. They said, "it's *my* car," "it's *my* game," and "*I* have a problem" or they used the collective pronoun "*we*" or "*our*" when they chose to work collectively. The participating children were visible upset when the LLR activities were canceled due to LACC activities or bad weather. Activities in the LLR lab provide attractors for all participants, including Mr. Steve. These attractors beg for the participants' *ontological attention*. When a child or Mr. Steve participated in an activity, their participation was apparently ontological because they could choose to participate in a different activity or just leave. The activity choice and the participants' commitment to the activities created possibilities for the participants' agency, motivation, and desire. The activity choices were often an intentional pedagogical design by Mr. Steve for emergence of student agency (this design could promote the student agency but could not guarantee its emergence or define its shape). This pedagogical design of multiple activities is in contrast with predominately mono-activity pedagogical design of a conventional classroom, in which the conventional teacher often has strong unilateral control promoting the only one legitimate activity in the classroom that is non-negotiable for the students (unlike audience in a movie theater who arguably are also involved in mono activity, students of conventional classroom cannot leave their classroom at their wish or not to come next time).

The ownership of LLR activities is often shared, but the ownership of the strategic transitions from one LLR activity to another often appeared unilateral: either by Mr. Steve or his aide, Jose Rosa. They often told the children directly what the children should do next, "I want you to…" I call this activity transition *strategic*, in contrast to a *tactic* transition, when this transition was not locally contextual and required some considerations disembedded from the activity's immediate contexts. For example, a transition from programming a car-robot to its testing on the mission table was a tactic transition because it was embedded in affordances of the local context (i.e., programming was accomplished and required testing). Questions of when to start a new mission, what kind of new mission task to start, or considerations of time before the competition were strategic transitions of activities. On first glance, all strategic transitions seemed to be made by Mr. Steve and Jose. There seemed to be little guidance and discussion of the decisions that involved the big picture of the project with students. However, on detailed observation of many LLR sessions, a different pattern emerges. Mr. Steve embedded an apprenticeship tacit model that helped to transfer responsibility for strategic transitions from Mr. Steve and Jose to the children. In the later sessions, I noticed that children sometimes chose a new activity strategically based on whether: 1) they wanted to help Mr. Steve or other participants, 2) they became interested in an ongoing activity, 3) they noticed a routine (e.g., setting the mission table or cleaning it at the beginning or the end of an LLR session), 4) they continued on previously worked activity, 5) they asked a question, "What am I supposed to do?", 6) they actively picked up the worksheet with the mission task guidelines and selected a new mission task for themselves.

I also noticed that Mr. Steve and Jose always provided their rationales for their own strategic decision making to the children, which provided the framework for an apprenticeship guiding strategic decision making. Sometimes these rationales generated discussions among the children and Mr. Steve or Jose. I have concluded that strategic decision-making was a tacit learning curriculum in the LLR club. Children's ownership for strategic decision-making makes their classroom *polyphonic* because the children learn to through themselves in *learning provocations*. However, I saw only once when their ownership reached the lever of *self-designed curricular journey*, when several years ago, a group of 12-13-year boys engaged themselves in a long-term project of making a dancing car like in a wrestling show of a Latino wrestler. At that time, they temporarily suspended Mr. Steve curricular journey of preparing to the Lego-Logo competition (with his permission and active support).

Often I saw children working intensively and sustainably on diverse LLR activities in the LLR lab without Mr. Steve and Jose being present in the room. This indicated their high level of overall ownership for the LLR activities and its overall practices. However, this freedom of participation in activities had its limitations. Some activities were in competition with each other for the participants. In one observed instance, a newcomer girl was reprimanded by Mr. Steve for not "coming back" to him with her attention to his mission instruction when Mr. Steve returned to the "Missions" group after he finished helping oldtimer children with testing their car-robots. The newcomer girl was consumed with observing her younger brother playing his computer game. Probably, from Mr. Steve's point of view, it was OK for her to observe the game while she was waiting for him to come back to his instruction, but she should have monitored his return and quickly moved back to the instruction activity when he was ready to resume instruction as some other newcomer children did. To my surprise, these incidences of the activity conflicts occurred rather rarely – only 2-3 times per a videotaped session.

Some of the activities competing for children's attention led to pedagogical violence, while others to negotiations. For instance, in the example above, Mr. Steve threatened the newcomer girl with possible expulsion from the LLR club by him emphasizing a (fake?) choice for her, "You will miss [the] whole thing again. Today is the last time you can come to the program, OK? Do you wanna do this or not? I don't want to force you to stay." The girl did not reply but looked upset, and she stayed silent for some time before she began to be active again in the LLR activities. In other cases, negotiations occurred and were between Mr. Steve and children because the children were involved in an activity which was competing with another activity that Mr. Steve had planned for them. Thus, an older oldtimer girl wanted to stay with the older girls and helped them assemble their car-robot and chat with them. Mr. Steve wanted her (and another oltimer boy) to program her team car robot at a computer. Both children complied to Mr. Steve's request, though accompanying their compliance with jokes -- the boy pretended to be crying like a reluctant baby and the girl made a joke exploiting Mr. Steve's confusing choice of words in his announcement and demand. Mr. Steve smiled at both jokes but kept directing the children to computers in a serious, business-like tone. The two children seemed to want to communicate to themselves, to Mr. Steve, and to the whole community that they accepted Mr. Steve's authority as legitimate at that time but their acceptance was not unconditional.

Yet, in many more cases when activities in the LLR lab might engage in competition for the participants' attention, Mr. Steve seemed to intentionally ignore the children in non-LLR activities (although he clearly noticed them) and instead strongly push his support for the LLR activities. For example, I observed that despite the fact that other children started working on their LLR activities, one of the children with 2-years of LLR experience continued playing a computer game. She was ignored by Mr. Steve and the other children. She played for about 12 minutes then switched off the computer and joined the LLR activities. I observed many incidences like that. In general, the LLR activities were much stronger attractors for the children in the LLR lab than competing activities. Even younger children who, according to the LLR official rules could not join the LLR activities because they were too young (younger than 9), eventually joined LLR activities on their own either by observing and peripheral participation or via parallel LLR activities such as building Lego cars and "testing" them through obstacle "mission tasks" which they invented. The availability of computer games eventually could not compete with the LLR collective project! Eventually, the non-LLR activities either peacefully co-existed with the LLR activities or were short lived without much enforcement from Mr. Steve. I call this observational pattern: *ecological eventualism*. Arguably, the non-LLR activities such as; chatting, computer games, phone calls, horse play, teasing, and so on might actually help the LLR project in the long run by helping the children to address their other needs to relax and regroup their attention (see my discussion below).

Was pedagogical violence necessary in the case of competing activities in the LLR lab? It seems to me, not. In my judgment, the observed pedagogical violence was caused by two main factors: 1) the deadline pressure from the official annual national competition and 2) Mr. Steve's apparent regression to a traditional adult-run transmission of knowledge educational philosophy in the face of the external time pressures (or just being tired). Let me justify my hypothesis with some evidence. In the accident of pedagogical violence described above, Mr. Steve threatened a novice girl simply because she did not return back to the mission instruction. It seemed that Mr. Steve was concerned that she might not learn about the mission tasks without his explicit instruction. However, a few weeks later, a young 9-year old boy joined the LLR club who had spent a session watching before joining. He learned successfully about mission tasks through his observation and participation in testing his team car-robot and other car-robots and the ongoing discourses about the LLR missions without having any formal instruction from Mr. Steve. Mr. Steve was aware of this boy's type of participatory learning, but he was very concerned that, unlike this boy, the novice girl would have to present mission tasks based on a selection contest in a local school. He seemed to worry that she might not learn fast enough or be able to publically present well all the required information about the mission tasks. Indeed, she made some mistakes during the contest's public presentation despite of his explicit instruction.

Diverse and Dynamic Membership in the LLR Club

My videotaped and non-videotaped observations and interviews with participants suggest a diverse and dynamic membership in the LLR club. First, it has ethnic diversity: the LLR club includes Puerto Rican, Mexican, and African American children. For the ten years that I have been involved in the LACC, I have observed tensions arise between Puerto Rican and Mexican children, and between Latino and African American children. In the four years of the LLR club's existence, I have never observed any racial or ethnic tensions among the diverse participants of the club. On the contrary, I have seen many lasting deep friendships being established as a result of participation in the club. This finding is in accord with the findings of social psychologists that suggest that cooperation leads to integration and friendship (Sherif, 1988). In the past, one of my undergraduate students, a preservice teacher Amy Spencer, established a "Girls' Club"[5] as a summer program at the LACC to promote the integration and friendship between "tough and difficult"[6] Puerto Rican and Mexican teenage girls who had been in constant fights before. The Girls' Club was designed after the LLR club copying Mr. Steve's dialogic pedagogy and use of collaborative long-term projects[7]. The success of the LLR club and Girls' Club[8] suggest that ethnic conflicts at afterschool programs are often a result of a lack of quality collaborative activities and projects for the youth. Mr. Steve also developed a humorous anti-violence curriculum to address the racial tensions when he initially started the club,

---

[5] The 10-week Girls' Club involved three long-term projects demanding coordinated efforts of all the participants (in time progression): 1) making a quilt blanket (Amy's unilateral idea), 2) designing a CD of the Club favorite music (Amy's and my idea based on observation on the girls' discourse and interests in music), and 3) organizing a carnival at the LACC (the girls' idea).

[6] The term "tough and difficult" was coined by LACC officers (however, not by Mr. Steve).

[7] Before that summer, Amy had participated in the La Red Mágica class, in which she went to a 9-week teaching practicum at the LACC. She closely observed the LLR club and pedagogy of Mr. Steve. In preparation and during her summer work, we reflected on the LLR club and Mr. Steve's pedagogy and thought how to use in her work with the Puerto Rican and Mexican teenage girls.

[8] The success of the Girls' Club is evident that the involved Puerto Rican and Mexican girls kept their friendships several years after the Club. They and the LACC officers still have fond memory of Amy's work. As one of LACC officers said in the time of the Club, "Amy's Club is the only leverage that we have to make these difficult girls behave. Before Amy, we had none."

Name-calling was a very big offense to them; they would be very negative and violent to any name-calling.... to each other or other kids from the outside. To the point where they, you know, they would strike, they would punch... violently. So we developed this little..., to get rid of some of this stuff and help them realize that these [potentially offensive] words [by themselves] are not that important. That it depends on the context of what's going on. I've proved them, I did a little group called the Techie club and this is on purpose for behavior to prove a couple of things to them...

We, the Techie club had a couple of components in it. One was that we would go in 'a therapy' type of setting with round chairs you know, chairs in a circle. And everybody would sit and to get over the name-calling part I asked them how they would feel about playing game called, *Your Mama Jokes*. And ah, "Man I play this one all the time, ah me too in school we." Okay, so this is what we're going to do, we're going to go to the computers, we're gonna look for all the Your Mama jokes that you can find. We're going to come back, we're going to have a seat, and everybody's going to take a turn saying a Your Mama joke to one another, right? And nobody can get offended; it's a joke, right? No matter how badly Your Mama joke is, you're not going to get offended. You gonna stay there and listen to that and laugh. And we did that, successfully, successfully without *any* repercussions and nothing behind closed doors. And ah, we you know, every two days in a row, every week, and after a while it became, and I see the difference it, you know. We did Yo Mama jokes we did um other types of um name-calling jokes and... Like ah, change the name of a, of the, call him, you know, like Taco [for a Mexican decent boy] for instance. It didn't bother; well, it bothered Taco in the beginning, the name Taco. Ah, you like booger face or um invalidate, I don't know, invalidating names. They used to call me the Pink Panther [laughs]. They call me ah Pickle Nose, Pink Panther [teasing names based on Mr. Steve's appearance]; they gave me a whole bunch of different names, in these groups, right? Because this is only for the groups, right? Outside we didn't practice that.

In the last two years the LLR club has diversified by gender and, in my judgment, this was entirely Mr. Steve's achievement. The LLR club started with almost 100% boys' participation. The girls were welcomed but they rarely become committed nor participated for any sustained time. They did not seem to have a sense of ownership of it either. In my observation, a part of that disturbing phenomenon was a sexist environment at the LLR club and beyond in the LACC and in the broader society. The girls seemed to receive a hidden, and at times not very hidden, message that the engineering practice of the LLR: assembling, programming, and testing car-robots was not for them -- not for girls. I remember one incident in which, in the first year of the LLR club, Mr. Steve was frustrated that the boys did not clean well at the end of the LLR session. He said jokingly to the boys and to me, "We definitely need more girls in the club!" and laughed. He apparently implied that girls would do cleaning job better than the boys but indirectly (or may be directly), his joke suggested that the gender place of boys was to do "real" work, while the gender place of girls was to clean up after them. I looked at Mr. Steve with surprise. I did not see any reaction from the boys nor the one girl who participated in the LLR activities at that time. Mr. Steve saw my discouraged reaction and, but also perhaps reflected at his own joke and added, "I probably shouldn't have said that." "Probably, not," I agreed. From time to time, I heard sexist comments from the LLR boys as well. We discussed the problem of engaging girls in the LLR club many times, however, I did not notice how Mr. Steve solved the problem -- but he did. Four years later, the LLR club has slightly more girls than boys in all the ages. In the interview, Mr. Steve could not pinpoint exactly what made girls to come to the LLR club, but they did.

The LLR club integrates children of diverse ages. According to the rules of the LLR national competition, only children of ages ranged from 9 to 14 could legitimately participate in the competition. In the LLC club, ages of the participating children at times were from 7 to 18. Though younger than 9-year old boys could not legitimately participate, those who came were allowed to stay in the computer club during the LLR activities. An "official" rule of the LACC was that all non-participating children could not come during LLR to avoid crowding in the rather small room. The boys developed their own alternative LLR activities, and peripherally participated in older LLR children's activities. Older children also participated in LLR from time-to-time, "In, behind the fact that, some of the kids, more of the kids in the Techie thing are still with us. Others have gone to [remote High] schools, one went to the Air Force. But these kids were consistent at coming here and doing the same thing time after time computers, rebuilding, programming, computers, rebuilding, programming. "Ah, helping Steve install games, helping Steve learn how to play shooting games, helping. And we were all, even networking and cabling, and we were a family, we were together, they're still with us, they even work with us. I mean some of these [older] kids [still] work with us" (Interview with Mr. Steve). At the time of this research, there was one 15-year old boy, a newcomer, and an oldtimer 18-year old Jose Rosa, a participant in the LLR club from its beginning, who was assisting Mr. Steve. The LLR girls were rather evenly distributed between 9- and 14-year olds[9].

The LLR club integrates children of different skill-levels. That phenomenon is apparently well-planned by Mr. Steve by ensuring that the participating children have diverse experiences at the club. Years each child has spent in the club was diversified, some children were newcomers and have just come to the club, others were in their second or third year. Jose was in his fourth year. The most experienced children usually (but not always!) had the most knowledge and skills in the LLR activities. The second reason for skill diversity was the emerging division of labor due to children's preferences (and, probably, commitments). Some children preferred the engineering activities of designing robots and solving mechanical problems, while others preferred assembling robots from Lego blocks, others preferred programming, while others preferred testing and improvising new LLR tasks outside of the annual mission contests, and still others were more or less "jacks of all trades." Mr. Steve supported the skill- and expertise- diversity at the LLR club, "Some of the kids specialize in programming and I have that now today. Some of the kids they specialize, you know, if they have what it takes to program. Other kids are better at, are inclined into the building of things. They're better with their hands, ah; other kids are better just at all around help. So, you know, I try to make them fit exactly where they are best at." Mr. Steve provides opportunities for newcomers to try diverse LLR activities, "The ones that have been there already, who are not new, who know, -- I let them choose what they want. The new kids, I don't know them, so I have to tell them, do this, do that, do this, do that. And I observe, and uh, they turn out that

---

[9] Probably, for a cultural reason, one can rarely see a girl at LACC older than 15-year old. Some LACC officers reported to me that the parents of these girls are afraid that the older girls might get pregnant as a result of mixing with teenage boys at the LACC. Ironically, I saw many former LACC girls in the LACC neighborhood got pregnant in their teen years after they dropped from the LACC participation. For the past 10 years of my affiliation with LACC, I have never heard any case of teenage girls becoming pregnant as a result of their participation in the LACC.

they like to build robots better, that they like to run their cars better. Other kids decide that they want to program the cars and they get good at it very fast and I, you know. At the beginning you gotta push 'em, tell them to do something, and then take it from there. You never know what, you know, exposure will turn into."

Some of the children in the past and present have achieved more expertise in the LLR practice than Mr. Steve who, accidently, also learned about the LLR practices with and from the children. The rich skill, expertise, age, and knowledge diversity in the LLR club created centers of autonomy and sources of distributed guidance throughout the LLR club time period. The presence of Mr. Steve was not even necessary for activities to run successfully and emergent problems to be solved. Within the diverse skill-levels and age community, the LLR children learn to solve technical, organizational, pedagogical, and interpersonal problems. They develop leadership skills in these areas under the guidance and modeling of Mr. Steve and Jose. Mr. Steve created ecology through the what activity performance can bring to relationship rather than vertical hierarchies alone (which often are divisive) -- being able to perform better is important for its added value to the quality brought to relationships – to increase the depth of another's expertise and enhance their value back and forth. The LLR children gain communal respect, status, and authority in the LLR club (and beyond at the LACC) not by their age, LLR seniority, physical strength, gender role, or attractiveness, but rather mostly by their ever increasing technical and social expertise exhibited through their ability and desire to help other people,

> Mr. Steve: Cris is, she's a pretty smart little girl. She is, I feel for her. She pays a lot of attention. She wants to help me all the time. She wants to help all the kids, and that's a special quality, I mean. Gail possesses that, she wants to help all the kids, also.
> Eugene (the author): I really like that here in this room that being smart mean being helpful.
> Mr. Steve: You got it right.

Finally, I want to comment on one more aspect of membership at the LLR club – its dynamism and asynchronicity. Children often join to the LLR club at different points in its annual work. Some children come to the computer lab during the LLR activities and decided to join the club after observing how "cool" it is. Some were invited by Mr. Steve. Some children were sent to the LLR club by their parents. The children's asynchronous entrance to the LLR club makes a pedagogical design "on the same page" organizationally unviable, actually, in my view, sameness is never viable. Observing Mr. Steve's pedagogical designs, I have come to a conclusion that he intentionally promotes asynchronicity in children joining his learning activities. This asynchronicity discourages vicious competitions and comparisons among children and promotes collaboration, mutual guidance, help, and autonomous activity centers. As I mentioned above, under time pressure sometimes, but relatively rarely, Mr. Steve regresses into a unilateral guidance pattern demanding that a group of his children be "on one page," but his pedagogical design resists this efforts to apply this philosophical approach to be applied on a systematic basis.

Transformation of Guidance

I argue that the main focus of any good pedagogy should not be on the guidance itself – how to give good, sensitive guidance and avoid pedagogical mistakes -- but on the adaptive transformation of that guidance in response to the attending participants. The difference between a good teacher and a poor teacher is not that the good teacher does not make mistakes – both do. Pedagogical mistakes are unavoidable. The difference between them in what happens after a pedagogical mistake is made: whether the teacher improves or worsens his or her guidance in response to a pedagogical mistake or remains the same. This point is somewhat analogous to the mechanical movement in physics. Before Galileo and Newton, scholars tried to explain movement and the causes for it. Galileo and Newton claimed that movement does not need to be explained because it is an aspect of all material objects. What has to be explained is the change of movement. Similarly, I claim that guidance, deliberate or unintentional, is an aspect of any human communication or activity and does not need to be explained[10]. What needs to be explained in the science of pedagogy is what force, if any, will creates a transformation of guidance.

The first observation about what creates transformation of guidance in the LLR club is that it is almost invisible and non-dramatic. Jose Rosa, Mr. Steve's aide, pointed out that this invisibility of guidance was a good thing, "kids can actually have fun ... learning -- this is a good way of teaching kids without them actually knowing that they are getting taught to do something." I speculate that this invisibility is a result of the fact that at the LLR club, the transformation of guidance is a big component of the guidance itself. Guidance at the LLR club was naturally somewhat transformative in nature as it coincided with the activity's problem-solving. For example, a child tested his car-robot after its programming to perform a mission task on the mission table (like on figure 9), but the car-robot stops before it should. The child was looked puzzled and stood in silence. Mr. Steve, observing the test, said, "One more second." The child smiled, took the car, and went back to programming. He increased the parameter of the movement for one more second and went back to testing. Of course, Mr. Steve's suggestion of one second was his guess (wild or informed), and factually wrong. The correct parameter was less than a second, which the child eventually came to, but it provided the direction (meta-guidance) for the child of how to approach the problem. This time the car-robot went too far. The child exclaimed, "Oh, too long!" picked the car up and went back to program to decrease the time parameter. Mr. Steve laughed and said, "You got it!"

However, in a similar case another boy did not do that but instead looked puzzled and a bit frustrated. In this case, Mr. Steve provided more extensive guidance, "This time, it's too long. One second is too much. Take ¾. Do you know fractions?" The boy nodded. Mr. Steve said, "How much is ¾?" The boy replied, "Point seventy five." Mr. Steve suggested seriously, "Enter point seventy five. I think it's enough…. But maybe not." He exploded in laughter looking around at the children and me. The boy also smiled at Mr. Steve's joke[11] and went to back to his computer to change the parameter. Of course, 0.75 second was not enough but the

---

[10] Like movement, guidance has a relative nature and "non-guidance" is a particular form of guidance (like, motionlessness is a particular movement with zero speed).

[11] My take on this is that Mr. Steve made a joke about his sureness of his own guess. I think he heard himself sounded almost arrogantly certain (how could he know for sure that ¾ second is enough?! Is he God?!). Arguably, the joke itself had a guiding property, communicating to the boy that the focus should be not on the exact number but on the process of approximating guessing.

boy was already involved in the action of approximation and made further approximations by himself. Mr. Steve transformed his guidance (i.e., extended it) in response to the children's educational needs. The first child got the idea of approximation from Mr. Steve's first suggestion but the second child required more help. In this sense, his initial guidance for the second child temporarily failed and Mr. Steve revised it. However, for an external observer this transformation of Mr. Steve's guidance seems almost invisible as if it were all an organic and smooth unfolding of his initial plan (which, of course, was not the case!).

I have noticed a few cases where a transformation of Mr. Steve's guidance was more visible. In one case, he was trying to prepare a group of novice younger children – whom he referred to as "Missions" -- for presentations of the LLR annual mission tasks at an upcoming local selection contest. He used conventional school guidance based on quizzing the group of the children by asking information-known questions like, "What's this for? What's the mission? What should we do [to perform the mission task]? But why?" The children provided their informed guesses based on their prior knowledge and experiences about energy and natural processes. They also focused heavily on the mission tasks that, in many cases, were arbitrary and disconnected from the underlining theme of the annual competition. The children were highly engaged and interested in their guess making despite the fact that (or even, maybe, because) Mr. Steve's quizzing was constantly interrupted by older children's testing their programmed car-robots performance of mission tasks. These interruptions arguably provided more guidance for the younger children about the mission tasks than Mr. Steve's quizzing. Mr. Steve was apparently puzzled why the children relied more on their own guesses and experiences in answering his quizzing questions than on the text of the official LLR worksheets that he provided to them. He asked them after their replies, "But is that what the worksheet says?" When children turned to the text, Mr. Steve seemed to notice that they had difficulties engaging in and understanding the monologic text of the LLR worksheets – the children started asking questions about the worksheets but their work with the text was not coordinated and remained accidental. When Mr. Steve realized fully the problem he said, "OK, we're going to do it this way." He assigned each child of the Missions group a presentation to prepare for the entire group about a particular mission task (e.g., moving trees to a power plant). The focus of the activity changed from replying to his quizzing questions to working with the text. It is interesting that in this case Mr. Steve, noting the emerging pattern of the children having difficulties working with the worksheets as an unplanned by-product of his initial guidance, transformed the problems with the worksheets into the main focus of his guidance. Although, each child learn only about one mission task, they all were learning how to work with the LLR official text and extract needed information. In a later session, I observed the new ease with which these children could work with the LLR worksheets and discuss them with each other. Paradoxically, it almost did not matter how the initial guidance had been organized – even though it was by a conventional transmission of knowledge educational philosophy as it was arguably done in the presented episode – as long as a "transformation of guidance" in response to students' educational needs is the overarching pedagogical practice.

Mr. Steve's guidance has a dialogic nature: it is suggestive, testing, explorative, addressive, and provocative. Although, Mr. Steve's guiding statements sound like commands, in my view, they are actually suggestions isomorphic to middle-class suggestive statements such as, "Why don't you try so and so..." Mr. Steve justifies his initially strong suggestive guidance by virtue that , "They get the..., they complete the missions. They change, their attitudes change when they see that it's successful. I give them every opportunity to think of how to make that mission execute. Every opportunity to do it on their own. When I see that they're stuck, that they're stuck, they can't make it work, I give them different options, 'Take the car; you can do it this way instead of that way. You can make the arm spin this way instead of that way because ah, by you spinning it that way it's breaking this other stuff or touching this other stuff. You'll get points disqualified for that. Or you know, if you....' I give them different option, 'you choose, do it this way try it this way first and see what happens.' So I give them different options." The children could and did question Mr. Steve's guiding options-suggestions. For example, when Mr. Steve suggested to a child that his car-robot should hit the wall with a sensor, *come back for 1 second*, and then spin to turn back; the child questioned Mr. Steve about the necessity to come back for 1 second before the car's spinning. Mr. Steve provided the explanation that if the car-robot tried to spin immediately after hitting the wall, the wall would prevent spinning and redirect the car from going back to the base according to the mission task. This time, the child seemed to agree with Mr. Steve and went back to programming according to his suggestion. In some rare cases, I observed children disagreed with Mr. Steve's suggestions after he explained his rationale to them. In these cases, Mr. Steve encouraged the children to try their own way and see what would happen. I have never observed a struggle for control of the activity between Mr. Steve and the children guided by him though I sometimes saw such struggles among the children.

Mr. Steve's suggestive guidance involves not only testing ideas to solve particular problems in the activity that the children faced, but also involves testing his own guidance. As I showed above, what might be good guidance for one child, might not be good for another. Mr. Steve did not just test his suggested idea about the car-robot but he also tested the child's understanding of his idea. If the child got his idea – the child could continue on his or her own. If not, Mr. Steve provided more and different guidance. The suggestive guidance creates ontological provocations for the object of the activity – e.g., the performance of the programmed car-robot – the problem-solvers (i.e., children and Mr. Steve), and Mr. Steve as the teacher. They all found themselves in a new situation that could not be fully predicted in advance: it was unclear how the robot-car would behave after a suggested change, what understanding of the problem and its solution the participants might have as a result of it, and how Mr. Steve should guide the children. The guidance goals were moving targets following the activity as it unfolded for the children rather than set rigidly sequential pedagogical targets in advance like in conventional schooling despite of the students' immediate needs,

> Oh frustration and, um, there's a lot of frustration in kids, they're, um, they get impatient. They start verbally complaining, you know uh, their behavior changes. ... Negatively, it's a minus, you know. ... You go to the, oh yea, oh yea, I try to get them back to the neutral zone [laughs].... Well, I motivate the, I give them options, I create jokes and talk to them. I've had sometimes... where I had to come out of the room one or two times with the kids and talk to them. You know, they want to give up. [I tell them,] 'It's easy, you know, how hard do you want to make this? Or how easy do you want to make this? I can make it very easy for you, tell me how, and you know, what is it that you want me to do for you?' And I help them but ah you know it, they do... they're frustrated, and I don't blame them. It's not, you know, easy... But I give them options, I mean when I see that they can't do, not even the option, then I'll sit with them. I'll sit with them and I'll guide them

through. I'll do the programming for them, until we execute a mission. Then their attitude is back on track! [Laughs]

As Mr. Steve pointed out in his interview, his pedagogical goal was not to have a child solve a problem on his or her own, or to do so independently in an activity (typical of conventional education) but rather to expand the child's participation in the activity. I wonder if this feature of Mr. Steve's guidance was similar to how parents in non-traditional cultures with little schooling provide guidance to their children (De Haan, 1999). Mr. Steve waived the children into an LLR activity that moved along while children gained in skill and responsibility for it. This growing responsibility of the children towards the LLR activity was not necessarily individualistic in terms of each child becoming more autonomous and independent as Vygotsky defined this notion in his famous "the zone of proximal development" (Vygotsky, 1978), -- but often was growing communal responsibility as interdependency increased as a result of it (Matusov, 1998; Matusov, St. Julien, Lacasa, & Alburquerque Candela, 2007). Thus, Mr. Steve explores with the children not only the problems with the car-robot not performing in the desired mission task at hand, but also into what kind of responsibility for the activity the child could assume in collaboration with Mr. Steve and other LLR participants.

Children's verbal and action replies to Mr. Steve's suggestions guided Mr. Steve in how to guide the children. His guidance was formative rather than pre-planned – the point that I have already addressed above. But in addition, it was formative dialogically rather than manipulatively – the point that I want to expand here. Mr. Steve worked *with* human agency of his students, not *on* them. His goal was not bring them to some conceptual, knowledge, or skill point that he had known from the beginning. Both problem solving process, definitions of problems, and activity goals were genuinely open for negotiation in the LLR club. Guidance and level of challenge is negotiated between Mr. Steve and the children. This is how this negotiation was described by 14-year old boy, a newcomer to the LLR club, in an interview, "First, they started me out with some big [project]... he [Mr. Steve] wanted me to program! But I was like, 'Nah not yet,' so I build a robot out the book, couldn't just do it, I read it out the book... then I was like, 'This should be somethin' like I'm into!' so then I started doing it [i.e., learning how to program car robots]."

It was true that both Mr. Steve and the other participants could be very passionate and committed in their particular actions, ideas, problems, and goals in contradiction to other participants but they were never forced out. "The last argument" for following his directions that I have heard Mr. Steve say is "you'll remember my words at the competition," but the children's own agency, and thus the responsibility for the consequences has the final say in any debate. He provides guidance to inform them of the possible consequences of their decisions, and to protect them from harm (potential harm seems to be the only place where he does not leave it open to a debate). Respect for human agency of his students and his genuine attention to and interest in the children's responses distinguished Mr. Steve's guidance as dialogic.

Discourses and Their Ecology

Synchronous and asynchronous diversity, dynamics, and fluidity of activities created synchronous and asynchronous diversity, dynamics, and fluidity of discourses and their themes at the LLR club. Fluidity of topical boundaries of these activities and their "official" legitimacy in the LLR lab promoted a sense of connection to the bigger world: the LLR activities could easily "spill out" outside of the LLR lab and the bigger world could legitimately "spill out" in the LLR lab as Mr. Steve and the children reported in their interviews. Mr. Steve valued non-LLR chats that the children were involved in the LLR lab, "I'm able to see what's going on with the kids. I'm able to help them with, if I can help them. Other times I try to, you know um, just let them work things out. Talk what it is that they need to talk about.... There's a psychological thing going on with that, you know, therapeutic value in them going to their peers and talking about their little or big issues. There's a trust building thing going on there. Sometimes I'll tell them, when I hear these little conversations going on about, you know, boys or girls..." Thus, some children reported during interviews that they valued the LLR club for opportunities to have fun with their friends. The LLR-related and non-LLR-related discourses seemed to have synergy: they apparently anchored each other. Children who came to the LLR club for having relations and fun with other children eventually got hooked on the LLR activities and discourses, and the reverse seemed to be true: children who engaged in the LLR activities and discourses eventually developed lasting and dynamic relations with other children in the LLR club. Let's consider the relationship between activity, social relations, and discourse in detail.

Types of Topical Density of Discourse

From a point of view of a discursive ecology, I think it is useful to differentiate five dimensions of discourse: I) its *topical density*, II) its *function*, III) its *topical and organizational ownership,* IV) its *locus of attention*, and V) its *inclusivity*. The topical density of a discourse can be: 1) sustainably mono-topic, 2) dynamically multiple-topic, and 3) fluidly diffused. A lecture or a clearly focused discussion often (but not always) represents sustained and prolonged mono-topical discourse. In mono-topical discourse, the participants agree about the main purpose of the discourse and its discussed problems and approaches. In this discourse, subtopics are subordinated to the main topic usually (but not always) in a hierarchical manner. At the LLR club, I observed both LLR-related and non-LLR-related mono-topical discourses between participants. An example of a LLR-related sustained and prolonged mono-topical discourse was the testing car-robots to perform a required mission. As I showed above, these mono-topical discourses had many subtopics that were subordinated to the main topic. An obvious example of non-LLR-related sustained mono-topical discourse was a discourse about a computer game that two younger boys were involved in during the entire videotaped LLR session.

In a multiple-topical discourse, there are several main topics that do not subordinate to each other. For example, the Missions group of children involved in their preparation for the high stakes contest to present the mission tasks. These tasks were presented a in the selective contest that provided access for these students to participate in the annual national LLR competition was such a multiple-topic discourse. The children were involved in two main LLR-related topics: 1) the preparation for the selective contest and 2) the testing car-robots of older and more seasoned children. Although, these two themes were not subordinated to each other, they had some synergy: participation in the testing of newly programmed car-robots clearly helped younger children better understand the mission tasks; while participation in preparations for presentations for the selective competition with the guidance of Mr. Steve arguably better prepared some of the younger children for their participation in making observations, judgments, and suggestions of the car-robot testing. Probably, because of this synergy, Mr. Steve prioritized car-testing and encouraged younger children's participation in it. In general, Mr. Steve liked the LLR-related mono- and multi-topic discourses and viewed them as the ideal communication at the LLR club, "there is a lot of communication going on between the kids or the adults regarding the programming or the, you know, the execution of the missions. There's a lot of communication going on, and there's no yelling there's no arguing. But we're all communication, you know, constructive communication. And when that happens I sit back and I watch it and I get self-satisfaction, you know, because they're doing the way that it's meant to be. And, you know, it's ah pretty awesome to see the kids interact with each other like that. Even when some of the kids don't get along but and then it happens."

In a topic-diffused discourse, there are no main topics at all – only the bubbling of proto-topics. It is rather easy to find numerous examples of a topic-diffused discourse in the children's horse playing, or Mr. Steve's joking, or in the teenage children's chatting – but these were mostly non-LLR-related activities. I most often observed a topic-diffused discourse in LLR-related activities when the participants got stuck in their LLR activity. For example, when two girls could not make their car-robot perform a mission task they tried several ways to reprogram the car-robot and change its position on the base from which the car-robot started its mission. They tried many disconnected proto-ideas some of which were "illegal" like redirecting their car with a hand during its mission, and some were in their fantasy world -- i.e., making jerky body movements[12] as if they were robots themselves who had to perform the mission on the mission table. Some of that discourse was done out of frustration and some in a playful, almost joking mood,

> Eugene (the author): Why is it fun, that it makes you laugh, or?
> Yasenia: Yea, we always do something stupid with the computer.
> Eugene: Okay, like what?
> Yasenia: Or make the robot do something retarded.
> Eugene: [Laughs] Okay, like what?
> Yasenia: I don't know, make it spin around, spin around, spin around, or like sometimes we make it go too long or too fast and it goes overboard.
> Eugene: That's cool. [Laughs] And do you do it on purpose?
> Yasenia: No, we do it on accident...

I think topic-diffused discourse has been noticed in past and diversely called by other scholars starting from Piaget calling it "ego centric speech" (Piaget, 2002), to "external speech for oneself" (Vygotsky et al., 1987), "children's chatter" (Jones, 1988), "mindstorming" (Baker-Sennett, Matusov, & Rogoff, 1992), "the third type of discourse" (Sidorkin, 1999), "on-task playful talk" (Wegerif, 2007), "topic mosaic" (Matusov & Hayes, 2000). As Sidorkin correctly points out, not only children are involved in topic-diffused discourse but also adults. For example, when Mr. Steve found a bizarre explanation in the official LLR mission worksheet that trees had to be moved to a power plant as a part of energy cycle, he got involved in a topic-diffused meaning-making exploratory discourse. The boundary between the three types of discourse based on topic density can be dynamic,

---

[12] After Bakhtin, I consider actions as a part of discourse when they address, respond to, and are responded by actions or utterances of others.

flexible, and diffused at times. In addition, several different discourses can overlap in , and participants can participate in different types of discourses at the same time. When topic-diffused discourses became prolonged and comprehensive, Mr. Steve often considered it as breakdown in the LLR club that has to be addressed, "[How does not good interaction at the LLR club look like?] Chaos, chaos, arguing, you know, too much joking around, nobody's paying attention and it's, you know, like an ADHD [laughs] and ADHD [Attention-Deficit Hyperactivity Disorder (ADHD)] anonymous is required in here. [Laughs] But you know it's hard to deal with them, you know its." However, at another place Mr. Steve talked about how the diffuse talk actually is important to keeping kids participating in the LLR. Maybe, he had ecology and a contextual role of diffused talk patterns in mind in the interviews. Probably LLR diffused talk wouldn't seem only as negative.

Functions of Discourse

Discourse always has two aspects: a goal-oriented activity and social relations. However, one of these two aspects can be prioritized in a discourse at expense of the other – discourse can serve different functions for participants. Thus, the function of a discourse can be: a) activity-based and b) relation-based. When asked what value the children see in the LLR club, the children were split between those who emphasized the LLR activities and projects and those who emphasized having fun and good time with their friends and other children at LACC (and with Mr. Steve). This ambivalence of the purpose is evident in the following my interview with a LLR girl who was in her 3rd year in the club:

> Eugene (the author): …So why did you sign up for this program?
> Diana: Because you know, um, my friends were here so then it made me think that I wanted to play. So like cause it looked fun, then it got then it got more endurance (interesting?) for me.
> Eugene: And who are they your friends?
> Diana: Gail, Alejandro, Mr. Steve, Jose, Cris.

When asked what she liked in the LLR program, Diana replied that: 1) "I like cause it gets harder every time they [the LLR organizers] try to make something [i.e., the LLR mission tasks]" – activity-based discourse, and 2) "I also like it because of my friends. They help me and it makes it easier for me when they help. And it's fun. That's why I like it," – both relation-based and activity-based discourse.

In an activity-based discourse, accomplishing something is more important than maintaining a particular relationship (although it can be also important, see for examples of the teacher focusing on social relations subordinated to guidance by the teacher in Lampert, 2001). The majority of the examples above are activity-based discourse. In a relation-based discourse, managing and maintaining particular relationship is in foreground while accomplishing something is in background of the discourse. The focus on social relations in the discourse can be individualistic – when participants try to achieve and bid for certain social positions in regards to the other participants such as "being your friend" or "knowing more than you" (see more on positioning in Davies & Harré, 2001) or collectivistic such as "having fun", "having laugh" (Willis, 1981), "off-task playful talk" (Wegerif, 2007), "being united against them", and so on. A good example of a relation-based discourse that I observed at LLR involved Mr. Steve and two young children. A boy came to Mr. Steve and insistently asked if the video camera that Mr. Steve set up earlier was running. The boy wanted to prove to another child that the camera was not actually running. His question to Mr. Steve was not seeking information, but Mr. Steve's confirmation of the boy's known truth. Initially, Mr. Steve seriously replied to the boy that the camera was running. But the boy insisted on asking again and again seeking a different answer from Mr. Steve. He wanted so much to hear that the camera was not running that he shook his head as if in negation while asking again his question, "Mr. Steve, it's not running, right?" as if he himself answered his own question. This funny mannerism was not unnoticed by Mr. Steve who changed his tone from serious to playful and replied to the boy, "Yes, it's not running" while shaking his head in negation and laughing. Then Mr. Steve turned to a novice 9-year old girl who came to the LLR club for the first time and said with smile, "No, it's running" while nodding his head in confirmation. The girl laughed in response to Mr. Steve's joke. Mr. Steve stretched his hand offering her "high five" and the girl gave her "five" to Mr. Steve. Later when I showed this videotaped episode to Mr. Steve, he commented that he wanted to build a rapport with the new girl to make her feel comfortable and welcomed at the LLR club, which was a clear indicator of a relation-based discourse.

The difference between an activity-based discourse and a relation-based discourse is relative, dynamic, and not absolute and each of them can have all three types of topic density. An activity-based discourse can easily become relation-based discourse and vice versa (and it can even be different for different participants) (Baker-Sennett et al., 1992). For example, I observed a dispute between two girls who were friends arguing about who was going to control my video camera next. At some point, their activity-based discourse about who was going to get the camera turned into a relation-based discourse about breaking their relations and moving away from each other and… the camera.

Types of Ownership in Discourse

Analyzing topical and organizational dimension of a classroom discourse, Gutierrez and her colleagues (1995) distinguish two types of unilateral (thus monologic) ownership of discourse: by the teacher (they called this discursive Space#1) and by the students (they called this discursive Space#2) and one collaborative ownership (discursive Space#3). In contrast with discourses found in traditional classroom research, I rarely observed extreme forms of unilateral discursive ownership at the LLR club. Any observed unilateral extreme discursive ownership was mostly related to strategic transitions from one mission to another or to the beginning of the activity as described above. Mr. Steve or his aide Jose Rosa might move a LLR team who, from Mr. Steve's and/or Jose's point of view, might be spending too much time on a mission to another mission because. This decision was based on the time pressure created by the closing in on the national annual LLR competition date. In most of the LLR club sessions' time, I observed alternations between shaper asymmetrical and more symmetrical collaborative ownership. In asymmetrical collaborative ownership, Mr. Steve, Jose, or a more knowledgeable child (or children) might take more or strategically different ownership in a discourse. For example, in working with the Missions group of novice children, Mr. Steve took the strategic ownership of quizzing the children about the missions. However, it was a child who started reading the LLR mission worksheet on her own, who then prompted Mr. Steve to change his guiding strategy and to distribute the missions among the participants of the group instead of quizzing them. While watching the testing of the car-robots all the observing children and Mr. Steve often had the same ownership for the discourse making evaluative judgments about the car's performance and suggestions for improvements to fix the observed problems.

Loci of Attention in Discourse

Discussing his three types of discourse in a conventional classroom, Sidorkin (1999) differentiates between whole group and small group discourses based on the participants' attention and speakers' intended audience. Sidorkin argues that the whole group discourse, especially, if a group is relatively big, like in a conventional classroom, is difficult to sustain for prolonged periods of time because it puts too much attention and articulation demands on the audience and speakers. In the LLR club, I observed a whole group discourse only during one videotaped LLR session, in which Mr. Steve made a whole club instruction about where information about the LLR national annual competition was located on the Internet. Even during this section, his whole club discourse was alternating with small group and solo discourses. The later involved, among other forms, a child quickly switching to an internet video game and talking to himself about the game. Mr. Steve's aide, Jose Rosa pointed out that this most monologic type of their activities was probably the most uninteresting for the children, "it's like homework to them, it's like doing a project for school and you know half of them don't like school work because it's not fun or interesting, so that's probably why they don't like it that much." I agree with Jose based on my observations. During Mr. Steve's monologic presentation of mission research on the Internet, I observed one older girl seasoned in the LLR club, at the computer who smuggled a message written on Notepad by hiding it behind the LLR official site page to her friend who visited the LLR club for the first time, "It's not usually like that here!" In my observation, these school-like monologic presentations by Mr. Steve were rare, not very prolonged, and accompanied with many "non-legitimate," "semi-legitimate," and "legitimate" parallel activities and discourses that the children either smuggled in or legitimately introduced during Mr. Steve's monologic brief presentations of his unilateral ownership.

In addition to Sidorkin's, whole group and small group discourses, I want to add solo discourse in which a participant engages in dialogue with him or herself. I observed not only children loudly talking and articulately acting for themselves but also Mr. Steve. Of course, we know that people involved in solo discourse where they address and respond to themselves or an imagined others occur in both silent and loud forms.

Exclusivity-Inclusivity of Discourse

The fifth, and the final, dimension of discourse that I have found useful for discussing the educational ecology at the LLR club is its inclusivity (or its exclusivity). An inclusive discourse is one that is open and welcoming for any available newcomer to join and/or attend. An exclusive discourse is one that prevents all or some available and willing newcomers to join and/or attend. There are never completely inclusive or completely exclusive discourses – this is always a matter of degree, although this degree can be dramatically different from one discourse to another. Discursive exclusivity can be factual or ideological. The factually exclusive discourses involve unintentional obstacles which prevent participation by others. For example, when some LLR participants switched to Spanish during emotional moments, it prevented non-Spanish speakers to attend and participate, including myself and other non-Spanish speaking children at the LLR club though of Latino-descent. Or some of discourse by the LLR seasoned children about programming their car-robots were so technical that it prevented more novice children (and me) to follow it. Also, far physical distances among the participants or lack of view of the objects involved into the discourse might prevent them from participation. In both cases, exclusivity was factual and unintentional.

However, in an ideologically exclusive discourse, exclusion is not accidental but intentional. I called this exclusivity "ideological" because it is usually accompanied with an ideological discourse that justifies the intentional exclusion (i.e., "the LLR club is not for kids younger than 9-years old", "our conversation is private", "you are not a part of our team"). Chatting teenage girls at the LLR club asked me to move my audio recorder away because they did not want me to record their "private conversation." In an interview, Mr. Steve pointed out the legitimacy of such ideologically exclusive private conversations during the LLR club sessions because they help the teenagers discuss their relational issues, but also protect younger children from inadvertently eavesdropping in on the older children's private conversations. According to him, this could occasionally cause damaging rumors and force adults to act punitively against the involved teenagers, "I say look, [whispers] keep your voice down, don't let other people hear this stuff 'cause it'll become gossip, and this should be a valuable conversation that you guys are having. Don't let nobody hear it, it's yours. It shouldn't interest or get into the ears of other people because, you know, other people here you know, young girl talking about kids, right away, 'Oh my god! I'm gonna tell her mom!' and it becomes like the pink thing, 'Oh no! Not my girl.' [But] It's not a big deal to me."

Often exclusive discourses are not appreciated by educators because they exclude other children and promote division among them and this is, of course, sometimes true (see Paley, 1992). However, exclusive discourses also often deepen relations among participants, make them special, and generate distinguished cultures (Matusov, Smith et al., 2007). They generate important rights, liberties, autonomies, and freedoms. Mr. Steve saw value in exclusivity discourse among the children, "I don't like to force too many kids to work with other kids that they do not know, they do not get along with, that they have bad feelings about, because that tends to close these kids minds up sometimes. If I can keep their minds open all the time, just by being with their friends that all work for me. That has worked for me. Prime example, Yasenia and Diana do not get along, they and they and they have been competing Legos for three year, well Diana two, Yasenia three and this happened before with other kids and you know. I have accepted the fact that I am not going to like everybody in this world and maybe a couple people maybe like ah… Like ah, but ah less of the world's population. So, if it's good for me, if it's good for the goose, it's good for the gander [laughs]. So if it works for me, it's gotta work for the kids." While inclusive discourses are sources for equality, exclusive discourses are sources of diversity and comfort.

Discursive Ecology in Education

Bakhtin (1991) argued that any discourse has two forces: centripetal – uniting, homologizing, and monologizing discourse and a community behind it, -- and centrifugal – diversifying, diffusing, and dialogizing discourse and a community behind it. He argued that each of the two forces put to the extreme – extreme monologism and extreme dialogism -- destroys its discourse (and a community behind it). Conventional pedagogy prioritizes the centripetal force of discourse and favorites a certain (with extreme monologicity) type of discourse in a classroom as the most educationally productive and efficient with the following dimensions: mono-topic, activity-based, unilaterally owned by the teacher, whole class, and inclusive – 100% of time on the teacher's task (Bakhtin, 1999; Gutierrez et al., 1995; Jackson, 1968; Kennedy, 2005; Lortie, 1975; Sidorkin, 1999; Skidmore, 2000; Waller, 1932). Critics of conventional pedagogy argue that this type of discourse especially as prolonged and prioritized by the conventional teacher has several problems. First, it is not as instructive and educational as the proponents of conventional pedagogy argue because unilateral topical and organizational ownership reduce intersubjectivity between the teacher and the students (and among the students) which makes the teacher's guidance blind without access to students' subjectivities and forces the students into passivity (Gutierrez et al., 1995; Matusov & Smith, 2007; Rogoff et al., 1996; Sidorkin, 1999). Second, the teacher's disregard to the relational aspects of the classroom discourse can block participation for some of the students who start feeling unwelcomed due to emerging negative positioning of the less advanced students – sending them and their classmates a message that they are dumb and/or that academic subjects are not for them (Lampert, 2001).

Third, the type of monologic discourse preferred by conventional pedagogy, when it is prolonged, puts tremendous demands on the students' psychology and physiology. This can easily make the students tired, bored, depressed, passive (not motivated), annoyed, disinterested, and agitated (one can find this argument in an indirect form in Sidorkin, 1999, 2002). Fourth, students not only learn in the classroom but also must live in it. Mono-topical activity-based discourses held by teacher ownership take a big chunk of the students' weekdays, robbing students of the kind of fullness intheir lives that require a diversity of discourses in which people may participate and enjoy (Jones, 1988; Sidorkin, 1999). Many students in conventional schools refer to recess and socialization with peers on non-academic matters as their favorite part of schooling (Jackson, 1968; Tenenbaum, 1940; Waller, 1932).

Finally, and fifth, Sidorkin[13] (1999, 2002, 2004) argues that this monologic type of discourse cannot be naturally sustained because it generates upheaval and rebellion in the students and which in response to or preemptively provokes the physical and psychological violence of the teacher who is supported and/or required by the school institution to suppress it. This violence is often mediated by classroom rules, school policies, and discipline and classroom management techniques. In his interview, Jose Rosa made a similar point, "If they're a hundred percent [focused]on [all the] time, I think that would make this become a little boring because it's just work, work, work, work. So like you know them you know talking about what they want to talk about, it's okay because as you know we can't force them to do a hundred percent of work because that's just going to make it boring and that's just going to make them like this less, and we don't want that you know we want them to have a good environment, to, you know, work well with others and to, you know, get along with each other and in order for them to do that they can't just constantly work." In sum, the type of discourse that is preferred, prioritized, and promoted by conventional pedagogy violates human ecology and is thus inhumane, besides being educationally ineffective.

The critique of the conventional classroom discourse based on excessive monologism leads to two mutually related questions: 1) what does an *ecologically valid* educational discourse look like and 2) what institutional design promotes an ecologically valid

---

[13] However in his latest writings (Sidorkin, 2002, 2004), after his first book (Sidorkin, 1999) based on his doctorial dissertation, Sidorkin seems to suggest that monologic instruction can be left intact and compensated by "economy of relations" based on exchange of favors between the teacher and the students (Smith & Matusov, 2009, in press) without much reform of the instructional discourse on the subject matter as his early book seems to suggest.

pedagogical discourse? How should centrifugal forces of monologicity and centrifugal forces of dialogicity be balanced in a classroom discourse? In a conventional school, human ecology is seen negatively as a recess or break from the productive but non-ecological activity of classroom instruction. Classroom ecology is preempted by a rigid decontextualized linear design: 45 minutes instruction plus 15 minute of recess. The exact time schedule can vary within the day but it is still decontextualized from the classroom discourse. I observed some long LLR club sessions that lasted almost 3 hours without the children having or needing any recess. When the LLR club session was over, the children were not happy that they were finished, but sometimes were upset because they had to stop working on their tasks. In the LLR club, the balance between the centripetal and centrifugal forces of discourse was not orchestrated in the institutional design but in the internal and situational negotiation among the participants themselves. The institutional design of the LLR club arguably supported negotiation of the discursive forces. I am turning to this issue the following section.

Pedagogical Design and Carnival

Pedagogical design is based on the degrees of freedom and restraints provided in the community. Degrees of freedom involve not only what is allowed but also what is available for participants. Based on my observations and interviews with the participants, I extracted several degrees of freedom at the LLR club that in my judgment supports the educational ecology of dialogic pedagogy:

1. Freedom to move in the LLR club;
2. Freedom to initiate conversation at any time with any person (through a negotiation of that, of course);
3. Freedom to choose a topic of conversation;
4. Freedom of (dis)association (although, it can or has to be negotiated);
5. Freedom of activity choice and direction (although, it can or has to be negotiated);
6. Freedom to leave the LLR lab (although, it has to be negotiated with Mr. Steve but not always);
7. Availability of non-LLR activities (e.g., computer games, Internet, chatting);
8. Availability of activities and peers outside of the LLR club.

All these degrees of freedom allow the participants to move out of temporarily dysfunctional LLR-related activities, engagements, and social relations which helps them not feel imprisoned or violated,

> Gail: Sometimes when I'm feeling upset or mad or I just feel like I'm all crowded in a small space. I probably won't feel welcomed because are harder for people and it's hard for them to get rid of what they are going through. It makes me feel as if I wasn't even part of the group, as if nobody was there with me, nobody there to help me in my times of need.
> Eugene (the author): Hmmm, and what would you do in this case?
> Gail: Probably hang out with a friend, talk to them a little, try to get away from everybody.

Having additional non-LLR activities available in the LLR lab gives room for the participants to negotiate their engagement in the LLR club and prevents the escalation of violence. As Mr. Steve pointed out in the interview, "Now, there are kids that I do have a hard time with, and I give them free time on the computers and I let 'em figure out, you know, on their own because I don't have the time to deal with them. That does happen, yea.... Well, I feel, I feel, like ah, that it's an issue that needs to be taken care of, but there are times, I guess I get moody sometimes. And there are times that I can't go ahead and deal with that. Sometimes what I'll do is I'll tell them to leave. I'll give them an extra fifteen minutes, an extra five minutes of playing, just so he can get satisfactory on whatever it is that he is playing. Then he'll bring 'em back and bring her back, or."

Many, if not all, of these freedoms are negotiable: Mr. Steve, Jose Rosa, or any other participants could make a demand of a child (or Mr. Steve) to be somewhere or talk (or not talk) or do something, but in my observation, all these demands are conditioned on reasons, explanations, and counter-argumentation by participants. Providing space for making choices and deciding on preferences, including the decision not to be at the LLR club, is very important to Mr. Steve, "I need to give them the space to think about what they're doing and if, whether or not there is value in what they're doing -- to them. They need to see value, and if they don't it's not for them. Maybe in that particular time and moment, they may not see the value. But who knows? Maybe a year later, they'll come back." In their interviews, both Mr. Steve and his aide, Jose, emphasized that it was important to them that the children felt free in their engagement at the LLR club, "I guess no one's ever gotten bored of doing the thing itself, but like if it had gotten done, it wouldn't been us. We'd a probably just told them, you know, if you think this is so boring why are you here? Like, you know, we're not forcing them to be here, we're not forcing them to be bored. Like all the kids who are only doing it are the ones who are interested and the one's who really do this and that's why they're there. So, if anyone got bored of it and didn't want to do it, like, we wouldn't stop them to leave. If they want to leave, they just don't come back" (interview with Jose Rosa). Jose also emphasized that he saw the success of the LLR program in the children being happy, "happiness, also and um, you know the urge to keep going after completing one thing, they just feel so overwhelmed that they can do it, so you could say happiness about it.... they scream with joy, they laugh, they're happy they're clapping they're running around a little bit saying, 'We did it!'"

However, all the participants reported about restrictive rules existing at the LLR during the interviews. Although, the participants did not list the same rules and their nature (for example, younger children saw the rules listed by them as unconditional and unreasoned – they could not explained a reason behind a particular rule -- while older children saw them as contextual, purposeful, and nuanced), there could be extracted several important restrictive rules in their discourse:

1. No disruptive movements in the LLR lab (e.g., no running);
2. No disruptive behaviors that make LLR activities more difficult (e.g., screaming, loud computer games);
3. No mean talk or bad words;
4. No gossiping;
5. No fighting;
6. No participation on porno Internet sites or MySpace.com;

7. No leaving the LLR lab without permission from Mr. Steve or Jose;
8. Be attentive to Mr. Steve and Jose;
9. Be respectful to everybody;
10. Do not talk on teen sensitive issues in the presence of younger children;
11. Children younger than 9-year old cannot participate in the LLR club;
12. No food at the LLR lab;
13. Computer games are allowed only for first 20 minutes of the LLR club session;
14. Prioritize the LLR club during its session hours over other activities available at LACC at that time.

These restrictive rules apparently prioritize participants' safety and well-being and promote the participants' commitment to the LLR club and its activities. The ownership of the rules seemed to be collective – all the participants seemed to support them -- but asymmetrical with the heaviest responsibility for designing and promoting these rules on Mr. Steve, Jose, and LACC staff. On numerous occasions, I observed a collective enforcement of some of the rules. A 7-year old boy was asked by a LLR girl to leave the LLR lab because he was too young for the LLR competition, but Mr. Steve allowed him to stay. Children reminded each other to stop saying bad words or being mean. I observed a group of boys getting on a sexually explicit website by chance. The page popped up while they were searching about for games; the boys did not see me observing them. One boy said, "It's nasty stuff" and closed the window of the site. When I came to the group and I asked why the site was nasty, several of them explained to me that, "It's mean to girls." The discourse about the purposes of the rules and their goals were open and public at the LLR lab, and at the LACC in general. When the children asked "why" questions, these questions were seen by Mr. Steve and Jose Rosa, and the other children as legitimate learning questions, and not seen as "challenging the authority." Mr. Steve and Jose Rosa often engaged in reasoning with the children and were careful in providing rationales for their actions and judgments. The children's questions and/or counter-arguments were often welcomed.

However, rules were violated and, what was even more interesting, some of these violations were ignored when noticed. Sometimes the rules were even suspended as it was in the case of Mr. Steve allowing a younger boy to stay on at the LLR lab in spite of the age requirement. Similarly, children could do their homework or play on computers for some of the time during the LLR sessions. In one case a child got under the LLR mission table and played there with Lego cars. These cases breaking the rules were clearly noticed by Mr. Steve or Jose, but the rules were not enforced. From the interviews with Mr. Steve and the older children and from my observations, it was clear that they saw the rules as conditional, instrumental, judgment-based, and reasonable when serving particular purposes rather than unconditional, absolute, procedural, and self-serving. Appealing to a rule did not automatically win an argument at the LLR lab. While younger LLR children saw the rules in absolute and unconditional terms, older LLR children saw the rules as conditional, requiring a judgment,

> Eugene (the author): What is allowed and not allowed [at the LLR lab] in terms of movement? Yesterday, I saw that Alejandro got under the table, right? Was it allowed? Or not? Nobody told him anything.

Cris: Mostly no because somebody can be like this... [makes kicking movements]
Eugene: Ah, kick himself, hurt himself?
Cris: And kick himself, yea.
Eugene: But yesterday it was fine?
Cris: Yea.

Apparently, rules were aimed at supporting a desired atmosphere in the community as was the use of authority not to enforce the rules but also to promote the desired atmosphere. Studying an Italian nursery, Corsaro (1990) noticed that the teachers often intentionally overlooked the rule that the teachers had established for the little children not bring toys from home in cases where the children did not know if the teacher had noticed their infraction. When asked by the researcher why they overlooked these infractions, the nursery teachers reported that the purpose of the rule was to prevent the children from engaging the teachers and their parents in their conflicts involving the toys brought from home. However, as long as the children could solve emerging interpersonal problems about the toys themselves (or did not have problems) the rules were not needed.

Similarly, the LLR rules were instrumental and conditional. For example, once Mr. Steve left the LLR lab during a LLR session to give me photos of LLR children getting trophies for participation in a recent local LLR selective competition. In his office, he gave me the photos and picked up a pile of candies. When he and I were entering the LLR lab, he heard his aide Jose Rosa reprimanding a child for bringing food into the LLR lab that could potentially mess up the computer and Lego-Logo equipment. Mr. Steve exclaimed, "Kids, who wants candies? Let's celebrate our trophies!" Then he laughed, looked at Jose and me, and added, "I guess I'm violating the 'No Food' rule." Food used as celebrations aimed at promoting communal solidarity and commitment to the LLR activities seemed to overweigh other possible concerns such about potential messiness or distraction of the children working on their LLR tasks. Also, eating a food collectively probably avoided typical concerns about food envy among the children, and promoted collective responsibility for the lab's cleanness and safety of the equipment – the primary concerns behind the 'No Food' rule.

Arguably, this type of rule breaking reinforces the general purpose of the community and the community solidarity. Such rule breaking sends a message to the participants that their community life cannot be reduced to something outside of them. Crowning and de-crowning rules – using Bakhtin's notions from his analysis of carnival as ecology of dialogue (Bakhtin, 1984, 1991, 1999) – enforcing and breaking the communal rules is important for promoting dialogic pedagogy. Communal discourse about rules can help to create, if not a communal consensus, at least a discourse about values in the community. The communal discourse about rules attracts the participants' attention to potentially problematic but important recursive situations in the community like pornographic web sites, eating in the lab, gossiping, fighting, and so on. Comunal discourse about rules also promotes a communal focus on the communal values: "what is important for us" and "where do we stay on this issue." When rules are fully understood and accepted by the participants, they can help save time on solving problems in a community because they automatically prescribe a solution without the participants' needing to reinvent it or consider the problem in depth (in the heat of the moment).

However, communal values, concerns, and purposes can come eventually in conflict with each other and local meanings can always escape rigid conditions of the rules. So, overreliance on rules can become dangerous for communal life. These situations require de-crowning and breaking the rules to revitalize a commitment to an unmediated communal life and its values. Internally persuasive discourse about the meaning of the events, communal prioritization of concerns, and communal values reemerges and overrules the rules. In this case, the rule breaking is not to destroy the rule but to subordinate the rule to the communal life and, thus, to regain its purposefulness. It is an ambivalent process that is usually accompanied by the participants' laughter, as the rule is killed in order to revitalize it. Mr. Steve's candy celebration in the LLR lab did not abolish the rule "No Food" at the lab but suspended it for a special occasion. This might be in part of why students want to both ceremonially extinguish Mr. Steve's command and follow it.

Besides the communal rules, I noticed that authority, frustration, failure, interpersonal tensions, and fear were crowned and de-crowned at the LLR club, "when I see the atmosphere getting a little bit too serious, I start making jokes. Ah, sometimes I create that seriousness, because I need to stop certain things that are happening. And ah, I, you know, just to relieve the pressure a little bit I start to [laughs] I start with my jokes." According to my observations, Mr. Steve is constantly involved in elevating and dismissing his own authority among the LLR children. As he pointed out in his interview, "I believe that all kids should get exposed to everything that they can 'til they find their passion. So you know it may be that you know they'll become game developers in computers or robotics ah creators, who knows? Maybe we have one, or maybe we'll find one in our kids, but you know one is big compared to none and worth the try is better than not trying at all [laughs] so we're not going to lose anything. I know that I'm pretty tough in my classes, I've been trying to be more lenient, and more like let them make their decisions, type of sessions that we have, and let them grow with, you know, their own help. A lot of times I just give them a green light to do whatever and I'll just monitor and look at how they're relating and helping each other with each other. You know it's tough with some of our kids, I'm not saying that it's a piece of cake, it's not it's tough so, we got a lot of static [Laughs]." On (rather rare) occasions, he threatened and actually suspended some children for disruptive behaviors that, from his point of view, make LLR activities more difficult for other children . Re-participation in the LLR club is determined by those suspended as Steve admonishes them to come back when, "they're ready" meaning that the children themselves could come back and report, "I'm ready to come back".

But more often, Mr. Steve made jokes about himself and his own limitations. For example, a girl complained to me that "Mr. Steve confused us" because his suggestion did not work for their car-robot to perform the desired mission task. Mr. Steve overheard this complaint and replied to it with laughter, "I never confuse nobody!" And then he added with a more serious tone but still smiling, "Listen, I'm just learning with you. I also don't know much about it either. What's *your* suggestion?" He seemed to emphasize that he is also a part of the community of learners – he is a learner as anybody else in the club. He seemed to want to empower the children not only about technology but also about the social world,

> They like to play Legos and discover at this set of Legos is a little bit different. It's more complicated because of the communication between the computer and the robot and what it takes to program it. It's actually easy. They like it, they like the fact that they can tell something what to do and it'll do it [laughs]. Unlike me, you

know, they tell me to do something; I won't do it [laughs]; well, it depends. It depends.

When Mr. Steve felt time pressure (i.e., a lack of time to prepare well for the national annual competition) he reminded the participants about their potential failure in a rather serious tone,

> The beauty of the program, what comes out of it, the outcomes of this whole thing is not just, ah, that we placed, you know 23rd or 50 [the kids' score on the national competeton], that is not my final outcome. My final outcome is that we successfully had kids from the beginning to the end. They completed the thing without quitting. They were exposed, they, you know, they competed against other people from other states, or other cities, or other schools, or other agency, and they went there. And no matter how much, how much, uh, fright and uncomfortability was in them, they still went through it they faced it, they dealt with it, and you know, and they learned, they learned. You know, it's one thing that I tell them, and I tell them often is, do not act or play around if it's not what you're going to do over there. Because over there you don't have time to do that. Everybody's going to be watching you. Don't get used to doing certain things here that you're not going to be (there). I want you to be the way you're going to be at the tournament. Because if you don't practice this now, if you don't practice ah self discipline now, when you get there you're gonna feel off, you know, totally uncomfortable. You're not gonna, 'cause you know, so, you know. I try to preach that to the kids, some will take it, some don't others you know will go through the motions of it, it has happened. Others will go through it over there and come back and say, "Mr. Steve, you were right." [laughter] see now, you know, what can I respond to that, "I told you so?" So, it's you know, next time, next time you'll do better.

Whenever unproductive or destructive chaos emerged for long time at the LLR lab, at least from Mr. Steve's point of view, he became serious and even angry, "When it's situation like that I get serious. I get angry. I, hey let's go! Cut it out! Cut it out! And I'm [yelling], 'Cut it at this and you going in a time out!' So, I have to make an example with one kid. I'm fair, part um, 'why?' they ask me 'why?' 'I'm gonna tell you why when I tell you to come off. So, you know why, but I'm going to remind you again.' And it works, you know. Kids will say, 'WOW, Mr. Steve will get you, don't do that.' [Laughs] So you know, being the disciplinarian is kinda ah, a responsibility that you have to take on there, too."

However, when a child was frustrated with his car not performing the desired task and told Mr. Steve in a bit of a whining tone, "It's very tough!" Mr. Steve replied, "Yeah, it's tough… until you solve it and then it's easy again!" and then Mr. Steve exploded in laughter while at the same time reducing the level of difficulty by engaging himself in the task. As the children reported during their interviews, they disliked LLR when the tasks become too hard for them, "Sometimes I don't like when it gets a little too hard" (Interview with a LLR child). During the interview, Mr. Steve acknowledged that he constantly monitored the children's engagement with the LLR tasks to promote a sense of progress and success for them while engaging them in challenges,

> I will approach him [a frustrated child] and ask him what's going on, and I'll take it from there depending on what his reaction may be. It may be that he's upset that he can't do certain things, so I'll go ahead and show him how to do it myself

and show him how easy it is. Thinks, sometimes you think that things are complicated and it's just that in their head they've created this big complex, little thing and ah. I try to make it look real easy so they can manage it as is, easy, so. ...

The fun, fun part [for the children at the LLR club], ahh, [is] making the robot move, and getting the robot to do exactly what they wanted it to do for a long time. I think they feel, they feel some type of gratitude behind that. Sometimes I make a lot of jokes to keep them laughing. Weird ones [laughs], but you know it makes them laugh. Maybe sometimes off the wall jokes, but you know, I try to keep them motivated, motivated. It's not all strictly directions and orders and, you know.

The LLR children were also visibly involved in the crowning and de-crowning of rules, frustration, authority, fear, and failure. They seriously controlled and playfully teased both each other and Mr. Steve. In my observations, Mr. Steve often took seriously the children's bids for control and supported their playful improvisations.

There were also rare but important abuses of crowning and de-crowning from both Mr. Steve and children's part in my judgment. Though exceptionally rare, I found points where Mr. Steve might abuse his laughter as I have reported in the one case when he made a joke about not having girls who would learn the lab in past years. Nearly all the time, Mr. Steve's jokes are very gentle and sensitive to the feelings of the children or to people in general. On rare occasions, Mr. Steve got angry, "I do get angry, you know, especially when they [the LLR children] are misbehaving and I'm tired, you know, I get angry, I get upset sometimes, you know, I don't deny that. I think they don't like that part, ah, especially the kids that have nothing to do with what happened with the other kids. I think they don't like me or the program, ah to have me angry in it. I think, I don't like people that get angry around me. I mean so I know that probably applies to them [the LLR children] too. And to, [I try not to] get angry too much, I don't get angry too much." When asked, some children reported that Mr. Steve could be mean (e.g., yelling at the children or being unfair) when he was tired or bad things happened, "Sometimes he's in a good mood, sometimes he's in a bad mood 'cause something bad happened. Usually, he's in a good mood" (interview with a LLR child), but they were very forgiving of his weaknesses. In all fairness, I have to admit that Mr. Steve is an exceptionally tolerant, patient, and sensitive teacher with the children and they clearly appreciated, attached to, and admired him.

As to the LLR children, they occasionally abused their seriousness and laughter especially in regard to each other. Surprisingly they were aware of their own potential to abuse in the interviews but they often are stopped by other children ,Mr. Steve, or even by themselves, "I talk to myself and I ask myself like why did I do that? Why was I mean? And I come back and say I'm sorry and like we just do whatever else we have to do" (interview with a LLR child). All interviewed children reported that they felt almost always welcomed at the LLR club.

Finally, I want to consider the following question. Can compulsive school with mandatory attendance be organized in a way that creates a learning ecology similar to the polyphonic LLR club at LACC? I think so. To a high degree, the children's attendance of the LACC is mandatory based on their parents' will -- this is especially true for the younger children. This might, of course, be more or less negotiable for the children depending on family circumstances and the parents' cultural beliefs in negotiability with their children. An innovative school could also be organized to promote a polyphonic learning ecology by having many centers of long-term projects (clubs) and activities in which children can volunteer their participation and growing expertise. Some of the centers, clubs, and activities can be adult-led and some children-led (with or without leaders) having open participatory structure such as in LLR club. The schedule of these centers, clubs, and activities can be diverse and comprehensive to allow children to experience diverse activities and settings. I participated (as a parent volunteer) in, observed, and studied one such schools (Matusov, 1999, 2001a; Matusov & Rogoff, 2002; Rogoff, Bartlett, & Goodman Turkanis, 2001; Rogoff et al., 1996). Of course, a school might not take a "one systems approach" as circumstances offer unique needs as well. However, Sidorkin's (2002) question about whether a polyphonic learning ecology can be introduced on a mass scale to public schooling remains open for practical experimentation.

Chapter 11

Designing the Students' Ontological Engagement and Ontologically-Oriented Teaching

Abstract

I reflect on my own and other educators' practice of ontologically-oriented teaching to find out what "ontologically-oriented teaching" is, why it is needed, and how to design it. Ontology refers to participants' commitment to what they do and say with their life, to taking responsibility for their own deeds and words, and the groundedness of what one says and does in his or her sociocultural circumstances of being and life. I contrast students' ontological engagement in academic subjects with non-ontological engagement and with ontological non-engagement and examine the consequences for education.

In my case, I hate everything that merely instructs me without augmenting or directly invigorating my activity.
Nietzsche (1983, p. 59)

Only in the stream of thought and life do words have meaning.
Wittgenstein (1967, p. 173)

I want to introduce the topic of this chapter – ontological teaching -- by providing a rather extended fragment of my videotaped lesson that I gave for preservice teachers for one of my method courses titled "Building Community of Learners" at the end of the semester. The fragment started at the beginning of a 3-hour classroom meeting. My students were 14 female white middle class students in their early twenties sitting in 4 small groups of rather big university Problem-Based Learning auditorium.

LESSON ON "DESIGNING STUDENTS'
ONTOLOGICAL ENGAGEMENT":
SETTING THE PROBLEM

EUGENE [Pointing at and reading the class topic from the long blackboard]: "Designing students' ontological engagement." OK, what's that? This is a very important topic, especially if you want to be a collaborative teacher. What's "ontological"? What does it mean "ontological"? "Designing students' *ontological* engagement." It's a Latin word meaning basically "life-based." Ontological engagement is extremely important for good teaching and learning. For example, right now... you guys, came to my class. And for some reason -- and we will discuss later in our class -- I have decided that *my* teaching about ontological engagement is very important for you. But did you decide that this topic is important for you to learn? Do you care about it? Probably *not*... And that will be the same about your students. Let me give another example. Imagine you are in your own future class... or even in, for that matter, in my class. I want to teach you about the Civil War [writes on the blackboard the topic]. Who is right now concerned about the Civil War, *right now,* in this given moment? Ok, Jamie, are you concerned about the Civil War?

JAMIE: No.

EUGENE: No. Thanks for your honesty. [The students are laughing. Eugene is pointing sequentially at other students -- they say no and Eugene is repeating after them]. No. No. No.... Please, some one here! Katey, how about you? Civil War? [Katey nods] *Really?* [with surprise and disbelief] Did you come to the class saying to yourself, 'Gosh, I'd really like to know more about the Civil War!'

KATEY: No. [smiling]

EUGENE: No? No. What about you? No..

LAUREN: Wait, what was the question?

EUGENE: Civil War? Lauren, are you currently concerned about the Civil War or not?

LAUREN: Nope.

EUGENE: No. [Eugene keeps pointing at and calling up other students. They reply "no" and he repeats after them]. No. Are you concerned about the Civil War right now or not? No. Meghan, are you concerned about the Civil War? No. [Eugene is pointing at Kristy and saying with sarcasm] Kristy, please, say "yes"!

KRISTY [smiling with sarcasm]: YES!

EUGENE [smiling and talking as if on behalf of Kristy]: "I'm really-really want to learn about the Civil War [Eugene moves his arms ...] The whole weekend I was thinking, all weekend I was thinking [Eugene demonstratively scratches his head to show theatrically his puzzlement], how much I want to come to Eugene's class to learn about Civil War!" [Kristy and other students are laughing. She says, no].

And, by the way, guys, this is what *you* will experience as future teachers. Your students came to your classroom not being concerned about lessons that you prepared for them... [points to Lauren] Right now Lauren is checking her cellular phone. [Eugene walks over to Jamie who is scratching her head and points at her and at the students around her who are eating food they bring to the class]. Someone's scratching her head. Someone's eating and someone feels hungry. [Eugene turns to another side of the class] Meghan is reading some notes. Jamie is um... where is your mind now? [says this as a genuine question. She points at the blackboard.] Ah, writing on what is on the blackboard. Um... That will be always like that for your future students – their minds can be in different places away from the targeted academic curriculum... [Lauren raises hand] Yes! [Eugene calls her.]

LAUREN: Actually, I'm making my mind about having a break [to have the class with a recess that runs longer or not have the recess and finish the class earlier – the concurrent theme for the students' discussion for several weeks, This topic was written on the blackboard as one item of the class agenda].

EUGENE: OK. You're making your mind up [about having or not having class break]. Thanks, no, that's good. OK. And you see the minds of your students will be like *that* as well. You, as are coming to your class only to see like Little Amanda might think about that [Eugene looks at what Amanda is doing at this moment]... she need to do something with her friend Little Sari, something good or bad, who knows? Little Julie will think about her birthday that's coming in two days [Julie nods. She told Eugene about her birthday before the class started and he put it on the class agenda on the blackboard.] Little Elizabeth thinks about... uh... that she forgot her sweater in another classroom [which was true and Eugene knew about that because Elizabeth asked Eugene to be a bit late for the class because of that] and just brought it back, and thought *'Oh, my God. Thanks, it's still there!"* - [to Elizabeth] Is it more or less what's on you mind?... Is this what you are thinking about now? [Elizabeth is nodding in agreement]. And yeah, you know, your minds are not there on what the teacher has prepared for you [Eugene points at the class topics written on the blackboard "Designing students' ontological engagement" and "The Civil War"].

And so, think about what the consequences for your teaching and your students' learning because of that. Look, at that right now [pointing at a couple of the students sharing something with each other], you guys are talking with each other, your mind is not there [Eugene now pointing on a group of other students who are talking at this moment with each other]. And if I, as your teacher, try to collaborate with you at this moment on the curriculum topic that I prepared for you, it would be very *difficult* for me to do that. Why? Because *you* guys are not *interested*. You're *disinterested* in the topic I brought to you. [Eugene writes on the blackboard "disinterested"]. You are disinterested in Civil War or in this topic as well [he points out at the topic "Designing students' ontological engagement" written on the blackboard]. *Right now* you're not interested in this topic. You are interested in plenty other topics now like eating, talking with your classmates, thinking about the deadlines for other classes, and so on but not about *my* topics that I prepared for you. My topics of my current interest are not yours and your topics of your current interest are not mine. And... if I'm a collaborative teacher, I want to collaborate with you but you do not want to collaborate with me. Not because you are kind of bad people or whatever, -- it's just your mind is not there. [pauses] OK?

I think you've experienced that when you give your writing lessons [during the ongoing teaching practicum]. How many of you did your writing craft lessons about writing letters? [A few students raised their hands.] You did. Did your students really were in their mind about writing letters or not? What do you think?

LAURA: Some of them were.

EUGENE: Some of them, some of them [nodding]

LAUREN: A few had like had no idea. [Some have difficulties with their writing but some not].

EUGENE: Yeah. It's not the issue of whether or not they could come up with any idea about their writing. They might have some ideas and some useful knowledge and some good skills and some relevant experiences. But it was difficult for them to put these ideas together for their writing because some of your students were probably disinterested in the writing you wanted them to do. It's like the topic of the Civil War for you right now. It isn't the case that you don't have any idea about the Civil War [points to the other side of the classroom, the table nearest the windows] -- it's just your mind, your *mind* is not there. And when your mind is not there and you need to write an essay, or discuss the Civil War, or whatever, it is *very* difficult to do -- *very* difficult to do. So, the question is *how* to create the students' focus on something like the Civil War (pointing out at topic on the blackboard) or like something else [pointing out the class topic about "Designing students' ontological engagement" on the blackboard]? *How* to move your mind, your focus, [Eugene outstretches arms across the room] so you start being really interested right now in something that the teacher prepares, that *you* will prepare for your future students? How to create that? How can I weave your current foci and interests into my topic that I prepared for you? Any ideas? How to do that? [some students raise hands] Yes.

INQUIRY OF REFLECTION ON THE PRACTICE OF ONTOLOGICALLY-ORIENTED TEACHING

The purpose of this chapter is to reflect on my own and other educators' practice of ontologically-oriented teaching to find out what "ontologically-oriented teaching" is, why it is needed, and how to design it. Ontology refers to participants' commitment to what they do and say with their life, to taking responsibility for their own deeds and words, and groundedness of what one says and does in his or her sociocultural circumstances of the being and life (Bakhtin used a similar term "participative," see Bakhtin et al., 1993).

For years, I have been struggling with making my teaching more and more ontologically-oriented (without even using this term). One of the major reasons of why I became a teacher was my High School physics teacher Alexey Korostelyev who often managed to successfully engage us in various topics of High School physics. I noticed that he asked questions and we replied and through this dialogue, we were somehow deeply engaged in study of physics. When I became a physics schoolteacher, I tried asking his questions but for some reason his questions did not make any magic in my class. Maybe I did not remember his questions well or did not ask them in the right moment. It took me many years to experiment, to read examples provided by excellent teachers (e.g., Freedom Writers & Gruwell, 1999; Korczak & Gawronski, 1992; Paley, 1992), and to observe many great teachers before I started getting a hint.

In discussing teacher education, Shulman defines "pedagogy of substance" as "assisting teachers to focus on the design aspects of teaching" (cited in Zlotkowski, 1999, p. 67). Understanding ontologically-oriented teaching is understanding of the design of this type of teaching: planning the design in preparation to the lesson and unfolding the design during the lesson. The main issue of the teaching design is how the academic curriculum, the students, and the teacher are connected during the lesson. In a conventional classroom, the teacher justifies the presented academic curriculum often by reference to the mandate from the school administration, the district, and the board. The teacher relates to the students through a system of rewards and punishments and not through the curriculum itself. Finally, the students relate to the academic curriculum as a mediator to the teacher's approval or disapproval that is often consequential for their well-being (institutionally as students and relationally with their peers and parents). In this conventional teaching design, ontological engagement for the students and the teacher is merely accidental if at all because the academic curriculum is not the major motivator for the students' engagement.

It took me many years to shift from this conventional teaching design of ontological disengagement and non-ontological engagement to ontologically-oriented teaching. At times, my teaching now is not successful either but, in contrast with past, I think I know how to start improving it. Here I present an analysis of videotaped lesson of how I taught ontologically-oriented teaching preservice teachers. This teaching pushed me to reflect more on the topic and promotes interesting inquiries about the notion of ontologically oriented teaching itself.

ONTOLOGICAL ENGAGEMENT, NON-ONTOLOGICAL ENGAGEMENT, AND ONTOLOGICAL DISENGAGEMENT

My early teaching was somewhat similar to one described Gutierrez, Rymes, and Larson (1995) mainly involving teacher's monologic official discourse and students' non-collaborative but dialogic unofficial counter-discourse. In the fragment below, the teacher organizes his teaching discourse around a guessing game about an article in Los Angeles Times that he expected his High School students read.

> TEACHER: We've got a- current events quiz, for those of you who are keeping up with the world. (pause) I've got some... I hafta read (pause). And we'll do some other nice things if I have time. Uhm. Start with some pretty easy ones here (pause). This week, for the last few days in fact. In fact it's on the front page of today's Los Angeles Times, there've been a lot of, uh, people pretty excited in Petaluma California. What are they excited about in Petaluma California.
> ...
> STUDENT: Isn't that guy going to jail or something?
> TEACHER: No...?
> STUDENT: Checkout.
> TEACHER: Yes?
> STUDENT: Is there a man getting executed or something?
> TEACHER: No-o-o!
> STUDENT (imitating the teacher): No-o-o!... (laughter)
> TEACHER: But that's a good guess, I'll give you another hint. There's a river that runs through Petaluma. That river drains out into the San Francisco Bay. Ugh, does anybody figure out, what's going on in Petaluma.
> STUDENT: They peed in the river (some laughter)
> TEACHER: Tania.
> TANIA: They're cleaning it? It's clean now
> TEACHER: Na::w, it's a good guess. (pause)
> TEACHER: Peter.
> PETER: Is there a new Dam, or something?
> TEACHER: No-o-o, it's-
> ...
> STUDENT: We don't know, no one knows.
> Tania: We don't know, nobody knows.
> TEACHER: Kathy?
> KATHY: Is the river polluted?

TEACHER: Probably, but that's not the answer, u:hhhh (Students are laughing)
Uh, Sara:?
SARA: They're gonna build houses on it.
TEACHER: No-o... I guess nobody knows.
...
TEACHER: No. There's a whale, in the river.
TANIA: I knew that.
STUDENT: I knew that.
TEACHER: Haven't you guys read about that?[1]

The teacher introduces his discourse without any regards to the students' interests and current foci. The students' participation in the discourse organized by the teacher is not motivated in the discourse itself and the students' past and anticipated experiences, interests, and needs. It is solely based on official power given by the school institution (also sanctioned by the broader society and parents) to the teacher. That is why the students' participation in the teacher-organized discourse is not ontological.

The teacher's discourse is monologic. Bakhtin (1999) defined a discourse as monologic when the speaker affirms or rejects replies from his or her addressees as being the right or wrong. In essence, in monologic discourse, addressees are not expected to say anything new that is unknown to the speaker. Rather they can say the right thing – the truth known to the speaker from the beginning – or wrong things (errors). Indeed, in monologic teaching, the student wither provides the right answer – expected by the teacher or the wrong answer that the teacher has to correct. This is how internationally recognized modern teacher, Vivian Paley, described her initial teaching experience, "In my haste to supply the children with my own bits and pieces of neatly labeled reality, the appearance of a correct answer gave me the surest feeling that I was teaching. Curriculum guides replaced the lists of questions, but I still wanted most of all to keep things moving with a minimum of distraction. It did not occur to me that the distractions might be the sounds of children thinking" (Paley, 1986b, p. 122). The teacher asks questions, the students reply, the teacher evaluates their responses: if the student provided the teacher-desired answer, the teacher can move on in the curriculum sequence; if not, the teacher has to provide scaffolding (Lemke, 1990; Mehan, 1979; Wells, 1992, September). There is not the teacher's interest in the students' answers. In the example of teaching presented above, the guessing game organized by the teacher is a classic monologic discourse. The teacher objectifies and finalizes the students treating them as source of errors rather than partners for a dialogue of a collaborative endeavor.

The students' unofficial counter-discourse (marked bold above) was dialogic with regard to the classmates but not collaborative with the regard to the teacher. The students made other students laugh very successful at expense of the teacher. Their dialogic discourse was not collaborative with regard to the teacher because not only they ignore the intent of the teacher's discourse but also they exclude the teacher from their discourse and promote adversarial relations toward the teacher in their dialogic turns treating him as an object of their discursive actions. They objectivized the teacher and made him the object of their discourse rather than another subject and addressee. They talked over him rather than with him. In this sense, their counter-discourse was also monologic with regard to the teacher. But

---

[1] I combined fragments presented by the authors (Gutierrez et al., 1995) and eliminated linguistic markers of the speech that are non-essential for our discussion.

it is dialogic with the regard to the other students. The students' counter-official discourse created a carnivalistic atmosphere (Bakhtin, 1984) in the classroom inviting other students to respond with laughter and more comments (serious or mock) about the teacher's monologic leash-like (cf. "adult-run" in Matusov & Rogoff, 2002; Rogoff et al., 1996) guidance – the guidance that forces the students to say what the teacher already knows but they do not (and then he apparently humiliates them for that). The second student's remark about people peeing in the river creates an interesting play with official culture being at the surface level a sanctioned guess among other guesses of the other students but deeply down it is defiance, non-participation, and active resistance to the official teacher-organized discourse. The teacher strategically chose to ignore both comments pushing the students' counter-official discourse on the margins of the classroom public space.

Studying working class Portuguese students marginalized in a Canadian catholic school, McLaren (1993) identifies in his ethnographic study four types of ontological engagement (which he called "states") some of which echo **Gutierrez, Rymes, and Larson's** research: (a) the *student state,* the 'default setting' in which the dominant theme is 'work hard' as students enter a highly ritualized space, where the emphasis is on being quiet, monothematic, serious, well-mannered and predictable, with movement and communication controlled by the teacher; (b) the *streetcorner state,* which is the flipside of the student state, the bottom-up, oppositional, parodic, resistive state, which is playful, improvisational, spontaneous, simultaneous, multithematic, flow-based, collective, often cathartic; (c) the *sanctity state,* with a sense of awe, with reverence, hierarchy, and subservience strong values, and (d) the *home state,* the latter not directly present at school, but often referred to by students, in which they evoke an experience of a sense of comfort and belonging, of being seen.

Gutierrez, Rymes, and Larson analyze discursive public spaces and define the teacher's official monologic discourse as "the first space". They define the students' dialogic but non-collaborative counter-official discourse as "the second space." If we focus on the students' engagement in both public discursive spaces, we can conclude that the students' engagement in the first space was non-ontological. The second space creates ontological participation for the students but this ontological participation in resistance to their engagement to the first space and not in the academic curriculum brought by the teacher. Thus, with regard to the teacher-organized discourse, the students' counter-official space can be characterized *ontological disengagement.*

From educational point of view, both non-ontological engagement and ontological disengagement are arguably undesirable because both of them have little educational value or even have anti-educational value. Non-ontological engagement, also known as "procedural participation" (Bloome, Puro, & Theodorou, 1989; Heath, 1978; Moll, 1990; Nystrand, 1997), when the students' participation is near-fully motivated by the institutional power transcendent to the discourse itself and its content often promotes surface learning based on memorization of unrelated (for them) facts (Rogoff, 1990; Rogoff et al., 1996; Scribner & Cole, 1981). Not only the students often forget what they learn in school through non-ontological engagement but they have difficulty applying what they have learned in school in non-school contexts (Lave, 1988; Nunes et al., 1993; Säljö & Wyndhamn, 1993). Besides, through non-ontological engagement many students have learned alienation from the academic subjects that the subjects are boring and irrelevant and that they themselves are not good at them. In other words, through non-ontological engagement they have learned non-academic identity (Lave, 1992a; Lave & Wenger, 1991; Wenger, 1998). In this sense, non-ontological learning is essentially anti-educational (rather than just non-educational or educational but not effective). Many students have learned in school to dislike school in school (I will provide evidence of that about my students, preservice teachers below). Arguably, they have learned disliking school through non-ontological engagement since many of them are institutionally very good students (but not necessary good learners) having very high GPA and passing exams very successfully. We know that non-ontological engagement created in psychological labs through extrinsic motivation decreases the students' interests (defined in the studies as "intrinsic motivation", cf. Subbotsky, 1995).

Ontological disengagement is arguably also anti-educational. Although non-ontological engagement mobilizes the students' interests and needs, it mobilizes the students to resist the academic curriculum – socially desirable learning – that is provided in a form of monologic and non-collaborative instruction. Like non-ontological engagement, ontological disengagement also alienates the students from academic curriculum (Eckert, 1989; Willis, 1981).

In their study, Gutierrez, Rymes, and Larson provide examples of discursive islands of the third space: collaborative dialogic public discourse involving both the teacher and the students as a spin-off of the teacher-organized topic on Brown vs Board of Education,

>   STUDENT1: What if they're half Black and half White?
>   TEACHER: What if who's (.) what?
>   STUDENT1: What if the kid's half White and half Black where do they g- what school do they go to?
>   STUDENT2: They don't have half Black .
>   TEACHER: In the South you weren't half anything.
>   STUDENT2: See?
>   TEACHER: In the South if you were even a teeny- weeny…-eentsy bit Black, you were Black. (Students are laughing). You were Black.
>   STUDENT3: Huh huh.

The student1's inquiry of how the segregation institutions in the US past dealt with mixed race people created ontological engagement into the academic curriculum for, arguably, all participants of the classroom including the teacher (we will return to this issue of later). The student1 using race categories like "mixed race" available to the student in the 1990s in California (the time and place of the lesson that Gutierrez, Rymes, and Larson analyzed) could not comprehend initially the dualistic "one drop" nature of the racist institutions during segregation. The student1 asked the teacher and the class a genuine information seeking question (Matusov & Rogoff, 2002; Rogoff et al., 1996). The teacher and the student2 provided their genuine answers to the genuine information-seeking question by the student1. This dialogic exchange of genuine information seeking question and answers is very different from the interaction occurred during non-ontological engagement and ontological non-engagement because in both cases, the students do not raise information seeking questions on the curriculum matters. In the former example of non-ontological engagement, the teacher did not seek information about the latest event in Petaluma reported by the Los Angeles Times – he had known the news before coming to the classroom. He just wanted to test if the student knew the news. He seeks information *about* the students – *not from* them. The teacher did not treat the students as his dialogic partners but rather as an object of his inquiry (compare with searching information about another object, for example, you may need to test if the door is locked: you try to push it back – you cannot, it means it is locked – the door is the object of your inquiry, not a co-participant in it). Similarly, the students did not seek information from the teacher when they mimic his intonation or made a joke at his expense. They just wanted to produce laughter from their classmates *about* the teacher. The do not treat the teacher as a dialogic partner but as the object of their joke. In contrast, the student1 treats the teacher and the other students as partners in the dialogue.

Bakhtin (1999) defined dialogue as information seeking from and with others. An individual's dialogic orientation involves self-acknowledgement that the individual is incomplete and need others. The student1's dialogic orientation to the classroom community, including the teacher and the other students, and to the curriculum is the essence of ontological engagement. As one of my students wrote in her final project for the EDUC390 class described above, "I ... know that when students are learning they are asking lots of questions because they want to know more" (from Dora Fernandez's Teaching Portfolio, 5/17/2005). She sees students' asking information seeking questions about academic curriculum is the evidence of their ontological engagement and learning. Likewise, Bakhtin (1999; Bakhtin et al., 1986) defined meaning of utterance as response to somebody's else question. Thus, teaching is meaningful only when it replies to the students' information seeking questions. Similarly, Greenleaf and Katz report that focusing on students asking question was important realization for English teachers working with minority High school students with limited reading abilities (and initially hating reading),

> When I first started asking students to pose questions about their reading, low and behold I got this absolutely incredible group of questions. I thought, "These are better questions that I would have ever asked if I were coming up with questions to lead a discussion." Day after day, I was incredibly impressed with the quality of the questions. *The kids seem to be much more engaged in the reading. That's part of what's exciting about it, is their level of engagement.* A very different dynamic happens when they're asking the questions than when a teacher does. When they're leading the discussion, leading the answers, the quality of the questions really indicates that they're thinking about they're reading (Greenleaf & Katz, 2004, p. 196, italics mine).

A student's information seeking question is probably the most explicit form of his or her ontological engagement. In ontological engagement, students' words are "populated with" students' "intentions" (Bakhtin, 1991, p. 293). A student's ontological engagement may take implicit, proto-dialogical, forms of puzzlement or any form of the student's "perezhivanie" ("experiential awareness", literally "living over" in Russian, see in Vygotsky & Kozulin, 1986) of some kind of cognitive, emotional, volitional, and/or relational discontinuity (cf. more cognitive versions of this notion "cognitive dissonance" and "cognitive disequilibrium", Festinger, 1968; Piaget, 1985). The puzzlement makes the student not equal with him or herself and potentially directs him or her to a dialogue with others.

As I discussed in previous chapters, many of Socratic Dialogues described or developed by Plato are ontologically charged exactly because they usually started with a "student" asking a question to the teacher (often Socrates). Meno asked Socrates if a virtue can be taught (Plato & Bluck, 1961). Through the whole dialogue, in which Socrates tried skillfully to redefine the question that Meno asked, remained interested and committed to his (transforming) inquiry. This was not necessarily true for two other participants in the Dialogue: the Slave and Anytus, a son of wealthy father. Socrates used the Slave to demonstrate to Meno that people do not learn from teaching but rather remember what they already know. The dialogue between Socrates and the Slave about areas of square revealed non-ontological engagement of the Slave into the mathematical issues of the square areas. The Slave cooperated answering to Socrates' questions probably because of his oppressed position of being Meno's slave. There is not any evidence that the Slave brought any of his own interests or tried to transformed ones by Socrates. Unlike Meno's contributions, the Slave replied with short up to the point answers – he never asked any question to Socrates, transformed a topic or introduced a new one. In addition, Socrates treats him more like a rhetorical tool, an argument, in his discussion with Meno. There were not attempts from Socrates to interest the Slave in the discussion of the math area (or about virtue). In contrast, Socrates tried to interest Anytus in the discussion of the virtue origin by asking him to help Socrates and Meno but Anytus ended with ontological disengagement. Initially, Anytus agreed to help Socrates and Meno with understanding of the notion of virtue. However, soon he seemed to recognize that Socrates did not want his help of sharing what he, Anytus, thought about virtue but rather tried to manipulate him forcing to say what Socrates wanted to hear. Anytus seemed to be more interested in Athena politics than to discuss if virtue can be taught or not. Anytus left Socrates and Meno not wanting to participate in dangerous and, probably, pointless, from his point of view, conversation. Leaving a conversation is one of manifestations of ontological disengagement along with resistance and ignoring.

It is hopefully clear that the student1 from Gutierrez, Rymes, and Larson's study and Meno from Plato's Dialogue were ontologically engaged. However, were the teacher and Socrates and the other students in the fragment from the social studies lesson about Brown vs Board of Education ontologically engaged in the discussion? How much ontological engagement was widespread in their "classrooms"?

In Gutierrez, Rymes, and Larson's study both the student2 and the teacher tried to provide the best answer to the information seeking question by the student1. In their desire to genuinely help the student1, the student2 and the teacher co-participated in the student1's ontological engagement and, thus, their engagement was also ontological. Ontological engagement are reflected in replies to an information seeking question involves similar principles as Gricean Maxims (Grice, 1975, p. 65) namely trying to be as helpful and truthful as possible. Socrates' response to Meno's information seeking question about the origin of virtue is also ontological because Socrates apparently believed that before considering the origin of virtues one must understand and define what virtue is – something that Socrates did not have answer by himself and suspected that Meno did not have either. Thus, from the presented evidence, we can conclude that the student2, the social studies teacher, and Socrates ontologically addressed the information seeking questions raised by the student1, the social studies teacher and Socrates. To the lesser degree, it can be said about the other students of the social studies lesson on Brown vs. Board of Education judging by their laughter and the comment by the student3. However, there was no evidence that the social studies teacher and

Socrates participated in an ontological collaborate inquiry in their "classrooms" – they were not ontologically engaged in any question or puzzlement themselves that they shared with their students.

In sum, ontologically-oriented teaching involves the teacher's addressing information seeking questions raised by the students. Non-ontological-oriented teaching involves the teacher's addressing questions that the students have not raised. However, the teacher cannot always reply on the students raising questions before each lesson. The pedagogical question is how to design for the students' ontological engagement into the academic curriculum? How can the teacher help to induce information-seeking questions in his/her students about the targeted academic curriculum? Is it possible and under what conditions?

DESIGNING STUDENTS' ONTOLOGICAL ENGAGEMENT INTO ACADEMIC CURRICULUM

The goal of designing students' ontological engagement into academic curriculum is to promote the students asking information seeking questions about the academic curriculum. Unlike Meno who came to Socrates with his question about origin of virtues, the students' minds are often not ontologically in the curriculum – they do not come to the classroom full of questions about the targeted curriculum. This is not a school-specific problem – any presentation faces with similar problem: a movie, a scientific conference, a fiction or nonfiction book, a documentary, a painting, a performance, a play, a song, and so on. Even in our everyday life, we face with such problem when we have to share something with our friends or loved ones. We have to draw our listeners into a presentation of our story, situation, joke, or problem. The only difference between school and all other contexts where a similar problem of designing ontological engagement emerges is that school can ignore it since its audience is captive. If a movie, or a book or a TV show, or a painting, or our conversation does not ontologically engage the audience, the audience can leave the cinema theater in the middle of the movie, change TV program, move to another painting, or change the topic of our conversation. Through this ontological disengagement, audience provides feedback that the design for ontological engagement is failed and needs serious modifications of the presentation. In practice these serious modifications are often followed the audience's feedback – sometimes, as in an everyday conversation, it is modified and adjusted on the flight when a speaker notices any verbal or non-verbal sights of the audience's disengagement. Using educational jargon, in everyday contexts, the problem of disengagement is addressed through change of the "instruction".

In contrast, in conventional school, teachers often do not recognize a problem of non-ontological engagement – students' boredom and disinterest are expected (see, for example, the beginning of the movie "Dead Poet Society" where this expectation of boredom and disinterest of school academic subjects accompanied with students' high (but non-ontological) engagement in their studies is nicely captured by the movie in their portrayal of this high class private boarding school at the beginning of the sixties). Instead, conventional teachers only recognize the students' ontological disengagement as a problem, but not a problem with their instruction but a kind of disciplinary problem rooted in the disengaged students themselves. The students' disengagement is often interpreted by the conventional teachers as some kind of classroom management, discipline, general motivation problem, or even asocial behavioral and medical problem within the "troubled students" themselves (Varenne & McDermott, 1998). The system of rewards and punishments and behavioral modifications are often applied for the disengaged students to address this problem (Doyle, 1986a). I would argue that even when successful in forcing the students to stay engaged, these non-instructional measures often lead to the students' non-ontological rather than ontological engagement. The instruction remains unimproved or even getting worse because classroom's time and the teacher's focus are dedicated to classroom management, discipline, and/or behavioral modification at expense of instruction and its necessary improvement. Conventional school regime shifts teachers' focus from establishment and maintenance of students' ontological engagement to teacher control over the students by setting regime of institutional and symbolic violence and bribes (e.g., so-called "token economy").

Since the conventional school in general and the teacher in specific are losing oppressive measures that can curtail the students' ontological disengagement (e.g., resistance, ignoring, smuggling non-academic activities into the classroom, tardiness) such as corporal punishment, mass dismissals of the disengaged students from school, punishment parents, and so on, there is a growing crisis of the teacher authority in the classroom (Sidorkin, 2002). About 50% of total number of new teachers nationwide changes their profession after 5 years of teaching in schools ("Campaign for Fiscal Equity, et al. v. State of New York, et al. defendants," 2001, January, p. 45). Based on exist surveys and interviews, one of the leading reasons for novice teachers' leaving teaching profession is classroom management (Weiss, 1999). My EDUC 390 students, preservice teachers, also focus their attention on the issues of classroom management as the most important teacher issue long before they start teaching. As one of my EDUC 390 students wrote in her Teaching Portfolio that she see her biggest challenge for her future teaching in, "making sure the students realize that the teacher... is the highest form of authority in the classroom."

The unique specific of the teacher preparation is that, in contrast with other professions, we, university professors, have to teach newcomers how to successfully socialize and participate in a *counter*-practice (and in a professional *counter*-culture). Preparation of novice practitioners in the other professions involves teaching the students, the future professionals, how to successfully engage in the existing practice. In contrast, in teacher preparation, the novice teachers learn what is wrong with the existing practice and how to change it. This puts the preservice teachers in a double-bind schizophrenic situation: to succeed in the university they have to learn to criticize the existing schooling practice but to succeed in their future conventional school, they have to learn how to align themselves with the existing practice. My EDUC 390 students often expect to learn tricks about classroom management (in its behavioristic interpretation) and instruction techniques from their general method class. As they told me, the issues of educational philosophy -- purpose of teaching, definition and evidence of learning -- they usually see as esoteric, irrelevant, and unimportant. This presents me, as their instructor, with an interesting teaching challenge of creating their ontological engagement around issues of educational philosophy. I want them to become puzzled about issues of educational philosophies.

At the first class meeting of the method teaching course, I briefly described above, I want to focus my students, preservice teachers, on the issue of what kind of teachers they want to be. This reflection that goes throughout the course leads to many important issues including the importance of educational philosophy perceived by many of my students as unnecessary bla-bla-bla before taking my class (in a survey I usually give my students at the beginning of the semester they rate learning about educational philosophy at the bottom of their importance scale with the issue of discipline leading their rating). For the four last years (equal 8 method courses with total 173 students), at the first class meeting, I give my students index cards and I asked them to write in one or two words their reaction to the following announcement, "The class is canceled." I ask my students not to sign the cards and collect them after minute or two. Then I draw smiling, neutral and upsetting faces. I ask one of the students to read the cards with "the right intonation" while together we code the students' reactions to the phrase. Out of 173 total responses that I keep for years, 6 were upsetting (e.g., "Yuak!"), 8 neutral (e.g., "it's OK", "Why?"), and the resent were enthusiastically happy (e.g., "Yeah!" "Sleep!" "Great!" "Good news!"). The 92% of future teachers are happy when their class is canceled.

Initially they are not surprised by the result because they consider it is normal to be happy when a class is canceled. They say, "We are happy because we can do something else at this time." I ask them if they would be happy when a movie is canceled. They unanimously reply "no". We discuss the contrast between their would-be reactions to a news of movie versus class being canceled. Why would all of the students without exception be unhappy when a movie that they are going to attend with their friends is announced to be canceled while they are happy when their class that presumably will help them to become good teachers is canceled? It becomes apparent for them that they dislike being students while they want to be teachers. I ask them why they want to inflict pain on their future students that they experienced themselves. "Are you sadists?" -- I ask them with irony. They are often puzzled by this question. They ask me how to become teachers whose students would be upset when their class is canceled. They ask me a question about the academic curriculum that I want them to teach. It means that they are ontologically engaged in the issues of good versus bad teachers and of how to become a good teacher. They are ready to be taught.

Figure 10. The preservice teachers' reaction to the statement "The class is canceled".

Since almost all my students (like me) have socialized in bad teaching (I coin a term "teaching by Dr. Evil" using famous movie "Austin Powers" as a descriptive metaphor), we investigate Dr. Evil teaching using the demonstrations of "typical bad teaching" designed by Richard Lavoie (Rosen & Lavoie, 1989) and discuss what should we, teachers, do to prevent that kind of "evil" teaching. We try to build what is "good teaching" as remedy to 'bad teaching" (cf. a similar approach to developing "good laws" Dershowitz, 2002). The undesirable "bad teaching by Dr. Evil" demonstrated by Lavoie and recollected by my EDUC 390 students becomes a guiding principle for our classroom community of teachers to develop "good teaching. For example, I ask my students, "If they have a choice of two workshops: one on 'the best instructional strategy' and the other on 'what kind of ed philosophy you like' – which workshop would you choose to attend?" I take a vote. My students predictably and unanimously choose the first workshop on the best instructional strategy. After the vote, I "invite" my students to "the best instructional strategy" workshop and ask, "We, as teachers, are often faced with a teaching dilemma – how to teach 2+2=4 or something that your students do not much care about? What is the MOST effective strategy for forcing the students to learn something they do no appreciate yet?" Very quickly the student start generating the best instructional strategies they have experienced as students like "assign readings and then test on it," "multiple choice exams", "random check-ups and quizzes with high stakes for the students," "make them compete with each other for grades" and so on. They begin to understand that all these strategies are powerful and very efficient but that is teaching by Dr. Evil – not the teaching they want. I ask them, "But you wanted 'the best instructional strategy' and you got it. What is wrong?" One of the students replies, "We don't want that 'best', Dr. Evil's 'best'." Another student asks, "Best for what?! Not best for Dr. Evil's teaching!" I ask them a counter-question of what their "best" is – they do not know but now eager to know. Again it was a moment of the students' ontological engagement in the academic curriculum that I prepared as they were puzzled by the main issue of educational philosophy about the purpose and quality of teaching rather than about how to get the best instructional technique.

Finally, in our second class meeting, I push further for what I call "ontological anxiety" in my students. I organize mock job interviews. I split my students in 4-5 small groups and give each group a real job description of a teacher position taken from the Internet. Each group becomes a mock school with unique features: some focuses on constructivism, some on integrated curriculum, some on individualized instruction, some on integration of special ed and regular students. I give my students general questions that many school administrators typically ask job candidates and they have to develop their own questions tailored to their particular school description. Also each group elects a job candidate who is going to go to the other groups for job interviews (the home group does not interview their own job candidate). Each school "administrator" and "teacher" has about 2-3 questions to ask the "job candidate". A job interview lasts about 10-15 min. Each "job candidate" has 3 interviews. After that, each "school" deliberates and selects "the best job candidate" and explains to the entire class their reason for their choice. We discuss the mock job interviews. Students ask many questions – they are anxious to realize how much they do not know yet about teaching (and especially about educational philosophies). They asked what constructivism is, what example of constructivism in language art curriculum, whether there other educational philosophies beside constructivism, what evidence of learning is, how to select good school for working, how good school look like, and so on. They have become ready to be taught.

Analyses of the Curriculum for Contradictions:
Historical, Epistemological, and Ontological

Unless students come to class full of questions like in many cases of Socrates' Dialogues described by Plato, preparation for ontologically-oriented teaching is needed. The question for the teacher is how to provoke students to ask ontological questions about the curriculum so ontological teaching can begin. McLaren formulates this task in the following way, "Since many symbols are polysemous and their interpretations and meanings are negotiable or 'up for grabs', teachers are thus challenged to repattern their classroom symbols so that they speak to the 'here and now' of their students – so that these symbols revealingly and magnetically relate to the students' life-world infusing them with a sense of hope and providing the with the ability to take control of their lives and relativize their condition of inequality" (McLaren, 1993, p. 244). In the design for ontological engagement in the academic curriculum, the students' past experiences, present flow, and the targeted academic curriculum come into a relationship (Dewey, 1998). In ontological engagement, the academic curriculum mediates emergent contradictions in the students' past and present experiences. In the example above of introduction of educational philosophies, the known educational philosophies such as constructivism, transmission of knowledge, community of learners (Rogoff et al., 1996) mediate the students' contradiction between wanting to be teachers and disliking to be students – the contradiction that becomes evident in their brief reactions to the announcement "the class is canceled" and the follow-up discussion about what kind of teachers they want to be and how to achieve that. In the class, the students experience the contradiction first induced by the teacher and the mediation by the academic curriculum second. This dialogic principle of problematizing the curriculum for the students was well developed and described by famous Japanese educator and theoretician of education Kihaku Saitou, "(Good classroom lesson) should be one in which there first occur some contradiction or tension between the teaching material, teacher, and students. Then, the teacher and students should get over the tension to discover and create something new (Saitou, 1969)" (cited in Miyazaki, 2006, p. 24). As Miyazaki points out, this contradiction has not only social and cognitive potentials driving learning but also engaging and motivating ones. In preparation for the lesson, the order for the teacher is reverse. First is to understand what contradiction the curriculum mediates and then to find where such contradiction is alive in the students' lives. Thus, the preparation for ontological teaching starts with the analysis of the targeted academic curriculum to reveal underlining contradictions it mediates.

The theory of how to reveal contradictions that the academic curriculum mediates has been developed by Davydov (Davydov, 1986, 1998; Davydov & Kilpatrick, 1990). Davydov recognized at least three types of contradictions associated with the curriculum: historical, epistemological (or "didactic"), and ontological (cf. "the life experiences of the children" in Davydov & Tsvetkovich, 1991, p. 15., he used slightly different terms). Historical analysis of the curriculum focuses on the historical origin of the concepts reflected in the targeted academic curriculum in human experiences. For example, the notion of "educational philosophies" emerged in the history of Western civilization when diverse schools with diverse pedagogies clashed among each other for which school is better (see, for example, debates between sophist and Socratic pedagogies reflected in Plato, 1984). Historical analysis of the curriculum can help to reveal the connection of the curriculum to the human practices and to the human needs and the historical process of its development. Epistemological analysis of the curriculum focuses on the ideas and concepts that constitute the targeted curriculum. Epistemologically, the concept of educational philosophy reveals the relationship between pedagogical ends and means and values. The epistemological essence of a civil war, another example of the development of ontologically-oriented curriculum that I used with my EDUC390 students, is in a passionate and unreconcilable conflict in a community, in which different groups in the community try to impose their ways of life on each other through fight.

Following Hegel and Marx, Davydov insisted that there is a strong relation between epistemology and history: (the correct) epistemology must reflect the logically abstracted history. For example, Davydov's historical analysis of the origin of fractions reveals that fractions emerged as a practical response to problems of measurement rather than a concept of a (rational) number. The latter is rather late development in math practice that was finalized only at the beginning of the 20th century (Davydov & Tsvetkovich, 1991). However, in traditional school, fractions are taught as numbers first (as a relationship between the whole and a part) and then, in a few years later, fractions are taught to use for measurements (as the relationship between a selected unit and a measured object). Davydov argued that in traditional school epistemology of fraction is wrong because it teaches product of math development (i.e., rational numbers) before the processes of their development (i.e., measurement). He argued that this wrong curriculum sequence is one of the major reasons of fractions are so difficult for many students to learn in school (Davydov & Tsvetkovich, 1991). Similarly, the historical origin of the concept of "educational philosophy" shows that the "correct" epistemology of educational philosophy is in its initial focus on a struggle among different educational philosophies for the teacher's heart and mind rather than the consistency between the pedagogical goals and means (that can come only as a by-product of this struggle). Traditionally educational philosophies are presented in educational textbooks as self-contained chapters without articulating their struggle with each other for the teacher's commitment (see, for example, Kauchak & Eggen, 2003).

Ontological analysis of the targeted academic curriculum focuses on where the epistemology of the targeted academic curriculum may "live" in the students' lives – in their past and present experiences. Ontological analysis goes much beyond of traditional "activation of the students' prior knowledge" (Kauchak & Eggen, 2003) because it focuses on contradictions and tensions in the students' lives and charged with potential social activism aimed at transforming their lives (Freire, 1986; Holzman, 1997) rather than just on "prior knowledge". For example, ontological analysis of the concept of educational philosophies focuses on where, when, and how the students might and may experience struggle of different pedagogies. My observation on undergraduate students in teacher preparation program is that all the students eager to become really good teachers. I have also noticed how much the high majority of them dislike being to be students. Studying in and out of the classroom is considered to be unpleasant work. These two observations of potentially conflicting positions that the high majority of my students have create a "natural" opportunity to induce a conflict of educational philosophies in them.

In my lesson on designing ontological engagement, I chose Civil War – one of the most remote curriculum topics for my students – to demonstrate what ontological engagement is, how to design it, and enact it in the classroom. Ontological analysis of the curriculum topic of the Civil War focuses on where, when, and how the students might and may experience internal unreconciled conflicts in their communities. I know that my students have "natural" anxiety about ontological engagement in general because they faced with the problem of ontological engagement while teaching language art lessons in their teaching practicum during this semester. I listened to them and read their reflections on this problem posted on the class web forum – many of them conceptualized and experienced the lack of ontological engagement that their teaching generated in their students as disciplinary problems of "unmotivated and noncooperative students."

As to finding an ontological contradiction of the curriculum topic of the Civil War in lives of my students, I was thinking that my students were currently involved at least in two conflicts tearing apart their local communities. The first one was related with choices of their boyfriends that, as I overheard them, they were discussing before and after class. The topic of boyfriends was one of the most popular one among my female students in their early 20s. My guess was that they probably had to navigate ethnic "appropriateness" of their boyfriends as potential spouses – some boyfriends can be ethnically more desirable than others for some of my students. The divide might reflect the American Civil War but even if it was not, I could use to induce puzzlement in my students. My expectation for this conflict as one that was ontologically important for my students could be wrong but this was something I planned to use in my classroom.

The other ontological conflict, I planned to use, was in my own class among the students who disagreed with each other about having or not having a recess in my 3-hour class. I knew that my students debated this issue in class, after class, and on class web forum. The reason of why I needed to introduce another example of ontological engagement to my students was that I also wanted to demonstrate my students how they could induce ontological puzzlement in their own future students – elementary school children – if my students want to teach them about the Civil War. Clearly using the issue of boyfriends may not effective for designing ontological engagement in the curricular topic of Civil War for elementary school children. For that purpose, I was thinking about a local conflict that our classroom community had about the issue of recess at that time. Our class was split whether to have a short recess in the middle of our 3-hour long class meeting or not to have and finish the class a bit earlier. The majority of the class did not want to have the recess to end the class earlier. The minority of the class wanted to have a recess to use bathroom. Although I told my class that they could leave the classroom for bathroom or could have food during the class any time, the minority did not want to miss anything in the class and argued that they needed a break. The discussion of this issue was on the class web forum (WebTalk) along many other professional discussions. My own position on this issue was that in this issue, I was just another member of the class and as another member of the class I also wanted to have a break to have some rest for myself. Since my students could not resolve the issue for several weeks, I thought that by my teaching ontological engagement it was a nice springboard to use this apparently irreconcilable problem in our local classroom community with diverse values for creating ontological puzzlement about the Civil War. I hoped that after experiencing and analyzing this design of ontological engagement, my students could understand how to design ontological engagement in the curriculum topic of Civil War and beyond for their own elementary school students in future.

My EDUC390 students also challenged me how to teach math and specifically fractions in a constructivist way so I was working hard to learn myself how develop ontologically-oriented teaching fractions. Ontological analysis of fractions focuses on where, when, and how the students might and may experience measurement demanding fractions that makes difference in their lives. One of many possibilities for ontological use of fractions as measurement and proportion is to reveal social injustice. For example, many American girls are involved in practices of monitoring and reducing their weight as "typical" and desired evidence of their femininity (Lyman, 2000) while many boys are involved in monitoring and increasing body muscle as "typical" and desired evidence of their masculinity (Schaefer, 2000). The fractions and proportions can reveal for the children that popular toys like Barbie doll targeted for girls and G.I. Joe targeted for boys violate human body proportions and can seriously damage children if they try to set Barbie doll and G.I. Joe toys as their body models (Mukhopadhyay & Greer, 2001).

What if a given curriculum does not correspond any ontological contradiction in the students' lives – can it still be taught in an ontological way? Davydov would argue "no" – it is not "developmentally appropriate" to teach the targeted curriculum to the given students. The students may need to learn some other curriculum first. In this case, the students' experiences in the classroom with one curriculum can become their ontological experience for another curriculum. For example, learning fractions as measurements can create ontological experiences for the students to learn about fractions as rational numbers later on (Davydov & Tsvetkovich, 1991).

Designing for Students' Ontological Commitment

To induce ontological puzzlement in students, the teacher has to commit the students to the ontological positions constituting an ontological contradiction in their lives. In other words, to be ontological the puzzlement involving the targeted academic curriculum has to be experienced by the students in the classroom "here and now" as their life experience. It is not enough for the teacher to say in the classroom, "I know that all of your want to be good teachers but I also know that many of your dislike being students, so there is a contradiction here: you want to do something to other people that you do not like yourself." The students have to experience and commit to the conflicting positions before reflecting on their contradiction and conflict. Otherwise, their engagement in the curriculum may be non-ontological (but purely intellectual) or non-engagement at all. Thus, the ontological analysis of the curriculum leads to design of students' commitment to the potentially conflicting ontological positions. For the example of teaching the educational philosophies described above, I designed two brief surveys of my students: 1) asking them to list topics they expect to learn in the class and 2) reacting to the phrase "the class is canceled". Both brief surveys that I took in the classroom committed my students to two conflicting positions: 1) wanting to become a good teacher and 2) disliking being a student.

For the topic of Civil War, I planned to commit my students to 1) a position of fairness and justice and 2) preference of ethnically particular boyfriend by showing them a few minutes fragment from the educational video "American Tongues" (Alvarez, Kolker, & Center for New American Media, 1987) in which a woman from New England told story of how she rejected her boyfriend because he came from deep South and had a strong Southern accent. I hoped that 1) the fragment would induce the sense of injustice while 2) their own discussion of how they select their own boyfriends would ontologically induce a position of ethnical exclusiveness. I also expected that my introduction of the topic of break for our class would split my students into two groups with irreconcilable ontological positions.

As for designing students' ontological commitment into fractions, proportions, and measurement, Mukhopadhyay & Greer (2001) designed a lesson in which they asked their students to measure Barbie doll body proportions and compare with their own – what kind of body the students would have if they had Barbie's body proportions. This measurement activity can commit the students into 1) liking Barbie doll and seeing her as a model of feminine beauty and 2) seeing how non-human and distorted her body is.

Designing for Students' Reflection on Ontological Contradiction

When the students are ontologically committed to conflicting positions, it is not always for the students that the positions they committed to are incompatible. For example, my students are often are not surprised that they dislike being students and want to become good teachers. They often see these two positions as being "normal." The contradiction behind these two positions that they ontologically experience in the class is not visible for them. It is a role of the teacher to help the students see the contradiction behind the irreconcilable positions experienced by the students. The preparation for this process involves visualization of the contradiction through classroom discussion and curriculum mediation. In the case of teaching educational philosophies, I ask my students series of questions to help them to reflect on the contradiction: 1) why they were upset if a movie is canceled while happy when a classroom is canceled, 2) if they ever experienced learning that they were not happy when it was canceled, 3) what they saw as desirable: their future students happy when their class is canceled or upset, 4) what have made them learn to be happy when their classes are canceled (my students remembered when they had been going to the first day of class how they were excited – how and why their excitement has gone), and so forth. It is difficult and probably unnecessary, if not totally counterproductive, to imagine[3] what kind of difficulties the students may face so the preparation for reflection is often limited by expectation of this work itself. The students' difficulties guide the teacher through the lesson.

Students' Guidance of the Teacher's Instruction

The purpose of the following lesson fragment in my overall lesson in EDUC390 class about designing students' ontological engagement was to demonstrate the students how they could have been ontologically engaged in a curriculum topic (Civil War) – the topic that they were not initially interested. I wanted them then to reflect after this learning experience on the teaching design that promoted their ontological engagement in this curriculum topic specifically and in any academic curriculum in general. I chose the topic of Civil War because I expected little immediate interest in this topic from my students. Also, as an immigrant from the Soviet Union to the United States, I was puzzled how and why this remote historical event is still well alive in regular lives of many Americans. This is especially true in comparison with Russian Civil War 1918-1921 – a more recent historical event but less alive in the Russian society than American Civil War 1861-1865 in the American society, in my view.

---

[3] Overzealous preparation may lead to teaching "imaginary students" when the teacher focuses on enactment of the preplanned lesson instead of tuning to the "here and now" ontology of the students.

In conventional, non-ontologically-oriented, teaching, activity that the students are involved mediate learning that is the immediate goal of the teacher. In ontologically-oriented teaching (like in many everyday activities), learning mediates immediate goals of the activity at hand (De Haan, 1999). My *immediate* teaching goal was a dialogic inquiry to learn from my students what they think about the Civil War and whether and how it may be still present in their lives. This immediate teaching goal could help me access my students' understanding of the topic, focus me on careful listening to them, and allow them guide me how to guide them since they, not I, have access to their knowledge of how conflicts of Civil War are still alive for them -- they knew something that I did not know.

My *mediated* teaching goal was for me to engage my students in problematics of the Civil War. I call this teaching goal "mediated" because it is mediated by my dialogic inquiry about the Civil War in American society. The goal of engaging students in problematics of Civil War should be a by-product of my dialogic inquiry rather than my immediate goal. Making engagement of my students as my immediate teaching goal would have shifted my attention from listening and authentic response to the students' contributions to my disinterested pedagogical manipulation of their subjectivities (see Matusov, St. Julien et al., 2005 for more discussion of the relationship between immediate and mediated teaching goals).

> EUGENE: ...Let me illustrate how the Civil War can be related *really* to you guys *right now*. To you guys. To you guys (almost whispering). Not to the kids with whom you worked in your practicum, but to you. Here and now. That's what I'm trying to show you. I do not know if my demonstration will work with you: it may or may not. Teaching is always magic for me – it always works unpredictably because it depends on you and me. I cannot predict you, my students. I cannot even predict myself (laughing). I don't know what I'm going to do when you response to my guidance in a certain way. Let me start with showing you some videotape and ask your opinion about this woman from New England rejecting her boyfriend, and what you think about her as well as what you take from the situation and whether it relates to you or not. [Pulls down screen and puts tape in VCR]
>
> EUGENE: Did you see the video that's called "American Tongues?" Anybody? No? You might see it in EDUC 258 class on cultural diversity.
>
> KRISTY: "American Tongues?" Oh yeah, I watched that movie, yeah. Is it a fragment about the guy from Boston?
>
> EUGENE: No, it's a fragment about the woman from New England.
>
> KRISTY: OK.
>
> EUGENE: If you know what I'm talking about now... You may remember it. The fragment about the guy from Boston is interesting as well.
>
> VIDEO (a White woman in her 40s talking to the interviewer): I was engaged for a while to a Yaley. Who sounded like a Yaley to me, although he had a trace of a Southern accent. I thought sort of a Bill Faulkner, Truman Capone accent. You know, when you're 20 you don't make these distinctions. And... I went home to meet his family at Christmas, and as we drove further South from New Haven, his accent got heavier and heavier. He became filled with all these hillybilly kind of regionalisms. You know, this real kinda "you all" stuff. And, as well, a lot of the... hand gestures. This man was becoming a different person as we're... mostly to language. By the time we got to Sparta, I had had it! I just knew that someone with those little accents was not going to crawl around inside of me! I was not going to have little Southern babies who talk like that! And I got a plane home. No question!

EUGENE: So, what do you think? So, what do you think about that movie? Why didn't she want to date the guy who had Southern accent? [Amanda raises her hand]. Hmm, hmm.

AMANDA: Um, I think she's very close minded, and she thinks that... like one way of talking is the appropriate way, and he has ...another way of talking, and it's considered uncultured...

EUGENE: Hmm...

KATEY: I think it's just a stereotype.

EUGENE: And what kind of stereotype would be that?

LIZ: ...Associated with being a stupid person or...

EUGENE: Any other association with a Southern accent? I remember watching a movie that's called "James Bond: Live and let die." The whole thing happens in Louisiana there. Well, not the whole thing, but a big part of that. Have you seen that movie? Well, anyway, there's a policeman from South and he's very stupid and he speaks this *heavy* Southern accent using constantly Southern accent, *"You boy!"* [Eugene now stands in front of the projector, resting on the table so that he is positioned more closely to the students]

SARI: Um... Well, I shouldn't say anything, but, I think there's also kind of a generalization that, they're sort of *racist*, or like the... that people from the South aren't liberal-minded at all, or... like that they're not cultured, or they're kind of like stick to themselves. Or like, that someone from the South would never be able to fit in [Eugene nods] or *want* to fit in [EUGENE: um, um] in, you know, like a city here. [Eugene write down the stereotypes listed by Sari on the blackboard.]

EUGENE: Any other stereotypes?...

I was both pleased and concerned with how the discussion was going so far. I saw that the issue brought by the video touched my students. I was right that the topics of selecting boyfriends and injustice evident in the video were highly relevant to my students. But I also saw how it was easy for my students to objectivize the New England woman and other people. I wanted to shift the conversation from "them" to "us." I wanted my students to commit so certain ideas than just to discuss some intellectual interesting but emotionally disengaging issues. I was also interested what *they themselves* really think about the issue.

...Let me ask you all, except Cora, of course, 'cause it's different for her [Cora is the only student is the class from South, Southern Delaware]. If you ... decided to date a guy from South, would there be any problems with your immediate family – parents, grandparents, siblings? Do you think it would be OK *for them* if you have a boyfriend with a heavy Southern accent? [There is silence in the class. Eugene is looking at his students. Some students negatively turn their heads but some are smiling in apparent agreement.] OK? You say 'no' [pointing to Elizabeth], not in your family. Do we have any other answers? Think about the situation: imagine that, you're bringing your boyfriend [moves arms to the left] with a heavy Southern accent to your family. Would it be a problem? [there is silence in the class]

SARI: Not if he's Jewish! [Sari and Laura and some other students laugh apparently easing the tension]

EUGENE: No, he's not Jewish! [Eugene smiles] He has a really *heavy* Southern accent. By the way, let me turn things around [points to Cora, who is from the South of Delaware] and ask about a guy from the North. And you're bringing him in your family. Would it be a problem? No?

CORA: No.

EUGENE: Who thinks that *may be* it would be a problem in your family [again there are students who are smiling conspiratorially but apparently do not want to reveal that a boyfriend from South may cause a problem in their families]. Or you might think about bring a boyfriend from South to you family twice? You need to think how to present the guy [moves hands and arms like a fish swimming against the current.] Or is it not a problem for you? [Long pause. Some students looked at Eugene with smile that suggests that some of them might have a problem but they don't want to talk about that] Well... think about that, it looks like South-North adversary is a problem *now* as well. It's not solved yet. Like uh, how many of you would think that if you bring Irish, let's say, boyfriend, it's a problem. [Katey raises her hand]. You'll have a problem?

KATEY: Well, I remember the first time, *I'm* dating a German guy, and I remember the first time that I said that I'm seeing him, my parents were like, don't even think about moving there [EUGENE: Ah!, nods head]. [?] don't even think of liking it, don't even think of... [being]

EUGENE: Right! Yeah, but this is about moving, not about necessarily even German descent guy. But, let me tell you, what... No go ahead...

KATEY: My dad said to me...

EUGENE: [?] German.

KATEY: Germans are cold.

EUGENE: Ah!

KATEY: Watch it! [with sarcasm, many students laugh]

It seemed that I managed to engage my students "proto-ontologically" into the topic. Although the students did not ask questions, their puzzlement promoted and maintained by the instructor seemed to be in "the zone of proximal development" (Vygotsky, 1978). The evidence of the "proto-ontological" engagement was in the students volunteering to share their experiences and their ease to alternate the instructor-initiated topic (by bringing issues of non-Jewish and German boyfriends). However, the students' proto-ontological engagement was not on the South-North issue. The students wanted to discuss family disapproval of boyfriends of certain ethnicities but not along the South-North divide. It seemed to me the issue of family disapproval of Southern boyfriends was apparently not safe for them to discuss publicly. From the students' non-verbal communication of tension, I suspected, although still without certainty, that the South-North issue existed and acknowledged by some of them but those students did not want to bring the issue to the public class discussion probably because they were afraid that their classmates (and the instructor?) my judge their families (and them?) as being closed-minded and prejudice. My goal was to *publicly* commit my students to the South-North issue if was apparently alive for them. I felt that I had to regroup and choose a safer issue for my students to promote them talking about the issue.

EUGENE: OK [nods]. OK. OK. But there was a time when Irish people were not considered to be white. There was time in the US when no, no way Irish people were treated like Anglo or more desired European descent immigrants [shakes head]. Do we have Irish descent people here? [Lauren, Kim and Liz raise their hands]. Yep. So, I would recommend you guys go, actually everyone, should go to the New Castle... uh... Have you been in New Castle? There is a nice little uh... plaza there. It's just where there used to be Delaware government, you know, the [old Delaware] capital, you now know the capital of Delaware used to be New Castle [the class discussed it a few lessons ago]. So there is a nice plaza where the government used to be.... And if you look around you will see a store with antiques, and one of the store windows displays, there is a... job announcement, very old job announcement, and it says "Irish please don't apply."

Figure 11. I showed this photo that I made several years ago to my students in next class meeting.

It's from the beginning of the century. Hmm, hmm. There used to be huge discrimination of Irish people in the United States. There is actually a book written about that. The book titled "When Irish became white." [pause]. So... at the beginning of the 20th century, Irish people were discriminated as well. *Now* – not anymore. Uh... at least I don't know about that. There may be some discrimination, but I don't know. Have you experienced discrimination because you are Irish? [points to Lauren, Liz and Kim]. Lauren, have you ever experienced any discrimination being Irish? No. So, you see, it's gone. It's not anymore an issue. You guys didn't even know about that, right? [the students nodding in agreement]. But maybe if you talk with your folks they might tell you. If you're going to talk with your grandparents, they might tell you about that [saying this with outstretched arms]. But, Southern and Northern... is a kind of interesting situation. It still seems to be with us. This type of things is confusing for me, a recent immigrant. So why is that? Why is the conflict still with us [long pause]. ...Yep, go ahead.
    SARI: Um... well I drove to Florida, and I stopped in Charleston. And they really are *different.* They're like... [laughs slightly, slightly nervously] I know I sound like the person on video, but like...
    EUGENE: Um, huh hum. Um, huh hum [arms folded].

I was glad that the conversation shifted – the students started talking about "us" and "them" and not about "some other people." They included themselves into reflection of the South-North issue. The students' proto-engagement shifted back to the South-North issue but this time it included them as the focus of their reflection rather than "other people" (e.g., the New England woman from the video).

    SARI: But like the accent is kind of *annoying.* [slight laughter in class; Eugene nods strongly, with arms folded]. It's, it's just like... insanity. It's like [?], they're so like *friendly,* and like [strong laughter]. It's just, personally, I didn't enjoy it.
    EUGENE: Um, huh hum. Yep.
    ELIZABETH: Well, I'm from Delaware, and my dad's side of the family is from Virginia.
    EUGENE: Uh, huh.
    ELIZABETH: And every time I go down there it's just *SO* different from people up here even though it's just 3 hours away.
    EUGENE: In what way? Do you remember?

ELIZABETH: Well, they talk about [?] down there, [?] and it's *so* different from here, it was a much *smaller* school, and suddenly, everyone was *so nice.* And everyone [?] back here, ... and when you come back here, people aren't really very friendly. [?]. Here, when people walk by you, they don't smile. There I just found that everywhere I walked, I feel being accepting.

EUGENE: Um, huh hum... [Liz and Amanda have their hands up, but Eugene doesn't see them]. Laura, did you raise your hand? Well... Well, if you interested, if you think about stereotypes, like [sees Amanda now], OK, Amanda.

AMANDA: Oh, well I was just going to say [Eugene is writing on front blackboard], I have a similar story to [?]

EUGENE: Um, huh hum.

AMANDA: I grew up here and then I moved to Alabama. And when I moved to Alabama, they really having an [?]. [?]. Their cousins and me are so different like, I got in trouble cause I didn't say "ma'am" after every sentence, like if you answer a question in class and you don't say "ma'am" you get your name on the board. Like they [?] so much like being... yeah like manners, and like being respectful to older people. It was just *so* different what I'm used to.

It was interesting for me that in their reflection on their perception of Southern people, my Northern students noticed the same differences between them and people from South but they judge the differences differently: Elizabeth seemed to valued Southern culture more than Northern while Amanda and Sari saw Southern culture negatively. There was not evidence for me that my students were aware of this difference. I thought that it was time to emphasize relativity of their observations and I wanted to switch my students to think how Southern people can see and stereotype them, people from North. I wanted to problematize my Northern students' experiences of South.

EUGENE: [Points to what he wrote on the front blackboard]. This leads me to what Amanda was just saying. OK, you just talked about stereotypes of North to the South, like most people talking about their impression of South. You heard that woman talking about, she said, "I don't want to have babies with this Southern accent!" And, what I heard from you, people from North, is how you see people from South. People from North say that they slow..., by the way, Cora, you know how some people from North of Delaware label Lower [Southern] Delaware?

CORA [uncomfortably]: Yeah.

EUGENE: OK. You know how they talk about, actually I learned it from my past classes, I had taught. Do you know how students from Upper [Northern] Delaware called Low [Southern] Delaware?...

MEGHAN: Slower Delaware.

EUGENE: Yep. Yep. Yeah, you said it! Some of my Northern Delawarean students thought that Southerners are slow and stupid.

MEGHAN: It's Slower Lower [laughs]. [some laughter in class; some else in class says softly "Slower Delaware"; Laura and Lauren laughing with each other].

EUGENE: So, it's the same thing as in the video. But let's consider the opposite thing: how people from South stereotypically think about people from North. Let me ask you, how do you think the people from South stereotype people from North [Liz and Lauren raise their hands]. Imagine that woman was not from New England but, let's say....

LAUREN: Yeah.

EUGENE: But from deep Georgia or Virginia. How would she talk about people from North? OK, Lauren?

LAUREN: Kind of something like rich...

EUGENE: Rich.

LAUREN: And yuppie. I don't know. [laughter]

[Kristy raises her hand]

EUGENE: Rich, yuppie. Interesting. This probably means that some people from North see many white Southerns as poor, "white trash" – have you heard about such derogatory label? And if we're talking about whites by the way, ...Rich, what else? Amanda?

AMANDA: Yankee.

EUGENE: Yankee. Which is what? [changes voice] Yankee. [Kristy raises her hand] [laughter] Yep. "You are such a Yankee!" What does it mean?

ELIZABETH: Not as respectful.

EUGENE: Disrespectful. That's interesting -- why is it disrespectful, by the way, any guesses? What Amanda's talking about is in a way related to that disrespect, I think. Why is it disrespectful? Uh, huh.

CORA: In the South, people listen to authority they don't really... [?] disrespect authority. People from North don't care about other people.

KRISTY: Unfriendly.

EUGENE: Let me put [translate to Southern perception of North]... "Selfish," right? [he writes that down on the blackboard] Northerners don't think about other people. OK, Other stereotypes? Kristy?

KRISTY: I wasn't going to say that they [Northerners] are mean, but I'm ...

EUGENE: No, no, no, you're right – "unfriendly" [nods]. This is actually what Liz was talking about, remember, unfriendliness [writes on board]. Some Southern people may stereotype Northerners as "unfriendly". Yes, uh, huh [points to Liz]

LIZ: Um, rude.

EUGENE: Rude, huh, huh [writes on blackboard].

SARI: I feel like people in the South are really like religious.

EUGENE: Um, hmm [writes on blackboard]

SARI: and like [?]...religious [?] faith and values [are important to them]

EUGENE: Yep, any other? [Cora raised her hand.] Yep.

CORA: I was just going to say, I think that people from the North think that people from the South are more like caring about family...

EUGENE: Uh should it go to here [pointing to the left side of the blackboard where negative stereotypes are written] or there [pointing to the right side of the blackboard where positive stereotypes are written]...

CORA: Yeah, in the right side.

EUGENE: Yeah, it's over here, right?

CORA: Like their family's *more* important than people in the North.

EUGENE: Would it be negative? [Eugene seemed to be confused the sides because his sides are opposite to the students' sides of the blackboard]

CORA: No, I think it would be positive.

EUGENE: On positive side. [I thought you may put it on negative side] 'cause Southern religious sentiments are often perceived as more or less negative as religious fanaticism by some people in the North. They see Southerners as more religious.

CORA: Depending on where you, I don't know.

EUGENE: Um, huh hum. Right, right.

CORA: I think it's personal.

The South-North divide issue still remained proto-ontological for the students because although they were publicly committed discussing it and shared their observations and knowledge of existing stereotypes rooted in Northers and Southerners about each other, they did not own the inquiry behind the discussion. By sharing all these stereotypes, the students re-experienced the South-North divide in the classroom. I felt it was time for the class to focus on reflection, on shaping and sharing the inquiry.

> EUGENE: Um, huh hum. Right, right. OK, any other... stereotypes?...[pause]... And the question of course, is why that is. [Eugene tells a story of first graders, he met in Utah, who knowingly used rhetoric of Civil War in their fight with each other]. And the war was ended 150 years ago. But we still have this problem... for Irish people, you know, that would not be like that at all because again, it's over for them! [pauses]. 100 years ago people would say some negative stereotypes about Irish people. But not anymore. Because it's irrelevant right now. And the question is why it is still relevant for *us*? And why yet it's not over? [pause]. Why we still use all these stereotypes about Southerners and Northerners -- you were born in early 80's, right? But the Civil War was ended almost 150 years ago, right? Why do we still *care*?! It's almost like if we start remembering, I don't know, [someone sneezes loudly, causing some students to talk, Eugene doesn't stop] if we start hating British, who hates British by the way? [he raises hand as if inviting other to do the same but nobody raises hand]. Who hates British 'cause of their wars against the United States? [by now the talking stops]. *Nobody!* 'Cause all that stuff was so *long time ago!* But not Civil War. Yes, Sari.
>
> SARI: Well, it [Civil War] really wasn't *that* long ago. I mean, if you think about it, like... *they* wanted to keep slaves, so like it's... I feel like it's a lot of animosity that *we* would have towards *them* just because like... *now* in the present time, *obviously* that sounds like the most idiotic thing ever and how *could* they have done it, and it's like how could *they* have been fighting so hard to, for it?

Sari presented the Civil War as a finalized and objectivized event common for traditional history school textbooks (Loewen, 1996): the war was "obviously" idiotic because we[4] (North) were obviously right and they (South) were obviously wrong. There was not place for uncertainty (inquiry) and addressivity to participants of the historical event. Bakhtin argued that people need to face conflicting discourses to come to new understanding, "The importance of struggling with another's discourse, its influence in the history of and individual's coming to ideological consciousness, is enormous" (Bakhtin, 1991, p. 348). I saw my role, as the instructor, in providing alternative and conflicting discourses to my students. I had to focus my students on the fact the Civil War was a particular war not like many other wars experienced by the US.

> EUGENE: Um, huh hum. But again, there have been so many years since then... Think about British, why don't we care about British? It also was "idiotic." The United States wanted to separate but the Great Britain kept trying and trying and trying to have American colonies. By the way, there were so many the wars with Britain uh... British wars were much longer than the Civil War.
>
> SARI [immediately answering]: Well, because racism is still such a big deal!
>
> EUGENE: Um, huh hum... [nodding head, pauses, thinking how to respond...]. Say more, please..

---

[4] It is interesting that Sari identifies herself to Northerners during the Civil War. Her ancestors arrived to the United States at the beginning of the twentieth century and did not participate in the Civil War.

I was pleased that Sari moved to historical particularity of the Civil War and its connection to the contemporary problems but she still was so certain about the war. I was searching for ways how to problematize the Civil War for my students. I was looking for guidance from my students to raise a "good" question that can problematize the Civil War for the students.

SARI: Well, I don't know, I just...

I was wondering what exactly she was not knowing or felt uncomfortable of talking about...

EUGENE: So you think the Civil War was about... what was the purpose of the Civil War? Is it about slavery? About racism? What was it? Katey [who was raising her hand], what do you think? What was it about?

KATEY: Well, I didn't [swallows this; she may be trying to say that she had her hand up earlier for something else, but decides to answer anyway], sorry. I was trying to say that, the South is kind of like seceding [can't make out next two words]... at that time. [Starts trying to say something else, but Eugene begins with a new question]

EUGENE: And why did South try to secede?

KATEY: They wanted their own government. They didn't want to deal with North...

EUGENE [interrupting]: Why? Why they were happy for 40 more years, 50 years almost [Kim raises her hand] since establishment of the Federation and then... they could have seceded at the beginning, but they didn't. Why is it they start seceding at that time? [Elizabeth raises her hand]

KIM: I think they were underrepresented and they didn't think [xxx] [North was] bossing them around and keeping them from doing their own way. And the South had no say in the Federal government...

EUGENE [question seems genuine, not treachery or for rhetorical effect]: But why was it in the middle of that century? Why wasn't it earlier? [questioning gesture suggests he wants students to answer this; Elizabeth has her hand raised high now]. Why didn't... -- why did they wait -- you know, if they didn't want it, they could have created confederacy from the beginning, they could just not sign the Declaration of Independence or, say [?] insist on other type of unity and then [?] Yep [to Elizabeth]. Why is it?

ELIZABETH: Because the North wanted to ... end ... slavery in South, new Western state did not want to have slavery ... and the Northern states ended slavery by majority anyway ...

EUGENE: But why is it the North decided to end slavery? [puts hands outstretched; good question -- this is a really interesting historical question probably, of course, without one answer. Looks around, long pause, then shrugs, with arms outstretched]. I mean, it was again, before that it was fine, right? [laughs slightly] But then suddenly, boom, "we want the slavery ended." [shrugs shoulders, suggesting to students he doesn't have an answer]

[Someone, I think Sari, is audibly confused, making an exasperated sound like, "Well..."]

The inquiry of why the Civil War started when it started – not earlier, not later – seemed to puzzle my students indeed. It seemed to become a "killer question" leading to the students' ontological engagement – raising the question in and by them. In the following fragment, the students were engaged in rapid and intensive brainstorming building on each other ideas in search for a satisfactory answer. "The third space" (Gutierrez et al., 1995) was firmly established in the classroom. Through the students' brainstorming I was learning how think about the Civil War. The students provided alternative and conflicting discourses for each other. My goal became to encourage them for further exploration.

> EUGENE: Um, huh hum... [points to Elizabeth as if to offer a perspective on the answer]
> ELIZABETH: I don't think [?] anymore, there were many things that led up to it, so... And I think that it's not as talked about as much, like there were ultimate [problems?]...
> EUGENE: Um, huh hum...
> LAURA [raising her hand, taking over the conversation as Elizabeth is talking]: Isn't it because, oh you're talking, I was just going to say I think they turned it around [?] people from North had majority because more states became against slavery...
> EUGENE: Um, huh hum.. But why did they become against slavery?...
> [Kristy and another student and Laura talking all at once. Sari's louder and more assured, taking over. It seems that as soon as Eugene makes a short response, another student takes a turn at contributing to the conversation...]
> KRISTY: ...factories in the North and cotton was in the South, and like the North wanted to have like that *dominance* over them. And they were going to get cheap labor and weren't they [EUGENE: Um...] exporting to England... [EUGENE: That's interesting, that's interesting.] in some of their factories?
> EUGENE: Hmm!
> KATEY: Isn't that it something?! [Lots of discussions now, involving many students split in small overlapping groups. It is difficult to hear what each student says. All students are involved in the discussions]
> SARI: It has to do with money, and that's like...
> KATEY: Yeah, It seems like it was more due to the money than than...
> SARI: And then like, oh, *we* [i.e., the North] feel really bad!
> [Elizabeth raises her hand]
> KRISTY: Yeah.
> [Eugene points to Elizabeth.]
> ELIZABETH: At first the North um... relied on the South for cotton [?]... and then um... when England started to produce cotton, the North started getting cotton from them, and they weren't real happy with the South.
> EUGENE [turning to the right side of the room]: Uhh!
> ELIZABETH: So, the South would lose money if they didn't deal with them.
> EUGENE: Hmm, um.
> ELIZABETH: And then wouldn't go for its wheat. So, it [?] 'cause they were losing money.
> EUGENE: OK.
> SARI [raising her hand]: Oh!! The machines were better! [long pause]
> EUGENE: Right, machines started developing at that time.
> KATEY: No, but when the cotton gin was developed, it increased slavery.
> EUGENE: Um?

In this brief but very rich exchange, the students provided a variety of rather sophisticated economic and political explanations of causes for the Civil War. Some of the explanations were compatible (e.g., North getting economically independent from South because of trade with England) but some were not (e.g., whether industrialization made slavery ineffective or, on the contrary, it could use slave more intensively than before). The class seemed to develop a regime of "internally persuasive discourse" (Bakhtin, 1991) where students themselves were testing each other's ideas (notice that Katey was arguing not only against Sari but also against the instructor who supported Sari).

> SARI [to Eugene]: Will you tell us?
> EUGENE [looking down at Sari]: You mean, "The truth"?! [Eugene smiles and says it with irony. Sari smiles in response, apparently appreciating the joke, and nods her head.] [pause]... It's actually an interesting question.

I was not ready to teach about the Civil War. The issues that my students brought were very interesting for me. I did not know about the cotton trade with England that made North less dependent on South. I also puzzled by Katey's point that industrialization and development of machines might not necessary make slavery ineffective. Modern-day sweatshops seem to prove that slave-like enterprises can successfully compete with companies based on free labor. I would like to educate myself together with my students. I, as the teacher, felt myself as a member of learning community about history of the Civil War (Greenleaf & Katz, 2004). If I chose guiding my students to address the historical issues they raised about the causes of Civil War, I would focus them on how to address them, where find the relevant sources, how to evaluate them, and where to find help. But my primary lesson was not about the Civil War...

> EUGENE: OK, guys, [lowered voice] back to our lesson on designing students' ontological engagement now! What was the point of that demonstration?! [Sari laughs; some other students laugh] Think of that. We came here to this class without much caring about Civil War. But now many of *you* start caring about that. [many more students are laughing] And you start asking me questions about Civil War – you are really interested in Civil War here and now. Now you're teachable about Civil War. This is the best way how you can teach students – when they start asking you questions about the topic you brought to the class. Right? [gasp, from Sari]. When your little students start asking questions, you say to yourself, [loudly] "Y-E-E-E-A-A-H!!!! Of course, my dear students, I'm happy to provide answers on this topic that I brought to you," right? And this is what designing ontological engagement is about. It's when your students start interested in the things that you brought to them to teach.
> SARI [upset]: You're not going to tell us about the cause of Civil War?!!
> EUGENE: No!!! You know, read books about Civil War. Check this out yourself. It's actually a very interesting question, and uh... I think it's very interesting. We need to know what causes the Civil War and why it is not fully over for us still after 150 years from its official end. But my lesson is not about Civil War. It is about how to make students care about academic curriculum. What made you start caring about Civil War. Let's reflect, how did we do that? [pointing at the relevant item on the side blackboard] Um... did I try something that affects your life? What did I try that affects your life? What do you think? [Laura raises her hand]
> LAURA: You asked us what a reaction our family would have to a Southern boyfriend.
> EUGENE: Right, right. Did you guys reply to my question? Did you answer to my question? [long pause] No!!! And some of you -- it's interesting -- some you gave me your non-verbal clues that your parents or grandparents may challenge

your *choice* if your boyfriend is from South. And, I saw that some of you hesitated to answer. 'Cause probably it's too personal for some of you. I did not insist because I didn't want you feel unsafe in our classroom. 'Cause it may be a personal thing. It's too close to home. It's too much ontological. But on the other hand, I wanted that tension because I *want* the topic to affect your lives. I want to *really* affect your life. 'Cause if I'm not affecting your life, you would not care about the topic and would not learn much from it. If you don't *care,* you will be not very much interested in the topic. OK? What else did I do? Do you have any other observations of how you become engaged in the topic of Civil War here and now? How else I managed to *trick* you in that topic, although you didn't care about that at the beginning whatsoever. Yes?

SARI: Ah, you made it *controversial.*

EUGENE: Exactly! Exactly! [goes to side blackboard to write the word "controversy" up there]. It's controversy that brings engagement... I want to engage you in controversy that still present in your life. [the discussion of how the teacher can design students' ontological engagement continues]

...

ELIZABETH: How can we create controversies for the students in our [future] classes?

DIALOGIC AND POLYPHONIC TEACHING

From a dialogic perspective, one of the most important evidence of learning is a student *voluntarily asking questions.* Sari's question to me about the major historical cause for the US Civil War turned her and arguably the rest of the class into learners of the history. Similar, Elizabeth's question about how to create controversies transformed her and, arguably, the rest of the class into learners of dialogic pedagogy. At this point, learning shapes an agency of the student and the student becomes a learner. The student's question mediates the student's own learning and creates the most meaningful educational event. A voluntarily asked question helps the student start taking in control of his or her own learning and thus to develop a learner's voice. By asking his or her own questions to other participants and to him/herself, a learner guides other participants how to guide him or her. The other participants recognize the learner's voice by treating it seriously, respectfully, and honestly – as coming from a consciousness with the rights equal (cf. Bakhtin, 1999) to them and to other respectful members of the broader community.

The teacher can promote the emergence of learners in his or her classroom by designing and arranging *learning provocations* before, in, and after the lesson and taking advantage of emerging "off-script" events – which are nothing more than emerging possibilities for learning provocations recognized by the teacher on-flight during the lesson flow. In the lesson above, I had several provocations both planned and emergent. My planned learning provocations involved exploitation of the existing North-South tensions in the US, possible tensions about the students' romantic relations existing it their families, and the whole lesson about the Civil War was one huge pre-planned learning provocation to focus my students on learning provocation themselves. One of the big emerging learning provocations that I recognized and exploited in the lesson flow was about the cause of the Civil War. I did not plan it. The teacher's provocations generate ontological surprises and tensions in the students that the students can translate and articulate into their own questions.

Systemically organized learning provocations constitute a *curricular journey*. I treated my whole class titled "Building a community of learners" as such a journey. In this journey that I organized for my students, I wanted them to explore what kind of teachers they want to be. This journey involved engaging my students into the historically unfolding discourses, debates, and ideas around controversial pedagogical ideas, philosophies, and practices. The journey goes not only about the pedagogical practices but through them when the students both participate in their own teaching practicum as novice teachers and in the class itself as a very experienced students (and emerging learners).

The described pedagogical practice, based on the students voluntarily asked questions, is dialogic. It stays in opposition to a monologic pedagogy in which learning is defined by the students' answers and demonstrated skills acceptable by the teacher (or any other institutional or epistemological authority) – by the preset endpoints. Dialogic pedagogy also stays in opposition to a polyphonic pedagogy in which learning is defined by the students' designing learning provocations and curricular journeys for themselves. In polyphonic pedagogy, the students learn to appreciate dialogue in its full might and became polyphonic learners involving in designing *their own* learning provocations and *their own* curricular journeys for themselves and others. This book is limited by a journey into dialogic rather than polyphonic pedagogy.

PROBLEMATICS OF ONTOLOGICALLY-ORIENTED TEACHING

Teaching, like any activity occurring "here and now," has an ontological aspect and influence on the students. The issue is whether this ontological aspect supports the instruction or not. For example, when a college professor lectures future teachers about advances of constructivism before giving a graded quiz testing if they can repeat the knowledge valued by the teacher (i.e., a transmission of knowledge and non-constructivist practice), the ontological aspect of his teaching involving traditional educational philosophy of transmission of knowledge may undermine his message about benefits of constructivism. His students may learn that constructivism is an unpractical bla-bla-bla that has little to do with their future teaching practice beyond passing a job interview. Of course, some other teaching may learn that the professor is not a good teacher and it is nothing to do with merits of constructivism. But even in this case, these students are not getting good grasp of benefits of constructivism as the instruction intended.

Even when teaching is ontologically-oriented – when teacher using the ontological aspect of teaching for instruction; – there are legitimate questions about how much it is desirable and practical. Here I am going to discuss problems that may emerge from ontologically-oriented teaching involving its possible negative side effects and feasibility of this type of teaching. One problem with ontologically-oriented teaching is about desirability of ontological engagement when it is not safe for the students or the teacher. An example of this problem was the described lesson when the instructor raised a question of whether the students' family may negatively react to the students' boyfriends from the South. It appeared through the students' non-verbal communication that some students might have such a reaction from their family but they did not want to discuss it in the class because probably they perceive this not being fully safe for them for some reasons. Another example is ontological teaching fractions through use of Barbie doll when students compare their own body proportions with ones of Barbie doll (Mukhopadhyay & Greer, 2001). When I replicated this lesson with my EDUC390 students, one of my students, who had slightly bigger body complexion, reflected on the lesson in the following way on the class web, "this activity was extremely intimidating. Being a girl who's measurements may be larger than average, I found myself embarrassed by the activity, and not wanting to take part in it at all. The major problem with this activity is that it causes some people to become intimidated. Who wants to take part in an activity that is embarrassing both physically and emotionally? Thankfully, there was someone in the group who was willing to measure herself, but for a few seconds I was panicking. I know that this is a true and valid problem due to the fact that I felt it myself, as I'm sure other girls in the class did as well. Because some students, such as myself, may not want to take part in this lesson their learning may be hindered. A student may choose to avoid the task by becoming disruptive or taking part in other problem behaviors." In a Michigan public school this type of lesson was forbidden by school administrators when some parents of 7th grader students protested because of their fear of this measurement activity was too sexual in its nature (Rombyer, 2004, February 26).

Ontologically-oriented teaching by its very nature involves a controversy that may split a local community. It is unavoidable. Communal conflicts promoted by ontologically-oriented teaching has been the main topic of most popular fictional movies about school: "Teachers", "Stand and Deliver", "Dangerous Minds", "Dead Poet Society", "To Sir with Love" and so on. Ontologically-oriented teaching is dramatic because it involves not only drama of ideas but people and communities. However, popular fictional movies about good teachers may give a wrong impression that the drama is temporary and involves a struggle between forces of good representing by good ontologically-oriented teachers[5] and evil representing conservative and insensitive teachers, school administrators, and parents. Ethnographic accounts of ontologically-oriented teaching (e.g., Freedom Writers & Gruwell, 1999; Paley, 1991, 1992) show that it is not the case – drama is a permanent, not temporary, aspect of such teaching. Dramas promoted by ontologically-oriented teaching occur not always between good and bad but at times among people of good will as well. Teaching without drama and risk associated with any drama and conflict is alienated teaching, boring, disinterested, uninvolved, and non-ontological.

The issue of ontologically-oriented teaching is how to manage risk and safety of such teaching. Ontological teaching that was aimed on using proportions to reveal unhealthy body images promoted in children popular toys should not induce pain in students suffered already from injustice of body politics promoted by the toys and discrimination based on health problems. Ontological teaching should not misfire. How to make ontological teaching safer for students without losing its dramatism? I do not think that there is a general receipt for that

---

[5] A 1969 movie "The Prime of Miss Jean Brodie" is an interesting exception from this grand narrative celebrating ontologically-oriented teachers. In this movie depicting a British private school for girls in the mid 1930s, ontologically-oriented teacher Miss Jean Brodie inspires her students to become fascists and join Spanish Civil War on Franco's side (among many other questional things that she inspires her students through her ontologically-oriented teaching). From this fictional but internally persuasive movie, it is clear that ontologically-oriented teaching by itself does not necessarily promote critical thinking and open dialogue. Ontologically-oriented teaching (and even social activism) is necessary but not sufficient for good teaching. Critical thinking, internally persuasive discourse, and open-minded dialogic public reflection are needed as well.

– honest discussions in professional communities and broader society and teachers' experimentation may be the communal way of solving this problem.

In another line of critique of ontologically-oriented teaching, Sidorkin (2002) argues that it is impossible to sustain intrinsic motivation in all students all time in mass schools. His argument comes from an economic ground focusing on essentially non-productive nature of school labor. In contrast to Marx who assumed that labor by definition is productive since it has to have exchange value, Sidorkin insisted that students' schoolwork is labor because it is organized by the societal need to have future workers and citizens, but this labor is not productive because its products cannot be consumed. When a patient pays for a doctor's diagnostics of his/her disease, s/he indirectly pays for essays about spent summer that the doctor did in her second grade – the writing skills that are necessary for the doctor to practice medicine were developed in part in her second grade writing projects. However, schoolwork is not productive – there is nobody interest in products of the students' assignments. Outcomes of students' learning projects have no pragmatic utilitarian value – it is a pure waste. Indeed, in many conventional schools, the product of students' schoolwork is graded and thrown away by the teacher (or by the students). The teacher her or himself often does not interested in consuming the students' work. The students work for essentially disinterested audience. Sidorkin argues that although some innovative schools can have productive projects that promote the students' ontological engagement by having utilitarian value for the students and others, on the mass scale, schools cannot compete with economy. Historically, mass schooling has been designed, in part, to keep children from productive labor and competition for jobs with adults. Thus, according to Sidorkin, ontologically-oriented teaching is impossible on a mass scale.

Sidorkin argues that based on economic laws when a product of activity does not have pragmatic utilitarian value, the activity can not generate motivation, and, we would add, to be ontological for the students (and teachers). To sustain, a non-productive (and, thus, non-ontological) practice requires motivation outside the practice itself. It cannot be self-sufficient and self-sustainable. Sidorkin's analysis shows that in the history of mass schooling, non-productive economy of schooling used punishments (violence) and rewards as the main means to sustain students' motivation: corporal punishment, expulsion, tracking, grades, access to prestiges institutions and practices, exclusivity, and so on. He convincingly shows that this system of rewards and punishments is in crisis now. His own proposal is to replace the system of rewards and punishments with a kind of exchange of favors system common in couch-trainee relations. The teacher can provide psycho-social and emotional support to the students while in exchange the students will keep doing non-productive work in school (like trainees may do unpleasant exercises for their favorite couch).

Sidorkin's economic analysis seems to be very fruitful. I agree with Sidorkin's analysis of conventional schooling that it is non-productive, does not generate motivation, and is based on a behavioristic system of rewards and punishments. I also agree that this system is moving to the crisis because the society does not tolerate institutional violence (corporal punishment) and injustice (exclusive education). However, I respectfully disagree with Sidorkin that a turn to a productive educational mass system is impossible. Using economic terms borrowed from Sidorkin, I argue that the mass system of formal education can be a hybrid of productive non-labor and productive labor.

Productive non-labor involves productive work for immediate consumption of the actor and the immediate community. The lesson above is, in my view, a good example of productive non-labor. The discussion of the Civil War – its causes and its roots in the contemporary society – was very productive for the participants in the classroom community. By its ontological authenticity, by its deepening interest, this discussion, although highly guided by the instructor, does not much differ from other sphere of productive non-labor -- other everyday discussions that the students and the instructor may be involved. Everyone was interested in everyone's else contributions. The instructor was not interested in seeing students' mistakes and misconceptions but rather was interested to know what his "community thinks" about the issues that he also thinks about. The product of the discussion – the growing uncertainty and problematicity about the causes of the Civil War and its current impact on the modern society had "use value", in economic terms, for the participants of the community (and probably beyond as the students and the instructor continue discussing the issues raised in the classroom).

Although, in my view, Sidorkin is probably right that mass school cannot compete with workplaces in promoting productive labor, mass school can and should be involved in different forms of productive labor. It can and should develop instruction through productive labor such as apprenticeship (Coy, 1989; Lave & Wenger, 1991), field practicums, service learning (Furco, 1996; Mettetal & Bryant, 1996; Zlotkowski, 1999). In all these instructional formats, students learn through participation in productive practice and through labor. Participation in productive labor promotes emergence of ontological puzzlement in students that the students can bring into the classroom or a reflective circle.

Sidorkin is correct that there is not a successful example of mass schooling based on ontological engagement involving a hybrid of productive non-labor and productive labor but so is his own proposal based on non-ontological engagement of exchange of favors. Further analysis of institutional demands and supports is needed to find out what kind of necessary resources ontologically-oriented teaching is required. For example, the instructor in the lesson analyzed above is an active participant of broader communities of educational researchers and educational practitioners that supported his practice along with his university. Further, ontologically-oriented teaching requires a political will from a broader society that may focus on other goals of schooling such as social mobility, credentialism, and completion for access for future better workplaces (Labaree, 1997).

Chapter 12

DIALOGUE AND ACTIVITY[1]

ABSTRACT

There is a growing concern in education in general and in dialogic pedagogy in particular that teaching design cannot guarantee learning. Learning is an emergent and, thus, probabilistic process. Similarly, how can the teacher design a dialogue? Learning and dialogue can be facilitated but cannot be designed. Both of them are relational processes that cannot be controlled by either party: the teacher or the students. Even a learner himself or herself cannot guarantee his or her own learning and what this learning will be about. But even more, as my colleagues and I have argued elsewhere (Matusov, St. Julien, & Hayes, 2005), the more educators focus on making particular learning happen in the heads of their students, the less effective their teaching usually is. Teaching seems to be a very different activity than many other activities we know. Sidorkin (1999) has developed an ontological approach to dialogic teaching that opposes an instrumental approach to dialogue in education. I consider the tension between the notions of learning and dialogue, on the one hand, and the notion of activity, on the other. I analyze educational practices of my own undergraduate teaching involving students' practicum in an afterschool program and teaching in the School of the Dialogue of Cultures pedagogical movement in Ukraine.

Teaching is a goal directed activity. Indeed, many educators want their students to know and to be able to do certain things by the end of a lesson, curriculum unit, term, year, or school. Teaching is mediated by design (Cole & Engeström, 2007; Hayes & Matusov, 2005a; Kafai & Resnick, 1996; Matusov, 2001b; Wiggins & McTighe, 2006). Traditionally, teaching design often involves:

- the teacher's self-questions (e.g., what themes am I going to cover during the lessons, how to present the material to the students, what learning materials to use, where to get learning supplies, how to fill out time of the lesson),

---

[1] I want to thank Olga Dysthe for inspiring me to work on this topic and for her tremendously helpful critical feedback on and discussion of earlier draft of this paper that really helped me think through many difficult topics discussed here. I also want to thank all participants of the Dialogue Seminar at the University of Bergen in January 2007 for discussing the presented issues.

- the teacher-students interaction scripts (i.e., the teacher's imaginary interaction with the students: what questions to ask the students and what kind of answers to expect from them) (Hunter & Hunter, 2004),
- learning activities and tasks (i.e., a sequence of specially organized activities and assignments),
- organizational structures (i.e., how will be students organized and structured during the lesson: seating arrangements, transitions, rules of interactions, and so on);
- contingency plans (i.e., what to do if something deviates from the expected script); and
- teaching objectives (e.g., "by the end of the lesson, my students will be able to do....").

Not all aspects of the teaching design have to be considered or are controlled by the teacher. For example, the time structure of the lesson or a day is sometimes controlled by the school or, in some countries, even by the ministry of education. The mandatory attendance of the students (another part of the teaching design) is often control by the law (although, at the university level student attendance still can be a part of the teacher-controlled design).

However, there is a growing concern in education in general and in dialogic pedagogy in specific that the teaching design cannot guarantee learning,

> Learning cannot be designed. Ultimately, it belongs to the realm of experience and practice. It follows the negotiation of meaning; it moves on its own terms. It slips through the cracks; it creates its own cracks. Learning happens, design or no design. And yet there are few more urgent tasks than to design social infrastructures that foster learning. This is true not only of schools and universities, but also of all sorts of organizations in the public and private sectors, and even of entities usually not called organizations, like states and nations. In fact, the whole human world is itself fast becoming one large organization, which is the object of design and which must support the learning we need in order to ensure there is to be a tomorrow. Those who can understand the informal yet structured, experiential yet social, character of learning - and can translate their insight into designs in the service of learning - will be the architects of our tomorrow (Wenger, 1998, p. 225).

Learning is an emergent and, thus, probabilistic process. Similarly, how can the teacher design a dialogue? Learning and dialogue can be facilitated but cannot be designed. Both of them are relational processes that cannot be controlled by either party: the teacher or the students. Even a learner him or herself cannot guarantee his or her own learning and what this learning will be about. But even more, as my colleagues and I have argued elsewhere (Matusov, St. Julien et al., 2005), the more educators focus on making particular learning to make it happen in the heads of their students, the less effective their teaching usually is. Teaching seems to be a very different activity than many other activities we know. Sidorkin has developed ontological approach to dialogic teaching that opposes instrumental approach to dialogue in education,

> My approach would be not to study dialogue in teaching, but teaching in dialogue. Burbules (1993) and others (see, for instance, Hull, 1985) convincingly show how using dialogical methods can improve teaching and learning. I make a stronger argument. These findings are indeed valuable, but they contain the seeds of self-destruction. Dialogue, which is being *used* for something ceases to be

dialogue. This is only a shell of dialogue, a conversation entirely within the *I-It* realm. No rules can guarantee that dialogue really happens, and dialogue may occur despite gravely monological forms of communication. Once dialogue begins, no one can channel it, or manage it, or transform it, even for the noble aims of education. I contrast the ontological vision of dialogue to a non-ontological one, which sees dialogue as a form of communication, as a means toward some other goal (Sidorkin, 1999, pp. 14-15, italics is original).

There seems to be some kind of tension between the notions of learning and dialogue, on the one hand, and the notion of activity, on the other.

My analysis of the notion of activity that I want to share here is that activity is responsible for the monologicity aspect of discourse. As such, it is not good or bad but a complementary and necessary aspect (see my discussion of this point in my previous chapter 5 on Bakhtin's polysemy of the notion of dialogue and monologue). Joint collective activity is about accomplishing something. The subject of such an activity is a unified, shared, common understanding – one consciousness, as Bakhtin would say. A joint activity becomes problematic when shared understanding is not achieved, partially achieved, or achieved about wrong things. Although heteroglossia can be viewed as a productive force in the activity at its initial and intermediary phases, at the final phase, it has to be eliminated. From this point of view, activity is essentially anti-dialogue (anti-heteroglossic). However, as Bakhtin showed, this unifying, centripetal force is an important aspect of any discourse defining one's voice, the recognized unity of consciousness. The problem starts when the other complementary and necessary aspect of discourse – namely dialogicity – is either ignored or attempted to actively exclude from the analysis (and design) or eliminate from the discourse, when *a* voice becomes *the* voice. In the latter case, there becomes a tendency to establish a regime of excessive monologism (see the previous chapter on Bakhtin's polysemy).

In social sciences – philosophy, political economy, psychology, sociology, education, sociolinguistics, and anthropology – there has been a long tradition of development of an activity approach (or an activity theory). No trying to be exhaustive (or even systematic), I impressionistically offer here the following list of names heavily contributing to the development of the activity approach in the social sciences: Spinoza; Hegel; Marx and Engels; Köhler (and German Gestalt psychologists); Vygotsky, Leontiev, and Luria (and their students and colleagues); Davydov (and his students and colleagues) and El'enkov; Engeström (and their students and colleagues) and Cole (and their students and colleagues); Wertsch (and his students and colleagues); Valsiner (and his students and colleagues); Rogoff (and her students and colleagues); Lave and Wenger (and their students and colleagues). Of course, the boundaries of this list are very arbitrary. As any social movement, it does not have the absolute beginning, the sharp border, and the ultimate end.

In my view, there are the three main principles of the activity approach that have been developed by the scholars listed above:

1.   Activity is defined by mediation;
2.   Human social and psychological phenomena is shaped by the humans' participation in the activities, practices, and institutions; and
3.   Activities transform and develop through dialectical contradictions.

In the activity approach, there is realization that the activity is not defined by its directionality but mediation. Marx (1990) argued that a human weaver differs from a spider because the weaver mediates his or her activity by the design (a weaving plan) while the spider's movements are guided by the instinct. Engeström (1987) argues, quite correctly in my view, that mediation is the key concept of the Activity Theory. Wertsch (1991b) insists that *mediated* action has to be *the* unit of analysis in human psychology. From Köhler's (1973) point of view, non-mediated action would be probably a misnomer. He would argue that without mediation, there are no actions but pure behavior guided by biologically pre-programmed instincts and/or by the psychologically charged environment: "positive or negative valences of the psychological fields" (Lewin & Cartwright, 1964) or "psychological affordances" (J. J. Gibson, 1979). Köhler defined intellect as a mediated action, as a special detour from the desire object. Even such a psychological phenomenon as stupidity he described through mediation arguing that stupidity is evidence of intellect that appears in inappropriate time and place (e.g., some apes tried to attach wooden boxes to the wall of their cage and jump on them to reach a banana hanging from the ceiling of their cage). Since Köhler could not observe mediation in chickens, he claimed that chicken cannot be stupid – only animals demonstrating mediation and, thus, intellect, (e.g., dogs, apes, humans) can be stupid (Köhler, 1973).

In humans, psychological processes and functions are regulated by cultural practices and institutions. Even such essential biologic functions as breathing is regulated by language and cultural norms not talking about such biological functions eating, defecating, or giving birth of a child (Rogoff, 2003).

Activities are charged with dialectical contradictions that push for transformation of the activities and development of new activities. For example, activity is driven by motives: by attraction to or by repel from some objects. However, mediation leads actors to focus on objects that they have not have interest before (i.e., tools, signs, environmental detours). A new motive emerges as a by-product of the activity: a reliable and better tool. Thus, through activity, actors develop a new motive: they may start building the tool – the tool becomes an object of new activity which, in its own turn, may require new tools (Köhler, 1973; Leontiev, 1981). Motive is both a pre-cursor and a by-product of the activity. In the activity, the actor does not only act on the objects but, through mediation, the actor acts on him or herself (especially through the use of signs, see Vygotsky et al., 1987). In activity, the motive and the tool are in a dialectical contradiction: the motive defines the tool and the tool defines the motive. This dialectical contradiction gives the impetus the activity for its transformation. To understand how and why activities change (or actively resist to change, or stagnate, or deteriorate), one has to do analysis of dialectical contradictions and tensions in the particular activities (Davydov, 1986; Davydov & Kilpatrick, 1990; Engeström, 1987; Engeström, 1990).

Studying psychology in the late 1970s – the early 1980s from Davydov, his students and colleagues, I was very attracted by the activity approach. The first blow I got from reading then published book by Bakhtin (1979) mainly consisting of fragments from his early and later work. I was surprised to find many negative and critical comments that Bakhtin made about dialectics, "Dialogue and dialectics. Take a dialogue and remove the voices (the partitioning of voices), remove the intonations (emotional and individualizing ones), carve out abstract concepts and judgments from living words and responses, cram everything into one abstract consciousness -- and that's how you get dialectics" (Bakhtin, 1986, p. 147).

Bakhtin saw Hegelian dialectics as some kind of deception[2] (Bakhtin, 1997, p. 666). However, the real blow to my attraction to the activity approach I got from a famous Soviet philosopher Anatoly S. Arsen'ev (Arsen'ev, Kedrov, & Bibler, 1967). In the early 1980s, together with my friends, I organized a Bakhtin-Kuzanskii short-lived seminar at the Institute of General Pedagogy led by Davydov. To my big surprise, Arsen'ev came to the seminar. He listened very tentatively to my presentation on differences and similarities between early Bakhtin and a medieval religious philosopher Nicholas of Cusa (1979) (whose two volumes were just published in Moscow) using the Hegelian activity approach framework. When I finished and invited comments from the audience, Arsen'ev pointed out that I misunderstood early Bakhtin who was, in Arsen'ev's view, neo-Kantian and anti-Hegelian (see Morson & Emerson, 1990 for more discussion of this point). I asked Arsen'ev to elaborate on why Bakhtin was anti-Hegelian. In his response, Arsen'ev claimed that, from quite early on, Bakhtin realized on the ethical grounds that Hegel and the activity approach in its logical conclusion lead to totalitarianism and genocide of any dissent. I was shocked. I do not remember well Arsen'ev's argumentation except his charge that Hegelian framework, which he equated with the activity approach, is about the expansion of one super consciousness (i.e., ultimate mutual understanding, "The Mind of Universe" in El'enkov's terms, "The Absolute Spirit" in Hegel's terms) trying to embrace the entire world (cf. Hegel & Baillie, 1967).

Later, I realized that the activity approach focuses on the monologicity aspect of discourse and if indeed it is pushed too far leads to excessive monologism as it happened with Marxism (Morson & Emerson, 1990 called Marxism "semiotic totalitarianism"). However, the activity approach does not need to be pushed to its "logical consequences." Monologicity has to be appreciated and recognized as an important and necessary aspect of discourse. For example, although Bakhtin criticized dialectics in many of his writings, he also acknowledged that dialectics can produce "a higher level dialogue," "dialectics was born of dialogue so as to return again to dialogue on a higher level (a dialogue of *personalities*)" (Bakhtin et al., 1986, p. 162). Activity approach has to be complemented by focus on dialogicity (Engeström et al., 1999).

CREATIVELY PRODUCTIVE ACTIVITIES: RE-PRODUCTIVE VERSUS BY-PRODUCTIVE ACTIVITIES

There is a Buddhist legend that an Indian raja asked Buddha how for him to reach nirvana. Buddha replied that to reach nirvana one should not think of a white monkey. "It's easy!" exclaimed the raja, "I never think about a white monkey." Of course, since then, each time the raja thought about nirvana, he unwillingly began thinking about a white monkey. My point here is that achieving learning and dialogue is like achieving nirvana in this Buddhist legend: the more one focuses on learning and dialogue, the farer they become. Dialogue like nirvana, like happiness, like love, like learning cannot be achieved by the direct desire to have a dialogue, to have nirvana, to have happiness, to have love, to have learning. In this sense, dialogue, nirvana, happiness, and learning (and teaching) are *not* goal-directed activities. They cannot be designed (Buber, 2000; Frankl, 1976; Frankl, Fairchild, & Ungersma, 1986;

---

[2] See also Wegerif (2007) for critique of dialectics (and of Vygotsky's dialectic psychology) from a Bakthinian dialogic perspective.

Sidorkin, 1999, 2002; Wenger, 1998). However, on the other hand, certain actions can increase possibility for engaging in dialogue, experiencing nirvana, love, happiness, desired learning and teaching. Similarly, some circumstances make dialogue, nirvana, love, learning, teaching more difficult, although never fully impossible. Thus, activity and design can be used for promoting these phenomena as their by-products.

The activity approach has rarely considered these types of byproduct-oriented activity processes. I propose, at risk being severely criticized by my colleagues, that activity approach mostly focus on *re*-productive activities, in which the issue of "how" (to achieve something known) is more important for the participants than "why" and "what" (they try to do what they do). In contrast, creatively productive activities develop a new product. Product is not just an object separated from an actor – outcome of a human activity, -- but, according to Marx (1990), it is *a use value*: an interest in this object by people (sometimes including the producer him, her, or themselves but not necessary). This use value is based on human interest in the new object that defines "the ideal" of the object-product (Ilenkov, 1977), or "meaningfulness" (Dewey, 1966). Thus, in a creative productive activity, an actor does not only create a novel object, but also a novel producer (a novel subject). And, what, perhaps, even more interesting in terms of consequences for dialogic pedagogy, creatively productive activity generates a new use value -- a new interest in people and, thus, a new community of such interest. For example, each radically new artwork, each radical theory, each radical technological invention visibly generate a new audience (less radical creative product also generates new audiences, consumers, practitioners but it can be less visible and dramatic). Modern capitalism has realized this communal aspect of creative productivity and promotes a new brand as a new communal lifestyle of a new, fabricated, desire (Gee, 2003; Glasser, 1972). If we apply this principle of creatively productive activity to education, it is possible that learning generates a new community, in which new products of this learning can be appreciated and desired.

Let me be clear on one point to avoid an unnecessary misunderstanding: there is no clear boundary between re-productive and creatively productive activities. Re-productive activities always have "disturbances" that require a certain degree of creative production (Engeström, Brown, Christopher, & Gregory, 1991; Wenger, 1998). Similarly creatively productive activities always use some more or less stable structures and traditions that they re-produce in their creative production (Bakhtin, 1991; Shklovskii & Sher, 1990). However, in re-productive activities the creative production is often perceived by the participants (and activity analysts!) as "disturbances" – a deviation for a desired norm, -- while in creatively productive activities, it is perceived as the main desired product, as creativity. It would be weird to imagine that scientists described their scientific findings as "disturbances" of their normal practice and neither artists, writers, composers, poets, inventors, and, arguably, learners and teachers.

Usually, the activities that the scholars guided by the activity approach have considered have more or less known product in advance (that is why I call them reproductive). In such activities, a direct focus on the more or less known product -- medical diagnosis and effective treatment (Engeström, 1990), effective court process (Engeström et al., 1991), effective insurance claim processing (Wenger, 1998), effective ship navigation (Hutchins, 1995), and so on – does not spoil the activity itself. The definitions and criteria for effectiveness (i.e., effective for what?) are more or less pre-existed in these practices. The "ideal" (in El'enkov's terms) endpoint of the activity is known: healthy person, resolution of a civil dispute, a processed insurance claim, the ship being safely navigated to the port or harbor. In re-productive activities, the "ideal," to a high degree, is Platonic and positivistic– it more or less pre-exists the activity itself (Whitson, 2007). The unknown is mostly about how to achieve this pre-existing ideal (e.g., how to teach all students to pass certain exams). Thus, I argue, these activities are *re*productive (they reproduce the known "ideal"). Reproductive activities are primarily based on instrumental mediation by tools, signs, and detours, well-described by the theoreticians of the activity approach.

Psychoanalysts have faced with a different type of activities that I would call *by*-productive (Bettelheim, 1960; Frankl, 1976; Frankl et al., 1986; Fromm, 1969; Neill, 1960). In such by-product-oriented activities, focusing on the final goal is ineffective if not dangerous for the participants. The goal of the activity is not to achieve some kind of a desired product but *to jumpstart an emergent process that can lead to some desired outcome*. For example, let's consider insomnia. To deal with some light forms of insomnia, the person has to relax him or herself. However, relaxation is arguably an anti-activity because it requires losing a concentration and thus one's control over him or herself. How can one use one's own control to lose it? This requires another and special type of mediation: mediation by another activity and an emergent process. In a case of insomnia, one can mediate relaxation by counting imaginary ship. This monotonous activity can help to relax and lose one's control (see figure 12).

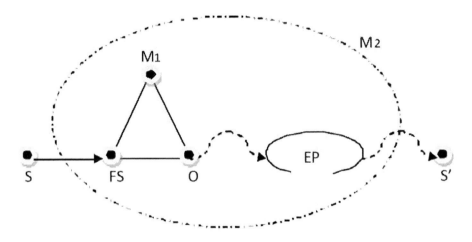

Legend:
S –   Subject (an insomniac);
FS –   Fabricated Subject (a counter of ship);
M1 – Instrumental mediation (number of ship);
O   – Object (imaginary ship);
EP – Emergent Process (relaxation);
S' – Transformed Subject (a sleeper);
M2 – Mediation by the activity and an emergent process (emergent mediation)

Figure 12. Model of by-productive activity of struggling with insomnia.

By-product activities are based on *double mediation*. First is usual instrumental mediation. For example, in the case of dealing with insomnia, one counts with numbers the imagined or mentally represented ship (the signs of them). The instrumental mediation involving tools, signs, and/or detours (in this case, number) is well described and studied by Köhler (1973), Vygotsky (1978), and Engeström (1987). The *instrumental mediation* involves full control by the participant and has the certain character (depicted with solid lines and arrows on figure 12). However, in the by-product activity, the subject of mediated activity (FS, see the triangle on figure 12) has a *fabricated*[3] character (S. J. Ball, 2004): an insomniac only *pretends* counting ship *as if* he or she is interested in the outcome of the count (actually he or she is not). Second is *emergent mediation* by an activity and by an emergent process. One has to design an activity of counting ship to mediate one's own relaxation and eventual sleep. Notice, that unlike the instrumental mediation which has often the deterministic character fully controlled by the participant, the emergent mediation by activity has the probabilistic and emergent character. It is not certain that counting imaginary ship would predictably lead the person to relaxation and that the relaxation would predictably lead to sleep. The mediation by activity is never certain and never fully controlled by the participant (as pointed by broken arrow lines on figure 12, see also table 12).

I argue that creative productive activities, like science, art, and dialogic education, are essentially *by*-productive. In creatively productive activities, the ideal endpoint of the activity is not known in advance. The goal is not known, the object is not known, the motive is not known, the definition of quality (i.e., definition of success) is not known, the audience for the product does not exist yet, – and thus, it is possible to say that the subject is not known either. Plato (1961) nicely captured this paradox of creative productive activity in the Meno Dialogue, a paradox of scientific search: if you know what you are looking for, why do you are looking for it (you have already found it); if you do not know what you are looking for, what are you looking for? One cannot answer to this question, until the one is transformed. Of course, in re-productive activities, the subject is transformed as well as many activity approach scholars have shown, but this transformation is less central, peripheral for the process of the activity and its goal. Transformation of scientists, artists, students (and I argue teachers) are essential for the creative productive practices. In creative productive activities, the participants *set themselves for a journey* to unleash emergent uncertain processes of fruitful self-transformations[4]. This idea of self-transformation as an adventurous jump into and navigation in uncertainty is different from Vygotsky's notion of self-mastery, self-control, and self-determination (Vygotsky, 1978, 1982; Vygotsky, Luria, Golod, & Knox, 1993).

Conventional education has been essentially *re*-productive by its nature. It focuses on producing pre-existing knowledge, pre-existing skills, pre-existing knowers (experts), and pre-existing doers (workers) (Lillejord & Dysthe, 2007, in press). The endpoint of conventional educational process is always known in advanced (Tolstoy, 1967). Fendler (1998) applied Foucault's genealogical analysis for deconstructing "an educated subject" in a historically developed Western education practice. He found that in the modern mainstream educational practice, "an educated subject" is manufactured from an ignorant and inept student. The student's subjectivity is supposed to be molded according the known certain end, "At the end of the lesson, the student will be able to…" Thus, in this pedagogical approach,

---

[3] The metaphor of "fabric" nicely reflects not only an artificial, illusory, non-authentic nature of the subject here but also the fact that multiple activities have to interweave each other to create this phenomenon.
[4] I see writing of this book as such a journey for myself so I called it "Journey into Dialogic Pedagogy."

the students' subjectivity becomes an object for the teachers (and, ideally, for the students themselves). Students are treated as objects of the teachers' pedagogical actions (Matusov, St. Julien et al., 2005). At the "end" of educational process, the students-objects are examined to see if they are well re-produced.

Sidorkin (2002) argues that conventional education is *non-productive* because nobody needs the students' schoolwork that usually ends up in garbage cans. As my colleague and I wrote in our review of Sidorkin's book, we both agree and disagree with him (Smith & Matusov, 2009, in press). We agree with Sidorkin that the students in conventional schools are forced to have *fabricated agency* (fabricated subjectivity): a student writes a persuasive essay of why the school recess has to be longer for the high stake test, *pretending as if* he or she is interested in the outcome of his or her persuasive speech (actually, he or she usually knows perfectly well that the essay was asked to be written not for the school administration to make any decision about the length of the recess but to assess his or her writing and persuading skills). However, we disagree with Sidorkin that conventional education is non-productive labor, – rather, we argue that it is re-productive. Products are not what the students produce, – we agree with Sidorkin that in conventional school students' schoolwork usually has very little use value (that is why it is so meaningless for the students), – but the students themselves. In conventional education, students are objects (and re-products) of the teacher's pedagogical actions. The students are required to cooperate in this re-production of their own objectivity, which makes their own agency fabricated. We also disagree with Sidorkin that, as he argues, this reproductive nature, and the student's fabricated agency associated with it, is unavoidable is institutionalized mass education (although this is an interesting hypothesis requiring a test by practice).

Table 12. Comparison of re-productive and by-productive activities

Activity aspects	Re-productive activity	Creative productive, by-productive, activity
The "ideal", the endpoint of the activity:	More or less known in advance	Unknown in advance
The primary goal of the overall activity:	Transformation of an object (re-productive) through instrumental mediation	Transformation of the subject (by-productive) through an emergent process
By-product:	Transformation of the subject	Transformation of an object
Deliberate focus:	On the desired goal through instrumental mediation	On the mediating activity, away from the desired goal
Mediation:	Single: instrumental	Double: both instrumental and by another activity and by an emergent process
Participants' control of mediation:	Full	Partial (only for mediation by another activity)
The character of mediation:	Certain, deterministic	Uncertain, probabilistic, emergent
Intersubjectivity is based on:	Mutual understanding	Heteroglossia based on gaps of interaddressivity

I argue that teaching has also to be a creative by-productive activity because learning is an emergent process stemming from the student's experiences organized (in part) by the teacher. As Lave (1992a) points out, teaching does not cause learning because learning is an aspect of any activity. It is not a question whether learning occurs or not – learning always occurs. The real question is what learning that has occurred is about. Some learning is neither socially nor personally valuable. For example, a person can learn to hate the academic subject or that he or she is not good at it and so on. Let me illustrate the by-productive nature of dialogic teaching using the following generative[5] example.

DIALOGIC TEACHING AS A CREATIVE BY-PRODUCTIVE ACTIVITY: A CASE OF DESIGNING ORDER WITH CHILDREN IN AN AFTERSCHOOL PROGRAM[6]

My students of a multicultural teacher preparation course participate in a service-learning practicum that is a part of the program called La Red Mágica ("Magic web" in Spanish) that I have organized in Fall 1998 with my colleagues as a partnership between the University of Delaware (UD) and the Latin American Community Center (LACC) of Wilmington, Delaware. The La Red Mágica involved UD undergraduate students, pre-service teachers, working with culturally diverse working class Latino/a children in an afterschool program twice a week for hour and a half during 9- to 10-week practicum (Renee DePalma, Santos Rego, & del Mar Lorenzo Moledo, 2006; Hayes & Matusov, 2005b; Matusov & Hayes, 2002; Matusov, Pleasants, & Smith, 2003; Matusov & Smith, 2008, submitted; Matusov, St. Julien et al., 2005).

The case I am about to describe here involved the very beginning of the practicum. It became a tradition by that time in Fall 2000 to start the practicum by a pizza party at LACC planned by the UD students. The pizza party usually starts with the UD students and LACC children making nametags for each other, than eating pizza while informally chatting with each other, and then playing games together. The UD class is split into two groups Monday-Wednesday and Tuesday-Thursday, so usually there are two pizza parties on Wednesday and Thursday of the first week (Monday and Tuesday of the first week of the practicum are reserved for LACC orientation for the UD students led usually by the LACC officers and children). The presented incident involved Monday-Wednesday group on the Wednesday pizza party, actually during the game that the UD students prepared for the LACC children to play. All preparations were done by the UD students in my class under my guidance. This Monday-Wednesday group prepared a game that is called "Indian Chief" (I had learned about this game in my 1999 class from my students). The game involved a person, called "guesser," who had to leave the group sitting on the floor in a circle ("the Indian tribe"), while the tribe elects its "Indian Chief" who would start certain movements (e.g., clipping, shaking the head) spreading across the whole tribe. When the guesser comes back, he or she should find who the Indian Chief is in the tribe by careful observing who starts a new pattern of the tribal

---

[5] *Generative* examples and cases are used to generate theory rather than just to illustrate it.
[6] I am thankful to John St. Julien for encouraging me to document and reflect on this case and for discussing earlier versions of the text.

movements. If the guesser finds the Indian Chief, the Indian Chief becomes the next guesser and the game continues.

On Wednesday, September 29th, 2000, three visitors decided to accompany the Monday-Wednesday group of the 8 UD students and me to the LACC to assist the students' work with the LACC children and observe the program in action: Oksana, a visiting professor from Ukraine; Manoli, a graduate student from Spain; and Samantha, my African-American graduate student and the teaching assistant for the class (all names here and further except mine and LACC Youth Director are pseudonyms to protect privacy of the participants) who had attended my class so the UD students had known them in advance. On that day, LACC had about 40 children of ages differed from 5-year old to 14-year old. Our students were all White middle-class females in their late teens (freshman and sophomore).

The incident occurred after the transition from us eating the pizza to playing the game "Indian Chief." As more and more LACC children finished eating and became restless (some UD students offered them playing the game Stone, Paper, Scissors as we discussed activity transitions in our class in preparation for the event). I suggested my students to move the LACC kids to the gym on the upper floor to play Indian Chief as we discussed, according to the students' plan. I volunteered to clean the recreational area, where we were eating pizza, with a small group of LACC children, who were eager to help me. The UD students moved the rest of the LACC children quickly and rather efficiently (I was pleased with that – although one of the UD student, Terry, disagreed with me about this account in her posting on the class web forum, see below). The 3 visitors followed them. This move of offering help with cleaning the recreational room was strategic on my side. I wanted to let my students, preservice teachers, to try to organize the activity with LACC children completely by themselves for the first time. I wanted to give time and space to experiment while being around and ready to come for help if things got deteriorated.

Things got deteriorated at the gym. When about 5-10 minutes later I came to the gym with a small group of kids who helped me with cleaning the recreational room, I found a troublesome picture. This was what I saw and heard. I heard a lot noise and angry yelling voices. I saw a lot of chaotic movements. A group of younger LACC children and older LACC girls with most of my UD students and 3 visitors were staying in the middle of the gym trying to start the game Indian Chief. Older boys were playing basketball running around the center of the gym where the others were staying. Two of my UD students were going after them begging to stop playing basketball and join the game of Indian Chief promising an exciting and interesting game ahead. The LACC boys either ignored them or promised to stop in a minute but they did not. Occasionally, disputes emerged among the older LACC boys about their basketball game and sometimes between the older LACC boys playing basketball and the older LACC girls who were staying in the center. I could hear a lot slurs and name calling like "hey, you, retired!" or "you, moron!" Some kids used Spanish and apparently not in a nice way (I could not understand but I could follow their angry non-verbal communication). A homework tutor (a young male adult in age of my students) interfered in the older boys' verbal fight in Spanish by yelling that if the kids did not stop talking like that they would be expelled from the program. Many separate short-living activities emerged and died. For example, a younger boy was running in the gym with his jacket waving it around his head in some kind of imaginary play, until he hit another boy who started chasing him trying to grasp the jacket.

My UD students in the center of the gym tried to silence the LACC children to explain the rules of the game "Indian Chief" by raising two fingers up as they saw the Youth Director, Galdys, was successfully doing in the recreational room. Very few young children followed and raised their two fingers up but majority did not. This strategy miraculously worked downstairs with Youth Director but it did not work with my UD students. Sometimes my students yelled, "Please be quite, please. We need to tell you the rules!" Some LACC kids try to help my UD students by trying to silence noisy kids around them and yell, "Shut up!" The other kids yelled back to them, "Shut up yourself!" or "No, you shut up!" My UD students did not support the children, who tied to help my students quiet the noisy kids, by asking these helpers not to yell. I noticed that many LACC kids allied themselves in this growing adversary along the gender, ethnic, school attendance, age, friendships, and family lines. With every second, LACC kids became less and less cooperative and more and more ignoring the adults' commands and demands.

Some UD students were trying to use "nice" voice to calm the kids down while begging them for attention, "You guys, please, let us talk, this is a really fun game." My students really tried hard to stay calm but it was clear to me that they were upset, frustrated, and even angry. Behind their artificial smiles, I saw boiling anger at the kids for being so uncooperative and at themselves for being so helpless. Sometimes, the UD students managed to gain quietness from the group for a few moments only to tell the children that the UD student would talk only when everyone would be quiet or to tell a particular rule of the game Indian Chief to the kids who did not hear this rules before. Usually noise and chaos remerged very quickly with a new strength immediately after.

I saw visitors Oksana and Samantha trying to discipline individual kids. Oksana, the Ukrainian visiting professor, came up to me and angrily told me in Russian that this was "a cuckoo house," ("сумасшедший дом") in her view, and that "all these kids are retarded!" ("они же все – придурки!"). She suggested to me to split the kids onto small groups. My student Amanda ran to me and suggested to call the LACC Youth Director so she could punished and expel unruly kids from the gym. She also suggested using candies that she brought with her to award well-behaving kids. Manoli, a graduate student from Spain, chatted with a few LACC children even during the time when the UD students tried to gain the LACC kids' attention and, thus, undermining their efforts to make all LACC kids quiet. But her engagement with the LACC kids seemed to be as real engagement. A few days later, Manoli described her feelings about the event in her follow-up fieldnote, "I felt so impotent! I did not know how to keep them interacted with everyone and what to do in this case" (Manoli's fieldnote, October 2, 2000).

It became very clear to me that the feelings of anger and helplessness were growing among many participants (both LACC kids and UD adults). Also, the adults (i.e., my 8 UD students and 3 visitors) were apparently exhausting their means of control of the LACC children and the whole situation. The tension, hostilities (i.e., horizontal, non-hierarchical, violence), and chaos at the gym were increasing, threatening to cross some kind of the invisible qualitative limit and explode. Paraphrasing Lenin's (1977) famous statement about the necessary conditions for revolution, there has been emerging a revolutionary situation in the gym when adults were unable to rule and govern in the old way and the children did not want to live in the old way (like becoming quiet and attentive when two fingers were up by an adult). I was afraid that not only something bad might happen with LACC children – somebody might be physically and/or emotionally be hurt, – or with UD students – someone might do something that would heavily regret later on, – but also that my UD students would develop phobia for being with the LACC children and even for teaching in general. I knew that I had to do something to stop this deterioration of the social fabric. Also, I felt that as their instructor, my students saw me as an educational role model. The kids also expected that some adult would interfere at some point. Some of them knew me from the previous year and expected an action. Although I also sensed that my three visitors expected some correcting action from me, they were my last concern. I felt being on the spot burden by responsibility. I had to act quickly and appropriately without having much space for an error.

I decided to act quickly and decisively. Abruptly I left the adults complaining to me at the kids and went to center of the gym. I quickly picked a few (5-6) younger kids whom I expected to be most cooperative. I invited them to play the game and without any explanation of the rules I commanded them to play in a rather dictatorial manner, "You will be a guesser," I said to an 8-year old boy, "Leave us so we can secretly select our Indian Chief. When we call you back, you have to find our Chief. Go!" The boy left. I turned the rest of the kids who were listening to me attentively despite the noise around. I looked at a 7-year old girl next to me, "You will be our Indian Chief. You have to order us new movements, like clapping or shaking your head, or something else creative. We will follow you." She silently nodded. I was not sure that she completely followed me but it did not matter. "Let's sit on the floor in a circle," I ordered rather than suggested and sat on the floor (I was sitting next to the Indian Chief). All 5 kids followed me. I tried not to pay my attention to what was going on around of me and avoided any eye contact with my students or the visitors. I could hear some of them saying to each other, "What's he doing?!" I turned to the girl whom I delegated the Indian Chief role, "Do something! Start a movement!" She looked at me with her open eyes smiling but not moving. I took her hands in my hands and started clapping them, "Do what she does! Follow her!" – I yelled to the other kids in the circle through the noise at the gym. They did. The Indian Chief girl continued clapping by herself by now. After a while, I order her, "Do something else!" She did: she started clapping on the floor with both her hands. "Follow the Chief!" – I order the tribe. The kids obeyed my order. Some of them start smiling with pleasure. They seemed to start liking the game. "Change," – I quietly whispered to the Indian Chief and she did by starting clapping on her head and giggling. "Change after a while, OK?" – she smiled at me and nodded. I noticed that all the tribe nodded to me after the Chief. The game started.

I stood up, "I'm going to call the guesser. Tribe, try not to look at our Indian Chief so the guesser would have tough time of guessing." I came to call the guesser. The guesser came very excited observing the tribe's movements from the distance. "Try to guess who our Chief is – who gives us orders to change the movements. Go!" The guesser boy looked around at the tribe kids, smiling, and selected me (of course, I was the boss!). Another boy next to me immediately reacted, "Nope, dummy!" The guesser stopped smiling. I reacted promptly but without turning my head to the offender – just by putting my hand on his shoulder, "Watch your language, young man!" I sensed with my peripheral vision that he turned his head to me, "Sorry, Mr. Eugene." I mediated this apology to the guesser boy, "He said sorry *to you*. Now guess again! You are a very smart observer!" The game continued.

A boy came to me from behind and asked to join the game. I did not reply verbally but just moved aside to give him a place. He watched the game for a while and then joined it. I could see that his neighbor whispered him something and he nodded in response – probably telling him who was our Chief. This modeled a few other kids, boys and girls, to join our circle on the floor. Our tribe grew rapidly. A few of my UD students come to the tribal kids and asked them if they could join the game. The kids did not answer but, like me, moved to give them place in the circle. At some point, we all have to move back to give more new kids to join. A few times, a ball got into our circle from older boys playing basketball all around us, we just threw the ball away from our circle to the boys and kept playing our game. The older boys apologized to me but I did not reply verbally -- only by nodding in acknowledgement and acceptance of their apology (and the fact that they did not do it on purpose trying to disturb our game). The tempo of the game rose.

Soon, the guesser correctly pointed at the girl next to me – our Chief was revealed. Everybody laughed. I praised the guesser and the Chief. The former Chief, a little 7-year old girl, became our new guesser and left the circle away from the center of the gym to wait when we would call her back. As soon as the new guesser left, many kids in the circle started yelling to me, "Me! Me! Me!", asking me to pick them up as our new Indian Chief. Some of them raised their hands as in school. They started moving closely to me. Some kids gave up on calling for my attention and moved further from me. I picked up a quiet girl which produced an uneasy sign in some boys showing publically that my decision was unfair in their view. I sensed the new problem but I did not know what to do yet.

We continued playing. Almost all my UD students were a part of the circle by now. Many of the older boys stopped playing basketball and joined us. Some of the older LACC boys apparently tried to flirt with my UD female students who were only slightly older than they were. But the overall attention was on the game itself and it was not disruptive or disrespectful (at least in my view). I made a mental note for myself to discuss it in the class at some point. One of my UD students, Elli, sitting in the circle, called the older boys who were stilled playing the basketball, "Common guys, join our game, it's fun!" I immediately looked at Elli with disapproval – you did not need to try to coerce the boys to join our game, they could see and judge for themselves, if our game had more fun than theirs did. I was afraid that in response the boys might do something opposite or even disruptive. But they did not – they just ignored my student's call. To my surprise, Elli seemed to fully understand my concern – she turned around and yelled back to them, "No pressure guys. Come when you feel ready!" Suddenly, the basketball players replied to the student, "Yeah, we will." They were listening to her after all and felt necessary to reply this time. Wow, I was very pleased and proud of Elli – we could professionally exchange arguments without use of words!

Suddenly the problem of selecting a new Indian Chief became a big threat of our new social regime of the game. The emerging sense of amity, community, and cooperation started deteriorating again. I was running out of the creativity and could not find a solution. So I decided to share the problem with the whole tribe. I asked, "Tribe, how can we select our next Indian Chief in a fair way?" The kids and my students were offering suggestions: alternating boys and girls, picking out only quiet kids, selecting kids who were not Indian Chiefs already, and so on. Suddenly I saw a little girl of 6 who was turning her fingers as if she was salting imaginary food with imaginary salt. I came closer to her and she said to me with a smile, "We need a spinner." It struck me. That was it – I would be this spinner! I went into the center of the tribe circle, asked all the kids and adults, who were staying and offering the suggestions, to sit down again (they did, probably being puzzled by my decisiveness). I closed my eye stretched my right hand as a clock arm and started slowly spinning around. I could hear again, "Me! Me! Me!" I opened my eyes, put down my hand, and said very quietly and slowly, "I will stop only at the quietest place. Yell if you do not want to be picked up." Many kids could not hear me because of the noise. They asked, "What did he say?" I did not repeat, instead I closed my eyes again, stretched my right hand, and started spinning slowly. I could hear that the kids were spreading my word with each other in whisper. Quickly, it got very quiet. We could hear only basketball hits of the three older boys, who still kept playing basketball around us. I felt a bit dizzy of spinning so I stopped at a most random place. The new game procedure worked.

Our next problem was on the way – kids wanted to be spinners. This time, I did not wait and asked them directly how to solve this problem. To my big surprise, the kids did not yell at once but start raising their hand. I turned to the little girl who suggested the idea of the spinner to call on the people who wanted to speak. At the end, we elected this girl to be our The Spinner of the Spinners who select a next game spinner. On that development, I felt that enough organization was done and it was a good idea for the kids and my students to take the control without me. I excused myself and left the gym under a fake urgency to speak with the LACC officers about future joint projects. When I came back after about 10 minutes or so of absence (I indeed went down to speak with some LACC officers), all LACC kids in the gym were playing the Indian Chief game[7]. The game had a nice natural rhythm of alternation between being quiet and being vigorous, which helped the kids to regulate themselves and their emotional states without getting tired quickly. It was time for UD students and the visitors to go. The UD bus was waiting for us to being us back to the UD campus. Many LACC kids hugged our UD students and visitors asking them when they would come back. I saw my students "melting" in the kids' hugs being overwhelmed emotionally (some had tears I noticed). This is how one of the student described her experienced on the class web to the other, Tuesday-Thursday, group immediately after she came from the LACC (notice, please the time of the posting, we came back from LACC at about 8:00pm),

HOW IT WENT   **From:** Terry   **Date:** 09/27/2000   **Time:**
09:15:55 PM

Hi everyone. I know you are anxiously awaiting to hear how it went today so here it goes... I will no doubt leave some things out so hopefully Leslie [another student from the Wednesday group – EM] will be able to fill in some of the gaps... and we will be talking A LOT about it in class tomorrow... because it turns out Eugene won't be able to make it Thursday (nor the other 3 adults we had with us) so it will likely just be you guys ... but you'll be fine. Really.

First of all, I had A TON of fun. The kids really look forward to us coming to play with them and they are very friendly. We ended up getting there a little late (10/15 minutes) because of an accident that was blocking traffic... but the time went by REALLY quickly. First Gladys [the LACC Youth Director at time – EM] introduced us, and that was very nice and she talked to the kids and had them give her the rules of being a La Red Magica Kid (respect, follow directions, etc...) and it was good to see the kids understood what was expected of them. And then we started making nametags and that went pretty well... one thing that was interesting,

---

[7] Spanish graduate student Manoli later reported in her fieldnote that it was not exactly how I perceived that at the moment, "We started to play Indian Chief, and after doing three times or four all the group was interested in that game except two kids. They came and told me that they just started to be boring. I did not how to engaged them in the game, because the rest of the group were involved on it!. So, what I did was to tell them that they could propose to the teacher [i.e., me – EM] to change the game...." (October 2, 2000). I did not know what happened with these two kids: did the return to the Indian Chief game or left the gym.

is that after seeing how I wrote my name, Randy [an LACC boy – EM] asked me to do his the same way, and I did, and all the sudden I was doing 5 kids nametags the same way... I suggested different colors, or using crayons or having them do it themselves... and some of them did choose different colors but yeah... I thought that was interesting... And I didn't mind doing it, but even while I was doing it I felt kinda bad because I had expected this to be an activity where they could each be creative in their own ways... but they asked and so since I had already did one, I did the others... Then we had pizza as people began finishing their nametags, and the kids really liked that... All of this was done in the "homework" room because it had tables which was nice, but it was a little small... but I didn't feel really as cramped as someone else had expressed. But anyway... it seemed these kids would eat as much pizza as you let them... but there was enough for everyone to have 2 and some had 3 I think and Gladys was very instrumental in making sure everyone helped to clean up... Oh, I almost forgot she showed us right in the beginning that when she wants quiet she will put one finger in the air and if you see that you should put one finger in the air and be silent... and if someone around you doesn't notice, she doesn't want them to say "shh." but to gently tap them with their one finger and show them that it is in the air so that they can do the same. It was pretty effective in that setting...

...but less so when we moved to the Gym... by the way, all of that took so long for us that we had only 40 minutes [I think actually it was even less – EM] to play up in the Gym so we played [only – EM] Indian Chief [they planned to play some other games as well – EM]... but when I went up to the Gym the lights were still coming on... (they take a few minutes...) so it was still relatively dark, and I thought someone had gone up with the kids but found only Leslie up there and the kids were running all over the place... so yeah, that transition didn't go super well... and even once the lights were on... (I have to apologize, I am horrible with remembering names, but do you all remember the woman that came to our class the other day from the Ukraine... I cannot remember her name...) Anyway she was there with us as well as another woman from Spain and Samantha (one of the women who played Rafa-Rafa[8] with us) were helping us get the kids together... and basically what worked the most effectively was just a few of us sitting down in a circle.... then the other kids just kind of followed along... Then I began trying to explain the game to the kids and I didn't realize it at the time, but I was trying to get everyone to understand, for instance one girl asked me to explain the game again and so I did... but Eugene pointed out [later on the bus – EM] that just like when I sat down and just started forming the circle hoping the others would follow... It's not necessary for everyone to fully understand before you start... Because they will catch on, and they can ask each other... so my advice to you would be to just get in there... explain it once so that at least a few understand, and let the rest catch on... Another minor thing we seemed to look over in planning the game was deciding how to choose a new Indian Chief each time... but Eugene came up with a good way in which he (or anyone else) gets in the middle, closes their eyes and spins around and stops... He mentioned once (after doing it a few times) that we would only stop at a quiet area... and the kids seems to pick up on that anyway without him telling... And Leslie made a good observation [on the bus, on our way back to the campus – EM] that showed the kids really were enjoying the game in that everyone wanted to be Indian Chief... It may have seemed a little crazy at times... but not out of control... you have to be on your toes, and I would

---

[8] A game simulating a sense of cultural shock of visiting another culture (see http://www.stsintl.com/schools-charities/rafa.html). We played this game in class at the beginning of the semester. The students started attending LACC on the 4th week of their class.

think with more of you there it will be easier to improvise and come up with ideas among you all... Basically, don't ever "panic" and just go with the flow... I know I'm forgetting some of the important things we were discussing afterwards... but that what class is for... All in all I had a GREAT time and the kids were adorable and wonderful :-) Good Luck to everyone going tomorrow :-)

Next day, on Thursday, in class, we discussed and analyzed our experiences at LACC. Our primary focus, of course, was on the problems emerged while starting and then playing the Indian Chief game at the gym. After we discussed in depth how we perceived and saw the initial problem in the gym (i.e., our emotions, observations, reasons for the problems, possible negative consequences of the problems, analysis of the tried approaches and reasons for their failure), we moved to the main interest of the students: what I did, why I did it, why it worked, why Gladys' approach of raising two fingers did not work at the beginning but worked at the end with the LACC kids, and what the students could do to be successful with the kids. It took me a while to convince my students that I did not have any of my solutions before entering the gym and that the idea of a spinner came initially from a little girl.

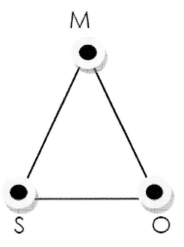

Legend:
S –   Subject (Gladys);
M – Instrumental mediation (two fingers raised in the air);
O   – Object (problematic LACC children);

Figure 13. Model of re-productive activity of Gladys disciplining LACC kids.

After we set all the students' questions about my actions at the gym on the blackboard, I asked them a guiding question that puzzled me since the day before. I asked the students why they wanted to play the Indian Chief game or any other game with the LACC kids on the first day of the LACC. I really wanted to know how they conceptualized the activity and its purpose. They replied that they wanted to have fun with the kids so they could start building good relations with them, to "break ice" with LACC kids, to start feeling comfortable around the kids, and so on. I was pleasantly surprised to hear that because their actions did not match what they were saying. I pointed at this saying that when I came to the gym I saw them attempting to install discipline, order, and silence on the kids – neither of which seemed to resemble collective fun that they were aiming at. They replied that they had thought that they had to establish the order and discipline and silence first to set up fun. I disagreed, saying, with a kind of tautology, that in order to set up fun, you have to have fun. They asked me but what creates fun. While I was being puzzled by this difficult question, a student offered an interesting answer: games create fun.

The class erupted. The students started talking interrupting each other while still attending to one another's ideas. I loved that thoughtful cacophony. This was what I could hear. "But we had a game – it did not work! There was not fun." "Yeah, but it did work for Eugene. Our game created fun!" "But what made it fun?!" "Rules! Good rules." "Nah-nah, rules are just stupid, like, 'you are the guesser.' What is fun in this? If I write the rules of Indian Chief, would you laugh?" "No, but when I play I would." "Not, all the time. Sometimes, we were serious in the game and still it was fun." I remembered Elli saying enigmatically, "Yeah, it's rules and not rules [that make games fun – EM]." Another student agreed, "Rules help but they cannot guarantee fun for sure. Like, we might have other 30 minutes of fun playing Indian Chief and then it would become boring for us. Then next day it can be fun again. It's in rules and not in rules." "Rules helped but…" "Rules trick us into fun!" "Yeah, rules help us have fun." "Rules create possibilities for something interesting to happen, for some joke to crack, for some kind of fun…" "And then, when the game routinized it becomes boring, plain boring." "Listen, guys, shh, quiet, please, listen, this is what Eugene did: he created possibilities for something fun to happen and this fun sucked the kids and us, us as well, I admit, in like a vacuum cleaner!" "You tricked us, Eugene!" "You guys, I saw it. It was like a crystal growing[9]." "I saw it as well, it was like a cancer[10] spread around fast! Nobody could stay out of the game, even the older kids who were playing basketball!" "Nobody forced them to stop playing the basketball but eventually they stopped and joined the Indian Chief game." Elli raised her hand and I gave her the class floor. She admitted, "You guys, at the beginning I tried to force [to join the Indian Chief game – EM] them [i.e., basketball players – EM] but they just ignored me. I looked at Eugene and he showed me to stop – I do not know how he showed but he did, right?" I nodded. "And then, guys, it daunted on me that I do not need to force them, that the game would do it itself. That I have to give them time. That I have to respect their own game. I have to respect them to make their own decision, to make their own move. I realized that you do not need to force kids and hover over them, you can control them by fun." Some students immediately disagree with Elli, "We do not need to control kids. We did not come to LACC to control kids – we came to have fun together, to build relations!" "If you start to do *'control thing[11]'* – it's not fun!" "Elli, if somebody starts doing this *control* shit with you, sorry Eugene, would you find it fun?" Elli retreated, "I didn't mean that, guys. You know, what I meant?! Eugene, I meant another type of order… the order based on fun." Melissa disagreed using her sarcastic voice, "*My dear*, fun does not have an order!" Leslie defended Elli, "Melissa, if you were yesterday

---

[9] The students seemed to use metaphors that remind me of the chaos theory – they try to describe an "attractor" (Prigogine & Stengers, 1984).

[10] This "cancer" metaphor brought by students bothered me then and bothers me now. Only after reading the dialogues many times, I have realized that it seemed to had hidden criticism of our UD colonization of the LACC. Jenny's criticism of our insistence on playing the Indian Chief game at the expense of the LACC kids' playing basketball reverberates with this important criticism.

[11] Double voicing, mocking Elli's voice.

at LACC, you'd have seen what real *dis*order means. Indian Chief [game – EM] created great fun order at LACC yesterday."

Listening to my students' excellent dialogue I realized that they collectively conceptualized pretty well the important tensions that could guide them in their work at LACC: control vs. fun, design vs. emergent process, being vs. instrumentality, the quality of alive and problematic relations vs. preset structure of the discipline, and so on. Some of these oppositions I was writing on the blackboard during the class dialogue when the students disagreed with each other. I felt that the second group was getting ready for taking responsibility for leading at LACC. I decided to help them to sum up (also, the time of the class meeting was running out), "So, Thursday group, how are you going to act at LACC today without 'adults,' as Terry wrote on the web yesterday? Do you feel confident? Are you scared to death? Should I cancel my other class and go with you today?"

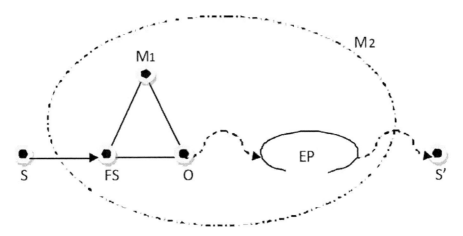

Legend:
S –   Subject (Eugene);
FS –   Fabricated Subjects (players obedient to the game rules);
M1 – Instrumental mediation (the game rules);
O   – Object (actions in the game);
EP – Emergent Process (fun);
S' –   Transformed Subjects (a new UD-LACC community);
M2 – Mediation by the activity and an emergent.

Figure 14. Model of by-productive activity of the Indian Chief game at LACC

"We're OK, Eugene!" "We've learned it today." "Start the game immediately – don't wait." "Do not silence kids, just start the game. No lengthy explanations of the rules. We can start the game even among ourselves and then the kids can join." "Like a vacuum cleaner!" "Yeah, plus many kids already know the game." "Practically, all." "We do not need to introduce a new game – we just need to have fun together." Terry from the Wednesday group offered them her help, "Guys, if you need help today, I can go with you – honestly." "No, we'll be OK, thanks." "We can do without 'experts'!" "We don't need a babysitter – I'm kidding." "Not funny..." "Sorry, Ter!" "We will be fine." "Just come with us!" "Yeah, let have fun at LACC!" "I will bring my boyfriend!" "There're we're talking, man!"

Suddenly, Amanda asked me a question that I did not expect, "Eugene, why didn't you guide us to join the basketball game yesterday with older boys? The game was fun, at least for the boys." I was puzzled by it, "Hmmm, indeed." I replied, "This is an excellent question. I don't know. To tell you the truth, I did not think about it at the moment. But thinking now, I see your excellent point. It would have been nice for all of us to learn how to join kids' own their territory, their game, not our game. And still, for some reasons, I'm now uneasy with that. I like what we did better. But I don't know why. Can somebody help? Am I defending a wrong decision or am I on something important?" The students were silently thinking. Then Amanda replied, "I feel that you might be right guiding us to initiate *our* game of Indian Chief rather than to join the *kids'* game. I'm a control freak and now I'm happy because I started seeing it [i.e., control, order] differently. As Elli said, 'fun order.' I love to be there, at LACC. I'm eager to come back now. It's not about 'you need to make the kids do this or that' when you're constantly doing some kind of tasks and not living there. You know what I mean? Yesterday, for 25 or 30 minutes I lived with the kids – the rest of the time I was busy [of thinking and worrying about] what to do and how to discipline them. Of course, I saw Eugene was working and we were working alongside with him even at the last minute at LACC but it was a different type of work. It was our work of taking care of kids and us and him. It was still living with all of us.... I don't know how to say it. But if you guided us to join the [kids'] basketball, I might have enjoyed it as well, but I would not have been happy as I'm now. No, I wouldn't. I mean it's nice to learn how to join kids' play and all that but I wouldn't happy. I'd have probably thought, 'Yeah, we had fun with the kids – but where is education here? What have I learned from it?!' I saw that magic of how to turn chaos and disrespect into a community and I have learned that I can do it myself. It's a bit scary but much more exciting. Don't get me wrong, I might need to learn how to join kids' activities as well[12], but I'm glad that Eugene did not start with that." Many students agreed with Amanda that they would not have been as happy as they were if I had guided them just to join the kids' playing basketball. I liked Amanda's answer a lot, "Thanks, Amanda, for your help. Now I know why I did what I did. And thanks, everybody, for the *beautiful* learning as, our Spanish friend Manoli often says. I don't know like you, but I've learned a lot yesterday and today!"

Jenny suddenly added a new twist to our discussion, just when other students started moving their bags to leave the classroom, "You know, guys, I was listening to all of us and I was thinking that we were wrong on insisting on *our* game and not joining *theirs*. We were just bragging, 'Our game has more fun than yours!' We're happy to break their game and their fun. I don't think it was right thing to do. We were their guests. I'm imagining them sitting in a class like ours at LACC and wondering why their game did not work for us. Now I feel a bit sad of what we did." Some students agreed with Jenny (including Elli) but some disagreed (including Amanda). The time of the class was over (which was very unusually that physical time corresponded to the psychological, social, and intellectual time – not that there was nothing to discuss for us but we did a great deal of work of becoming a professional

---

[12] In this class, the role of UD students at LACC in their context of work with LACC children is a recursive topic in the class. In one of the first of my classes at US, one of my students coined a negative term of "glorified babysitters" referring to their role at LACC (Matusov, St. Julien et al., 2005). I think that Amanda raised a similar concern here.

community on that day)[13]. While I was collecting my teaching stuff in the classroom, through a classroom window, I saw them passionately talking on the street in small groups outside our Willard Hall Education Building. I was thinking that maybe we did a wrong thing at LACC, as Jenny stated, but I loved to be at LACC with my students and with the LACC kids and I liked to be in our class. I thought that we seemed to be passing Amanda's test of good pedagogy so far. I wondered if the LACC felt the same or not.

Next day I saw the following report about how things went at LACC on Thursday evening,

> Re: Thursday at LACC **From:** Tommy **Date:** 09/29/2000 **Time:** 03:16:19 PM
>
> I had a really good time at the LACC on Thursday. Everyone seemed very relaxed and no one even hesitated to go right over and start working with the children. I think that we had a good handle on things. I would definitely have to thank the Wed. group for letting us in on the best way to get the kids involved..... That is to just begin the game. That tactic seemed very successful and after a few moments most of the children were engaged in the activity. I was actually quite surprised at how effective that was. I did notice that there were a handful of boys that were becoming violent with each other and running around the gym. I know that a bunch of us asked them to calm down, but that was not too effective. Does anyone have any suggestions what we could do in this situation? I tried asking them what games they were interested in playing and we could play them, but they said they didn't want to do anything. Just interested what anyone else thought about it.

POLYPHONIC MEDIATION TO SUPPORT DIALOGUE

Activity approach is very helpful for starting and supporting dialogue in order to move, paraphrasing Gadamer (1975), from "conducting a lesson" to "falling into dialogue." Activity approach helps to design dialogue and to maintain it. Of course, a lot of mediation happens during the dialogue itself but it is embedded into heteroglossia and dialogicity and not in instrumentality. Dialogic flow is similar to everyday conversations with their multiple and overlapping foci and themes (Linell, 1998; Morson, 2004; Rorty, 1979; Sidorkin, 1999). However, Bialostosky (1989) disagrees with this statement arguing that dialogue is a special artwork different from the flow of everyday conversation (see also pedagogical notion of instructional conversation discussed in, Echevarria et al., 1995; Tharp & Gallimore, 1988). I feel truth in both sides that requires more investigation. In this section, I will discuss supportive aspect of polyphonic mediation.

What was my role during the discussion? Of course, I was listening to the students very carefully. I felt myself participating in the discussion in two roles: one as a co-participant equal to my students and the other one as an instructor having a special role of supporting the dialogue and guiding the process. Here I want to focus on this latter role because arguably it

---

[13] The dialogues were reconstructed a couple of weeks after the class meeting occurred on Thursday, September 28th 2000, based on the TA notes on the class. The presented verbatim approximates the students' and mine actual utterances and our mannerisms.

involved polyphonic mediation. While I was listening to my students and myself, I was sensitive to *emerging moments of dialogic tensions*. These moments can be responsible for shaping the participants' communal experiences by creating dramatic collective being or communal dramatic events. Bakhtin (1999) played with the Russian word "событие" ("event") to show that you can read it as two words "со-бытие" – literally co-being, or being together. Event also refers to something happing out of ordinary, something remarkable, something almost exotic, out of routine of the life. These are points of transformation of the community and relations in the community (Matusov, St. Julien et al., 2005).

The emergent points of dialogic tension can be mediated and mastered by the participants. When the purpose of such mastery is to promote, support, and deepen the dialogue, *this mediation becomes polyphonic*. The concept of dialogical mediation has been developed recently in several related terms: "boundary object" (Star & Griesemer, 1989), "interobjectivity" (Latour, 1996), and "intersubjectivity without agreement" (Matusov, 1996, 2001b). Dialogical mediation differs from monological mediation in communication by the type of participants' (and/or observers') project it used to. The participants' project in monological mediation (what makes the mediation monological) is to establish, maintain, repair, and promote shared, common, meaning and mutual understanding in order to accomplish something together (Reddy, 1979; Schegloff et al., 1996; Wittgenstein & Anscombe, 2001). In contrast, the participants' project in dialogical mediation is to keep distance of incomprehensivety ("transgradience" in Bakhtin's terms, Bakhtin et al., 1990) and boundaries of distinguished voices for the sake of dialogue and its emergent by-products. Monological mediation promotes sharedness while dialogical mediation promotes heteroglossia. By themselves, dialogical and monological mediations are neither good nor bad. They both constitute aspects of any discourse. However, in some types of discourses, one dominates over the other. In conventional pedagogy, monological mediation dominated over dialogical one. I argue that in polyphonic pedagogy, polyphonic mediation should dominate over monological one.

I use "polyphonic mediation" and "dialogical mediation" here not as synonyms. Polyphonic mediation is a subclass of dialogical mediation in which dialogue is consciously valued by the participants as its final goal (Morson & Emerson, 1990) while in other type of dialogical mediation it is not necessary the case. For example, Star and Griesemer (1989) describe a case of collecting rare animal species for a museum in California, when the rare species ("boundary objects) mediated and coordinated the discourses and discursive actions among many participants (e.g., hunters hunting for the museum for profit, biologists interested in research with the species, local preservationists, philanthropists financially supporting the project, museum workers, reluctant farmers hunting the annoying animals) without these participants valuing the dialogue as their goal. But, on the other hand, they did not try to achieve mutual understanding and shared vision either.

By the definition of the term, emergent moments of dialogic tension refer to a problem, a threat, and/or a creative possibility that polyphonic mediation tries to address. In my teaching practice, I have noticed that my students and I are faced with several distinguished types of emergent moments of dialogic tension.

Dialogic Opposition: Interaddressivity

Dialogic opposition involves an irresolvable confrontation of person-ideas. The person-ideas (Bakhtin, 1999) and their confrontation are deeply rooted in both ideology and ontology of the participants and their relations. Kuhn (1996), who studied the practice of science and scientific debates, might call dialogic opposition a "confrontation of paradigms" but, in my view, it misses a bit ontological and political aspect (see Latour, 1987). Dialogic opposition involves whole-person commitment with their life-trajectories into to the opposition. It is not a pure intellectual game that does not commit the participants to certain life situations. But it is not a pure ontological and relational conflict that does not have strong ideological and intellectual component either.

At the beginning of our class discussion about the gym incident presented above, I wrote on the blackboard, "Focus on discipline (Gladys) vs. Focus on having immediate fun (Eugene)" as one of the first dialogic opposition as an emergent moment of dialogic tension. Gladys, the LACC Youth Director at the time, and I were the opposite idea-persons. Gladys was a person of structure while I was a person of dynamics and relations. As Gladys mentioned on one of interviews that we took with her, when she had arrived at the LACC as the Youth Director, she had set up one of her first urgent goals to expel me, personally, and the La Red Mágica program, in general, from LACC. However, we finished up working in a very close collaboration without compromising our ideological differences and our fruitful dialogues (Matusov & Smith, 2008, submitted). Our dialogue opposition was irresolvable not in a sense that we could not agree with each other on every issue – we did occasionally (often because of very different reasons, although). It was (and still is) irresolvable in a sense that for us to deeply agree with each other, we have to transform on the onto-ideological levels and become basically different people than whom we were (and probably still are). However, probably because of our dialogical irresolvable opposition not only we worked well with each other but we enjoyed working and being with each other, tremendously enjoyed each other, and benefited from each other's contributions (although we struggled as well).

By putting on the blackboard (public space) the text capturing the dialogic disagreement in the class, I wanted to attract the students' attention on both permanence and importance of this disagreement. Although at the end of the class many (if not all) of my students were leaning toward my dynamic position rather than Gladys' structural, during the rest of the semester many students revisited this tension. They also noticed and commented on complexities they noticed later on. For example, they noticed that I used discipline with the kids as well (even in the described case) by promoting and engaging the kids into certain procedures, while they learned that Gladys was the LACC champion in Pokemon and NeoPets games that were highly popular among LACC kids (she even bargained with the kids for certain disciplinary favors in exchange for neopet money she gave to the kids).

During the class, I listed several dialogical oppositions. The last one I placed on the blackboard when the students were leaving the class, "Learning how to design new activities with LACC kids (Amanda, Eugene) vs. colonizing LACC kids (Jenny)." This was another dialogic opposition that defined our discussions and our work at LACC (and us as a learning professional community). Arguably, it was this dialogic opposition that seemed to force Tommy to engage into a dialogue with the LACC boys about what kind of game they wanted to play, "I did notice that there were a handful of boys that were becoming violent with each other and running around the gym. I know that a bunch of us asked them to calm down, but that was not too effective. Does anyone have any suggestions what we could do in this situation? I tried asking them what games they were interested in playing and we could play them, but they said they didn't want to do anything. Just interested what anyone else thought about it" (WebTalk posting, 9/29/2000). Tommy seemed to want to follow Jenny's position by talking with the boys about their preferences but it was not very successful. It is also interesting that the students were engaged in testing their actions for or against the dialogical positions in the disagreements.

Finally, it was not always my responsibility to mark publically a dialogic opposition. Although it did not happened during this class meeting, sometimes my students asked me to write down (since I controlled the class blackboard) an important dialogic opposition they noticed. Some dialogic oppositions were recognized publically on the class WebTalk (the class asynchronous forum) by them or me (Matusov, Hayes, & Pluta, 2005; Matusov, St. Julien et al., 2005).

Orchestration of Dialogue

Orchestration of dialogue involves mediation of issues of exclusion involving the participants' access to and comfort in the dialogue and its fragmentation. Although I taught a relatively small class of young adults, there are always emergent organizational issues of dialogue (see our discussion and analysis of how the teacher deals with organization of dialogue with younger students and big classroom in Matusov, Smith et al., 2007). Some students might be systematically excluded from a classroom dialogue despite their desire to participate, some students do not listen to each other, and sometimes the participants stop replying to each other by trying to promote their own agendas, sometimes the class splits onto small discussion groups, and so on. Some of these developments might not necessary indicate a problem of deterioration of dialogue and/or might not require any mediation but some do.

In the described class meeting, orchestration of dialogue was often a shared responsibility between the students and me. To get class floor, the students could do it in several ways: 1) speak loudly after waiting for a pause without raising their hand and being called by me, 2) speak after bidding and negotiation with each other (e.g., "You speak"—"No, you speak, please, I'll speak after you"), again without raising their hand and being called by me, 3) raising hand and waiting when I give the class floor to them, 4) speak loudly interrupting other speaker(s). According a tacit rule, I could speak at any time and interrupt anyone. Sometimes a student could interrupt me with a question, a comment, or a challenge as well and it was always fine with me.

I use many non-verbal signs that were clear to my students for orchestration of dialogue. For example, if the students spontaneously split onto many small informal discussion groups and I moved to the corner of the class away from the center of the blackboard, the students often realized that by this move I was giving legitimacy of their small groups' (often passionate) discussions. If however, I moved to the center of the blackboard and raise my both hands up (as if catching a ball), they knew that I demanded their attention (I could also use a small bell that I carry with me). Some students felt necessary to assist me by saying "shhh" (like LACC kids) or saying, "You guys, Eugene is waiting for us." I also use index finger to acknowledge somebody to speak next (and to show all other students that I did that) and nodding to acknowledge that I saw their bids for the class floor by placing them in my mental queue for the class floor and they did not need to attract my attention any more. Sometimes, the students also use their fingers to point at another student to me who, in their view, had to take the class floor either because they had to say something important but too shy or because did not have the floor for long time and too shy. Having, asynchronous class web forums where students can initiate any topic broadly relevant to the class or reply to postings are others is one of the modes of dialogic orchestrations. The students in my undergraduate classes are required[14] to post minimum two postings (initiations or replies) per week (see Matusov, Hayes et al., 2005, for analysis of dialogic orchestration using these web forums).

Let me illustrate how orchestration of dialogue works using the example from the class meeting that I described above. In the middle of our discussion, I saw Elli raised her hand. Elli was a student who usually did not feel necessity to raise her hand but skillfully joined the class discussions. Once I remember, I asked the students to raise the hand who felt that she was shy (I was making some point with that demonstration). Elli raised her hand first before anyone could even think which made everybody laughed because Elli was so an outgoing, extrovert person. She was openly embarrassed and then told us, "You do not know me, guys. Sometimes I have zero confidence in myself." Our laughs and smiles disappeared at once. Anyway, when I saw Elli raising her hand, I realized that she wanted to change our dialogue and/or offer some serious self-disclosure. I nodded her in acknowledgement but let the conversation continued a bit until I felt it had right intellectual and emotional mode. Then I called out Elli who said, "You guys, at the beginning I tried to force them but they just ignored me. I looked at Eugene and he showed me to stop – I do not know how he showed but he did, right? …And then, guys, it dunned on me that I do not need to force them, that the game would do it itself. That I have to give them time. That I have to respect their own game. I have to respect them to make their own decision, to make their own move. I realized that you do not need to force kids and hover over them, you can control them by fun." Arguably, without this Elli-Eugene orchestration (i.e., polyphonic mediation), Elli's important contribution might be lost and did not give birth Amanda-Jenny dialogic disagreement.

Dialogic Addressivity of Respect

Dialogue is mediated by prolepsis of respect. Rommetviet (1979) introduced the notion of "prolepsis" to refer to something that is taken for granted by participants of communication. When this prolepsis of respect is getting undermined, the dialogue is in jeopardy and to save it the participants try to mediate the prolepsis of respect through

---

[14] Can something be required of the students in a polyphonic classroom? As I argue further about dialogic authority, I would say 'yes' only if the teacher's unilateral requirement is expected eventually to die out. As Morrison wrote in the early 1930s, "In the sense, the fundamental problem of teaching is to train the pupil, so arrange his studies and so apply an effective operative technique that he will eventually be able to become so absorbed in any study which in itself is worthwhile [for the pupil]" (Morrison, 1931, p. 135). In my class, the requirement is never died out and thus was essentially monologic in its nature (I have never tried to abandon my requirements at the end of the class – I think it is worth trying although one semester of dialogic classroom might not be enough for the students to understand and value dialogic pedagogy). I have never seen my classroom as polyphonic but rather as a dialogic-monologic hybrid. I see myself as a forever-monologic teacher who tries to develop innovative dialogic educational practices (I borrowed this approach from Alcoholic Anonymous practices). Being raised in monologic educational institutions, I do not expect anything else from myself but excessive monologism. My own excessive monologism upsets me but it does not surprise me. This realistic approach prevents me from becoming paralyzed (or feeling self-betrayed) when I noticed

addressivity of their dialogic contributions. *Dialogic addressivity of respect involves the issues of promoting respect of the dialogic partners as the final agency for their deeds and actions and avoiding humiliation* (cf. Rorty, 1999). In the previous quote by Elli, the issue of addressivity was raised with all its acuteness. Elli tried to force boys playing basketball in the gym to join the UD-organized game of Indian Chief. She used a fake invitation masking an actual command, "Common guys, join our game, it's fun!" The boys replied to the command by ignoring it. Of course, this is just my interpretation (alternatively, the boys did not notice or hear Elli's bid although she yelled it very loudly) but it is plausible because when Elli changed her strategy and said, "No pressure guys. Come when you feel ready!", they positively acknowledged her bid, "Yeah, we will." I argue what made her second bid successful was the change of addressivity from Elli's pressure on the boys that treated the boys as resisting objects without much of their own agency to Ellis' respect of the boys' decision making process that treated them as "the consciousnesses equal to the consciousness of" Elli (Bakhtin, 1999).

Bakhtin argued that the issue of addressivity of how to address others without denying their agency and their responsibility for their own deeds (ethically good or bad) is one of the most central in the Dostoevsky work (Bakhtin, 1999, p. 60, the italics is original),

> Truth is unjust when it concerns the depths of *someone else's* personality.
> The same motif sounds even more clearly, if in somewhat more complex form, in *The Brothers Karamazov,* in Alyosha's conversation with Liza about Captain Snegirev, who had trampled underfoot the money offered him. Having told the story, Alyosha analyzes Snegirev's emotional state and, as it were, *predetermines* his further behavior by *predicting* that next time he would without fail take the money. To this Liza replies:

>> . . . Listen, Alexey Fyodoruvich. Isn't there in all our analysis -- I mean your analysis . . . no, better call it ours-aren't we showing *contempt* for him, for that poor man-in *analyzing his soul like this,* as it *were, from above,* eh? In deciding so certainly that he will take the money? [SS IX, 271-72; *The Brothers Karamazov,* Book Five, I]

When other people determine one's behavior and the person notices that, he or she often feels humiliated. This is probably universal human feature common to all cultures. Of course, in different cultures there might be different responses and different level of determination after which the person might feel humiliated. This bold hypothesis of mine requires empirical investigation.

Conventional monologic education does not often recognize the problem of addressivity and respect for the students (and even the teacher's) agency. Recently, I noticed the following (homework) assignment in a social studies textbook for middle school students, "Compare these two texts and find similarities." The assignment uses genre of command, there is no even the mediator of conventional politeness "please" recognizing agency of addressee's at least in a ritualistic way. Further, there is no any attempt to explain the students why they should compare the texts and find similarities, what for. There are zero attempts to share a bigger project (of course, if it actually exists) with the students. Finally, there is no

---

monologic aspects in my own teaching practice and does not force me to rationalize these aspects but to work hard on addressing my excessive monologism in my own teaching.

assumption that the students might be needed to convince to join this project. All these three aspects of *dialogic* addressivity: respect for the agency, sincere sharing the project and its goal, and feeling for necessity to convince the addressee to participate in the project are necessary aspects of dialogic addressivity. Addressivity dialogically mediates human relations that become by-products of this negotiation. When, for example, the teacher asks the student in the classroom, "Two plus two equals...?", the teacher promotes and mediates the teacher-student relationship between the expert and the ignorant whose knowledge is tested. One of the three (if not all three) aspects of dialogical addressivity is violated in this example.

Math teacher and educational researcher, Lampert (2001) insists that, in feedback or guidance, the teacher has to not only intellectually guide the students but also be concerned about the students' their own self-image and image of others with regard to being mathematicians and members of the classroom community. In my view, Lampert talks about the issue and problem of dialogic addressivity. In the classroom discussion described above, the students ran into problem of addressivity several times. At the end of my undergraduate classroom meeting that I described above, Jenny suggested that we did not address LACC children respectfully by insisting our own activity, the Indian Chief game, and by not joining to their activity, the basketball game. Similarly, when Terry offered Tuesday-Thursday group her help but some people from this group rejected the help apparently feeling that Terry was hovering over their agency and responsibility (my interpretation),

> Eugene: "So, Thursday group, how are you going to act at LACC today without 'adults' as Terry wrote on the web yesterday? Do you feel confident? Are you scared to death? Should I cancel my other class and go with you today?"
> "We're OK, Eugene!" "We've learned it today." "Start the game immediately – don't wait." "Do not silence kids, just start the game. No lengthy explanations of the rules. We can start the game even among ourselves and then the kids can join." "Like a vacuum cleaner!" "Yeah, plus many kids already know the game." "Practically, all." "We do not need to introduce a new game – we just need to have fun together." Terry from the Wednesday group offered them her help, "Guys, if you need help today, I can go with you – honestly." "No, we'll be OK, thanks." "We can do without 'experts'!" "We don't need a babysitter – I'm kidding." "Not funny..." "Sorry, Ter!" "We will be fine." "Just come with us!" "Yeah, let have fun at LACC!" (Terry,) "I will bring my boyfriend!" "There're we're talking, man!"

In a half-serious, half-joking form, I tried to provoke the Thursday group to assume responsibility for their own preparation for their first independent actions at the LACC. As I expected, my half-joking provocation produced reassurances and solidarity from the Thursday group that they were ready. Terry's serious offer of help, however, eliminated a sense of carnivalistic atmosphere from our discussion and strengthened its serious mode of (Eugene's and Wednesday group's) doubting in the ability of the Thursday group to manage the situation at LACC independently. I do not mean to say that Terry implied that doubt but she was apparently understood by the Thursday group as such. The Thursday group understood Terry as distrusting their agency and attempting to hover over their shoulder with her "expert opinion," "No, we'll be OK, thanks," "We can do without 'experts'!", "We don't need a babysitter ...." I speculate that not only the Thursday group got offended by the Terry's but they also jumped quickly on an emerging opportunity of creating an oppositional solidarity against Terry (and possibly the entire Wednesday group, who remained silent during this fast exchange) turning her into their group scapegoat – I am judging it by a nasty twist of their attack s by using negative labels: "expert," "babysitter." Terry responded with her public expression of pain, "Not funny…" At this point, the community would either reunite or split further. Terry set a test. It was a dramatic event. The Thursday group backed off from their assaults on Terry (and, indirectly, on the Wednesday group), accepted responsibility for intentional causing pain, and apologized in a sincere and emotionally affectionate way, "Sorry, Ter!" However, they still seemed to continue interpreting Terry's offer of her help as doubting in their abilities to independently handle the situation at LACC by trying to reassure Terry (and the rest of the class?) that they would be fine. But they also were changing her addressivity to Terry (and indirectly to the Wednesday group) by now by inviting her as a peer (not as a helper) to LACC with them, "Just come with us!" Finally, when Terry suggested that she would bring her boyfriend, everybody seemed to relax, "There're we're talking, man!" – they accepted that Terry's offer for help was sincere, coming from "an equal consciousness" (Bakhtin, 1999), and not from an expert doubting in their agency. Addressivity of respect meditating a dialogue was restored.

Dialogic Epistemological Authority of Trust

Dialogue is mediated by epistemological authority of trust. Morson (2004) and Sidorkin (1999) argue that dialogue is impossible without organizational (i.e., orchestration, see above) and epistemological authority is creates a shared focus. Here I want to argue that dialogic authority is needed for dialogue because it: 1) creates shared focus (i.e., *important* issues to discuss), 2) connects to important voices of broader dialogues (i.e., network of *important and most influential* voices), and 3) introduces relevant facts (i.e., a network of *important and most relevant* facts). The teacher's epistemological authority is rooted in the classroom internally persuasive discourse: it is its precursor and by-product. The students' trust in the teacher legitimizing his or her authority is based on the internally persuasive discourse on that everything can be tested and questioned. But it does not mean that everything has to be tested and questioned – it is impossible for the students to repeat by themselves all the history of the Dialogue in the history of the humankind: to find out by themselves what important issues are, what important voices are, and check all the facts. They have neither time for that nor the societal machinery based on the network of distributed practices.

In my review of Morson's position, I argue that dialogue does not eliminates the need for authority but changes its purpose and nature (Matusov, 2007). On the first glance, this statement is paradoxical and contradictory to Bakhtin's (1991, 1999) notion of the "internally persuasive discourse" that defines dialogue as essentially authority-less discourse in the opposition to the "authority discourse." Indeed, the notion of authority seems to contradict Bakhtin's (1999) idea of discourse among "the consciousnesses with equal rights." Bakhtin's dialogic principle of equal rights of consciousnesses is not based on any epistemological symmetry among the participants but rather on the regime in any statement is legitimately open for challenge and testing by anybody.

However, as Morson points out, dialogic authority can facilitate and promote these equal rights, even more without dialogic authority these equal rights are impossible because the participants will not have shared focus. "Why would I have to listen to you, if I have my own ideas?" Dialogic listening and attending to contributions of others involves temporary withholding of one's judgment giving an opportunity the author to express him, her, or themselves. This temporary withholding of judgment is based on trust that the other person might present something important and worth. Dialogic listener gives legitimacy of this temporary inequality of the consciousnesses and, thus, epistemological authority to the author based on trust. Although, temporarily, the consciousnesses of the author (i.e., speaker, writer) and the audience (i.e., listener, reader) do not have equal right, as dialogue demands, -- this inequality promotes and makes possible the dialogue. ""In order for me to engage readers in an internally persuasive discourse regarding this essay, for instance, they must trust my assertion that investing their attention, time, and effort in reading it is worthwhile. In other words, readers must trust my authority at least to some extent. This trust is not unconditional; it must ultimately be rooted in the authority-less internally persuasive discourse that I have tried to weave into my essay…. the teacher must gain [dialogic authority – EM] over the classroom in order to lose it through the development of internally persuasive discourse" (Matusov, 2007, pp. 232-233). Bakhtin also seemed envision dialogic authority in internally persuasive discourse as he wrote,

> Both the authority of discourse and its internal persuasiveness may be united in a single word [i.e., discourse -- EM] -- one that is simultaneously authoritative and internally persuasive -- despite the profound differences between these two categories of alien discourse. But such unity is rarely given -- it happens more frequently that an individual's becoming, an ideological process, is characterized by a sharp gap between these two categories: in one the [authoritarian -- EM] word (religious, political, moral, the word of a father, of adults and of teachers etc.) that does not know internal persuasiveness, in the other the internally persuasive word that is denied all privilege, backed up by no authority at all, and is frequently not even acknowledged in society (not by public opinion, nor by scholarly norms, nor by criticism), not even in the legal code. The struggle and dialogic interrelationships of these categories of ideological discourse are what usually determine the history of an individual ideological consciousness (Bakhtin, 1991, p. 342).

Morson argues that the fact that the teacher (or another student) may create a shared focus or bring certain ideas for a class discussion based on conditional trust – dialogic epistemological authority – does not undermines the dialogue because everything still remains "tested and forever testable" (Morson, 2004, p. 319). For example, in a so-called "the School of the Dialogue of Cultures" – Ukrainian-Russian educational movement based on Bakhtin's ideas of dialogue – two social sciences teachers Kurganov and Kurganova "invite" two experts on culturology Mikhail Bakhtin and Oswald Spengler [the author of "The decline of the West", (Spengler, 1939) —EM] in their sixth grade classroom to present their students about these authors' views on the notion of culture,

> A mini-lecture was presented to the students on behalf of M.M. Bakhtin. Sitting on the "logical chair," a teacher outlined the following main principles of Bakhtin's understanding the notion of "culture":

Civilizations and peoples disappear -- they are not eternal. Culture lives forever – it is immortal.

Culture lives eternally in cultural artifacts and artwork.

The time of life of culture is always the present time.

Culture does not have its own internal territory. Culture exists only where two cultures present. Culture exists on the border of two cultures.

Nikita, Serezha, Andrey immediately raise questions.

Nikita [boy]: Why are two cultures needed for existence of one?

Serezha [boy]: Heavenly (medieval) culture is an exception. It is culture by itself. Because culture created by the God's Word is perfect: it has only its own internal territory and it does not have boundaries with any other culture equal to the God's one.

Andrey [boy]: Perhaps, the virgin-primary culture is also an exception. Because it was the only culture at the time and, thus, did not have boundary with any other.

Ksyusha [girl]: I'm ready to reply to you, Nikita. For any culture, two are needed because if the first culture lives on some separate island and does not communicate with anybody, then it cannot reveal [actualize – EM] itself, it cannot self-express: they do not have anybody to fight or to exchange goods. For example, if Ancient Greeks had lived alone [without any contact with other cultures – EM], and nobody lived around, then there would not have been the great Greek-Persian War, even the word "barbarian" would not have existed (nobody would have been around to call this name). Culture with all its customs, creative art, and worldview can reveal itself only in the contact with others. Science of this culture develops in this way: someone communicates with other cultures, learns their customs, like Herodotus, and, thus, a series of books about history is developed. Without others, Herodotus would not have been able to do that and, thus, another piece of culture would not have existed. This was why Bakhtin insisted on this point.

Denis [boy]: For each culture, a rival emerges and each culture tries to become more perfect than its rival is. It is exactly because of that, cultures invent new and very interesting things.

Rita [girl]: I don't think that for existence of a culture, there are two cultures necessary. In my homework assignment asking what culture is, I replied that culture is a custom. If each people has its own custom (culture), then why to mix them? There is nothing good can come out of this!

Matvey [boy]: One culture is not a culture.

Maxim [boy]: For existence of a culture, two cultures are needed because one culture has to cooperate with other cultures. [Otherwise -- EM], nobody could have strived for the throne of the world culture. There would not have been development of the humankind.

Serezha [boy]: As a person cannot become famous without making something [remarkable EM], a culture cannot be called "culture" until it initiates a contact with another culture. Faith is an exception from this principle [although – EM] – the heavenly culture. It is culture by itself.

Andrey [boy]: I disagree with Bakhtin. Because at the very beginning of the evaluation of the humans, there was only one culture. And it was. And we studied it. There was no any other one. And then this First Culture split onto numerous cultures. My question to Bakhtin: why don't cultures have their internal territories?

Katya Sveridova [girl]: I agree with Bakhtin. I understand him this way. In order for one to become a person of a culture, another person is needed.

Vitalik Kalinichenko [boy]: In a dialogue of cultures, two cultures have two different pasts, but one common future.

Rita [girl]: A culture does not need another culture. Two cultures, like two different peoples, have different rituals. There is always the gap between two cultures and cannot be understanding.

Teacher Kurganova [woman]: German philosopher Spengler thought this way. Perhaps, we can talk with him and explore his understanding of culture.

Ruslan [boy]: Only in the XX century, the dialogue of cultures has begun. Before the XX century, each culture was independent of each other.

Teacher Kurganova [woman]: Some scientists of culture say that either the XXI century will be century of dialogue of the cultures, or it won't make it at all[15]...

Kate Koryagina [girl]: I don't understand: how can peoples protect their freedom and independence of their cultures in the condition of dialogue of the cultures[16]?

Teacher Kurganova [woman]: You will think about that at home."

Then the teachers introduced Spengler by letting Katya Koryagina sit on "the logical chair" and read a list of Spengler's 6 principles, extracted and prepared by the teachers in advance, to the class. After listening to the Katya Koryagina, the students jumped into a lively discussion (and testing) of Spengler's ideas by their comparisons his idea with Bakhtin's and their own ideas (Solomadin, 2004, translation from Russian is mine). The Kurganov teachers used their epistemological authority to select particular scientists, specialists on the notion of culture, who, in their view, were important voices for the students to talk with. The 6th grade students listen carefully to the teachers, Bakhtin and Spengler, presented by the teacher, because their trust the teachers that these presentations are very relevant and useful for them and will be open for upcoming public scrutiny, investigation, questioning, and testing. On the long run, the consciousnesses of the teachers, Bakhtin, and Spengler are equal to the consciousnesses of the 6th grade students (later in the year, the students were exposed with fragments from the original texts by Bakhtin and Spengler). As a reader of this pedagogical dialogue, I found myself impossible not to consider my own position in the relationship with the children's and the teachers' dialogical contributions about Bakhtin and Spengler (see my colleagues' and mine discussion of this issue in Matusov, Smith et al., 2007). Authentic learning dialogue is always inviting, being hungry for new audience-participants, and creatively productive.

In my own teaching, I use dialogic epistemological authority of trust a lot. Some of that is similar to the presented fragment from the School of the Dialogue of Cultures, when I, like the Kurganov teachers, introduce another influential author or text for our collective exploration. I also often define initial topics for the class discussions but my students can bring their own and we can collectively overrule my initial topics due to urgency of the students' ones (see Matusov, St. Julien et al., 2005, for a good example of that process). At the beginning of each class meeting, we develop a class agenda collectively.

Valuing and Recognition of Dialogue

---

[15] Probably, it is a reference to Bakhtin (1986) and Soviet philosopher Bibler (1991) who insisted on this notion.

Finally, I want to briefly touch upon another polyphonic mediation that I call appreciation of dialogue. *Valuing dialogue involves public recognition and value of the dialogue and the dialogic community.* Appreciation of dialogue can be as simple as participants' comments how fun their dialogue was and how much they enjoyed time. This sounds like an "abnormal mediation" because it is not aiming at addressing problems threatening the life of dialogue or dialogic community per se as other types of polyphonic mediation. Meanwhile, it is a very important type of mediation transforming dialogue into polyphony (Morson & Emerson, 1989).

Only recently, I have become to realize its importance as I have noticed that some of my students struggled with appreciation of dialogic pedagogy and dialogue itself. For example, in each of my undergraduate classes, I gave students "mind-attendance" index cards to write about what they have learned in the class, questions, and feedback on the class. Some students write sometimes, "I like our class discussions today but I don't understand where Eugene tried to lead us" (index card, September, 2006) or "I feel like I did not learn a lot but rather just expressed my opinions" (class evaluation, December 2006), or "I feel like I did not learn how to incorporate diversity in the classroom, but rather figured out my opinions and heard other students' expression" (class evaluation, December 2006). This feedback shares the students' frustration with, distrust of, and disvalue of dialogue as the existence of truth despite the fact that they intensively and successfully participated in it. These students seemed to value monologic truth as something that can be separated from dialogue and dialogic community. For these students, class was dialogic but not polyphonic. Some become appreciating the dialogue as the place where truth lives only at the end of class, very few come valuing the dialogue from the beginning, I know some students who realized that only after some time when the class was long over (as they told me when they took another class with me), some probably never, and some in the class. For example, this is what one student wrote in her anonymous class evaluations that our university requires, "The honors section of this course did not differ in any way from the regular section. However, I feel that Prof. Matusov runs his class in a way that I wish all my honors classes (and non-honors classes) were run. It is always discussion based, he is very open to students' opinions, and we are able to discuss issues that directly relate to our practicum experiences. I grew professionally and personally. I met so many minds inside and outside the class – my mind is blossoming" (class evaluation, December 2006).

In the case above of a dialogue in my class, the issue of appreciation of dialogue surfed only three times, in my view. First, very tacitly, in the discussion by Amanda about what kind of learning she would be happy about, second, when Eugene tried to sum up the dialogue saying how much he learned from it, and third, when Jenny implied that we had to know the LACC children's perspective on our entrance to their community. However, appreciation of dialogue did not directly enter the shared focus of the class. Appreciation of dialogue is an interesting and important problem of polyphonic mediation in pedagogy.

---

[16] I can hear in this utterance a discourse of nationalism that is very strong in Ukraine in the last 15 years or so. I am curious if the School of Dialogue of Cultures explores this issue with the children.

DESIGN FOR EDUCATIONAL POLYPHONY

At the beginning of the chapter, I discussed teaching as a goal directed and planned activity. What can plan or design for polyphonic classroom? Design for polyphonic lesson is design for a "classroom" dialogue (granted that education occurs not only in the classroom). This design for dialogue involves provocations. Educational dialogic practices know several types of such provocations. First is provocation by a disagreement. For example, Zimbabwean science teacher Mr. Moyo asked his new 7th grade South African students in Black township school new Pretoria at the beginning of school year to list basic human "needs" and "wants" to introduce them to fundamental economic concepts. When the students brainstormed an initial list, he focused their attention on some apparent contradictions because some items (like "money", "education", "love", "God") were listed twice which provoke the students to split on opposing sides and to passionately debate the issues (Matusov, Smith et al., 2007). Similarly, the introduction of Bakhtin's and Spengler's opposing views on the nature of culture in the sixth grade generated lively discussions in the School of Dialogue of Cultures (Solomadin, 2004).

Second is provocation by a paradox. For example, in my brief science teaching in South Africa, I asked Black South African middle school students in a science class why I had white color of skin and they had black color of skin. Initially, the students did not see any paradox in that fact but when they realized that white color more reflects light and black color more absorbs light, they became puzzled of why light-skinned people traditionally live in geographical areas with relatively a lower level sun exposure (too little sun, lack of vitamin D as a possible health problem) while dark-skinned people traditionally live in geographical areas with relatively a higher level of sun exposure (too much sun, skin burn and skin cancer as a possible health problem). These groups of people are supposed to live in the opposite geographical areas, according to biological adaption and the physical features of the colors. The debates and experimentations emerged in the class with light reflection and absorption after the students realized the paradox.

Third is provocation by a problem. This is a common design of dialogue in "problem-based learning" approach. It can involve solving a particular problematic case. Solving a specific legal case of a pedestrian being hit by a car requires the students to discuss diverse aspects of the case: legal, physical, medical, ethical, and so on to approach the problem (Duch, Groh, & Allen, 2001).

Finally (but not exhaustively), it is possible to place the students into practice so their participation in this practice (so-called "service-based learning", see Furco, 1996; Mettetal & Bryant, 1996) will generate in the students their own questions for whole class discussion. An example of that was Tommy's web posting above in which she asked the classroom community how to act with the LACC boys who "were becoming violent with each other." These dilemmas emerged in the students' practice can generate important classroom dialogues. Thus, in dialogic pedagogy, lesson plans are designs of learning provocations for dialogue (see Suchman, 1987, for analysis and discussion of the provocative nature of plans).

CONCLUSION

I agree with Engeström's (1999) call for focusing the Activity Theory on dialogic aspects of activity: multivoicedness, heteroglossia, questioning, and goal defining processes. Furthermore, I think that it has to be realized that teaching, in general, and dialogic pedagogy, in specific, is a special activity. It is not a reproductive activity, but rather by-product-oriented, type of activity. It has its own mediation that is not fully instrumental but also based on mediation by entire activities and by emergent processes. Also, this mediation has always discourse properties. Appreciation of dialogue is itself a curriculum in a polyphonic classroom.

Arguably, Bakhtin spent a lot of his focus on considering and discussion the relationship between dialogue and activity. In his literary work, this focus was articulated itself as the issue of plot in a polyphonic novel and the issue of chronotope in a polyphonic novel. It is interesting that one of the most reworded and added place in his 1929 book on Dostoevsky for the second edition in the early 1960s was about what became Chapter 4 of his second edition book, "Characteristics of genre and plot composition in Dostoevsky's works" (Morson & Emerson, 1990). Bakhtin argued that the plot of polyphonic novel can be better characterized through development of the genre of Menippean satire (Bakhtin, 1999). On pages 110-118, he listed 19 specific features of Menippean genre, which as I have argued in my early chapters, is another, more developed, term for "internally persuasive discourse" that Bakhtin developed earlier in his career. According to Bakhtin, Menippean genre focuses on collective search of the truth and going to the ultimate questions, on discursive provocations for and in dialogue, on the ontological and ideological nature of the participants' commitment to dialogue, on its dramatic and eccentric nature, on plot being used to give new dialogic opportunities rather for some kind of action outcome, on multiple themes and multiple nature of discourse, and so on. Full translation of Bakhtin's idea of the relationship between dialogue (i.e., Menippea, polyphonic novel) and plot into educational context is need. In this chapter, I just started this work.

Chapter 13

CONCLUSION: LIMITS OF DIALOGUE AND DIALOGIC PEDAGOGY?[1]

ABSTRACT

There is growing interest among educators in dialogic pedagogy influenced by Bakhtin's notions of "dialogue" and "internally persuasive discourse" (IPD) -- discourses focusing on search for truth, in which all involved "consciousnesses have equal rights." However, there are concerns that these notions and pedagogical practices behind them that are value-loaded. The suspicion is that for some social groups (or circumstances) Bakhtin's framework promotes, or even normalizes, a certain way of life, arguably Western, feminine, and middle-class which prioritizes verbal negotiation over physical action, and runs against the diverse cultures of other social groups. I examine this suspicion in detail for two types of social groups based on age (specifically, young children) and individuals with autism.

There have been growing concerns that the notions of dialogue, dialogic pedagogy, internally persuasive discourse are culturally biased. There are claims made that dialogue is biased against shy people, males, working class people, non-Western cultures, non-verbal communication, action, antagonistic relations demanding violence and/or coercion, and non-truth seeking activities. It has been argued that dialogue is a particular cultural construct rooted in feminine, bourgeois parliamentism, Western middle class, verbalism, and philosophical intellectualism cultures (Casey, 2005; Delpit, 1993; Ellsworth, 1992; Laclau & Mouffe, 2001; Rogoff, 2003). For example, Casey writes,

> Experts have pointed out that far less talking takes place in working-class homes than in middle-class ones. The irony, of course, is that our diversity initiatives place a premium on discourse. While a mere statistical increase in nonmainstream students hardly guarantees cross-group dialogue, the academy's dedication to diversity assumes precisely that model. Yet working-class students may be far less likely than others to talk, either about course material or about themselves—and not only because they are often unpersuaded as to the value of

---

[1] I am thankful to Tara Ratnam and Kathy von Duyke for providing their supportive feedback and helpful suggestions to early drafts of this chapter.

what they perceive as open-ended conversation. They also [p.35] intuit that academic culture—which invites alternative perspectives but overlooks the possibility that sharing perspectives is itself a class-inflected activity—doesn't recognize their difference. For working-class students, an inability or unwillingness to crack the cultural code that demands their speech, coupled with the sometimes acute embarrassment associated with their particular brand of difference, may result only in continued silence.

What is to be gained by speaking about or through a less privileged experience in a selective college setting? Diversity imperatives assume that both minority and majority groups will benefit equally from a heterogeneous student body, that somehow a productive tension can and should be maintained among the differences that students bring to the educational table. But working-class students come to college for the purpose of *entering into* a class and culture from which their families have been previously excluded.

Indeed, educational rhetoric generally, both at the high school and college levels, has long celebrated college as the way up and out of the working class. For the less privileged student, *that* rhetoric—the rhetoric of the American Dream, of achievement, of assimilation—is far more immediately compelling than the diversity rhetoric that purports to value difference, including class-based difference. Hence the working-class student feels pressured not to differentiate him or herself, but to conform to a middle-class academic norm. That such conformity might be best approximated through quiet watchfulness in both classroom and social settings is obvious: in this way, the student risks revealing neither lack of academic preparation nor awkward details of a personal nature. (Casey, 2005, pp. 34-35)

These are very important and serious charges against dialogic pedagogy that have to be investigated and addressed. This task, however, probably requires its own monograph. In this chapter, my goal is just to start this discussion about possible limitations of dialogue and dialogic pedagogy rather than to address the listed concerns in detail.

In my view, Bakhtin's insight equating the nature of humanity with dialogism is both inspiring and potentially dangerous. It is inspiring because dialogism emphasizes open and humble aspect of humanity constantly seeking for contact and dialogue. It views any discourse as dialogic (in a broader sense) even when this dialogue is bad and oppressive one. Students' resistance to the teacher's institutional oppression is a part of discourse as well (Eckert, 1989; Gutierrez et al., 1995; McLaren, 1993; Willis, 1981). Bakhtin's approach is potentially dangerous because it can exclude some people, cultures, and practices from realm of "the humane" as it has happened in past with other attempts to develop universal concepts defining humanity (see Rogoff, 2003, for more discussion of this historical phenomenon).

Dialogism is a particular cultural value because it does not just try to describe the world (i.e., what is the nature of humanity) but also prescribes of how the world should be (Maranhão, 1990). It tries to inform the will and argues against some other cultural values that it treats as "monologic" and oppressive. For example, dialogism, as goal and design, is incompatible with racism (although dialogic analysis will reveal dialogic aspects of racism as any human phenomenon). From this point of view, dialogism is a cultural bias. However, since dialogism is arguably a part of any culture, communication, action, practice, this cultural bias is compatible with them in a sense because it is rooted in them. As Hegel pointed out, even in such oppressive practice as slavery, there is a dialogic basis (Hegel & Baillie, 1967). Dialogic pedagogic approach involves expanding the already existing dialogic aspects in a practice or in a community and engaging them in dialogic forms of other communities. Using Casey's example of working class students, it is not assimilation to middle class of dialogue that dialogic pedagogy calls for but to explore dialogicity of working class community: its interactional forms, contents, and contexts (see Shor, 1987, for detailed description of such pedagogical efforts) and inviting them into the classroom to create creole classroom communities.

It is important to acknowledge that my claim rooted in Bakhtinian scholarship that dialogism is not alien bias to any culture or practice is problematic and requires further empirical testing. I think that unless there will be a definitive proof that the claim is wrong, we never will come to a definitive proof that it is correct and this is even undesirable. Through this testing, we will develop better understanding of the notion of dialogue based on diverse practices and relations (that even can be unthinkable now).

One of the concerns about dialogue and dialogic pedagogy that I shared with many critics of dialogism is equating *a* particular cultural form of interaction with *the* dialogue and equating *a* particular cultural form of instruction with *the* dialogic pedagogy. It is easy to develop erroneous normalcy of dialogue and dialogic pedagogy and then judge certain, usually marginalized, social groups as not being able or compatible for dialogue. Below, I will provide two examples of such erroneous normalization and my analysis of them.

AGE: "TOO YOUNG TO DIALOGUE"

Some educators think that learning dialogue is very difficult if not impossible for younger children because they do not have necessary social and verbal skills and special orientation for dialogue and/or learning. Let us bring a long quote from one of the founders Ukrainian and Russian School of the Dialogue of Cultures, teacher Sergey Kurganov (2005). He discusses why dialogic learning is so difficult for six-year old children in comparison with seven-year old (In Ukraine there is a transition of shifting from the beginning of primary school from 7 to 6 years old),

> If a child comes to school at 6-year old, the process of the child's dialogical education becomes essentially more complicated. The absence of the desire of all children to get "the status of student" does not allow performing manipulative strategies of "pulling in" the child into school learning. ...
> What prevents the 6-year old child to engage in learning a dialogue immediately in the "class room"?

> The teacher is closed by the children' play community. The children become acquainted, immediately find their own cozy place in the classroom, without understanding and listening to the teacher. The 6-year old children have not gone through the 7-year old age crisis. The school is not desired. They have not played in school yet. There is not yet an image of the desired teacher (and a desired student). The teacher is not an authority person for 6-year old, a peer is.
> The children are closed from each other by pre-school problematics (genital, oral). Teachers do not accustom to work in the conditions of absence of "sexual moratorium." One of our 6-year old female students assumed that she came to school because school allows "making sex." Children kiss each other, hug, cannot walk orderly from school to woods – they cannot hold orderly lines and directed

movement. Walking class of 6-year old children in September [the beginning of school year in Ukraine – EM] immediately because a horde of kissing kids. They go not in the right direction and not even in one direction creating a big circle.

There is not a "lose of immediacy" (Vygotsky). A child says first thing that comes to the child's mind. The toilet theme prevails. The most "difficult" children represent their own sexual organs, label them, draw on the blackboard, and then on the desks and hands. We have never met 7-year olds drawing pictures on their desks. For 7-year olds, desk is a sacred place. For 6-year olds toilet is a puzzled and extremely interesting place. They visit toilet with peers in groups. Dressing and undressing for PE classes is accompanied with their acute interest to naked legs and joyful laugh about that. I have never observed anything like that among 7-year olds.

Kurganov asks, "Is it possible to teach 6-year olds at all?" He continues elaborating on the difficulties,

In school, the 6-year olds' consciousness is got arrested at its most primitive forms. The children do not starve to a shift of their consciousness to the pole of cognition:

The 6-year old children do not see the blackboard. The do not see learning ("working") line in the notebook. They write and draw in any place on the page without submitting to the rhythm of the page format. They do not have an image of a writing person (Shuleshko). While 7-year old children played a lot by posing themselves as if they were writing when they were in kindergarten before school.

Not only 6-year old children do not see and understand writing of another child on the blackboard but they do not see the teacher's writing on the blackboard and cannot copy it in their notebooks. They seemed to think that they have their own space (a notebook page) and the teacher has their own space (the class blackboard). These two worlds do not touch each other. Even more, the world of the notebook page is not appropriated yet by the child, they write whenever they might want at the moment. We have not noticed this problem in 7-year old children (like a mother does not notice how she teaches to see a visual able child in contrast to teaching a blind-mute-deaf child).

Children who are able to read are not able and do not want to read books in the classroom because they cannot orient themselves in a book. As soon their finger is taken off the book, they start discussion of the read – they are not able to return back to the book. That is why to do reading "charged with literary analysis" in the first semester of the school as it is common in the School of the Dialogue of Cultures. The children cannot, are not be able, and do not want to do robin reading in "a chain."

6-year old children who are able to count orally and orally solve math problems are not able to use writing to facilitate their calculations and problem solving (brief notation, use of graphs, schemas, and so on). The teacher cannot teach math 6-year old children by using accustomed forms of instruction.

...Six-year old children cannot be engaged in a direct dialogue with the teacher because the other children are offended that they are not called, are not listened, and, thus, are not loved. When one 6-year old child speaks something to the teacher, the other children pull up their hands saying by that, "I'm also good, please call up on me!" (Let's remember the fragment from the documentary film by

A.K. Dusavitsky "Two plus two is x"). In September, learning dialogue in "the class room" is impossible for the six-year olds. Although, seven-year old children also do not accustom rapidly to the fact that first of all they have to learn by ears, listening to another student. But for 7-year olds, this norm is enforced by the authoritative teacher and, while with squeaking, it is still accepted by them. In six-year old age, to make this norm accept without rather intense amount of pedagogical violence cannot be done. In order to enforce this [dialogic] norm for the six-year old students at once, the teacher has to be not just authoritative but authoritarian. I rejected this possibility [for myself as a dialogic teacher – EM]" (Kurganov, 2005).

Kurganov provides many keen observations about younger children's socialization, interests, ways of communicating, and activities. Many of these descriptions presented as children's deficits. Of course, the background of the deficits is the norms of the educational practices that, unfortunately, Kurganov does not analyze. The educational practices implicitly presented by Kurganov that make the younger children so deficient are very conservative, monologic, and even outdated (e.g., robin reading), including his insistence on students learning mainly by their ears, although, to give Kurganov his credit, listening to the peers and not the teacher. However, what makes Kurganov an authentically dialogic teacher is his conclusion that he would rather reject dialogue than impose pedagogical violence and an authoritarian regime on the children.

But is Kurganov right that learning dialogue for six-year olds is very difficult and even has to be postponed for at least a semester? Should skills and dispositions necessary for dialogue be taught first (i.e., non-dialogically) and only then the ready students be introduced dialogue? Is dialogic pedagogy instrumental -- a way among other ways to organize instruction and curriculum, -- or ontological – a way of life and relating to students and the world (Sidorkin, 1999)?

Kurganov painstakingly shows how his pedagogical chronotope supporting his dialogic teaching and learning dialogue in his work with older students collapses with 6-year olds. There are three main possibilities. First, suggested by Kurganov, is that younger children do not ready for learning dialogue. This has deep consequences suggesting that Bakhtin was wrong that dialogue equates with humanity itself (Bakhtin, 1986). Second, Kurganov's pedagogical chronotope for support of dialogic pedagogy with younger students is wrong. There is evidence coming, for example, from Paley that learning dialogue among 5-year old (and even younger) students is possible (Paley, 1984, 1986a, 1986b, 1988, 1991, 1992). Third, it is possible that Kurganov's definition of learning dialogue might be too narrow.

Another founder of the School of the Dialogue of Cultures' (SDC) Igor Solomadin made a very good observation about the DCS definition of learning dialogue, "SDC has not developed the problem of dialogue 'horizontally,' – the problematics that is often called 'political cultureness'" (Solomadin, personal communication, February 5, 2007). The School of the Dialogue of Cultures developed *a "vertical model" of dialogue*: dialogue of past cultures with the children. For example, SDC teachers organized dialogues between Heraclites and 6-graders asking the students to discuss the meaning of Heraclites' famous statement that it is impossible to enter twice into the same river. The sixth graders use their own experiences "Efim [a male student]: What is unclear here?! The river has a current which makes water always different," to make sense of Heraclites' philosophical statement and through this are engaged in a philosophical discussion with each other and the teacher, "Olya [a female student]: 'Into the same river...' It is strange... On the one hand, he says that everything changes, but on the other hand, that the river is the one and the same. It is some kind of a contradiction" (Kuznetsova, 2005).

Vertical dialogue is a dialogue *about* epistemological authority and, to a lesser degree, is a dialogic *with* epistemological authority. The students try to make sense, put together, and collide with each other fragments of knowledge that they got from the epistemological authority (e.g., parents, adults, books, experts, full participants) recognized as such by students. For example, Kurganov (2005) describes the first spontaneous and self-initiated (vertical) dialogue that he overheard among his six-year old students outside of the classroom about whether the biggest number exists or not (the dialogue about "The Red Point" the biggest number as one student of Kurganov claimed). In this vertical dialogue, fragments of diverse information that the children have heard from the adults (and possibly older siblings) actively examined and collided with each other: mathematical proofs and counter-proofs, Gothic stories, Soviet-Russian cosmonauts, the mathematical sign of infinity, geometric figures, Bible, the notion of the Universe, and so on. I call these fragments of knowledge deriving from the epistemological authority as "authority texts," in which the students are very peripheral participants, to distinguish it from participative experiences in which the students are "full participants" (cf. Lave & Wenger, 1991). In a vertical dialogue, the students are often guided by the teacher first to find a puzzle point in the authority text and then to discuss it. Vertical dialogue is about a problem-in-authority-text. It is about a dialogue between the past and the present (sometimes addressing the future).

In contrast, the horizontal dialogue focuses on the problems of the students' ontological present – their participative experiences. It can be a problem of systematic exclusion of some children from games (Paley, 1992, p. 20), *"Lisa:* I could play alone. Why can't Clara play alone? *Angelo:* I think that's pretty sad. People that is *alone* they has water in their eyes." The problems of horizontal dialogue are often interpersonal (what Solomadin called nicely "political cultureness") but they can also be experiential with the world of objects. Thus, I discussed with a small group of three-year olds why when they put a finger in a glass of water their finger looks like broken (or is it really broken?). Horizontal dialogues can also involve texts. Paley developed her own fairytale for discussion in her class. In my own teaching experience, I used Leo Tolstoy's moral fables to discuss some moral issues with four-year olds. However, in contrast to vertical dialogues, in horizontal dialogues, these texts usually model students' ontological experiences and problems, in which they are full participants, and do not represent any epistemological authority for the students.

The boundaries between so-called vertical and horizontal dialogues are not sharp but, in my view, it is useful to distinguish them. In horizontal dialogues of contemporary cultures, learners' ontology is primary while intellectual sphere is secondary and requires development. In vertical dialogues of past-present cultures, learners' intellectual sphere seems to be primary while the ontological sphere is secondary and has to be developed and addressed ("why should I care what Heraclitus said about rivers?! – this type of questions does not often emerge in horizontal dialogues).

I am not saying here that horizontal dialogues should be present for younger learners and vertical dialogues have to be present for older learners. No. Both types of dialogues have to present for older students. As to younger students, it seems to me that vertical dialogues to which Kurganov so accustomed might have very limited use if at all (more research and pedagogical experimentation is needed to investigate this issue). Again, it is not the case, that younger children cannot be involved in philosophical discussions – they can (e.g., Subbotsky, 1993) but their philosophical discussions are often rooted in the present, "horizontal", ontology rather than in an intellectual dialogue with past cultures.

It sounds like I am saying that dialogue is possible for learners of all ages. What about toddlers, what about infants, what about newborns?! I am not a specialist in this area but cross-cultural work shows that traditional Japanese, Mayan, and some African cultures have more dialogic respect to infants than many North American and European cultures do. They show much more respect to infants' wishes and distresses (Rogoff, 2003). I hypothesize paraphrasing the famous controversial statement made by Jerome Bruner (1986, p. 129) about teaching that *any child can be dialogued at any age in some form that is honest.* The million-dollar question is, of course, what the honest way for any child at any age is.

Autism: "Being Cut off from Human Communication"

Autism represents another concern about limitations for dialogic pedagogy. Autism is often described as self-absorption and isolation, which makes communication impossible. How can the teacher dialogue with an autistic student, if the student cannot participate in communication? A famous psychotherapist Oliver Sacks described autism as,

> The autistic, by their nature, are seldom open to influence. It is their 'fate' to be isolated, and thus original. Their 'vision', if it can be glimpsed, comes from within and appears aboriginal. They seem to me, as I see more of them, to be a strange species in our midst, odd, original, wholly inwardly directed, unlike others.... The autistic would complain- if they complained-of absence of influence, of absolute isolation. (p. 230)...
>
> Is being an island, being cut off, necessarily a death? It may be a death, but it is not necessarily so. For though 'horizontal' connections with others, with society and culture, are lost, yet there may be vital and intensified 'vertical' connections, direct connections with nature, with reality, uninfluenced, unmediated, untouchable, by any others. This 'vertical' contact is very striking with Jose, hence the piercing directness, the absolute clarity of his perceptions and drawings, without a hint or shade of ambiguity or indirection, a rocklike power uninfluenced by others (Sacks, 1990, p. 231).

What is striking in the case of the autistic patient Jose that Sacks described in his book is that although the patient could not talk, he and doctor Sacks communicated rather well although probably mostly in a non-verbal way but it was not completely clear,

> 'Draw this,' I said, and gave Jose my pocket watch.
>
> He was about 21, said to be hopelessly retarded, and had earlier had one of the violent seizures from which he suffers. He was thin, fragile-looking.
>
> His distraction, his restlessness, suddenly ceased. He took the watch carefully, as if it were a talisman or jewel, laid it before him and stared at it in motionless concentration.
>
> 'He's an idiot,' the attendant broke in. 'Don't even ask him. He don't know what it is-he can't tell time. He can't even talk. They says he's 'autistic', but he's just an idiot.' Jose turned pale, perhaps more at the attendant's tone than at his words--the attendant had said earlier that Jose didn't use words.

'Go on,' I said. 'I know you can do it.'

Jose drew with an absolute stillness, concentrating completely on the little clock before him, everything else shut out. Now, for the first time, he was bold, without hesitation, composed, not distracted. He drew swiftly but minutely, with a clear line, without erasures....

I was puzzled by this, haunted by it as I drove home. An 'idiot'? Autism? No. Something else was going on here... (pp. 214-215).

The third time I saw Jose, I did not send for him in the clinic, but went up, without warning, to the admission ward. He was sitting, rocking, in the frightful day room, his face and eyes closed, a picture of regression. I had a qualm of horror when I saw him like this, for I had imagined, had indulged, the notion of 'a steady recovery'. I had to see Jose in a regressed condition (as I was to do again and again) to see that there was no simple 'awakening' for him, but a path fraught with a sense of danger, double jeopardy, terrifying as well as exciting-because he had come to love his prison bars.

As soon as I called him, he jumped up, and eagerly, hungrily, followed me to the art room. Once more I took a fine pen from my pocket, for he seemed to have an aversion to crayons, which was all they used on the ward. That fish you drew,' I hinted it with a gesture in the air, not knowing how much of my words he might understand, 'that fish, can you remember it, can you draw it again?' He nodded eagerly, and took the pen from my hands. It was three weeks since he had seen it. What would he draw now? (p. 223)

I am surprised that the doctor Sacks, who showed through his book as being a keen observer, did not notice that he and his patient Jose were in communication, in the "horizontal" connection with people, culture, and society. It is amazing how he could overlook his own dialogic relations with the autistic patient and the "steady recovery" of the human world in which they both engaged! In his book, Sacks provided thoughtful analysis of the patient's drawing and even discussed their communicative potential. However, he did not discuss and analyze oppressive, monologic nature of the hospital attendant calling the patient "idiot" in the presence of the patient himself (notably, Sacks did not apparently intervene on the patient behalf). Sacks did not discuss his own emerging relations with Joe, in which Oliver Sacks increasingly treated Joe as a skillful artist with a message while for Joe, Oliver's request for drawing apparently became special moments in his otherwise hospital dull and miserable life of labeled "idiot." Throughout the book, I felt that Sacks almost intuitively wanted to reach to his patient and arrange the meeting of the consciousnesses with equal rights (Bakhtin, 1999). Sometimes he could achieve it, like in the case of autistic Joe, in many cases he could not. However, there was very little reflection (if at all) on his intuitive efforts, successes and failures, and values behind them.

Although, some therapeutic approaches may acknowledge dialogic aspects in their work with autistic people, as for example, "We emphasize individualized assessment to understand the individual better and also 'the culture of autism,' suggesting that people with autism are part of a distinctive group with common characteristics that are different, but not necessarily inferior, to the rest of us" (http://www.teacch.com/welcome.html), it rarely goes beyond this lip service of vision statements and quickly focus on how to adapt autistic people to the mainstream world, "To enable individuals with autism to function as meaningfully and as independently as possible in the community" (http://www.teacch.com/mission.html). There is often little realization in autism therapists that the world belongs to autistic people as well and that the disorder is relational and goes across the "normal" mainstream community as well: self-absorption and impaired social communication – typical description of autism -- involves at least two people.

Reading literature on mental handicaps (Coplan, 2006; Grandin & Scariano, 2005; Mattingly & Garro, 2000; Sacks, 1990; A. Young, 1995) and numerous professional organizational websites (e.g., http://www.autism-society.org/site/PageServer? pagename= about_treatment_learning), I have came to a conclusion about overwhelming prevalence monological approaches to autism (and to other mental differences) and to autistic people in general. These monological approaches vary in their severity (i.e., oppressive power) and function:

1. Classificatory: sorting autistic people according medical diagnosis;
2. Disciplinary: domesticating autistic people and making them manageable, less demanding (i.e., "independent"), and less disruptive for the "normal" mainstream people;
3. Curing: making autistic people the "normal" mainstream people;
4. Colonizing: make autistic people an exotic object of an enlightened curiosity.

In all these monological approaches, autistic people are treated as medical, therapeutic, pedagogical, or curiosity objects rather than as consciousnesses with equal rights to be addressed and replied. Let me bring words of an autistic activist Amanda Baggs to illustrate this problem (http://ballastexistenz.autistics.org/):

> Autism expert: Do "normal people" sometimes scare you?
> Amanda Baggs No, normal people don't trouble me, but people who wished that I was normal — that is, people who see me as only a broken normal person rather than as an intact autistic person — do hurt me.
> Autism expert: Describe one or two things that people can do to help you.
> Amanda Baggs: They can have utter respect for diversity, and they can understand that diversity leads a tattered life when not wedded to tolerance.
> Autism expert: Do you think it would be a good thing if researchers found a cure for autism and Asperger's?
> Amanda Baggs: The road to Hades is paved with good intentions.
> Autism expert: Would you want to be cured?
> Amanda Baggs: I would rather be cured of bigotry before being cured of autism.

I wonder if the road to Hades (i.e., hell), referred by Amanda Baggs, is paved with bodies of objectivized and finalized people who are viewed as "they" for "us, good people." "We," i.e., neurologically typical, want to push and challenge "them," i.e., autistic, to become as good as "we" are ("we" are do not have problems requiring "our" therapy and education – "they" do). I think that if "we" start addressing people like Amanda Baggs, children, clients, and students about the issues of how we want to live together, how we want our world to be – these are unresolved issues among us, -- then I think genuine education or therapy can occur. When autism is a problem, it is not a problem of a child but a problem of the broken, often violent, relations. In my view, "our" statements about "our" work cannot be without addressing our collaborators.

Not only autistic people have to learn to function in OUR world in order, for example, to buy a loaf of bread but we, neurologically typical people, have to make OUR world livable for autistic people and make it THEIR world as well (cf. Kauffmann, 1990, p. 171). By the way, not everything can be learned and should be learned: it is impossible to teach blind people how read print text – rather literacy practice has to be changed. Learning has its limitations. The focus has to be on access to socially desired practices and activities through changing infrastructure (e.g., talking ATMs), providing social networks of support (e.g., car garages for fixing cars), demanding human rights (e.g., access codes for buildings), inventing new tools (e.g., Brielle's literacy system), developing new drugs, and, yes, learning.

We, neurologically typical people, have to learn from and with the different others (e.g., autistic kids) how they sense, know, and experience the world and themselves and then we have to learn how to share with them how we sense, know, and experience the world. And then, in order to be in a relationship with them, we together need to negotiate a creole way of sensing, knowing, and experiencing the world that is neither fully "ours" nor "theirs." As they "normalize", we "autisticize." Sensing the world as an autistic person does make our perception of the world richer (see http://www.youtube.com/watch?v=JnylM1hI2jc , http://inquiring-nick.net/videos/TheLivingCamera.wmv). Through this creole process, we together become enriched and better humans (more humane). I think it is more humane and interesting to treat students, clients, and patients as dialogic partners to be addressed and replied than objects of pedagogical or therapeutic actions.

We might have to change our convenient ways of doing things and accommodate other people that requires us to change "the" world and OUR comforts. We should probably stop our unilateral demands from autistic people to "learn ways of how they should be able to express their love and caring for those around them." "We" also have to learn ways of how we should be able to express our love and caring for those around us (including autistic people). Watching Amanda Baggs' videos on YouTube.com, I have realized that it would be probably difficult for me to be with and relate to her. This means that I have to learn how to be with autistic people, relate to them, and perceive our shared world differently.

To illustrate this building a creole community with an autistic child, please consider the following example. Jacob is a 7-year old second grader who was kicked out from several schools. He was mild autism and also has been diagnosed with "alphabet cocktail" of disabilities: "PDD/NOS, ODD, MD/NOS, and ADHD." He is sitting on the floor with his teacher in small private multiage school that he entered about two months ago. According both of them, it is a private session. When another child tries to join them, Jacob tells to the child, "This is private." They constantly alternate playing Lego and discussing recent incidents, in which Jacob hit a few younger kids in the school. This is not the first private session like this. In one of the previous sessions, Jacob suggested his teacher holding his armpits when he gets out of his own control. Although this helped to reduce damage that Jacob could make to another child, it did not reduce the number of incidents. According my interviews with the teacher, she tries to engage Jacob in learning empathy to younger children and self-control. The teacher is aware that it can be a long process before Jacob might be able to sufficiently control himself to prevent himself from aggressive outbursts and that he might need help for that from people around him. However, she believes that Jacob has to become an active ally, if not the primary agent, in this process. She wants to work *with* him rather than *on* him.

Before the following fragment, the teacher introduced the topic of boxing to separate mean, antisocial intention from violent behavior. Although boxing involves violence, aggression, fight, and making deliberate pain to another, it is a kind of sport based on rules and consensus between players about the purpose and conduct of the activity. The teacher tries to engage Jacob to contemplate what kind of consensus and rules of conduct he would like for the school community to establish. She appeals to fairness: one of 3F that so important for young children, according to Paley (1986b, the other 2F are "friendship" and "fantasy")

Teacher: How about if you hit Ken and he doesn't like that? Is that a good idea?

Jacob: (in a quiet voice) No, but it isn't a good idea for you to be pinching me, so I don't want you to be pinching me even if either I hit or pinch Ken [6-year old boy in the Montessori school].

T: Ah, that's not fair. If you hit and pinch Ken I think you are saying it is okay to hit and pinch and I should be allowed to hit and pinch you. That's not fair, I don't want to play that game, that's the game where you get to do all the punching and nobody else gets to punch. I wouldn't play boxing games like that. I wouldn't go in the ring with somebody and they said, "I'm going to punch you but you can't hit me." That would just tire me out and wear me down. That's not a fair game. I don't agree with that game Ken. I don't like the rules of your game. Can we think of something that I think is fair, too?

J : Uh, I can't think of anything else. But not pinching and I'm the only one.

T: So you want to play the game where you can just punch somebody, and I'm supposed to just let you?

J: You can just hug me, but not pinch me back. Like that. (Makes an arm squeeze)

T: Yea but, you hurt somebody, and hugging doesn't hurt you. Hugging is nice actually, but...

J: But you are holding me so I can't move.

T: But that's not my job to hold you. I don't really like that game either and the reason I don't like it is because the other child is hurting and you are being hugged. That doesn't feel like a good game, they are hurt, and you are getting a nice hug.... and you aren't controlling yourself, somebody else has to have the job of controlling you. That's too much work for somebody else. I don't like that game either.... What's a better game that we could do, I don't like the rules of that game.

J: I think um, I don't know.

T: Hmm. What if you didn't hit people? You could do boxing with them.

J: Then they could hit me back.

T: Well, you wouldn't have to play that game unless you wanted too. They don't have to play unless they want too. What if you don't hit people unless they agree to have a hitting game with you?

J: I want to have a hitting game where they don't hit me.

As Bakhtin (1999) would say, the teacher and Jacob enter the zone of the Final Questions in their dialogue. Jacob wants to have a game recognized by the community, in which only he can hit anyone at his will at any time. And why not?! Why would not community accept this game?! The teacher's previous argument of fairness based on Kantian ethical relativism, "treat other people how you want the other people treat you" was rejected by Jacob's absolutism, "nobody should be like me. I have the exclusive right to hit others with impunity." What the community and the society at large can ultimately offer in response to this absolutism to violence? The teacher's answer to Jacob's final ethical question, which she regretted afterwards, her reference to the violence chain: for each bully, there is always a stronger bully and the ultimate bully is the society at large, "Well, that's not the way life works, Jacob. Somebody is either going to hit you back, or make you go away, like jail, like a corner, or when you are bigger they put you in a big jail and don't let you out for a long time." After exploring the issue of jail, Jacob introduces a compromise, how about him hitting only older kids in impunity, "What if I punch someone like Bob [10-year old boy in the school]? It doesn't even hurt, he's way bigger." The teacher rejects the compromise because Jacob's punch still can be very hurtful, "Well, it… it, like you are pretty strong, and if you punch Bob, it is going to hurt, and when you punch your mom it hurts her, even though she is way bigger than you. So, especially if people aren't expecting it, it is a shock." After this rejection, Jacob could find any other suggestion of compromise for the communal consensus and the teacher could not offer a better argument against Jacob's monopoly on violence. The discussion again shifts to Lego and when the teacher tries to return back to the discussion of "the fair game," Jacob asks to finish the session, "Can I go downstairs now?"

There are many questions remained unanswered in this dialogue. Why does Jacob want to hit people? Does he like to hurt people? If so, why? Is it pleasurable for him? If so, always? If not, under what conditions? What would Ben and Jacob's mother say about his compromised proposal? What would other members of the community say in response to Jacob's main proposal of hitting them on his will with impunity? If they decide to reject his proposal for "the game," what would be their arguments? What are the societal ultimate (i.e., non-reducible) arguments against absolutism on violence? What should others *do* in the community when they are hit by Jacob?

The latter question is important to stop Jacob from hurting other members of the community (especially younger children) on the short run. Dialogic pedagogy is action-based and not only word-based. Actions are also utterances in a dialogue. But does dialogue has its limit in the context of violence? Gee argues that dialogue has its limit, "All I or anyone, can say it that people do not accept it, (first principle, to do no harm), or if they act as though they do not accept it, then I and most others are simply not going to interact with them. We have come to a point at which one must simply offer resistance, not argument" (Gee, 1996, p. 20). Freire (1986) made a similar point about limitation of dialogue that at some point dialogue with oppressors is not possible and only violent revolution is the right course of action, "dialogical encounter cannot take place between antagonists" (p. 110). In other words, dialogue requires a dialogic regime, in which, at its very minimum, the existence and well-being of the participants is not threatened. The struggle for a dialogic regime might require counter-violence. However, this resistance and counter-violence in struggle to establish a dialogic regime are themselves embedded in the Big Dialogue demanding to answer important questions, "What is the meaning of this resistance? How different are you from one you oppose in your violent struggle?" Although, counter-violence may be reasonable at time, it does not escape a dialogic judgment for its excessive monologism. Counter-violence and resistance is not a good alternative to a bad one but rather it is a bad alternative to a worse one. In other words, the end does not justify its means. Even when violence is reasonable and the best solution, it cannot be taken easily as it always involves a partial defeat of dialogue[2].

---

[2]In the 1971 Russian fictional movie "Andrei Rublev" by the director Andrey Tarkovsky about a XV century icon painter and a monk, Rublev, a person of dialogue and peace, had to kill a Russian soldier during a feudal

In the case of Jacob, the threat of him hurting other members of the community forces the teacher to use short-term actions of violence to stop Jacob's aggression again other members of the community (especially younger children) embedded in ongoing dialogue with him and other members of the community about how they want to live together. The question, "What should others do in the community when they are hit by him?" should not exclude Jacob from answering to it. The idea of the dialogue is not to exclude the member through a communal unilateral ostracism using a discourse of consequences or rules that is often in traditional school. Rather dialogue is aimed at preventing everyone from being entrapped and imprisoned by others members of the community. There are no rules that are given in advance but rather always worked out in the process. For a communal rule to be meaningful, it has to be a reference to a communal consensus but a communal consensus has to be established and supported first. When a child says that he wants a game of hitting other people with impunity, there is no such a consensus yet.

Although Jacob's teacher stops short to introduce these and other questions in the dialogue with Jacob, in her interview with me, she expresses her strong desire to continue the dialogue. However, what is even more important, in my view, she has successfully engaged Jacob in a genuine dialogue about his relationship with other people based on a consensus. From Jacob's own account in this session, this type of dialogue is pretty novel for him because in his previous schools the teachers seemed to focus mainly on conforming, taming, fixing, domesticating, if not breaking, Jacob to their rules. Paraphrasing Bakhtin's characterization of Dostoevsky's relationship with his characters, it is possible to say that apparently for the first time, "the the autistic student interests the teacher not as some manifestation of reality that possess fixed and specific socially typical or individually characteristic traits, nor as a specific profile assembled out of unambiguous and objective features which, taken together, answer the question, 'Who is he?' No, the student interests the teacher as *a particular point of view on the world and on oneself*, as the position enabling a person to interpret and evaluate his own self and his surrounding reality. What is important for the teacher is not how her student appears in the world but first and foremost how the world appears for her student, how the student appears to himself" (Bakhtin, 1999, p. 47, the italics is original, in the quote I substitute Dostoevsky for "teacher" and hero for "autistic student"). From this transformed quote, it becomes clear that the teacher and her autistic student Jacob were successfully engaged in dialogic relations. The dialogic journey for the teacher and Jacob has started…

CONCLUSION

Here, in this chapter, I do not mean to dismiss scholars' concerns about limitations of dialogue and dialogic pedagogy. Rather I try to redefine the 'struggle with the limits of dialogic pedagogy' as a struggle to explore its potential possibilities by stretching our limited understanding of it as a resource and how to use it to understand the other (both mainstream

---

sedge of a Russian city to save a mentally retired woman from rape during a war battle. In a scene with his teacher, Rublev asks how to reconcile his faith with his deed. The teacher replies, "God forbids you but you do not forbid yourself. So, this way, you have to live between the great mercy and great remorse."

and the non-mainstream)[3]. Not only I think these concerns are real and important for the dialogic approach, but also I think these challenges can push dialogic approach in pedagogy and elsewhere to new exciting conceptual and practical journeys and discoveries. Considering apparent anomalies and difficult cases can be very productive for development of dialogic pedagogy.

How to dialogue with people who do not value dialogue? Is possible to dialogue with infants, animals, texts, objects, imaginary people, the nature, and god? How much these heavily asymmetrical interactions can be called real, rather than metaphorical, dialogues? Already Socrates (through Plato) complained at apparently monological nature of written texts that a reader can question but are always silent in response. However, paradoxically, Bakhtin developed his notion of dialogue based on his analysis of Dostoevsky's literary texts (see Mecke, 1990, for more discussion of this issue). What is non-verbal dialogue and how to capture it? How much such dialogues are limited and in what sense they are dialogues?

How much the notion of dialogue is Western, bourgeois, historically developed, and middle class? It is interesting that I observed most developed classroom dialogism in South Africa, in the science classroom taught by a Zimbabwean teacher who, according to his account, learned teaching in a traditional African way (Matusov, Smith et al., 2007). Also, historian argue that the US form of parliamentarism has been heavily influenced by tribal federalism of the Five Nations (Weatherford, 1988).

---

[3] I am thankful to Tara Falcone for making this point to me.

REFERENCES

Adler, M. J. (1982). *The Paideia proposal: An educational manifesto* (1st Macmillan paperbacks ed.). New York: Macmillan.

Adler, M. J., & Paideia Group. (1984). *The Paideia program: An educational syllabus.* New York: Collier Macmillan.

Afary, J., Anderson, K., & Foucault, M. (2005). *Foucault and the Iranian Revolution: Gender and the seductions of Islamism.* Chicago: University of Chicago Press.

Akhutin, A., & Bibler, V. S. (1993). Bakhtin's legacy and the history of science and culture: An interview with Analotlii Akhutin and Vladimir Bibler. *Configurations, 1*(3), 335-386.

Al'brekht, V. (1981). *Kak byt' svidetelem (How to be a witness).* Paris: Izdanie zhurnala "A-IA".

Alcoff, L. (2006). *Identity politics reconsidered* (1st ed.). New York: Palgrave Macmillan.

Allen, B., Getzels, P., & Getzels, H. G. (1992). Summerhill at 70 [videorecording]. New York; Princeton, NJ: Middlemarch Films for Channel 4; Films for the Humanities & Sciences, Inc.

Allen, R. E. (1959). Anamnesis in Plato's Meno and Phaedo. *Review of Metaphysics, XIII*(1), 165-174.

Alvarez, L., Kolker, A., & Center for New American Media. (1987). American tongues [videorecording]. New York: The Center.

Anderson, J. R., Reder, L. M., & Simon, H. A. (1997). Situated versus cognitive perspective: Form versus substance. *Educational Researcher, 26*(1), 18-21.

Appiah, A. (2006). *Cosmopolitanism: Ethics in a world of strangers* (1st ed.). New York: W.W. Norton.

Archambault, R. D. (1967). Introduction. In R. D. Archambault (Ed.), *Tolstoy on education* (pp. v-xviii). Chicago: University of Chicago Press.

Argyris, C., & Schön, D. A. (1978). *Organizational learning: A theory of action perspective.* Reading, MA: Addison-Wesley Pub. Co.

Aristotle, & Apostle, H. G. (1966). *Metaphysics.* Bloomington: Indiana University Press.

Aristotle, & Freese, J. H. (2000). *The "art" of rhetoric.* Cambridge, MA: Harvard University Press.

Arsen'ev, A. S., Kedrov, B. M., & Bibler, V. S. (1967). *Анализ развивающиеся понятия [Analysis of the developing concept].* Moscow: Nauka.

Asterhan, C. S. C., & Schwarz, B. B. (2007). The effects of monological and dialogical argumentation on concept learning in Evolutionary Theory. *Journal of Educational Psychology, 99*(3), 626–639.

Atweh, B., Forgasz, H., & Nebres, B. (2001). *Sociocultural research on mathematics education: An international perspective*. Mahwah, N.J.: Lawrence Erlbaum Associates.

Ayala, F. J. (2006). *Darwin and intelligent design*. Minneapolis: Fortress Press.

Bagley, W. C. (1907). *Classroom management: Its principles and technique*. New York; London: The Macmillan company.

Baker-Sennett, J., Matusov, E., & Rogoff, B. (1992). Sociocultural processes of creative planning in children's playcrafting. In P. Light & G. Butterworth (Eds.), *Context and cognition: Ways of learning and knowing.* (pp. 93-114). Hillsdale, NJ: Lawrence Erlbaum Associates, Inc.

Baker-Sennett, J., Matusov, E., & Rogoff, B. (1993). Planning as developmental process. In H. W. Reese (Ed.), *Advances in child development and behavior, Vol. 24.* (pp. 253-281). San Diego, CA, US: Academic Press, Inc.

Baker-Sennett, J., Matusov, E., & Rogoff, B. (1998). Sociocultural processes of creative planning in children's playcrafting. In D. Faulkner, K. Littleton & M. Woodhead (Eds.), *Learning relationships in the classroom* (pp. 237-257). London ; New York: Routledge in association with the Open University.

Bakhtin, M. M. (1979). *Эстетика словестного творчества (Aesthetics of word art)*. Moscow: Iskusstvo.

Bakhtin, M. M. (1984). *Rabelais and his world* (H. Iswolsky, Trans. 1st Midland book ed.). Bloomington: Indiana University Press.

Bakhtin, M. M. (1986). *Speech genres and other late essays*. Austin: University of Texas Press.

Bakhtin, M. M. (1991). *Dialogic imagination: Four essays by M. M. Bakhtin* (C. Emerson & M. Holquist, Trans.). Austin, TX: University of Texas Press.

Bakhtin, M. M. (1997). *Собрание Сочинений [Collected Work]* (Vol. 5). Moscow: Russkie slovari.

Bakhtin, M. M. (1997a). Из архивных записей к работе "Проблема речевых жанров" (From archieve notes for manuscript "The problem of speech genres") (E. Matusov, Trans.). In *Собрание сочинений в семи томах (Collected work in seven volumes)* (Vol. 5). Moscow: Русские словари (Russian dictionaries).

Bakhtin, M. M. (1997b). Проблема текста (The problem of text) (E. Matusov, Trans.). In *Собрание сочинений в семи томах (Collected work in seven volumes)* (Vol. 5). Moscow: Русские словари (Russian dictionaries).

Bakhtin, M. M. (1999). *Problems of Dostoevsky's poetics* (Vol. 8). Minneapolis: University of Minnesota Press.

Bakhtin, M. M. (2004). Dialogic origin and dialogic pedagogy of grammar: Stylistics in teaching Russian language in secondary school. *Journal of Russian & East European Psychology, 42*(6), 12-49.

Bakhtin, M. M., Duvakin, V. D., & Bocharov, S. G. (2002). *М.М. Бахтин: Беседы с В.Д. Дувакиным [M.M.Bakhtin: Conversations with V.D. Duvakin]*. Moskva: Soglasie.

Bakhtin, M. M., & Emerson, C. (1999). *Problems of Dostoevsky's poetics* (Vol. 8). Minneapolis: University of Minnesota Press.

Bakhtin, M. M., Holquist, M., & Emerson, C. (1986). *Speech genres and other late essays* (1st ed.). Austin: University of Texas Press.

Bakhtin, M. M., Holquist, M., & Liapunov, V. (1990). *Art and answerability: Early philosophical essays* (1st ed.). Austin: University of Texas Press.

Bakhtin, M. M., Holquist, M., & Liapunov, V. (1993). *Toward a philosophy of the act* (1st ed.). Austin: University of Texas Press.

Ball, A. F., & Freedman, S. W. (2004). *Bakhtinian perspectives on language, literacy, and learning.* Cambridge, UK ; New York: Cambridge University Press.

Ball, D. L., & Cohen, D. K. (1999). Developing practice, developing practitioners: Toward a practice-based theory of professional education. In L. Darling-Hammond & G. Sykes (Eds.), *Teaching as the learning profession: Handbook of policy and practice* (1st ed., pp. 3-32). San Francisco: Jossey-Bass Publishers.

Ball, S. J. (2004). Performativities and fabrications in the education economy: Towards the perfomative society. In S. J. Ball (Ed.), *The RoutledgeFalmer reader in sociology of education* (pp. 143-155). London: RoutledgeFalmer.

Barnacle, R. (2005). Research education ontologies: Exploring doctoral becoming. *Higher Education Research & Development, 24*(2), 179-188.

Bartolini Bussi, M. G. (2000, May). *The theoretical dimension of mathematics: A challenge for didacticians.* Paper presented at the Canadian Mathematics Education Study Group, Montreal, Quebec, Canada. The paper is available online: http://www.eric.ed.gov/ ERICDocs/data/ ericdocs2/content_storage_01/0000000b/80/28/00/1e.pdf.

Bateson, G. (1987). *Steps to an ecology of mind: Collected essays in anthropology, psychiatry, evolution, and epistemology.* Northvale, NJ: Aronson.

Baumrind, D. (1971). *Current patterns of parental authority.* Washington, DC: American Psychological Association.

Beall, J., Crankshaw, O., & Parnell, S. (2002). *Crisis States Programme.* London: Development Research Centre.

Beatty, J. (1984). The complexities of moral education in a liberal, pluralistic society: The cases of Socrates, Mrs. Pettit, and Adolf Eichmann. *Soundings, 67*(4), 420-442.

Beckwith, F. (2003). *Law, Darwinism & public education: The establishment clause and the challenge of intelligent design.* Lanham, Md.: Rowman & Littlefield.

BenHabib, S. (1992). *Situating the self: Gender, community, and postmodernism in contemporary ethics.* Cambridge, UK: Polity Press.

Bennett, W. J., Finn, C. E., & Cribb, J. T. E. (1999). *The educated child: A parent's guide from preschool through eighth grade.* New York: Free Press.

Berlyand, I. E. (1996). *Puzzles of the number.* Moscow: Academia.

Berlyand, I. E. (2009, in press). A few words about Bibler's dia-logic: The School of the Dialogue of Cultures conception and curriculum. *Journal of Russian & East European Psychology.*

Bettelheim, B. (1960). *The informed heart: Autonomy in a mass age.* Glencoe, IL: Free Press.

Bialostosky, D. H. (1986). Dialogics as an Art of Discourse in Literary Criticism. *Publications of the Modern Language Association, 101*(5), 788-797.

Bialostosky, D. H. (1989). Dialogic, pragmatic, and hermeneutic coversation: Bakthin, Rorty, and Gadamer. *Critical Studies, 1*(2), 107-119.

Bibler, V. S. (1991). *Михаил Михайлович Бахтин или поэтика культуры (Mikhail Mikhailovich Bakhtin or the poetics of culture).* Moscow: Progress.

Billig, M. (1996). *Arguing and thinking: A rhetorical approach to social psychology* (New ed.). Cambridge, UK: Cambridge University Press.

Bloome, D., & Katz, L. (1997). Literacy as social practice and classroom chronotopes. *Reading & Writing Quarterly, 13*(3), 205-225.

Bloome, D., Puro, P., & Theodorou, E. (1989). Procedural display and classroom lessons. *Curriculum Inquiry, 19*, 265-291.

Boghossian, P. (2002). Socratic pedagogy, race, and power: From people to propositions *Education Policy Analysis Archives, 10*(3), available: http://epaa.asu.edu/epaa/v10n13.html.

Bogomolov, Y. (1993, October 17). Mass riots as means of communication. *Moscow News, 42*.

Booth, W. C. (1979). *Critical understanding: The powers and limits of pluralism*. Chicago: University of Chicago Press.

Boyer, E. L. (1983). *High school: A report on secondary education in America* (1st ed.). New York: Harper & Row.

Brady, J. (1994). Critical literacy, feminism, and a politics of representation. In P. McLaren & C. Lankshear (Eds.), *Politics of liberation: Paths from Freire*. New York: Routledge.

Bransford, J. D., Brown, A. L., & Cocking, R. R. (1999). How people learn: Brain, mind, experience, and school [microform]. Washington, D.C.: National Academy Press.

Brockman, J. (2006). *Intelligent thought: Science versus the intelligent design movement* (1st Vintage Books ed.). New York: Vintage.

Brown, A. L., & Campione, J. C. (1994). Guided discovery in a community of learners. In K. McGilly (Ed.), *Classroom lessons: Integrating cognitive theory and classroom practice.* (pp. 229-270). Cambridge, MA, US: The MIT Press.

Brown, A. L., & Palincsar, A. S. (1987). Reciprocal teaching of comprehension strategies: A natural history of one program for enhancing learning. In J. D. Day, J. G. Borkowski & et al. (Eds.), *Intelligence and exceptionality: New directions for theory, assessment, and instructional practices.* (pp. 81-132). Norwood, NJ, USA: Ablex Publishing Corp.

Brown, C. (1978). *Literacy in 30 hours: Paulo Freire's process in North East Brazil.* Chicago, Ill.: Alternative Schools Network.

Brown, J. S., & Burton, R. R. (1978). Diagnostic models for procedural bugs in basic mathematical skills. *Cognitive Science, 2*(2), 155-192.

Bruner, J. (1986). *Actual minds, possible words*. Cambridge, MA: Harvard University Press.

Bruner, J. (1996). *The culture of education*. Cambridge, MA: Harvard University Press.

Buber, M. (2000). *I and Thou* (R. G. Smith, Trans. 1st Scribner Classics ed.). New York: Scribner.

Buber, M. (2002). *Between man and man*. London: Routledge.

Bukovsky, V. K. (1979). *To build a castle: My life as a dissenter*. New York: Viking Press.

Burbules, N. C. (1993). *Dialogue in teaching: Theory and practice*. New York: Teachers College Press.

Burbules, N. C., & Callister, T. (2000). *Watch IT: The risks and promises of information technology for education*. Oxford, UK: Westwood.

Burke, K. (1969). *A rhetoric of motives*. Berkeley, CA: University of California Press.

Bykov, R. (1966). Aybolit-66 (movie). Moscow, USSR: Mosfilm.

Campaign for Fiscal Equity, et al. v. State of New York, et al. defendants (Supreme Court of New York 2001, January).

Candela, A. (1999). Students' power in classroom discourse. *Linguistics and Education, 10*(2), 139-163.

Carson, T. R., & Sumara, D. J. (1997). *Action research as a living practice*. New York: P. Lang.

Casey, J. G. (2005). Diversity, discourse, and the working-class student *Academe, 91*(4), 33-36.

Castañeda, J. G. (1997). *Compañero: The life and death of Che Guevara.* New York: Knopf.

Caulfield, P. J. (1991). From Brazil to Buncombe county: Freire and posing problems. *Educational Forum, 55*(4), 307-318.

Chang, K.-E., Lin, M.-L., & Chen, S.-W. (1998). Application of the Socratic dialogue on corrective learning of subtraction. *Computers & Education, 31*(1), 55-68.

Chapman, M. (2007). *40 days and 40 nights : Darwin, intelligent design, God, Oxycontin, and other oddities on trial in Pennsylvania* (1st ed.). New York, NY: Collins.

Clark, K., & Holquist, M. (1984). *Mikhail Bakhtin.* Cambridge, MA: Belknap Press of Harvard University Press.

Clow, F. R. (1920). *Principles of sociology with educational applications.* New York,: The Macmillan company.

Cole, M., & Engeström, Y. (2007). Cultural-historical approaches to designing for development. In J. Valsiner & A. Rosa (Eds.), *The Cambridge Handbook of Socio-Cultural Psychology.* Cambridge, UK: Cambridge University Press.

Colvin, S. (1919). The most common faults of beginning high school teachers. In G. M. Whipple & H. L. Miller (Eds.), *The professional preparation of high school teachers* (pp. 262-272). Bloomington, IL: Public School Publishing.

Comfort, N. C. (2007). *The panda's black box: Opening up the intelligent design controversy.* Baltimore: Johns Hopkins University Press.

Cooney, T. J., Davis, E. J., & Henderson, K. B. (1975). *Dynamics of teaching secondary school mathematics.* Boston: Houghton Mifflin.

Cooper, P. (2005). Literacy learning and pedagogical purpose in Vivian Paley's "storytelling curriculum". *Journal of Early Childhood Literacy 5*(3), 229-251.

Coplan, J. (2006). The national history of autism spectrum disorders: A new diagnostic model. *Autism Advocate, 41,* 26-30.

Corsaro, W. (1990). The underlife of the nursery school: Young children's social representations of adult roles. In G. Duveen & B. B. Lloyd (Eds.), *Social representations and the development of knowledge* (pp. 11-26). Cambridge, UK: Cambridge University Press.

Corser, J. K., Gardner, S., & University of Michigan. (1989). The Polished stones: K-5 math achievement in Japan & Taiwan [videorecording]. Ann Arbor, MI: University of Michigan.

Coy, M. W. (1989). *Apprenticeship: From theory to method and back again.* Albany: State University of New York Press.

Crapanzano, V. (1990). On dialogue. In T. Maranhão (Ed.), *The interpretation of dialogue* (pp. 270-291). Chicago: University of Chicago Press.

Davies, B., & Harré, R. (2001). Positioning: The discursive production of selves. In M. Wetherell, S. Taylor & S. Yates (Eds.), *Discourse theory and practice: A reader* (pp. 261–271). London: SAGE.

Davis, R. B. (1983). Diagnosis and evaluation in mathematics instruction: Making contact with students' mental representations. In D. C. Smith (Ed.), *Essential knowledge for beginning educators* (pp. 101-110). Washington, DC: American Association of Colleges for Teacher Education: ERIC Clearinghouse on Teacher Education.

Davydov, V. V. (1986). *Проблемы развивающего обучения (The problems of instruction that promotes development).* Moscow, USSR: Pedagogika.

Davydov, V. V. (1998). The concept of developmental teaching. *Journal of Russian & East European Psychology, 36*(4), 11-36.

Davydov, V. V., & Kilpatrick, J. (1990). *Types of generalization in instruction: Logical and psychological problems in the structuring of school curricula*. Reston, VA: National Council of Teachers of Mathematics.

Davydov, V. V., & Tsvetkovich, Z. (1991). On the objective origin of the concept of fractions. *Problems in Mathematics, 13*(1), 13-64.

Dawkins, R. (2006). *The God delusion*. London: Bantam Press.

De Haan, M. (1999). *Learning as cultural practice: How children learn in a Mexican Mazahua community*. Amsterdam: Thela Thesis.

De Laat, M., & Wegerif, R. (2007). Argunaut deliverable D5.1: Perspectives/rules to evaluate discussion. *Journal*. Retrieved from http://www.argunaut.org/publications/Members/ rakheli/publications/Argunaut%20deliverable%20D5.1%20-%20Perspectives-rules% 20 to%20evaluate%20discussions.pdf

De Lauretis, T. (1986). *Feminist studies, critical studies*. Bloomington, IN: Indiana University Press.

De Soto, H. (2000). *The mystery of capital: Why captitalism triumphs in the West and fails everywhere else*. New York: Basic Books.

Delpit, L. D. (1993). The silenced dialogue: Power and pedagogy in educating other people's children. In L. Weis & M. Fine (Eds.), *Beyond silenced voices: Class, race, and gender in United States schools.* (pp. 119-139). Albany, NY, US: State University of New York Press.

Delpit, L. D. (1995). *Other people's children: Cultural conflict in the classroom*. New York: New Press: Distributed by W.W. Norton.

DePalma, R., Matusov, E., & Smith, M. (2009, in press). Smuggling authentic learning into the school context: Transitioning from an innovative elementary to a conventional high school. *Teacher College Record*.

DePalma, R., Santos Rego, M. A., & del Mar Lorenzo Moledo, M. (2006). Not just any direct experience will do: Recasting the multicultural teaching practicum as active, collaborative and transformative. *Intercultural Education, 17*(4), 327-339.

Dershowitz, A. M. (2002). *Shouting fire: Civil liberties in a turbulent age* (1st ed.). Boston: Little, Brown and Co.

Dewey, J. (1956). *The child and the curriculum and the school and society* (Combined ed.). Chicago: University of Chicago Press.

Dewey, J. (1966). *Democracy and education: An introduction to the philosophy of education* (1st Free Press paperback ed.). New York: Free Press.

Dewey, J. (1998). *Experience and education* (60th anniversary ed.). West Lafayette, Ind.: Kappa Delta Pi.

Dostoyevsky, F. (1996). *The brothers Karamazov* (1996 Modern Library ed.). New York: Modern Library.

Doyle, W. (1986a). Classroom organization and management. In M. C. Wittrock & American Educational Research Association (Eds.), *Handbook of research on teaching* (3rd ed., pp. 392-431). New York, London: Collier Macmillan.

Doyle, W. (1986b). Content representation in teachers' definitions of academic work. *Journal of Curriculum Studies, 18*(4), 365-379.

Du Bois, W. E. B. (1961). *The souls of black folks*. New York: Dodd, Mead & Company.

Duch, B. J., Groh, S. E., & Allen, D. E. (2001). *The power of problem-based learning: A practical "how to" for teaching undergraduate courses in any discipline* (1st ed.). Sterling, VA: Stylus.

Dyson, A. H. (1997). *Writing superheroes: Contemporary childhood, popular culture, and classroom literacy*. New York: Teachers College Press.

Echevarria, J., Silver, J., Hayward, D., National Center for Research on Cultural Diversity and Second Language Learning., University of California (System). Regents., Center for Applied Linguistics., et al. (1995). *Instructional conversations: Understanding through discussion*. Santa Cruz, CA: Regents of the University of California.

Eckert, P. (1989). *Jocks and burnouts: Social categories and identity in the high school*. New York: Teachers College Press.

Edwards, A. D., & Furlong, V. J. (1978). *The language of teaching: Meaning in classroom interaction*. London: Heinemann Educational.

Edwards, C. P. (1995). Book review: You can't say you can't play. *Journal of Moral Education, 24*(1), 80-82.

Eemeren, F. H. v., & Grootendorst, R. (1992). *Argumentation, communication, and fallacies: A pragma-dialectical perspective*. Hillsdale, NJ: L. Erlbaum.

Einstein, A. (1950). *Essays in physics*. New York: Philosophical Library.

Elias, J. L. (1976). *Conscientization and deschooling: Freire's and Illich's proposals for reshaping society* (Original ed.). Philadelphia: Westminster Press.

Elias, J. L. (1994). *Paulo Freire: Pedagogue of liberation* (Original ed.). Malabar, Fl: Krieger Pub. Co.

Ellsworth, E. (1992). Why doesn't this feel empowering? Working through the repressive myths of critical pedagogy. In C. Luke & J. Gore (Eds.), *Feminisms and critical pedagogy* (pp. 90-119). New York: Routledge.

Emerson, C. (1997). *The first hundred years of Mikhail Bakhtin*. Princeton, NJ: Princeton University Press.

Engels, F. (1978). Letter to Mehring. In K. Marx, F. Engels & R. C. Tucker (Eds.), *The Marx-Engels reader* (2d ed., pp. 766-766). New York: Norton.

Engeström, Y. (1987). *Learning by expanding: An activity-theoretic approach to developmental research*. Helsinki, Finland: Orienta-Konsultit Oy.

Engeström, Y. (1990). *Learning, working, and imagining*. Helsinki, Finland: Orienta-Konsultit Oy.

Engeström, Y. (1999). Innovative learning in work teams: Analizing cycles of knowledge creation in practice. In Y. Engeström, R. Miettinen & R.-L. Punamäki (Eds.), *Perspectives on Activity Theory* (pp. 377-404). Cambridge: Cambridge University Press.

Engeström, Y., Brown, K., Christopher, C. L., & Gregory, J. (1991). Coordination, cooperation and communication in the courts: Expansive transitions in legal work. *The Quarterly Newsletter of the Laboratory of Comparative Human Cognition, 13*(4), 88-97.

Engeström, Y., Miettinen, R., & Punamèaki-Gitai, R.-L. (1999). *Perspectives on activity theory*. New York: Cambridge University Press.

Enos, R. L. (1993). *Greek rhetoric before Aristotle*. Prospect Heights, Ill.: Waveland Press.

Erickson, F. (1986). Qualitative methods of educational research. In M. C. Wittrock & American Educational Research Association. (Eds.), *Handbook of research on teaching* (3rd ed., Vol. 3, pp. 119–161). New York: Macmillan.

Erickson, F. (2003). Forward. In K. Schultz (Ed.), *Listening: A framework for teaching across differences* (pp. ix-xi). New York: Teachers College Press.

Fábri, Z. (Writer) (1976). The fifth seal [VHS]. In Mafilm (Producer). Hungry: Facets Video.

Facundo, B. (1984). Freire-inspired programs in the United States and Puerto Rico: A critical evaluation, Available from http://www.uow.edu.au/arts/sts/bmartin/dissent/documents/ Facundo/Facundo.html

Fantini, M. D., & Weinstein, G. (1969). *Toward a contact curriculum*. New York: Anti-Defamation League of B'nai B'rith.

Felman, S., & Laub, D. (1992). *Testimony: Crises of witnessing in literature, psychoanalysis, and history*. New York: Routledge.

Fendler, L. (1998). What is it impossible to think? A genealogy of the educated subject. In T. S. Popkewitz & M. Brennan (Eds.), *Foucault's challenge: Discourse, knowledge, and power in education* (pp. 39-63). New York: Teachers College Press.

Fernandez, E. (1994). A kinder, gentler Socrates: Conveying new images of mathematics dialogue. *For the Learning of Mathematics, 14*(3), 43-47.

Festinger, L. (1968). *A theory of cognitive dissonance*. Stanford, CA: Stanford University Press.

Feuchtwanger, L., & Josephy, I. (1937). *Moscow, 1937: My visit described for my friends*. New York: The Viking press.

Fiore, K., & Elsasser, N. (1982). 'Strangers no more': A liberatory literacy curriculum. *College English, 44*, 115-128.

Fishman, E. M. (1985). Counteracting misconceptions about the Socratic method. *College Teaching, 33*(4), 185-188.

Fogel, A. (1993). *Developing through relationships: Origins of communication, self, and culture*. Chicago: University of Chicago Press.

Ford, M. J., & Forman, E. A. (2006). Chapter 1: Redefining disciplinary learning in classroom contexts *Review of Research in Education, 30*(1), 1-32.

Fordham, S., & Ogbu, J. U. (1986). Black students' school success: Coping with the "burden of acting White.". *Urban Review, 18*(3), 176-206.

Forrest, B., Gross, P. R., & NetLibrary Inc. (2004). *Creationism's Trojan horse the wedge of intelligent design*. Oxford ; New York: Oxford University Press.

Foster, D., Haupt, P., & Beer, M. D. (2005). *The theater of violence: Narratives of protagonists in the South Africa conflict*. Cape Town, RSA: HRSC press.

Foucault, M. (1984). *The Foucault reader*. New York: Pantheon Books.

Foucault, M. (1988). The ethic of care for the self as a practice of freedom: An interview. In J. W. Bernauer & D. M. Rasmussen (Eds.), *The Final Foucault* (pp. 1–20). Cambridge, MA: MIT Press.

Foucault, M. (1995). *Discipline and punish: The birth of the prison* (2nd Vintage Books ed.). New York: Vintage Books.

Foucault, M., & Gros, F. (2006). *The hermeneutics of the subject: Lectures at the College de France, 1981-1982*. New York: Picador.

Frankl, V. E. (1976). Man in search of meaning [sound recording]. Waco, Texas: Word Inc.

Frankl, V. E., Fairchild, R. W., & Ungersma, A. J. (1986). Logotherapy [sound recording]. Berkeley, Calif.? ;.

Freedman, S. W., & Ball, A. F. (2004). Ideological becoming: Bakhtinian concepts to guide the study of language literacy, and learning. In A. F. Ball & S. W. Freedman (Eds.), *Bakhtinian perspectives on language, literacy, and learning* (pp. 3-33). Cambridge, UK ; New York: Cambridge University Press.

Freedom Writers, & Gruwell, E. (1999). *The Freedom Writers diary: How a teacher and 150 teens used writing to change themselves and the world around them* (1st ed.). New York: Doubleday.

Freire, P. (1976). *Education: The practice of freedom*. London: Writers and Readers Publishing Cooperative.

Freire, P. (1978). *Pedagogy in process: The letters to Guinea-Bissau*. New York: Seabury Press.

Freire, P. (1986). *Pedagogy of the oppressed*. New York: Continuum.

Freire, P., & Freire, P. (1973). *Education for critical consciousness* (1st American ed.). New York: Seabury Press.

Freire, P., & Macedo, D. P. (1987). *Literacy: Reading the word & the world*. South Hadley, Mass.: Bergin & Garvey Publishers.

Fromm, E. (1960). Foreword. In A. S. Neill (Ed.), *Summerhill: A radical approach to child rearing* (pp. ix-xvi). New York: Hart Publishing Company.

Fromm, E. (1969). *Escape from freedom*. New York,: Avon Books.

Fry, P. (1996). The status of human rights organizations in Sub-Saharan Africa Guinea-Bissau. Retrieved December 18, 2006, from http://www1.umn.edu/humanrts/africa/gbissau.htm

Furberg, A., & Ludvigsen, S. (2008). Students' meaning-making of socioscientific issues in computer mediated settings: Exploring learning through interaction trajectories. *International Journal of Science Education, 14*(1), 1-25.

Furco, A. (1996). Service-learning: A balanced approach to experiential education. In *Expanding boundaries: Serving and learning* (pp. 2-6). Washington, DC: Corporation for National Service.

Gadamer, H.-G. (1975). *Truth and method*. New York: Continuum.

Gagarin, M. (2001). Did the Sophists aim to persuade? *Rhetorica, 19*(3), 275-291.

Galilei, G., & Drake, S. (2001). *Dialogue concerning the two chief world systems, Ptolemaic and Copernican*. New York: Modern Library.

Gardiner, M. (1992). *The dialogic critique: M. M. Bakhtin and the theory of ideology*. New York: Routledge.

Garlikov, R. (1998). Contributed Commentary on Volume 5 Number 20: Rud "The use and abuse of Socrates in present day teaching.". *Educational Policy Analysis Archives* Retrieved April, 5, 2005, from http://epaa.asu.edu/epaa/v5n20c1.html

Gee, J. P. (1996). *Social linguistics and literacies: Ideology in discourses* (2nd ed.). London: Taylor & Francis.

Gee, J. P. (2003). *What video games have to teach us about learning and literacy* (1st ed.). New York: Palgrave Macmillan.

Giangrandi, P., & Tasso, C. (1997). Managing temporal knowledge in student modeling. In A. Jameson, C. Paris & C. Tasso (Eds.), *User modeling: Proceedings of the Sixth International Conference* (pp. 415-426). New York: Springer Wien New York.

Gibson, J. J. (1979). *The ecological approach to visual perception*. Boston: Houghton Mifflin.

Gibson, M. A., & Ogbu, J. U. (1991). *Minority status and schooling: A comparative study of immigrant and involuntary minorities*. New York: Garland.

Gide, A. (1937). *Back from the U. S. S. R.* London: Secker and Warburg.

Gilligan, C. (1993). *In a different voice: Psychological theory and women's development.* Cambridge, MA: Harvard University Press.

Glaser, B. G. (1967). *The discovery of grounded theory: Strategies for qualitative research*. Chicago: Aldine Publishing Co.

Glasser, W. (1972). *The identity society* ([1st ed.). New York: Harper & Row.

Goldman, L. (1984). Warning: The Socratic method can be dangerous. *Educational Leadership, 42*(1), 57-62.

Goodlad, J. I. (1984). *A place called school: Prospects for the future*. New York: McGraw-HIll Book Co.

Gould, S. J. (1996). *The mismeasure of man* (Rev. and expanded. ed.). New York: Norton.

Graff, G. (2003). *Clueless in academe: How schooling obscures the life of the mind*. New Haven, CT: Yale University Press.

Grandin, T., & Scariano, M. (2005). *Emergence: Labeled autistic, a true story*. New York: Warner Books.

Greenleaf, C. L., & Katz, M.-L. (2004). Ever newer ways to mean: Authoring pedagogical change in secondary subject-area classrooms. In A. F. Ball & S. W. Freedman (Eds.), *Bakhtinian perspectives on language, literacy, and learning* (pp. 172-202). Cambridge, UK ; New York: Cambridge University Press.

Greeno, J. G. (1997). On claims that answer the wrong questions. *Educational Researcher, 26*(1), 5-17.

Grice, H. P. (1975). Logic and conversation. In P. Cole & J. L. Morgan (Eds.), *Syntax and semantics* (Vol. 3, pp. 41-58). New York: Academic Press.

Griffith, W. S. (1972). Paulo Freire: Utopian perspective on literacy education for revolution. In S. M. Grabowski (Ed.), *Paulo Freire: A revolutionary dilemma for the adult educator* (pp. 67-82). Syracuse, NY: Syracuse University, Publications in Continuing Education.

Gulley, N. (1968). *The philosophy of Socrates*. London: Macmillan.

Guterman, N. (1990). *The Anchor book of French quotations: with English translations*. New York: Anchor Books.

Gutierrez, K., Rymes, B., & Larson, J. (1995). Script, counterscript, and underlife in the classroom: James Brown vs. Board of Education. *Harvard Education Review, 65*(3), 445-472.

Hall, E. B. (1906). *The friends of Voltaire*. London: Smith.

Hall, E. T. (1983). *The dance of life: The other dimension of time* (1st ed.). Garden City, N.Y.: Anchor Press/Doubleday.

Hansen, D. T. (1988). Was Socrates a "Socratic" teacher? *Educational Theory, 38*(2), 213-224.

Harasim, L. M. (1983). *Literacy and national reconstruction in Guinea Bissau: A critique of the Freirean literacy campaign*. Unpublished Thesis (Ph.D.), University of Toronto, Toronto.

Hargreaves, A. (1989). *Curriculum and assessment reform*. Toronto: OISE Press.

Hargreaves, A. (1994). *Changing teachers, changing times: Teachers' work and culture in the postmodern age*. London: Cassell.

Harrist, A. W., & Bradley, K. D. (2003). "You can't say you can't play": Intervening in the process of social exclusion in the kindergarten classroom. *Early Childhood Research Quarterly, 18*, 185-205.

Hartmann, D. P. (1992). Design, measurement and analysis: Technical issues in developmental research. In M. H. Bornstein & M. E. Lamb (Eds.), *Developmental psychology: An advanced textbook* (3rd ed., pp. 59-151). Hillsdale, NJ: Lawrence Erlbaum.

Havel, V., & Vladislav, J. (1989). *Living in truth: Twenty-two essays published on the occasion of the award of the Erasmus Prize to Vaclav Havel* (Paperback ed.). London: Faber and Faber.

Hayes, R., & Matusov, E. (2005a). Designing for dialogue in place of teacher talk and student silence. *Culture and Psychology, 11*(3), 339-357.

Hayes, R., & Matusov, E. (2005b). From 'ownership' to dialogic addressivity: Defining successful digital storytelling projects. *Technology, Humanities, Education, Narrative Journal, March 3*, available online: http://thenjournal.org/feature/75.

Heath, S. B. (1978). Teacher talk: Langauge in the classroom. *Language in Education: Theory and Practice, 1*(1), 1-30.

Hegel, G. W. F., & Baillie, J. B. (1967). *The phenomenology of mind*. New York: Harper & Row.

Heinze, T. F. (2002). Answers to my evolutionist friends: Who designed woodpeckers? . *Journal*. Retrieved from http://www.creationism.org/heinze/Woodpecker.htm

Herrnstein, R. J., & Murray, C. A. (1994). *The bell curve: Intelligence and class structure in American life*. New York: Free Press.

Hirsch, E. D. (1996). *The schools we need and why we don't have them* (1st ed.). New York: Doubleday.

Hirsch, E. D., Trefil, J. S., & Kett, J. F. (1988). *Cultural literacy: What every American needs to know* (1st Vintage Books ed.). New York: Vintage Books.

Holquist, M. (1990). *Dialogism: Bakhtin and his world*. London: Routledge.

Holquist, M. (1991). Introduction (C. Emerson & M. Holquist, Trans.). In *Dialogic imagination: Four essays by M. M. Bakhtin*. Austin, TX: University of Texas Press.

Holzman, L. (1997). *Schools for growth: Radical alternatives to current educational models*. Mahwah, NJ: L. Erlbaum Associates.

hooks, b. (1993). Speaking about Paulo Freire. In P. McLaren & P. Leonard (Eds.), *Paulo Freire: A critical encounter*. New York: Routledge.

Houghton Mifflin Company. (2000). *The American Heritage dictionary of the English language* (4th ed.). Boston: Houghton Mifflin.

Hull, R. (1985). *The language gap: How classroom dialogue fails*. London ; New York: Methuen.

Hunt, M. W. (1969). Tips for beginning teachers. In National Education Association of the United States. (Ed.), *Discipline in the classroom: NEA journal, selected articles of continuing value to elementary and secondary school teachers*. Washington: National Education Association.

Hunter, R., & Hunter, M. C. (2004). *Madeline Hunter's Mastery teaching: Increasing instructional effectiveness in elementary and secondary schools* (Updated ed.). Thousand Oaks, CA: Corwin Press.

Hutchins, E. (1995). *Cognition in the wild*. Cambridge, Mass.: MIT Press.

Ilenkov, E. V. (1977). *Dialectical logic: Essays on its history and theory*. Moscow: Progress Publishers.

Jackson, P. W. (1968). *Life in classrooms*. New York: Holt Rinehart and Winston.

Johnson, D., & VanVonderen, J. (1991). *The subtle power of spiritual abuse*. Minneapolis, MI: Bethany House Publishers.

Jones, P. (1988). *Lipservice: The story of talk in schools: Reflections on the development of talk and talk opportunities in schools 5-16*. Philadelphia: Open University Press.

Kafai, Y. B., & Resnick, M. (1996). *Constructionism in practice: Designing, thinking, and learning in a digital world*. Mahwah, N.J.: Lawrence Erlbaum Associates.

Kameen, P. (2000). *Writing/teaching: Essays toward a rhetoric of pedagogy*. Pittsburgh: University of Pittsburgh Press.

Kauchak, D. P., & Eggen, P. D. (2003). *Learning and teaching: Research-based methods* (4th ed.). Boston: Allyn and Bacon.

Kauffmann, R. L. (1990). The Other in question: Dialogical experiments in Montaigne, Kafka, and Cortázar. In T. Maranhão (Ed.), *The interpretation of dialogue* (pp. 157-194). Chicago: University of Chicago Press.

Keneally, T. (1993). *Schindler's list*. New York, NY: Simon and Schuster.

Kennedy, M. M. (2005). *Inside teaching: How classroom life undermines reform*. Cambridge, MA: Harvard University Press.

King, N. R. (1993). You Can't Say You Can't Play (Book review). [Book Review]. *Educational Studies, 24*(4), 333-338.

Klag, P. (1994). A new look at Invitational Education. *The Collaborator, 5*(14), 1-2.

Kleindienst, B. (1998). The children of Summerhill. New York: Cinema Guild.

Klinghoffer, A. J. (2006). *The power of projections: How maps reflect global politics and history*. Westport, CT: Praeger Publishers.

Kogon, E. (1947). *Der SS-Staat*. Stockholm,: Bermann-Fischer Verlag.

Kohlberg, L., & Ryncarz, R. A. (1990). Beyond justice reasoning: Moral development and consideration of a seventh stage. In C. N. Alexander & E. J. Langer (Eds.), *Higher stages of human development* (pp. 191-207). New York, U.S.A.: Oxford University Press.

Köhler, W. (1973). *The mentality of apes*. London: Routledge and Kegan Paul.

Koppel, T., Bury, C., Will, G. F., Thomas, C., ABC News Productions., & Films for the Humanities & Sciences (Firm). (2006). Intelligent design vs. evolution [videorecording]. Princeton, N.J.: Films for the Humanities & Sciences.

Korczak, J., & Gawronski, G. (1992). *When I am little again and "The child's right to respect"*. Lanham: University Press.

Koshmanova, T. S. (2006). Teaching for democracy in Ukraine: Activity-based developmental and dialogical education. *International Journal of Educational Reform, 15*(1), 80-96.

Kotek, J., & Rigoulot, P. (2000). *Le siècle des camps: Détention, concentration, extermination, cent ans de mal radical*. Paris: Lattès.

Kuhn, T. S. (1996). *The structure of scientific revolutions* (3rd ed.). Chicago, IL: University of Chicago Press.

Kurganov, S. Y. (2005, September). Шестилетние первоклассники [The six-year old first graders]. *Детский сад со всех сторон [Kindergraten from all angles], 34-35*, 190.

Kurosawa, A. (Writer) (1970). Dodesukaden (Clickity Clack) [DVD]. Japan: Toho Company.

Kuznetsova, N. I. (2005). "Выслушав не мою, а вот эту речь...": Опыт понимания Гераклита ["Listening out to not my but this speech...": Experience of understanding Heraclites]. In I. E. Berlyand (Ed.), *«Архэ». Труды культурологического семинара ["Arkhe". Works of the culturology seminar]* (Vol. 4, pp. 353 – 367). Moscow: RGGU.

Labaree, D. (2003). The peculiar problems of preparing educational researchers. *Educational Researcher, 32*(4), 13-22.

Labaree, D. F. (1997). *How to succeed in school without really learning: The credentials race in American education*. New Haven, CT: Yale University Press.

Laclau, E., & Mouffe, C. (2001). *Hegemony and socialist strategy: Towards a radical democratic politics* (2nd ed.). London: Verso.

Lampert, M. (2001). *Teaching problems and the problems of teaching*. New Haven: Yale University Press.

Latour, B. (1987). *Science in action: How to follow scientists and engineers through society*. Cambridge, MA: Harvard University Press.

Latour, B. (1996). On interobjectivity. *Mind, Culture and Activity, 3*(4), 228-245.

Latour, B., & Woolgar, S. (1979). *Laboratory life: The social construction of scientific facts*. Beverly Hills, CA: Sage Publications.

Lave, J. (1988). *Cognition in practice: Mind, mathematics, and culture in everyday life*. Cambridge, UK: Cambridge University Press.

Lave, J. (1992a). *Learning as participation in communities of practice*. Paper presented at the meeting of the American Educational Research Association, San Francisco, CA.

Lave, J. (1992b). Word problems: A microcosm of theories of learning. In P. Light & G. Butterworth (Eds.), *Context and cognition: Ways of learning and knowing.* (pp. 74-92). Hillsdale, NJ: Lawrence Erlbaum Associates, Inc.

Lave, J., & Wenger, E. (1991). *Situated learning: Legitimate peripheral participation*. Cambridge, UK: Cambridge University Press.

Leander, K. (2002). Silencing in classroom interaction: Producing and relating social spaces. *Discourse processes, 32*(2), 193-235.

Lemke, J. L. (1990). *Talking science: Language, learning, and values*. Norwood, NJ: Ablex Pub. Corp.

Lenin, V. I. i. (1977). May day action by the revolutionary proletariat. In *Lenin Collected Works* (Vol. 19). Moscow: Progress Publishers.

Lensmire, T. J. (1994a). *When children write: Critical re-visions of the writing workshop*. New York: Teacher College Press.

Lensmire, T. J. (1994b). Writing workshop as carnival: Reflections on an alternative learning environment. *Harvard Educational Review, 64*, 371-391.

Leontiev, A. N. (1981). The problem of activity in psychology. In J. V. Wertsch (Ed.), *The concept of activity in Soviet Psychology* (pp. 37-71). Armonk, New York: Sharpe.

Lewin, K. (1948). *Resolving social conflicts: Selected papers on group dynamics 1935-1946*. New York: Harper.

Lewin, K., & Cartwright, D. (1964). *Field theory in social science: Selected theoretical papers*. New York,: Harper & Row.

Lewin, K., Lippit, R., & White, R. K. (1939). Patterns of aggressive in experimentally created "social climates". *The Journal of Social Psychology, 10*, 271-299.

Liddell, H. G., Scott, R., Jones, H. S., & McKenzie, R. (1948). *A Greek-English lexicon* (New ed.). Oxford: At the Clarendon Press.

Lillejord, S., & Dysthe, O. (2007, in press). Productive learning practice: A theoretical discussion based on two cases. *Journal of Education and Work*.

Linder, S. B. (1970). *The harried leisure class*. New York,: Columbia University Press.

Linell, P. (1998). *Approaching dialogue: Talk, interaction and contexts in dialogical perspectives*. Philadelphia: J. Benjamins Publishing Company.

Lipman, M. (2003). *Thinking in education* (2nd ed.). New York: Cambridge University Press.

Lobban, R., & Lopes, M. (1995). *Historical dictionary of the Republic of Cape Verde* (3rd ed.). Metuchen, N.J.: Scarecrow Press.

Lobban, R., & Mendy, P. K. M. (1997). *Historical dictionary of the Republic of Guinea-Bissau* (3rd ed.). Lanham, Md.: Scarecrow Press.

Loewen, J. W. (1996). *Lies my teacher told me: Everything your American history textbook got wrong* (1st Touchstone ed.). New York: Simon & Schuster.

Lortie, D. C. (1975). *Schoolteacher: A sociological study*. Chicago,: University of Chicago Press.

Lotman, Y. (1988). Text within text. *Soviet psychology, 24*(3), 32-41.

Luria, A. R. (1976). *Cognitive development, its cultural and social foundations*. Cambridge, MA: Harvard University Press.

Lyman, K. (2000). Girls, worms, and body image. *Rethinking schools, 14*(3), available online http://www.rethinkingschools.org/archive/14_03/girl143.shtml.

Macedo, D. P. (1994). *Literacies of power: What Americans are not allowed to know*. Boulder: Westview Press.

Machiavelli, N., & Donne, D. J. (1985). *The prince*. New York: Bantam Books.

Macmillan, C. J. B., & Garrison, J. W. (1988). *A logical theory of teaching: Erotetics and intentionality*. Boston: Kluwer Academic Publishers.

Mandela, N. (1995). *Long walk to freedom: The autobiography of Nelson Mandela*. London: Abacus.

Maranhão, T. (1990). Introduction. In T. Maranhão (Ed.), *The interpretation of dialogue* (pp. 1-22). Chicago: University of Chicago Press.

Marx, K., & Engels, F. (1990). *Karl Marx, Capital* (2nd ed.). Chicago: Encyclopµdia Britannica Inc.

Mashayekh, F. (1974). Freire -- the man, his ideas, and their implications. *Literacy Discussion*(Spring), 1-62.

Mattingly, C., & Garro, L. C. (2000). *Narrative and the cultural construction of illness and healing*. Berkeley: University of California Press.

Matusov, E. (1996). Intersubjectivity without agreement. *Mind, Culture, and Activity, 3*(1), 25-45.

Matusov, E. (1998). When solo activity is not privileged: Participation and internalization models of development. *Human Development, 41*(5-6), 326-349.

Matusov, E. (1999). How does a community of learners maintain itself? Ecology of an innovative school. *Anthropology & Education Quarterly, 30*(2), 161-186.

Matusov, E. (2001a). Becoming an adult member in a community of learners. In B. Rogoff, C. G. Turkanis & L. Bartlett (Eds.), *Learning together: Children and adults in a school community* (pp. 166-174). New York: Oxford University Press.

Matusov, E. (2001b). Intersubjectivity as a way of informing teaching design for a community of learners classroom. *Teaching and Teacher Education, 17*(4), 383-402.

Matusov, E. (2004). Bakhtin's debit in educational research: Dialogic pedagogy. *Journal of Russian & East European Psychology, 42*(6), 3-11.

Matusov, E. (2007). Applying Bakhtin scholarship on discourse in education: A critical review essay. *Educational Theory, 57*(2), 215-237.

Matusov, E. (2008a). Applying a sociocultural approach to Vygotskian academia: "Our tsar isn't like yours, and yours isn't like ours". *Culture & Psychology, 14*(1), 5-35.

Matusov, E. (2008b). Dialogue with cultural-historical Vygotskian colleagues about a sociocultural approach. *Culture & Psychology, 14*(1), 81-93.

Matusov, E., Bell, N., & Rogoff, B. (2002). Schooling as cultural process: Shared thinking and guidance by children from schools differing in collaborative practices. In R. Kail & H. W. Reese (Eds.), *Advances in Child Development and Behavior* (Vol. 29, pp. 129-160). New York: New York: Academic Press.

Matusov, E., DePalma, R., & Drye, S. (2007). Whose development? Salvaging the concept of development within a sociocultural approach to education. *Educational Theory, 57*(4), 403-421.

Matusov, E., & Hayes, R. (2000). Sociocultural critique of Piaget and Vygotsky. *New Directions in Psychology, 18*(2-3), 215-239.

Matusov, E., & Hayes, R. (2002). Building a community of educators versus effecting conceptual change in individual students: Multicultural education for preservice teachers. In G. Wells & G. Claxton (Eds.), *Learning for life in the 21st century: Sociocultural perspectives on the future of education* (pp. 239-251). Cambridge, UK: Cambridge University Press.

Matusov, E., Hayes, R., & Pluta, M. J. (2005). Using discussion world wide webs to develop an academic community of learners. *Educational Technology & Society, 8*(2), 16-39.

Matusov, E., Hayes, R., & Smith, M. (2005, September). *Smuggling authentic learning into the school context: Learning-loving minority in conventional US high schools (a response to John Ogbu)*. Paper presented at the International Society for Cultural and Activity Research, Seville, Spain.

Matusov, E., Pleasants, H., & Smith, M. P. (2003). Dialogic framework for cultural psychology: Culture-in-action and culturally sensitive guidance. *Review Interdisciplinary Journal on Human Development, Culture and Education, 4*(1), available online: http://cepaosreview.tripod.com/Matusov.html.

Matusov, E., & Rogoff, B. (2002). Newcomers and oldtimers: Educational philosophy-in-actions of parent volunteers in a community of learners school. *Anthropology & Education Quarterly, 33*(4), 1-26.

Matusov, E., & Smith, M. P. (2007). Teaching imaginary children: University students' narratives about their Latino practicum children. *Teaching and Teacher Education, 23*(5), 705-729.

Matusov, E., & Smith, M. P. (2008, submitted). Ecological model of inter-institutional sustainability of after-school program: The La Red Mágica community-university partnership in Delaware. *Anthropology & Education Quarterly.*

Matusov, E., Smith, M. P., Candela, M. A., & Lilu, K. (2007). "Culture has no internal territory": Culture as dialogue. In J. Valsiner & A. Rosa (Eds.), *The Cambridge Handbook of Socio-Cultural Psychology* (pp. 460-483). Cambridge, UK: Cambridge University Press.

Matusov, E., & St. Julien, J. (2004). Print literacy as oppression: Cases of bureaucratic, colonial, totalitarian literacies and their implications for schooling. *TEXT: International Journal, 24*(2), 197-244.

Matusov, E., St. Julien, J., & Hayes, R. (2005). Building a creole educational community as the goal of multicultural education for preservice teachers. In L. V. Barnes (Ed.), *Contemporary Teaching and Teacher Issues* (pp. 1-38). Hauppauge, NY: Nova Publishers.

Matusov, E., St. Julien, J., Lacasa, P., & Alburquerque Candela, M. (2007). Learning as a communal process and as a byproduct of social activism. *Outlines: Critical Social Studies, 1*(1), 21-37.

Matusov, E., & White, C. (1996). Defining the concept of open collaboration from a sociocultural framework. *Cognitive Studies: The Bulletin of the Japanese Cognitive Science Society, 3*(4), 11-13.

Maynard, D. W. (1980). Placement of topic changes in conversation. *Semiotica, 30*(4), 263-290.

Mayo, C., Alburquerque Candela, M., Matusov, E., & Smith, M. (2008). Families and schools apart: University experience to assist Latino/a parents' activism. In F. Peterman (Ed.), *Partnering book: Community activism in partnering to prepare urban teachers* (pp. 103-132). Washington, DC: American Association of Colleges for Teacher Education.

McAdams, D. P. (2006). *The redemptive self: Stories Americans live by.* New York: Oxford University Press.

McDermott, R. P. (1988). Inarticulatedness. In D. Tannen (Ed.), *Linguistic in context* (pp. 37-68). Norwood, NJ: Ablex.

McDermott, R. P. (1993). The acquisition of a child by a learning disability. In S. Chaiklin & J. Lave (Eds.), *Understanding practice: Perspectives on activity and context* (pp. 269-305). New York: Cambridge University Press.

McLaren, P. (1993). *Schooling as a ritual performance: Towards a political economy of educational symbols and gestures* (2nd ed.). London ; New York: Routledge.

McLaren, P., & Lankshear, C. (1994). *Politics of liberation: Paths from Freire.* New York: Routledge.

McLaren, P., & Leonard, P. (1993). *Paulo Freire: A critical encounter.* New York: Routledge.

McNeil, L. M. (1986). *Contradictions of control: School structure and school knowledge.* New York: Routledge & K. Paul.

Mead, G. H. (1956). *On social psychology.* Chicago: University of Chicago Press.

Mecke, J. (1990). Dialogue and narration (the narrative principle). In T. Maranhão (Ed.), *The interpretation of dialogue* (pp. 195-215). Chicago: University of Chicago Press.

Medvedev, P. N. (1985). *The formal method in literary scholarship: A critical introduction to sociological poetics* (A. J. Wehrle, Trans.). Cambridge, Mass.: Harvard University Press.

Mehan, H. (1979). *Learning lessons: Social organization in the classroom*. Cambridge, MA: Harvard University Press.

Mettetal, G., & Bryant, D. (1996). Service learning research projects: Empowerment in students, faculty, and communities. *College Teaching, 44*(1), 24-28.

Metz, M. H. (1978). *Classrooms and corridors: The crisis of authority in desegregated secondary schools*. Berkeley, CA: University of California Press.

Michaels, S., & Cazden, C. B. (1986). Teacher/child collaboration as oral preparation for literacy. In B. B. Schieffelin & P. Gilmore (Eds.), *The acquisition of literacy: Ethnographic perspectives* (pp. 132-154). Norwood, NJ: Ablex.

Minick, N. (1993). Teacher's directives: The social construction of "literal meanings" and "real worlds" in classroom discourse. In S. Chaiklin & J. Lave (Eds.), *Understanding practice: Perspectives on activity and context* (pp. 343-374). New York: Cambridge University Press.

Miyazaki, K. (2006). Another imaginative approach to teaching: A Japanese view. *Academiea, 4*(5), 22-31.

Miyazaki, K. (2007, July). *Teacher as the imaginative learner: Egan, Saitou, and Bakhtin*. Paper presented at the the 2nd annual research symposium on imagination and education, Vancouver, Canada.

Moerman, M. (1988). *Talking culture: Ethnography and conversation analysis*. Philadelphia: University of Pennsylvania Press.

Moll, L. C. (1990). *Vygotsky and education: Instructional implications and applications of sociohistorical psychology*. Cambridge ; New York: Cambridge University Press.

Morrison, H. C. (1931). *The practice of teaching in the secondary school* (Rev ed.): The University of Chicago press.

Morse, R. A. (1994). The classic method of Mrs. Socrates. *The Physics Teacher, 32*(May), 276-277.

Morson, G. S. (2004). The process of ideological becoming. In A. F. Ball & S. W. Freedman (Eds.), *Bakhtinian perspectives on language, literacy, and learning* (pp. 317-331). Cambridge, UK; New York: Cambridge University Press.

Morson, G. S., & Emerson, C. (1989). *Rethinking Bakhtin: Extensions and challenges*. Evanston, Ill.: Northwestern University Press.

Morson, G. S., & Emerson, C. (1990). *Mikhail Bakhtin: Creation of a prosaics*. Stanford, CA: Stanford University Press.

Mukhopadhyay, S., & Greer, B. (2001). Modeling with purpose: Mathematics as a critical tool. In B. Atweh, H. Forgasz & B. Nebres (Eds.), *Sociocultural research on mathematics education: An international perspective* (pp. 295-311). Mahwah, NJ: Lawrence Erlbaum Associates.

Murphy, D. (1992). *Tolstoy and education*. Blackrock, Co. Dublin: Irish Academic Press.

Myers, G. (1990). *Writing biology: Texts in the social construction of scientific knowledge*. Madison, Wis.: University of Wisconsin Press.

Neill, A. S. (1960). *Summerhill: A radical approach to child rearing*. New York: Hart Publishing Company.

Newman, D., Cole, M., & Griffin, P. (1989). *The construction zone: Working for cognitive change in school*. Cambridge, UK: Cambridge University Press.

Nicholas. (1954). *Of learned ignorance*. London: Routledge & Paul.

Nicholas, Tazhurizina, Z. A., Bibikhin, V. V., & Sokolov, V. V. (1979). *Sochineniya [Collected work]*. Moskva: Mysl'.

Nietzsche, F. W. (1956). *The birth of tragedy* (F. Golffing, Trans. 1st ed.). Garden City, NY: Doubleday.

Nietzsche, F. W. (1983). *Untimely meditations.* Cambridge Cambridgeshire; New York: Cambridge University Press.

Nightingale, A. W. (1999). *Genres in dialogue: Plato and the construct of philosophy.* Cambridge: Cambridge University Press.

Numbers, R. L. (2006). *The creationists: From scientific creationism to intelligent design* (Expanded ed.). Cambridge, Mass.: Harvard University Press.

Nunes, T., Schliemann, A. D., & Carraher, D. W. (1993). *Street mathematics and school mathematics.* New York: Cambridge University Press.

Nussbaum, E. M., & Sinatra, G. M. (2003). Argument and conceptual engagement. *Contemporary Educational Psychology, 28*(3), 384-395.

Nystrand, M. (1986). *The structure of written communication: Studies in reciprocity between writers and readers.* Orlando, FL: Academic Press.

Nystrand, M. (1997). *Opening dialogue: Understanding the dynamics of language and learning in the English classroom.* New York: Teachers College Press.

Ogbu, J. U. (1987a). Variability in minority responses to schooling: Nonimmigrants vs. immigrants. In G. Spindler, L. Spindler & et al. (Eds.), *Interpretive ethnography of education: At home and abroad.* (pp. 255-280). Hillsdale, NJ, USA: Lawrence Erlbaum Associates, Inc.

Ogbu, J. U. (1987b). Variability in minority school performance: A problem in search of a solution. *Anthropology and Education Quarterly, 18*(4), 312-333.

Ogbu, J. U. (2003). *Black American students in an affluent suburb: A study of academic disengagement.* Mahwah, NJ: Lawrence Erlbaum Associates.

Ogbu, J. U., & Stern, P. (2001). Caste status and intellectual development. In R. J. Sternberg & E. L. Grigorenko (Eds.), *Environmental effects on cognitive abilities* (pp. 3-37). Mahwah, NJ: Lawrence Erlbaum Associates, Inc., Publishers.

Ohliger, J. (1995). Critical views of Paulo Freire's work. *Journal.* Retrieved from http://www.uow.edu.au/arts/sts/bmartin/dissent/documents/Facundo/Ohliger1.html

Olson, D. R. (1981). Writing: The divorce of the author from the text. In B. M. Kroll & R. J. Vann (Eds.), *Exploring speaking-writing relationships: Connections and contrasts* (pp. 99-110). Urbana, IL: National Council of Teachers of English.

Olson, D. R. (1994). *The world on paper: The conceptual and cognitive implications of writing and reading.* New York: Cambridge University Press.

Orwell, G. (1992). *1984.* New York: Knopf.

Ongstad, S. (2007, January). *Argument(s) and/as utterances, genres and context.* Paper presented at the Argumentation in (con)text, Bergen, Norway.

Oxford University Press. (1989). Oxford English dictionary. from http://dictionary.oed.com/

Paley, V. G. (1984). *Boys & girls: Superheroes in the doll corner.* Chicago: University of Chicago Press.

Paley, V. G. (1986a). *Mollie is three: Growing up in school.* Chicago: University of Chicago Press.

Paley, V. G. (1986b). On listening to what the children say. *Harvard Educational Review, 56*(2), 122-131.

Paley, V. G. (1988). *Bad guys don't have birthdays: Fantasy play at four.* Chicago: University of Chicago Press.

Paley, V. G. (1989). *White teacher.* Cambridge, MA: Harvard University Press.

Paley, V. G. (1991). *The boy who would be a helicopter* (1st Harvard University Press pbk. ed.). Cambridge, MA: Harvard University Press.

Paley, V. G. (1992). *You can't say you can't play*. Cambridge, MA: Harvard University Press.

Paley, V. G. (1995). *Kwanzaa and me: A teacher's story*. Cambridge, MA: Harvard University Press.

Paley, V. G. (1997). *The girl with the brown crayon*. Cambridge, MA: Harvard University Press.

Paley, V. G. (1998). *Wally's stories*. Cambridge, MA: Harvard University Press.

Paulston, R. G. (1992). Ways of seeing education and social change in Latin America: A phenomenographic perspective. *Latin American Research Review, 27*(3), 177-202.

Pekarsky, D. (1994). Socratic teaching: A critical assessment. *Journal of Moral Education, 23*(2), 119-134.

Petto, A. J., & Godfrey, L. R. (2007). *Scientists confront intelligent design and creationism*. New York: W.W. Norton & Co.

Philips, S. U. (1993). *The invisible culture: Communication in classroom and community on the Warm Springs Indian Reservation*. Prospect Heights, IL: Waveland Press.

Phillips, C. (2002). *Socrates café: A fresh taste of philosophy*. New York: W.W. Norton.

Phillips, D. C. (1995). The Good, the Bad, and the Ugly: The many faces of constructivism. *Educational Researcher, 24*(7), 5-12.

Phillips, D. C. (2000). *Constructivism in education: Opinions and second opinions on controversial issues*. Chicago, Ill.: National Society for the Study of Education : Distributed by the University of Chicago Press.

Piaget, J. (1985). *The equilibration of cognitive structures: The central problem of intellectual development*. Chicago: University of Chicago Press.

Piaget, J. (2002). *The language and thought of the child* (3rd ed.). London: Routledge.

Piaget, J., & Elkind, D. (1968). *Six psychological studies*. New York: Vintage Books.

Pijanowski, C. M. (2004). Education for democracy demands 'good-enough' teachers. In C. W. Bingham & A. M. Sidorkin (Eds.), *No education without relation* (pp. 103-120). New York: Peter Lang.

Plato. (1984). *Great dialogues of Plato* (W. H. D. Rouse, Trans.). New York, NY: Mentor.

Plato. (1997). *Complete works* (J. M. Cooper & D. S. Hutchinson, Trans.). Indianapolis, IN: Hackett Pub.

Plato, & Bluck, R. S. (1961). *Meno*. Cambridge, UK: University Press.

Plato, & Riddell, J. (1973). *The Apology of Plato, with a revised text and English notes, and a digest of Platonic idioms*. New York: Arno Press.

Pólya, G. (1954). *Induction and analogy in mathematics*. Princeton, N.J.,: Princeton University Press.

Popper, K. R. (1966). *The open society and its enemies* (5th ed.). Princeton,: Princeton University Press.

Popper, K. R., & Bartley, W. W. (1993). *Realism and the aim of science*. London ; New York: Routledge.

Porter, A. P. (2006). *Where now, o biologists, is your theory?: Intelligent design as naturalism by other means*. Eugene, Or.: Wipf & Stock Publishers.

Powell, A., Farrar, E., & Cohen, D. K. (1985). *The shopping-mall high school*. Boston: Houghton Mifflin.

Prigogine, I., & Stengers, I. (1984). *Order out of chaos: Man's new dialogue with nature* (1st ed.). Boulder, CO: New Science Library: Distributed by Random House.

Purkey, W. W. (1992). An introduction to invitational theory. *Journal of Invitational Theory and Practice, 1*(1), 5-15.

Rappaport, R. A. (1978). Adaptation and the structure of ritual. In N. B. Jones & V. Reynolds (Eds.), *Human behaviour and adaptation* (pp. 77-102). London: Taylor & Francis.

Reddy, M. J. (1979). The conduit metaphor -- a case of frame conflict in our language about language. In A. Ortony (Ed.), *Metaphor and thought* (pp. 284-324). Cambridge, UK: Cambridge University Press.

Renshaw, P. (2004). Dialogic learning, teaching and instruction: Theoretical roots and analytical frameworks. In J. L. v. d. Linden & P. Renshaw (Eds.), *Dialogic learning: Shifting perspectives to learning, instruction, and teaching* (pp. 1-15). Boston: Kluwer Academic Publishers.

Richards, J. (1991). Mathematical discussions. In E. v. Glasersfeld (Ed.), *Radical constructivism in mathematics education* (pp. 13-51). Dordrecht, The Netherlands ; Boston: Kluwer Academic.

Rockwell, E. (2000). Teaching genres: A Bakhtian approach. *Anthropology & Education Quarterly, 31*(3), 260-282.

Rogoff, B. (1990). *Apprenticeship in thinking: Cognitive development in social context.* New York: Oxford University Press.

Rogoff, B. (2003). *The cultural nature of human development.* New York: Oxford University Press.

Rogoff, B., Bartlett, L., & Goodman Turkanis, C. (2001). Lessons about learning as a community. In B. Rogoff, C. G. Turkanis & et al. (Eds.), *Learning together: Children and adults in a school community.* New York: Oxford University Press.

Rogoff, B., Matusov, E., & White, C. (1996). Models of teaching and learning: Participation in a community of learners. In D. R. Olson & N. Torrance (Eds.), *The handbook of education and human development: New models of learning, teaching and schooling.* (pp. 388-414). Malden, MA, US: Blackwell Publishers Inc.

Rogoff, B., Turkanis, C. G., & Bartlett, L. (Eds.). (2001). *Learning together: Children and adults in a school community.* New York: Oxford University Press.

Rombyer, P. (2004, February 26). Barbie gets booted from 7th grade Concord math class. *The Jackson Citizen Patriot. The Associated Press,*

Rommetveit, R. (1979). On the architecture of intersubjectivity. In R. Rommetveit & R. M. Blakar (Eds.), *Studies of language, thought, and verbal communication* (pp. 147-161). New York: Academic Press.

Rommetveit, R. (1984). The role of language in the creation and transmission of social representations. In R. M. Farr & S. Moscovici (Eds.), *Social representations* (pp. 331-359). Cambridge, UK: Cambridge University Press.

Rommetveit, R. (1992). Outlines of a dialogically based cognitive-social apporach to human cognition and communication. In A. H. Wold (Ed.), *The dialogical alternative: Towards a theory of language and mind* (pp. 19-44). Oslo: Scandinavian University Press.

Rorty, R. (1979). *Philosophy and the mirror of nature* Princeton: Princeton University Press.

Rorty, R. (1999). *Achieving our country: Leftist thought in twentieth-century America* (1st Harvard University Press pbk. ed.). Cambridge, MA: Harvard University Press.

Rosen, P., & Lavoie, R. D. (1989). How difficult can this be? Understanding learning disabilities: Frustration, anxiety, tension, the F.A.T. city workshop [videorecording]. Arlington, VA: WETA [distributor].

Rosenberg, M. B. (2001). CNVC founder Marshall Rosenberg's response to the events of September 11, 2001. *Journal.* Retrieved from http://www.cnvc.org/responmr.htm

Rossetti, L. (1989). The rhetoric of Socrates. *Philosophy and Rhetoric, 22*, 225-238.

Rossmeissl, J. W., & Webber, F. A. (1969). Incommensurables and irrational numbers. In J. K. Baumgart & National Council of Teachers of Mathematics. (Eds.), *Historical topics for the mathematics classroom* (pp. 70-72). Washington: National Council of Teachers of Mathematics.

Rud, A. G. (1997). The use and abuse of Socrates in present day teaching. *Education Policy Analysis Archives, 5*(20), available: http://epaa.asu.edu/epaa/v5n20.html.

Ryan, R. (2003). Anatomy and evolution of the woodpecker's tongue. *Journal.* Retrieved from http://www.talkorigins.org/faqs/woodpecker/woodpecker.html

Sacks, O. W. (1990). *The Man who mistook his wife for a hat and other clinical tales* (1st Harper Perennial Library ed.). New York: Harper Perennial Library.

Saitou, K. (1963). *Jugyo [The classroom lesson].* Tokyo: Kokudo-sha.

Saitou, K. (1964). *Jugyo no tenkai [Development of classroom lesson].* Tokyo: Kokudo-sha.

Säljö, R., & Wyndhamn, J. (1993). Solving everyday problems in the formal setting: An empirical study of the school as context for thought. In S. Chaiklin & J. Lave (Eds.), *Understanding practice. Perspectives on activity and context* (pp. 327-342). New York: Cambridge University Press.

Sánta, F. (1986). *The fifth seal: A novel* (A. Tezla, Trans.). Budapest: Corvina.

Saperstein, A. M. (2007). Teaching science to biblical literalists. *Academe, 93*(1), 43-45.

Sapon-Shevin, M., Dobbelaere, A., Corrigan, C., Goodman, K., & Mastin, M. (1998). Everyone here can play. [Article]. *Educational Leadership, 56*(1), 42-45.

Sarason, S. B. (1983). *Schooling in America: Scapegoat and salvation.* New York: Free Press.

Savinkov, B. V., & Shaplen, J. (1931). *Memoirs of a terrorist.* New York,: A. & C. Boni.

Schaefer, A. C. (2000). *G.I. Joe meets Barbie, software engineer meets caregiver: Males and females in B.C.'s public schools and beyond* (Vol. The British Columbia Teachers' Federation). Vancouver, BC.

Schegloff, E. A., Ochs, E., & Thompson, S. (1996). Introduction. In E. Ochs, E. A. Schegloff & S. Thompson (Eds.), *Introduction and grammar* (pp. 1-51). Cambridge, UK: Cambridge University Press.

Schultz, K. (2003). *Listening: A framework for teaching across differences.* New York: Teachers College Press.

Scott, E. C., & Branch, G. (2006). *Not in our classrooms: Why intelligent design is wrong for our schools.* Boston: Beacon Press.

Scribner, S. (1977). Modes of thinking and ways of speaking: Culture and logic reconsidered. In P. N. Johnson-Laird & P. C. Wason (Eds.), *Thinking* (pp. 483-500). Cambridge, UK: Cambridge University Press.

Scribner, S., & Cole, M. (1981). *The psychology of literacy.* Cambridge, MA: Harvard University Press.

Shanks, N. (2004). *God, the devil, and Darwin: A critique of intelligent design theory.* Oxford; New York: Oxford University Press.

Sen, A. (1999). *Development as freedom.* New York: Anchor books, a division of Random House, Inc.

Sherif, M. (1988). *The Robbers Cave experiment: Intergroup conflict and cooperation.* Middletown, CT: Wesleyan University Press.

Shermer, M. (2006). *Why Darwin matters: The case against intelligent design* (1st ed.). New York: Times Books.

Shipman, M. D. (1971). *Education and modernisation.* London: (3 Queen Sq. W.C.1) Faber and Faber Ltd.

Shklovskii, V. B., & Sher, B. (1990). *Theory of prose* (1st American ed.). Elmwood Park, IL: Dalkey Archive Press.

Shor, I. (1987). *Critical teaching and everyday life.* Chicago: University of Chicago Press.

Shor, I., & Freire, P. (1987a). *A pedagogy for liberation: Dialogues on transforming education.* South Hadley, Mass.: Bergin & Garvey Publishers.

Shor, I., & Freire, P. (1987b). What is the "dialogical method" of teaching? *Journal of Education, 169*(3), 11-31.

Sidorkin, A. M. (1999). *Beyond discourse: Education, the self, and dialogue*. Albany, NY: State University of New York Press.

Sidorkin, A. M. (2002). *Learning relations: Impure education, deschooled schools, & dialogue with evil*. New York: P. Lang.

Sidorkin, A. M. (2004). Relations are relational: Toward an economic anthropology of schooling. In C. W. Bingham & A. M. Sidorkin (Eds.), *No education without relation* (pp. 55-69). New York: Peter Lang.

Silberman, C. E. (1971). *Crisis in the classroom: The remaking of American education* (Vintage Books ed.). New York: Vintage Books.

Simon, S., Erduran, S., & Osborne, J. (2006). Learning to teach argumentation: Research and development in the science classroom *International Journal of Science Education, 28*(2 & 3), 235-260.

Sinclair, J. M., & Coulthard, M. (1975). *Towards an analysis of discourse: The English used by teachers and pupils*. London: Oxford University Press.

Skidmore, D. (2000). From pedagogical dialogue to dialogical pedagogy. *Language and Education, 14*(4), 283-296.

Smith, D. E. (1998). Bakhtin and the dialogue of sociology: An investigation. In M. Mayerfeld Bell & M. Gardiner (Eds.), *Bakhtin and the human sciences: No last words* (pp. 63-77). London: Sage Publisher.

Smith, M. P., & Matusov, E. (2009, in press). A proposal for a new schooling: Hybrid of reciprocity and authentic dialogue. Review of the book [Sidorkin, A. M. (2002). Learning relations: Impure education, deschooled schools, & dialogue with evil. New York: P. Lang.] *Mind, Culture and Activity*.

Smutny, J. F. (1993). Book reviews: You can't say you can't play. [Book Review]. *Roeper Review, 16*(2), 135-136.

Snyder, D. H. (1985). The problem of evil and the paradox of friendly atheism *International Journal for Philosophy of Religion, 17*(3), 209-216.

Solomadin, I. M. (2004). История мирной культуры как учебный предмет в контексте интегрированного гуманитарного курса [History of the World Culture as an academic curriculum in the context of an integrated liberal art course]. *Директор Школы [School Principal], 7*(September), 37-86.

Solzhenitsyn, A. I. (1974). *The Gulag Archipelago, 1918-1956: An experiment in literary investigation* (T. P. Whitney, Trans. 1st ed.). New York: Harper & Row.

Spengler, O. (1939). *The decline of the West*. New York: A. A. Knopf.

Star, S. L., & Griesemer, J. R. (1989). Institutional ecology, "translations" and boundary objects: Amateurs and professionals in Berkeley's museum of vertebrate zoology, 1907-39. *Social Studies of Science, 19*(3), 387-420.

Stein, P. (2004). Representation, rights and resources: Multimodal pedagogies in the language and literacy classroom. In B. Norton & K. Toohey (Eds.), *Critical pedagogies and language learning*.

Still, A., & Costall, A. (1991). *Against cognitivism: Alternative foundations for cognitive psychology*. New York: Harvester Wheatsheaf.

Stock, P. L. (1995). *The dialogic curriculum: Teaching and learning in a multicultural society*. Portsmouth, NH: Boynton/Cook Publishers.

Subbotsky, E. (1995). Development of pragmatic and non-pragmatic motivation. *Human Development, 38*, 217-234.

Subbotsky, E. V. (1993). *Foundations of the mind: Children's understanding of reality*. Cambridge, Mass.: Harvard University Press.

Suchman, L. A. (1987). *Plans and situated actions. The problem of human machine communication.* Cambridge, Mass: Cambridge University Press.

Sunderland, L. D. (1976). Miraculous design In woodpeckers. *Creation Research Society Quarterly, 12*(4), 186.

Suoranta, J., & McLaren, P. (2006). Socialist pedagogy: It's not what the ideologues taught you. *Journal, 2*(1). Retrieved from http://web.mac.com/publicresistance/iWeb/2.1/2.1-2%20Suoranta%20%26%20McLaren.html

Tamruchi, N. O. (1995). *Moscow conceptualism, 1970-1990.* Roseville East, NSW, Australia: Craftsman House.

Tenenbaum, S. (1940). Uncontrolled expressions of children's attitudes toward school. *Elementary School Journal, 40*(May), 670-678.

Tharp, R. G., & Gallimore, R. (1988). *Rousing minds to life: Teaching, learning, and schooling in social context.* Cambridge, New York: Cambridge University Press.

Thomas, D. W. (1985). The torpedo's touch. *Harvard Educational Review, 55*(2), 220-222.

Thorne, B. (1993). *Gender play: Girls and boys in school.* New Brunswick, NJ: Rutgers University Press.

Tisa, L., & Matusov, E. (2001). [Review of the book Watch IT: The risks and promises of information technology for education by N. Burbules and T. Callister]. *Educational Review* (Available on-line at http://coe.asu.edu/edrev/reviews/rev107.htm).

Todorov, T. (1984). *Mikhail Bakhtin: The dialogical principle.* Minneapolis: University of Minnesota Press.

Tolstoy, L. N. (1967). *Tolstoy on education* (L. Wiener, Trans.). Chicago: University of Chicago Press.

Tolstoy, L. N., & Blaisdell, R. (2000). *Tolstoy as teacher: Leo Tolstoy's writings on education.* New York: Teachers & Writers Collaborative.

Tolstoy, L. N., Maude, L. S., Maude, A., & Gifford, H. (1983). *War and peace.* New York: Oxford University Press.

Tolstoy, L. N. (1985). *Tolstoy's diaries* (R. F. Christian, Trans.). New York: Scribner Press.

Torres, C. A. (1994). Paulo Freire as Secretary of Education in the municipality of São Paulo. *Comparative Education Review, 38*(2), 181-214.

Toulmin, S. (1981). The tyranny of principles. *The Hastings Center Report, December 1981.*

Toulmin, S. E. (2003). *The uses of argument* (Updated ed.). Cambridge, UK: Cambridge University Press.

Tyler, S. (1990). Ode to dialog on the occasion of the un-for-seen. In T. Maranhão (Ed.), *The interpretation of dialogue* (pp. 292-300). Chicago: University of Chicago Press.

van der Veer, R., & Valsiner, J. (1991). *Understanding Vygotsky: A quest for synthesis.* Oxford, UK: Blackwell.

Varenne, H., & McDermott, R. P. (1998). *Successful failure: The school America builds.* Boulder, CO: Westview Press.

Vitanza, V. J. (1997). *Negation, subjectivity, and the history of rhetoric.* Albany: State University of New York Press.

Vlastos, G., & Burnyeat, M. (1994). *Socratic studies.* Cambridge; New York: Cambridge University Press.

Voloshinov, V. N. (1973). *Marxism and the philosophy of language.* New York: Seminar Press.

Vygotsky, L. S. (1978). *Mind in society: The development of higher psychological processes.* Cambridge, MA: Harvard University Press.

Vygotsky, L. S. (1982). *Sobranie sochinenii v shesti tomakh [Collected work in 6 volumes].* Moskva: Pedagogika.

Vygotsky, L. S., & Kozulin, A. (1986). *Thought and language* (Translation newly rev. and edited / ed.). Cambridge, MA: MIT Press.

Vygotsky, L. S., Luria, A. R., Golod, V. I., & Knox, J. E. (1993). *Studies on the history of behavior: Ape, primitive, and child*. Hillsdale, NJ: Lawrence Erlbaum Associates.

Vygotsky, L. S., Rieber, R. W., & Carton, A. S. (1987). *The collected works of L.S. Vygotsky: Volume 1: Thinking and speech* (Vol. 1). New York: Plenum Press.

Walker, J. (1981). The end of dialogue: Paulo Freire on politics and education. In R. Mackie (Ed.), *Literacy and revolution: The pedagogy of Paulo Freire*. New York: Continuum.

Waller, W. W. (1932). *The sociology of teaching*. New York: J. Wiley & sons.

Walton, D. N. (1996). *Argumentation schemes for presumptive reasoning*. Mahwah, NJ: L. Erlbaum Associates.

Walton, D. N. (1998). *The new dialectic: Conversational contexts of argument*. Toronto: University of Toronto Press.

Weatherford, J. M. (1988). *Indian givers: How the Indians of the Americas transformed the world* (1st ed.). New York: Crown Publishers.

Wegerif, R. (2004). Towards a account of teaching general thinking skills that is compatible with the assumptions of sociocultural theory. In H. Brighouse, R. Curren & J. Justin (Eds.), *Theory and research in education* (Vol. 2, pp. 143-159). London: Sage.

Wegerif, R. (2007). *Dialogic, educational and technology: Expanding the space of learning*. New York: Springer-Verlag.

Weiler, K. (1994). Freire and a feminist pedagogy of difference. In P. McLaren & C. Lankshear (Eds.), *Politics of liberation: Paths from Freire*. New York: Routledge.

Weiss, E. M. (1999). Perceived workplace conditions and first-year teachers' morale, career choice commitment, and planned retention: a secondary analysis. *Teachers and Teacher Education, 15*(8), 861-879.

Wells, C. G. (1992, September). *Re-evaluation of the IRF sequence: A proposal for the articulation of theories of activity and discourse for the analysis of teaching and learning in the classroom.* Paper presented at the Conference for Sociocultural Research, Madrid, Spain.

Wells, C. G. (1999). *Dialogic inquiry: Towards a sociocultural practice and theory of education*. New York: Cambridge University Press.

Wenger, E. (1998). *Communities of practice: Learning, meaning, and identity*. Cambridge, UK: Cambridge University Press.

Wertsch, J. V. (1985). *Culture, communication and cognition: Vygotskian perspectives*. New York: Cambridge University Press.

Wertsch, J. V. (1991a). The voice of rationality in a sociocultural approach to mind. In L. Moll (Ed.), *Vygotsky and education: Instructional implications and applications of sociohistorical psychology* (pp. 111-126). Cambridge, MA: Cambridge University Press.

Wertsch, J. V. (1991b). *Voices of the mind: A Sociocultural approach to mediated action*. Cambridge, MA: Cambridge Press.

Wertsch, J. V. (1995). Sociocultural research in the copyright age. *Culture and Psychology, 1*(1), 81-102.

Wertsch, J. V. (2002). *Voices of collective remembering*. Cambridge, UK: Cambridge University Press.

Whitson, J. A. (2007). Education *à la Silhouette*: The need for semiotically-informed curriculum consciousness. *Semiotica, 164*(1/4), 235–329.

Wiggins, G. P., & McTighe, J. (2006). *Understanding by design* (Expanded 2nd ed.). Upper Saddle River, NJ: Pearson Education, Inc.

Willis, P. E. (1981). *Learning to labor: How working class kids get working class jobs* (Morningside ed.). New York: Columbia University Press.

Wiltz, N. W., & Fein, G. G. (1996). Evolution of a narrative curriculum: The contributions of Vivian Gussin Paley. *Young Children, 51*, 61-68.

Wittgenstein, L., & Anscombe, G. E. M. (2001). *Philosophical investigations: The German text, with a revised English translation* (3rd ed ed.). Oxford ; Malden, Mass.: Blackwell.

Wittgenstein, L., Anscombe, G. E. M., & Wright, G. H. v. (1967). *Zettel*. Berkeley: University of California Press.

Wood, D., Bruner, J. S., & Ross, G. (1976). The role of tutoring in problem solving. *Journal of Child psychology and Psychiatry, 17*, 89-100.

Woodruff, P. (1998). Socratic education. In A. O. Rorty (Ed.), *Philosophers on education: Historical perspectives* (pp. 14-31). London: Routledge.

Woodward, T. (2006). *Darwin strikes back: Defending the science of intelligent design*. Grand Rapids, Mich.: Baker Books.

Yalom, I. D. (1995). *The theory and practice of group psychotherapy*. New York: Basic Books.

Young, A. (1995). *The harmony of illusions: Inventing post-traumatic stress disorder*. Princeton, NJ: Princeton University Press.

Young, M., & Edis, T. (2004). *Why intelligent design fails: A scientific critique of the new creationism*. New Brunswick, N.J.: Rutgers University Press.

Zacharakis-Jutz, J. (1986). Review of [Issues for an Evaluation of Freire-Inspired Programs in the United States and Puerto Rico by Blanca Facundo, 1984]. *Adult Literacy and Basic Education, 10*(3).

Zappen, J. P. (2004). *The rebirth of dialogue: Bakhtin, Socrates, and the rhetorical tradition*. Albany: State University of New York Press.

Zerubavel, E. (1985). *Hidden rhythms: Schedules and calendars in social life* (1st California pbk. ed.). Berkeley: University of California Press.

Zinchenko, V. P. (1985). Vygotsky's ideas about units for the analysis of mind. In J. V. Wertsch (Ed.), *Culture, communication and cognition: Vygotskian perspectives* (pp. 94-118). New York: Cambridge University Press.

Zlotkowski, E. (1999). Pedagogy and engagement. In R. G. Bringle, R. Games & E. A. Malloy (Eds.), *Colleges and universities as citizens* (pp. 96-120). Boston: Allyn & Bacon.

Медведев, Ж., & Медведев, Р. (2004). *Солженицын и Сахаров. Два пророка*. Москва: Время.

Name Index

SUBJECT INDEX

Alienation
Antagonism
Argumentation
    authoritarian
    dialogic pedagogical
    in traditional education
    traditional outside of education
Assessment
    formative
    summative
Awarness without responsibility
Authority
    authoritarian
    authoritative
    dialogic
    discourse
    epistemological
    expert
    learning
    pre-dialogic
    post-dialogic
Authorship
Autism
Boundary object
Carnival
Circular self-deception
Chronotope
    assigned task
    didactic
    ontological
    semiotic
Chronotopic compartmentalization fallacy
Consciousness
    dialogic
    equal
    monologic
    non-trasparent (opaque)
    transparent
Community
    behind
    of learners
Conflict
Contradiction
Conventional
    education
    schooling

INDEX

B

C

D

E

N

Q

R

S

U